The Mexican Nation

Historical Continuity and Modern Change

Douglas W. Richmond

University of Texas at Arlington

Prentice
Hall

UPPER SADDLE RIVER, NEW JERSEY 07458

Library of Congress Cataloging-in-Publication Data

RICHMOND, DOUGLAS W., [date].
  The Mexican nation: historical continuity and modern change / by DOUGLAS W. RICHMOND
    p. cm.
  Includes bibliographical references and index.
  ISBN 0-13-092227-7
  1. Mexico—History. I. Title.
  F1410 .R397 2002
  972—dc21   2001021523

VP, Editorial Director: *Charlyce Jones Owen*
Acquisitions Editor: *Charles Cavaliere*
Associate Editor: *Emsal Hasan*
Editorial/Production Supervision: *Joanne Riker*
Prepress and Manufacturing Buyer: *Tricia Kenny*
Director of Marketing: *Beth Gillett Mejia*
Cover Art Director: *Jayne Conte*
Cover Designer: *Bruce Kenselaar*
Cover Images: *from top, Pan American Union, Library of Congress, Mexican National Tourist Council, and Mexican National Tourist Council.*

This book was set in 10/12 Times Roman by East End Publishing Services, Inc. and was printed and bound by RR Donnelly & Sons Company. The cover was printed by Phoenix Color Corp.

 © 2002 by Pearson Education, Inc.
Upper Saddle River, New Jersey 07458

ISBN 0-13-092227-7

Pearson Education LTD., *London*
Pearson Education Australia PTY, Limited, *Sydney*
Pearson Education Singapore, Pte. Ltd
Pearson Education North Asia Ltd, *Hong Kong*
Pearson Education Canada, Ltd., *Toronto*
Pearson Educación de Mexico, S.A. de C.V.
Pearson Education — Japan, *Tokyo*
Pearson Education Malaysia, Pte. Ltd
Pearson Education, *Upper Saddle River, New Jersey*

To
Soraya and Belinda

Contents

Preface

Three basic factors stimulated the formation of a Mexican nation. The interaction of regional, religious, and ethnic elements and their relation to economic as well as international forces both reveal and clarify the continuity of Mexican history. Continuity slowed and shaped these factors, but they remained constant features of the Mexican past. Scholars have begun to interpret continuity in the context of historical themes. Recent studies, for example, emphasize greater continuity in economic history. The 1910 revolution interrupted the development of the Mexican economy more than changing its essential nature. The theme of continuity in modern Mexican intellectual history has become entrenched since 1985.

This book emphasizes how some leaders have succeeded and others failed. Rulers who interpreted the needs of regions, religion, and ethnicity and responded to them within a nationalistic criteria by the eighteenth century usually did well. Nationalism can be defined simply as the urge of every society to live according to its traditional customs and to be governed responsibly. The most successful nationalist leaders were the statesmen who harmonized religious, regional, and ethnic sensitivities while molding Mexico into a connected body as much as possible.

Until the nineteenth century, political leaders represented their regions, and scholars of Mexico have noted the power of regional identities in shaping Mexican history. The dominant trends, particular in the early periods, have moved through regional variants. Gradually, modern Mexico found itself locked in a struggle between provincial elites and groups in Mexico City attempting to displace established regional structures. Cultural, economic, and political trends complicated the process, but geography also imposed a tremendous burden upon Mexico. High mountain ranges and the lack of navigable rivers made it difficult to link various regions. These two physical obstacles increased regional transportation expenses, consequently raising labor costs and lowering productivity, and ultimately, impeding national integration.

An appreciation of the significance of religion is essential to understanding Mexican history. When the sacred and daily routines were still fused, religion pervaded daily life. The sustaining rituals of existence were spiritual, and people's understanding of politics, war, economics, justice, literature, and art, as well as their concepts of death and their aspirations for life, were usually shaped within a religious context. The Church provided continuity through its traditions, rituals, and services and appealed to all groups, indigenous peoples as well as *mestizos* and whites.

Ethnicity is the other vital theme in Mexican history. The indigenous foundation of the nation in large part explains much of its uniqueness. The Spanish invasion resulted in the fusion of Europeans and Africans with native peoples. Colonial society was dynamic in part because the Church adopted culturally inclusive strategies and consciously retained many indigenous traditions. Consequently, Mexico possessed a national culture long before a sense of political nationalism emerged.

At various times in Mexican history, ethnic, religious, and regional tensions subsided sufficiently to permit the formulation and implementation of national programs. Particularly notable are the pre-Hispanic era, the seventeenth century, the Porfiriato, and the period of confidence between 1940 and 1967. Few regimes succeeded if they failed to respect the religious, ethnic, and regional continuities that bound the country together. The pre-Hispanic centuries were notable for scientific and technological breakthroughs, economic success, and healthy living. Religion, however, had become a fundamental weakness of this epoch by the time Spaniards arrived. The seventeenth century witnessed the establishment of institutions that provided stability during a century of unusual change. Mexico adapted itself to the transatlantic system, while the interaction between religion and region became practical as well as harmonious. Perhaps the Porfiriato (1876–1911) succeeded more than any other system. During this era, the north and south experienced far greater economic growth than the center. Religion no longer divided society as it had during Mexico's tempestuous first half century of independence. Favoritism, however, became the fatal weakness of the Porfirian era. Between 1940 and 1967, Mexico enjoyed an era of self-confidence; civilian leaders placed economic growth at the head of their agenda and minimized ideological zeal and social conflict. The political crisis of 1968, however, soon brought economic as well as fiscal nightmares that plagued Mexico in the final decades of the twentieth century.

As the twenty-first century begins, Mexico appears to be entering a new age under recently elected President Vicente Fox. Sensitive to religious tradition, determined to balance regional growth, and promising a more harmonized relationship with the United States, Fox offers great hope. Mexico seems to be passing from an authoritarian, one-party state to a more complex and sophisticated society empowered by representative government, economic freedom, and social equality. As a leader who favors local and regional industrial development to complement Mexico's abundance of export-related plants, Fox seems to understand the continuities of the past while articulating the necessity for sensible change.

Acknowledgments

Three remarkable history professors from the University of Washington provided the foundation for graduate studies. I will forever be indebted to Dauril Alden, Carl Solberg, and Joan Connelly Ullman. The University of Texas at Arlington provided a faculty development leave to research and write the colonial section of this book during the pleasant winter and spring of 1995.

There are some kind people who provided most of the photo illustrations in this book. Kit Goodwin, a cartographic archivist, of the Special Collections Division at the University of Texas at Arlington (UTA) Library, hustled up several items relating to the U.S.–Mexican War from 1846–1848. Benito Huerta of the Gallery at UTA kindly signed off on artwork reproductions from an exhibition relating to Mexican art held in Arlington back in 1978. The illustrations from the revolutionary era, particularly the Carranza items, came from my old friends at the Centro de Estudios de Historia de México in Mexico City.

Richard Francaviglia, director of the Center for Greater Southwestern Studies and the History of Cartography here at the University of Texas at Arlington, provided travel funds to present papers about various aspects of Mexican history. One of the privileges of being a Center Fellow has been the opportunity to utilize the Center research assistants. Four of them were very helpful in my endeavor to uncover new information: Jimmy Bryan, José Delgado, David Filewood, and Linda Pelon were immensely valuable.

Four people went to the trouble to read portions of the manuscript. Malcolm McLean and Bruce Winders read Chapter 8 and furnished wonderful suggestions. Dale Story, likewise, grappled with Chapter 17 and, although he counseled me to be less critical, Dale also gave me the benefits of his extensive knowledge of both the political and economic realities of modern Mexico. Roberto Treviño critiqued the migration section in Chapter 16 very thoroughly.

And then there are two fine ladies named Josefina. Josefina Zoraida Vásquez has been coming to this campus since the 1970s to enlighten us about the early nineteenth-century events of Mexican history. Gracious and stimulating, she has vast knowledge and she has provided many original insights during the many years I have been privileged to know her. Josefina Moguel Flores encountered me when I was a young graduate student as we both worked at the archive of the Mexican Foreign Relations Secretariat. Later she moved over to the Centro de Estudios de Historia de México, where she supervised the archives. A delightful and intelligent person in every respect, she has nurtured my historical formation in countless ways.

Of the many peers in the business of Mexican history who have helped me, I must first mention my two best friends in this profession. Mike Smith and Joe Stout of Oklahoma State University have provided many a laugh, drink, and shrewd insights in the course of thinking about the Mexican past. Through almost weekly contact, they have both helped me untangle knotty historical problems since I first met them at a 1993 conference in Stillwater, Oklahoma. Others who have aided me are Ward Albro, David Bailey, Francisco Balderrama, Joe Bastien, Bill Beezley, Tom Benjamin, Lyle Brown, Don Coerver, Mark Gilderhus, Miguel González, George Grayson, Linda Hall, Charles Harris, John Hart, Sam Haynes, Peter Henderson, Laura Herrera, Alusine Jalloh, Gil Joseph, David LaFrance, Bill Meyers, Suzanne Pastor, Jeffrey Pilcher, Terry Rugeley, Jim Sandos, Pedro Santoni, Gerald Saxon, Miguel Soto, Lawrence Taylor, Mark Wasserman, David Weber, Allen Wells, Berta Ulloa, and David Walker. I know I have forgotten a few, so please forgive me if you are not on this list.

Several students formulated original and stimulating insights. Chief among them are Kim Henke Breur, Joe McCambridge, Rob Robinson, Scott Roden, and Cubie Ward.

My wife Belinda and my daughter Soraya forgave me many times for having my nose in a book or typing too many times. It was not easy to go about the lonely endeavor of history when I would rather have spent time with them because they are my world.

Last but by no means least, my thanks to Alta Vick, who typed this narrative for me.

1

Mexico's Indigenous Roots

At the time of the Spanish invasion, a rich and complex civilization flourished in the Valley of Mexico. The brilliant Maya kingdoms of the southeast collapsed somewhat earlier. The accomplishments of the Aztec, Maya, and other indigenous civilizations rank among the greatest achievements in world history. Early Mexican societies designed agricultural, artistic, and social systems which reveal their continual search for order. Early Mexican society was not based on the individual but revolved around the good of the community. Dietary, medicinal, and scientific studies provided a high standard of living for pre-Hispanic Mexico.

By contrast, contemporary European peasants lived in dank, vermin-infested hovels and knew little of the world outside their villages. Their precarious existence was so empty of promise that most had no surname to pass on to their offspring. Early Mexico had its own shortcomings, but the positive attributes certainly exceeded the negative aspects.

ANCIENT MEXICO

Mexico's First Inhabitants. The slow interaction between nature and humans gradually produced the first Mexicans. The land bridge between Central and South America lay underwater for several million years during the Cenozoic period. The most important land connection extended over the Bering Strait, when cold weather lowered world water levels. Frigid climate encouraged large land mammals, such as camels and horses, to leave the Americas for Asia. The first signs of human activity on the American continent indicate that life goes back 35,000 or 40,000 years.

The traditional theory is that Mexico's first inhabitants were Amerind hunters and food gatherers. From what is now Japan and China, these Stone Age hunters followed game trails across the Bering land bridge before it subsided underwater, approximately 10,000 years ago. The cold climate eliminated germs on the continent as well as anyone who suffered from diseases. The presence of 13,000 year old bones discovered on an island off the California coast suggest that Amerinds must have had seafaring capabilities by the end of the last ice age. People may have also come from Europe more than 12,000 years ago. The first groups of New World people hunted in the tall grass lands, but they could not make pottery, spin cloth, or even use bows and arrows. As herds dwindled, they journeyed to Appalachia, Florida, and Cuba. Many Amerindians preferred milder climates near deserts and rocky slopes. As the

1

Amerindians settled in specific regions, they evolved into different physical types.

Agriculture was the most compelling innovation during the ancient period. In locations such as the Tehuacan valley of Mexico, farmers began planting seeds from wild plants such as teosinte as early as 7200 B.C. By at least 2500 B.C., agriculture appeared in many areas. Squash, maize, and beans became prominent crops. New World agriculture produced a wider variety of plants than the Old World. Maize became the most abundant food source and diverged into 700 varieties throughout Latin America. Corn cobs in Mexico date back to 6,300 years ago. Potatoes, tomatoes, and sunflowers were among the nearly one hundred different types of cultivated plants which the Spaniards eventually encountered. The indigenous people also ate anything that crawled or walked. But the ancient diet was nutritious. Squash and beans supplied protein. Chiles, which appeared later, provided cellulose as well as vitamins A and C. Pulque, an alcoholic drink made from the agave plant, furnished vitamins C and B as well as fiber.

Until 900 B.C., Mexican society consisted of individual households and very small villages not responsible to any government. At this time most Mexicans planted seeds in their *milpa* (fields) by means of the slash-and-burn method. Cutting and burning the foliage provided short-term harvests but did not replenish the soil quickly. After 900 B.C., food surpluses became trade items. Hunting declined in importance while the cultivation of food stabilized. Increasing numbers of craftsmen produced pottery, shells, jade, jewels, and feathers for barter in the bustling markets. Families now elaborated burial techniques. Kinship bonds possessed more authority than did the nuclear families that married couples and their children formed. Kinship relations settled homicide, divorce, and other social problems. Religion also assumed a greater social role. Public ritual characterized religion. Priests began to furnish calendars for planting crops. The priests also inspired confidence by encouraging *ofrendas* (offerings) to the gods.

Offerings became feasts for the spirits of the dead who would return and be nourished on certain nights during observances of what became a national observance, the Day of the Dead. The feasts involved spending a day at family burial grounds, remembering departed loved ones. Feasts eventually involved *calavera* skulls and round loaves of *pan de muertos* (bread of the dead) accompanied by chocolate, tamales, and bananas.

Celebrations varied from one region to another; they all focused upon a spiritual covenant between communities and supernatural entities of deceased family members and friends. The act of decorating clay skulls with flowers enabled villagers to confront their fear of infinity. To pre-Columbian people, death was simply a door, part of an unending cycle that represented a transition from one life to another. A tomb, burial mound or a cave was merely a point of departure from one plane to another. Spiritual values became a natural part of daily living, as religion, medicine, and art combined to form a holistic system of life.

Villages began evolving throughout Mesoamerica (the lands from Central Mexico to the edge of today's Costa Rica) by 2500 B.C. Public works and government became more fully developed. As villages became more complex, temples appeared and writing facilitated various tasks. Not surprisingly, villagers located markets near worship centers. Irrigation appeared in various areas, either in the form of terracing or as *chinampas*. Often referred to as floating gardens, the *chinampas* were limbs, boughs, and twigs on which farmers piled fertile soil from lakes and rivers. The highly productive *chinampas* furnished three or four harvests yearly. But the ancient societies had neither large animals that could be domesticated, nor the wheel or metal.

Olmec Society. The Olmecs became the first fundamental civilization in Mexican society. They provided all of the basic elements of Mesoamerican civilization that would reoccur in later ones. As the Trojan War ended, the Olmec culture began about 1200 B.C. in the Veracruz-

Tabasco region. The Olmecs are undoubtedly responsible for extending as well as emphasizing intensive corn cultivation in the lowlands. Because many Olmec centers were in the vicinity of rivers as well as swamps that rise and fall annually, the Olmecs utilized this natural irrigation system with its rich supply of silt. This development supported a large population. Recent discoveries of hoes and human refuse used for fertilizer indicate extensive agricultural skills.

Fabulous stone architectural achievements reflect a rigorous sense of planning and order, the hallmarks of Olmec culture. Massive stone carvings, monuments, civic centers, ball courts, and temples indicate the Olmec penchant for public works projects. Able to construct colossal heads weighing several tons and transport them on sledges, the Olmecs were also exceptional engineers. Stone-lined ritual ponds and earthen platforms also attest to an Olmec florescence.

The subtlety and artistic achievements of Olmec craftsmen are quite substantial. Olmec art became very widespread and is notable for its historical themes as well as realism. Beginning in Olmec times, mastery of stoneworking techniques existed for even the hardest of stones. The large basalt sculptures had a theatrical presence; their melancholy yet expressive force could impose, impress, and overwhelm. Delicate jade statuettes demonstrate that no other Mesoamerican people rivaled the Olmec mastery of this gemstone.

The Olmecs constituted a nonegalitarian society with definite social ranking. The Olmecs became highly organized with a well-tuned division of labor. Middlemen, merchants, and creditors became local leaders after they controlled river levees. Although it is unclear whether the Olmec seat of power was a monarchy or an elite leadership, it may also have been a theocracy.

The Olmecs introduced ceremonial centers and formulated the first Mexican deities. The major ceremonial center was a two-mile island known as La Venta. Near a coastal estuary, La Venta enjoyed rich food resources and salt. A 100-foot pyramid, the first large pyramidal structure in Mexico, dominates the center with a ceremonial court nearby. As a demonstration of faith, Olmec worshippers left behind wonderful mosaics, exquisite jade carvings, striking tombs, and marvelous altars within the various mounds at La Venta. Perhaps the most significant Olmec contribution of Mesoamerican religion was an elaboration of the cult of Quetzalcoatl, the benevolent Feathered Serpent, as well as the rain god Tlaloc. A jaguar cult represented the rise of an increasingly influential warrior class.

Once the production of jade and ceramics encouraged long-distance trading networks, commerce and conquest went hand-in-hand. La Venta was a prosperous community of fishermen, farmers, traders, and artists. Active Olmec merchants obtained iron ore from Oaxaca. Extensive trade relations reached into El Salvador, Honduras, and Costa Rica. Scholars such as Ignacio Bernal believe that trade ranked second only to agriculture in terms of producing income.

Quetzalcoatl, god and legendary ruler of the Toltecs in Mexico, c. 1500 A.D. *The Granger Collection.*

Other accomplishments included the development of a calendar, mathematics, and writing. The Olmec concern for dating their products motivated them to create a long-count calendrical system. Undoubtedly, the Olmecs discovered the length of a year and the lunar month, making them the first to use a calendar. The 1986 discovery of the La Mojarra stone in Veracruz indicates that the Olmecs were probably the first literate society in Mexico. Astronomical observations necessitated the bar and dot mathematical system which evolved under the Olmecs. The Olmecs also devised a shell-like representation for zero, a feat that the Europeans would not duplicate until Arabs introduced it during the Middle Ages. Although Olmec mathematics were rudimentary, their system could carry out routine calculations, mainly calendrical in nature.

The Olmecs finally passed from the scene about 400 B.C. in a spasm of violence. Perhaps the Olmec system demanded too much from its totally stratified underlings because the destruction of the temples indicates pent-up hatred. But their influential legacy would characterize more impressive successors.

Teotihuacán, Cholula, and Monte Albán.

The city of Teotihuacán became a ceremonial and social center of major significance. Teotihuacán evolved from a beautiful, well-watered valley. Irrigation, an obsidian industry, its strategic location as a marketing center, and the growing importance of its religious shrines enabled Teotihuacán to become the greatest city in the Americas from A.D. 100 to A.D. 750. Massive temples and royal palaces indicate the cosmopolitan nature of Teotihuacán which had about 200,000 inhabitants. Its Ciudadela was a vast religious complex highlighted by the temple of Quetzalcoatl. An enormous market center, the Great Compound, is the other feature of the east-west road. Both the Ciudadela and the market intersect with a north-west avenue, the Pathway of the Dead. At both ends of this avenue are the Pyramid of the Moon, 495 feet by 405 feet at the base and 140 feet high, and the massive Pyramid of the

Sun, which is 700 feet on each side and 210 feet high. The Pyramid of the Sun served as a temple base but also had astronomical functions. It faces a point on the western horizon where the western star cluster Pleiadades sets and where the sun goes down during summer and winter solstices. Religious articles found in a four-chambered cave deep within the pyramid's base suggest that it was once a sacred shrine that attracted pilgrims from throughout Mesoamerica.

Within its impressive center, Teotihuacán vibrated with tremendous energy until its demise. It was Basically a theocracy, and the priests lived along the Pathway of the Dead with most of the upper class. Average people lived within more than 2,000 walled compounds of varying size and character. The Teotihuacanos brought craftsmen from across Mesoamerica to manufacture their specialized goods. Teotihuacán's craftsmen and artists enabled it to influence distant cities, particularly the Maya kingdom at Tikal, in northeastern Guatemala. The first truly urban Mesoamerican civilization collapsed mysteriously in the eighth century.

Cholula became a notable successor to Teotihuacán. Survivors from Teotihuacán stimulated the emergence of Cholula, where the largest pyramid in Mexico emanated. Larger than the Cheops pyramid in Egypt, the Cholula pyramid covered 40 acres. Like many other Classic era cities, Cholula claimed Quetzalcoatl as its patron god. Cholula's religious spirit also attracted great wealth, since the city's rulers proclaimed Quetzalcoatl as the god of wealth. Merchants attempted to follow Quetzalcoatl's example. Pilgrims poured into Cholula to view the great pyramid dedicated to Quetzalcoatl. Many pilgrims came from as far as 300 miles away. The priests sacrificed at least 6,000 people a year in order to satisfy the gods.

Built in 500 B.C. by Zapotecs near present-day Oaxaca City, Monte Albán began its rise to power when the Olmecs declined. Originally a fortress until priests expanded it, Monte Albán was an early theocracy. Monte Albán depended upon water from nearby ravines and natural springs. Once the recipient of Olmec culture, Monte

Albán devised a form of writing, a calendar, and produced a distinct artistic style which reflects its pristine natural surroundings. Unlike other Classic era civilizations, Monte Albán became a strong monarchy. The Zapotecs used their kingdom to control nearby areas so that allied villagers as well as conquered subjects paid tribute. Monte Albán's influence eventually extended into the Valley of Mexico, Chiapas, Veracruz, and Teotihuacán. About 250,000 inhabitants lived in Monte Albán during its peak, from A.D. 200. to A.D. 750. The city consisted of one layer of settlements built upon another. Monte Albán finally collapsed about A.D. 900. when Mixtecs overran it. Deforestation and overuse of water are probably the critical factors that led gradually to an inability to provide food, like most other early Mexican civilizations.

The Toltecs represent the rising resentment of an underclass of laborers and noncivilized groups against the Classic-era cities. As order in the interior broke down, warrior societies such as the Toltecs dominated the final pre-Hispanic centuries. The Toltecs emerged from a rough Chichimeca background, probably somewhere near Zacatecas. Despite their barbarian origins, the Toltecs benefited from Teotihuacan's influence. Eventually, the Toltecs became proficient artisans, fine architects, and enjoyed a successful agricultural life. Rich maize and cotton harvests enabled Toltec society to maintain a legendary standard of living that many envied, particularly after the Toltecs established their capital at Tula. The Toltecs, however, remained militarists with a strong priesthood.

The dual nature of their early religion reflected a rivalry that proved fatal. The Toltec kings insisted that their monarchy maintained a direct line of descent to Quetzalcoatl. At the same time, the Toltecs worshipped the sun and emphasized sacrifice to the warrior god Tezcatlipoca. Both gods fought one another in order to be associated with the sun, the ultimate symbol of supremacy. Eventually, the warrior faction promoted the legend that Tezcatlipoca persuaded Quetzalcoatl to become intoxicated from pulque and to seduce his sister. The shame of incest forced Quetzalcoatl to flee to the east although his return would occur during a critical reed calendar year, when significant events would take place during 52-year calendrical accumulations of time.

Although, the aggressive Toltecs expanded to five new centers, they could not contain the fierce Chichimecas. Living north of the Toltecs, the primitive but fierce Chichimecas were a society geared for warfare. Motivated by harsh twelfth-century droughts, the Chichimecas crushed the Toltecs and seized Tula, forcing the Toltecs to migrate to Chapultepec, within present-day Mexico City.

Agriculture encouraged the appearance of rudimentary civilization in faraway locations such as the Gila River and Salt River valleys of southern Arizona. About 300 B.C. farmers known as Hohokam began weaving and making pottery. The Anasazi civilization appeared in the Four Corners area by the sixth century A.D. Then irrigation systems and elaborate canals supported permanent Anasazi villages. Ball courts, feathers, and copper bells attest to Mexican influence. Although the Anasazi borrowed little from their immediate neighbors, Mexico inspired them. Drought finally destroyed their society in the twelfth and thirteenth centuries.

THE WORLDLY MAYA

Possessed with universal human traits, the great Maya civilization rose and declined long before Europeans entered the Americas. Maya literary endeavors mean that the written history of the New World began in 50 B.C., not 1492. There is a clear continuity between the ancient Maya and today's Maya. But the technological capabilities of the Maya far exceeded their ability to establish a lasting community.

The Maya created the most advanced civilization in the pre-Columbian Western Hemisphere. Many of their achievements took place upon the limestone foundation of the Yucatecan peninsula. Somehow the Maya converted a landscape of poor soil and scant water into massive cities by at least 600 B.C. The Pre-Classic era, which began about 1100 B.C., included intensive agriculture, fishing, artistic skills, and impressive architectural endeavors among its accomplishments.

The social system created a tightly stratified culture. Women could not own property or hold public office. After baptism, children learned to be courteous and highly respectful. Boys lived in communal dormitories apart from their families for a social and religious education. Professional matchmakers arranged marriages after which couples resided in the bride's home for six years. Males could carry out divorce by means of simple repudiation.

Peasants were the foundation of Maya society. The Maya understood and respected nature. It is no coincidence that the Maya clustered their settlements along fracture zones, formed millions of years ago by faults in the bedrock, where easier access to water and better soil conditions existed. Maya farmers enjoyed the security of various fields on which to grow crops. The diet of deer, turkey, stew, fish, rabbit, armadillo, iguana, and chocolate definitely surpassed the quality of European meals. Clans administered the communal lands. Despite having no plows or shovels, the Maya farmers often achieved better results than those in the modern era, because of their efficient agricultural techniques.

Peasant life centered around the family home and its agricultural fields. The overriding significance of the farmer's residence was due to the tradition that the bones of ancestors were buried within, thereby legitimating family rights. Each household maintained different types of land in dispersed patterns. The fields farthest from the home were the *k'ax* fields that lay fallow, only partially cleared of trees and yielded a number of crops as well as serving as a source of herbs, wild game, and raw material for construction. When working the land, Maya farmers built huts on or near these fields for temporary residences or to store surplus. These distant fields are considered *milpas*. Closer to the residence were fields under continual cultivation, which also grew a variety of crops. Gardens and orchards surrounded the home. The Maya prized their orchards since they were inherited as the living symbols of family lineage—they were planted by ancestors and descendants enjoyed the fruit.

As the Maya population expanded—it reached three million by A.D. 800—agricultural production became critical. In populated areas, the Maya terraced nearly every hillside; farmers constantly enlarged waterholes. Virtually all major Maya communities had large rivers, lakes, or a seacoast nearby in order to cultivate fields or obtain fish. The maintenance of a communal land system obligated the masses to labor on public works projects. Droughts necessitated a cooperative labor program because natural catastrophes could be severe. Therefore the Maya drained the swamps by means of a system of canals to build raised *chinampas* fields.

Often stocked with fish and wide enough for vital canoe traffic, the canals served trade as well as agriculture. The canals controlled water flow with the aid of stones built into the sides, which kept the fields intact and allowed for drainage in rainy seasons. The Maya also constructed dams in order to utilize water during dry periods. These reclamation projects conserved the rich jungle soil; two or three crops per year were the norm. The anthropologist Richard Adams estimated that this extensive canal system covered 11,000 square miles in Guatemala alone. Moreover, the canals help explain how the Maya could feed such a large population.

Trading was another important economic activity. The highland Maya traded obsidian, jade, quetzal feathers, incense, cedar, mahogany, flint, dyes, and millions of tools as well as medicinal herbs. The lowland groups provided purified salt, honey, wax, cotton, chocolate, dried fish, and smoked deer. It was almost a purely barter economy. Well-regulated markets and an excellent infrastructure of roads and canals moved goods smoothly. Artisans provided outstanding pottery and basic household goods.

Slaves were another commodity in great demand. Slavery existed in part because the Maya had a rigorous sense of justice. Debtors, thieves, and prisoners of war became enslaved. Generally, crimes such as homicide and adultery resulted in death. Little crime seems to have existed. Few questioned the law. Those who attacked the nobility could expect to have their navel cut open and their intestines pulled out.

The Ruling Class. The Maya were a dynastic society with definite levels of authority which indicated to whom the masses should bow. The nobles, known as *ahau* (lord), were also gods. The upper class distinguished themselves by elaborate dress and feathered headgear. Flattened skulls, hooked noses remade with putty, and nostrils filled with jade gave the *ahau* an imposing appearance.

But the upper class had clear responsibilities. They controlled trade and the economy. *Ahau* supervision of the markets clarifies this role. Cultural endeavors distinguished the nobility from the farming masses. United by an appreciation for art, capable of reading hieroglyphic texts, and fascinated with astrology, the *ahau* also enjoyed privileges. They departed the world amid elaborate funeral rites. Confined to one legal wife, they could also maintain concubines. The political function of the nobility meant that they administered regions while local nobles with less prestige, known as *cahal*, controlled villages and neighborhoods. A *cahal* received aid from both a council of elders and wealthy individuals; neighborhoods usually selected their representatives to the *cahal*.

Maya society became a class system controlled by powerful monarchs working in conjunction with an active military. Decentralization of authority resulted in a lack of overall unity because a single city-state rarely controlled Maya society. The Maya were not a democracy or a theocracy. Since an *ahau* normally inherited his status, Maya society often resembled the Japanese shogun dynasties or medieval Europe. The maintenance of power also depended upon the ability of the nobles. The monarchs forged alliances by setting up marriages between members of two kingdoms. Maya kings also led armies into battle while at the same time they interpreted the cosmic rituals of Maya religion. Although the monarch had unquestioned authority, the king had to earn the respect of his followers. Blood sacrifice accompanied important events in each kingdom. Monarchs, the nobility, and commoners gave their blood in addition to sacrificing captives. Kings usually pierced their penises with spines while queens pulled barbed ropes through holes in their tongues. Blood sacrifices had the effect of uniting small as well as large kingdoms in rituals that provided a collective sense of mission.

Urban and Military Life. As in the Olmec society, urban ceremonial centers manifested a central power connected to the management of an intensive agricultural system. Successful agriculture accelerated the tempo of urban life. During the Classic period, the Maya built at least 200 cities.

Towns and cities had common features similar to Spain. Most notable is the ceremonial center within a large plaza. Markets functioned in this area. Unique to Mesoamerica was the ball court. Ball courts celebrated fertility and the afterlife as well as war and peace. This exciting mass spectacle became an evolving institution that resolved conflict within and between groups. The losing team understood that they would be sacrificed.

As in Iberia, the upper class lived near the plaza. Their homes were often stone palaces with apartments containing built-in beds. The masses enjoyed bright, clean homes with thick, cool plaster floors. Open-air terraces with thatched canopies were pleasant accompaniments. The walled nature of the cities and their impressive architecture depicting throngs of prisoners indicate that the Maya were hardly peaceful, quiet types.

Historians now consider the Maya as bloody and warlike as the Aztecs. Military life became increasingly significant in Maya society. In fact, warfare became a highly stylized undertaking. Maya writings celebrated victories of one feuding city-state after another. Such conflict became inevitable when one considers the need for slaves, vague boundaries, and the shifting nature of agriculture. Armed with obsidian-edged clubs, flint knives, spears, and short swords carved out of shells, the lightly armed Maya fell below European standards. Their inability to fight at night, the constant need to plant and harvest, and the reluctance of the troops to carry on when chiefs died, weakened Maya military organization. Such liabilities became critical when Spaniards arrived.

Religion and Culture. Religion was fundamental in Maya life because it influenced birth, death, and agriculture. It also oriented astronomy and architecture. Maya religion was complex if only because of its numerous, capricious gods who could be benevolent as well as evil. Moreover, the gods inhabited the sky, earth, and underworld.

The Maya view of the cosmos was as hierarchical as their society. The Maya envisioned the earth as square with each cardinal direction possessing great ritual significance. The Maya believed that there were 13 heavens and 9 hells sustained by four major gods who stood at the cardinal directions and held up the world. Like the Greeks in their mythology, the Maya emphasized a pantheon of gods in their folklore.

Popul Vuh is the epic of Maya literature. It describes the creation of the Maya world, the birth and death of the first underworld fathers, the defeat of evil by the sacred mother, and the birth of the Hero Twins. Like many medieval European epics, *Popul Vuh* follows the Hero Twins—sacred figures throughout North and Central America—from boyhood trials to their discovery of a true calling and descent into the underworld, their ultimate victory over its evil lords, and their final deification as the sun and moon.

Since gods existed for everything from ropemakers to suicide, the Maya attempted to be on as good terms as possible with them in order to avoid natural disasters and personal trauma. Thus Maya religion often consisted of complex ceremonies, precisely supervised in order to please the gods.

Maya religion accentuated a circular relationship among humans, nature, and gods. The gods grew the crops, which supported humans, who in turn sustained the gods by means of offerings. The Maya believed that they re-created the universe each day, even in the simplest tasks. They respected a life system that created them. The Maya assumed that humans existed to acknowledge the divine force that permeated their lives. They accepted a responsibility to participate in the universe and thus part of the totality of life. The Maya witnessed the act of creation in their *milpa*, kitchens, and working areas. Ritual helped them see that what they did every day replicated the birth of the universe.

Sacrifice opened the way to be with the gods and to view the pattern of destiny. Above all, the gods cherished pounding hearts and human blood. Many sacrificial victims went to their deaths peacefully when the priests pried out their hearts with flint knives. Participants often enjoyed a meal of the victim's flesh. Prisoners of war received more brusque treatment.

Not surprisingly, Maya religion was hardly cheerful. Convinced that the world would come to an end during a struggle between good and evil, most Maya became pessimistic. The Maya assumed that they were destined for an underworld where the dead faced trials devised by lords of death. If victorious, the deceased emerged as a powerful ancestor spirit able to influence the living. Naturally, the Maya like the Chinese, became involved deeply in ancestor worship. They buried the placenta of newborn babies to return them to mother earth. Everyone believed that he or she carried a second soul, that of an animal, as protection from evil. Therefore the Maya, like other pre-Hispanic Mexicans, believed that death was part of the transition cycle from one life to another.

For the Maya, art was as real as nature; its concerns helped define the world. The large, sculptured pyramids on which the artists used plaster and stucco to produce multicolored masks and friezes are unlike anything else in the world. Maya stucco sculpture represents a technically exact and orderly endeavor in which each motif is bound to a specific category of the chromatic spectrum. The tough, pulverized limestone cement formed a tight bond. After polishing and glazing the cement, technicians applied tree bark to the walls to make their buildings rain resistant.

After the techniques arrived from Ecuador about 2500 B.C., the earliest pottery appeared. Exquisite pottery, fine carvings, and lavish murals attest to the high level of Maya artists and artisans. Although working within the limited medium of limestone and stucco, the Maya utilized them to provide a sense of movement. By the end of the Classic period, their style had shifted to more abstract, geometrical patterns. The generally realistic painting retained an emphasis upon symbolism and religion without being merely decorative. The Maya also utilized classic fresco painting methods on wet cement walls. In addition to incorporating people and movement into their paintings, the Maya became masters of line and color. The various murals, paintings, and figurines indicate that the Maya participated in drama, dance, music, poetry, and epic tales.

Science and Communication. The belief that past events would duplicate themselves motivated the Maya to measure time carefully. Calculating the omens and determining suitable responses became a major concern. Not surprisingly, Itzamna, the inventor of writing and patron of science, became the supreme deity. Therefore astrology was the chief science; it enabled the Maya to count millions of years into the past as well as the future. Many Maya temples had specific astronomical functions. Edzna is the oldest lunar observatory in the Western Hemisphere because it is the only place where the sun would rise directly overhead on the Maya New Year. Eventually, precise calendars dictated religious ceremonies. The passage of time occurred in cycles which necessitated the appropriate festival.

Maya priests took careful note of the sky, using their observations to develop one of the world's most sophisticated calendars. Their solar calendar had 18 months, each of which comprised 20 days. Five left over days also occurred. Each month possessed deities who influenced people and events. But the true function of the solar calendar served agriculture as well as religion. The precise calendar predicted full moons for sailors. The other important calendar was a ritual almanac consisting of a 260-day cycle. The ritual calendar scheduled ceremonies; each day had a number between 1 and 13. Each day also had a set of 20 names associated with a god; both the number and the god's name defined a cycle. The combination of the solar and ritual calendars allowed names in each calendar to reappear together every 52 years. The famous long count, a seriously measured accumulation of years, led to cyclical infinity. The astrologers eventually calculated that Venus required 584 days to revolve. Today's figure is 583.90 days.

The Maya road system was the best in the hemisphere until the completion of the Lancaster Turnpike in 1792. The Maya built elaborate roads in order to facilitate trade as well as travel to religious sites. The broad, level paved roads sometimes had causeways at least 50 feet wide. The roads connected all inland cities. Excellent roads supplemented human carriers who hauled everything on their backs—no large beasts of burden existed.

Writing and mathematics coordinated trade, science, and religion. The Maya were the only indigenous group to develop a sophisticated writing system. Like the Chinese and Egyptians, the Maya had no alphabet. Only recently did scholars realize that Maya writing is basically phonetic—pictures represent sounds or syllables instead of meanings. Some items are pictographic or ideographic (representing ideas instead of syllables), but the writing could also be logographic, indicating words. The Maya system is confusing because instead of using a single form of writing, the Maya used dozens of applications in whatever fashion the individual writer chose.

The Maya published many books as part of their concern to maintain historical events. After perfecting the use of paper, the Maya wrote books known as a codex for over 800 years, far more than any other indigenous group. Unfortunately, only a few of these writings survived the Spanish invasion. Nevertheless, the Maya recorded their history on monuments or in songs and in verses, normally discussing the birth of a god or a king's accession. Concerned with what the past's impact would have upon the future, the Maya recorded early events, current experiences, and prophesies. Entire communities listened to readings of their books and participated in the revisions in order to provide newly reasoned goals. Such a unique intellectual outlook enabled communities to debate their future while they discussed their history.

Although inferior to the Arab mathematical system, Maya arithmetic far surpassed the clumsier Greek, Egyptian, and Roman methods. Within the highly rational Maya computation, a dot equaled one and a bar equaled five. Thus $\underset{=\!=\!=}{\bullet\,\bullet}$ equals 17 and combined forms provide larger totals. The Maya also discovered zero, which enabled them to produce astronomical calculations almost impossible for the Eastern world to duplicate.

Decline of the Maya. The Classic Maya culture fell a millennium ago and scholars remain unsure in deciding why this descent occurred. Single-case theories do not present a realistic view of how the Maya disintegrated; but they highlight Maya problems which existed by the eighth century.

Overpopulation and food shortages certainly contributed to the end of the Maya civilization. Soil erosion and loss of water were critical factors. Evidence of overpopulation and ecological stress come from population estimates and anthropological studies. Skeletal remains suggest that malnutrition appeared as the Classic period ended. An overburdened and fragile agricultural system could not hold up, particularly when an excessive number of farmers continued to employ slash-and-burn techniques. Clearly the intrusion of militarized societies, such as the Toltecs, also disrupted the Maya because the somewhat more secular outsiders demanded more sacrifices. A form of total warfare began to destroy cities and kill civilians, somewhat as in World War II. The disruption of long-distance trade may have isolat-

ed the southern lowland Maya. The cost of providing more defense weakened monarchies to some extent. And it is possible that natural disaster struck, mass starvation occurred, or disease appeared on a large scale. A violent peasant revolt can be considered the possible response to agricultural failure, excessive taxes, or disillusion with rulers. Whatever the causes, there is no question that the highlands decayed first and general decline took place by A.D. 800. The Maya abandoned the civic core of most southern cities by the tenth century.

THE AZTEC HEGEMONY

The Aztecs developed from nomads into the builders of a great as well as complex civilization. In less than 200 years, they emerged from aggressive warriors into a highly organized society. By 1519, the Aztec empire stretched from the Gulf of Mexico to the Pacific coast and from the Isthmus of Tehuantepec north to the Panuco River.

Origins and Expansion. The Aztecs became an amalgamation of several groups who shared the Nahuatl language. The Aztecs used the term Nahua for all those who spoke the empire's official language. Like the Christian conquerors of Iberia, who emphasized continuity with the Visigothic crown, the Aztecs created a legend of their origins in Aztlán, an appropriately vague place, in order to integrate the many tribes within their system. Aztlán is probably one of the northern provinces of the Toltec empire.

Chichimecas were the source of Aztec life. Tough, resourceful huntergatherers, the Chichimecas foraged for roots and vegetables or ate raw meat, human or animal. Attracted by the fertile land and abundant game of Tula, the Aztecs began migrating into the Toltec capital by about A.D. 1168. Constant intertribal warfare involved women who fought as individuals with males and participated in all-female units.

Although the Toltec empire lay in ruins when the Aztecs arrived, Toltec accomplishments generated basic characteristics which became merged into Aztec civilization. The Aztecs admired the grand architecture and military organization of the Toltecs as well as innovations in hydraulic agriculture, achievements in astronomy, and the establishment of a tribute system. At this point, the Aztecs allied with the Otomi, an old but less developed group whom the Toltecs considered ignorant.

Struggling to survive as mercenaries and bodyguards, the Aztecs moved into the Valley of Mexico in 1253 near Chapultepec. After seeing an eagle with a serpent in its beak while perched on a cactus, the Aztecs decided to take up permanent residence. This legendary symbol became the modern national emblem that appears on official seals as well as the national flag. By now a heterogeneous group that included Chinampecs, Toltecs, and Mexitin, the Aztec nation became quite pluralistic. But their new neighbors despised and distrusted them, often accusing the Aztecs of coveting local wives. Defeated in several encounters, the Aztecs moved onto a swampy islet in Lake Texcoco and established Tenochtitlán in 1325. They then became known as the Mexica. Apparently *azteca* referred to an interethnic communal relationship. Aztec is still the term used to designate their entity.

The organizational structure inherited from the Toltecs coalesced with warlike Chichimeca instincts to form a cohesive kinship system. The *calpulli* predated Aztec contact with the Toltecs, but became crucial to the development of Mexican society. Related by kinship ties and connected to chiefs whom they elected, *calpulli* groups of families possessed hierarchical structure that endured for centuries. Acamápichtli became the first Aztec ruler of prominence by emphasizing the Toltec origins of the royal dynasty. His Toltec mother presided as a princess of the realm. More importantly, Acamápichtli enhanced his power by marrying the daughters of all the *calpulli* chiefs. A triple alliance with the cities of Texcoco and Tlacopan became the foundation for an Aztec hegemony. By 1434, the Aztecs created a single government for the entire Lake Texcoco area. The Aztecs became the most powerful entity in Mesoamerica when Motecuhzoma I, beginning in the 1440s, raised Tenochtitlán to a position of power in many regions. General Tlacaélel extended Aztec military victories thereafter.

Experts in war and administration, the Aztecs closely resembled the Romans and Incas. Envoys usually offered "friendship treaties" whereby war god Huitzilopochtli would be admitted to rival temples even though locals could maintain their other gods, customs, and rulers. After constructing loose local alliances, the Aztecs built an empire that was actually a mosaic of 28 cities. Yet all citizens understood that their primary duty was service to the state. Once they trained their boys for war, the Aztecs became the superior military group. The Aztecs could amass a large army on short notice. Never a true dominion, the Aztec hegemony retained local leadership in conquered states. The search for a broad expanse of tribute areas ruled out direct territorial control. The Aztecs learned to generate resources from the broadest possible base at minimal cost to themselves. In general, the Aztecs influenced a limited range of subordinates' activities until the 1440s when Aztec emperors replaced local leadership after various conquests. Women could no longer be warriors after the Aztecs dethroned the ancient Earth Mother (war goddess) and introduced a male-dominated society. Like the Romans, the Aztecs maintained their empire through political control rather than military occupation. Both empires emphasized internal security by co-opting local rulers. The early Aztecs adapted their imperial system uniquely to the geographical and regional realities of Mexico.

Aztec administration succeeded in Tenochtitlán and throughout the empire. Judges had to be impartial and underwent careful scrutiny. There seems to have been very little corruption among public officials; future Mexicans would ascribe public malfeasance to Spaniards. Crime barely existed. Homes had no locks because the authorities acted swiftly but severely. Those guilty of drunkenness, rape, and homosexuality received death sentences.

Most important was the emperor. Elected by nobles in the early period, Aztec rulers had many tasks. The emperor led armies in the field, interpreted the law as supreme judge, and directed administration. Everyone expected the monarch to have speaking ability, set an example of self-control, and maintain respect for the collective welfare. The emperor bonded his subjects together by means of trade, intermarriage, and a common language.

Society. At the center of Aztec society was its magnificent capital, Tenochtitlán; soon the fifth largest city in the world. Its 200,000 people spread over five miles in a process of controlled growth. The huge tax revenues and tribute which poured in attracted a large influx of skilled laborers and artisans. By 1521, the *calpullis* increased to 20 when the city defined eight districts. Three wide causeways connected this island metropolis to Lake Texcoco's shoreline. It was an active, interesting, and beautiful city. The massive Tlatelolco market serviced about 20,000 people daily and 60,000 on market day. A theater, lordly homes, and impressive public buildings sparkled in their whitewash splendor. A thousand employees swept Tenochtitlán clean daily. An aqueduct provided clean drinking water and numerous fountains for bathing. Small latrines constructed over canoes collected human excrement which enriched agricultural productivity.

As asthetics, the Aztecs believed beauty to be pervasive; it was central to artistic expression. Magnificent stone sculptures, gardens, and flowers made everyday life attractive. Public buildings represented artistic splendor. The lovely jewelry sold in the streets centuries later is based upon ancient forms. Aztec painting reflects an art of tremendous spirituality with a dark yet potent power.

Preimperial Aztec society comprised farmers, fishermen, merchants, and warriors who were relatively evenly balanced until tribute wealth enabled the military to dominate. Moreover, the conquest of enemies always resulted in land distributed to the *calpulli* chiefs. The nobility devel-

oped from a warrior class. Gradually, the majority of the ruling class became nobles. Early Aztec society prided itself upon a meritocracy that bestowed power and privileges upon the upper class. The nobles fulfilled many duties. They collected taxes, supervised the collective labor projects, and distributed nonagricultural employment to those in need of work. Closely related were the approximately 5,000 priests, virtually all of whom came from the nobility. Often dressed in black robes as well as hoods ornamented with skulls and entrails, the priests were a vital component of education and public ceremonies. They guided scientific and intellectual endeavors skillfully. Prolonged fasting, constant vigils, and continual laceration of their bodies sharpened their loyalties to the Aztec nation.

Partially because the military provided a source of upward mobility, social distinctions evolved into a class system with hereditary privileges. Farmers comprised the majority; but commoners could increase their status by becoming warriors. The empire demanded great services from the ambitious. Moreover, the state expected a bare minimum of devotion to duty. Fathers could put their sons to death if they considered their offspring reluctant to fight in war. All citizens adhered to a strict moral code regardless of class.

Compulsory education fulfilled imperial as well as social needs. The nobles used full-time *calmecac* boarding schools, which became necessary for most nonmilitary positions in Aztec administration. Priests staffed the *calmecacs* in order to inculcate the rigorous ethical system. Here strict discipline, duty, and the broader features of Aztec knowledge received attention. Exceptional commoners gained admission as part of the Aztec policy of co-opting bright males. Commoners attended *telpochalli* schools for males and *ichpocacalli* schools for females within their *calpulli*. Students in these schools went home regularly, mainly to assist parents with harvests. The *telpochalli* emphasized citizenship, history, art, and weaponry. The females learned childraising and household skills. At both levels of schooling, youths studied until the age of 20 unless military service took the males.

Women had benign attitudes but tremendous personal status as the crucibles for human regeneration within the cosmic Aztec ideology. Most women aspired toward marriage. Marriage was a social role rather than a sacred bond; but giving birth and breast-feeding paralleled the spectacles of sacrifice in terms of the regenerative forces deep within Aztec beliefs. Marriage brokers, usually older women, arranged marriages by following *calpulli* customs such as making certain that each partner came from a different clan. Unlike Spain, divorce existed and women could initiate separation because of beatings or a spouse's inability to provide for his family. On the other hand, males viewed women suspiciously, in part because of their conviction that sexual relations had to be controlled in order to preserve the hierarchy. Therefore women generally became isolated behind domestic boundaries. Few women held public office although some served as priestesses. Other females, particularly widows, worked as healers, traders, midwives, and matchmakers.

The excellent Aztec medical service became closely related to religion. Like other Mesoamericans, the Aztecs believed that the human body linked itself to the universe. Therefore bodily functions affected cosmic events. Aztec society always assumed that the stability of the universe depended upon proper human activity. The Aztec state responded intelligently to the need for health facilities. After Motecuhzoma I established botanical gardens, the Aztecs had the capacity for precise clinical diagnosis and prognosis. The gardens stimulated medical research. The Aztecs utilized 1,500 plants for herbal remedies. Patients received free plants with the understanding that they report the results back to the researchers. Physicians experimented with various plants so that an accurate botanical and zoological taxonomy resulted.

The Aztecs innovated several medical procedures. Physicians excelled in the use of traction as well as splints. Mexican doctors often treated disabled Spaniards during the early invasion period because of Aztec superiority in treating wounds. With obsidian blades, physicians performed cosmetic surgery on noses, lips, and other areas. Brain surgery was available, but the treatment of bone injuries became the most advanced form of surgery. Polishing teeth and scraping tartar were significant dental accomplishments. Another area of outstanding medical procedures was obstetrics. The use of midwives, a high state of sanitation, and encouragement of the squatting position to induce birth proved highly effective.

The well-balanced Aztec diet surpassed what modern Mexicans ate in the twentieth century. Maize, beans, squash, and peppers nourished society for centuries. Lake algae, high in protein and amino acids, became an excellent addition. People also enjoyed hairless dogs, snakes, insects, grains, vegetables, and wild game. In general, Mexico suffered less from organic and infectious diseases than Europe. Influenza and rheumatism were problems in Mexico. Halucinogenic treatments cured some ailments, but the widespread use of soap and deodorants attest to the higher level of hygiene in Mexico than virtually the entire world.

Economic Forces. A well-diversified economy converted the Valley of Mexico into a symbiotic region, based on regional tribute obligations and economic interdependence. Highly productive agriculture became the foundation. Some well-managed *chinampas* produced seven crops a year. The interplanting of corn and beans proved to be a fine technique. In 1450 the *chinampas* became part of a massive public works program established in response to devastating droughts and frosts. Dams, dikes, irrigation, and terracing also evolved. At least 50 percent of the cultivable land became irrigated. The empire divided cultivated areas into (1) communal lands, (2) land belonging to the nobility, and (3) state land.

Land use underwent many changes. In the Valley of Mexico and Tula, at least half the population depended upon *calpulli* relations. *Calpulli* land decreased in the periphery because military conquests resulted in awards and booty. Imperial desires to appease the nobility of newly conquered groups usually overrode common needs. This manifested the state's typical desire to maintain land ownership and manage it directly. Because of heavy casualties among the warriors, new nobles had to be recruited and given land in state-controlled areas. Commoners who distinguished themselves in battle not only received noble title but also, fairly often, land with usufruct status. These *cuauhpipiltín*, as they were termed, virtually became a separate class. Although no private ownership of land existed in theory, a growing scarcity of land and the rise in population led to smaller plots used for collective needs. Polygamy among the upper class led to overpowering demands for land because of the rapidly expanding number of young nobles demanding property. As primogeniture restricted land ownership, those who remained, noble or common, fell into *mayequé* status, thus working the land as sharecroppers. The *mayequé* comprised 30 percent of central Mexico's population by 1519. The conquest of new areas forced non-Aztec farmers to work the land as tenant farmers or servants. In addition to labor requirements on state land or the property of nobles, administrative centers used forced labor as well.

Slavery was the lowest form of labor. *Tlachotin* (slaves) could be resold without their consent but could at least contract themselves as laborers and servants. Slaves, who gradually amounted to 5 percent of the empire, lived unpleasant lives. Nevertheless, slaves could purchase land, save money, own homes, and even acquire their own slaves. Those who failed to repay debts or who sold themselves, which assured food and clothing, often became slaves. Judges could sentence criminals to toil as slaves.

Industries were an important feature of the early economy. Well-paid artisans known as *amanteca* maintained fine guilds. Goldsmiths, jewelers, feather workers, and weavers acquired great distinction. Membership in the artisan or merchant guilds appears to have been based upon heredity. But promotion to the upper rungs of the guilds depended upon individual effort, accomplishment, and education, similar to most positions within the Aztec meritocracy.

Pochteca merchants became the most prominent vocational group. Excluded from high-ranking administrative and political positions, the *pochteca* nevertheless assumed great responsibilities. The state expected the merchants to enter neutral or even hostile areas first, which often led to war. The pochteca traded in Central America, normally offering medicinal herbs, dyes, and industrial goods such as gold, cotton, and cacao beans. Eager to acquire the status of nobles, apprentice merchants provided expensive offerings to gods as well as banquets for their peers. Some of these ceremonies required flesh-eating functions where the most ambitious merchants sacrificed slaves during banquets.

Aztec merchants deserve some of the credit for a reorganized and autonomous system of markets which integrated the empire. Well-maintained rest homes and shrines provided havens for road travelers. *Tlamemes*, the workers who carried merchandise on their backs, became the primary road commuters over the long distances to Oaxaca, Tehuantepec, and the Pacific coast. The *tlamemes* became a separate, hereditary occupational group. As the empire expanded, the ranks of *tlamemes* increased to include those dispossessed by conquest. Runners carried messages, news, and small cargo rapidly in relays from stations 2.6 miles apart, often traveling 13 miles in one hour. Coastal tribes handled sea trade in canoes. Hewn from single trees and propelled by oars or poles, the Aztec dugouts did not have sails. Nevertheless, an extensive system of canoe transport enabled the efficient transport of foodstuffs with the result that the Aztecs supported a large population in a relatively small area.

Tribute and taxes fueled the Aztec hegemony. Most tribute items collected as foodstuffs remained in warehouses. Like the Incas, the Aztecs stored food in case of poor harvests for use by the army and government and as gifts to favored groups. The government distributed gold, cotton, and precious stones to artisans for processing into industrial goods exported by merchants. Tribute hit commoners the hardest because labor formed the basis of most tribute payments, especially on the hydraulic system. Conquered regions also provided warriors for imperial campaigns. Taxes increased the prosperity of the empire greatly. Taxes on farm produce, market transactions, and the use of physical labor as a form of tax payment amounted to enormous assets. The regime spread most tax revenues throughout the empire rather than only supporting the needs of Tenochtitlán.

Religion. Religion and government bonded themselves tightly, as in contemporary states throughout the world. The heterogeneous, dynamic nature of Aztec society resulted in an ever-changing religion. The preservation of a well-balanced cosmic system was a basic premise of Aztec life. The Aztecs raised solidarity with the universe to a degree unmatched by other civilizations. The Aztecs were atavistic in their desire to satisfy their gods, but religion became the weakest feature of the Aztec hegemony.

Despondency and fatalism gradually characterized Aztec religion. The somewhat hopeful tendencies became muted. Overall, a negative religious atmosphere prevailed. Graves remained unmarked because death destroyed everything, including the soul. People gave little thought to the future because the gods had unpredictable characteristics of destruction and creation. Most considered divine punishment a major source of ailments and associated cures for certain diseases with particular deities. A particularly ominous conviction maintained that the world had already been destroyed four times earlier. Everyone assumed that the final destruction of the fifth sun would occur in the not-distant future.

Aztec religion did not have the vitality of contemporary beliefs. It shared with Islam the concept of self-sacrifice for future generations, sin, a lost paradise, and predestination. But unlike Islam, Aztec religion lacked a comprehensive concept of social justice and true egalitarianism. The major difference between Christianity and Aztec religion is that Christ's blood sacrifice became a benevolent gift from a kind god while the

Aztec gods demanded blood for the sun. Hindu and Buddhist beliefs projected a strident humanism within an optimistic ethical framework.

The most significant Aztec gods associated themselves with earlier cosmic systems. During the first sun, Tezcatlipoca assumed powerful proportions. This god corresponds to Jupiter and Lucifer in Western culture. Tezcatlipoca dominated early Aztec life because he created the first sun as well as war. He practiced black magic and most feared that he would eventually plunge the world into permanent nightfall. Tezcatlipoca was aggressive but capable of forgiveness despite horrid acts attributed to him.

The second sun was the pleasant period of Quetzalcoatl. Quetzalcoatl was a former Toltec leader who underwent transfiguration as the god of kindliness, holiness, and beauty. The only god humane enough to be idealized with a mortal body, Quetzalcoatl had fair skin and a beard. Quetzalcoatl was also a morning star and lord of wealth. Aztec society rejoiced in rituals which maintained that he would reclaim his imperial power.

Ominous events followed in Aztec lore. Tlaloc presided over the third sun because he was the rain god. The agricultural cycle obviously required a central deity and the Aztecs placed Tlaloc into their pantheon in order to validate Mexica dominance within the Aztec coalition. Tlaloc's female counterpart created the fourth sun, but Huitzilopochtli actually directed it. Huitzilopochtli was the sun god and god of war, the primary Aztec deity. Huitzilopotchli was the transfiguration of Tezcatlipoca, who had taught the necessity of sacrifice.

The rationalization for sacrifice was that various gods had created humans with their own blood and sacrificed themselves to maintain the fifth sun, which Huitzilopotchli gradually controlled outright. Therefore society assumed the responsibility to provide blood in order to feed the sun since the earth swallowed the sun each day. The Aztecs interpreted the daily drama of the rising and setting of the sun in terms of Huitzilopotchli's struggle to defeat darkness. As in Roman spectacles, many of the victims were condemned criminals and prisoners of war, although sacrifices may also have been a method for unhappy people to gain eternal life. Sacrifices normally took place at the temple of the appropriate god.

Extracting hearts became the key step. The flint knife itself became a god. Cannibalism existed, but priests normally burned women and children intact rather than have them eaten afterwards. Sacrifice and cannibalism usually occurred at harvest time; famine did not motivate these essentially religious untertakings. Never a truly vicious group, the Aztecs were horrified by torture. Professional musicians performed during sacrifices and other religious ceremonies.

Flower wars took place mainly in order to take prisoners of war who could be sacrificed. The flower wars consisted of battles designed to furnish worthy victims when ordinary methods of tribute collection failed. These ceremonial en-

Human sacrifice was practiced by the Aztecs to pay tribute to the gods. *Culver Pictures, Inc.*

gagements resulted in an invitation to actual combat; the participants set the time and location, often exchanging weapons in the process. Volunteers generally took part because any warrior taking a prisoner enhanced his career. Although the flower wars enabled the Aztecs to distract strong opponents while their army campaigned elsewhere, constant Aztec victories increased enmity with rivals as well as those who had been previously conquered.

Pessimism pervaded the twilight of the Aztec period because of an increasingly uncertain future. Unable to conquer the Tlaxcalans and Tarascans, the Aztecs increasingly relied upon the flower wars for a new supply of sacrifical victims. A key event occurred in 1487 when Motecuhzoma II decided to sacrifice 30,000 people to honor Tlaloc and Huitzilopochtli's new pyramid in Tenochtitlán. Constructed in seven major stages over the course of 200 years, the *templo mayor* was the center of state-sponsored religion and re-created the triumphs of Huitzilopochtli over his rivals. The *templo mayor* also glorified imperial expansion and sought to obtain plentiful harvests. Dated plaques for the *templo mayor* commemorate the onset of solar cycles as if to equate the ascendancy of the Aztecs with the sun's appearance.

Aztec religion was a cosmic endeavor. Drugs enabled the individual to gain entrance to the magical concept that each person is associated with animal counterparts that accompany each individual destiny. Most people, however, expected to live in a dreary underworld after death. The Aztecs did not believe that their lives or their deaths were really theirs. Space and time were bound together to form an inseparable whole. Religion and destiny ruled their lives, and they spent much of their time investigating the uncertain will of the gods. Only the gods were free, and only they had the power to choose. The possibility of a degree of happiness depended upon the sign under which one was born. The sign would decide one's death and afterlife. Therefore astrological influences determined occupations. Even the state of the universe affected one's body.

The concept of an all-encompassing, eternal chronology superceded everything. Even the gods subordinated themselves to time. After observing the sun and the stars, the Aztecs based such predestination upon their calendar system. The *tonalpoalli* was a 260-day ritual calendar with a particular sign, number, and deity for each day. The total number of days came about by multiplying 20 times 13, the 20 sacred numbers and the 13 levels of the supernatural. The *xiuhpoalli* solar calendar contained 365 days, consisting of 18 intervals of 20 days plus 5 "unlucky" days. A bundle or reed event occurred every 52 years when the beginning of the natural and sacred years coincided. Twenty-day cycles had less importance; on these occasions, the nobles and masses participated in feasts held 18 times each year. Calendar rituals therefore cemented internal as well as external groups together at Tenochtitlán. The elaborate temple dedications specified the exact role each calpulli would assume. The counting of years in each region varied because the solar year did not begin on the same date everywhere.

Aztec religion was even more complex than the society which it dominated. But religion became a liability by the end of the fifteenth century. Fear of natural forces with an elaborate polytheism resulted in the creation of explanations so elaborate that they became convoluted and demonic.

By 1519, Mexico featured the rise and fall of great civilizations that often combined distinctive features. Pre-Columbian traits of material culture in the form of home construction, furnishings, cookery, diet, and clothing would persist into the late twentieth century. Ancient languages, birth customs, and religious features would not disappear in rural Mexico. The Maya achieved a high level of philosophical and spiritual development in addition to their skills in communication and art. The pre-Hispanic era in Mexican history is the one where scientific achievements stand out more than in any other period. The Aztecs combined administrative and technological skills to allow their citizens to enjoy high levels of diet, medicine, and artistic skills. The Aztecs empha-

sized ideology to a greater degree than people in other parts of the world. As the Aztecs attempted to bridge the gap between the cosmos and daily life, religion assumed a primordial function. Ideology would remain vital in Mexico well into the modern period. Finally, Mexican influence throughout Mesoamerica would never again equal the ancient period.

SUGGESTED READING

Aveni, Anthony F. *Skywatchers of Ancient Mexico.* Austin: University of Texas Press, 1980.

Berdan, Frances F. *The Aztecs of Central Mexico: An Imperial Society.* New York: Holt, Rhinehart, and Winston, 1982.

Bernal, Ignacio. *Mexico Before Cortéz: Art, History, and Legend.* Garden City, NY: Doubleday and Company, 1975.

———. *The Olmec World.* Berkeley: University of California Press, 1969.

———. *Literaturas indígenas de Mexico.* Madrid: Editorial Mapfre, 1991.

Bray, Warwick, Ian Farrington, and Earl H. Swanson. *The Ancient Americas.* New York: Peter Bedrick, 1989.

Broda, Johanna, David Carrasco, and Edward Matos. *The Great Temple of Tenochitlán: Center and Periphery in the Aztec World.* Berkeley: University of California Press, 1988.

Brundage, Burr Cartwright. *A Rain of Darts: The Mexican Aztecs.* Austin: University of Texas Press, 1972.

———. *The Fifth Sun.* Austin: University of Texas Press, 1979.

Carrasco, David. *Religions of Mesoamerica. Cosmovision and Ceremonial Centers.* Prospect Heights, Il: Waveland Press, 1998.

Clendinnen, Inga S. *Aztecs: An Interpretation.* New York: Cambridge University Press, 1991.

Coe, Michael. *The Maya,* 4th ed. London: Thomas and Hudson, 1987.

Coe, Michael, and Richard Diehl. *In the Land of the Olmecs.* Austin: University of Texas Press, 1981.

Conrad, Geoffrey W., and Arthur Demarest. *Religion and Empire: The Dynamics of Aztec and Inca Expansionism.* Cambridge, UK: Cambridge University Press, 1984.

Culbert, T. Patrick. *The Classical Maya Collapse*. Albuquerque: University of New Mexico Press, 1973.

Davies, Nigel. *The Aztec Empire—The Toltec Resurgence*. Norman: University of Oklahoma Press, 1987.

———. *The Toltecs: Until the Fall of Tula*. Norman: University of Oklahoma Press, 1977.

Gillespie, Susan. *The Aztec Kings: The Construction of Rulership in Mexica History*. Tucson: University of Arizona Press, 1990.

Grove, David C. "Altars and Myths." *Archaeology* 26 (April 1973).

Guerra, Francisco. *The Pre-Columbian Mind*. New York: Seminar Press, 1971.

Hammond, Norman. *Ancient Maya Civilization*. New Brunswick, NJ: Rutgers University Press, 1982.

Hassig, Ross. *Aztec Warfare: Imperial Expansion and Political Warfare*. Norman: University of Oklahoma Press, 1988.

———. *Trade, Tribute, and Transportation: The Sixteenth Century Political Economy of the Valley of Mexico*. Norman: University of Oklahoma Press, 1985.

Henderson, John S. *The World of the Ancient Maya*. Ithaca, NY: Cornell University Press, 1981.

Henke Breuer, Kimberly. "'Which comes down to us from ancient times.' The Conception of Space and Maya Self-Identity in Early Colonial Yucatan, 1540-1650." Paper present at the Social Science History Association in Fort Worth, Nov. 13, 1999.

Luckert, Karl W. *Olmec Religion*. Norman: University of Oklahoma Press, 1976.

McAnany, Patricia. *Living with the Ancestors: Kinship in Ancient Maya Society*. Austin: University of Texas Press, 1995.

Ortiz de Montellano, Bernard. *Aztec Medicine, Health, and Nutrition*. New Brunswick, NJ: Rutgers University Press, 1990.

Schele, Linda, and David Freidel. *A Forest of Kings: The Untold Story of the Ancient Maya*. New York: William Morrow, 1990.

Sharer, Robert J. and David C. Grove. *Regional Perspectives on the Olmec*. New York: Cambridge University Press, 1989.

Soustelle, Jacques. *The Daily Life of the Aztecs on the Eve of the Spanish Conquest*. Stanford, CA: Stanford University Press, 1970.

Tedlock, Barbara. *Time and the Highland Maya*. Albuquerque: University of New Mexico Press, 1981.

Thompson, J. Eric. *Maya History and Religion*. Norman: University of Oklahoma Press, 1970.

Van Zantwijk, Rudolph. *The Aztec Arrangement: The Social History of Pre-Spanish Mexico*. Norman: University of Oklahoma Press, 1985.

Von Hagen, Victor. *The Aztec: Man and Tribe*. New York: Mentor Books, 1961.

2

The Spanish Invasion, 1519–1598

The Spanish assault upon Mexico reduced most indigenous societies to scattered vestiges of their former glory in less than 30 years. More than any other European power, Spain possessed unique qualities and experiences which enabled its conquerors to defeat the Aztec empire. Spain's medieval legacy of cultural splendor and constant warfare proved unsurmountable when the Aztec leadership hesitated and Mexican subject states became seduced by the Spanish conquerors. Soon an impressive imperial apparatus of administrators began reshaping Mexico into a colonial appendage of its Iberian masters. The Spanish invasion did not conquer Mexico completely but instead resulted in a European hegemony that changed Mexico considerably.

THE IBERIAN BACKGROUND

Ancient Iberia. The first people in Iberia bestowed upon it an unmistakable military legacy. After the appearance of Cro-Magnon peoples at about 35,000 B.C., the chisel enabled Iberians to become great hunters. Although fishing, herding, and growing crops characterized the coastal areas after the Stone Age ended, ancient writers exalted Iberians for their ability in war, particularly guerrilla tactics. Iberians won fame as cavalry, since

horses abounded on the peninsula. Mounted warriors became so skillful that their horses could kneel upon command.

Celts entered Iberia through the Pyrenees in the eighth and ninth centuries B.C. They introduced iron metallurgy and cremated bodies for burial. Both groups began to merge during the next 300 years as organized religion gradually became accepted, alphabetical languages appeared, and village life spread. Tribal organizations prevailed, but minor kings began to control various monarchies in southern regions, often on a semi-democratic basis. Mining and textiles became major industries.

Tin, copper, and silver soon attracted eastern traders. In 1100 B.C., Phoenicians established Cádiz and Málaga and thus forged commercial and cultural contacts that made a deep impression on eastern Mediterranean ports. Some scholars credit the Phoenicians with initiating the first bull fights. More importantly, the ports connected Iberia with international trade permanently. Greeks came to Murcia about 800 B.C. and established themselves in the Barcelona area. The iron ore mined in Catalonia became known for producing high-quality weapons. The Greek historian Polybius formally gave the name Iberia to the entire peninsula. Not surprisingly, the Greeks introduced the tradition of city-states. Essentially trading posts, the Greek settlements clung to the coast line. From there, Greek settlers introduced wine-producing techniques with imported vines. Iberians cherished Greek pottery for its beauty and symmetry. Moreover, the mathematical works of Pythagoras and Homerian epics provided important contributions to Iberian culture.

Carthaginians arrived shortly after the Greeks. With Roman sanction, they began to dominate southern Spain. Eager for Iberian resources and manpower, the Carthaginians founded Spania, a powerful kingdom which became exploited directly by foreigners for the first time. The Second Punic War, however, resulted in the permanent defeat of Carthage and the rise of Rome.

Roman Hispania. Economic considerations motivated Rome to incorporate what they called Hispania into their empire. Foodstuffs and ores paid for the cost of invading legions. An important aspect of Roman rule was the increase of Spanish mining technology. Silver became the most important Roman product from Spain. The Romans introduced to Hispania the concept of deep shaft mines dug by workers with 150-pound iron rods into the mountains. Direct state exploitation of mines became the rule; Rome maintained that the country's subsoil wealth belonged to the state.

Rome's success in colonizing Spain was symbolized by the steady appearance of cities. Here the Hispanic city dwellers worked with Roman educators, judges, and bureaucrats to incorporate Spain into the Mediterranean world. Great roads, incredible bridges, and aqueducts bringing fresh water spurred the growth of cities along the Spanish coastlines. More loyal Hispanics sought Roman citizenship because Romans did not have to pay taxes during difficult times.

In general, Roman administration became efficient by the time Augustus emphasized rule by law. A 5 percent inheritance tax helped reduce the gap between rich and poor. The Romans dug the first sewage systems. Formerly fierce Iberians gradually entered the cities once the magnificent roads enabled farmers and shepherds to prosper.

Schools in Hispania enabled many of Rome's greatest literary figures to emerge from Iberia, such as Seneca the younger and Quintilian, allegedly the first teacher publicly paid in Europe. Trajan and Hadrian, two great Roman emperors, had Hispanic backgrounds as did Theodosius and Magnus Maximus.

Christianity represents the great religious triumph of the late empire. Spaniards believed that St. James preached the gospel in Iberia—hence they established Santiago de Compostela because Christians considered James the brother of Christ. Others claimed that St. Paul also preached in Spain. Although usually limited to urban areas, Christianity spread rapidly in the second and third centuries. Despite periodic persecutions, nearly all Spaniards embraced Christianity when Emperor Constantine officially recognized the new doctrine. The Hispanic church had distinctive rites by the fifth century with bishops in the provincial cities. Most Spaniards in the periphery now spoke Latin although this trend took place slowly in the central, agricultural zone. Wheat, wine, and olive oil flowed back to Rome from large landed estates known as latifundia.

The appearance of latifundia agriculture heralded the decay of Roman rule. As Rome declined, small farmers toiled to pay heavier taxes while inflation handicapped their standard of living. Jews experienced persecution as the long period of peace and prosperity ended. The collapse of Roman rule resulted in large groups of Germanic tribes moving into Hispania through the Pyrenees by A.D. 409.

The Visigoths emerged as the dominant rulers of early medieval Spain and established several characteristics of Hispanic culture that would reappear in Mexico a few centuries later. Faced with strong regional and ethnic differences within Iberia that not even the Romans could eliminate, the Visigoths relied upon regional dukes and heads of smaller districts known as counts to administer Iberian villages. As a pastoral people, Visigoths had little interest in the Hispanic cities and withdrew into landed estates. The Christian church became the only unifying link between the masses and its rulers once the monarchy accepted orthodox Christianity. Establishing a central capital at Toledo reinforced the monarchy. The upper class collaborated with the Visigoths and, not by coincidence, the church sanctified the kings with divine right rule. The other great Visigothic achievement was their legal system. The judges applied the law to everyone with the same weight and emphasized consistency in terms of punishment. Carefully prescribed rules covered all acts of the courts; moreover, the burden of proof fell upon the plaintiff. Women and children enjoyed unusual legal protection from disinheritance, rape, and forced marriages.

But the Visigoths created several weaknesses. The warrior aristocracy could never amalgamate itself to the urban Hispanic elite. Peasant revolts broke out against high levels of taxation, which often reached levels of 70 percent of the harvested crops. Savage attacks upon the Jewish minority evoke comparisons to Nazi policies. Jews had to pay special taxes, suffer travel restrictions, and undergo holiday surveillance. Sexual relations with non-Jews could result in scalping. Jewish refusal to convert to Christianity eventually led to their enslavement. Large and growing numbers of slaves accentuated the growing class differences within Visigothic society. Such social differences encouraged an intense local parochialism in early medieval Spain. Frequent dynastic changes, often by means of murder, ruled out an orderly transition from Roman rule.

Islamic Rule in Al-Andalus, 711–1031.
Muslim forces quickly overpowered the weakening Visigoth monarchs. A strong ideology of social justice enabled the fast-moving light cavalry of Arab forces to reach North Africa by early in the eighth century. After a short raid across the channel into Spain in 710, the Muslim commander Tariq decided that Iberia could be conquered. Tariq also took advantage of a Visigothic dynastic struggle. Dissidents led Tariq across the water and diverted reinforcements with the result that Berber mercenaries from North Africa defeated Visigothic forces. But like Hernán Cortés and Christopher Columbus later, Tariq was poorly rewarded by his master, the caliph of the Umayyad dynasty in Baghdad, with the result that Tariq died in obscurity.

The Islamic policy of toleration consolidated their rapid conquest. Lack of manpower meant that the Muslims had to be practical. Therefore those who accepted Islamic rule retained control over community affairs, churches, and land. In addition, Spanish villagers not only retained their land but also paid lower taxes to the Muslims than to the Visigoths. Jews also aided Muslim rulers, often being the first to open their city gates to Islamic armies. Since they brought no women, the Muslims married Spanish women and many Hispanic Catholics assumed the culture of their Muslim rulers. Within a few years, Islamic forces penetrated all the way to the Pyrenees.

Under various emirs and caliphs, Al Andalus (land of the Goths) surpassed the cosmopolitan centers of eastern Islam as well as all of Europe. Wealthier inhabitants enjoyed cooling systems, lighting mechanisms driven by mercury basins, and clockwork toys. Stimulated by Sudanese gold, the economy advanced consistently. Most importantly, Islamic toleration permitted a degree of cross-cultural fertilization unheard of elsewhere.

The Muslims utilized a concept of enlightened diversity to maintain social control. They began by rebuilding the Roman roads and cities. Córdoba became the greatest city in Europe by the early ninth century. One hundred thousand inhabitants enjoyed its rich bazaars, excellent schools, clean drinking water, and good health. Mosques, palaces, and literary contests attest to a high standard of living. Moreover, the court at Córdoba attracted merchants, musicians, sages, and poets from the east. Not surprisingly, it became the premier center for scholarship. Christians, Jews, and Muslims worked together in a variety of disciplines. Their collaboration in medicine, astronomy, and mathematics gave Christian Europe access to advanced concepts. In addition, the scholars reintroduced many classical Greek and Roman works to Europe. The Arabs preserved, for example, Ptolemy's astronomical findings.

This work later inspired Columbus; a miscalculation, however, led him to believe the earth smaller than it actually is, making his westward route to India believable.

Notable achievements accelerated economic change. In agriculture, the Muslims introduced such products as citrus fruits, rice, sugar cane, bananas, almonds, figs, and watermelons. Lower taxes resulted in surplus production of wheat by Hispanic sharecroppers. The Muslims also built an extensive irrigation system which became the best in the world, enabling Spain to produce silk, hemp, and wool. The arrival of mules also aided agriculture. At this time, Spain made great progress in industrial growth. Notable products later to appear in the New World were ceramics, textiles, leather goods, ivory work, perfumes, weapons, dyes, furniture, and crystal. The Toledo ironworks actually originated from Baghdad foundaries. The Muslims facilitated commerce by introducing modern coinage and a mint. Spain also possessed Europe's only paper factory. During the period of Muslim rule, trade never declined; commerce increased steadily. The flourishing economy resulted in much prosperity and little poverty.

Cultural vitality characterized this period. Great works of art and architecture with careful attention to an appreciation of nature appeared. The Islamic sensitivity to aesthetics enhanced this period. They loved water and therefore built fountains all over Spain. Windows placed in buildings gave the best possible view. Inns and public baths became comfortable as well as sensual delights. Scholars such as S. M. Imamuddin claim that nearly every Hispanic could read and write—unlike the rest of the Europeans. Rich, lusty poetry based on love themes became popular. The Muslims also introduced the guitar. Women enjoyed greater freedom in Spain than the rest of the Islamic world; they could manage property and administer offices on behalf of their sons. Great advances in surgery and medicine enriched society. The Muslims understood the use of herbs and conducted brain surgery. Hospitals nurtured many cities. Relations with Europe, Africa, and Con-

stantinople demonstrate that Spain became the most cosmopolitan part of Europe during the Middle Ages.

Wise administration and cultural magnificence could not produce political order forever. In the early eleventh century, smaller Islamic kingdoms broke away from the capital in Córdoba after a conference of local leaders held in 1031. Soon an age of toleration and pluralism gave way to hate and religious warfare. But before the Christian kingdoms were swept into the idea of crusades and conquest, Islamic Spain bestowed upon Hispanics a solid legacy of inquiry, industry, and intelligence.

The Christian Reconquista. In northern Spain, several Christian kingdoms developed Hispanic traditions during their reconquest (*reconquista*) of the peninsula which greatly affected their subsequent imperial control of Mexico. The crusade mentality entered from France, brought by Frankish Knights. It began when Basques in Asturias finally defeated Muslims at Covadunga in 922. The victory enabled the Asturian king to claim that he had inherited the Gothic throne. Religious fervor added to the expansion of Asturias. Although it is very unlikely that St. James or his disciples ever proselytized in Hispania, a bishop of the ambitious Asturian church announced the excavation of the saint's body in the early ninth century at a place in Galicia. Miracles took place at the shrine which drew pilgrims from all over Europe. Popular devotion to Santiago Matamoros (St. James the Moorslayer) originated in the *reconquista* and continued with the invasion of the Americas. In addition, large numbers of Christian immigrants from southern Spain as well as French settlers doubled the Asturian population.

Castile soon became the dominant Hispanic kingdom. It emerged as a frontier south of Asturias in north-central Spain. So many castles predominated that this no man's land became known as Castile. The Asturian kings created the Castilian nobility by awarding them land on which to build their fortifications in exchange for *fueros* (privileges) which exempted feudal lords from taxation. The multitude of free peasants created by the *reconquista* defended their rights and allied or submitted to nobles only after negotiations and an articulation of peasant rights as well as noble obligations to defend them from other aristocrats. Peasants working the lands of the nobility normally had few rights, but in frontier zones such as Castile, the use of *encomienda* provided protection from marauding warriors in return for village land coming under control of the nobility. As would be the case in the New World, hostile frontier regions resulted in the lower classes obtaining greater freedom. For Muslims communities, *encomienda* meant having to provide labor to Christian conquerors. Serfdom began to disappear by the twelfth century as villages received written *fueros* of self-government from the monarchs.

Military success finally enabled Castile to dominate Spain. With the use of heavy armor and double-edged swords, Castilian cavalry began to control the weaker Muslim kingdoms, exacting tribute in exchange for peace. The most famous Castilian knight was Rodrigo Díaz, better known as El Cid. El Cid became the national hero of Spain and the subject of the country's first national epic. A mercenary from modest origins, he rose to become wealthy and powerful as the ruler of the eastern seacoast city of Valencia, which he captured and ruled until his death in 1109. Warriors like El Cid received land grants as did monasteries and religious orders as the Muslims retreated south. Wealthy Catalonia also joined in the *reconquista* but the eventual triumph resulted largely from the efforts of Castilians. Castilians valued wealth as a result of conquest more than any other medieval entity. Adventurers and mercenaries who experienced military participation in the *reconquista* would again repeat these efforts as sixteenth-century conquistadors in Mexico.

Compelling medieval events continued to transform Hispanic life. A Muslim revolt in 1263 against harsh Christian policies resulted in the Muslims being driven out of the cities or into Granada, the last Muslim kingdom. The church, nobility, and crusading orders received most Muslim land. Because the Christians did not understand how to manage the complex irrigation system, Castile became a ranching society. A syndicate of sheepowners known as the *Mesta* acquired great power. The relative egalitarianism of Castile became codified into laws known as the Siete Partidas in 1265. This royal law outlined the rights of commoners and *fueros* of the aristocracy. It is also notable for harsh punishments. Thieves had their hands cut off, men could accuse women with adultery without furnishing testimony, and sodomizers were executed. Moreover, Europe's first medieval parliament convened in 1188; the Cortes enabled the three estates to consult with one another, present grievances to the king, ratify succession to the throne, and vote on taxes. Its fervent support for the church also unified Castile. Perhaps one church existed for every 100 inhabitants. Religious orders added to the prestige of Catholicism. Friars and monks preached social service, developed land, and directed new universities, but the church advocated tighter restrictions upon Jews and Muslims. Patriotism became associated with religion.

Fernando of Aragon and Isabella of Castile consciously created a sense of Spanish identity previously lacking in Hispania. Their 1469 marriage established a strong state. During their reign, traditionally Iberian regional loyalties became slowly transformed into a shared allegiance to the mystical notion of a greater Spanish homeland, a powerful monarchy, Christian universalism, and a sense of honor, xenophobia, and racial purity. This dual heritage of *patria chica* (region) and *patria grande* (nation state) became transmitted to Mexico during its initial exploration and invasion.

The sense of purpose that defined their marriage made Fernando and Isabella overwhelmingly popular. During a ten-year war against Granada, Isabella and Fernando shaped the government into an effective bureaucracy. *Corregidores* now exercised decisive influence over Spanish municipalities. Members of the nobility who defied royal officials could be mutilated. Trained in law and usually with previous military experience, *corregidores* indicated the rise of an intelligencia loyal to the crown. Rural police forces known as *hermandades* also enforced order. Created in the Middle Ages by towns and cities, the *hermandades* came under national control. Isabella destroyed many of the castles owned by the nobility and forced them to surrender land seized illegally. In return for *mayorazgo*, the privilege of the aristocracy to maintain ownership of its land, the nobility lost about half its wealth. In fact, the Council of Castile had nine middle-class *letrados* (educated degree holders) serving on the all-important body that acted on all matters. In essence, the monarchs used royal law to unite Spain. The Aztec policy of political control and religious piety shows similarities with the practices of the Catholic kings.

But unlike Motecuhzoma, Isabella became an extraordinary ruler whose uncompromising zeal, ambition, and purpose won the respect of her subjects. Simple and hard working, Isabella and her husband traveled tirelessly and listened to suggestions as well as complaints. The green-eyed, blond Isabella became such a workaholic that she invented an alarm clock in 1496. Because the petty nobility and town dwellers looked to the monarchy for unity and protection, the rise of the Ottoman Turks, particularly after their capture of mighty Constantinople in 1453, raised the fear of Muslims again. The 1492 surrender of Granada therefore represented a great victory. In that same year, Isabella and Fernando enforced Christian orthodoxy in the belief that Spain had become God's chosen people. The Inquisition began to seek out heretics in 1480. Religious unity became the goal which resulted in the edict that all Jews convert or leave Spain. Sponsoring Columbus' search for Asian trade and potential converts, Isabella astutely improvised an empire in the Americas when Asia proved elusive.

The Middle Ages thus ended with extraordinary diversity but an unmistakable continuity toward unity. Nowhere had Judaism, Christianity, and Islam coexisted and influenced one another as in Spain. Later, Christians struggled to vanquish the others during their rise to power. Many characteristics fashioned during the medieval epoch affected the colonization of Mexico: a preference for investment in land rather than commerce or industry; the belief that manual labor should be carried out by inferiors because Christian Hispanics had won the right to rule; and the idea of gaining wealth by tribute based upon superior military power. Spaniards learned how to treat conquered peoples who had a higher civilization and technology. The crusading fervor of the *reconquista* appeared countless times during the invasion of Mexico. Once the nobility drove Muslims from Granada, soldiers in Spain became eager for continued conquest and glory. Because the nobility of Castile lived off warfare in order to increase the size of their landed estates, many Spaniards headed eagerly for the New World in search of opportunity and wealth.

DEFEAT OF THE AZTECS

The invasion of Mexico redefined its nationality into a Hispanic variant. This produced many of Mexico's problems as well as qualities. Claiming vast territories and all its inhabitants, Spain ushered in the first large-scale attempt at colonization since the fall of the Roman Empire. The Spanish invasion of Mexico became the most spectacular event during the Hispanic intrusion into the New World. Superior leadership, the devastating appearance of disease, and the negative aspects of Mesoamerican religion enabled Spain to triumph from 1519 to 1521.

Aztec religion had weaknesses which enabled the Spanish conquerors to take advantage of critical miscalculations by Motecuhzoma II, the Aztec ruler. A series of omens that indicated negative occurrences on the horizon startled Motecuhzoma. Strange and ominous events plagued Tenochtitlán for a number of years prior to Cortés' arrival: boiling waters in Lake Texcoco; two-headed people wandering the streets; incessant disembodied voices crying, "My children, we are lost"; and strangest of all, a bird with a mirror on its head. Motecuhzoma even gazed upon strange, armed men riding beasts that resembled deer. When the high priests looked in the same mirror, they saw nothing. The omens created such panic that unrest seized the commoners as well as the Aztec royalty. Fires, floods, apparitions of sunless skies and mysterious invasions placed the Aztecs in a vulnerable position. His soothsayers and interpreters mistakenly convinced Motecuhzoma to send gifts and invite the Spaniards to Tenochtitlán. Motecuhzoma also became captivated by the belief that Hernán Cortés was Quetzalcoatl. The year 1519 happened to occur on a one-reed year, when a 52-year cycle had just finished, which portended ominous events.

Unlike Motecuhzoma, Cortés acted decisively. Cortés had quick intelligence, imagination, and adaptability. His background enabled him to become a consummate leader and skilled self-promoter, who distorted events and undermined his rivals' credibility to enhance his own status. Cortés studied law at Salamanca, which sharpened his skill in speech and debate. His adept speaking ability saved him many times, enabling Cortés to assure followers of his loyalty and support. Cortés' mother was the daughter of Diego Pizarro Altamirano, thereby making Cortés a relative of Francisco Pizarro. Martin Cortés de Monroy, Cortés' father, achieved the status of a minor hidalgo noble because he served as an infantry captain against the Muslims. Afterwards, the elder Cortés socialized with prominent nobles. These connections enabled Hernán Cortés to receive an invitation to join Nicolás de Ovando to leave for the conquest of Hispaniola in the Caribbean.

In Hispaniola, Cortés established himself as a leader who intended to seek his fortune. In return for the unusual military skill that Cortés demonstrated, Ovando granted him an *encomienda* tribute of indigenous laborers and appointed Cortés as a notary. Later, Diego de Velásquez, the governor of Cuba, promoted Cortés to head the municipality of Santiago and then to captain-general. The 15 years spent in Hispaniola gave Cortés invaluable administrative and political experience. Upon learning of two successful expeditions to the coast of Yucatán in 1517 and 1518, Cortés solicited Velásquez for the command of a fleet to sail to Mexico. Velásquez, seeking to increase his power, planned to send his eager lieutenant to explore the coast but reserved the actual conquest for himself. Velásquez could not fool Cortés, however, who courted Velásquez by offering to marry his daughter in order to reassure him of his allegiance. Cortés kept up the ruse until he sailed safely out of the governor's reach.

After landing at Veracruz, Cortés gained an interpreter who would play a major role in the coming campaign. This interpreter, Malinalli Tenepal, became one of the mistresses of Cortés who provided key information to the Spanish invaders. A noble from Coatzacoalcos, she had been sold into slavery and given to Cortés. Tenepal spoke Nauhuatl and Maya. She learned Spanish quickly and advanced to the position of head interpreter. The Spaniards baptized the beautiful and outgoing Tenepal and gave her the name Marina (from the sea). Mexicans called her Malinche, a pejorative that came to refer, centuries later, to Mexican women who favored foreigners. Cortés quickly realized her shrewdness and employed Marina as his diplomat. Marina's intimate knowledge of indigenous psychology and customs made her invaluable to Cortés' mission. She apprised Cortés of the legend of Quetzalcoatl and the Aztec belief that Cortés was the god-king returning to claim his throne.

His good luck and willpower enabled Cortés to pacify the unhappy Aztec vassals. Local chieftans soon realized the difficulty in defeating the Europeans. Resentful of having to provide sacrificial victims to the god of war as well as high taxes, groups such as the Tlaxcalans enabled Cortés to have enough military support to overpower Aztec armies. Cortés pulled down their idols and denigrated their gods, while extolling the virtues and superiority of the Christian god. When the fearsome retribution of their angered gods did not materialize, indigenous groups began backing Cortés.

Aztec military techniques and strategy were wholly inadequate when faced with European martial technology and their disciplined tactics.

Aztec armor was merely quilted cotton soaked in brine to stiffen the fabric. Spanish swords sliced through it with ease. Wooden clubs, darts, and blowpipes were often useless against the steel cuirasses worn by Spaniards. Aztec tactics also failed. The Aztecs employed their traditional strategy of capturing the enemy alive for later sacrifice; but this approach broke down in long-term warfare. The use of massed, frontal assaults by the Aztecs against the coordinated infantry and cavalry tactics of the Spanish did not permit them to bring the full weight of their vast numerical superiority into play.

Cortés, on the other hand, enjoyed a decided military advantage. The Spanish soldiers were the best in Europe and would not suffer defeat until 1643 at Rocroi, France. Mesoamericans always announced their wars; the Spanish did not. The metal swords, horses, cannon, ships, and aggressive Spanish tactics carried Cortés to victory. Crossbows and harquebuses gave the Spaniards a tremendous superiority because of their great range and striking power. Some of Motecuhzoma's emissaries fainted when the Spanish fired their cannon. The *conquistadores* were generally tough adventurers from southwestern Spain in the prime of their lives. Very few upper-class *hidalgos* came along, probably only 5 percent. A few women and two Africans also participated. Regular Spanish army officers did not take part, although some *conquistadores* had prior experience on European battlefields. Most sought wealth and a better life although few profited. Many ended their lives in poverty and 60 percent of the Spanish forces perished in the final assault upon Tenochtitlán.

Powerful religious motives also inspired Spanish invaders. In the Catholic mind at this time, the masses attempted to do God's will. They assumed that God allowed Spain to arrive in lands previously unknown and deduced that God had chosen them to perform divine labors. The Spanish concluded that individuals who did not follow God's precepts peopled the Aztec empire because they offered human sacrifice to graven images. Perhaps the most famous of these soldiers was

Bernal Díaz del Castillo, who became disgusted with the sodomy of the Aztec priests. Spanish judgments upon the invasion answered their moral and political needs. Diaz's conviction that the Spanish attacked Mexico to do God's work seems somewhat plausible in that Spaniards rarely stole from or plundered villages after taking them.

Ever since the first reports of mountains moving off the coast, which turned out to be Spanish ships, Motecuhzoma became increasingly irresolute. He unwittingly drew Cortés to Tenochtitlán by plying him with fantastic gifts meant to placate the Spanish lust for gold. This decision only increased the Spanish desire to move inland. Motecuhzoma feared the unrelenting approach of Cortés so much that he became progressively less able to rule. When Cortés arrived at Tenochtitlán, Motecuhzoma blundered by allowing him to enter unopposed. This reduced Motecuhzoma's stature in the eyes of his fellow Aztecs. To make matters worse, the commoners had to harvest the crops when the nobility should have fought with recruited soldiers. Cortés' unyielding approach and the ease with which he defeated or enlisted Aztec subjects only added to Motecuhzoma's consternation. After Cortés took Motecuhzoma hostage for eight months in the Aztec plaza, Motecuhzoma tried to discourage Aztec desires to resist, even burning to death those leaders whose forces attacked Spanish troops. Before his own citizens stoned him to death, Motecuhzoma had, in effect, surrendered the Aztec empire to Cortés.

The astute and beguiling Cortés continued to quickly ascertain the realities and opportunities presented by his opponents. He continued to protest his loyalty to the Spanish king by means of skillfully written letters. The Veracruz town council appointed by Cortés ruled that his expedition had accomplished Velásquez's mandate and therefore elected Cortés to be directly under the king's authority. His election as mayor of Veracruz was a legalistic maneuver that allowed Cortés to avoid the authority of Velásquez. Cortés had revived the precedent for conquest established during the drive against the Muslims. After

The capture of Mexico City by Cortes as depicted in this steel engraving by an unkown American artist, c. 1870. *The Granger Collection.*

imprisoning Motecuhzoma, Cortés learned of the arrival of Pánfilo de Narváez, sent by Velásquez to capture Cortés. With only 266 soldiers, Cortés overwhelmed Narváez's force of 800 by means of a midnight assault. Cortés imprisoned Narváez in Veracruz and he returned to Tenochtitlán with reinforcements; but Cortés soon learned of Aztec preparations for combat in Tenochtitlán. Pedro de Alvarado, who had stayed behind as commander-in-chief during Cortés' absence, claimed to have uncovered a secret insurrection under the guise of a fiesta and proceeded to massacre women, old people, warriors dressed in festive costume, as well as large numbers of children. The slaughter infuriated the Aztecs, who drove Cortés and his forces out during the *noche triste* (sad night) of June 30, 1520. Although Cortés' army appeared to be on the verge of extermination, a natural element turned out to be his principal weapon.

Smallpox and measles epidemics soon resulted in almost unbelievable devastation of the indigenous population. Disease weakened Aztec resistance to a critical level. The decimated indigenous ranks could not mount an effective response against the Spaniards. In the darkness of the *noche triste*, the Aztecs gathered thousands of corpses which had been scattered through forests and over plains. The Aztec warriors had abandoned their weapons and did not pursue Cortés' decimated forces in order to recover their dead. Among the Spanish cadavers was a black man brought by Narváez who coughed and bled from the nose as large ulcers spread through his body. The nameless African soon transmitted smallpox, which had devastated the Caribbean islands from 1507 to 1517. Smallpox spread quickly with lethal consequences. Tens of thousands died within a few weeks. By 1630, over 90 percent of Mexico's indigenous groups would die of European disease.

When Cortés and his forces regained their strength, they constructed ships and seized Tenochtitlán from Lake Texcoco. The attack determined the ultimate capture of the city and other allied capitals that obeyed Chitlahua, the younger brother of Motecuhzoma, whose subjects elected him king and formally invested him on September 16, 1520. The Spaniards sunk the small Aztec boats and bombarded Tenochtitlán cruelly until virtually destroying it. The Aztecs refused to surrender until the final land assault into the city. Despite a formal capitulation on August 13, 1521, the Spaniards and their allies continued to attack and slaughter innocents for several days, looting and enslaving many in the process.

The outcome of the Spanish invasion was inevitable. A different leader or more decisive action against Cortés may have delayed but could not have prevented the eventual demise of the Aztec empire. Aztec military techniques and strategy eventually failed. Moreover, the subjugated peoples under Aztec rule resented and rebelled against sacrifice and taxes. A diplomat and genius, Cortés encouraged 200,000 discontented Indians to unite with the conquistadors which gave the invasion the necessary impetus to topple the Aztec hegemony. Their hatred provided a driving force that Cortés harnessed to crush the Aztecs. Historians such as Ross Hassig attribute Spanish victory to the fragmented organization and divided aims of the Mexican population. The fragile Aztec alliance simply broke down when faced with superior Spanish power. Their limited form of transportation augmented the Spanish invasion. Moreover, the Aztec fear of regional autonomy and democratization would continue to characterize governments in Mexico City thereafter. One of the great consequences of the Spanish invasion was that Mexico became much more rural once the indigenous cities collapsed. In crossing the ocean, mastering unknown cultures, and claiming huge territories, the Spaniards cleared the way for new and more destructive acts by others; the English were more oppressive and less tolerant toward indigenous groups than the Spaniards.

The Spanish invasion of the rest of Mexico proceeded less rapidly. Francisco de Montejo, one of Cortés' lieutenants, penetrated the Yucatán peninsula in 1527. Spaniards crushed a major revolt in 1547 but remained in the northwestern corner of the peninsula. Because the Maya had no gold, many Spaniards lost interest in Yucatán and actually withdrew somewhat. A similar pattern developed in Oaxaca, where social and landholding patterns endured to a degree unknown in other Mexican regions. With an imposing geography, diverse indigenous groups, and a simple occupational structure, Oaxaca had little to offer. Only the discovery of mineral wealth in the Guadalajara and Zacatecas regions motivated large-scale attempts to settle the area north of Mexico City. In order to consolidate central Mexico and the rapidly emerging mineral districts of the north, Spain fashioned governmental traditions that persist today.

ADMINISTRATION OF NEW SPAIN

For three centuries, Spanish officials ruled Mexico, changing profoundly the lives of its indigenous people. Spaniards sought to impose a semifeudal structure upon Mexico, requiring all inhabitants to assume a special obligation to the Crown, in exchange for royal protection. Notaries accompanied bands of adventurers to read conquest proclamations and create records that would verify Hispanic claims. Unlike the Romans, however, the Spaniards were not content with imposing civil order on Mexico. Spain sought also to change the inner life of Mexicans—to reap a harvest of souls for the church. One of the underlying assumptions within Hispanic administration was the conviction that Spain's governmental system, social patterns, and cultural values could be transplanted successfully to remote Mexican regions. Finding little in terms of existing trade patterns, Spain installed medieval institutions to gather tribute and labor.

Colonial administration had several characteristics. Clearly, an authoritarian flavor permeated the softly polished exterior of professional public servants. The theory behind government maintained that a divine right monarch ruled Mexico as his personal domain by means of a papal grant to Christianize the population. Officials operated as very paternalistic representatives of the Spanish monarch and the structure of Spanish administration changed very little until the eighteenth century.

Royal statecraft underwent three distinct phases. First, a creative period characterized the years 1520 to 1600. During the sixteenth century, royal officers gradually replaced the *conquistadores*. The Crown introduced Castilian institutions throughout Mexico much in the way that Christian kingdoms reconquered Spain. From 1600 to 1700, abuses, corruption, and loss of royal control over the administration indicate a decline in Hispanic energy. King Felipe II began the sale of public offices after consolidating the state from the threat of a new nobility. Finally, the period of Bourbon rule from 1701 to 1800 is notable for general revival of the economy and an improvement in administrative efficiency. The eighteenth century is discussed in Chapter 4.

Early Centralization. As part of the largest empire in history, Mexico experienced constant supervision from Spanish administrators. Created in 1503, the Board of Trade became a royal bureau that examined licenses, crews, and the ships that sailed to Mexico. This agency also trained and licensed pilots, who guided the ships by maneuvering them into harbors or along shorelines. The Board of Trade also drew up the latest, up-to-date navigational charts.

The Council of the Indies began with 4 members in 1524 but increased to 20 because it wrote minute laws in great detail. Its *Recopilación de las Indias* was a 73-year project for establishing colonial legislation, and was eventually completed in 1681. In the *Recopilación's* 11,000 chapters were no less than 400,000 laws. Its great authority mandated the Council of the Indies to send numerous instructions and royal proclamations, particularly after this body studied various reports and recommendations. The Council of the Indies also made appointments, even for church positions, and reviewed the conduct of every significant royal official in Mexico. In addition, it served as a court of last resort for civil disputes when lower courts sent up legal decisions.

Lawyers and clergy served as the original members of the council, but it soon included retired viceroys and judges. A very able and hardworking agency in the sixteenth century, the council became responsible for garrisons and fortifications until the formation of a Council of War in the seventeenth century. Although the Council unofficially sold imperial offices by auction and by means of graft, its great power endured until the eighteenth century.

The Crown established a Royal Exchequer in Mexico because general fiscal incompetence and the farming out of contracts created havoc with administrative accounts until auditors restored order. A royal treasurer paid bills and salaries as part of a lifetime appointment. The comptroller, known as a *contador*, served as accountant. The *factor* resembled both a business manager and purchasing agent because he converted Indian tribute into cash and administered the royal monopolies. The *vedor* exercised responsibility for mines and assay offices. Then as now, the aduana customs officials assessed official duties upon foreign and domestic trade. The *casa de fundación* applied royal seals to silver and gold bullion. The *casa de moneda* mints were in private hands until the establishment of a royal mint in the eighteenth century. Thus the structure of a bureaucratic officialdom appeared in the sixteenth century; the attitudes and procedures would not change a great deal after independence. Officials had little accountability and tended to regard public office as their personal domain. True loyalty went to immediate superiors.

The Viceroy. Ultimately responsible for carrying out orders from Spain, the viceroy became the most important person in colonial Mexico. During the colonial epoch, 61 viceroys ruled Mexico with varying degrees of effectiveness. As personal representatives of the king, they usually represented the cream of Spanish society, such as Antonio de Mendoza, the first viceroy sent to Mexico.

Viceregal responsibilities varied. First of all, the viceroy supervised administration in all phases and headed the audiencia law court. In this position, he could issue pardons. The viceroy was always the senior military commander. He regulated economic life in order to increase royal revenues. The viceroy represented the king in all church matters by controlling the religious orders and the bishops. Finally, the viceroy served as a protector and confessor. He listened to everyday problems and frustrations. The viceroy reserved one afternoon a week in order to hear Indian complaints.

The General Indian Court established in 1573 distinguished Spanish administration. The court traced its origin to both Muslim and Castilian traditions of conserving the right of conquered people to adjudicate offenses committed within their communities. This remarkably innovative institution arose out of the difficulty in handling Indian grievances. Because the courts recognized Indian laws and customs as precedents, indigenous people won lawsuits consistently. To support court expenditures, each indigenous family paid a tax amounting to one-sixteenth of a peso, thus resulting in a form of legal insurance. Although the viceroy exempted certain areas of New Spain from the court's jurisdiction, its indigenous agents labored hard to protect Indians from excessive cruelty and exploitation. The court maintained Indian rights to property and assured the cultural survival of many indigenous communities until its demise in 1820.

Actual viceregal power was more apparent than real. The king forbade the viceroy to intervene in treasury affairs. Moreover, the viceroy could not really control patronage because these appointments emanated from Spain or others purchased them during the seventeenth century. The viceroy's military was weak because no Spanish armies were garrisoned in Mexico until well past the mid-eighteenth century, aside from presidio forts. The viceroy really had little more than a personal guard of 50–150 soldiers and the generally undependable militia hardly inspired fear.

Audiencia. These courts handled appeals from religious tribunals and royal officials. It was an outgrowth of medieval theories of kingship which held that the sovereign's prime duty consisted of dispensing justice. The audiencia also served as a sort of viceregal cabinet that shared power with the viceroy. Its judges helped formulate policy, toured regions, and issued laws while monitoring their implementation. The audiencia advised the viceroy when laws conflicted or when precedent lacked. These *oidores* (ears) were highly trained magistrates as well as clerks and surgeons. The monarchy isolated them from other colonials in order to maintain judicial loyalty. Therefore judges could not marry local women or even attend bullfights. Nevertheless, they became involved in local economies and arranged marriages. The *oidores* wielded great power because they often served their region for 15 to 20 years and held supreme authority during a corregidor's absence. They quarreled frequently with viceroys because although they were from the upper class, Spaniards born in Mexico gradually served on the audiencia, particularly when this office could be purchased from 1687 to 1750. Not surprisingly, a policy of *obedezco pero no cumplo* appeared. This phrase meant that officials such as audiencia judges would promise to obey royal policy but often did not comply in order to satisfy regional needs during periods of social discontent.

The second audiencia, dating from 1530 to 1535, understood the need for striking a balance between the moral and legal requisites of the crown and the interests of the treasury as well as the colonists. In doing so, the second audiencia laid the foundation for subsequent colonial policy. Viceroy Mendoza realized that land grants had to complement positions of authority. Mendoza rewarded his inner circle but also used his authority to encourage the rapid adoption of livestock ranching in New Spain and expansion northward. Despite restrictions upon the *oidores*, the private economic activities of leading royal officials provided a crucial aspect in the economy.

Corregidores. Transplanted from Spain, these urban governors served as judges on the local level. They enforced labor relations, regulated mining claims, led the colonial militia, and concerned themselves with religious duties. Employed by means of term appointment, *corregidores* are sometimes referred to as *alcalde mayor* or *gobernador*. The first *corregidores* appeared as royal substitutes for *conquistadors*. After 1550, *corregidores* collected tribute and helped centralize Spanish control. At this time, *corregidores* also assumed civil and criminal jurisdiction over indigenous people as well as Spaniards. About 200 *corregidores* ruled throughout various Mexican regions during the colonial period. The provincial district controlled by *corregidores* are occasionally termed *alcaldias mayores*.

Corregidores usually had little personal contact with Indians because they preferred using Hispanized Indians as caciques in the villages. Restoring indigenous caciques strengthened Spanish control. Caciques in the periphery became an integral part of the economic system. This was not a difficult transition because many Indians saw little difference between paying Spanish officials and Indian caciques. Therefore the *corregidores* often preserved the original boundaries of indigenous towns and villages. Early *corregidores* sought to minimize the disruption of Indian congregations by discouraging Spanish cattle from trampling village fields.

The *corregidor* position sold for a high price but required energy and tact. The *corregidor's* salary depended upon how much tribute he collected. Although they were supposed to be fair in dealing with Indians, *corregidores* gradually used their positions to exploit Indians for personal gain. By the seventeenth century they extorted indigenous produce for resale at a higher markup. In return, the *repartimiento* of merchandise resulted in a policy whereby the provincial administrators forced Indian communities to purchase useless items such as eye glasses without lens, wigs, canes, and umbrellas. What motivated *corregidores* to engage in such a contemptible practice was the reality that many provincial administrators borrowed money from influential merchants to purchase their offices. Naturally, merchants expected favored treatment in return. Strapped for funds, the Spanish government objected little because of the financial crisis that

gripped Spain beginning in the second half of the sixteenth century. Because New World *corregidores* had less legal training than their Spanish counterparts, their military backgrounds served to emphasize their authority over Mexican regions.

Cabildos. These municipalities, also known as *ayuntamientos*, covered large tracts of land as a sort of combination of city and county government, mainly because Spanish colonies became more urbanized than British or French possessions. Also, miners, ranchers, and planters maintained homes in towns and cities as part of the urban Iberian heritage.

In the beginning, *cabildos* exercised virtually sovereign powers over sizable areas. They defined the judicial duties of the *corregidores* until the Council of the Indies transferred much of their authority. *Cabildos* organized militias and gave out large land grants. An annual vote of all property holders determined municipal officers. The undemocratic elections denied voting rights to gamblers, day laborers, blasphemizers, women, debtors, and illegitimates (often considered mixed bloods). During the sixteenth century, cabildos became the main area of colonial administration that Mexican-born Spaniards could control, since Europeans received most of the provincial appointments.

A typical *cabildo* consisted of aldermen, a justice of the peace (*alcalde ordinario*), secretary, and constable. Some held these positions for 20 years or longer. *Cabildos* normally met twice a week. Those who missed gatherings received fines. Fortunately for historians, *cabildos* carefully recorded the minutes of their meetings. *Cabildos* closed their sessions to the public except in times of crisis. Then a *cabildo abierto* (open municipality) took place, although usually for prominent citizens.

Among its many functions, *cabildos* maintained Indian authority. Defense became the most important duty; but *cabildos* also regulated the price of meat, wine, and other foods. They discussed the impact of cash crops upon their communities. The *cabildos* also took control of

Indigenous governments, which often remained largely unchanged. Some Indians had more autonomy than others. Many of traditional indigenous governing systems in Cuernavaca, for example, survived more or less intact and continued to function effectively until the 1820s. Spaniards usually did not interfere with local government once idolatry had been exterminated or unless Indians became obstreperous. Spaniards also enforced the procedures for self-government indifferently so that indigenous practices became preserved. In the indigenous *cabildo* of Tlaxcala, its members decided that plantings of cochineal cactus would be limited to ten persons because the mania for this cash crop had resulted in a decline of food production, traditional rituals, and excessive drinking of alcoholic beverages.

But Spanish officials and priests irreversibly undermined the old order as they went about selecting principal towns (*cabeceras*) to serve as administrative and ceremonial capitals of the new colonial regime. Despite successful Indian resistance in the south and north, the forced resettlements (*congregaciones*) of the mid-sixteenth century further altered central Mexico. But Indian families often left their new communities to form more remote but constantly diminishing localized cults as part of a desire for social cohesion. Another factor that motivated Indian flight into fragmented pockets in the mountains was the arrival of Spanish settlers, usually petty merchants and small farmers, into the indigenous communities. By the late sixteenth century, most of the differences which may have characterized native groups in central Chiapas had disappeared under the combined pressure of demographic and political collapse. Only during the nineteenth century did these communities acquire the distinctive Tzotzil and Tzeltan characteristics.

Whatever possibilities that existed for true democracy died by the middle of the seventeenth century. Because the Crown feared an independence movement led by *cabildos*, the colonial administration attempted to install its favorites as

Spaniards Destroying Mexican Idols. *Culver Pictures.*

aldermen. Gradually, the prestige of senior royal officials dominated Mexican towns. Even so, the Mexico City municipality and several others could be assertive and even forceful. Perhaps more fundamental, prominent families stayed in power in order to make sure that property taxes remained low. This satisfied the Crown because it feared that local rights might have to be extended in return for the tax increases of the sixteenth and seventeenth centuries.

Administrative Checks and Balances. Spain maintained very elaborate checks and balances throughout its colonial apparatus. The Church, treasury, judiciary, and political offices all had some form of autonomy and checked each other's power. Moreover, the king permitted appeals over the heads of superiors in order to eliminate conspiracies and discourage graft at the top levels of government. The Crown also encouraged judicial review. The prospect of legal appeals and the power of the Council of Indies meant that a viceroy seldom had the satisfaction of knowing that his decisions would be final.

Overlapping branches of government occurred because the monarchy believed that checks and balances would forestall the growth of regional power bases. Therefore the Inquisition often dueled with the audiencia courts. Meanwhile, judges pressured viceroys with their views because the crown expected audiencias to keep their eyes on the viceroy. To maintain viceregal influence, the crown expected each viceroy to carry out inspections. Viceroys wrote a memoria for successors which recapitulated a term of office. They were 300–400 pages long by the eighteenth century.

Residencias and *visitas* were official inquiries made into the conduct of important authorities. The *residencia* and *visita* evolved as two methods used by Spain to check on officials and ensure efficient as well as stable administration. The *residencia* consisted of a formal hearing at the end of an official's term; the *visita* was a secret surveillance that resulted in official action of one kind or another. A set of questions arising from complaints of various people could be presented against any official in what amounted to a trial. It was a stressful procedure because the possibility for revenge among various citizens was great, particularly in land disputes. Death sentences could result for guilty parties, but, in most cases, blemishes upon Hispanic honor or fines usually took place. The excessive cost of *visitas* and *residencias* as well as their long duration and meager results often makes them seem ineffective. Actually, the Crown appeared more interested in obtaining additional revenues and eager to settle disputes between Spaniards over the allocation of jobs and other issues. Pursuing justice often seemed a secondary issue of colonial administrators during the imperial period.

Although the bureaucracy seems inefficient by modern standards, it achieved Spanish goals. Caution became a major factor that limited effectiveness; time and distance also retarded timely responses. Sales of public offices, stagnation, and resignation became negative features. But the 30 million documents in the colonial archives at Sevilla attest to the dedication of many imperial officials. Without massive armies or fortifications, the bureaucracy enabled Spanish rule for three centuries. Royal authorities channeled wealth from Mexico and enhanced Hispanic prestige as well as Spain's strategic goal as a world power.

SUGGESTED READING

Arribas, Antonio. *The Iberians.* New York: Praeger, 1968.

Borah, Woodrow. *Justice by Insurance: The General Indian Court of Colonial Mexico and the Legal Aides of the Half-Real.* Berkeley: University of California Press, 1983.

Chejne, Anwar. *Muslim Spain: Its History and Culture.* Minneapolis: University of Minnesota Press, 1974.

Collins, Roger. *Early Medieval Spain: Unity in Diversity, 400-1000.* London: Macmillan, 1983.

Cortés, Hernán. *Letters from Mexico.* Trans. and ed. by A. R. Pagden. New Haven, CT: Yale University Press, 1986.

Díaz del Castillo, Bernal. *The True History of the Conquest of New Spain, 1517–1521*. New York: Farrar, Straus and Giroux, 1966.

Elliott, John H. *Spain and Its World, 1500–1700: Selected Essays*. New Haven, CT: Yale University Press, 1989.

Fletcher, Richard. *The Quest for El Cid*. New York: Oxford University Press, 1991.

Greenberg, Bernhard. "Origins of the Conquistadores of Mexico City." *Hispanic American Historical Review* 74:2 (May 1994), 259–83.

Haring, C. H. *The Spanish Empire in America*. New York: Harcourt, Brace and World, 1963.

Haskett, Robert. *Indigenous Rulers: An Ethnohistory of Town Government in Colonial Cuernavaca*. Albuquerque: University of New Mexico Press, 1991.

Hassig, Ross. *Mexico and the Spanish Conquest*. New York: Longman, 1994.

Imamuddin, S. M. *Some Aspects of the Socioeconomic and Cultural History of Muslim Spain, 711–1492*. Leiden, The Netherlands: E. J. Brill, 1965.

Jackson, Gabriel. *The Making of Medieval Spain*. New York: Harcourt Brace Jovanovich, 1972.

Kamen, Henry. *Spain, 1469–1714: A Society of Conflict*. 2d ed. New York: Longman, 1991.

King, P. D. *Law and Society in the Visigothic Kingdom*. Cambridge: Cambridge University Press, 1972.

Leon-Portilla, Miguel, ed. *The Broken Spears: The Axtec Account of the Conquest of Mexico*. Boston: Beacon Press, 1972.

Liss, Peggy K. *Isabel the Queen: Life and Times*. New York: Oxford University Press, 1992.

———. *Mexico under Spain, 1521-1556: Society and the Origins of Nationality*. Chicago: University of Chicago Press, 1975.

Lockhart, James. *The Nahuas After the Conquest: A Social and Cultural History of the Indians of Central Mexico, Sixteenth Through Eighteenth Centuries*. Stanford, CA: Stanford University Press, 1992.

———. and Frances Berdan with Arthur J. O. Anderson. *The Tlaxcalan Atlas*. Salt Lake City: University of Utah Press, 1986.

Marks, Richard Lee. *Cortes: The Great Adventurer and the Fate of Aztec Mexico*. New York: Knopf, 1993.

Nicolini, Gerard. *The Ancient Spaniards*. Westmead, England: Saxon House, 1974.

Padden, R. C. *The Hummingbird and the Hawk: Conquest and Sovereignty in the Valley of Mexico, 1503–1541*. New York: Harper and Row, 1970.

Payne, Stanley G. *A History of Spain and Portugal*. Madison: University of Wisconsin Press, 1973.

Vicens Vives, Jaime. *Approaches to the History of Spain*. Trans. Joan Connelly Ullman. Berkeley: University of California Press, 1970.

3

Society and Culture

Shortly after their arrival, Spaniards established a social structure based upon racial as well as class features. Mexican society underwent seismic transformations as the indigenous population, although virtually wiped out in many areas, slowly merged with Spaniards. Racially, it was one of the most diverse and complex societies in the world. A blending of race and culture resulted in a new society because the transformation of Hispanic culture in Mexico, racial mixture, and growing *criollismo* all strengthened regionalism, a progenitor of Mexican nationalism. The new culture retained many indigenous features while adopting Spanish traits that resulted in the initial appearance of national traditions that retained their vitality for centuries.

SOCIAL STRUCTURE

Sources of Immigration. Spaniards came to Mexico for a variety of reasons. For one thing, Mexico became a sanction for misfits who could not accept Iberian roles. A love of adventure and romance also motivated many to leave Spain. After all, the Renaissance inspired many to gamble everything. Finally, Mexico represented a new opportunity for rusty soldiers, disinherited sons, and those who yearned to end unhappy marriages.

A high degree of internal social mobility characterized early modern Spain and represents the restless nature of many Spaniards.

Most colonials came from western Spain as well as the southern region of Andalusia. The Spanish empire belonged technically to Castile until King Fernando IV allowed unlimited immigration from all of Spain in 1756. In the early sixteenth century, the crown offered inducements to have settlers populate critical areas and many Spaniards responded, despite the efforts of the Spanish nobility to restrict immigration.

Spanish Restrictions. Spain barred many types of people from entering Mexico, but numerous illegal entries got through anyway. The crown forbade Muslims to enter Mexico as well as orthodox Jews. Many converted Jews practiced Christianity loosely but remained Catholics. Authorities always sent gypsies back to Europe when they discovered them in Mexico because the crown disapproved of their unconventional lifestyle.

After 1580, Spain tried to restrict foreigners from coming to Mexico. Spain simply assumed that all foreigners were spies and that they would lower the high standards of colonization. Therefore, Protestants especially were kept out. The Spaniards made exceptions only for those foreigners possessing needed skills, such as in mining, metallurgy, medicine, artillery, and various crafts. One way for foreigners to enter Mexico was by marrying Spanish women and waiting ten years for citizenship papers to be initiated.

A few other groups slipped through. Joining religious orders became another method to enter Mexico. The crown exerted great pressure upon the orders to keep foreigners out. Even though all but Jesuits agreed, because they wanted their best people in Mexico, the other orders smuggled foreigners into Mexico anyway. Seamen became another source of foreign immigrants. Since other European nations carried most of Spain's merchandise once the seventeenth-century wars took their toll, abundant opportunities for jumping ship presented themselves. Spain apprehended very few foreign spies even though the crown took such drastic steps as evicting all Portuguese after 1640.

The Caste System. Initially, Spanish law ranked people according to their skin color—which resulted in a pigmentocracy of certain privileges and restrictions. Status, coming from the medieval concept of estate, became a social barrier in Mexico that has persisted beyond the colonial period. Society became composed of groups with few shared values or collective goals. Racism resulted but Spaniards did not mind because they wanted to divide Mexico on a social basis. The Spaniards elaborated a caste system which featured Spaniards born in Europe (*peninsulars*) on top of the social pyramid followed by *criollos*, *mestizos*, *mulatos*, and Africans. Skin color determined the status of each group.

Peninsulars enjoyed the top of the caste system by virtue of their European birth. Virtually all *peninsulars* considered themselves hidalgos and assumed that an allegedly superior culture and intelligence entitled them to the most privileges—only four viceroys were not *peninsulars*. Few grandees came to Mexico because of their unwillingness to abandon comfortable landed estates in Spain. The upper echelon of Hispanic society considered farming in Mexico a servile pastime.

Spaniards monopolized appointments in the bureaucracy because fairly significant numbers of Spanish officials came to Mexico. Spaniards became particularly prominent in wholesale commerce. Most *peninsulars*, however, were from the Spanish working class. They took advantage of the extraordinary social mobility for whites to establish themselves as wholesale merchants, foremen, managers, and clerks. Nearly all peninsulars dreamed of returning to Spain.

Criollos, Spaniards born in Mexico claimed Hispanic status but the crown considered *criollos* untrustworthy as well as unreliable, extravagant, and unorganized. Spanish law drew no distinctions between *criollos* and *peninsulars* but in practice, *peninsulars* obtained about 80 percent of the appointments made as bishops. European-born candidates won two-thirds of church positions despite a concession to *criollos* of alternating *criollos* and *peninsulars*. Although favoritism annoyed *criollos*, they imitated haughty *gachupines*, a pejorative still applied to Spaniards, in clothing, language, and culture while looking down upon mixed bloods and Africans. As *gente de razón* (people who reason), *criollos* and *peninsulars* created a chasm between themselves and the masses that persisted for centuries. Discouraged from positions in government and the church, successful *criollos* prospered eventually as landowners, silver miners, and local retailers. In the course of the seventeenth century, *criollos* became the predominant owners of estates in the countryside. The persistent insecurity that characterized *criollos* manifested itself in purchases of certificates of whiteness, a documentation of unquestioned white European background, that had become popular in Spain itself.

Mestizos (mixed Spanish and Indian) became the intermediaries in Mexican society. The shortage of Spanish women led to micegenation and creation of numerous *mestizos*. A ten to one ratio of men to women existed in the early colonial era, partially because Spaniards considered Mexico morally unsafe. In theory, *mestizos* had legal equality but in practice whites rejected them as did Indians below *mestizos*. Born of illegitimacy and sexual violence, *mestizos* became extremely insecure. Lumped with the lowest groups, royal law prohibited *mestizos* from being notary publics or from entering religious orders. They could serve in the Spanish church but quite often *mestizos* confronted tremendous obstacles toward advancement. Frequently orphaned and abandoned, many became *vagabundos*, or vagabond drifters.

Indians had to pay tribute as a sign of their social inferiority. Because Spaniards considered Indians legally subordinate, they excluded Indians from most government positions. In many instances during court proceedings, testimony of three Indians was the equivalent of one Spaniard. But as the indigenous population rapidly declined, authorities favored intermarriage in order to repopulate communities devastated by disease. By 1540, the crown ruled that those Spaniards living with Indian women had to marry them or lose labor privileges. The idea of the sacredness of marriage at first collided with indigenous customs. But the slow recovery of the Indian population arose partially from the fact that Indians married more frequently than whites and became parents at an earlier age. Indians in Oaxaca and other remote regions preserved their customs, but loss of land forced many Indians to look for work in urban areas and live in Hispanic towns and cities. The creation of the *república de los indios* and the *república de los españoles* became the first attempt to distinguish between indigenous and European societies.

Mulatos, sometimes referred to as *pardos*, were the combination of Spaniards and Africans. The rapid death of many indigenous communities resulted in the importation of African slaves. Although mulatoes were commonly believed to be physically stronger than whites or Indians, Spaniards barred *mulatos* from militia groups until they obtained the right to join segregated units later on. Most *mulatos* toiled as manual workers although some became artisans and priests. Spaniards esteemed *mulato* women as mistresses.

Africans served as slave laborers once Indians could not be enslaved legally after 1542. Africans had to pay tribute and Spaniards prohibited them from wearing extravagant clothing, carrying firearms, and, in some municipalities, umbrellas or being on the streets after dark. Spaniards considered blacks culturally and ethnically inferior. Because Hispanics often considered physical labor degrading, they forced Africans to do it. Africans could not marry whites or Indians by law; rarely did they marry other blacks, but freed blacks married at rates similar to whites.

The class factors that defined Mexican society became more apparent as the social pyramid began to break down through intermarriage. Here the concept of *gente decente* still commands attention today when people refer to themselves as respectable, home-owning, and hard-working with a certain educational level which differentiates middle-and upper-class status from the sweaty masses. The class aspects of social decline meant that a Spaniard could be considered an undignified plebian if he or she became associated with *castizo* (any kind of mixed blood) and in any way fell into a working-class lifestyle. Family, place of birth, and one's marriage also determined class status. Earning a certain salary or becoming wealthy could also raise one's status even if that individual were a *casta*. Anyone who did not work with their hands commanded a certain respect not given to everyone.

Cultural determinants maintaining class status as well as achieving social advancement consisted of wearing European clothing, particularly shoes, speaking Spanish, and eating non-Indian food, particularly wheat. Miscegenation may actually have worked to create social classes since the kind of work that one performed often had a class criteria that became fairly precise.

Scholars such as Douglas Cope conclude that Hispanic racial domination faced limits. The construction of the central plaza mayor in Mexico City attempted to segregate Indians, but indigenous people lived there in fairly noticeable quantities anyway. *Castas* became more independent than Spaniards desired, because *castas* could bargain and manipulate for favors given the characteristic labor shortages that affected Mexico.

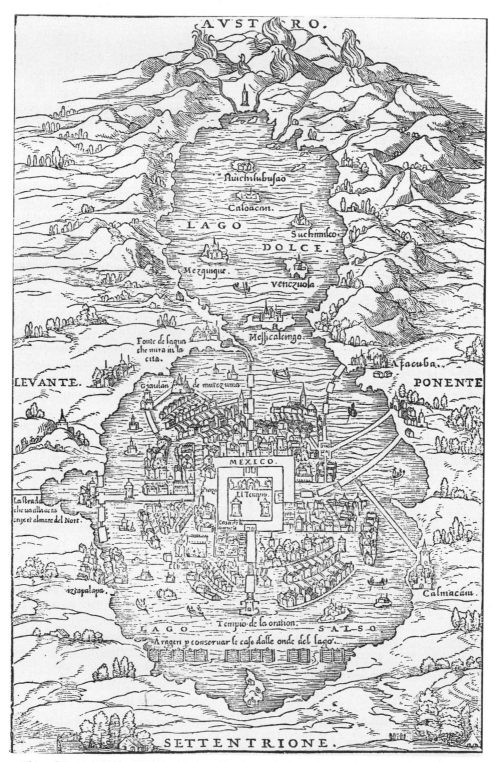

Plan of Tenochtitlán (Mexico City) at the time of the Spanish conquest as depicted in this woodcut, c. 1556. *The Granger Collection.*

Even the indigenous population had its own caste system, according to local Mexican documents, but the rigid social system eventually produced riots in Mexico City because the social pyramid became a tight cork upon social mobility. The 1642 and 1692 *tumultos* riots in Mexico City reflected interclass hostility that had racial overtones. Angry at an increase in corn prices and convinced that authorities had abused an indigenous woman, a mob of largely artisan Indians attacked the viceregal palace in 1692 and burned it when royal officials could not maintain order. Unlike rungs on a ladder, the social pyramid enabled elites to use patronage to foster a class structure. At least the Spaniards did not enforce the caste system's social regulations consistently.

MESTIZAJE

During the first two centuries of Spanish rule, the number of persons from racially mixed backgrounds remained small. Beginning in the seventeenth century, however, *castas* began to grow rapidly until they numbered about one quarter of colonial society by the end of the eighteenth century. As the quantity of mixed bloods increased, *mestizaje*, as this process is called, acquired distinctive traits which became venerable features of Mexican society and culture.

Status and Discrimination. Although they acquired Christian surnames from Hispanic fathers, the majority of *mestizos* endured poor social status. Stung with the stigma of illegitimacy, *mestizos* suffered a heavy drawback since good jobs and educational facilities required birth certificates. Some *mestizos*, such as the son of Cortés, enjoyed exceptional circumstances and even became knighted in Spain. And, unlike blacks and Indians, they did not have to pay tribute. But *castas* in comfortable surroundings were exceptional. Only *mestizos* from notable families—such as the daughters of wealthy merchants or miners—were sought after by Spaniards for wives, particularly if they could provide a rich dowry. *Castas*

were not vecinos—Spanish citizens—and hovered between both republics created by Spain for Mexican society. Because of similar employment trends, *mestizos* and other *castas* interacted with Indians more than blacks or whites. Another source of tension resulted from the desire of some *mestizos* to pass as *criollos* or even Spaniards if they were sufficiently light skinned.

Mestizos experienced tragic prejudice in the early colonial period. By the seventeenth century, *mestizos* came to mean acculturated natives at the bottom of society; the Spaniards considered Indians hopeless wards of the state incapable of ever fitting in. Spaniards often abandoned the Indian mothers of *castas* so that offspring grew up insecure and hostile. Many terms were applied to racially mixed children with connotations of contempt and mockery. Sons of *mestizos* became known as *tente en el aire* (suspended in air) to indicate that such persons could never be whites. Children of *mestizo*-Indian couples became known as *salta atras*, meaning a step backward, because the racial trend of children would be toward Indian. Mixtures of Africans, Indians, *mestizos*, and other combinations resulted in such pejoratives as mule, wolf, and cow. Mutual animosity and ethnic confusion created a society divided and suspicious of one another, which is what Spaniards usually desired.

Spaniards considered marriage to Indian women dishonorable. If they did take indigenous spouses, they married daughters of Indian nobility when they could. In order to acquire prestige, Indians often sought casual unions with *conquistadors*, and these liasons produced a *mestizo* population that began to appear before the fall of Tenochtitlán.

In the sixteenth century, *mestizos* did not yet form a community distinguishable from indigenous or Hispanic society. They either lived as Spaniards or Indians. Those born within wedlock or adopted by Hispanic fathers became absorbed into the first generation of *criollos*. The population actually labeled *mestizo* in the sixteenth century grew up around the fringe of Spanish society and in the shadow of the African community. By the seventeenth century, *mestizos* became catagorized as a mere subsection of the African population and were always listed last in census reports.

The rise of *mestizos* as a subsection of the African community did not improve their position or enhance their reputation. Although *mestizos* were theoretically equivalent to whites, in actuality, officials identified *mestizos* with *gente vil*, base folk, a category of non-Indians, mainly Africans. The Spaniards could not decide where—at some point between the white apex and the African base—to place *mestizos* in the social hierarchy. Nevertheless, they became the main building block of the Mexican nation.

Despite constant reprobrations from Europeans, *castas* by the seventeenth century became a more distinct social group. Clearly, *castas* dominated urban areas numerically by 1650. *Mestizos* finally became a more separate group at this time. They married among themselves more than with other groups. *Mestizos* numbered about 130,000 by 1650. They were also the hardiest group in terms of their resistance to diseases. Therefore they grew faster, to the point that they numbered 2.2 million by 1800. Mexico is unique in terms of the significance of *mestizaje* in determining its society. *Mestizaje* did not occur in Peru until well into the second half of the nineteenth century.

Economic Role of Mestizos. *Mestizos* lacked the stability of the Hispanic legal system yet gained limited opportunities within the generally restricted economic system. In this sense, *mestizos* faced the opposite situation of Indians. As early as 1540, Spaniards barred *mestizos* from public offices and certain professions, such as lawyers. Most guilds would not accept *mestizos*, but many became artisans anyway. Spain also enacted laws stating that *mestizos* could not use cattle branding irons or carry knives and weapons. Cities prohibited *mestizos* from living in the better residential areas.

Most *mestizos* had to accept lowly kinds of work. Since Spain barred them from religious orders, some became priests of the church. Many more worked as peddlers, *arrieros* mule train drivers, *tlamemes,* who carried cargo on their backs, and servants. The toughest jobs were in the mines or the early textile mills. Industrial development at this time was too weak to provide a feeling of class solidarity.

The frontier experience of shared dangers and isolation from the rigid rules of Spanish etiquette created a more open situation. The frontiers enabled *mestizos* to become more accepted than in areas closer to royal supervision. *Mestizos* became important in settling the north as well as southeast; here more of them became priests and fought as soldiers. Since most colonials had little interest in military service, *mestizos* often joined military units when officials made them liable for duty. Since the poor quality of most recruits disturbed authorities, many *mestizos* became attracted to the possibility of serving as officers. Some contributed money to establish their own units; such effort resulted in *fuero* tax exemptions, fancy uniforms, and status.

Mestizos, however, had few opportunities to acquire land. Fights between *mestizos* and Spanish communities became common by the end of the seventeenth century. The consolidation of the hacienda estates meant that haciendas sought to acquire *mestizo* holdings which had previously been unchallenged. Some *mestizos* roamed the rural areas until they became caught up as peons on the great estates. At first, day laborers in free villages hired themselves out to estate owners for two reales a day. *Mestizos* worked on irrigation ditches, aqueducts, buildings, and dams as well as tending animals.

Alienation and Protest. As *mestizos* increased in numbers, their status declined, particularly in central Mexico. Because they could not reside in decent residential areas, *mestizos* wound up living in slums. Demoralized and defiant, many *mestizos* became drunks, beggars, robbers, and the street people of colonial Mexico. Even the church used *mestizo leperos* (riffraff) whenever they wanted to protest against viceroys or grafting *criollos*. Since *mestizos* had no legitimate recognition or stake in the social system of the central highlands, they sometimes drifted into crime. Some became bandits, a profession that maintained itself into the early twentieth century. Others became professional body guards and assassins. With the commercialization of pulque, alcoholics appeared. Poor health and little education increased *mestizo* resentments. In the countryside, they lived in *jacales*, flimsy dirt-covered shacks with thatched roofs, and took to cattle rustling in some localities.

A tragic insecurity caused numerous *mestizos* to seek to manipulate others. Face-to-face manipulation became the norm since legality existed only for the protection of Indians and Hispanics. The *mestizo* quest for power derived from an intense personalism. Therefore *mestizos* accelerated the growth of machismo as a way to control and express their hostility. Here the ultimate manifestations of power in males are sexual prowess, courage, and action. Unlike Indians, who reluctantly changed many of their basic attitudes, *mestizos* became dynamic and disruptive. For *mestizo* leaders, the group served the individual rather than the reverse. With little to lose, many *mestizos* became skilled in the use of double talk and false promises. *Mestizos* reasoned that since the possibility of becoming a property owner remained elusive, particularly in urban areas, stability should be challenged. *Mestizos* became leaders because they were in a position to argue against a system of privileges that the Spaniards never really reformed. Therefore, *mestizos* demanded a more egalitarian society, like those that existed on the borderlands. Northerners would style themselves as redeemers throughout much of modern Mexican history.

INDIAN-WHITE RELATIONS

Indigenous governmental and cultural patterns survived largely intact until about 1550. As during the Spanish *reconquista*, orders such as Franciscans and Dominicans maintained their tradition of missionary goals among newly conquered subjects. Hispanic efforts to missionize and impose tribute led to alternating periods of widespread indigenous rebellion or partial submission.

The search for mineral wealth motivated early Spanish encounters with indigenous people beyond the Aztec capital. After the conquest of Tenochtitlán, explorers eagerly sought to find an advanced culture similar to the Aztecs. Marcos de Niza first triggered news of such a people in 1539. De Niza, a Franciscan priest, had traveled into the northern country and, from a distance, caught a glimpse of the Zuni pueblos. He returned without setting foot in the villages, but his tale of cities and riches led the viceroy to authorize an expedition under the command of Francisco Vásquez de Coronado in 1540. Leaving Mexico City with 300 Spaniards and a large group of Indian allies, Coronado and his followers, the first Europeans to explore what is now Arizona and New Mexico, continued on to the buffalo-covered plains of Texas and into Oklahoma and Kansas. Initially, Coronado's group enjoyed friendly relations with New Mexico Indians, but as demands for provisions began to increase, the Pueblo Indians forced the Spaniards out of their headquarters, near today's Bernalillo, New Mexico. Coronado crushed the revolt and executed several hundred Pueblos, which laid the foundation for the antagonism that thereafter characterized relations between the Pueblos and Spaniards. Two subsequent expeditions to New Mexico failed, partially because the southwestern United States began to suffer a severe drought that persisted throughout the seventeenth century. Thus the increased burden of supporting Spanish explorers pushed the resources of a horticulturalist society beyond the limits of its capacity to support the local environment.

The Mixtón War was the most serious conflict between Spaniards and Indians in the first half of the sixteenth century. It was partially motivated by religious factors, because the Indians reacted strongly against the cruelties of Nuño de Guzmán, a lawyer who headed the first audiencia and used his authority to attack Cortés and his adherents since Nuño de Guzmán owed his position to governor Velásquez of Cuba. Opposition from

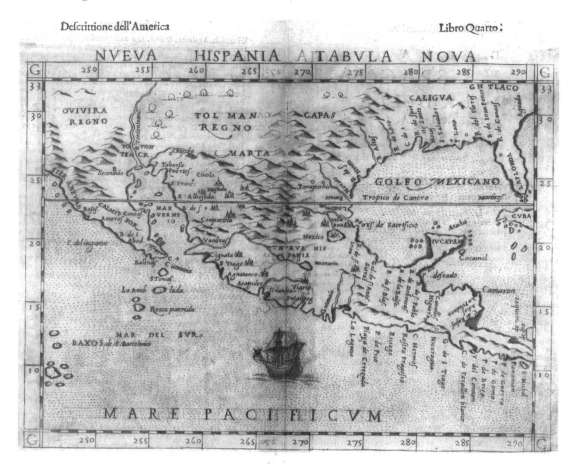

Descrittione dell'America

Libro Quarto:

Mexico in 1599, Nueva Hispana Tabula Nova. (Venice: Giordano Ziletti, 1599). This Italian map is one of the few which was compiled from information provided by various expeditions and travelers. It emphasizes mountain ranges in order to highlight Mexico's mineral wealth. *Courtesy of Special Collections Division, Virginia Garrett Cartographic History Library, University of Texas at Arlington, Arlington, Texas.*

clerics and Spaniards forced Nuño de Guzmán to flee west, where he cut a bloody trail. Attempts to enslave large numbers of Indians led to attacks on Spanish ranches near Guadalajara. As the war evolved into an attempt to drive all Spaniards from Mexico, viceroy Mendoza sent in Pedro de Alvarado when governor Juan de Oñate could not maintain order. When Alvarado himself failed, Mendoza recruited an army of 30,000 Tlaxcalans and Mexica who finally crushed the resistance. Indian insurrectionaries fought in the mountains until 1541 when they fled to Nayarit and the cen-

tral plateau. They mixed with other Indians, particularly the dreaded Chichimeca.

The Chichimecas, defined as "dirty, uncivilized dogs" by their neighbors, controlled the northern area on the basis of their warlike disposition. They danced around captives before killing them and sought the desirable qualities of selected individuals or animals by eating them, usually raw. Chichimeca shamen venerated the drug peyote and encouraged its use. Diversions included wrestling, drinking, and archery. Often credited for introducing bows and arrows into the Valley of Mexico, young males received instruction in this weapon at an early age. Chichimecas made alcoholic drinks from maguey, cactus pears, and mezcal. Hunting provided them with the bulk of their food.

The Chichimecas geared their society almost completely to war. If they happened to be clothed before going into battle, they undressed. Warriors often wore scalps hanging from their backs as well as arm and leg bones as trophies. Absolutely cruel, fearless, reckless and skillful, the Chichimecas earned fame with unusually thin arrows that had incredible penetrating power. The carefully constructed bow equalled two-thirds the length of an average body. Frightened Spaniards soon realized that Chichimecas could release arrows faster than Spaniards could manipulate their harquebuses or crossbows. Chichimecas were ferocious at hand-to-hand combat, especially after a dose of alcoholic beverages and peyote. Their expert knowledge of terrain and ability to survive in the desert made them difficult to pursue. When Chichimecas adopted horses, they became even more dangerous. Infamous for torture, Chichimecas slowly removed various body parts or cut off genitals and stuffed them into a victim's mouth. Children had their heads bashed against rocks.

In 1539, Spanish friars conducted cautious probes into the Bajío region north of Mexico City, which covers the modern states of Guanajuato, Hidalgo, San Luis Potosí, and Querétaro. In return for not paying tribute for ten years, the Chichimecas pledged peace. Beginning in the early 1540s, cattle ranchers and additional friars began a discreet settlement on the fringes of this ominous stronghold. Soon a semicircle of Spanish outposts appeared on the generally unknown frontier; but silver strikes in Zacatecas initiated a heady rush into the northern wonderland in 1549 and 1550. The *camino real*, a royal highway from Zacatecas to Mexico City became vitally important, especially after the discovery of other silver mines.

By 1550, the Chichimecas had initiated large-scale attacks upon roads and settlers. Africans who escaped from slavery also joined in attacking caravans and waylaying solitary travelers.

After 1560, Chichimecas assaulted towns, churches, and even came close to Mexico City a few times. By the late 1570s, Chichimeca raids extended farther south than ever before. As the Chichimecas experienced the delights of beef, horses, mules, and Hispanic clothing, they raided almost to the point of recklessness. Between 1580 and 1585, the Chichimeca threat reached its most dangerous zenith. Highway travel beyond Zacatecas became almost nonexistent and cooperation among the four principal Chichimeca tribes reached a high point. The fear of Chichimecas assumed almost panic proportions. By 1585, pacification of the northern frontier had become the outstanding problem of New Spain, Mexico's official name. The vaunted Spanish military and administration seemed doomed to failure.

By 1589, Viceroy Alvaro Manrique de Zuñiga decided upon a policy of peaceful conquest. He deployed soldiers who raided merely for obtaining slaves and set up investigations to punish wrongdoers. And Manrique agreed with the archbishop, who demanded that friars be used more extensively for the conversion of Chichimecas into pliable citizens.

The pacification of the Chichimecas resulted largely from the brilliant plan that brought sedentary Indian allies to settle hostile areas. These Tlaxcalans as well as Tarascans often received titles of nobility, military commissions, Spanish military protection, and exemption from tribute as well as labor service. Eventually, the nomadic groups virtually disappeared once the northward-moving groups absorbed them. Attracted largely because of their desire to use Spanish weapons and horses, Otomies and other allies became the auxiliaries which formed the bulk of Spanish military forces.

The strategy to attract Chichimeca submission eventually paid dividends. The Spaniards finally realized which chiefs and tribes were important and what they wanted. In November 1589, peace negotions opened with the principal Chichimeca leaders. Here the Spaniards promised food, clothing, land, religious (as opposed to civil) administration, and agricultural implements. Food and gifts soon placed Chichimecas onto level settlements with livestock, maize, and clothing for an indefinite period. Occasionally, reluctant Chichimeca leaders appeared before the viceroy, who took many of the enslaved Chichimeca away from their holders and put them into the hands of the various religious orders. Many friars had an excellent knowledge of the various Chichimec dialects and became vital interpreters.

The pacification program continued well into the next century to prevent new hostilities. Then the distribution of meat and maize, the basic items, came more and more into the hands of religious authorities. Within three-quarters of a century, rapidly multiplying Tlaxcalans pushed the Chichimecas off the best lands. Other Chichimecas drifted throughout New Spain; some arrived in Mexico City where they established their own barrio.

Although the loss of life and property during the Chichimeca war exceeded any other Spanish-Indian conflict in North America, this campaign is another blow at the black legend of Hispanic misdeeds against supposedly peaceful, innocent Indians. Other European conquests at this time and even later became much more brutal. The Italian invasions of Ethiopia and Libya seem to be a particularly ugly modern comparison. The Spaniards had a legalistic sense of justice that no other colonizers possessed as well as an excellent administrative system fashioned from medieval experiences in Iberia. Gold and silver certainly motivated Spaniards, but the humane friars eventually won the confidence of Indians. Even today, the United States cannot administer Native Americans effectively despite significant wealth.

After pacifying the Chichimecas, the rugged country along the boundary of Durango and Sinaloa became the scene of protracted clashes with the Acaxee and Xixime. A major Acaxee revolt in 1601 required the services of Governor Francisco Urdinola, who carried out harsh retribution. Nevertheless, the Xixime and Tepehuans subsequently revolted. Before the Spaniards finally subdued the Sierra Madre tribes, their attention shifted to the headwaters of the Conchos River in southern Chihuahua. There the Tobosos and Salineros presented problems in a valuable mining region as well as a staging area for *entradas* into New Mexico and Texas in the 1580s and 1590s.

Southeastern Resistance to Spanish Colonization. Yucatán and other southeastern areas became colonial backwaters. Spain transformed other regions into maximum production of natural resources, but few opportunities for wealth presented themselves in the southeast. The Spaniards took what they needed from the indigenous tribute system and left the means of production largely up to the Maya. The modest Maya economic existence consisted of coastal trading areas and corn production. Corn required much land and dispersion of the population. Food could be supplied with minimal effort. Also, the southeast differed from the central plateau and the north because the indigenous population greatly outnumbered the few Spaniards. Little mixing took place between Maya and Spaniard. Spanish and Maya leaders failed to form a partnership, which resulted in a strict caste separation. Initially, the church educated Maya nobles who became influential but the Spaniards feared the possibility of powerful native leaders challenging them and therefore ceased educating the Maya.

The Spanish invasion produced a fragile social order. Most Maya preferred appeasing the Spaniards rather than military clashes. The fighting that took place occurred on the seacoast and eastern frontier. Flight became much easier when conditions worsened. A very mobile people, the Maya could leave any area on foot at a moment's notice. Population movements became frequent. Often Maya simply relocated to a neighboring community. Colonial labor tribute and taxes produced even more movement. The Spanish invasion forced many Maya to flee southeastward. For the next 150 years, refugees in modern Quintana Roo, Belize, and the Petén area of Guatamala carried out a sustained resistance by means of retreat and rebellion to frustrate Spanish control. Since the Maya frontier had little attraction for Spaniards, the Maya refugees succeeded. Lacking resources and convinced that the eastern zones of the former Maya empire offered few economic rewards, Spain did little. Resistance took the form of revolts when the Maya massacred Spaniards in 1624 and 1638. Only with great effort were *conquistadors* able to establish some order, and they had still not brought the Maya under their control by the late seventeenth century.

Following the initial invasion, struggles developed between settlers and friars over who would have ultimate authority in the region. The appointment of Diego de Landa in 1562 as Provincial of the Franciscan mission placed Franciscan authority firmly in place. The order strictly regimented the towns and villages. Forcible introduction to Christianity devastated Maya society more than any other aspect of the invasion. Even though social fragmentation did not proceed as deeply as in other parts of Mexico, authorities replaced indigenous leaders who at least continued to enjoy authority within their communities. The Franciscans moved the Maya out of the wilderness and into cities created by fusing hamlets, villages, and towns.

The Maya preserved the most important aspects of their culture despite Hispanic influence. A strong bond with their natural habitat distinguished Maya civilization and developed its unique social organization. Yet individual survival during the invasion depended upon mutual aid. The Maya remained communal, only opting for flight in crisis situations. A godparenting system helped in times of famine or epidemics. This became significant once the Maya realized that the colonial tax system could not adapt to famine. Communal entities also carried valuable benefits. *Cajas de comunidad* became community funds which Spaniards tolerated. The funds provided indigenous elites with resources to manage fiestas, community events, or family needs. Underground Maya trade networks linked communities together on an interdependent basis. The Maya maintained a sense of autonomy by continuing to rely on their priests and lords to interpret events, perform traditional rituals, chant their sacred histories, and maintain a proper balance with nature. With each retelling, their histories evolved, as they incorporated new experiences. Through this

systematic process, the Maya continued to develop a coherent cultural system and maintain a distinctly Maya identity while adapting to the Hispanic world around them.

The Spaniards never "conquered" Mexico. Indigenous revolts continued through the seventeenth and eighteenth centuries. A particularly intense Zapotec insurrection shook the southern part of Oaxaca from 1660 to 1661. The ultimate loss of political and economic autonomy often incited rebellions. Throughout the colonial era, Indians usually targeted local authorities rather than the imperial apparatus. This distinction is important, because it reveals the extent of indigenous adaptability to Hispanic norms. Yet far fewer rural revolts took place in Mexico compared to Peru because taxes and labor services were less onerous. Moreover, Mexico contained far more ethnic groups with no common language or traditions to unite them.

Social Implications of the Invasion. Indian villagers adopted to their Spanish overlords by preserving some village customs, creating new ones, and strengthening ties within their villages.

In order to survive the Spanish invasion and preserve traditional social practices, Indians adopted many Hispanic conventions. Wills preserved individual properties and their division among offspring. Last wills and testaments enabled villagers to express their love or contempt for one another and their allegiance to older ways of doing things. Land transactions and the concept of title and nobility had precedence within indigenous practices and they continued. Soon frequent land sales took place. The appearance of a complete real estate market represents a major accomplishment introduced by Spanish officials.

The impact of the invasion upon individuals and families imposed a common strain throughout daily life that required flexibility. In towns such as Culhuacan in the valley of Mexico, most residents added Nahuatl surnames to their chosen Hispanic names. Towns and villages also utilized coats of arms to legitimatize land titles. Indigenous groups learned to fabricate land taxes. The spread of education in the second half of the sixteenth century reached many Indians regardless of social class. After 1550, alphabetic writing replaced pictographics. Nobles and plebians often learned to read and write together with the result that plebians increasingly gained access to positions such as *alcaldes*, *regidores*, and even governors. Many Indians could work where they pleased and began borrowing Spanish nouns; from 1630 to 1660, they added verbs, prepositions, and idioms. After 1650, bilingualism appeared. Educated Indians tended to defend their privileges and rank, particularly those educated by the Franciscan college established at Tlatelolco. After 1571, Indians came under exclusive jurisdiction of civil courts.

Like the *reconquista* invasions in Iberia and the Aztec assaults, the new victors altered the lives of the defeated. The original stones of indigenous buildings were used to construct Spanish churches. The Spaniards crushed the indigenous ruling elite and only those who collaborated with Spain retained their old positions, titles, and land. These caciques became Hispanized on the surface in terms of dress, language, and economic outlook. They slept on beds with mattresses and pillows while using Spanish furniture. They cooperated with royal officials until pushed aside in the seventeenth and eighteenth centuries.

But old boundaries persisted. Tlaxcala enjoyed relative autonomy in New Spain because of Spanish gratitude for Tlaxcalan aid during the victory over Tenochtitlan. Cultural traditions also lived on. A multitude of painted and written memories reveal that indigenous traditions survived during the sixteenth century.

As in the past, idolatry responded to basic needs within many indigenous communities. Idolatry continued to answer questions concerning ancestrality, reproduction, and natural forces, a summary of beliefs that historian Serge Gruzinski terms "the substance of existence." The indigenous *curandero* faith healers passed on oral idolatry by means of song, custom, and ritual. By means of practices, gestures, words, and beliefs, *curanderos* bound individuals as well as commu-

nities to the concept of time. People ranging from *voladores*—who dangled upside down from rotating wheels in Veracruz—to governors believed in idolatry for centuries. Laying food offerings on tombs persisted in indigenous areas. Offerings could be gourds full of water, kernels of corn, plants, fishing rods, or nets. In terms of regional manifestations, Guerrero and Morelos particularly embraced idolatry. Idolatry continued to mandate that Indians maintain figurines, terracotta vases, and dried plants to maintain domestic prosperity.

The white religion encouraged religious improvisation. Fortune tellers and Catholic rituals became formidable threats to idolatry once *mestizos* and blacks rejected purely indigenous ritual during the seventeenth century. Christian miracles became particularly attractive to Indians. Moreover, Iberian as well as African magic became potent rivals to indigenous beliefs. *Curanderos* responded by taking on Christian aspects of supernatural orientation, integrating it into their rituals. At first the use of hallucinogenic drugs terrified Spaniards almost as much as cannibalism and human sacrifice. Nevertheless, the use of hallucinogenic drugs became common for broad sectors of colonial society by the beginning of the seventeenth century.

COLONIAL CULTURE

The blending of indigenous and Hispanic traits soon produced a distinctly Mexican culture that became more unique as time went on. This syncretic amalgamation became most pronounced in the central region, less so in the south where indigenous traditions remained powerful. The north remained a warlike frontier zone.

Tone of Life. Colonial cities and towns appeared quickly and established characteristics that persist today. The Spanish grid pattern, promulgated by King Felipe II in 1573, established a central plaza that dominated urban environments. Here the administrative headquarters of the royal officials dominated one side with the cathedral juxtaposed on another flank. The plaza, sometimes referred to as the *traza* or *zócalo*, became the place where bullfights, executions, religious festivals, and bartering took place. Impoverished barrios of ordinary persons grew up farther away from the central plaza on narrow, unpaved streets because wealthier citizens preferred to live near the plaza. The majority of urban working-class families lived in single rooms or chambers divided by a blanket and shared with other families. The constant shortage of adequate family housing resulted in a lack of privacy; sexual assaults upon women and children reflected the pressure of unpleasant living standards for the majority of urban inhabitants.

Colonial cities became quite colorful and lively. During the sixteenth century, religious celebrations, such as the Corpus Christi festivals, dominated the urban scene. But the proliferation of civic festivals reflected elite fears of social and economic instability in Mexico City and other cities. In order to combat urban dissidence, state and church decided to acculturate diverse ethnic groups in order to avoid dissidence and to reaffirm the legitimacy of colonial institutions during a period of increasing miscegenation. By the seventeenth century, as many as 90 days of civic festival and religious holidays took place in Mexico City each year. Therefore, *cabildos* became financial organizers of Corpus Christi rites in order to entertain or even captivate urban *castas*, in particular.

The numerous festivals gave colonials a feeling of importance and participation. That so many responded enthusiastically suggests that the holidays provided a key link between ordinary Mexicans and their rulers. Expensive and generally paid for by *cabildos* or influential rural leaders in smaller villages, the festivals normally assumed lavish proportions. Each town had its own saint whose residents celebrated its day with *juego de cañas* games to commemorate the town's founding. This medieval jousting event featured spear throwing to break the ranks of opponents. Placing the municipal banner on a velvet pillow on a church altar during mass preceded the *juego de cañas* games. Bullfights, open to all, concluded the festivities. The arrival of a new viceroy became another important event. Citizens greeted him by erecting paper arches on the route from Veracruz. Officials monitored these celebrations carefully; they reported protocol mistakes to the Council of the Indies. The new viceroy exchanged coaches with the retiring one and read his instructions after greeting the bishop. When a viceroy died, the funeral train could sometimes extend as long as a mile. Notices of Spanish victories on European battlefields or royal weddings also became accompanied by mass celebrations, sky rockets, and orations by professors. The consumption of food, alcohol, music, and noise approximated rural festivities in early modern France.

Health became a serious social question. A smallpox epidemic devastated New Spain from 1518 to 1525; four additional outbreaks of sickness occurred from 1530 to 1581. In addition, flu, measles, typhus, various plagues, and fevers became the most dreaded diseases. The number of Indians fell from roughly 22 million at preinvasion time to less than 3 million by the middle of the sixteenth century. Poor hygiene and dirty water spread disease quickly; soap and clean clothes represented luxuries for most. Mexicans generally believed that when a person became ill, the situation was hopeless and lay in God's hands.

Remedies for illness did not provide optimism. Quacks and frauds outnumbered competent physicians. Many immunized themselves by taking crab eyes, dragon blood, and other useless prescriptions. The best doctors remained in urban areas, as is the case today. Town barbers, therefore, usually served as local surgeons. Phlebotomists (bleeders) were usually illiterate and had sparse training other than a knowledge of veins. Indigenous herbs often proved to be the best solution to illness.

To provide some relief, cross and crown provided hospital care. The epidemics that killed huge numbers of Nahuas throughout the Valley of Mexico motivated officials in Mexico and Spain to construct hospitals quickly. The religious orders, particularly Franciscans, Augustinians, and Benedictines, drew upon their medical experience to establish over 120 hospitals. In the beginning, these hospitals restricted care to Spaniards but eventually extended their services to Indians. Religious orders continued to provide health facilities throughout Mexico. The Franciscans, for example, established the famous San Juan de Montesclaros in 1584 as a hospital for seafarers in Veracruz.

The government provided unique services in Mexico City. One of these was the Royal Pharmacy. But more impressive is the Royal Indian Hospital, whose construction began in 1554 near the *plaza mayor*. With eight infirmaries by 1650, the hospital battled smallpox, venereal disease, tuberculosis, and rabies. Rabies afflicted many because rabies-infected rats passed the malady on to dogs and cats. Because few Indians recovered from rabies, the hospital persuaded the viceregal authorities to rid the capital of its dogs and cats periodically by authorizing bounties for the unlucky animals. But after each outbreak subsided, canines and felines reappeared. By the early seventeenth century, the hospital employed 80 people and cared for as many as 2,500 Indian patients per month. The first secular hospital under Spanish rule, the Royal Indian Hospital, relied basically on herbal medicines that came from the pharmacy.

Society usually enjoyed plentiful supplies of food during the sixteenth century. Despite long distances from population centers, arable land became readily available. Both colonists and indigenous peoples enjoyed a diet of unprecedented diversity once European and local crops combined. Corn became the Mexican grain adopted by Spaniards for fodder as well as food. Because the newly arriving cattle, hogs, chickens, and sheep could eat it, corn not only boosted Europe's supply of meat and dairy produce but also survived in Africa and eventually spurred population growth there. Chile peppers gave flavor to Italian sauces while American tomatoes provided the substance. Paprika became the hallmark of Hungarian stews. In exchange, Indians enjoyed the large domesticated European animals; meat became plentiful for everyone. Mixed bloods and Africans gradually acquired an interest in rice, wheat, limes, and bananas brought in from the Canary Islands. Clearly, European domination did not result in hunger. Only the commercialization of sugar, cacao, and wheat, at the end of the sixteenth century, reduced the tremendous volume of food supplies generated by the sixteenth-century Spanish onslaught.

Alcoholic beverages also had a tremendous impact upon society. Officials legalized pulque in 1608 after failing in attempts to prohibit it. *Pulquerías* appeared in urban areas beginning in the seventeenth century and increased in number in the eighteenth century. Beaten women, abortions, and drunken brawls became a key element of *mestizo* culture in drinking establishments. Transvestites and other sexual outlaws attended taverns. Rowdy behavior associated with alcoholic drinks challenged the colonial hegemony. Constant alcoholic consumption increased during the seventeenth century as Spanish brandy, wine, and sherry as well as *aguardiente* from sugar cane became popular. The regional dimension indicates less alcoholism and drinking away from Mexico City. In areas like Oaxaca, communal traditions remained powerful and drinking continued to be carried out for social purposes. Catholic rituals in rural provinces provided social cohesion often lacking in urban areas. Indeed, the violence that resulted from drinking excessively was individualized rather than becoming an expression of communal resentments. Alcohol, according to historian William Taylor, became related to over 60 percent of the homicides in central Mexico.

Harsh living standards took their toll. Despite plentiful food and numerous hospitals, illness and squalid living conditions resulted in frequent death. As late as the eighteenth century, census takers considered males who had reached 50 years of life to be aged and women old at 40.

Love and Marriage. The rules governing Christian marriage altered the social structure profoundly. Similarities between Hispanic and Mexican cultures eased social adjustment because both upheld male-dominated societies with traditions of lineage and extended family kinship systems.

Hispanic notions of romance and matrimony are unique. Marriage without parental consent became valid in Spain where love determined the wishes of young couples about to marry—unlike the rest of Europe. Moreover, Hispanic culture supported the ideal of free love in plays and catechisms; most Hispanics opposed coercive parental control. Males usually proposed verbally rather than in writing; men who backed out of oral commitments wound up in prison or pulling an oar in the galleys.

The same traditions appeared in Mexico. In Mexico City, secret marriages formed the majority of weddings from the late sixteenth century to 1689. When contested legally by parents, ecclesiastical judges ruled in favor of couples 92 percent of the time. Rural females married as early as 12 to 14 years old; in urban areas, 20 to 21 was the typical age. A lavish ceremony sealed most weddings; brides presented a dowry payment to their grooms who in turn bestowed gifts known as *arras*. The Spanish instituted an inheritance procedure so that widows received property and a portion of their husband's valuables. Hispanic law guaranteed female widows half their spouse's assets; children divided the rest. Isolation became the norm for many married women, particularly Spanish. Working women characterized the lower classes who needed extra income from market sales, work as maids, and whatever opportunities availed themselves. Affluent females who desired social interaction or intellectual stimulation entered convents. Here making preserves and prayer took up time but so did charitable activities. Mexican society considered childbearing the supreme function for most women. Unfortunately, a high mortality rate for both mothers and children resulted. And husbands often treated wives roughly. Beatings and mistreatment became an unpleasant part of *la mala vida* (a rough life). Men spent most of their time out of the home, frequently in the plaza, playing cards or attending cock fights.

Many colonials had love affairs. Accepting an offer of marriage usually initiated sexual rela-

tions. And there were many who did not bother with nuptial vows. In Mexico as well as Spain, the illegitimacy rate was much higher than the figure in Europe. In Guadalajara, the percentage of the illegitimate population began at 40 percent in 1600, rose to 60 percent in the 1650s, and leveled off at 50 percent by 1700. Similar figures characterize San Luis Potosí, Oaxaca, and Lima, Peru, but less illegitimacy appeared in rural areas because of the conservative Indian presence and the high prestige of the religious orders. Most bigamists moved around rountinely in rural areas. Lechery did not motivate most men although sexual favors were readily available.

The Hispanic nuclear household gradually became the family norm. *Compadrazgo*, where a close family friend sponsored children during religious sacraments, became a vital element in colonial life. *Compadrazgo* served as a social device for acknowledging mutual obligations in the social as well as economic spheres. Godparenthood enabled Spaniards to give easier access to Indian labor. Through *compadrazgo* as well as intermarriage, elite families formed a tight network that utilized patronage and ritual kinship to dominate the masses. Fortunately, indigenous culture also honored extended families, but with important distinctions.

The indigenous tradition of having more than one wife or a concubine was something Spanish officials had difficulty in stamping out. Maintaining several wives denoted high status and baptism did not always deter couples from living in polygamous relationships. Irritated, the crown in 1530 attempted to punish men who acquired additional wives. In response, many males married sacramentally their first or favorite wife. Also, Christian monogamy tended to diminish the role of uncles in indigenous kinship systems. The requirement for mutual consent among couples, the prohibition of kin as marriage partners, free choice for daughters, and the termination of marriages between political allies became sharp blows to Indian customs. Gradually, Hispanic norms prevailed.

Marital stability and the integrity of nuptial rituals began to break down by the late seventeenth century. At this point, interracial marriages began to occur in modest numbers for the first time. Although marriage became more common for non-whites, tension became noticeable when Hispanic males began to back out of betrothments in significant numbers. Frequently, men offered financial inducements to walk away from unions with pregnant females and got away with it. Once the economy improved after 1670, material motives became more notable in marriages or general relationships. Romance and love lost their esteem, to a certain point.

Despite the tight control Spaniards maintained over African slaves, blacks managed to live vibrant family lives as much as possible. Huts where slaves lived often became the centers of private life. Here slaves tried to raise children and developed a modest number of nuclear families, despite white attempts to break them up. Marriage became an effective defense against the continuation of slavery. At first, marriage was uncommon for blacks, although the marriage rate for African females rose sharply in the seventeenth century. Although Spanish law prohibited intermarriage between Indians and Africans, it became inevitable. Since only one-third of the Africans brought into Mexico were female, black males took up with Indians instead. Intermarriage weakened slavery because, after 1542, Spain did not consider Indians slaves. To improve the lot of their children, African men married Indian females, knowing their offspring would not live in bondage. To cite one region, from 1646 to 1746, priests of the Santa Veracruz parish married 1,662 couples, of whom one or both persons were of African descent. African males also married *mestizas* and free *mulatas*, who became a major portion of seventeenth century *mestizaje*.

Education. After an auspicious beginning, Spanish educational policies never fulfilled expectations. A coherent and sustained plan for educating indigenous peoples never appeared. Although every municipality had the obligation to provide a minimum of one primary school, reality dictated otherwise.

Education in Mexico began with a racial divergence. Unlike the settlement of North America, Spain assumed that the indigenous population would form a vital part of society as workers and tribute-paying Catholics. Officials decided early that education would play an integral role in assimilating Indians. But uprooting the indigenous way of life became frustrating. Indians did not show much interest in learning Spanish, growing wheat, and accepting new trade concepts. The persistence of idolatry became particularly unnerving, especially when Franciscan friars assumed that their progress in Yucatán would never end. The 1562 discovery of idols in caves resulted in vengeful inquisitorial persecution of hundreds of Maya. The early utopian hopes of religious orders to produce a puritanical society received an additional blow when epidemics nearly wiped out the indigenous population. Thus a full process of Westernization in the frontier zones gave way to the simple desire for control. By the beginning of the seventeenth century, the orders concentrated upon educating the urban European settlers.

The colonists obtained basic education in a variety of settings. Young girls attended private secular schools staffed by female instructors in several municipalities. Others lived in convents or enrolled in day schools operated by nuns. Wealthy and well-to-do Spaniards used tutors, who were often retired soldiers and priests. Particularly in remote villages or isolated towns, parish schools became major providers of education. In all these surroundings, rote memorization under the instructor's firm hand remained a ritual for centuries. The whip, which each parish school teacher wielded, symbolized his authority.

Colegios and other secondary schools existed on a higher level. *Colegios* abounded in the cities and correspond with modern U. S. high schools. Some females attended religious establishments shortly before the invasion, but secondary education was more pronounced for young males. Shortly after their arrival in Mexico, the Jesuits opened the first of many *colegios* in 1574. These schools offered studies in law, theology, and medicine. The Jesuit *colegios* surpassed others in quality and thus became by far the most popular institutions of secondary education. As with the universities in Spain and throughout Latin America, the basis of colonial education reflected the philosophy of Thomas Aquinas, the leading Catholic philosopher, who subordinated philosophy to theology; natural law to the revelations of Christ; human society to religious dogma. Thomistic teaching endeavored to demonstrate that these approaches would benefit philosophy, natural law, and human society.

The royal pontifical university of Mexico served Mexico well during the colonial epoch. Guided by traditional Spanish academic patterns as part of an attempt to tie the colony to the motherland, little change took place in its environment until the nineteenth century. The Mexican upper class provided generous contributions to the university as well as other institutions of higher learning. Only a university degree would entitle aspirants to hold positions in the ecclesiastical and bureaucratic positions which the elite coveted.

Founded in 1553, the university contained mostly part-time, ill-paid faculty who eventually granted some 30,000 degrees. Modeled after Salamanca and Alcala de Amores universities in Spain, the curriculum stressed philosophy, medicine, theology, rhetoric, and law. The lectures prepared students for degree exams during a six-month school year with no regular examinations. Part of the university's role was maintaining the status quo. Therefore students could not smoke or wear colored socks or they would be put in the university dungeon. In order to receive their degrees, students had to swear a loyalty oath to the king, viceroy, and other officials as well as proclaim that the Virgin Mary was conceived without sin.

As a reflection of restrictive colonial practices, the university had limitations. No females could attend. Africans and *mulatos* at best received discouragement. Indians could legally apply for admittance, particularly if they had descended from the nobility, but few entered. In reality, the university existed mainly in order to train clergy. But the Church's own reluctance to open its ranks to indigenous people is a clear demonstration of the gap between whites and nonwhites. Only a few faculty demonstrated genuine interest in indigenous peoples. In fact, the positions in Indian languages recorded the most severe violations of academic integrity at the university. The inability to include indigenous students in higher education restricted Mexican intellectual growth until the 1920s.

Intellectual Trends. National identity existed long before the successful completion of the independence war. Although national awareness concerned primarily only an intellectual elite, the first signs of a Mexican consciousness appeared, however latent, as early as the latter sixteenth century when writers began to differentiate between the quality of life in Mexico and Spain.

Despite attempts by church and state to maintain a dogmatic intellectual life by minimizing science as well as empirical methods, a rich literary tradition unfolded. Verse writing became very popular and many aspired for recognition as poets. Chivalrous romances such as *Amadis of Gaul* and *Don Quijote* dominated reading tastes along with medieval Christian literature. Nationalist trends emerged with Bernardo de Balbuena's *Grandeza Mexicana*, which extolled the floral luxuriance of the Valley of Mexico and sketched the universe required for the appearance of the Virgin of Guadalupe. In this poem, the roses which nurtured the madonna's creation and the stars on her mantle are related to the women of Mexico City. The first Mexican writer to extoll the intellect of Mexican women, Balbuena also authored the only real colonial novel, *El siglo de oro en las selvas de Erifile*. Until the 1640s, all significant Mexican intellects resided in New Spain as well as the mother country.

Juan Ruíz de Alarcón is one of three outstanding intellects who represent the transition from a purely Hispanic to a more Mexican emphasis. Born in 1581 to well-established parents in Mexico City, Ruíz de Alarcón studied at the university before sailing off to Spain in August 1600. After studying canonical law in the University of Salamanca, Ruíz de Alarcón practiced law in Seville. In 1600, his literary life began when he had to write a work for the festival of San Juan de Alfarche. Ruíz de Alarcón returned to New Spain but failed to obtain his doctoral degree or obtain a teaching position at the university. After his return to Madrid in 1614, critical themes, characterized by an uncanny sense of rhyme, also embellished his various comedies.

One of Ruíz de Alarcón's masterpieces is *La verdad sospechosa* (1621), a poetic comedy based upon mental and artificial constructions, yet expressed in free verse with a joyful vitality. It was the first time in Europe that a work represented the triumph of character comedy over intricate structures. Irony and criticism of King Felipe III as well as the Spanish aristocracy antedated social unrest in Mexico. Dishonesty is a constant theme that Ruíz de Alarcón condemns. His demand for honesty would characterize *criollo* complaints against the rising corruption of the seventeenth century. Similarly, his play *El examen de los maridos* exalts sincere love. After Ruíz de Alarcón, Mexico's two major writers never lived in Spain.

The most famous Mexican scholar is the multi-talented Carlos de Sigüenza y Góngora. His father tutored King Felipe IV and his mother was related to a famous Spanish poet. After the family immigrated to Mexico, their son enrolled with the Jesuits but his superiors ousted him for indiscipline. Life as a priest failed to satisfy his remarkable intellect until Sigüenza y Góngora obtained the chair of mathematics and astrology at the University of Mexico at the ripe age of 25. Corresponding with his peers in Europe, Sigüenza y Góngora achieved outstanding contributions to astronomy and various engineering projects. By using a telescope with multiple lenses, he gauged the motion of the planets and stars, much in the Maya tradition. His scientific endeavors resulted in a fiery exchange against the well-known Jesuit, Eusebio Kino, who attempted to maintain traditional theology and antiquated assumptions against Sigüenza y Góngora's scientific, rational approach.

Unlike most other intellectuals, Sigüenza y Góngora possessed an active interest in Mexico's pre-Hispanic past. He learned indigenous dialects while collecting documents and artifacts. He studied the Aztec dynasties and the Mesoamerican calendar. Most experts consider his repository of indigenous items the most inclusive in the world. His imaginative, interpretive ability struck a prophetic nerve when *Phoenix of the West* hypothesized a link between the apostle Saint Thomas and Quetzalcoatl. The few hundred or so intellectually active persons in Mexico City began to ponder his theory as a way to consider a distinct Mexican uniqueness, particularly in the eighteenth century. The contradiction between faith and reason did not unravel the brilliant Sigüenza y Góngora, who believed in miracles and never intended to upset the established order although much of his research did so indirectly.

Sor (sister) Juana Inés de la Cruz was an amazing intellect who became a symbol of Mexican dissatisfaction with the stratified Spanish system. She became a nun because that was the only way to be allowed to study on a serious level. Her ambition in writing and energy in researching wide-ranging topics are as notable as her courage to take on such tasks.

Born southeast of Mexico City into a family of small landholders between the volcanoes of Popocatepetl and Ixtacihuatl, Juana Ramírcz was illegitimate, beautiful, brilliant, and poor. Her grandfather taught her to read at the age of three. Seven years later, her mother sent Juana to live with an aunt in Mexico City. Largely self-taught, she progressed rapidly in her studies and Juana came to be regarded as a child prodigy. Juana's relatives presented her to the Marquise Mancera, whose husband became viceroy in 1664. The lack of a formal education resulted in unusual originality that immediately motivated the viceregal court to hire Juana as a maid-in-waiting.

At this point, Juana's individuality asserted itself. Juana may have feared that she might not be able to live in the court beyond the end of the viceroy's term. Despite her beauty, it is doubtful that she could have married, given her illegitimacy and lack of a dowry. Moreover, she opposed marriage because she could not have been both a wife and scholar. Yet, to pursue intellectual tastes rarely became an option for colonial women. Therefore Juana entered the Jeronymite order in 1669, where she pursued her scholarship and writing. The somewhat superficial court atmosphere had distracted her from undisturbed intellectual forays. Lacking a family, Juana was attracted to the communal cloister. She lived the rest of her life at the Santa Paula convent, and Juana's parlor became a study where she amassed a library and carried out extensive correspondence. At the same time, Juana assumed teaching duties and maintained the convent's accounts.

But Sor Juana was an unusual nun whose attitudes and accomplishments kindled envy. Unlike most clergy, Juana justified the study of logic, rhetoric, physics, music, history, and other subjects to enhance an understanding of the Bible. She became famous in Spain when the viceroy's wife published her poetry in Madrid. Such an accomplishment enhanced her fame but increased jealousy of her status as well as her gender. She also acquired jewels, money, and notes that accumulated in her cell.

A skilled prose writer, poet, and musician, Juana oriented the intimate portion of her work toward new knowledge rather than reaffirming her Catholic surroundings. The range of her poetry is unusually wide, balancing passion and reasoned intellect. Her witty, well-crafted dramas for the public theater as well as the court charmed nearly everyone. The dexterity and polish of her work made Juana a world figure. Yet humor as well as technical skill became her legacy.

Juana's skill in stylizing the popular lyricism of song and dance is particularly notable. Sor Juana possessed an unusual ability to empathize with the feelings of average people. Therefore she composed lyrics for various dances and songs during religious festivities. She did this for 15 years. Cathedrals in Oaxaca and Puebla also commissioned her to write, indicating an appeal beyond Mexico City. These *villancicos* lyrics are characterized by a religiosity adjusted for the needs of commoners, often witty and capable of satarizing prominent figures. In addition to *villancicos*, Sor Juana produced one-act plays for the feast of Corpus Christi. Many of her poems reflected the outlook of everyday Mexicans because she utilized indigenous phrases, African languages, Latin, and Basque dialects. Her interest in Mexican diversity can be interpreted as a concern for embryonic Mexican nationality.

She elaborated universal themes generally removed from the classical approach. Juana dedicated love poems to women although no evidence of lesbianism or bisexuality has appeared in her life. The hundreds of poems she wrote are considered a manifesto of early feminist literature. During her lone meditation on theology, Sor Juana seemed to push the concept of free will to the limit at a time when authority and traditionalism began to seize the initiative in social matters. More than any of her Hispanic peers, she championed individuality. Her attacks on the sexual double standard and defense of rights of women make her relevant to today's readers.

Sor Juana's quest for knowledge ended in bowing to pressure from the Catholic hierarchy. The bishop of Puebla published something that surprised Juana: her theological critique of a sermon that had been delivered decades before. To this, the bishop appended a letter in which the bishop claimed that God disapproved of vanity in females; he suggested that Sor Juana had read too much philosophy and not enough scripture.

Sor Juana's reply is an eloquent statement on behalf of a woman's right to receive a formal education, to express her opinions, and to create literature. Since so many women have practiced verse "in a fashion so evidently praiseworthy," she stated, "what can be so wrong about my being a poet?" Her 1691 reply proclaimed that the gift of intelligence carried with it the responsibility to use it, whether the possessor is male or female.

The exchange deepened the animosity that the archbishop and other religious leaders felt toward Sor Juana—partially because of her writings and because a woman had produced them. By the end of the 1680s, the archbishop objected to Juana's plays written for public performance. Probably succumbing to church pressure, Sor Juana took the first of several steps by which she renounced her lack of religious devotion. She gave up much of her library and other possessions and retired to prayer, fasting, and tending to the sick. She died during a 1695 epidemic while caring for plague-stricken sisters in the convent. By then, the impact of Sor Juana had become compelling. Some sermons in the second half of the seventeenth century contained a strong dose of *criollo* nationalism.

Art and music that appeared in the middle of the colonial era also exhibited a subtle sense of nationality. Colonial art exhibits a vital link between the preHispanic epoch and modern Mexico. Viceregal painting also displays an ambiguity typical of colonial culture: the emulations of European styles by artists detached from the sources that originally inspired them. In New Spain, both indigenous and external forces produced this art. The struggle for national identity was not simply among Indians, Spaniards, and colonials born in Mexico but a contest among all three. Powerful and often solid artistic results appeared during the colonial period. During the sixteenth century, many paintings depicted the Spanish invasion but also the survival of the Aztec past. Although missionaries destroyed art they considered pagan, they also preserved pre-Hispanic artistic techniques. The art of New Spain strongly bore the imprint of the Renaissance and the Counter-Reformation in Europe until the seventeenth century witnessed the emergence of a conscious Mexican style from 1650 to 1715. Despite the eradication of the indigenous sites and practices, the spirit of the old religion persisted, in turn imbuing Mexican art with distinctive characteristics that still survive.

Music in New Spain derived from three sources. Spanish composers in Iberia wrote much music which was carried in manuscript or printed book form to the New World. Missionaries disseminated the music throughout Mexico City. Monks became successful in using music to convert Indians. Several famous Spanish teachers came to Mexico with Baroque and Renaissance styles. Transplanted Spanish composers in Mexico wrote a second category of musical works in either Latin, Spanish, or indigenous dialects. Splendid composers such as Juan Gutiérrez de Padilla, Francisco López Capillas, and Juan de Lienas crafted excellent seventeenth-century works. Indians composed a third musical repertoire in European style. Franciscan and Jesuit monks translated the liturgy into indigenous tongues, wrote devotional music in Indian languages, and taught the Indians to make and play the recorder, violin, trumpet, and organ as well as to compose music after European models. Delightful works, blending European musical forms with New World vitality, utilized pre-Hispanic affinities for song, flutes, and drums.

The cultural foundation of colonial Mexico had a strong Hispanic imprint. The transmutation of Spanish dance techniques surfaced quickly in public festivals, theater, and the court. The *conchero* dance developed after the Spanish invasion and incorporates indigenous and Spanish cultural elements. This dance has been performed continually for more than 450 years. The evolution and repertoire of the guitar and opera became significant events. At the same time, the development of *mestizo* and *criollo* musical traditions from the fusion of indigenous and Hispanic cultures rounded out a zesty cultural panorama.

SUGGESTED READING

Aiton, Arthur Scott. *Antonio de Mendoza.* Durham, NC: Duke University Press, 1921.

Beezley, William H., Cheryl Martin and William French, eds. *Rituals of Rule, Rituals of Resistance.* Wilmington, DE: Scholarly Resources, 1994.

Boyer, Richard. *Lives of The Bigamists: Marriage, Family, and Community in Colonial Mexico.* Albuquerque: University of New Mexico Press, 1995.

Castro Leal, Antonio. *Juan Ruíz de Alarcón: Cuatro comedias.* Mexico City: Editorial Porrua, 1969.

Clendinnen, Inga. *Ambivalent Conquests: Maya and Spaniard in Yucatán, 1517–1570.* New York: Cambridge University Press, 1987.

Cline, Sarah. "The Spiritual Conquest Reexamined: Baptism and Christian Marriage in Early Sixteenth Century Mexico." *Hispanic American Historical Review* 73:2 (August 1993), 453–80.

———. *Colonial Culhuacan, 1580–1600. A Social History of an Aztec Town*. Albuquerque: University of New Mexico Press, 1986.

Cope, R. Douglas. *The Limits of Racial Domination: Plebian Society in Colonial Mexico City, 1660–1720*. Madison: University of Wisconsin Press, 1994.

Curcio-Nagy, Linda. "Giants and Gypsies: Corpus Christi in Colonial Mexico City." In Beezley et al. *Rituals of Rule, Rituals of Resistance*, pp. 1–26.

Driver, Harold, ed. *Americas on the Eve of Discovery*. Upper Saddle River, NJ: Prentice Hall, 1964.

Farriss, Nancy. *Maya Society Under Colonial Rule*. Princeton, NJ: Princeton University Press, 1984.

Gibson, Charles. *The Aztecs Under Spanish Rule*. Stanford, CA: Stanford University Press, 1964.

Gonzalbo Aizpuru, Pilar. *Historia de la educación en la época colonial: La educación de los criollos y la vida urbana*. Mexico City: El Colegio de México, 1990.

Gruzinski, Serge. *The Conquest of Mexico: The Incorporation of Indian Societies into the Western World, 16th–18th Centuries*. Cambridge: Blackwell, 1993.

Jones, Grant D. *Maya Resistance to Spanish Rule: Time and History on a Colonial Frontier*. Albuquerque: University of New Mexico Press, 1989.

Kamen, Henry. *Spain, 1469–1714: Society and Conflict*, 2d ed. New York: Longman, 1991.

Leiby, John S. "The Royal Indian Hospital of Mexico City, 1553-1680." *The Historian* 57:3 (Spring 1995), 573–580.

Leonard, Irving A. *Baroque Times in Old Mexico*. Ann Arbor: University of Michigan Press, 1959.

Liss, Peggy. *Mexico Under Spain, 1521–1556: Society and the Origins of Nationality*. Chicago: University of Chicago Press, 1975.

Love, Edgar F. "Marriage Patterns of Persons of African Descent in a Colonial Mexico City Parish." *Hispanic American Historical Review* 51:4 (February 1971), 84–96.

MacLachlan, Colin M. *Spain's Empire in the New World*. Berkeley: University of California Press, 1988.

MacLachlan, Colin, and Jaime Rodriguez. *The Forging of the Cosmic Race: A Reinterpretation of Colonial Mexico*. Berkeley: University of California Press, 1980.

Noguera, Eduardo. *El horizonte Tolteca-Chichimeca*. Mexico City: Ediciones Mexicanas, 1952.

Paz, Octavio. *Sor Juana or the Traps of Faith*. Cambridge, MA: Harvard University Press, 1982.

Powell, Philip Wayne. *Soldiers, Indians and Silver*. Berkeley: University of California Press, 1982.

Seed, Patricia. *To Love, Honor and Obey in Colonial Mexico: Over Marriage Choice, 1574-1821*. Stanford, CA: Stanford University Press, 1988.

Steck, Francis B. *Motolinia's History of the Indians of New Spain*. Washington, DC: Academy of American Franciscan History, 1951.

Super, John. *Food, Conquest and Colonization in Sixteenth Century Spanish America*. Albuquerque: University of New Mexico Press, 1988.

Wolf, Eric. *Sons of the Shaking Earth*. Chicago: University of Chicago Press, 1959.

4

Hispanic Foundations

The consolidation of the Spanish invasion resulted in the establishment of semifeudal institutions that transformed Mexico permanently. Many Mexican products entered the world economy on a lasting basis while various labor practices endured until the twentieth century. Catholicism became a spiritual lifeline throughout the country and a successful system of social mobilization.

MEXICO'S MERCANTILIST ECONOMY

System of Mercantile Colonialism. Mercantilism always characterized Spain's approach to managing the Mexican economy. Mercantilism defined Spain's goals of self-sufficiency and enhancement of state power by means of maintaining a higher level of exports than imports. Spain needed substantial revenues from Mexico to help finance its European wars. The Mexican colony also furnished large amounts of bullion and raw materials which enabled Spanish merchants to enter lucrative markets. Mercantilism also became a system of monopoly control because only Spaniards could take part in trade with Mexico. Spain's privileged groups successfully insisted that Mexican items which competed with Spanish industries be discouraged. Until the eighteenth century, only Castile enjoyed complete access to Mexican specie and agricultural commodities because Seville and Cádiz were the only Spanish ports that could trade with Mexico. Up to the very end of the colonial epoch, the closed Mexican markets remained off limits to European rivals. Spanish merchants maximized their profits even more by limiting the quantity of goods sent to Mexico so that they could charge higher prices.

Agriculture soon surpassed the market value of the more famous mines in terms of the value of its overall production. Upon their arrival in Mexico, Spaniards soon realized that it would be imperative to bring trees, cattle, and other European items in order to establish a self-sufficient but noncompetitive economy because the difficulties which arose by provisioning Mexico from Spain became costly. The Spanish also began to understand the necessary geographical conditions. To cite a few examples, sheep and wheat thrived in Oaxaca but failed in Yucatán. Nevertheless, Spaniards planted everything that grew in Iberia, such as olives, limes, and oranges.

Particularly important to the Spanish was the export of luxury items from which a great deal of money could be made in Europe. Therefore plantation agriculture, characterized by a high volume of exports to the world economy, became important early in the colonial economy and would characterize the propensity of modern Mexico to export goods from its choicest growing areas rather than foodstuffs for the national economy.

Cacao became an extremely vital export. The pulverized seeds of the cacao tree—*chocolatl*—made a dark drink enjoyed originally by the masses in Aztec days. Mixed with other ingredients, the creamy beverage dazzled Cortés, who sent the beans back to Europe. Tabasco enjoyed a dynamic cacao industry during the colonial era. The Spaniards grew cacao in large quantities and created a large demand for it throughout Europe.

Sugar also became important. Eventually, sugar emerged as the second most important agricultural product. To encourage its growth, the viceroy granted a ten year tax exemption for all sugar producers, who argued that they merited special attention because of the expense of the mills, labor costs, pirate attacks, and irregular rainfall. To maintain interest in sugar growing, the crown declared sugar plantations inalienable from creditors when planters went into debt. Such favored treatment resulted in latifundia, because the plantation owners required large amounts of land.

Tobacco became another moneymaker after Columbus sent samples back to Spain from where its use spread all over Europe. Tobacco at this time was thought to have medicinal powers. It could be grown freely all over Mexico until Spain established a monopoly over it in 1764.

Vanilla beans became valuable exports. In addition to enjoying vanilla's rich sweetness, Europeans rubbed it on their heads to cure baldness, mixed it with tobacco for smoking and chewing, and considered it a miracle drug. At one time or another vanilla was used to lower fevers, cure hysteria, impotency, and rheumatism, and many thought it would prevent sleep and serve as an antidote to poison and the bites of venomous animals.

Mexican agriculture flourished on a diversified basis. Spanish settlers developed substantial regional export trades in honey, wax, and countless other items, despite having to transport their goods with Indian porters until sufficient numbers of mules and horses became available. The crown encouraged the efforts of Spanish farmers be-

cause royal officials feared the possibility of a rival landowning class emerging as feudal rivals who would challenge royal hegemony.

But the tendency to concentrate on agricultural exports resulted in a food production crisis by the end of the sixteenth century. Although the pasture land of the American continent was so rich that range animals multiplied rapidly, food supplies declined in many rural areas. Therefore the Spanish established regional *alhóndigas* (graineries) beginning in 1578 to sell grains at fixed prices. The viceroy established prices and forbade the hoarding of corn. European agricultural techniques and livestock raising increased production but could hardly fulfill the needs of larger numbers of colonists. Fortunately, large haciendas began making their presence felt by raising food supplies so that the worst shortages ended by the 1650s. At this time, the Hispanic economic center of gravity shifted from Spain to Mexico.

Industry and Manufacturing. The Spaniards gradually developed a lucrative dye industry. Cortés introduced mulberry trees in order to obtain a yellow dye. Cochineal became a lucrative red dye which came from insects resembling lice that fed on cactus. Only female insects could be utilized; it required 100,000 of them to be baked and dried in order to produce a pound of the much sought-after dye. Producers maintained a natural monopoly which the Spaniards guarded carefully. In Yucatán, an indigo industry flourished briefly until competition from Central America overwhelmed this source of blue dye. Campeche logwood produced a solid purple and black dye. In 1576, the Spanish crown declared the logwood trade a royal monopoly.

Silk raising succeeded only in Puebla after the Spaniards tried to introduce silk industries in several regions. The problem was finding balanced weather conditions and intermediate altitudes, between 5,000 and 7,000 feet. Cortés established the silk industry in 1527 and it remained profitable until the 1580s. Silk declined in Mexico because the Indians revolted and destroyed trees as well as looms. Moreover its high cost meant that Mexico could not compete with superior silk brought in from China. Finally, Seville merchants pressured the crown to stop the Mexican silk industry.

Manufacturing had a tremendous effect upon the spread of cities and the economic development of various regions. Mining communities stimulated the growth of Zacatecas, Guanajuato, and other cities as the need for commodities developed. But Mexico City, Puebla, and Querétaro developed craft mills and processing plants. Many other localities took part in the large colonial market economy as opposed to isolated subsistence modes of production. Community and kinship often determined which businesses expanded and diversified and provided the stability that held complex as well as diverse businesses together.

Regions and cities specialized in certain goods. In northern Mexico, furniture made at Jesuit missions evolved into what came to be known as the hardy, austere colonial Mexican style. Puebla produced porcelains, tiles, and blown glass. The talavera style blended Muslim, Hispanic, and indigenous ceramic techniques into a unique as well as beautiful medium that made Puebla famous for centuries. Guadalajara specialized in textiles while Querétaro produced jewelry and leather goods. Querétaro also became well known for its woolen goods. The colonial division of labor gave rise to local manufacturing outlets. One can still see how this is internalized within the towns themselves. With medieval taxing and regulatory practices in mind, jewelers would be established in one area, dry goods in another. Colonial officials could supervise industries easier if all of them resided on a particular street or in a certain area of town.

The most common industry was textiles. It was easy to maintain given preHispanic traditions of weaving. Its long strands made Mexican cotton ideal for smooth cloth and superior to coarse European materials. Now, Europe did not have to depend upon earlier cotton imports from India and the Middle East. Mexican *obrajes* (textile facto-

ries) used children as young as ten to produce coarse sheep cloth for the masses. Shipbuilding was another common industrial activity, particularly after the decline of the Spanish navy. Soap making also became prominent, as well as the production of alcoholic beverages and matches.

Commerce and Trade. Mexican merchants exercised considerable influence over Atlantic and Pacific trade during the colonial period. The merchants influenced socioeconomic life throughout Mexico in innumerable ways.

The merchants operated on a large scale. An elite group of prominent shippers controlled about 70 percent of Mexico's overseas trade. A merchant's career normally followed a regular course: A period of apprenticeship in a family business and a junior partnership of considerable duration; then the status of independent trader once the merchant acquired a well-dowried wife and Mexico City residence; finally, with expanded business activities and purchase of public office, the merchant eventually became a public figure of status and influence. Although operating out of Mexico City, the merchants maintained kinship linkages to Spanish ports because most of them were born in Spain. Content with their control of the economy, merchants did not particularly innovate because the dynamic scale of operations across two oceans called for systematic long-term ventures. Profits ranged in the 30 to 70 percent category. Merchants concentrated upon importing Asian and European goods while exporting large quantities of indigo, cochineal, and other agricultural items.

Since there were no banks in colonial Mexico, the merchants often possessed the only local investment capital. They loaned it out to miners, sugar plantation owners, textile producers, and those who purchased urban real estate. Residing in impressive homes, merchants maintained the continuity of wealth and status for their offspring. Children and grandchildren accumulated civil and ecclesiastical titles. Their wealth equaled or exceeded that of the most esteemed landowners. Even though the economic downturn between 1640 and 1660 became severe and resulted in reducing the number of merchants to about 250 by the late 1630s, the business community did not suffer permanent damage. Some regions experienced ruin and depression in the middle of the seventeenth century, but the continuity of merchant operations remained relatively unchanged.

Because of the rapid expansion of trade with Mexico, the structure of Spanish commerce expanded accordingly. The size of Spanish ships increased from 70 tons in 1504 to 400 tons by 1641. Not surprisingly, the gross tonnage of these ships also increased from 15,000 tons in 1510 to 273,000 tons by 1606. Although slow in the beginning, the mean time for crossing the Atlantic eventually was reduced to 67 days.

Mexico also became more integrated into the world economy as Spain failed to build up her own industries and had to rely upon purchases of manufactured goods from northern Europe. Merchants sold these items on consignment to Mexican customers at very inflated prices. Thanks to the industrial decline of Iberia, northern Europe acquired Mexican gold and silver and used them as the investment capital of the Industrial Revolution. Despite the fluctuations of the seventeenth century, Mexican trade across the Atlantic became lucrative although tightly regulated. The Spanish organized a flota system whereby heavily armed escorts of Hispanic warships protected merchant ships after the 1560s. Annual convoys arrived in Veracruz each spring before departing to Havana for the return trip to Spain.

In the Pacific, no other line of ships endured as long or were as exposed to as many dangers and temptations as the Manila galleons. The Philippines were always the center of Spanish trade in Asia and Mexico City administered it. The demand for Chinese silks, opium, porcelain, and spices became great in Mexico. Clerical interests and cautious Manila merchants controlled the trade under careful supervision by the Spanish governor since the ships of the Manila trade were royal property. Leading citizens placed their goods onto the ships for sale in Mexico's port of Acapulco. Profits ranged from 100 to 300 percent; the sixteenth century was the most lucrative period. The six-month voyage to Acapulco was extremely dangerous; the overloaded and unescorted galleons faced hurricanes, monsoons, overcrowding, and scurvy. Not surprisingly, 30 ships sank. The return voyage provided better winds and lighter hulls; therefore it required only three months.

The merchants enjoyed friendly relations with colonial officials and prominent *criollos*. To facilitate amicable links to the administration, merchants financed the purchase of high as well as lower government posts. This enabled them to pressure administrators to avoid tax payments. Lax officials could also be bribed in order to smuggle in contraband goods. Increased convoy taxes often motivated the smuggling of silver. *Criollo* mining and pastoral ventures resulted in juicy dowries from marriageable daughters. The crown itself did not want to alienate holders of liquid capital such as the merchants and therefore issued pardons for contraband seizures when Spanish governmental deficits mounted in the war-plagued atmosphere of Europe. And throughout Mexico, the forced sale of goods to Indians and compulsory production of commodities became the motor of the regional economies. Local merchants often advanced goods and cash to *corregidores* who then distributed them to Indians in return for cotton, wheat, cochineal, and whatever the market required, thus creating a commercial monopoly.

The Mining Cycle. Although agriculture always surpassed mining in terms of the value of economic production, silver mining fueled the growth of the colonial economy and always remained at the center of royal attention. For this reason, the crown upheld Roman tradition, which maintained that the subsoil rights of the country belong to the state. This meant that colonists could acquire concessions but never outright ownership of any mines that they developed. Moreover, miners had to pay a royal *quinto* (fifth) and then a *diezmo* (tenth) after 1548 on all the wealth they mined. Spain received about $5 billion in ores from all of Latin America during the colonial period, about $2.25 billion from Mexico.

A silver boom soon engulfed Mexico. At first many hoped that large amounts of gold could be found. Mexico legally exported more than five million pesos in gold before 1550. But only about one million pesos left from Veracruz from 1550 to 1650. The first notable silver strike occurred about 1530 in Sultepec and Zumpango near Mexico City. Taxco and Tlalpujahua strikes occurred shortly afterward. But the conclusion of the Mixtón War enabled the settlement of the northwest where silver fever soon took hold. In 1543 an Indian maid serving a woman rancher in Guadalahjara brought her some ore from near the provincial capital of Compostela. Espiritu Santo became the first great silver strike. Thousands flooded in; many barely knew what they were doing or looking for.

The majority of large mines evolved north of Mexico City. Juan de Tolosa, sent to crush Indian rebels in the northwest, succeeded. His true reward came when Indians guided him to the hills of Zacatecas where he found the San Bernabé vein. With three other Basques, Tolosa formed a partnership which initiated the silver aristocracy of Mexico. He lost a great deal of money fighting military campaigns, developing other mines, and putting up with costly relatives and wound up as a royal pensioner. But Zacatecas had 50 silver processing plants by 1550. In addition, Zacatecas could boast of 500 churches, 300 households with African slaves, and a European population exceeded only by Mexico City. Zacatecas became extremely productive, providing about one-fifth of the world's silver supply from the mid-sixteenth to the end of the eighteenth century.

As the Spaniards found more silver, they colonized the central and northeastern regions. In 1550, a Spanish convoy saw the famous "hill of light" in Guanajuato when a full moon alerted them to huge silver veins. Eventually, the most productive mine of all, Guanajuato yielded a mother lode comparable to the famous Comstock Lode in Nevada three centuries later. In 1545,

Francisco de Urdiñola established the San Luís Potosi mines; later he initiated the Santa Barbara enterprise at Parral, Chihuahua. Northwest of Zacatecas, at Sombrerte, campers started a forest fire that became so hot that the silver ore formed nuggets which the explorers eagerly scooped up. A brilliant mining prospector, Francisco de Ibarra, supervised the Sombrerte mines. In the 1560s, he became the unpaid frontier governor of Nueva Vizcaya. Here he founded towns and ranches throughout the Durango area before turning them over to inhabitants. Near Mexico City, sites such as Real del Monte and Pachuca became well-known silver producers after the 1550s.

The patio process characterized the production of silver until the late nineteenth century. Initially, Spaniards used smelting methods to produce silver because this simple technique was relatively inexpensive. But smelting required large quantities of wood to fuel the burners and became labor intensive. Because of the isolation of areas such as Zacatecas from forested areas and the rapid decline of indigenous communities, the patio process soon filled Spanish needs. Implemented by Bartolomé de Medina from Spain, the patio process made the processing of Mexican silver much easier. The patio process became more costly than smelting but it raised production and increased profits because it did not require large amounts of water, normally a severe problem in northern areas. The key difference from older techniques was that the patio process utilized mercury from the Almadén mines in southern Spain and then, after their development, the Huancavelica operations in Peru. The crown maintained very low as well as stable mercury prices from 1617 to 1767 as a subsidy for Mexican miners.

The production techniques varied little for centuries. Workers brought the ores out of shafts in leather buckets, each holding 150 to 300 pounds of ore. They crushed the ores into a fine powder and washed them down into cakelike *tortas* about 100 feet wide and 2 feet thick on stone patio floors. At this point, the *azoguero* (mercury man) took over, adding salts, limes, and copper

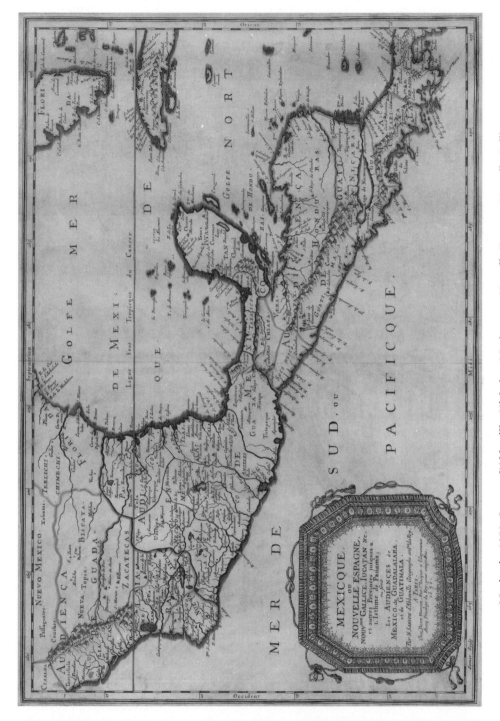

Mexico in 1650. Sanson d'Abbeville, Nicholas. *Mexicque ou Nouvelle Espagne, Nouvelle Gallice, Iucatan.* (Paris: Sanson d'Abbeville, 1850). The French court cartographer prepared this map. The French were the finest map makers of the seventeenth century, usually relying on data provided by travelers, military officers, and clerics. *Courtesy of Special Collections Division, Virginia Garrett Cartographic History Library, University of Texas at Arlington, Arlington, Texas.*

pyrites to heat and determine the proper heating time as drops of mercury acting as a catalyst attracted the silver metal away from the ore so that the mercury and pure silver bonded together. At the proper time, the *azoguero* added more salts and limes before washing the *tortas* in vats so that only the silver residue remained. Although time-consuming, the patio process became necessary because Mexican ores were not high grade; only 1 or 2 percent were silver bearing.

Miners, merchants, and the crown attempted to control the distribution of silver. Early in the colonial period, most miners maintained refineries known as *haciendas de mina*. Eager to monopolize silver production, the Spanish monarchy decreed the establishment of the Casa de Moneda (mint) in May 1535. Only a year later, the first coins in the American hemisphere rolled off the wooden machinery of the Moneda. The Carlos and Juana coins, named in honor of the Castilian rulers, were silver until the Moneda minted gold coins in 1675. During the reign of Felipe II, the Mexican pesos, which became the first coins with universal acceptance, appeared. Despite severe penalties for smuggling and the necessity of royal seals for all bullion, the crown lost control of the silver trade to merchants. Because of their decisive role in financing miners, the silver merchants forged tight links with Moneda officials and avoided taxes wherever possible. During the mid-seventeenth century, the Spanish government virtually surrendered control of mint operations, since public purchase resulted in generally private control.

Mining affected Mexico greatly. By 1600, gold and silver accounted for 80 percent of Mexico's exports; they retained this high level for most of the colonial period. Because the use of gunpower and more efficient mining methods, the value of mining increased throughout the eighteenth century. Moreover, the mining boom occurred just as the Central European mining expansion tapered off. Mining also stimulated interest in New Mexico and other portions of the southern United States because many assumed this area contained huge wealth. Yet New Spain's

bullion set off tremendous inflation in Spain itself. Commodity prices in Iberia tripled between 1501 to 1650. Spanish industry declined and Hispanic rulers did not invest their treasures wisely; too much silver fueled wasteful European wars. But the mines encouraged the growth of great landed estates in the north and the settlement of buffer areas. Finally, Mexico became dependent on mining for its economic wellbeing for many years. The economy became more regionalized as a result of mining and was not well integrated. For example, Puebla's initial advantages of location and ability to supply wheat, livestock, and textiles attracted Spaniards; but because Puebla lacked minerals, other regions, particularly in the north, competed successfully against Puebla to the point where Puebla began to decline before independence.

LABOR SYSTEMS AND LAND OWNERSHIP

Working conditions and landowning patterns varied greatly from one region to another, usually because of economic changes and social structure. Church protests and the decline of the indigenous population gradually resulted in improved labor systems. Land ownership, on the other hand, became increasingly monopolized in the north while the communalized indigenous land holdings usually managed to survive in the south.

Coercive labor exploitation characterized early Hispanic treatment of indigenous populations in Mexico. Under the Maya and Aztecs, Indians carried out collective labor tasks with obedience and even pleasure. Under Spanish rule, Indians soon lost any sense of joyous participation when slavery became the early norm. Spanish settlers often assumed possession of slaves held by indigenous communities and rulers since slavery had been a part of pre-Hispanic Mesoamerica. Furthermore, Indians who resisted the imposition of Hispanic authority could be legally enslaved in the early years of the Spanish invasion. In fact, the sale of Indian slaves by Spanish military leaders financed a good portion of the Chichimeca war. The need for food and labor resulted in hundreds of thousands of indigenous laborers being marched off to the north or to Yucatán, never to return.

The *encomienda* served as the initial means of enslaving the indigenous population. This medieval Spanish institution first appeared in the Caribbean before its conception in Mexico. In Mexico, the *encomienda* became a trusteeship of Indians, usually in one or more villages, from the crown to various Spaniards. As it was basically a grant of tribute labor, Indians had to provide commodities and service in return for religious instruction and a vague form of civilization, neither of which the indigenous population received consistently.

The Spanish government disliked *encomienda* distributions but understood that settlers as well as invasion veterans pressured Cortés and subsequent Spanish authorities to receive laborers. Therefore, in October 1523, Cortés received authority to specifically award and reassign *encomiendas*. Combat experience was the primary prerequisite for labor grants; two-thirds of those taking part in the siege of Tenochtitlán received *encomiendas*. Andalusia provided the largest number of Spanish *encomenderos*, followed by Extremadura. Among recent arrivals to Mexico, members of the nobility received preference in *encomienda* awards. Thus the *encomenderos* represented a broad selection of Spanish society. Most *encomenderos* resided in areas within a three-day march from their *encomiendas*. The early towns and cities of New Spain served primarily as headquarters of the *encomenderos*.

The 1521 to 1555 period seemed to promise much for conquistadors but ended with rewards for relatively few. Losing most of the indigenous population made Spanish rulers pause because disease killed four out of five Indians in Central Mexico from 1545 to 1548 as Spanish cattle swarmed over the corn patches. The Indians did not object to tribute, except when they believed that it exceeded fair levels. Since few Indians volunteered to serve Spaniards during the early invasion, it is not difficult to imagine their reluctance

to mix with Hispanics. In 1528, Cortés received the title of Marqués del Valle de Oaxaca and confirmed his request for large estates and an *encomienda* of 100,000 Indians. But in 1529, Mexico became the viceroyalty of New Spain and Viceroy Antonio de Mendoza told Cortés to stay out of Mexico City. Cortés eventually returned to Spain and fought in Algeria in 1541, before dying deaf and blind seven years later.

The *encomienda* system soon generated critics who produced legislation designed to curtail its abuses. Most Spanianrds, particularly those who aspired to *hidalgo* status by having servants and peons, considered Indians morally inferior and worthy of enslavement. Gonzalo Fernández de Oviedo y Valdés articulated those views in his *General History of the Indies*, which accused the Indians of being lazy and shiftless. But Bartolomé de Las Casas and Antonio de Montesinos spoke for those in the Spanish Church who sought to save the souls of the indigenous peoples, partially because they became convinced that the world would not last much longer. Las Casas defended the Indians as obedient, faithful, and virtuous. Because the crown had a papal mandate to Christianize the Indians, it attempted to satisfy both sides by summoning a council which resulted in the Laws of Burgos.

This 1512 legislation outlined proper relations between Indians and Spaniards. The preface stated that Indians were inclined toward vile practices and lacked interest in Christian virtue. That meant they had to be under "Christian lords," should pray in Latin, and stop heathen practices such as bathing and painting themselves. As part of this farcial attempt to justify the invasion on moral grounds, Spanish military officials had to read a *requerimiento* (requirement) that explained the nature of Christ, the Castilian king, and the dire consequences of not submitting to Hispanic rule.

The Crown came under increasing pressure to mitigate treatment of the Indians. Vasco de Quiroga, an audiencia judge, founded a communal settlement and hospital for indigenous peoples in 1532 and then another during a formal *visita* to Michoacán from 1533–34. His concern for Indians in that region earned him gratitude that persisted for centuries. In 1537 Pope Paul III issued a bull in which he protested that Indians were rational and should be Christian. Las Casas continued to study and write, insisting that Indians should be pacified without force. Finally, he returned to Spain in 1540 in order to lobby for the end of *encomiendas*.

Concerned about the possibility of budding feudalism, the Crown established legislation designed to end *encomiendas*. The regulations pleased Las Casas but angered soldiers, ecclesiastics, and bureaucrats who felt they deserved their *encomiendas*. This 1542 legislation ordered that all *encomienda* grants would end upon the death of present holders and revert to the crown. Moreover, Indians now had to be paid for their labor and these New Laws limited the type of warfare that could enslave hostile Indians. No one could require personal services from Indians.

Yet the colonies opposed the legislation boldly. A delegation of friars informed the Spanish king that the maintenance of *encomiendas* was vital to defense and labor supplies. *Cabildos* attacked the New Laws in an unprecedented storm of protest that caught Spain by surprise. Viceroy Mendoza simply suspended the legislation until *encomenderos* could present their views to the king. The result was modification of the New Laws in 1545 so that *encomenderos* could keep their grants if the crown believed the Indians were well treated; but the prohibitions against royal officials owning Indian vassals remained as did the requirement to pay for labor. The debate over treatment of the Indians continued as the golden age of the *encomenderos* waned by the 1550s; about half the *encomenderos* kept their grants within the family line after their initial bestowal. Reluctant to enforce the laws, royal officials endeavored to avoid a civil war among the whites, as had occurred in Peru. Therefore, enforcement was lax and *encomiendas* managed to survive another one hundred years.

Several factors resulted in the establishment of the *repartimiento* system in the middle of the sixteenth century. For one thing, forced labor meant that the dwindling number of Indians paid less attention to raising badly needed crops. Meanwhile the arrival of increasing numbers of whites resulted in even more labor demands by increasingly dominant royal officials. As the Spanish Crown tried to eliminate outright slavery as well as unrecompensed labor, royal judges controlled labor as the shortage of workers mandated the need for tighter regulation.

The *repartimiento* became a system of rotational labor which distributed Indian laborers on a more rational basis. It lasted for about 75 years and benefited more Spaniards than the *encomienda* system. It satisfied the demands of mine operators as well as farmers, ranchers, and the royal government.

The origins of *repartimiento* came about by improvisation. Its first use occurred during the summer of 1550 when the viceroy sent an unspecified number of Indians to work on wheat farms. Started in order to ease food shortages in Mexico City, it served as a labor draft for five years. Another ad hoc *repartimiento* took place during Mexico City's flood crisis in 1555 when exceptionally heavy rains raised the level of the surrounding lake, damaging streets and bridges. The viceroy therefore summoned a large force of Indians to close up the sluice openings of walls and causeways, to shift the course of streams, and construct a massive dike which eventually covered four miles. Many Indians died, since much of the work took place underwater. At this point, the Spaniards decided to implement the *repartimiento* on a mass basis throughout Mexico.

By the early 1560s, *repartimiento* engaged the labor of thousands of Indians who were distributed among 114 Spanish farmers, each of whom received an average of about 20 Indian laborers. A *juez repartidor* (*repartimiento* judge) administered indigenous workers on the district level in weekly shifts to Spanish farmers and miners in the same area. After taking a careful census of all Indian villages, a quota of 2 percent had to report to local caciques for work assignments. Every Monday morning, *repartimiento* Indians assembled inside a corral where the *juez repartidor* assigned them on the basis of what wheat or corn had to be harvested. Spanish farmers then paid the *juez repartidor* an allotted sum for each worker plus an extra amount for the cacique who mobilized them. The Indians received their wages after a week of work before being released back to their communities.

Therefore Spanish colonists received an assured labor supply in weekly rotation while quotas minimized the strain on Indian communities. Those who did work received a receipt from the *juez repartidor* which prevented them from being called again unfairly. Moreover, the system adopted itself to past and present indigenous organizations. In addition to assuring food and labor, the *repartimiento* provided workers for public works projects. *Repartimiento* labor rebuilt Mexico City, churches, convents, and public buildings on a grand scale. Colonial officials invoked *repartimiento* labor in Guadalajara and Oaxaca during the second half of the eighteenth century. The rotational system served elites in the northwestern Nueva Vizcaya region for over a century and a half. The *repartimiento* also enjoyed a long tenure in Yucatán, partially because it did not disrupt production methods during the rise of local haciendas.

Debt Peonage. Landowners far from *repartimiento* labor pools began resorting to debt peonage, a procedure whereby laborers toiled on the holdings of landowners in return for cash advances in the form of loans. The crown did not object and established new regulations which usually encouraged debt peonage, such as making land transfers legally valid if they included the transfer of debt laborers. Debt peonage developed rapidly, becoming a major source of labor in the seventeenth century.

Debt peonage had important ramifications for Mexican character. It attracted large numbers of *mestizos* and helped form a Mexican sense of nationality by drawing workers away from large indigenous centers. It may have improved the lot of many by isolating them from the demands of exploiters in the central plateau. Indians could also work where they pleased and began to speak Spanish and gravitate, to some extent, to the Catholic Church as a symbol of Mexican unity. During the early seventeenth century, alphabetic writing replaced pictographic traditions for Indians in many regions. These changes would not have occurred so quickly had not large landowners sought workers to leave traditional villages.

Debt peonage had characteristics that persisted until outlawed in 1915. Most landowners preferred not to have large numbers of resident workers, but as the competition for labor became intense, ranchers and *hacendados* offered contracts and advanced money in the form of loans in areas where Indians and *mestizos* did not exist in great numbers, particularly in the north. But the loans could rarely be repaid because workers received wages lower than their standard of living. Under Spanish law, Indians and *mestizos* could not leave their places of work until they repaid their debts. Holding workers in bondage became reinforced when *hacendados* helped one another by never accepting runaways and sending fugitives back to the original owners for harsh punishment. The system reinforced itself by maintaining a *tienda del raya* (company store) that charged high prices for food, clothing, and other necessities, all carefully recorded in the account book and added to an individual's total debt.

The personal relationship that many workers enjoyed with their bosses (*patróns*) is one of the few benefits of this system. The *patrón* became the godfather to many workers, paid for weddings and burials as well as many other personal expenses. All that he asked for in return were dependable work and personal loyalty. Colonial and republican governments allowed the *patróns* to control workers by acting as lawyer and judge in terms of punishment. Many Indians left their villages to avoid *repartimiento* toil in return for the somewhat greater freedom offered by debt peonage.

Convict and Free Labor. Forced labor and free workers also existed in various regions of Mexico. Convicts guilty of particularly nasty crimes often found themselves placed in *obraje* sweatshops. Often locked in at night and beaten until textile quotas became produced, they suffered miserably. The *obrajes* featured inexpensive wooden machinery. Although the typical owners were fairly humble persons, they profited from cheap labor provided by colonial officials. Likewise, Yaqui and Maya rebels in Sonora and Yucatán also found themselves forced into long hours of grinding toil until they revolted. Never conquered until the twentieth century, such regions of continual warfare made the Spaniards quick to punish recalcitrants.

Once the recovery of the indigenous population made itself felt after 1650, prominent groups of salaried workers appeared. In Tehuantepec, pastoral activity on those haciendas owned by the Cortés family depended upon free *mulato* labor as well as African slaves. As in the north, marginal social types enjoyed more responsibility, good wages, and better working conditions because of the labor shortage in Oaxaca. Indians hired as free wage laborers constituted over two-thirds of the mining force in the northern mining districts. In addition to high wages, mine workers enjoyed a *partido*, which amounted to a share of the ore gathered from a day's work. Not all workers received *partidos*, and the *partido* varied from camp to camp. Nearly 45,000 workers toiled in the mines in the seventeenth century and enjoyed better working and living conditions than their peers in other sectors of the colonial economy. Free labor resulted in stable wages for less dynamic labor markets. Most hacienda peons in the Valley of Mexico earned two reales a day by 1650, a wage that still prevailed by 1800. By 1630, free and debt laborers outnumbered those bound by *repartimiento* labor.

African Slaves and Mulatos.
At one point, Mexico contained the largest number of slaves in the New World. Mexico is unique because of its total absorption of Africans into an increasingly heterogeneous society.

An intense human drama characterizes the arrival of Africans into Mexico. The Spanish simply tapped into an ongoing system in Africa after the Portuguese opened it up. Slavery had been fundamental in African society because land could only be owned by individual rulers or various polities. Landlord-peasant relationships characterized West African society after European monopolies organized the slave trade. First the Portuguese, then Dutch, French, and British traders received *asiento* contracts to sell slaves from Africa. Most of the slaves who arrived in Mexico came from Guinea, Niger, the Congo, and Angola. The first slaves accompanied Cortés and other invaders as personal attendants, guides, laborers, and farmers. The bishop of Chiapas, Las Casas advocated the idea that Africans instead of Indians should be enslaved, though he regretted his views later. The Catholic Church never concerned itself with Africans as it did with Indians; with Africans there were no moral or legal restrictions to enslavement.

The slaves suffered from cruel treatment during the voyage from Africa to Mexico. After being kidnapped from areas within two hundred miles of the West African coast, their captors shackled the naked Africans together on bare wooden boards in the ships' holds. As little as 40 inches separated each level. Crews forced the slaves to stay prostrate throughout most of the

Spaniards supervising slaves that were brought to work in the mines are depicted in this engraving by Theodore de Bry (c. 1596). *The Granger Collection.*

voyage. Only women and children could stay on the deck. Because of being cramped the slaves were prevented from performing basic body functions comfortably—breathing, moving, expelling waste. Packed into multidecked holds, the Africans tried to endure the pestilent, poisonous air, extreme heat, and the stench of their own defecation. The blood and mucus covering the floor spawned numerous illnesses. To dissipate sadness, the merchants unchained the slaves from their prone positions and forced them to dance. Nevertheless, losses during the sixteenth century averaged 15 to 25 percent.

After surviving the infamous "middle voyage," Africans had to submit to colonial regimentation. The first slaves arrived in Veracruz and other tropical regions where the indigenous labor force had declined greatly. Sugar caused slavery to flourish. Once slaves arrived, sellers auctioned them off on trading blocks or included them in sales of equipment and property, just like most other commercial items. Slaves often had owners waiting for them when they docked. The Spanish usually mixed and scattered various tribes in order to weaken African religion and political organizations. Age and physical condition determined the prices of slaves; therefore individuals in their teens or early twenties comprised the majority of Mexican slaves, although whole families could be sold together. Slaves became an expensive investment, partially because they provided great prestige to owners. The cost varied between 150 to 300 pesos. The slaves received new names and lost much of their culture. Spaniards scorned them as racially inferior and assumed that most were infidels. Priests did not try to convert blacks with the same zeal as Indians but provided lay brotherhood organizations known as *cofradías* and sponsored mutual aid societies. That slaves accommodated themselves to bondage without losing their dignity, esteem, and African traits demonstrates their remarkable ability to survive brutal conditions.

Slave labor enabled Mexico to become a world leader in sugar and gold trading as well as to establish a diversified regional economy. Africans served in such varied occupations as muletrain drivers, carriers, ranch hands, guards, and tax collectors. By the beginning of the seventeenth century, the Royal Indian Hospital employed African slaves and *mulatos* as attendants, due mainly to the difficulty in getting others to work because of the hospital's high mortality rate. Most urban slaves became servants although some worked in guilds. Black slaves comprised 14 percent of the labor force in the mines. Female Africans became highly coveted in convents or as mistresses. Gradually, many Africans became free wage proletariats. Obtaining freedom often resulted from the desire of owners to reward favorites in wills or to get rid of older slaves. Some slaves simply bought their way out of bondage. In general, freedom depended on good behavior. The more fortunate worked their way into positions as artisans, mine foremen, and caravan traders.

The Africans exerted a tangible impact upon colonial society. During the sixteenth century, African immigration was quantitatively greater than white. In Mexico City, for example, Africans outnumbered whites during the late sixteenth century. Nevertheless, African males usually had Indian wives; the number of *mulatos* grew faster as a group than pure Africans because women and children comprised only 20 percent of the slave population. The number of *mulatos* grew so quickly in the early colonial period that they often outnumbered *mestizos*. Priests encouraged marriage as long as it was to other blacks; upsetting the caste system was more than frowned upon. Because of the intermingling between *mulatos*, Indians, Africans, and Hispanics, some slaves took on a white complexion. Slave holders handled this situation ruthlessly. To prevent light-skinned slaves from being mistaken as pure whites, slave holders often branded them, preferably on the forehead. Others were branded on the shoulder with humiliating messages.

Social restrictions encouraged defiance. Africans could not wear gold, pearls, silk, or shawls. They could not go out after dark, ride horses, live in Indian villages, or attend burials in groups larger than four. Officials denied certain fields of commerce to African Mexicans. Blacks and *mulatos* could not sell chickens, fruit, and vegetables although Indians could. Punishment became harsh and sadistic. Slaves found guilty of mistreating Indian women received 100 lashes; ears would be chopped off for repeat offenses. *Cimarrones* (runaways) missing for six months or more could expect death or castration. Never granted full citizenship, Africans in Mexico became the first slaves on the American continent to revolt. Riots shook Mexico City in 1546 and 1570; a severe response to an African female being flogged to death resulted in 1,500 Africans rising up in 1612. Mexico City authorities hanged 29 black men and women in retribution. But *cimarrones* continued to flee and often instigated slave rebellions. A serious *cimarron* challenge broke out from 1607 to 1611. Yanga, a *cimarron* who claimed to be a Congoese prince, organized sustained revolts along the road from Puebla to Veracruz. Once their efforts to crush the unrest failed, whites arrived at a compromise with the *cimarrones*. Authorities allowed them to settle a town; but in return, the newly free runaways agreed to submit to Spanish authorities and act as slave catchers. Four other major *cimarron* uprisings occurred in the seventeenth and eighteenth centuries. The propensity to flee altered the social structure of Veracruz greatly. From 1640–1659, 50 percent of all African residents in Veracruz estates were free; by 1680, 70 percent enjoyed free status. But because of the shortage of African women, the males took Indian wives, thus losing their African identities.

The Landowning System. The structure of the various landed units depended upon market opportunities and imperial policies. The characteristics of the landowning system would have an enormous effect upon the regional development of Mexico. The north, with its emphasis upon free labor and local markets, became more egalitarian. The plantations of the south and, to a lesser extent, the central plateau depended more upon plantation slavery and international marketing of their luxury exports.

Initially, medieval Spanish *reconquista* attitudes enabled the *conquistadores* to receive the first land awards. King Carlos V allowed Hernán Cortés to distribute *caballerias* properties. Measuring about 40 hectares, *caballerías* became the standard unit of royal land awards. But fearful of an independent nobility arising in Mexico, royal policy encouraged farmers rather than conquerors to settle the land. Spanish farmers in Puebla received one or two *caballerias* in a successful attempt to initiate wheat farming there. To encourage farming, the crown also granted town lots to those farmers who decided to live in Puebla, founded in 1532. The farmers also received *ejido* grants near whatever municipality they lived. As in the pre-Hispanic period, *ejidos* functioned as public lands which could not come under private control. They became useful for Spanish farmers to use as grazing lands for livestock. *Ranchos* were the medium to large agricultural properties on which the owner resided. Often the most productive landholding system, *labores* were smaller agricultural units, usually measuring about one or two *caballerias*. *Chacras* were the smallest of agricultural holdings, many of which gained fame (or notoriety) for raising pigs. Owners tended to be poor Spaniards or even *mestizos* and *mulatos*. As in medieval Spain, the crown provided open range land for general use known as *terrenos baldios*. These holdings would remain under state control until the late nineteenth century. Wealthy individuals in Spain were another group that received land awards. Few members of the Spanish nobility had any interest in living in Mexico; but there were a number of court parasites whom the Spanish monarchy wanted to get rid of. Since they had enough money to invest in large-scale enterprises, they could be more useful in Mexico as part of colonial consolidation rather than plotting with rivals and eating up revenue. In fact, the Crown became so concerned about treasury shortcomings that it regularly sold grants of land directly in order to increase royal revenues.

Another early Crown policy was its decision to preserve indigenous towns and villages as a check against the possibility of a feudal class. Tax revenue and labor from Indians had become vital to royal interests. And the Church had successfully demanded that most indigenous areas should come under their supervision. Therefore, the Spanish prevented any expropriation of most indigenous lands. By Hispanic law, Mexican estates or properties had to be at least a few thousand feet away from indigenous communities. Colonial tradition in much of Mexico enabled the recipient of Crown land grants to take possession of them only in the event that, passing along the grant boundaries, the grantee encountered no opposition from the indigenous population. The Indians understood the procedure quite clearly and frequently appeared, shouting "and we come to object." Indian town sites and *ejidos* received legalization with Spanish titles.

Viceroys also possessed the ability to award royal land grants, known as *mercedes,* to notable individuals or budding settlements. To attract settlers to the Bajío region north of the Lerma River, the former home of the Chichimecas, the viceroy awarded land in small portions of 265 acres. The emerging municipalities, which also received the right to award land in the colonial area, usually received about 20,000 acres each in the Bajío for this purpose. In this way, many viceroys settled the areas north of Mexico City with hard-working and often deserving colonists.

But the operation of mines in the north motivated the Crown to decide that large landed estates would be necessary for settling the northern wonderland. Haciendas, as they came to be known, were basically the largest of all rural properties. The largest ones existed in the north, because the lack of water and adequate grazing sites necessitated haciendas controlling large areas of any particular region. Often evolving from *encomienda* grants, which never included property but only labor, the haciendas served the mining areas by providing a diversified production of grazing animals or grains. Sheep and cattle gradually predominated on hacienda lands. Haciendas often dominated local markets because the indiscriminate grazing of sheep made moderate landhold-ings uneconomical in many northern areas. Thus overstocking led to environmental degradation that shaped local circumstances rather than the nature of the Hispanic colonial system.

The Crown did initiate policies that favored the increasingly large size of properties. By 1550, hacienda land became legally impregnable when *mayorazgo* became established. *Mayorazgo* meant that landed properties became legally entailed so that heirs could not divide or sell the property. Although all wealth and property acquired during marriages was divided so that half went to the surviving spouse, *mayorazgo* normally functioned as a system of primogeniture so that the oldest son usually operated a hacienda with the consent of other family members. By paying a title verification fee known as the *composición,* hacendados confirmed boundaries as well as titles beginning in the seventeenth century. Another source of land for *hacendados* was their control of the municipalities. Since a rich upper class eventually controlled the *cabildos* by the seventeenth century, they passed laws so that hacendados bought more land that actually fell under municipal control.

The power of hacendados increased throughout the colonial era. Because poor transportation and communications increased the isolation of many regions, haciendas exercised a tighter grip on local markets. Their *casa grande* (big house) often became the most notable landmark in many rural areas even if the hacendado lived in regional capitals or Mexico City much of the time. Ties with other elites became vital. Hacendados often obtained credit from wealthy merchants and the Church. The Crown approved the withering away of the *encomienda* class, which it always feared, when hacienda owners married into mining and merchant families in order to expand or even stay afloat.

Plantation owners were the other large landowners. They became the most heavily capitalized estates because of their machinery, irrigation, labor expenses, and integration into a competitive world economy. They tended to characterize Morelos, near Mexico City, and the other sugar-producing areas in the south, particularly Veracruz, Michoacán, and Yucatán. Tobacco and cochineal plantations also evolved in the southeast and, like the sugar plantations, dropped slave labor in favor of *mestizo*, *mulato*, or Indian workers, who received relatively good pay.

Within 100 to 150 years after the invasion, much of Mexico's land had fallen into private hands. Haciendas appropriated much of the land not under title, grant, or in the *terreno baldio* category. The rapid decline of the Indian population left many indigenous lands vacant. After 1603, the crown often let landowners bully Indian landowners and acquire their land legally, either by means of public auction or by permitting Indians to sell their land. Many Indians believed that selling land was the only way to pay the tribute. But the land represented indigenous connections to their gods and their opportunity for rebirth. Many assumed that they could not be saved without their lands. Thus the Spanish failed to recognize the spiritual significance between the Indians and the land; by taking the land, colonial as well as future rulers failed to gain loyalty and real submission from the indigenous communities. *Estancia* holders, a sort of medium-sized ranching group, profited greatly in central Mexico where sheep and cattle ranching also predominated. Small landholdings continued to exist in Oaxaca and other indigenous areas in the south. The sparseness of some markets prevented latifundias from operating. Moreover, the incredible activity of the religious orders often operated as an effective barrier to settler demands upon indigenous landholdings.

THE CATHOLIC CHURCH

The social vitality provided by the Church became as important to Mexico as a beating heart is to its body. The Catholic Church maintained a strong position of authority because it held the deed to many homes and the key to salvation. Religion, in a new Hispanic structure, continued to be the foundation of Mexican culture. On the other hand, it remained a colonial rather than a Mexican church since a domestic clergy never really took definite shape.

The early relationship between Church and state represented a compromise. As the Spanish monarchy became stronger, it demanded the *patronato real*, which meant that Spanish kings presented the candidacy of bishops and other ecclesiastical appointments. In addition, the crown collected the Church tax known as the tithe, restricted the movements of Church officials as it saw fit, and won the right for the Council of the Indies to approve papal decrees in order for them to be enforced in Mexico. The papacy recognized the effort involved in the Spanish *reconquista* and the establishment of the American empire. For these two reasons, Rome agreed that the Crown could control all aspects of Church activity in Mexico except doctrinal matters. In return, the Spanish government assumed the obligation to defend the faith and assist the Church in general. Therefore the Church received many privileges, such as obtaining the best areas in all towns, particularly the highest elevations, and receiving tax exemptions.

Religious Orders and the Spanish Clergy. The Crown controlled the Church in Spain while the religious orders operated under separate organizations for their own administration. The Spanish clergy had such a low reputation that Cortés did not even want them to take part in the 1519 invasion. The priests tended to stay in cities and towns. Many colonials became obsessed with guaranteeing the prompt release of their souls from purgatorial agony. They lavished their funds on Church-related good works. Depending upon their ethnic and social origin, chaplains and priests often worked outside the Church and had varied careers. Many appeared before courts in secular matters. The organization of the clergy in Mexico began with the establishment of dioceses, the introduction of the *ordenanzas del patronazgo*, and three church councils held in 1555, 1565, and 1585. By the 1570s, the structure of the Catholic hierarchy remained virtually unchanged.

Associations of communal piety, the *cofradías*, help us understand the popularity of the Catholic Church. Organized by priests, the *cofradías* carried out elaborate rituals and practices of community solidarity manifested in processions, devotions, and the public dispensation of charity to the poor. Stressing deeds rather than contemplation, the *cofradías* represented intense local Catholicism derived from the grass roots. The vitality of local religion based on external works of piety and mercy help account for the immunity of the Mexican population to the Protestant Reformation or other religious movements. Indeed, the *auto sacremental*, a play with religious themes, often became the most emotional event in many Mexican villages. Taking part in the *auto* became enormously important for many.

Criollo citizens increasingly identified themselves closely with the Church. The predominantly *criollo* clergy worked with civic officials to organize Corpus Christi festivals during the seventeenth century. The elites encouraged fiestas to stratify Mexico quickly, combat dissidence, and reaffirm the institutional social order during a time of rapid social change. Directed at Indians and *castas*, the *cabildos* used their role as financier and organizer of Corpus Christi to legitimize the pigmentocracy. On the other hand, the clergy ministered to the Indians in localities besides the Hispanic centers of the cities. They also had experience with indigenous Catholicism and its religious, emotional needs. The priests understood the necessity for a powerful imagery if they were to achieve their aim of extending their hold over the general Indian population. But administrative reforms and new economic demands imposed by authorities at the end of the seventeenth century challenged many indigenous norms about the ritual obligations of community leaders, the need for reciprocity in political affairs, and the supernatural origins of power. Moreover, ecclesiastical politics appeared in the seventeenth century which tended to pit *criollo* colonials against peninsular interests. Even the orders became divided into *criollo* and peninsular factions.

The acrimony between *criollos* and peninsulars also arose within the convents. Many women traveled from Spain to Mexico in order to establish the first convents. They regarded their courage and fortitude as especially notable. The contradiction between the requirement to remain cloistered and removed from contact with the outside world and the nuns alternate role as ideal symbols and transmitters of Hispanic culture was immense. They created a new type of writing which recorded physical movements as well as their spiritual journeys.

The texts written by both men and women at San José, the first Carmelite convent in Mexico City, became particularly notable. Convent writings were designed to be read by specific audiences, including the nun's confessor, her convent community, and, on occasion, the general public. Striking contradictions emerged. Although female spirituality and rationality were regarded as inferior to those of males, public speaking by females was discouraged. Saintly women living under a rule of silence were nevertheless encouraged to write as well as meditate between the earthly and the divine. Moreover, nuns always remained aware that they walked a very fine line, which the Inquisition watched, between vain, posturing self-expression and speech truly inspired by God.

Eventually the San José convent went on trial for heresy. The Inquisition began a thorough investigation after several complaints that its nuns had rejected the efficacy of confession to non-Carmelite fathers, a direct conflict with official Catholic doctrine. One of the informers, a nun who supported the Spanish clergy, was interrogated and her testimony revealed the profound social and economic divisions between the *peninsulars* and *criollas*. The convent therefore reflected the cultural disputes with the church itself.

Another issue provoked dissent. Although designed for high-ranking *criollas*, a proposal within San José to establish a convent for promising indigenous females aroused heated debate. Many considered Indians to be ignorant barbarians and minors before the law. Others assumed that women were not fully rational, therefore removing any legal standing they had. Reformers argued that because women were the opposite of men and that indigenous males tended to be evil, that indigenous females were undoubtedly inclined to be good. Eventually, piety and orthodoxy triumphed, symbolizing the general success of the Spanish colonial hegemony.

Each religious order adopted a distinct posture toward evangelization according to its peculiar philosophic traditions. Directly responsible to the pope, a general usually commanded the orders. In general terms, the Franciscan defense of Indians followed the course of charity and love, while the Dominicans pursued a more theoretical and judicial route. In the words of Mexican historian Edmundo O'Gorman, eulogizing Las Casas and the Franciscan Toribio Motolinía, an exceptional early missionary who eventually wrote the monumental *Historia de los indios de Nueva España*, "Motolinía was a father to the Indians and Las Casas was their lawyer."

Evangelization began in 1522 when three friars arrived to establish a mission in Tlaxcala. Their *doctrina* school established the precedent for Franciscan efforts to understand Indian languages and customs while schooling them in writing, singing, and the gospel. More impressive was the arrival of ten friars and two lay brothers in 1524 who became known as the Twelve Apostles. Spiritual reformers hand-picked for their skill in missionaries, they proceeded to walk barefoot from Veracruz to Mexico City where Cortés and other *conquistadores* knelt to kiss their hands. The Franciscans emphasized ethnographic and linguistic studies along with a deep concern for training a native clergy. A dozen Dominicans disembarked in Mexico in 1526. More attached to orthodoxy and less optimistic about the Indian's religious capacities, the Dominicans concentrated upon Oaxaca and Chiapas. Las Casas called for compassion and peace as before. At Oaxaca, he composed *The Only Way* in 1539, a treatise that influenced mission theory and prac-

The First Mass in the Temples of Yucatan. *Culver Pictures.*

tice by calling for Christian charity. In 1533, Augustinians arrived and concerned themselves mainly with organizing indigenous communities, building monasteries, and providing spiritual training. Jeronymites also came to participate in converting Indians.

Finally, the great rivals of the Franciscans, the Jesuits arrived in 1572. Starting with very little capital in the late sixteenth century, the Jesuits developed their wealth in rural estates by taking underused properties in strategic locations and exploiting them systematically. With exceptional management skills, the Jesuits developed *colegios* in the cities but wisely divested themselves of useless lands donated to the *colegios*. They rented properties near their profitable estates as regional markets dictated, practiced specialization, and transported their own goods. The Jesuits also devoted themselves to missionary work in the northwest. Although most Indians mounted bloody attacks against Spaniards on the northern border, the Yaquis humbly gave in to the Jesuits in the early colonial period. The Yaquis maintained their cultural identity for four centuries because the Jesuits insulated them from society and provided them with economic and political stability. Similar to the way the Indians of Paraguay developed under the Jesuits, the Yaqui became self-sufficient, determined not to be displaced from their homes, and resolved to maintain their separate identity.

Relations between Indians and the religious orders remained close during the sixteenth century. However, the same cannot be said for ties between friars and the Spanish clergy. By the 1570s, friction became acute. The priests believed that indigenous parishes such as Mexico City and Puebla, with large concentrations of Spaniards, should be self-administered. The friars refused to surrender their buildings, lands, and rights to food as well as labor. But the clergy continued to increase during the heady boom of 1580 to 1620 while the orders merely held their own. With little support from the *criollos*, the orders doubled and trebled their requests for labor and food and charged exorbitant fees for the sacraments. Nevertheless, the friars expressed concern for the de-

spair and alcoholism rampant among many indigenous areas. To restore meaning to the Indians lives, the friars intended to revive the Indian Catholicism that had sprung up in the wake of the initial mass conversions. This was the basis of the friars' refusal to relinquish their control of indigenous parishes.

The greatest success of Catholicism was its rapid conversion of perhaps six million Indians in the early sixteenth century. Friars as well as priests sought to save as many souls as possible. Franciscans were convinced that the end of the world was close at hand. The spirit of Reformation and their fear of Protestants motivated priests. In an attempt to lift themselves from the spiritual void left by the invasion, Indians grasped desperately at the emotional and spiritual path that the friars offered them.

Many Indians became fervent Catholics and remained the most religious sector of Mexican society. Eventually, the majority of indigenous peoples seemed to accept the Church's teachings. Sometimes they took the path of least resistance and renamed their pantheon of deities for Jesus, Mary, Joseph, and various Catholic saints. This arrangement seems to have satisfied most. Over time, Maya and Christian traditions blended into current practices. The nobility more or less accepted conversion to Christianity, but this did not commit their subordinates to accept a new religious affiliation, as in Europe. Shocked by the demographic disaster, Franciscans and Dominicans returned to their tradition of conversion, as they had in Iberia.

There is no question that conversion succeeded. The Spaniards encouraged Indians to continue following aspects of their religion that did not conflict with Catholicism. Therefore each village continued to maintain its own deities using community resources. A patron saint represented its community in communicating with a divine power. The friars set up *congregaciones* of dispersed indigenous peasants around monasteries and other doctrinal centers in an almost medieval pattern. Similarities eased the process. Spaniards were almost as supernatural (or superstitious) as the Indians. Both used omens, folk medicine, and priests. Hispanic and Mexican religion had great similarities in ritual and symbolism: confession, communion, the use of a cross, the concept of original sin, fasting, penance, pilgrimages, and celibate virgins.

Although it represented a more unsettling change, the baptismal process did not require coercion. Other family members often recommended the names given at baptisms. Sometimes census takers offered suggestions. The Spaniards considered baptism such an important act that census takers appeared to record it. Baptism and Christian marriage varied greatly from place to place within a given region after 1521. In Morelos there was greater choice of male names than female ones, which was standard Hispanic practice. In Morelos and other central plateau regions, Nahuas accepted Christianity more readily than the Maya in the south or indigenous groups in the north. The Spaniards succeeded in grasping the essentials of Nahua political systems in order to rule the Indians.

Although the friars' task was enormous, they converted Indians with zeal as well as practicality. The Indians had a completely different worldview; it was very difficult for the friars to express and articulate concepts such as sin and evil in Nahuatl language. Nevertheless, Indians found the message of salvation attractive. The promise of a bountiful and blessed future was a benevolent replacement for the pessimistic Aztec religion.

New rituals and artistry eased the transition to Catholicism. Although the Spaniards burned chronicles and idols, the production of pictographic productions continued under Spanish rule. Alphabetical writing began as did general learning. Spanish frescoes, paintings, and sculptures played an important role in conversion because preaching could not allow necessary visualizing. Painted altar pieces were particularly effective once the Indians approached to burn incense. *Cofradías* appealed to some Indians because they offered some autonomy from clerical jurisdiction. Brotherhoods restored sanctuaries and organized feasts so as to preserve continuity with the past.

When Spanish priests arrived in Chalma in 1537, they found Indians worshipping the god Tezcatlipoca in a cave. A band of Catholic hermits moved into the cave in 1623 and built a chapel nearby. Such usurpation of indigenous sites by the church was common in colonial Mexico. Dances in the postinvasion era celebrated the arrival of friars and defeat of non-Christians amid sumptuously clothed figurines on feast days.

Posada festivities became an integral part of Mexican Catholicism at this time. When Spanish friars accompanying the *conquistadors* attempted to convert Indians, they found the task easier when they incorporated a key element in the indigenous belief system—reenactment. Pre-Hispanic peoples believed strongly in reenacting the drama and forces that brought about the universe. Each step signified a spiritual ascent or a physical descent as the forces of creation battled for the soul.

During the late 1550s, a friar decided that a simple story, along with food, music, and games would attract the attention of the indigenous population away from ancient rituals usually observed at that time. The friar divided his flock into *peregrinos* or pilgrims and *posadero* innkeepers. The pilgrims, representing Joseph and Mary, went from door to door, usually in the neighborhood, asking in song for *posada* lodging. Twelve verses had to be sung until the doors opened amid joyous refrain and festivities.

The Mexican piñata also appeared at this time. Early piñatas made their way into Mexico by way of Spain, which drew upon the Italian game of *pignatta*. But in Spain, the game took on religious meaning and the first day of Lent traditionally was designated piñata Sunday. The piñata pot, called an *olla*, represented evil and was a squat, ugly water vessel. To disguise its homely appearance, the Spaniards added layers of clay to make it look like a religious symbol. In Mexico, the piñatas were created by covering a clay jar with brightly colored paper. They were fashioned into celestial bodies, such as the sun, moon, and stars, which were pivotal in the Indians' cosmic hierarchy. Shattering these ancient symbols became a crucial goal for the friars, and breaking the piñata became a dramatic act of destruction—a symbol that God is giving good things.

Missionaries. The Europeans who colonized northeastern America bought land from the Indians for a few trinkets. They then forced the "savages" to move away so more colonists could sail to America and settle on former Indian territory. In Mexico, the Spaniards tried to change indigenous lifestyles by means of missions. Missionaries introduced the Indians to Christianity as well as the language, laws, and culture of Spain. The Spaniards hoped that converted Indians would become loyal Spanish subjects.

By the 1570s, the Spanish clergy had won the argument over who should be first to enter pacified areas. Therefore the friars had to either give up control of their *doctrina* indigenous villages and retreat into monasteries or move into untamed areas. At that point, the orders decided to move into the north and southeast.

The missionaries made the most of the aid offered them. A 1573 law which ruled that the padres could no longer rely on *adelantado* explorers forced the orders to rely on poor quality mercenary soldiers. To mitigate the high costs of establishing missions, the Spanish crown provided an initial subsidy, items such as tools, and a tardily paid stipend. The Church also convinced wealthy landowners to turn over land and money for mission endowments.

Establishing a mission required much labor. The missionaries usually scouted selected areas before settling in. The missions produced their own food and usually had chapels, pens, and barns. The missionaries offered prospective Indians trinkets to enter and more or less bribed them to stay. The friars realized that to achieve success in Christianizing Indians, they needed a thorough knowledge of indigenous traditions and language. The friars also wanted to perpetuate the severity of missionary morals. Hostile areas forced the construction of thick walls to keep converts inside, since they could not legally leave the mission once they entered. Sedentary Indians accepted Catholicism at least superficially, but

slavehunting thugs often victimized nomads. Indigenous groups also suffered psychological trauma, abortions, miscarriages, and death in childbirth. The unhealthy conditions in missions sometimes resulted in 90 percent of the infants dying before their eighth year. Not surprisingly, Indians often rose up and destroyed missions.

Contradictions characterized the relationship between the Indians and their European overlords. In the sixteenth century, the friars assumed that Indians could be nominally civilized after ten years. In theory, the missions belonged to the Indians. But in fact, padres became virtual monarchs of the missions as well as nearby areas. The work day began at dawn with lashes for those who did not get up. Despite occasional cruelty, most missionaries were high-quality individuals, particularly the Jesuits. The Jesuits attracted Poles, Czechs, Germans, and Irish friars. Sophisticated as well as idealistic, many missionaries were trained linguists. It was difficult to learn indigenous tongues but the friars often succeeded while carrying out scientific as well as engineering projects. Missionaries also became outstanding explorers and counselors to high royal officials. Nevertheless, they invariably regarded Indians as inferiors and never thought they could be integrated into white society.

Missionary relations with society became ambiguous. Sometimes the missions flourished while the poor white settlers struggled. Many Spaniards resented the Church privilege of not paying taxes and often considered the missions a haven for Indians who escaped from settler properties. In the far north, colonizers valued the missions because of the protection afforded them from Apaches, Comanches, Chichimecas and meddling European rivals of Spain. The orders themselves underwent changes; the Jesuits aroused envy when they, as well as the Spanish church, became interested in making money. The Franciscans, however, maintained their lofty ideals.

The Inquisition. The Inquisition served a police function. Most of the Spanish population supported its activities because the average colonialist was very religious—most would fall to their knees upon hearing the church bells ring. Independent of civil and clerical courts, the Inquisition is a good example of Spain's divide and rule policies as well as the checks and balances that helped control social groups.

The Inquisition assumed its duties in Spain in 1480 as part of its task to homogenize religious beliefs. Before the Holy Office, as it was known officially, came to Mexico heads of religious orders campaigned against blasphemy, idolatry, and Protestantism. Then the archbishop delegated such powers to other bishops from 1535 to 1571. Finally, in 1571 the Inquisitor General established the Holy Office in Mexico City at the Plaza de Santo Domingo.

The Inquisition's official purpose consisted of protecting Mexicans from relapsed Jews, foreigners, and those who were disloyal to Spain. The most spectacular and repressive actions focused upon foreigners and Indians in the Tribunal's early years. The Holy Office also spied on and punished those charged with sodomy, adultery, blasphemy, sorcery, witchcraft, and heresy. The Inquisition interrogated and prosecuted hundreds of bigamists. As a result of the Inquisition's investigation of unorthodox sexual practices, in 1658 the Holy Office had 16 males burned after they had been accused of homosexual behavior. Most of the 123 accused were ordinary artisans, servants, slaves, and *obraje* laborers although two priests and a Pueblo councilman escaped punishment. In addition, mostly white *curanderos* suffered persecution in the seventeenth and eighteenth centuries.

The impact of the Holy Office became somewhat limited by the mid-seventeenth century. After 1575, the crown exempted Indians from Inquisition trials because of their allegedly "weak minds." Although the Inquisition could not persecute Indians, other church bodies continued to have jurisdiction over offenses committed by indigenous people. Inquisition officials occasionally boarded ships in search of scandalous books on a papal list. But efforts toward censorship proved ineffective in halting the spread of new ideas. The prosecutorial role diminished after 1650 when the

Holy Office began handling cases that private parties brought rather than pursuing cases on its own initiative.

The extensive structure of the Holy Office resulted in considerable expense. Large staffs aided the Inquisition, particularly regional commissioners, who gathered evidence throughout Mexico. With the help of lay police known as *familiares*, who enjoyed exemption from secular authorities, the Inquisition relied upon denunciations of fellow citizens. This meant that *familiares* agents could not be charged with smuggling, murder, or serving in the colonial militia. Therefore the Holy Office became a costly operation. Gossip and curiosity about the operations of the Inquisition provided swift communication about the fate of suspects or the condemned. Despite their role in ferreting out nonconformists, *familiaes* had status similar to holding a seat on a local *cabildo*.

Inquisition trials are not as horrible as commonly imagined. Denunciations of alleged crimes resulted in the collection of evidence before arrests took place. Inquisition prisons tended to be better than others. Torture was limited and controlled carefully. Nevertheless, tribunals operated in secrecy; the accused became cut off from society completely. Torture squeezed out testimony and confessions. Defendants could not have legal aid or know the names of accusers. Sometimes the charge was not made for months and years after the arrest. Trials were conducted by two inquisitors, a chief prosecutor, an expert who examined evidence, a constable and a notary. Truth-seeking ordeals became common among many staffs. Water torture, racks, and thumbscrews became standard tortures employed, although other methods of inhumane treatment persisted. Confiscation of property and heavy fines became typical penalties. *Auto de fé* (public act of faith) became the usual punishment. These spectacles often consisted of forcing the guilty person to walk down the streets shouting out the crime committed, wearing a dunce cap or having the charge engraved inside the church where the unfortunate person worshipped. All such verdicts had the intention of stripping the individual of their honor, a devastating indictment in Hispanic society. More unfortunate were those who became imprisoned in jail cells where it was impossible to sit. Exile, gagging, and service in the galleys also awaited those found guilty. Rarely did someone suffer being burned at the stake; only 30 or 40 individuals suffered such a fate during the entire colonial epoch. Typical of the victims were a Dominican monk who, in 1578, was burned for having fathered a child, reporting visions, and declaring that Spain would be punished for its cruelty to Indians. In another case, the Indian cacique of Texcoco was burned in 1539 for objecting to virtually every aspect of colonialism. Such cases illustrate how the Inquisition served the needs of the Spanish state more than anyone else.

Economic Role of the Church. The enormous amount of money spent on the conspicuous consumption of the Churches succeeded in impressing all colonial Mexicans. An obvious question that must be answered is the source of the great wealth enjoyed by the Catholic Church.

The tithe paid by all Spaniards, most *mestizos* and certain products submitted by Indians provided a steady flow of income. Tax farmers collected the tithe, usually assessed as 10 percent of one's property or produce, and turned it over to the Church. An excessive burden on the Mexican economy, the tithe fell heavily on the majority who were marginal.

Ecclesiastical fees for baptism, confirmation, and marriage remained very high until the early twentieth century. Because many parents could not afford to pay what often amounted to half a year's wages for marriage expenses, children suffered the humiliation of illegitimacy. The Church maintained virtually all social records until the 1880s because the government did not involve itself with births, marriages, and deaths until well into the nineteenth century.

Partially because the Church paid no taxes, it became the greatest property holder in Mexico by the eighteenth century. *Adelantado* explorers and those who hoped to receive honorific titles pro-

vided the initial land grants. But the Church obtained much land particularly because it served as the colonial banker, charging 6 percent on most loans. And if a person defaulted on a lien payment, the Church seized the land in question. More income resulted because the Church's land was usually urban property; religious authorities rented it out to Mexican citizens and obtained even more money. According to an 1856 government census, the Catholic Church owned almost 50 percent of all real estate in Mexico City by that year. The Jesuits soon enjoyed the reputation of using their property most profitably. They organized sugar refining, plantations, and various agricultural enterprises to finance their carefully organized undertakings. Soon they became the largest slaveholders in Mexico. They also built their own ships, mills, tanneries, and textile mills.

Gifts and bequests became the major source of Church wealth. Charitable foundations and borrowers of Church capital enjoyed a comfortable as well as spiritual relationship. Priests often swooped down on the death beds of prominent citizens to offer perpetual prayers in exchange for earthly belongings. Perhaps the most famous episode occurred when a seventeenth-century miner gave 225,000 pesos. Therefore the Church established chaplains and other pious foundations to say masses in return for donations. The Church loaned these sums to others while the interest supported many priests and established their careers in countless communities.

Guardian of the Social Order. The Church had a deep impact upon colonial society. In addition to assuming an obligation to provide education and recreation, the Church established countless hospitals, orphanages, and asylums for the blind as well as insane. The most destitute, hungry members of society could usually count on a priest ringing the church bell and providing free bread, soup, or other edibles. A tremendous number of monastery churches, one for each provincial unit, appeared during the 1570 to 1620 period. Convents of nuns also became visible and both provided countless acts of charity. Thus the social role of the Church made it a permanent feature of Mexican culture.

But by inculcating fatalism and demanding submission, the Church played a key role in consolidating the material exploitation of the masses by Spaniards. Fatalism suited the upper-class colonial rule stressed by the Church: obedience to the monarchy and acceptance that the duty of an individual was to suffer, endure difficulties, and wait for the afterlife. The Church enjoyed enormous advantages unmatched by other institutions. Many churchmen became viceroys or key advisors given their long tenure in Mexico. And because Church and state often disagreed—Hispanic legislation attempted to limit the number of Church lands—the ecclesiastics could use the threat of excommunication or an interdict (the stoppage of religious services) in order to attack government officials. In general, Church and state enjoyed a medieval partnership that did not experience major difficulties until late in the eighteenth century.

The Virgin of Guadalupe. For centuries myths have been created concerning appearances of the Virgin Mary. These myths often resulted in symbols which encompassed Europe. Poland has its Black Madonna of Czenstochowa and Spain had our Lady of Guadalupe in Extremadura. In the New World, there are similar symbols in Peru, Argentina, and Bolivia. In all instances, the Virgin appeared as intercessor between God and humanity. The Madonnas have the same message—faith, hope, and peace.

None of these symbols have yielded such national authority as in Mexico. The Virgin of Guadalupe became the first symbol of Mexican identity and nationality. In no other part of the world has a myth so strongly influenced religion, politics, and culture to encompass an entire society. How did this happen? Why does the image appear in homes, churches, bull rings, taxis, restaurants, and even houses of ill repute?

The Spanish invasion coincided with the culmination of the cult of two Aztec masculine divinities: Quetzalcoatl and Huitzilopochtli. The indigenous people concluded that the defeat of

those gods represented the end of a cosmic cycle and the inauguration of a new divine kingdom. They returned to the ancient feminine deities, a development which would prove to be of great importance. Immediately after the 1521 Spanish invasion, reports of people seeng Mary and God appeared. Newly converted Indians previously believed in Tonantzin, the pre-Hispanic mother of the goddess of moon, earth, and corn, which made it simple for them to embrace the concept of Mary. Their state of turmoil had made them ripe for miracles. With the Spaniards had come cataclysmic change and heaven was empty.

Shortly after the fall of Tenochtitlán, the Franciscans established a shrine dedicated to the Virgin of the Apocalypse on Tepeyac Hill slightly north of the city, which had previously been the site devoted to the worship of Tonantzin. On December 9, 1531, the legend of the Virgin of Guadalupe began. That morning, Juan Diego, a recently baptized Indian, began picking cactus apples on the foothills of Tepeyac. After he crossed the hill, he claimed to see an apparition of the Virgin Mary before him. That image became the beautiful, brown-skinned Virgin of Guadalupe. She spoke to Juan Diego in Nahuatl and said, "I desire that you build me a temple on this spot, to show the world my love and compassion." Juan took the message to Bishop Zumárraga, who did not believe the story. Three days later, the Virgin reappeared. As a sign of proof for the bishop, the apparition told Juan to cross the field and pick roses, even though it was winter and cactus covered the hillside. Juan found lovely Castilian roses and filled his cloak with them. When he opened the cloak to the bishop, a brilliantly painted image of the Virgin appeared emblazoned on it.

Zumárraga became a believer and ordered a chapel to be built on Tepeyac Hill. This shrine has been rebuilt several times and is now a monstrous structure of wood, cement, and plastic that holds 10,000 people. The cloak is enclosed in a gold-framed case and shows no signs of age. The colors are as brilliant as they were in 1531, and the picture reveals an image of a young Virgin. Unlike traditional European Madonnas who usually carry

The Virgin of Guadalupe. *The Granger Collection.*

from a mid-seventeenth century invention that has no historical authenticity.

The Virgin's presence underscores her role as mother of the nation. Clearly, the Virgin of Guadalupe began forging Mexico's *mestizo* culture. Mexicans' belief in the Virgin's powers contributed to colonial stability and helped merge the Hispanic and indigenous cultures after the Spanish invasion. Catholic saints began to replace older customs and offerings. The Virgin represents a cultural nationalism as well as the recovery of indigenous oral traditions. Indians brought offerings that had once been given to the old goddess to the Virgin of Guadalupe. Yet most of the Virgin's devotees were primarily *criollos* from Mexico City. She remains as the archetypal image of motherhood while incorporationg indigenous beliefs and European practices. Many Mexican Indians continue to worship Tonantzin. The Virgin phenomenon has been powerful throughout history because it is a female representation of the divine, bearing attributes otherwise excluded from mainline Christian perceptions of God as Father, Son, and Spirit. For all these reasons, no other saint or Christ himself inspires more public displays of devotion than the Virgin of Guadalupe.

SETTLEMENTS EAST AND NORTH

The frontiers beyond Mexico became the setting for contention and transformation. By means of force, conversion, and persuasion, the Spanish enjoyed varying degrees of success in subduing indigenous resistance. The relentless efforts of clergymen and religious orders converted many indigenous peoples to Catholicism but eventually resulted in ecological and demographic disaster for the Indians. Nevertheless, administrators often demonstrated exceptional ability, and the establishment of presidio fortresses and hundreds of towns and villages anchored Hispanic life for centuries.

The prospect of Asian wealth lured Spanish forces to the Philippines. After Magellan's sortie,

the Christ child, the Virgin of Guadalupe stands alone, as Tonantzin. She wears an open crown with cosmic stars in it and a flowing gown. She stands on a half-moon symbolizing the Immaculate Conception. The shrine became popular to all, partially because of the Virgin's similarity to the image of Guadalupe in Extremadura, Spain. As a result, the Virgin began to be called Our Lady of Guadalupe. For almost a hundred years, until the seventeenth century Maria of Guadalupe remained a local phenomenon. The Church promoted it, although friars disapproved of the cult and considered it idolatry. The traditional narrative resulted a 1542 expedition from Mexico under Ruy López de Villalobos attempted to conquer the Philippines but failed. Then Miguel López de Legazpi finally subdued the islands, naming them for King Felipe II. From the colonial capital of Manila, imperial rule controlled the coasts but not the southern island, where Islam entrenched itself. Yet the viceroyalty of New Spain administered the Philippines, whose prosperity depended upon exchange of Mexican silver for silk from China. Intermarriage between Spaniards, the indigenous population, and Chinese immigrants produced *mestizos* who developed a distinctive new culture. Attempts to trade in China and Japan ended by 1632; Japanese efforts to trade in Mexico had concluded in 1620.

The first Spanish explorer to study the southwest was Alvar Nuñez Cabeza de Vaca. Shipwrecked after setting out to Florida from Cuba, Cabeza de Vaca symbolizes Spanish toughness by walking from the Texas coast to the gulf coast of California. The Spanish king, impressed by such heroics, named Cabeza de Vaca as governor of Paraguay. Dropped off at the east coast of South America, Cabeza de Vaca walked inland to take up his new position.

Don Juan de Oñate colonized New Mexico, which became the foundation of Hispanic life in the southwest before California and Texas became effectively colonized in the eighteenth century. But the Indians resisted the Spanish because they feared labor exploitation, physical punishment, and restrictions upon their religious practices. In 1610, Oñate moved the provincial government to Santa Fe as he embarked upon a vigorous campaign of Christianizing the Pueblo Indians. The director of the missionary program reported in 1630 that 60,000 Indians had been converted and that 90 chapels had been built. But Oñate dealt brutally with villages that resisted, burning them, ordering the feet amputated for each surviving male, and forcing all into 20 years of personal service.

Franciscan missions anchored New Mexico. From 1609 to 1674 a triennial mission caravan to Santa Fe brought supplies and new settlers. Mis-

sionary workshops taught the Indians weaving, leatherwork, blacksmithing, and a variety of other tasks. But the Franciscans became disturbed by the persistence of Indian ceremonies that they considered idolatrous. The Franciscans whipped indigenous religious leaders and executed repeated offenders so the Pueblos became more covert in their concealment of ritual practices.

Determined to maintain their communal independence, the Pueblos achieved an unprecedented unity of purpose to force the Hispanic missionaries and settlers out. The leader of the revolt was Pope, a medicine man from the Tewa pueblo of San Juan. The nature of Pueblo ceremonial associations and the secret character of the meetings allowed Pope to map out the revolt's strategy and enlist the aid of virtually every Pueblo. The general instructions that Pope conveyed were simple: Kill all friars and colonists at a set time, which was August 10, 1680. Santa Fe soon came under siege and the beleaguered colonists departed 11 days later. But the Pueblos did not attack the retreating force and the unity of the Pueblo villages broke off.

Diego de Vargas became governor of New Mexico in 1690 and reoccupied it a few years later. In 1692 De Vargas made a preliminary expedition into the Pueblo area and received the formal submission of 23 villages. Dissension among the Pueblos enabled the Spaniards to recruit some as allies. On October 4, 1693, Diego de Vargas left El Paso del Norte with 800 settlers and soldiers. Many of those he led were survivors of the Pueblo revolt. Vargas had spent eight months in northern Mexico recruiting settlers and attempting to secure financing from the royal treasury. When no funds arrived, De Vargas nevertheless departed before winter arrived, reaching the capital and defeating the Pueblos who had occupied Santa Fe. Despite promises to the contrary, De Vargas executed 70 Pueblo leaders. He also turned over a large number of the defenders and their families and colonists as slaves. During his second term as governor, De Vargas brought the Pueblos into a partnership with the colonists against nomadic enemies. In addition, the Franciscans and civil authorities modified their treatment of the Pueblos; coercive policies gave way to more humane treatment.

Texas soon occupied the attention of the viceroy. After the Pueblo revolt, difficulties with the Sumas and Pimas served to divert attention away from New Mexico and led to the etablishment of two Franciscan missions near Presidio, Texas, in 1683. In the well-watered valley the mouth of the Conchos River pours into the Rio Grande. Farther south, Indian warriors succeeded in convincing friar Juan Larios to convert them to Christianity. During the 1670s, he ministered to Coahuiltecans. Then, after several attempts at founding a mission, San Juan Bautista appeared on the banks of the Rio Grande, followed by San Francisco Solano, both in 1700.

The activities of French rivals in Texas soon concerned the viceroyalty more than the Indians. The foremost French explorer, René Robert Cavelier LaSalle, took possession of the Mississippi delta in 1682. This placed French ambitions next to the northern borderlands. King Louis XIV made La Salle governor of Louisiana and approved LaSalle's plans to expand French influence. But LaSalle's next expedition became shipwrecked off Texas in late 1684. The attempt to form a French colony failed. LaSalle explored the Trinity River in north Texas but some of his men killed him near present-day Arlington, Texas. News of LaSalle's expedition alarmed the Spanish who sent several expeditions to locate him as well as the origin of the Mississippi River. In 1690, a basically missionary group settled into east Texas along the Neches River. Mission San Francisco de los Tejas became the first Texas mission far from the Río Grande. The Spaniards encountered no French enemies in the area, much to their relief. But a weakening financial situation, as well as hostility from the Indians, motivated the viceroy's decision to pull the settlement out; it was finally terminated when its battered remnants stumbled into Monclova in 1694.

Thus after establishing the basic foundations of Hispanic institutions in Mexico, the viceroyalty also extended its domain into the northern borderlands. Although Spain could never establish harmonious relationships with the indigenous peoples on a consistent basis, Hispanic culture remains as a vibrant legacy several centuries later.

SUGGESTED READING

Aguirre Beltran, Gonzalo. *La poblacion negra en Mexico*, 2d ed. Mexico City: Fondo de Cultura Económica, 1972.

Bannon, John F. *The Spanish Borderlands Frontier, 1513–1821*. Albuquerque: University of New Mexico Press, 1974.

Brading, D. A. *Haciendas and Ranchos in the Mexican Bajío: Leon, 1700–1860*. New York: Cambridge University Press, 1978.

Carroll, J. Patrick. *Blacks in Colonial Veracruz*. Austin: University of Texas Press, 1991.

Chevalier, Francis. *Land and Society in Colonial Mexico*. Berkeley: University of California, 1970.

Chipman, Donald E. *Spanish Texas, 1519–1821*. Austin: University of Texas Press, 1992.

Cline, Sarah. "Conquest and Aftermath: Center and Periphery in Colonial Mexico." *Latin American Religious Review* 27:3 (1992), 244–253.

Curtin, Philip D. *The Atlantic Slave Trade, A Census*. Madison: University of Wisconsin Press, 1969.

Davidson, David. "Negro Slave Control and Resistance in Colonial Mexico, 1519–1650." *Hispanic American Historical Review* (August 1966), 235–253.

Diggs, Irene. "Color in Spanish America." *Journal of Negro History* 28:4 (October 1953), 401–423.

Elliott, John H. *Spain and Its World, 1500–1700*. New Haven, CT: Yale University Press, 1989.

Fariss, Nancy. *Maya Society Under Colonial Rule*. Princeton, NJ: Princeton University Press, 1984.

Gibson, Charles. *The Aztecs under Spanish Rule: A History of the Indians of the Valley of Mexico*. Stanford, CA: Stanford University Press, 1964.

Greenleaf, Richard. *The Mexican Inquisition in the Sixteenth Century*. Albuquerque: University of New Mexico Press, 1969.

Hamilton, Earl. *American Treasure and the Price Revolution in Spain, 1501–1650*. New York: Octagon Books, 1965.

Himmerich y Valencia, Robert. *The Encomenderos of New Spain, 1521–1555*. Austin: University of Texas Press, 1991.

Hoberman, Louise. *Mexico's Merchant Elite, 1590-1660*. Durham, NC: Duke University Press, 1991.

Inikori, Joseph. "Slavery in Africa and the Trans-Atlantic Slave Trade." Paper at 30th Annual Walter Scott Webb Memorial Lectures, University of Texas at Arlington, March 9, 1995.

Israel, Jonathan. *Race, Class, and Politics in Colonial Mexico, 1610–1670*. London: Oxford University Press, 1975.

Jackson, Robert H. *Indian Population Decline: The Missions of Northwestern New Spain, 1687–1840*. Albuquerque: University of New Mexico Press, 1995.

Kamen, Henry. *Inquisition and Society in Spain*. Bloomington: Indiana University Press, 1985.

Love, Edgar. "Negro Resistance to Spanish Rule in Colonial Mexico." *Journal of Negro History* 61:2 (April 1967), 87–103.

Lynch, John. *The Hispanic World in Crisis and Change, 1598–1700*. Cambridge, MA: Blackwell Press, 1991.

MacLachlan, Colin and Jaime Rodriguez. *The Forging of the Cosmic Race*. Berkeley: University of California Press, 1980.

Martin, Norman F. *Los Vagabundos en la Nueva España*. Mexico City: Editorial JUS, 1957.

Olivera, Mercedes. "Posada Resists Secularizing." In the *Dallas Morning News*, December 23, 1990, p. 34A.

Ortega, Sergio, ed. *De la Santidad a la Perversión: O de prorque no se cumplía la ley de Dios en la sociedad novo Hispano*. Mexico City: Grijalbo, 1986.

Palmer, Colin A. *Slaves of the White God: Blacks in Mexico, 1570–1650*. Cambridge, MA: Harvard University Press, 1976.

Perry, Mary E., and Ann J. Cruz, eds. *Cultural Encounters: The Impact of the Inquisition in Spain and the New World*. Berkeley: University of California Press, 1991.

Poole, Stafford. *Our Lady of Guadalupe: The Origins and Sources of a Mexican National Symbol, 1531–1797*. Tucson: University of Arizona Press, 1995.

Powell, Philip Wayne. *Mexico's Miguel Caldera: The Taming of America's First Frontier, 1548–1597*. Tucson: University of Arizona Press, 1977.

Ricard, Robert. *The Spiritual Conquest of Mexico*. Berkeley: University of California Press, 1966.

Schwaller, John F. *The Church and Clergy in Sixteenth Century Mexico*. Albuquerque: University of New Mexico Press, 1987.

Sampson Vera Tudela, Eisa. *Colonial Angels: Narratives of Gender and Spirituality in Mexico, 1580–1750*. Austin: University of Texas Press, 2000.

Shurz, William Lyle. *The Manila Galleon*. New York: Dutton, 1939.

Taylor, William B. *Landlord and Peasant in Colonial Oaxaca*. Stanford, CA: Stanford University Press, 1972.

Thornton, John. *Africa and the Africans in the Making of the Atlantic World, 1400–1680*. New York: Cambridge University Press, 1992.

Warman, Arturo. *Y venimos a contradecir: los campesinos de Morelos y el estado nacional*. Mexico City: Ediciones de las Casa Chata, 1976.

Zeitlin, Judith Francis. "Ranchers and Indians on the Southern Isthmus of Tehuantepec: Economic Change and Indigenous Survival in Colonial Mexico." *Hispanic American Historical Review* 69:1 (February 1989), 23–60.

5

Revival, Restriction, and Crisis, 1700–1810

Once thought of as something of a golden era in Mexican history, the eighteenth century was an incongruous blend of economic growth, imperial centralization, and acute social crisis. The period begins with the newly installed Bourbon monarchy revitalizing Spain. By means of administrative, fiscal, and military reforms, Spain once again became a major world power. The new dynasty took a keen interest in Mexico, which soon felt the impact of Bourbon desires. Institutional restrictions and complex socioeconomic changes, however, gradually alienated many Mexicans. Spain's participation in European wars finally disrupted her ability to trade and even communicate with Mexico. The demise of the Spanish monarchy and French occupation of Spain produced a confusing climax to Mexico's colonial epoch.

THE BOURBON DYNASTY REVIVES SPAIN

The Bourbon Agenda. Before he died, Carlos II decided that Philip of Anjou, grandson of Louis XIV, would represent the Bourbon dynasty as king of Spain. Fearful that Britain and Austria would divide Spain's colonies, Carlos wanted Philip to preserve the empire, which was a source

of Spanish wealth as well as pride. Although Philip renounced his rights to the French throne, most of Europe feared an amalgamation of French and Spanish power. The War of Spanish Succession began in 1700 and finally concluded after a bloody stalemate. The Treaty of Utrecht in 1713 had the virtue of ridding Spain of costly possessions in Italy and Belgium. Thirty-year old Philip made sure that he retained his valuable American empire, but England obtained Gibralter and trading rights in the New World.

Felipe V (1714–1746) reduced clerical privileges and revived the economy. Increasing taxes, stimulating agriculture, and promoting as well as subsidizing luxury industries also strengthened the monarchy. The Crown began to object to land held in mortmain by the Church, demanding that it be put on the market in order to increase agricultural production. Felipe reasserted the monarch's rights to appoint bishops, control ecclesiastical taxes, and approve papal publications that circulated in Spain and Mexico.

Acting as a catalyst for ideals of European Enlightenment, Felipe's French and Italian advisors introduced the Enlightenment to Spain. The new philosophy asserted that experiments guided by reason and logic would produce natural laws which new leaders would implement in order to perfect society. These optimistic thinkers believed that people were a product of their environment. Therefore, religion became less important than empirical research in attempting to modernize society.

Perhaps only 1 percent to 5 percent of the population knew the ideas of Montesquieu, Rousseau, Voltaire, and other philosophes, but their writings had a tremendous impact upon the administration, which championed the idea of a royal despot who would strengthen the ideal of a nation-state. The Enlightened spirit was eloquent and inspiring, washing away the gloom of Hapsburg decline, while encouraging public participation.

New ideas challenged traditional assumptions. In 1739, the dean of the Spanish Enlightenment, Gerónimo Feijoo y Montenegro, argued that females were equal to males in terms of intellectual ability. To demonstrate his concern for learning, Felipe created the Palace Public Library during the war, which eventually became an autonomous national library.

Spanish diplomacy revolved around the family pact ideal, so that Spain's alliance with France could overcome Britain, now recognized as Spain's real enemy. Determined to avenge the War of Spanish Succession, Felipe prepared to invade Britain in 1719 in order to back up Stuart claims. To illustrate Spain's new capabilities and self-confidence, Spain fought wars in Italy which resulted in reacquisition of Sicily and Parma.

Felipe asserted royal power by centralizing the monarch's authority. The French ambassador encouraged the use of new administrators known as intendants. In this rearrangement, authority responded to the king and his secretaries. Intendants concerned themselves primarily with extending royal law, resolving legal disputes, and expanding the tax base. Therefore building roads, bridges, and canals not only revitalized the economy but also increased royal budgets and enabled political centralization to expand. Intendants also encouraged the *ayuntamientos* to assert themselves. Well paid and assisted by subdelegates, the intendants were often former military officers and had no limit on their terms of office. Replacing the *corregidores* with intendants generally

succeeded. Remaining Jews and *moriscos* enjoyed full legal equality while revenues increased.

Fernando VI (1746–1759), like Felipe V, recognized the need to stimulate Mexico. Eager to preserve peace, Fernando rebuilt the navy but continued the policy of domestic reform. A particularly beneficial development was the *sociedades económicos del pais* in 1748. Motivated by the Enlightenment, these elite groups devoted themselves to mathematics, physics, history, geography, and current events as well as a market economy. Concerned about the lack of Spanish industry, the *sociedades* opposed idle land and emphasized local development. They discussed their new ideas in papers which they presented as well as in various publications. Spreading rapidly, 5,000 of these groups existed by 1805 with several branches in Mexico.

Carlos III (1759–1788) represents the apex of Bourbon reforms. Carlos personally patronized the arts and encouraged the tapestry as well as porcelain industries. The manufacture of *indianes* (printed calicoes) began in Catalonia in the early 1730s. Eventually, Spain produced most of the products sent to Mexico. Carlos established tariff protection for the consolidation of low-quality cloth industries, reduced foreign dependence in general, and wiped out external debts. Inflation almost disappeared, stable currency encouraged investment, and paper money circulated for the first time. New joint stock companies and partnerships emerged to sell various goods. Determined to prepare Spain for modern capitalism and an industrialized society, Carlos curtailed aristocratic privileges. The king selected ministers on the basis of talent rather than lineage.

A crisis in 1766 represents the authoritarian style by which the Bourbon changes became implemented. Carlos removed price controls on grains in order to encourage profits and production as part of overall plans to expand agriculture, but riots broke out when feeble harvests resulted in high bread prices. Meanwhile, an Italian minister, the Marques de Esquilache, attempted to reduce crime in Madrid by prohibiting floppy hats and capes, unaware that these items protected their owners during cold Madrid winters. When police attempted to enforce this unrealistic regulation, Madrilenos revolted. As mobs demanded an end to dress regulations and lower bread prices, the king fled. Carlos dismissed Esquilache and distributed bread, claiming that Jesuits had stirred up the rioters. This accusation is partially true, but basically it served as a pretext to outlaw the Jesuits, banish them from Spain, and dissolve their order in 1767.

Civil and religious restrictions resulted in rural unrest. The king knew that the Church owned about one-seventh of the land, with the remainder in noble hands. Therefore the government enacted a law which stated that unused land would be seized and put into productive use. Little happened because aristocrats in control of local municipalities thwarted reformers who wanted to put land on the market. Nevertheless, landless peasants attacked the nobility in areas such as Zaragoza.

Spain benefited from a successful foreign policy. The family pact continued; Carlos aided the 13 colonies against the British. As a result, Spain recovered Florida as well as Minorca. The key to Spain's enhanced international presence was the vast improvement of the navy and army. Spain's military was one of Europe's best by the 1780s.

Despite their open-mindedness to reform, the Bourbons were never democratic and insisted that Mexico subordinate itself to imperial needs, particularly when war in Europe necessitated more colonial revenues. The interesting changes that Mexico experienced in the eighteenth century must be understood within the context of Spanish reforms. In their endeavor to sanctify science and create a market economy, the Bourbons unleashed dynamic social forces within Mexico.

CONTRADICTIONS OF IMPERIAL REFORM

Administrative Centralization. Bourbon reforms strengthened royal authority throughout New Spain and increased economic growth. As the innovations succeeded in Spain, the Crown decided to create more uniformity between Mexico and Spain, particularly in political and economic systems. Although New Spain generally benefitted, Madrid nevertheless sought to increase dependence and continue mercantilism.

The Bourbons realized quickly that Mexico was rich but administered by self-seeking, ineffective individuals. Disturbed by reports of inefficiency, corruption, and sales of public offices, royal officials decided to introduce the intendancy system into Mexico. A *visitador general*, José de Gálvez, arrived at the end of the Seven Years' War in order to obtain more revenues for the defense of the Philippines, Cuba, and Louisiana. After a 1760s trial in the Mexican northwest, Gálvez established the intendancy system throughout Mexico in 1786. The intendants would not only provide more revenue but also improve administration. A shocked Gálvez concluded that the *alcaldes mayores* pocketed 50 percent of the Indian tribute. Subdelegates administered a new jurisdictional unit, the partido, which replaced *alcaldias mayores*. Twelve intendants, carrying their new 325-page handbooks, replaced 200 *corregidores*.

In their attempt to make local administration directly responsible to Madrid, the Bourbons reduced viceregal authority. This decision had unpleasant consequences. Many of the eighteenth-century viceroys became very popular figures. Viceroy Marqués de Valero, for example, established an Acordada in 1722 in order to apprehend criminals and bandits. The efficient Acordada assumed an unlimited territorial jurisdiction and handled four-fifths of all criminal cases by the 1780s. By 1808, the viceroys acquired a reputation for giving *criollo* needs careful attention. Viceroy José Iturrigaray became a nationalistic leader for many Mexicans, partially because of his ability to connect with other regions and social groups outside Mexico City. Disturbed by reports that royal hospitals turned away soldiers and Africans, Iturrigaray directed an intendant to improve medical care in the Veracruz region and then inspected Monteclaros Hospital in May 1805. Once viceregal authority declined, the late colonial administration became quite autonomous because the Crown valued bureaucratic experience.

Administrative reforms improved local government, but often at the expense of *criollos*. The Bourbons reduced the sale of public offices but replaced *criollos* in the *audiencias* with loyal *peninsulares*. The Crown employed more bureaucrats after 1750, yet the majority of new appointments were born in Spain rather than Mexico. Turned away from public administration, many *criollos* pursued positions in the *cabildos*, the Church, or economic endeavors.

Commercial and Mining Reforms. Free trade undeniably created greater opportunities for Mexicans as well as Spaniards. A new Board of Trade, impressed with British free-trade policies during its occupation of Havana in 1763, decided to reduce traditional trade restrictions. The Bourbons also abolished the *flota* system because no matter how well organized, the *flota* contradicted the needs of Mexican merchants. Faster moving, private commercial vessels not only eluded enemy warships but also collected warehouse goods more efficiently. English slave traders, French smugglers, and United States merchants had become accustomed to dealing with Mexico. Numerous trade breakdowns with Spain caused by war in Europe also hastened the inevitability of free trade. In 1789, a newly created Junta del Estado in Madrid finally freed trade between Mexico and Spain on a complete basis. Instead of only two consuls and one *consulado* in Mexico City, the Bourbons created *consulados* in Veracruz and Guadalajara. Imperial needs remained paramount. Spain promoted commercial reforms in order to discourage smuggling with other Europeans, particularly the British in Jamaica. Trade incentives also strengthened the Spanish economy by creating a large Mexican market for textiles and other goods.

Spain continued to control international trade in Mexico. Despite the appearance of new *criollo* merchants, most Mexico City merchants were Spanish immigrants who married wealthy, status-conscious *criolla* women. Aggressive new Mexico City merchants continued to market the Manila trade and increase sales to miners while selling more cochineal dye in Spain. Merchants prospered more than ever by diversifying their assets and using bullion as capital to invest in mines, agriculture and pulque production.

Mining reforms enabled a great increase in silver production. One of Spain's notable achievements was a tenfold increase in mercury production throughout the eighteenth century after the Bourbons took control of the Almaden mine from German investors known as the Fuggers. The Crown granted tax exemptions for miners, cut production costs, and reduced the price of mercury as well as gunpowder. Spain encouraged new technology by means of a Royal School of Mines staffed with foreign experts. Free trade had the tendency to ease the importation of mining machinery. Miners also organized themselves into guilds and enjoyed legal jurisdiction within a Tribunal de Minería. These efforts resulted in the value of Mexican silver production increasing from 3 million pesos in 1700 to 13.5 million pesos in 1750 to 27 million pesos in 1804. The total production of silver quadrupled during the eighteenth century. The Crown also doubled copper production in Michoacán in order to mint coins and manufacture armaments.

Social and Intellectual Changes. The monarchy continued to perceive the Church as a rival and decided to make itself supreme, thus dissolving the traditional Church-state partnership. The Bourbons promoted science and encouraged educational as well as economic opportunities for women but maintained rigid social values that Mexicans began to question. Many mixed-blood individuals had become wealthy during the economic boom and began to marry white women. Social tensions began to take on an increasingly strong racial connotation.

Tensions between Church and state reached a climax during the reign of Carlos III. Although religious himself, the king placed matters of state foremost and appointed deists as ministers. The

Crown restricted the use of royal police by clerics, limited asylum to only a few Mexican Churches, upheld the monarch's right to limit papal publications, and removed tax exemptions. Royal courts assumed jurisdiction over matters such as inheritance and couples living together informally that had previously been the sole jurisdiction of the Church. Finally, the Bourbons attacked mass culture relentlessly. Officials ridiculed miracles and restricted dances and feast days. They prohibited religious dramas in 1756 and abolished the brotherhoods in the 1790s. Idolatry declined somewhat but persisted stubbornly in isolated areas. Many Mexicans now began to believe that Spanish monarchs viewed religion less favorably than they should have.

Carlos III expelled the Jesuits from Mexico as part of a carefully executed plan conducted on the morning of June 24, 1767. The king's drastic measure against the Jesuits took place because Carlos began to fear anyone not totally loyal. In addition, complaints about Jesuit wealth had accumulated in Spain. Royal officials seized Jesuit properties in the countryside that brought in five million pesos. The Jesuits aroused royal suspicion because several taught modern social contract theories of government. Beginning in the seventeenth century, theologian and political commentator Francisco Suárez claimed that the king was subject to law and that tyrannicide was justifiable if the king became a despot. Other Jesuits insisted that political power derived from God through the people and not a monarch.

The Church-state crisis during the 1760s aggravated the Church's role in mediating disputes from indigenous communities and mixed bloods against royal authorities. Outbursts over local issues characterized most eighteenth-century village revolts. But in 1761, Antonio Pérez, a local indigenous leader, opposed royal attempts to reorient religious practices in the Morelos highlands toward traditional Catholicism. Pérez formed a millenarian cult with himself as a self-proclaimed God who acted as a priest but called on indigenous groups to refuse monetary contributions to the Church. Disturbed by the expulsion of Catholic orders, Pérez symbolized the profound insecurity troubling Catholic indigenous communities. In fact, colonial reliance upon forceful administrators caused many clergymen to question the new authoritarianism and to consider supporting mass groups against the Bourbon system.

On a positive note, the Bourbons patronized science. Advances in health care proved particularly beneficial. By the late eighteenth century, Mexican doctors established new preventive health measures such as a general vaccination program. Once the College of Surgery established itself in Mexico City, ceasarean section operations became available. The college also trained new physicians. In 1768, a chair of anatomy, which included a dissecting room, was established at the national university. Four years later, José Ignacio Bartolach founded the first medical journal in Mexico. In 1787, Spain established a botanical garden and added an Institute of Biology to the university. Carlos III also promoted a wide variety of scientific research. The Malaspina expedition of 1789–1794 was the greatest of many attempts to collect data in Mexico. The botanical work of these naturalists was enormous, and thousands of specimens were collected.

The construction of observatories and the trend toward discovering new knowledge accelerated intellectual activity. José Velázquez de León was one of the brightest stars on the *criollo* intellectual scene. De León organized a scientific expedition to Baja, California, wrote several tracts on mining, and penned a long report on the physical features of the Valley of Mexico. Sympathetic to the Bourbons, he created allegorical themes for triumphal arches utilized for three viceregal receptions. By means of his *Gaceta de Literatura*, José Antonio Alzate y Ramírez advocated a scientific approach to life by writing a series of articles on agronomy, medicine, and industries designed to improve Mexican life. José Mariano Moziño Suárez became such an acclaimed naturalist in Mexico that he later served as president of the Royal Academy of Medicine in Madrid. Foreign technicians, administrators, and specialists arrived in greater numbers and imparted the latest European ideas. Mexican intellectuals took more pride in local life and approached indigenous culture with a more objective curiosity than in the past. In 1784, the Bourbons established the Royal Academy of San Carlos in order to provide instruction in painting, sculpture, and architecture. This Mexico City institution would wield considerable artistic influence beyond the nineteenth century.

But Spain also attempted to place restrictions upon a changing society. Spaniards had no desire to modify the caste system. Only 1,500 foreigners immigrated to Mexico from 1700 to 1760, but many more arrived within the next 40 years. The Mexico City elite, who formed the apex of colonial society, combined speculation with secure land investments in order to remain at the head of the hemisphere's largest city. These one hundred families protected their status by means of intermarriage, absorbing successful newcomers and competitors; they entered public service through the purchase of titles, administrative offices, and military rank. Marriage patterns in Oaxaca and Mexico City reveal that Spaniards strongly favored marriages within their own group be they *criollos* or *peninsulares*.

Nevertheless, a new Mexican society was taking shape whether Spaniards liked it or not. Mixed bloods accounted for 20 to 25 percent of Mexican society during the eighteenth century. A dramatic increase occurred in interracial marriages. *Mulatos* began a gradual merging with *mestizos*, who had low levels of endogamy. Many Spanish men now married women who had formerly been considered lovers only. Spanish women began to take an interest in wealthy males with African or indigenous blood. The caste structure could not be maintained if intermarriage began to eliminate the quantity of pure whites. As blacks began to diminish and *mestizos* multiplied more rapidly, the caste system came under attack. Growing miscegenation with Indians and whites led to several pitched battles fought in the Veracruz area from 1725 to 1741. Four encounters were severe with significant losses of life and property. This was a potentially disastrous conse-

quence for a social structure based upon racial differences.

Concerned about the fluid nature of marriages, the Bourbons restrained nuptial aspirants motivated by love. Until the 1720s, couples could marry for love despite parental objections. Priests performed secret marriages and nearly always responded to the needs of couples who appealed for marriage when parents objected. After 1730, however, priests abandoned secret marriages after pressure from Spanish authorities and upper-class desires for status influenced a clerical hierarchy now structured to the liking of Madrid. Men who violated a woman's virginity no longer had the obligation to marry; they needed only to provide financial compensation instead. A 1776 Royal Pragmatic encouraged civil authorities and the Church to allow parents to forbid marriages based upon racial distinctions.

Opportunities for women opened up despite the rigid racial policies of Church and state. The Bourbons revealed their contradictory notions toward reform by interpreting expanded female opportunities as more for the benefit of state and society than personal independence. To the Bourbons, educated women were superior mothers. Women's charitable organizations pleased Spain because these outlets provided relief for much needed social services. In 1784, the Bourbons lifted guild restrictions against women workers as part of an attack upon the monopolistic guild system. Females began to participate more actively in the economy. Recognition of their competence was a positive development for Mexican women.

Women also received the right to public as well as private elementary education, although secondary and university education continued to be denied. In 1754, the foundation of the first convent school of the Order of Mary, known as La Enseñanza, institutionalized women's education in Mexico. Convents of La Enseñanza became more numerous in Mexico than anywhere else in the Spanish empire. For the first time, an institution solely devoted to feminine education imparted the task. La Enseñanza not only became the first school to admit boarders on a regular basis, but it also offered free public classes to females of all social backgrounds. This innovative concept, however, limited itself to urban women.

The first labor strikes broke out under the Bourbons. The labor conditions for mine workers deteriorated in the eighteenth century. In 1730, Chihuahua mine workers struggled with owners over the issue of being able to take home ores, but the workers lost. The first successful strike in Mexico occurred at Real del Monte in 1765 after Pedro Romoreo de Terranos cut the wages of mine workers by 25 percent and restricted the right of these peons to retain ores after fulfilling their daily quotas. Another issue which motivated strikers was the role of labor recruiters, who forced inactive males to toil involuntarily.

The Bourbon response was contradictory but fairly enlightened. The viceroy's representative decided to maintain the heavy-handed press gangs and restricted workers from taking the best ores, but he restored wages to earlier levels, fired unpopular managers, and stopped a recent speedup in work routines. Moreover, the custom of taking ores home became a legal right. Confronted by a determined strike and concerned about labor scarcities, the regime decided upon a repressive but flexible policy to maintain mining revenues.

In 1774, Mexico City leaders created the Mexico City Poor House, the centerpiece of a bold experiment intended to eliminate poverty and impose a new work ethic on former beggars by constructing a forcible internment policy for some and putting others to work. The asylum, however, functioned primarily to indoctrinate white orphans instead of discouraging begging and regulating the *casta* community from whom it was designed. Although Mexico had traditionally regarded the impoverished as having the right to receive charity and affluent citizens felt obligated to provide alms, the Poor House was doomed from the start mainly because the Bourbons underestimated the tenacity of begging traditions.

Military Expansion. The 1762 disaster at Havana shocked Spain into building up Mexican defenses. Mexico had always been garrisoned

lightly, but now it became highly vulnerable to world conflicts. Spain had stationed only 3,000 regular army troops in Mexico by 1758 and the provincial militia lacked discipline. Actually controlled by guilds and merchants, the militia responded only in emergencies. The Bourbons increased the number of soldiers who served but in the process weakened the Crown's legitimacy.

Like other Bourbon innovations, negative factors paralleled positive results concerning military improvements. By 1800, Spain had approximately 6,150 regular army troops in Mexico, half of whom served in 20 presidios along the northern border. In addition, 25,762 militia protected various regions. But mass desertions, high mortality rates, poor equipment, and substandard training reflected the fact that the masses disliked military service. The Bourbons created animosity among the *castas* when they demanded that mixed bloods serve but allowed blacks and Indians to enjoy exemption until 1807. When press gangs forced commoners into units, these unfortunates frequently witnessed their families beg and suffer because of the poor pay that soldiers received.

The fact that large numbers of *criollos* entered the officer corps was a temporary Bourbon triumph. Serving in the militia gave insecure *criollos* great prestige. An impressive uniform and a day on the parade ground mitigated *criollo* social frustrations. Even more enticing was the opportunity to become officers in regular Spanish army units. By the end of the eighteenth century, more *criollos* served in regular regiments—about two-thirds in those units—than in the militia, where slightly over half the officers were *criollos*. Many *criollos* took great pride in the 1807 field maneuvers when Viceroy José de Iturrigaray mobilized 15,000 troops to prepare for an expected British invasion. Many *criollos*, however, would later employ their military experience against Spain during final stages of the independence struggle.

Renewed Colonization in the North. Increased imperial competition forced Spain to create northern buffer zones that could protect Mexican mines. Spain became particularly concerned when France founded New Orleans in 1718. The British caused more apprehension by moving into Georgia by 1733. In 1725, Catherine the Great sent Vitus Bering to search for a northern route to Europe. By the 1760s, Russian fur hunters had established camps in the Aleutians; permanent settlements in Alaska soon followed.

The colonization of Texas began after French traders shocked Mexico City when they appeared on the Red River as well as the Rio Grande. The viceroy immediately ordered that Texas be reoccupied. After the wealthy Marquéz de Aguayo pledged to finance the recovery of east Texas, 76 soldiers, priests, and colonists departed Saltillo in 1716. They arrived in the Nacogdoches area and established four missions. In 1721, the Aguayo expedition set up a mission at nearby Los Adaes, which were the colonial capital of Texas. San Fernando de Bexar (later San Antonio) was a way station between the Río Grande and the Red River. Industrious Canary Islands farmers and ranchers became the settlement's core. A successful cattle industry and several missions resulted in San Antonio installing its first civilian *ayuntamiento* in 1731.

Missions became the hub of life in San Antonio. The most famous was productive San Antonio de Valero, better known as the Alamo. By 1745 it had 300 Indians within its walls with several thousand head of cattle and annual harvests of 2,000 bushels of corn and 1,000 bushels of cotton. The other missions also flourished. San Francisco de Espada featured a mile-long aqueduct while Mission San José bustled with carpenters, blacksmiths, and tailors; most of its indigenous inhabitants practiced a trade by 1777. As in Paraguay, resident Indians spoke Spanish, played musical instruments, and performed Spanish dances. The San Antonio missions symbolize Spain's ability to implant deep Hispanic roots in Texas.

By far the most successful colonization project occurred in the lower Río Grande valley. José de Escandón explored the area in 1747 and established friendly relations with local Indians. In 1749, Escandón departed Queretaro with 3,000

settlers who received free land, travel expenses, and tax-exempt status for ten years. By 1757, the settlement had 200,000 livestock and 6,300 pioneers in 23 towns and 18 missions along both sides of the Río Grande. Royal policy enabled colonists to obtain individual land grants as well as communal ejidos. The land grants strengthened the north because settlers spread out over large areas near San Antonio and east toward Louisiana. Eventually, an 1805 royal decree established the Nueces River as the border between Nuevo Santander and Texas.

As Texas forged a more open society, Bourbon regalism provoked protests. Texas maintained a less rigid caste system. At least 20 percent of all births were illegitimate. Greater upward mobility enabled mixed bloods to own property and serve as public officials. *Cabildos* objected in 1778 and 1783 when Bourbon officials declared royal ownership of all ownerless stock and insisted that those who took such animals would pay fines. Although the military obtained a Comanche peace treaty in 1785, royal authorities angered many by secularizing the San Antonio missions. The demise of the missions, symbols of prosperity and religious tradition, is another example of Bourbon insensitivity to cultural norms.

The Bourbons strengthened Mexico's eastern flank by using Louisiana to weaken British influence. When Spain lost Florida as part of the Seven Years' War, France offered Louisiana to console Madrid. Bernardo de Gálvez, a commander of several Texas presidios, became the governor who fulfilled Spain's strategic objectives. He sent crucial supplies to rebels in the 13 colonies fighting Britain. New Spain also provided Gálvez with 9,000 cattle which enabled his 7,000 troops to defeat Britain at Biloxi, Baton Rouge, Natchez, Mobile, and Pensacola. The Treaty of Paris restored Florida to Spain and Gálvez returned to Mexico where he became the viceroy.

By 1768, Spain finally decided to colonize Alta, California. After he arrived in San Diego, Junípero Serra began to build several missions. Traditionally, missions allowed Spain to control land and Indians, but in California, the missions failed to assimilate the indigenous people. By 1832, the Franciscans had baptized nearly 80,000 Indians in their missions but about 60,000 of them died. Father Serra was excessive in his use of corporal punishment by the standards of his time. Not surprisingly, lack of food and disease caused Indians to revolt and burn the San Diego mission in 1775. Meanwhile, Spaniards settled Monterey in 1770 and established new communities in San José (1777), Los Angeles (1781), and Santa Barbara (1782). Juan Bautista Anza began colonizing San Francisco in 1776 after traveling up the beautiful Camino Real. In 1778, the viceroy ordered a sea expedition to Vancouver Island where colonists established themselves at Nootka Sound.

But thinly populated California became isolated from Mexico. By 1800, only 1,200 Spaniards lived there. California found that it could not depend upon overland trade with New Mexico or through Sonora. The towns struggled to survive because the northern frontier attracted few settlers. Free trade after 1786 did not integrate California into the Mexican economy. Its destiny appeared to be tied to the sea. California sent mission produce out and imported manufactured goods. By century's end, the ranchers began smuggling cowhides and tallow to foreign traders, but California remained a mission frontier.

Apache warfare and lack of water restricted Spanish success in New Mexico. Deportation programs and Spanish reinforcements wore the Apaches down. Eventually, they accepted food rations in return for peace. An elaborate missionary system gradually characterized administration in New Mexico. Albuquerque settlers expanded indigenous irrigation ditches for agricultural purposes. Sheepherding became a bastion of Hispanic communities throughout New Mexico. And local officials exhibited flexibility on the alcalde level because their rulings generally conformed to community expectations of justice.

To tie New Spain's northern frontier together, José de Gálvez eventually created a Comandancia General in 1776; this new administrative unit covered California, Sonora, New Mexico, Coahuila,

and Texas. The Bourbons hoped to consolidate the Rockies, Plains, and Pacific Northwest under their control. Demographic and cultural progress occurred, but the distances remained great and success was elusive. In Mexico, pioneer life never became idealized as it later did in the United States. The hostile, arid north failed to stimulate a sense of mission. Northern frontiersmen enjoyed greater opportunity and egalitarianism, but the central plateau remained the foundation of Mexican life.

The Bourbons rarely fashioned a coherent policy to assimilate or even understand indigenous peoples. Chiapas is a case in point. In the summer of 1712, a Maya woman experienced a fantasy with the Virgin Mary in the forest. The miracle attracted indigenous pilgrims throughout the Chiapas highlands. When Spanish officials attempted to stop the popular cult, they ignited a full-scale rebellion by 5,000 Tzeltal rebels.

Expanding haciendas and tightly centralized rule threatened the autonomy of many indigenous communities, thus precipitating bloody clashes. After Indians built up immunity to European disease, their increased numbers during the eighteenth century necessitated more areas to provide food. But the need for land also resulted in confrontations with whites. By 1740, a severe famine in Sonora triggered a serious Yaqui revolt against their Jesuit administrators, who had been sending grain to California. Indigenous revolts also flared up in the central valley. In 1761, an even bloodier Maya insurrection broke out in Yucatán. Events began with the murder of a white merchant during a drunken revelry. Afterwards, the Maya decided to oppose higher tribute taxes until authorities suppressed the revolt.

Regional social and economic integration slowly began to emerge in northern Mexico as the colonial period reached its twilight. Only after the Jesuit expulsion did northern Spanish settlers profit from agriculture and stock raising. This encouraged the rise of Guadalajara as a significant grain producer. Farther west, the Sánchez Navarro family managed huge flocks of sheep in Coahuila. Increases in population, mining, and trade led to social changes that varied according to local circumstances. Limited *mestizaje* finally occurred in Sonora, although Yaquis and Seris did not participate. But many Yaquis began working in the mines. Anchored by the cities of Chihuahua and Durango, the province of Nueva Vizcaya had 140,000 inhabitants by 1740. Military colonists sponsored by Spain appeared to defend the border.

MEXICO BY 1810: CAUSES FOR UPHEAVAL

Intellectual Ferment. New Spain's thinkers became more aware of their differences with Europe as international events undermined traditional monarchies. The revolt of the 13 colonies had a striking effect upon Mexico. That fellow Americans could defy the greatest European power encouraged many Mexicans to consider the concept of liberty. The demand for knowledge about the process of North American independence resulted in the translation and publication of Benjamin Franklin's work in Mexico City. The American Philosophical Society promoted several *criollos* to its society. The "Black Legend" of Spanish cruelties spread as New Englanders and *criollos* exchanged books. A decade later, the French Revolution questioned the foundations of imperial rule.

Now the *criollo* intellects possessed more confidence than ever. New professors in Mexico continued to correspond with their European counterparts, discussing enlightened ideas and scientific research. Adam Smith's *Wealth of Nations* influenced Hispanic thinkers to accept a free market approach. As the century ended, however, Mexicans disagreed with Spaniards. Sensitive to the disregard that Europeans often exhibited toward New Spain's society, Mexican intellects shed their insecurity once it became clear that change would be inevitable.

The visit of Alexander Baron von Humboldt was a great event. Humboldt, a German scientist, spent five years in the Hispanic dominions of the New World from 1799 to 1804, gathering infor-

mation and material for a systematic, scientific examination of the geography, flora, and fauna of the regions through which he traveled. It was the obscurity of mining in New Spain that first drew Humboldt into the project. The director of the Royal School of Mines in Mexico City, M. d'Elhuyer, persuaded the scientist to take the information he had collected regarding the country's national industry and produce a map depicting the thirty-seven mining districts, as well as the location of the major mines. d'Elhuyer lamented that he could not locate one map published in Europe that even noted the city of Guanajuato. Humboldt responded to the request and completed the mining map after his departure from Mexico City in 1804. It was this initial request that led to the comprehensive publication about conditions in New Spain.

During his journey, Humboldt encouraged more critical thinking on the part of Mexican intellects. He often seemed to indicate that Mexico

Baron Alexander von Humboldt. *Corbis.*

Mexico in 1811. Poirson, J.B. *Carte du Mexique et des Pays Limitares Situes Au Nord et a l'est.* (Paris: F. Schoell, 1811). The Royal School of Mines requested von Humboldt to produce this map, which became a major cartographical step because it was the first accurate map of Mexico in over 100 years. *Courtesy of Special Collections Division, Virginia Garrett Cartographic History Library, University of Texas at Arlington, Arlington, Texas.*

could get along better without Spain. Encouraged toward a more independent point of view, Mexican scholars provided much of the data to Humboldt that appeared in his monumental *Ensayo político de la Nueva España*.

The Military Fuero. Although entrenched privileges became unpopular, the Bourbons unwisely decided to extend *fueros* to the military in 1768. Here is another example of Bourbon reforms becoming obstructive and incoherent. The *fuero* allowed officers to assume control of municipal offices. Officers who incurred debts no longer had to fear imprisonment or property loss. Moreover, military courts suddenly possessed dominant jurisdiction over officers involved in crime. The Bourbons extended these privileges to provincial units and the militia; but defiant officers disrupted royal law and used *fueros* as a pretext not to pay taxes.

Alienation of the Church. The Bourbons not only enraged the clergy but also angered landowners once war in Europe heightened Spanish tendencies to exploit the colonists. The Crown began borrowing large sums of money from the Mexican elite in 1795 but never obtained sufficient amounts. In 1804, the Bourbons decreed that liens and mortgages whose interests supported the pious works of the Church should be redeemed. Eventually, the Crown appropriated 10.5 million pesos from this source, which it never returned. In addition to taking a profoundly anticlerical position, Bourbon authorities disrupted the financial system of New Spain since pious foundations supplied much of Mexico's investment capital. About 25,000 to 30,000 of Mexico's leading landowners suddenly became obligated to repay clerical loans on their generally indebted haciendas. Moreover, many resentful priests derived a large share of their income from pious works such as chaplaincies. The clergy, along with many other Mexicans, now believed that Spain could no longer be trusted. Although many paid with promissory notes, the actual financial effects were not as severe as commonly feared. Eventually, energetic mer-

chants picked up much of the demand for capital as they had begun to do early in the eighteenth century. The Bourbons hastily suspended the hated decree in 1808, but incensed colonials learned that Napoleon's authorities in Spain received at least five million pesos of the funds collected in Mexico. A profound mistrust of Bourbon Spain never faded away.

For health and hygiene reasons, King Carlos IV decided to ban burials inside churches throughout the Spanish empire in 1804. The release of noxious gases from rotting corpses exacerbated by burning candles, darkened buildings, closed doors, and poor ventilation had made many Catholic churches unsanitary places to worship in the minds of Bourbon officials. Therefore the king ruled that new cemeteries would have to be built on the outskirts of towns. But priests objected, fearing that such a change would cut into their incomes. Religious devotees considered burial under altars and pews their supreme act of salvation as well as achieving enormous social status. But the Bourbons persisted and reiterated their unpopular ban on church burials in 1819.

The Crown alienated the Church further by actively intervening in other clerical affairs. Secular courts assumed increasing jurisdiction over the clergy, strictly regulating their travel, declaring their property temporal, expelling all foreign ecclesiastics, and taxing mortmain property. An 1812 *bando* eventually removed the last vestiges of the Church *fuero*. Publicly and behind the scenes, the Church resisted and it is no wonder that at least 400 priests took part in the independence movement. Probably a majority of Mexicans outside the Church resented Bourbon attempts to "destroy religion."

International Factors. Late in the eighteenth century, Spain began to experience difficulty in protecting herself during several European wars. Mexicans became alarmed when Spain's northern borders in the New World began to crumble. The Nootka Sound crisis in 1789 compelled Spain to withdraw from Vancouver Island when Paris would not support Madrid. The ratification of

Pinkney's Treaty in 1795 gave the fledgling United States unprecedented trading rights in New Orleans and throughout the Mississippi River area. In 1799, Napoleon started forcing Spain to relinquish the vast Louisiana territory.

By April 1799, Spain was 150 million pesos in debt by and suffering serious military defeats, such as Cape Vincent in 1797. A British blockade of Cádiz forced Spain to permit neutral nations to trade with Mexico from 1797 to 1802. Nearly half of all U. S. exports went to Latin America after 1800. When the naval disaster at Trafalgar occurred in 1805, Spain lost the ability to protect or even communicate with Spanish America. British smugglers and U. S. merchants appeared to trade, especially after Spain restored free trade in 1804. The tendency of U. S. merchants and consuls to bring copies of the Declaration of Independence and to encourage the ideal of freedom added to tensions in Mexican society.

Spain found itself without a monarch when Napoleon attacked Madrid in May 1808. Earlier, Spain and France decided to divide up Portugal between themselves. After allowing French forces to pass through Spain in order to invade Portugal, Carlos IV resigned in favor of his son, Prince Fernando. The French, however, attacked Spain in order to install Napoleon's brother, Joseph, on the Spanish throne. Instead of fighting back, Fernando abdicated and retired to pleasant surroundings in France. The corrupt monarchy urged the Spanish people to accept Joseph, but when citizens realized that their Bourbon authorities had abandoned them, massive riots broke out in Madrid. Various juntas throughout Spain temporarily resisted Napoleon's armies as the Bourbon monarchy lost prestige that it would never recover.

The collapse of Bourbon integrity in Spain accelerated the tempo of *criollo* demands in Mexico. *Criollos* now insisted that the temporary disappearance of the Bourbons provided Mexico a certain amount of sovereignty. The Mexico City *cabildo* became increasingly defiant. Although most *cabildo* members were rich, particularly the overseas merchants who dominated its proceed-ings, some had lost their wealth as a result of the 1804 financial crisis. War in Spain soon became the *cabildo's* immediate concern and resulted in its insistence that the *cabildo* represented all of Mexico. An almost daily exchange of letters and proposals to the audiencia and other royal officials took place after news of Napoleon's invasion reached Mexico City. In July 1808, the *cabildo* urged Viceroy José de Iturrigaray to take charge of New Spain in the name of the king with a junta composed of municipal representatives as part of a regional congress. Iturrigaray, after listening to the autonomist point of view, merely recognized Fernando VII as king.

The *cabildo* also made it clear that it wanted to remain with Spain but that it also wanted to be considered an analogous partner. This was not an unusual request because Brazil had won the status of an equal kingdom shortly after the Portuguese monarchy arrived from Lisbon. *Cabildo* members became increasingly aware of the trappings of their social status and radicalized their rhetoric to demand limited sovereignty. After 1808, regional support for the *cabildo* against the audiencia became widespread. Therefore a political consensus among the elite vanished in 1808 while *cabildo* members articulated notions of self-determination that eventually triumphed in 1821.

To forestall the threat of a *criollo* takeover, *peninsulares* forced the popular viceroy Iturrigaray out in favor of two hard-liners, Francisco Javier de Lizana y Beaumont and Pedro de Garibay. To make matters more confusing and to further weaken royal legitimacy, the anti-French Cádiz regency appointed Francisco Xavier de Venegas as its viceroy in Mexico. Such was the chaotic situation when the call for revolt finally rang out on September 16, 1810.

Commercial, Financial, and Economic Crisis.
Events in Europe precipitated the formation of a more national economy as warfare tore Spain apart. *Criollo* merchants and landowners formed a Mexican market now that international trade became less a factor during the late eighteenth-century crisis.

Regional economies continued to grow for a number of reasons. For one thing, Spanish attempts to end the *repartimiento de comercio* failed because the subdelegates never received salary increases and because the *repartimiento* served as the only source of credit for Indians and the rural poor. Because of their increasing influence, Mexican merchants successfully forestalled ordinances against the *repartimiento de comercio* from 1792 to 1800. Encouraging the formation of regional economies was the difficulty Spain faced in absorbing Mexican produce during periods of international or internal conflict. Therefore, the Mexicans received access to better markets and prices in the world economy as well as increased sales of their own goods.

The regional economies not only grew but also increasingly became drawn into an incipient colonial economy that initiated the slow integration of the national economy generations later. The economic growth did not cause the general standard of living to rise nor did it lead to structural transformation. New Spain experienced a narrow consumer market, an unskilled labor force, high levels of debt, low commodity prices, and high transportation costs as well as an unfavorable ratio of prices to costs. Loans to Spain, taxes, and monopolies too often retarded economic growth.

Urbanization created changes that shook the broad spectrum of the socioeconomic structure. Guadalajara is a prime example, growing sixfold from 1700 to 1800. The increasing urban market for foodstuffs resulted in grain cultivation replacing livestock as the primary mode of production in the last third of the eighteenth century. Landowners committed higher capital investments to irrigation as well as storage facilities. More importantly, *criollos* gradually gained control of supply and marketing, frustrating royal attempts to control wheat production through public granaries. Merchants and *hacendados* rather than Bourbon administrators began to dominate various regions and cities such as Guadalajara. Economic autonomy in the interior was the prelude to economic motivation for independence during the early nineteenth century.

Market pressures encouraged greater concentration of land in other regions. Eager to promote sugar and henequen on the world market, Yucatecan landowners initiated land seizures in the 1780s. The expansion of the *haciendas* left less land for indigenous populations. The Maya lost much of their communal autonomy as well as their *ejidos*. The same conflict appeared in Morelos when landowners seized property in order to increase sugar exports. Similarly, wheat-growing areas in Puebla were a source of unrest. Large landowners tended to infringe on small and medium landowners' water supplies, which resulted in cumbersome as well as expensive litigation throughout Mexico.

Although the Mexican population doubled during the Bourbon century, food supplies declined. Agricultural production in the first half of the century remained above the rate of population growth, but it fell behind the rising rate of demographic growth in the second half. Maize production actually declined in central Mexico. Agriculture's failure to supply growing needs occurred for several reasons. Agriculture underwent few technical changes. In Puebla and the north, Spanish deforestation decreased irrigation reserves which led to a scarcity of water. Indigenous desires to sell firewood and livestock consumption of ground cover increased soil erosion tremendously. After the 1780s, merchants and landowners began holding grain from the Guadalajara and Mexico City markets. The tendency toward speculation and withholding grain supplies by large landowners became common toward the end of the colonial period.

The colonial economy was a paradox. Its impressive extractive powers matched those of contemporary absolutist states in Europe. Yet this very success limited innovation and efficiency and it drained a high level of economic surplus from Mexico. The result was a system whose nonextractive capacities became limited and whose weaknesses soon became revealed in the independence struggle.

Inflation suddenly halted economic growth after the 1770s. Inflation appeared partially because Spain diverted increasingly large amounts of capital from Mexico to pay for imperial defenses. In Mexico, as in Chile, grain prices rose after the 1760s. The simultaneous growth of the money supply accompanied rapid population growth. Silver prices increased, allowing relative price levels to rise.

Stagnant economic conditions added to social miseries. Mexican per capita income probably did not grow over the course of the century and certainly declined by the 1770s. The great mass of rural inhabitants experienced poverty because food prices went up quickly. Indigenous peasants gradually became integrated into plantations, textile mills, and restrictive systems which they resented. Less purchasing power led to a decline in pulque production after 1785. By the 1790s, maize and bean prices reached a critically high level.

The inability of the economy to produce balanced growth reflected social difficulties. As the income of the masses declined, they purchased cheaper cottons produced in Europe. Many *obraje* workers lost their jobs because of Catalonian and British imports. Closely bound to the cities, Mexican textiles necessitated high transportation costs. Internal markets required more integration, but the Bourbons failed to improve the local infrastructure. Scarce investment capital frustrated Mexican entrepreneurs because mining profits generally went to Spain instead of being reinvested in Mexico.

Criollo Resentments. Mainly due to their numerical ascendancy and wealth, *criollos* became increasingly estranged from Spain. As can be seen from Table 5–1, *criollos* outnumbered *peninsulares* heavily by 1803 when Mexico's population reached 5.8 million. Humboldt overestimated the number of *mulatos* and *peninsulares*, but his figures are fairly accurate. Based on Humboldt and other sources, it is clear that *criollos* formed the majority of the richest, most prominent families by 1803. *Criollo* estates often became the basis for family enterprises. *Criollo* haciendas provided the collateral for credit-hungry *peninsulares*. Therefore *compadrazgo* func-

TABLE 5–1 Population of New Spain in 1803

Indigenous	3.0 million
Mestizos	1.2 million
Criollos	1.1 million
Mulatos	500,000
Africans	25,000
Peninsulares	15,000
Asians	10,000
Total	5,850,000

Source: Alexander von Humboldt, *Political Essay on the Kingdom of New Spain*, Vol. 1, p. 356 and elsewhere.

tions in the credit system became critical, because credit increasingly became the foundation for local economies. As borrowing by the white oligarchy increased and the Church approved disproportionately fewer loans, Mexico experienced an increasingly national consciousness that *criollos* understood.

In 1789, however, the Bourbons restricted *mayorazgo* privileges in order to restrain the propensity of *criollo* families to maintain large landed units. *Criollo* elites objected because they needed collateral to obtain loans in order to diversify economic activity and protect themselves from bankruptcy. In an increasingly capitalistic Mexico, the *criollos* often lost fortunes and sold haciendas.

Criollos particularly resented newly established monopolies. The tobacco monopoly dedicated to imperial revenue needs, provoked bitter indignation as did the prohibition of Mexican vineyards. The Crown sold cards, gunpowder, and even snow for high profits. The copper distribution monopoly became self-defeating because technical improvements that led to the revival of copper production were not cost efficient; Spain abandoned its copper monopoly in 1809. Attempts to reform mercury distribution eventually failed because shortages appeared after temporary increases in supply. New Spain could have mined its own mercury under a more liberal policy. Unlike Portugal and Brazil, Spain had little ability to work in harmony with the colonial Mexican elite.

The Enlightenment strengthened *criollo* thought by attacking the Hispanic social hierarchy and its preoccupation with preserving a caste system that suited Spanish interests. For one thing, *criollos* began to lose interest in classical knowledge imported from Spain. Led by Francisco Javier Clavijero, *criollos* attempted to recover the indigenous past. They turned increasingly to art and science and wrote a new literature that emphasized Mexico's physical beauty, much as Brazilians did. An incipient nationalism began to characterize *criollo* attitudes once they took pride in their cultural variations—harsh *peninsular* voices, delicate, high-pitched *criollo* language, cuisine, dress, and flora.

Social Inequalities. Humboldt noted that nowhere in the Hispanic world did he see such vast differences between wealthy and poor as in Mexico. The poverty of Indians shocked travelers. Once the indigenous groups doubled from 1740 to 1810, their presence became increasingly visible. The humiliating payment of tribute continued, denying the social integration of Indians. Although debt peonage helped to form a Mexican nation by drawing workers away from large indigenous areas, inequalities persisted. The caste system meant that Indians could not wear Spanish clothes, own horses, and possess weapons. Royal policies excluded indigenous people from receiving credit even though indigenous people retained much of their land, particularly in the south. Because the Bourbons would not permit Indians to purchase cotton, the textile industry languished. By the late 1750s, most indigenous women and children had to work if they lived in Mexico City. Indian women worked more frequently and at more difficult tasks than *mulatos*. Although some Indians aspired to *mestizo* status, Spaniards contemptuously segregated *mestizos* and Indians from Hispanic neighborhoods.

Marriage patterns indicate a decline in Hispanic institutions and a growth in Mexican values. After 1725, endowed marriages among the rural poor and urban families decreased in Guadalajara and Puebla. Indians and *castas* never involved themselves in dowries. That rural *criollos* and Indians married within their own groups is not surprising. But when *mulatos* and *mestizos* married outsiders, this change in marriage patterns demonstrated that the racial definitions of castes were breaking down at the base of the social pyramid. Nearly all Africans, for example, had been absorbed by the end of the century. The caste system weakened more rapidly on the frontier. A pronounced decline in the endogamy rate occurred in Nueva Vizcaya because race was less important in defining status. Increasing mobility meant that property and wealth became crucial factors that enabled concepts of class to challenge race as the prevailing norm in Mexican society.

Declining social conditions provoked drinking and defiance. Educational facilities never satisfied public demand. The La Enseñanza convent closed in 1785 after earlier success. The 1714 and 1750 famines were quite serious, but the Matlazahuatl epidemic from 1736-1739 took an especially heavy toll among indigenous groups, causing a permanent population decline in some areas. Smallpox and measles were severe problems after 1740. The 1786 famine was the worst of all, killing about 300,000. The Bourbons could not rid the Mexico City food stalls of animal carcasses and excrement. Increased consumption of alcoholic beverages reflected social strife. By this time, each block in Mexico City had at least one pulquería or tavern in which to drink and socialize. To avoid heavy taxes, many drinking establishments operated without the necessary licenses. As part of their attempts to reduce drinking, authorities expanded the size of the police force in 1783 and 1790 because drunkenness became excessive and weakened economic productivity.

The late colonial period was notable for general crime after 1750. Police placed into the stocks those guilty of fornication or defecation in public. Lewd songs and crude dances became mass protests to elite values, particularly during public ceremonies. Higher taxes and clerical fees provoked a great deal of spontaneous violence at the community level. Apparently willing to recognize that bloody outbursts were an inescapable means of manifesting local grievances, the Bourbon courts were surprisingly lenient.

In Mexico City, crime intensified and the authorities responded more severely. Part of the problem was that young poor males and females migrated from rural regions and swelled the numbers of the unemployed in the capital. With rapid population growth and economic insecurity came an increase in street crime, providing a constant flow of criminals to Mexico City's jails. Women accounted for 30 percent of all convicts. Attempts at rehabilitating female criminals resulted in placing them in separate facilities, or in private homes, to serve as maids for *gente decente*. Unfortunately, this often amounted to their exploitation as unpaid laborers. For men, jail became a temporary stop followed by severe corporal punishment, forced labor, or military service. Criminals frequently died before completing their sentences.

The rich lived well. The wealthiest Mexican families often had incomes of 200,000 pesos compared to a high of 35,000 in Cuba and 10,000 in Venezuela. Silverware and table settings cost as much as 35,000 to 40,000 pesos and such luxuries sold frequently in Mexico City. Further dividing society was a royal decision to grant 49 titles of nobility. *Peninsulares* received 29 titles, usually to merchants. The titled *criollos* yearned to legitimize their status despite possessing investments in mines, agriculture, stock raising, commerce, and finance. For a short period, titles gave Mexican as well as Spanish elites something in common, but the presence of a titled nobility caused resentment throughout the remainder of Mexican society. Church inequalities became even more glaring. The Archbishop of Mexico had an annual income of 130,000 pesos while priests earned only 100 to 120 pesos a year.

The birth of *criollo* Mexican statehood now approached. The Hapsburg era evolved into flexibility and compromise based upon an appreciation for economic growth and social stability. The Bourbons, however, seemed to evoke a rigid centralism that became less acceptable to many Mexicans during the rapid socioeconomic changes of the eighteenth century. The idea of the nation as a natural polity was fashionable in Europe and manifested itself in protests from *criollo regidores* in Mexico City as well as writers such as Alzate. The emerging Mexican economy not only established itself in key regions, but also entrepreneurs, clerics, and landowners began to question the ability of Spain to protect their vital interests.

SUGGESTED READING

Archer, Christon I. *The Army in Bourbon Mexico, 1760–1810.* Albuquerque: University of New Mexico Press, 1977.

Arrom, Silvia M. *The Women of Mexico City, 1790–1857.* Stanford, CA: Stanford University Press, 1985.

———. *Containing the Poor: The Mexico City Poor House, 1774–1781.* Durham: Duke University Press, 2000.

Brading, David. *Miners and Merchants in Bourbon Mexico, 1763-1810.* Cambridge: Cambridge University Press, 1971.

Carrol, Patrick. *Blacks in Colonial Veracruz: Race Ethnicity and Regional Development.* Austin: University of Texas Press, 1991.

Chance, John. *Race and Class in Colonial Oaxaca.* Stanford, CA: Stanford University Press, 1978.

Coatsworth, John. "The Limits of Colonial Absolutism: The State in Eighteenth Century Mexico." In Karen Spalding, ed. *Essays in the Political, Economic, and Social History of Colonial Latin America.* Newark, NJ: University of Delaware Press, 1982.

Chowning, Margaret. "The Consolidacíon de Vales Reales in the Bishopric of Michaocán." *Hispanic American Historial Review* 69:3 (August 1989), 451–478.

Cutter, Charles. *The Legal Culture of Northern New Spain, 1760–1810.* Albuquerque: University of New Mexico Press, 1995.

Engstrand, Iris H. "Mexico's Pioneer Naturalist and the Spanish Enlightenment." *The Historian* 53:1 (Autumn 1990), 17–32.

Farriss, Nancy M. *Maya Society Under Colonial Rule.* Princeton,NJ : Princeton University Press, 1984.

———. *Crown and Clergy in Colonial Mexico, 1759–1821: The Crisis of Ecclesiastical Privilege.* Albuquerque: University of New Mexico Press, 1968.

Fox y Fox, Pilar. *La revolucíon pedagógica en Nueva España (1754–1820).* 2 vols. Madrid: Instituto Gonzalo Fernández de Oviedo, 1981.

Garner, Richard L. "Price Trends in Eighteenth Century Mexico." *Hispanic American Historical Review* 65:2 (May 1985), 279–326.

———. "Prices and Wages in Eighteenth Century Mexico." In Lyman Johnson and Enrique Tandeter, *Essays on the Price History of Eighteenth Century Latin America*. Albuquerque: University of New Mexico Press, 1990, 73–108.

———. *Economic Growth and Change in Bourbon Mexico*. Gainesville: University of Florida Press, 1993.

Gonzalez Claverán, Virginia. *La expedicíon scientífica de Malaspina en Nueva España, 1789–1794*. Mexico City: El Colegio de México, 1988.

Gosner, Kevin. *Soldiers of the Virgin: The Maya Economy of a Colonial Maya Rebellion*. Tucson: University of Arizona Press, 1992.

Gruzinski, Serge. *Man-Gods in the Mexican Highlands: Indian Power and Colonial Society, 1520–1800*. Stanford, CA: Stanford University Press, 1989.

Hamnett, Brian R. "The Appropriation of Mexican Church Wealth by the Spanish Bourbon Government: The Consolidacíon de Vales Reales, 1805–1809." *Journal of Latin American Studies* 1 (1969), 85–113.

Haslip-Viera, Gabriel. *Crime and Punishment in Late Colonial Mexico City, 1692–1810*. Albuquerque: University of New Mexico Press, 2000

Herr, Richard. *The Eighteenth Century Revolution in Spain*. Princeton: Princeton University Press, 1958.

Humboldt, Alexander von. *Political Essay on the Kingdom of New Spain*. 4 vols. London: AMS Press, 1966.

Jackson, Jack. *Los Mesteños: Spanish Ranching in Texas, 1721–1821*. College Station: Texas A&M University Press, 1986.

Ladd, Doris. *The Making of a Strike: Mexican Silver Workers' Struggles in Real del Monte, 1766–-1775*. Lincoln: University of Nebraska Press, 1988.

Lipsett-Rivera, Sonya. " Puebla's Eighteenth Century Agrarian Decline: A New Perspective." *Hispanic American Historical Review* 70:3 (August 1990), 463–481.

McAlister, Lyle N. *The "Fuero Militar" in New Spain, 1764–1800*. Gainesville: University of Florida Press, 1957.

MacLachlan, Colin M. and Jaime E. Rodriguez O. *The Forging of the Cosmic Race: A Reinterpretation of Colonial Mexico*. Berkeley: University of California Press, 1980.

Ouweneel, Arij. *Shadows over Anáhuac: An Econological Interpretation of Crisis and Development in Central Mexico, 1730–1800*. Albuquerque: University of New Mexico Press, 1994.

Seed, Patricia. "Social Dimensions of Race: Mexico City, 1753." *Hispanic American Historical Review* 62:4 (November 1982), 569–606.

———. *To Love, Honor, and Obey in Colonial Mexico: Conflicts Over Marriage Choice, 1574–1821*. Stanford, CA: Stanford University Press, 1988.

Stein, Stanley. "Bureaucracy and Business in the Spanish Empire, 1759–1804: Failure of a Bourbon Reform in Mexico and Peru." *Hispanic American Historical Review* 61:1 (February 1981), 2–28.

Swann, Michael M. *Tierra adentro: Settlement and Society in Colonial Durango*. Boulder, CO: Westview Press, 1982.

Taylor, William B. *Drinking, Homicide, and Rebellion in Colonial Mexican Villages*. Stanford, CA: Stanford University Press, 1979.

Thompson, J. K. J. *A Distinctive Industrialization: Cotton in Barcelona, 1728–1832*. New York: Cambridge University Press, 1992.

Van Young, Eric. *Hacienda and Market in Eighteenth Century Mexico: The Rural Economy of the Guadalajara Region, 1675–1820*. Berkeley: University of California Press, 1981.

Weber, David. "Turner, the Boltonians and the Borderlands." *American Historical Review* 91:1 (February 1986), 66–81.

———, ed. *New Spain's Far Northern Frontier: Essays on Spain in the American West, 1540–1821*. Albuquerque: University of New Mexico Press, 1979.

Will, Martina E. "At the Intersection of the Here and Hereafter: New Mexico Deathways, 1760–1850." Paper presented at the Social Science History Association in Forth Worth Texas, November 13, 1999.

6

Independence from Spain, 1810–1821

After centuries of domination, Mexicans developed a sense of identity that alienated them from their Hispanic rulers. In many ways, the independence movement became a continuation of the unhappy response to Bourbon repression. Like patriots in the United States, Mexican rebels initially sought local autonomy rather than independence. The French invasion of Spain allowed the Mexican elite to displace their colonial masters. After two priests initiated regional insurrections, the independence struggle often became local conflicts rather than a movement for national liberation. This was particularly evident when upper-class forces battled the masses, who attempted to use the unrest to obtain redress of their socioeconomic problems. In addition to becoming a war for social emancipation, independence struggles also involved the construction of regional centers of power by local elites. Eventually, the *criollo* determination to control Mexico triumphed when Iturbide provided the formula for consensus.

HIDALGO INITIATES SOCIAL REVOLUTION

Compared to the rest of Spanish America, independence in Mexico took on unique characteristics. For one thing, no cabildo-based junta emerged in Mexico as was the case in Chile, Buenos Aires, Caracas, and Lima. Dormant during the colonial era, sentiment for sovereignty was never totally obliterated by the sixteenth-century Spanish invasion. Revolutionary leaders glorified the Aztec past and emphasized that Mexico had been independent prior to the Spanish invasion. Writers such as Carlos Maria de Bustmante proclaimed that the insurgents were liberators dedicated to restoring the Mexican nation. Mexican independence was atypical in that clerical intellectuals interpreted Mexican yearnings for separation from Spain. Juan Benito Díaz de Gamarra y Dávalos, who taught in present-day San Miguel Allende, challenged authoritarian scholasticism in favor of reason, empirical research, and a quest for truth in accordance with reason. Miguel Hidalgo y Castillo read his writings carefully. Francisco Xavier Clavijero glorified the abilities of indigenous Mexicans and denounced Spanish cruelties before being exiled to Italy with other Jesuits. Tremendously successful in Europe, Clavijero sent and dedicated his book *Storica Antica del Messico*, to the University of Mexico, where it was received with great applause. From this tradition of clerical protest, Hidalgo and José María Morelos led the early phase of Mexican independence.

Hidalgo's Intellectual Background. An intelligent *criollo*, Hidalgo realized eventually that a change in the socioeconomic structure of the colonial system had to take place. One of the most complex leaders in Mexican history, Hidalgo represents the explosive mixture of ethnicity, region, and religion that has always generated Mexico.

Hidalgo was born on a hacienda southwest of Guanajuato in 1753. On his mother's side was the Spanish founder of Valladolid (now Morelia) in the sixteenth century. Hidalgo's father managed the Corralejo hacienda. Unconcerned with social status, Hidalgo's parents enjoyed respectability but were far more interested in educating their sons. Hidalgo also experienced an early concern for the indigenous population that was unusual. In addition, his family owned five African slaves.

Hidalgo came into contact with clerical ideas at an early age. After he learned how to read and write, Hidalgo's father sent him to the Jesuit *colegio* of San Francisco Xavier in Valladolid. The Abbot Clavijero was its most brilliant teacher before being transferred to Guadalajara. Although unable to directly absorb Clavijero's reviving message which permeated the school, Hidalgo eventually owned a copy of *Storia Antica del*

Miguel Hidalgo y Castilla as a young man. *Culver Pictures.*

Messico. Hidalgo's instructors were reformers, interested in promoting science and reason, familiar with enlightened European thinkers, and fluent in Otomi, Nahuatl, and Mixtec languages.

After witnessing the expulsion of the Jesuits two years later, the 14-year-old Hidalgo entered the Colegio de San Nicolás, also in Valladolid. Here Hidalgo blossomed into a brilliant student and studied philosophy, Latin, literature, Italian, French, Tarascan, and Otomi. Finally, in 1770, he received his bachelor's degree from the University of Mexico. Because of his excellent record as a student, particularly his awards and students electing him to be president of his class, as well as various literary societies, Hidalgo won an appointment to teach at San Nicolás.

Once again, Hidalgo distinguished himself with his teaching skills and interest in ideas. At the age of 31, Hidalgo entered a contest sponsored by the dean of the Cathedral of Valladolid for the best paper on the true method of studying methodology. Hidalgo's thesis postulated that speculative theology would be supplanted by empirical approaches as well as a critical approach applicable to all academic fields. In other words, Hidalgo advocated a form of free investigation similar to what Sor Juana had wanted a century earlier. Popular with students, Hidalgo received promotion to rector in 1790. At this point, he began to spend time with the local bishop, Manuel Abad y Queipo. Abad y Queipo was a reformer who encouraged Hidalgo's concern for equality and fairness. But Hidalgo resigned suddenly in 1792, partially because he was a poor administrator. Many of his peers disliked Hidalgo because of his passion for gambling as well as women. Certainly his detractors envied Hidalgo's obvious intellectual talent.

More controversy followed. Hidalgo's superiors, weary of jealousy and intrigues against Hidalgo, transferred him to two relatively obscure parishes, Colima and San Felipe de Torresmochas. In both places, Hidalgo brought about a cultural renaissance by promoting plays, music, and philosophical discussions. Hidalgo particularly enjoyed staging the works of Moliere and Racine because of their emphasis upon hypocrisy. By now Hidalgo attempted to encourage equality in all dealings. Because of his lengthy sojourns among Indians, Hidalgo became unequaled at identifying with them. He also fathered two illegitimate sons.

Eventually, the Inquisition investigated Hidalgo. Reports streamed into the Inquisition concerning Hidalgo's views on sexual relations, French liberty, criticism of Church officials, and unorthodox religious views. Hidalgo's belief that *criollos* should have increased access to office and that an interregional economy needed to be established stamped him as a potentially dangerous individual. Fortunately for Hidalgo, his lovers swore under testimony to the Inquisition that Hidalgo was an upright individual. The tendency to show off his intellectual skills, his critical temperament, and an impatience with narrow-minded outlooks caused problems with most superiors. But the usually jovial Hidalgo had a sense of humor that enabled him to charm critics when danger approached.

Hidalgo's last assignment occurred in August 1803 when he succeeded his brother in Dolores, Guanajuato. The city of 15,000 represented an improvement because the lucrative parish had a healthy climate and solid revenues. Here Hidalgo began to receive poor Indians into his home and became more concerned about developing social consciousness and economic progress. Gradually, Hidalgo resolved to free indigenous groups from Spanish control. As a result he encouraged indigenous industries by establishing grape presses for wine production, planting illegal mulberry trees for silk manufacture, and setting up pottery factories. Beekeeping and ceramics also received Hidalgo's patronage. He clearly began to attack the caste system and its inequalities by providing workshops for carpentry, harness making, blacksmithing, and wool weaving. Here the years of Jesuit training manifested themselves because Hidalgo was attempting to establish a miniature Paraguayan republic of self-sufficiency. By this time, Hidalgo's only religious undertaking at Dolores was morning mass. He spent the rest of his time on industrial training or reading.

Conspiracy in the Bajío. Despite the controversial nature of his activities, Hidalgo enjoyed popularity with the masses and even with a portion of the upper class. In Dolores, Hidalgo became a good friend of the enlightened Spanish intendant Juan Antonio Riaño. Riaño supported the candidacy of Hidalgo as a representative of Guanajuato to the Cádiz Cortes. Although Hidalgo could not attend, he agreed with those in the Mexico City cabildo who argued that town councils truly represented the people, and that since the Spanish king was imprisoned, the cabildo should rule. After the Junta Central of Spain and the Indies consolidated regional Spanish juntas, it gave way to a regency in 1810—which called for a meeting of the Cortes, which included American representatives. The cabildos of each Mexican provincial capital elected provincial representatives to the Cortes, which met in Cádiz. In the meantime, the regency appointed General Francisco Javier Venegas as viceroy to Mexico, who arrived at Veracruz on August 15, 1810. Determined to restore Spanish power, Venegas confronted Hidalgo's revolution on the second day of his residence in Mexico City.

Hidalgo's membership in a conspiratorial group placed him in contact with those eager for autonomy. Already Mexican coins circulated and had the words "Rex Hispaniarum et Indiarum" engraved upon them, meaning that Mexico was a separate kingdom from Spain. After the 1790s, the French Revolution inspired several secret societies which planned for revolt. In addition to Hidalgo's Querétaro group, another conspiracy took place in Valladolid. Within Hidalgo's group, he met dissatisfied *criollo* officers such as Ignacio Allende, Juan Aldama, and Mariano Abasolo. Like Allende, Hidalgo lost his hacienda when the 1804 Consolidación loans were called in. The three landowning *criollo* captains liked Iturrigaray because he mobilized the militia in 1806 for large field maneuvers. Therefore, they resented the 1808 Yermo *golpe* directed against Iturrigaray as well as the Mexico City cabildo and autonomists. But since the next three governments before Venegas failed to provide leadership, the *criollos* decided that the opportunity to establish autonomy had arrived. Another important person was Miguel Domínguez, the boss of Querétaro and a native of Guanajuato. Domínguez was a very enlightened lawyer who ended obraje abuses. His wife Josefina also became active in the conspiracy.

This Querétaro group was enlightened and wealthy but not part of the aristocracy. They simply hated the gachupines and, like many other *criollos*, wanted to abolish the Spanish tradition of metropolitan control from Madrid. By March 1810, the plotters persuaded Hidalgo to join them. Fearful that autonomy might not be acceptable to all within Mexico, their plan called for various juntas to seize power and aid Spain against France. Afterwards, the juntas would expel the Spaniards from Mexico so that provincial juntas could elect a national junta. Their scheme envisoned raising a large indigenous army because the conspirators were unsure if the colonial militia would support their revolt.

The dissidents eventually chose Hidalgo to lead the rebellion because of his learning and popularity with *castas* and Indians. It seemed obvious that indigenous revolts could become widespread. In 1802, el Indio Mariano led a rebellion in Tepic and Nayarit, which proposed restoring the empire of Motecuhzoma II. Eventually the Spaniards captured and executed Mariano, a leader like Hidalgo who had the potential to mobilize angry indigenous uprisings. The Querétaro conspirators scheduled their revolt for November. They planned to take advantage of the San Juan de los Lagos religious ceremonies when Hidalgo would ride in and call for indigenous support. Soon Hidalgo instructed his factory workers to manufacture weapons. Once that occurred, the overconfident plotters moved the date of the rebellion back to October 2 under the assumption that mass support would be theirs.

Regional and Social Phase of the Struggle.
The impetus for the revolutionary period of the independence conflict was regional in origin and social in terms of mass motivation. By 1800, Mexico had been decapitalized and bankrupted

by Madrid. Recession, the famine of 1808–1810, and the momentary royal loss of control combined to convert regional tensions into revolution. Thus, the largely Hispanized Bajío rose up against the center of Mexico. A similar cycle occurred in South America; the areas conquered last during the sixteenth century eventually became the first to rise up. In Mexico, a racial conflict quickly emerged from the Querétaro conspiracy. Instead of a relatively bloodless upper-class transfer of power, *mestizos* soon set the tone of the early struggle against Spain.

Why did revolution break out from the Bajío? Among many factors, certainly the growth of commercial agriculture threatened the Bajío masses as well as peasant communities in the Guadalajara-Jalisco region. The indigenous population of Bajío was largely transplanted from other regions. This made it easier for Hidalgo to organize them, since the Indians had no fixed ties to the local environment or established authorities. Rapid population growth placed additional pressure upon indigenous communities. Much litigation between peasants and landowners over marginal lands by the 1780s indicated an intense demand for land. Thus many Indians became laborers rather than farmers. Therefore, resident peons on haciendas constituted the core of the regional labor force. Adding to mass discontent was the inflation that resulted in a fall of living standards because wages remained the same. Although the prices for maize, beans, and wheat had been stable for 120 years, they skyrocketed after 1786. All of this increased frustration because indigenous leaders continued to acquire land unavailable to most. Having to pay fees for the census count particularly angered Indians. Meager opportunities for the younger generation added to resentment.

Many of the rebels emerged from expanding urban centers. Vagrants flocked to Guanajuato, Celaya, Guadalajara, and other cities in search of employment. But when Spanish wars disrupted the mines and the flow of capital, unemployment led to desperation. The Bajío experienced widespread bandit activity after the 1780s, particularly from

1805–1807. Highway robbers generally had backgrounds as criminals from the poorest socioeconomic groups. Military deserters from the militias also added to a highly inflammable social crisis.

Religion also became a vital factor. After 1750, Spanish officials removed most of the Franciscan monks from Lake Chapala and Jesuits from other areas. Replacing the monks with Spanish priests failed as attested by numerous complaints. Many villagers, eager for any kind of land, sought *cofradía* lay brotherhood properties, which the Church refused. Old customs and traditions put in place by the religious orders began breaking down and many became distraught.

How did Hidalgo mobilize supporters from this unhappy set of circumstances? It began when the intendant discovered the plot and reluctantly closed in on the conspirators, who were formerly his friends. Josefina Domínguez directed Aldama to wake up Hidalgo at two in the morning so that he could escape. Hidalgo decided to start the revolt in Dolores.

Nobody really knows what Hidalgo actually said on September 16, 1810, but his manifesto appealed to many. Hidalgo undoubtedly called for vivas to King Fernando, America, and religion as well as "death to bad government!" In the early days, Hidalgo used the name of Fernando VII as a screen, primarily to win support from the royal militias, because they would not have followed the Dolores priest without the king's name. Both Spain and Mexico wanted freedom from France. Therefore, Hidalgo did not demand independence but called for liberty. Hidalgo gained mass support by announcing the end of the tribute system, emancipation of all slaves, and the termination of liquor taxes. When he appealed for equality before the law, Hidalgo satisfied many demands to end the privileges which Spaniards primarily enjoyed. Even *criollos* wanted to preserve Mexico from peninsulars who had overthrown Iturrigaray. Hidalgo definitely favored a separate nation, but *criollos* interpreted autonomy to include a preponderance of power in their hands alone.

Hidalgo's famous *grito* immediately triggered a social revolution. If a revolution is understood as a mass social movement that changes the socioeconomic and political order by means of violent, radical change, then Hidalgo's unleashing of a savage conflict that lasted until 1821 certainly fits the definition of social revolution. Hidalgo offered a peso a day to those who could provide horses and weapons, but most who joined the movement had few weapons. They followed Hidalgo to Atotonilco where they adopted the Virgin of Guadalupe as their symbol, indicating that the insurrection was not directed against the Church. The Virgin of Guadalupe represented the religious nationalism of the colonial period. As a patroness of indigenous hospitals, chapels, and *cofradías*, the Virgin of Guadalupe was the most potent religious figure in rural Mexico. She represented the struggle for the Indians to maintain their identity and recover their lands. The Virgin of Guadalupe symbolized the struggle for *criollos* to identify with the land of their birth, and she epitomized the desire of *mestizos* to be guaranteed a place in society. But the insurgents showed no mercy when they sacked San Miguel. They also killed about 250 royalists at Zacoalco, Jalisco.

By the time Hidalgo's forces reached Guanajuato, they were ready to attack Spaniards openly. In demanding that the Spanish officials surrender, Hidalgo escalated the nature of his demands:

> I am at the head of more than 4,000 men, and in accordance with their will, we wish to be independent of Spain and to govern ourselves. We have been in the tremendously humiliating and shameful position of 300 years of dependency under Spain, and the Spaniards' totally unjust profiteering from the wealth of the Mexicans…. (Antonio Gomez Robledo, "Ideological Roots of Mexico's Revolution for Independence," *The Mexico Forum*, 1985, p. 13.)

The apprehensive Spaniards holed up in the *alhondiga* (public granary), hoping that they could weather the storm. But Hidalgo's furious forces set fire to the *alhóndiga* and slaughtered 500 Spaniards. It was an event that made the white upper class determined to preserve order. Hidalgo could not discipline his followers and made little attempt to stop them for two days. Another Hidalgo mob sacked Celaya similarly two days later.

The rapid growth of the insurrection represents mass grievances. Indian peasants made up the bulk of Hidalgo's forces as they did in other independence era armies. By 1810, there were at least 2.5 million indigenous people in Mexico – about 60 percent of the population. Indigenous areas south of Guadalajara and throughout the Bajío played a decisive role. A number of highwaymen and robbers also joined the insurrection. Cattle rustlers participated, especially when insurgents freed them from local jails. Communities which participated often did so on the basis of local conflicts and grievances.

With such a large group, Hidalgo confronted royalist forces in the capital. One army captured Valladolid, San Luis Potosi, and Zacatecas. Hidalgo then approached Mexico City with about 80,000 followers. Viceroy Venegas acted decisively. Venegas ordered all *criollo* and peninsular males to report for military service if they could provide their own uniforms and weapons. Although handbills in favor of the rebels appeared all over Mexico City, timely royalist propaganda responded effectively. Royal officials decreed the end of indigenous and *casta* tribute payments and barricaded the streets. On October 30, a few thousand Spanish regulars went out to fight Hidalgo's forces. They succeeded in slowing down the insurrectionaries at Las Cruces, but nearly all died in the process. Meanwhile, Venegas promoted Félix Calleja, a Spaniard living in Mexico since 1789, as the highest ranking royalist field commander. Until Calleja's arrival, however, Mexico City trembled in fear. Venegas proclaimed the Virgin of Guadalupe as generalissima and captain general of the royal army before a nearly hysterical crowd.

With the capital at his mercy, Hidalgo made the astounding decision to retreat. Uneasy about having his troops sack Mexico City, Hidalgo pondered what to do as his ammunition ran low. Hidalgo became disappointed that no uprising took place inside the capital. Messengers informed him that local indigenous communities were not interested in joining his forces. Unnerved by the concentrated artillery fired at them during the Las Cruces battle, many of Hidalgo's followers deserted. A large number had joined merely for looting and had become bored with the tedium of military life. Aldama and Allende wanted to attack, but Hidalgo stunned them with his disastrous decision to retreat. This event prolonged the independence struggle up to 1821.

Disunity among the insurrectionaries doomed their future. Hidalgo himself began to lose faith in his hordes but was willing to allow pillage as a reward and even a lure in order to hold his forces together. Aldama and Allende lost much of their confidence in Hidalgo. Allende considered his throng of followers as merely a means for *criollo* ends. Mob violence, he believed, went beyond the scope of his military code. But the elaborate and bloody violence against whites reveals pentup *casta* as well as indigenous resentments. Thus the insurrectionaries became confused and distrustful of one another and allowed victory to slip from their grasp. Calleja's forces soon relieved the capital and on November 7, they crushed Hidalgo decisively at Aculco, near Querétaro. Calleja also established a regionalized military command that cleverly decentralized the movement of royalist forces.

The royalists countered Hidalgo by appealing successfully to *criollos*. The Church leadership accomplished much by excommunicating the rebels. Clerical pamphlets attacked Hidalgo as a symbol of disorder; appealing to the insecurities of the *criollos*, the Church stressed the Hispanic heritage of peninsulars as well as *criollos*. Most whites agreed with Spanish officials that Hidalgo's mass support was dangerous as well as disorderly. Moreover, many *criollos* expected the Congress at Cádiz to improve Mexico's relationship with Spain. Within six weeks after Hidalgo's *grito*, the vast majority of *criollos* supported the royal government or remained neutral. Few *criollos*, except priests, supported the insurrectionaries. When Hidalgo spoke about a *reconquista*, virtually all Spaniards considered this a caste mutiny. The army and militia remained loyal.

Indigenous support beyond the Bajío rarely materialized. The Bajío was unusual because its indigenous population had generally arrived after the sixteenth century and had become more urbanized than the rest of Mexico. But in other regions, indigenous cultural and political autonomy had survived to a striking degree since the Spanish invasion. Although the cold wind of economic decline had hit the Bajío hard, the rest of Mexico's indigenous communities, and even many within the Bajío, did not respond to Hidalgo. Eliminating the tribute convinced many to remain loyal. But the indigenous communities strongly desired to preserve their communities within a modified order under a Spanish or even indigenous king. Communal landholding continued to anchor indigenous villages.

Articulation of the Hidalgo Insurrection.
The defeat at Aculco weakened rebel confidence considerably. Unhappily, they divided forces. Hidalgo journeyed to Valladolid to reorganize, recruit, and terrorize, while Allende headed for Guanajuato. As Hidalgo retreated toward Guadalajara and more of his forces deserted, Hidalgo restored *criollos* to various municipalities. Hidalgo preserved the records of seized peninsular properties and tried to protect *criollo* wealth as much as possible. But at the same time, he lacked a clear notion of what he wanted to do with Mexico after driving the Spaniards out.

Hidalgo's outlook changed considerably once he and his followers realized that a large army could be raised in Guadalajara. By the time he arrived in Guadalajara, Hidalgo began ordering the executions of Spaniards to please his indigenous and *casta* followers. Indians under Jose Antonio Torres killed about 250 Spaniards at Zacoalco, Jalisco, on November 4. These intensely ideological followers wanted swift changes. Hidalgo followers killed one out of eight peninsulars in Mexico until the revolution collapsed. This explains the intensity of the fighting and the tumultuous welcome that Hidalgo received upon entering the city.

Amid these strong expectations, Hidalgo articulated the program of his revolution. First, he began

to plan for a proposed congress and a vague form of representative government. Hidalgo also announced a desire to banish poverty and promote science, art, and industry while developing agriculture. Still uncertain as to how he would implement his objectives, Hidalgo at least called for unconditional independence. To consolidate his appeal, Hidalgo reiterated a ban on indigenous tribute, stopped unpopular taxes upon liquor and tobacco, and ended slavery. Hidalgo decreed that slaveowners not releasing their slaves within ten days would be executed. Only about 10,000 African slaves existed at this time, but Mexico became the first country in the Americas to abolish slavery.

In line with his Jesuit notions of economic independence, Hidalgo attempted to end the colonial system quickly. *El despertaodor americano* was Hidalgo's newspaper, which articulated radical reforms. He ended Spanish restrictions upon

Miguel Hidalgo y Castilla, who led the first Mexican war for independence was executed in 1810. *Culver Pictures.*

industry and agriculture while putting an end to state monopolies. The first land reform took place under Hidalgo when he attempted to return land belonging rightfully to indigenous communities. On December 5, 1810, Hidalgo decreed that rents due indigenous landowners should be paid. To prevent Indians from losing their lands to *hacendados*, Hidalgo ruled that indigenous lands could no longer be leased. *Ejidos* had to be returned to the "communities of natives." Hidalgo wanted to end the fear of community lands being usurped by hacienda owners.

The first diplomatic mission of independent Mexico left from Guadalajara when Hidalgo appointed Pascasio Ortiz de Letonio as envoy extraordinary and plenipotentiary to the United States. Recognition of a state of war and cooperation would have helped Hidalgo greatly. Unfortunately, this first mission failed because the young diplomat was arrested when he attempted to cross the northern border. Faced with the prospect of humiliation and torture that lay in store for him, Ortiz de Letona preferred to take his own life by drinking a poison that he carried.

Collapse of the Hidalgo Movement. Within four months, the Hidalgo revolution disintegrated. After proclaiming reforms, Hidalgo mobilized a new army of 40,000 followers. But this group faced Calleja's royalists at the Bridge of Calderón on the outskirts of Guadalajara. During the battle on January 17, 1811, a chance explosion of Hidalgo's ammunition wagon from a lucky artillery shot caused the rebels to panic. They made the mistake of trying to run from professional cavalry forces in an open field. Defeat became a confused rout. An angry Allende stripped Hidalgo of his command but retained him as a puppet. The desperate rebel leaders drifted north into Coahuila, hoping to reach the United States. Instead, a local hacendado captured them in Monclova on March 21, 1811, and handed them over to Spanish authorities. Hidalgo's revolution did lead to the overthrow of Spanish rule in San Antonio, Texas, until General Joaquin de Arredondo snuffed out the revolt.

The end came quickly. Hidalgo and his principal supporters were transferred to Chihuahua for a military trial, where nine *criollos* judged them. The judges ruled unanimously for death sentences. Allende, Aldama, and the others were executed promptly. During his four-month trial and imprisonment, Hidalgo admitted the revolution was a mistake and prepared himself to die because of it, but not for it. Since he was a priest, Hidalgo received the right to be shot in the chest and in privacy, which took place on July 30, 1811. The Spaniards displayed the severed heads of the four leaders in cages at the Guanajuato *alhóndiga* until the independence struggle finally ended.

Hidalgo had initiated Mexico's first social revolution. It would be another one hundred years before a similar revolution would take place. By the time his movement ended, Hidalgo had attracted two million Mexicans into his movement. Alfonso Reyes, a great philosopher of the next century, concluded that

> In Hidalgo, history has combined the features of mythology: the book and the sword, the plow and the loom, the smile and blood. (Gomez Robledo "Ideological Roots," p.14)

Hidalgo's insurrection was also a reflection of the increasing gap between upper and lower clergy. Hidalgo and reformists such as Manuel Abad y Queipo articulated a sense of nationality and social justice that represented a dynamic form of Mexican patriotism unique in the Americas.

MORELOS CONTINUES THE INSURGENCY

José María Morelos y Pavón. Morelos took over the independence cause. He defined his aims more clearly than Hidalgo, which included complete independence, social justice, and racial equality. These goals inspired his indigenous and *mestizo* followers but met the firm opposition of *criollos* as well as peninsulars. Morelos, however, provoked a broad conflict because his interpretation of a new nationality based upon socioeconomic reforms and pride in the Mexican past appealed to many insurgents.

The background of Morelos resembles the life of Hidalgo. He was born in Valladolid in 1765, his *mulato* father was a former hacienda worker who became a carpenter; his mother influenced Morelos as a strong-willed schoolteacher. After an elementary education, he worked on his uncle's hacienda near Apatzingán as a laborer and then became an *arriero* muleteer. Morelos worked the China road from Acapulco to Mexico City until his mother convinced him to study for the priesthood in 1790.

The church defined the early outlook of Morelos. At the age of 25, he enrolled in the Colegio of San Nicolás, when Hidalgo served as rector. The exact relationship that Morelos formed with Hidalgo is unclear, but Hidalgo undoubtedly impressed him strongly. Morelos distinguished himself at San Nicolás and studied an additional two years as a seminary student. He received his bachelor's degree at the University of Mexico and obtained a clerical appointment in 1795. He enjoyed teaching in the beautiful city of Uruapan, but his superiors transferred him a few years later to the parish of Tacámbaro, in the heart of the *tierra caliente* of Michoacan, the unpleasant hot lands. The area was so rough that Morelos's mother died there. Morelos naturally requested an area with a cooler climate but was assigned instead to Curácuaro, only 30 miles east. The municipality of Curácuaro became a center of tropical fruit and sugar cane cultivation as Morelos established himself there from 1799 to 1810. But injustices and general inequality infuriated Morelos. Paid merely 24 pesos a month, Morelos had to collect his salary by knocking on local doors. His parishoners were so poor, miserable, and ill that they chafed at having to pay. But Morelos administered the sacraments dutifully and built one of the best churches in the area with the aid of an inheritance that he finally secured after 16 years of litigation. Morelos also used his new funds to develop a successful livestock business and enjoyed relations with women.

The turbulent events beginning in 1804 motivated Morelos to rebel. Already resentful of his repressive superiors, Morelos suffered decreases in income because of the 1804 Consolidación. The idea of an independent Mexico excited him. The absence of the Spanish king in 1808, he argued, meant that the authorities representing the monarchy represented nothing but themselves. Morelos probably had no knowledge of the Hidalgo plot, but when contacted, he did not hesitate to join.

Morelos enjoyed instant success. He first met with Hidalgo on October 20, 1810, to offer his services as a chaplain, but Hidalgo insisted instead that Morelos serve as a commander. Specifically, Hidalgo persuaded Morelos to collect weapons, organize a provisional government, seize Europeans and their property, and to deport peninsulars before seizing Acapulco. Morelos started out with only 20 recruits but had 2,000 before arriving on the outskirts of Acapulco. The ability to mobilize so many on a revolutionary course indicates the high level of mass dissatisfaction and frustration with the Spanish order. But over one hundred guns and twelve-foot thick walls defended Acapulco's garrison. The arrival of royal reinforcements turned the struggle into a stalemate that endured for six months. Unable to win, Morelos headed north in mid-1811.

Victory at Chilpancingo demonstrated Morelos's ability to form a disciplined army. Captured weapons provided the means to fight. Most importantly, Morelos selected excellent officers who became important nineteenth-century leaders. Vicente Guerrero eventually became the real heir of the independence movement. The highly religious Mariano Matamoros served as Morelos's best field commander, whose troops carried a black banner with a crimson cross, the arms of the church, and the slogan "Die for Ecclesiastial Immunity." Guadalupe Victoria later became Mexico's first president. Morelos also possessed a supurb knowledge of the terrain and topography where he operated. Unlike Hidalgo, Morelos paid close attention to detail, training, and discipline. He emphasized surprise, deception, and mobility—the hallmarks of modern warfare.

Administrative and organizational ability became evident in the first set of reforms that Morelos decreed. Although radical, these measures had a somewhat practical tone. First, Morelos announced that *criollos* who cooperated with his movement would retain their positions and have their interests protected. Those *criollos* who resisted would lose everything, including their lives. Morelos declared null and void all debts to Spaniards. He also stressed the concept of independent nationhood more than Hidalgo by decreeing that all people except Spaniards would be known as Americans. In other words, nationality now determined citizenship instead of skin color. To abolish the caste system, Morelos ended slavery along with indigenous tribute payments. As a priest, Morelos never lost sight of his religious principles. And the lower clergy supported him because Morelos defended religion publicly but attacked the unpopular Spanish hierarchy within the Church.

Despite a promising beginning, Morelos temporarily lost his military initiative. Riots that began in central Mexican villages throughout 1811 and early 1812 became a critical factor until they declined. Viceregal forces crushed Ignacio Rayón in the north, which allowed them to isolate Morelos. Calleja, always superior in military leadership against the insurgents, began surrounding Morelos in Cuautla. A lengthy as well as expensive siege forced Morelos to evacuate the city, but not before a royalist attack cut his army to pieces. During the year that followed, Morelos remained in the Tehuacan-Orizaba area, achieving only minor success.

Events in Spain once again threatened the viceregal government, particularly the promulgation of the new constitutions. The need to coordinate military activities against the French, together with a British demand for a formal government with which to ally, led to the organization of the Junta Suprema Central in December 1808. The government of Joseph Bonaparte, whose brother Napoleon had appointed him king of Spain, claimed to be based on a constitution, although it had been prepared in Bayonne, France. Thus Joseph's constitution is the first written constitution to be applied to Spain and its empire. Opportunistic bureaucrats, several army officers, and radical liberals backed Joseph, claiming that the Bourbon monarchs could not be trusted to enact serious reforms. Therefore, the Peninsular War not only became an international conflict, but also a civil war within Spain itself. The war caused enormous destruction of property and life; it destroyed the fabric of personal security. Guerrillas could not protect city dwellers from French reprisals and cruel atrocities, particularly the burning of villages.

As the war continued in Spain, the monarchy's lack of prestige resulted in demands for the enactment of radical measures in the form of a constitution. Therefore, the junta transformed itself into a Council of Regency, acting for the exiled King Fernando in France, and convoked the Spanish parliament to write a new constitution. The Cortes met in Cádiz, one of the few cities not captured by Napoleon's forces, where this unicameral, elected body of 100 individuals declared that national sovereignty resided in the Cortes. Despite colonial revolts against Spanish rule breaking out in 1810, debate over the new constitution went on from August 1811 until its promulgation on March 19, 1812.

The features of the 1812 Constitution affected Mexico profoundly. Before establishing the constitution, the Cortes allowed priests the right to vote in elections for local officials. The new charter was very liberal, certainly the most democratic in Europe. It proclaimed universal male suffrage and abolished privileged properties which could no longer be kept off the market. In an attempt to weaken the aristocracy, the 1812 Constitution instituted municipalities in any settlement above 1,000 inhabitants. The law now required each municipality to provide primary education. *Jefes políticos* would be appointed by the king to integrate regions with the national government. One of the constitution's most radical provisions was that the Cortes reserved the right to alter the royal succession if the heir became incompetent or had "done something to deserve losing the crown." The deputies also mandated that the royal ministers were now responsible to the Cortes. Of great interest to the 30 American deputies was the decision that the Council of State would have 12 of its 40 members elected from overseas. Previously, Spain functioned as a series of regional parliaments, but the new constitution established one law for Spain and all of its empire.

Other privileges came to an end. The 1812 Constitution distributed taxes among all citizens without any exemptions. This became very important in Mexico because it would nullify the tribute paid by Indians. The Cortes also reserved the right to establish the size of the army and navy on an annual basis. The deputies encouraged the formation of national militias to maintain order within the towns. And the king could not use them outside any province without authorization from the national legislature. One of the more democratic features was Article 10's proclamation of the right of any individual to demand of the Cortes or the king that an infraction of the constitution be corrected. Another limitation on the king was the proviso that all public officials swear allegiance to the Cortes.

Since it was written in Cádiz, the 1812 Constitution overrepresented liberal ideas; it basically reflected the thinking of new commercial and middle-class groups. For this reason, they ended aristocratic privileges but demonstrated some concern for peasants and workers by limiting peasant taxes and labor drafts. The Cádiz deputies were more concerned with middle-class civil liberties such as religious tolerance, a free press, and the right to political association. All persons became subject to civil and criminal jurisdiction. No longer did the Church, universities, and guilds have the privilege of passing judgment on persons who were active members. The *audiencia* lost its administrative functions and acted solely as a high court. The electoral regulations established in Mexico under the 1812 Spanish constitution specifically included Indians and *mestizos* among eligible voters. Regions would elect provincial deputies to govern provinces with royal officials.

But the Spanish liberals never lost sight of traditional imperialism. Twenty-one of the thirty representatives from America were Mexicans who joined other deputies from the empire in demanding autonomy. The Spanish liberals, however, refused to treat seriously the moderate reforms requested by the colonials. The Cortes denied Americans equal representation and their requests for social and economic reforms were lost in the confusion created by the establishment of new and conflicting institutions to administer Mexico. The Cortes, for example, would not consider allowing the provincial deputations to be local legislatures representing each province. The provincial deputations, insisted the Spaniards, would have to be administrative councils with no legislative function. Although the 1812 Constitution withheld autonomy, *criollos* of Mexico City greeted it with enthusiasm after its promulgation on September 30, 1812, amid a magnificent ceremony. Although the office of viceroy disappeared on a legal basis, Venegas and Calleja never intended to step down peacefully. By 1814 enthusiasm for the constitution had cooled once the *cabildo* of Mexico City fought with Calleja and mismanaged funds.

Neither Venegas nor Calleja supported the 1812 Constitution. The authoritarian Venegas had never allowed a free press, even when told to do so by the regency. Determined to exercise complete control, Venegas decided by December 1812 that the 1812 Constitution presented a real danger. The November 1812 voting for electors resulted in all 25 chosen being *criollos*, even though the *audiencia* had criticized the entire constitutional system a few weeks before. Therefore, Venegas annulled the elections and ordered the hereditary *cabildo* of Mexico City to remain in office. The more astute Calleja finally replaced Venegas on March 4, 1812. Calleja pretended to acquiesce in supporting constitutional reforms. He allowed the electors chosen in November 1812 to meet on April 5, 1813, and they selected a new *cabildo*, all of whom were *criollos*. The emerging *criollo* differences with the motherland became more apparent when the regency would not support American delegates to the Cortes, who insisted that a free press article in the constitution be respected.

Calleja became more authoritarian. He attempted to usurp control of the police by removing its jurisdiction from the cabildo. This allowed him to arrest many suspected traitors although the cumbersome Spanish legal system produced few convictions. The return of King Fernando to Spain in the spring of 1814 revived the prospects of authoritarian rule when Fernando annulled the constitution. Overcome with joy, Calleja told the *criollo cabildo* that their days were numbered. Soon the *cabildo* had little to do other than plan bull fights and fiestas to honor the king's return. Calleja even reestablished the Inquisition, and formally dissolved the elected *cabildo* in December 1814. With no one to stand in his way, Calleja arrested many more *criollo* suspects to the point that by mid-1815, the government no longer feared the prospect of local uprisings, which had been a major preoccupation for the previous five years. But even Calleja recognized that the 1812 Constitution had damaged Spanish authority permanently, particularly in the capital. Calleja admitted to the new king that the old institutions had lost their legitimacy. What Calleja did not understand was that the elites merely desired reform, preferably on a modest scale, rather than revolutionary insurgency. By opposing the constitution and any change at all, Venegas and Calleja doomed the royalist cause. Their only defense was brute force, a militarism not seen in Mexico since the 1519 Spanish invasion.

Food shortages weakened the royalist cause as well. They occurred in two phases: one from 1803 to 1815 and the other from 1819 to 1821. In both cases, refugees flocked to cities and marauding armies carried off whatever supplies they could from farms and ranches. Corn supplies were in acute shortage, but so were needed quantities of meat and fuel as well as currency. Shortages in turn led to inflation. Contributing to diminished

supplies were problems with transportation. Rebel leaders such as Nicolás Bravo could wipe out royal expeditions and disrupt the road from Veracruz to Mexico City at critical times.

With its revenues lowered and high war costs escalating, the regime alienated many by means of its fiscal coercion. The first phase of the independence movement aroused such fears among whites that voluntary loans could be obtained successfully. The pressure for more money to be sent to an increasingly desperate Spanish government soon exhausted the willingness of donors in Mexico. The first forced loans took place in February 1812. Special war taxes on chiles, beans, and corn followed, along with property taxes earmarked for general revenues. Despite the mortgaging of silver and tobacco monopoly funds, the viceroy could not repay earlier obligations. Even a national lottery emerged, with half the sales earmarked for prizes. Nevertheless, the viceregal debt doubled from 1813 to 1816.

To make matters worse, over half of Mexico City's population fell ill with plague in the summer of 1813. Many victims were buried in the streets or in vacant lots. At one point, no worker would clean the streets for fear of losing his life. Packs of wild dogs roamed the streets, attacking domestic animals as well as their owners, until the city council finally ordered the night watchmen to slaughter the canines. Eventually, one out of eight inhabitants of the continent's greatest city died that summer.

Morelos Interprets the Insurgency, 1812– 1815. Swift victories enabled Morelos to become the undisputed leader of the independence movement. He revived the insurgency by taking Oaxaca. By means of a surprise attack that few expected, Morelos occupied this vital city in November 1812. But Morelos could not prevent his 15,000 troops from sacking Oaxaca due to months of hunger and the humiliation they had suffered. Ignoring pleas to attack Mexico City, which Morelos wanted to isolate, he set out for Acapulco with 3,000 soldiers in February 1813. After a siege that lasted until August 1813, Morelos finally gained complete control of the port. He extended his control to both coasts and as far south as Guatemala.

Morelos offered insurgents a clear program of ideas that were actually radical changes. As part of his demand to cut ties with Europe, Morelos called for unconditional independence. He also planned to end Mexico's export economy so that it would be self-sufficient. Therefore, Morelos sought to destroy the tobacco and sugar plantations along with royal buildings. Even the archives were to be burned, symbolizing a complete break with Spain. Of course, ending foreign trade would have resulted in extreme isolation. The early radicalism of Morelos also manifested itself when he proclaimed that the land was to be owned only by those who worked it. Morelos believed that workers should receive the income derived from land ownership. Moreover, the rich would have their land confiscated because Morelos considered them enemies of the people. Specifically, Morelos insisted that haciendas larger than six square miles be broken up and divided. This ruling also included unused Church lands.

Morelos was very religious but can also be considered something of an anticlerical. In other words, Morelos believed that the Church had to be reformed as an institution. As part of his populistic nationalism, Morelos disliked the European hierarchy of the Mexican Church. High-ranking ecclesiastics lived well, but they provided only 6,000 priests for a population that had quadrupled since 1650. The badly paid priests supported an early form of Mexican nationalism and participated actively in the independence struggle. Superiors could not control the priests and an 1812 viceregal decree abolished the last of the church *fueros* in order to authorize military trial and executions of captured rebel priests. This fatal move drove more priests into the insurgent ranks.

Part of Morelos's appeal derived from his strong religious views. To maintain mass identification with Catholicism, Morelos ordered public masses honoring the Virgin of Guadalupe each month. All his soldiers wore images of the Virgin of Guadalupe on their sombreros; officers swore an oath of eternal loyalty to her. A zealous Catholic who would not tolerate other religions, Morelos wanted to maintain the payment of tithes in order to support the Church.

Morelos also attracted support from women. Prominent among them was Leona Vicario, a wealthy heiress in Mexico City. Unknown to her family in Mexico City, Vicario used her home to deliver coded information to the insurgents, send money, and recruit troops. Escaping from prison after her capture, doña Leona joined Morelos. There she married Andrés Quintana Roo, rode with Morelos's forces, administered their finances, and oversaw the care of sick and injured partisans. Other women in rural areas seduced royalist soldiers in order to persuade them to desert. Many others smuggled weapons and messages under their skirts or prepared food and nursed wounded soldiers. The angry government responded by jailing, deporting, and even executing numerous insurgent women.

Unlike Hidalgo, Morelos attracted support from various professionals, intellectuals, landowners, and entrepreneurs. Acapulco merchants hurt by Bourbon economic regulations provided key financial support as did *mulato* cotton farmers. Foremost among them was the Guadalupes, a clandestine organization based in Mexico City which enabled disaffected members of the Mexico City elite the opportunity to communicate with and influence Morelos as well as other insurrection groups. Conspirators used picnics, family reunions, literary gatherings, and the city council to plan and carry out their missions. They prepared daily reports describing important events in the capital while arranging the defection of those who sought to join the insurgents. Most were not discovered and apprehended until the defeat of Morelos.

Despite his success in attracting allies to his mass-based following, Morelos fell victim to bad judgment. Of particular concern was the group of *criollos* led by Ignacio López Rayón, a lawyer who set up a rebel junta in Zitácuaro, Michoacán. Rayón's people had little interest in the populistic notions of social justice that Morelos supported. Born into a lower social group than Hidalgo and, undoubtedly, insecure when dealing with Rayón's educated subordinates, Morelos slowly accepted them into his inner circle and established a *Junta Suprema Americana*. These advisors convinced Morelos to hold a constituent congress, partially because the 1812 Constitution promulgated in Spain seemed to threaten the validity of the insurgent demand for representative government. Concerned that Rayón's junta at Zitácuaro was becoming a semi-independent power, Morelos agreed that several of Rayón's followers could participate in the Chilpancingo congress.

The attempt to establish a national political structure at Chilpancingo failed. Part of the problem was that Morelos had become egotistical and authoritarian. Morelos instructed the 13 hand-picked members of the congress to elect him as generalissimo for life; he accepted their offer to become the "Servant of the Nation." The September 1813 congress also rejected Morelos's early, radical program of reforms and did little other than proclaim a heady declaration of independence, end the sales tax, abolish torture, and limit the emigration of foreigners. Thus the rebel leaders failed to form a constitutional government at a critical moment because of attempts by Morelos and Rayón to monopolize power.

The downfall of Morelos accelerated with military defeat. In November 1813, Morelos headed for Valladolid with 6,000 troops, the largest army he had ever commanded. But the attack turned into a disaster; royalist forces commanded by Agustín de Iturbide crushed Morelos's army convincingly. After giving up Acapulco, Morelos lost his political leadership to the congress at Chilpancingo, which assumed overall authority of the insurgency.

Pursued by Calleja's forces, the congress fled to Apatzingán where they finally produced a constitution and declared a republic on October 22, 1814. The first constitution articulated in Mexico featured a separation of powers, popular sovereignty, and indirect elections. Articles 24 and 39 granted free public education without regard to

gender. Catholicism became the state religion and Morelos demanded that the new charter be consecrated to the Virgin of Guadalupe. Private property received strong sanction and only out of extreme public need could anyone lose their land. Although it condemned the colonial order and called for egalitarianism, the 1814 constitution failed. Its most interesting reform was a 5 percent income tax, but the document basically emphasized individual freedom and property rights—in reality the thoughts of about six men. The Constitution of 1814 attempted to replace the discredited despotism of Hidalgo, Rayón, and Morelos, but attempts to divide and limit power had not worked since 1810. Moreover, the 1814 Constitution failed to secure foreign aid or shift the thinking of most *criollos*, who wanted autonomy within a secure socioeconomic order. Morelos actually had little influence on shaping the constitution. But without mass support and regional leaders, the constitution and its backers could not endure much longer. Throughout 1815, the Congress had to flee from royalists constantly.

In November 1815, the Spanish finally captured Morelos. After being forced to view the execution of 27 followers, Morelos was taken to the Inquisition dungeons in Mexico City. Church officials tried him first, then the Inquisition. Morelos claimed that since Fernando VII had surrendered Spain to France, he was not guilty of treason:

> Treason toward the king? Fernando's flight gave Spain its freedom and the Americans were in no way at fault by rising up against the authorities who were representing the monarchy; on the contrary, they were exercising a sacred right. (Gomez Robledo, *Ideological Roots,* p.12.)

Morelos believed that the authorities representing the monarchy represented nothing but themselves. These trials were hard on Morelos, who began to fear for his salvation. Morelos admitted that he had carried out many executions and began to divulge military information. After undergoing an *auto de fe*, the clerics turned Morelos over to the viceroy. When Morelos coughed up more information, Calleja provided that he be executed outside Mexico City and that his body would not be dismembered before burial.

The significance of Morelos and his movement is great. Morelos failed partially because he had regional rather than national support. His was the last revolutionary movement that would emerge in Mexico until 1910. Morelos resembles José Artigas, the egalitarian caudillo of Uruguay, in terms of an attempt to classify *castas* as "Americans," who could participate in political elections and hold public office. Morelos claimed equality for all, but his version was not true egalitarianism; his hatred of Spaniards was well known. Thus the theme of class alliance along economic and racial lines which emerged under Hidalgo ended with the demise of Morelos. The Mexican upper class became determined to maintain the socioeconomic status quo; they did not view independence as paramount due to the bloodshed of Hidalgo and Morelos.

SPANISH HEGEMONY AND COLONIAL STALEMATE

As Spain's domestic stabilization proceeded during the war against Napoleon, the viceregal regime gained the momentum against the insurgents. With the death of Morelos, rebel leadership fractured more than ever. *Criollos* either waited in vain for autonomy to be accepted by Spain or actively fought against the insurgents. Despite its mounting difficulties, the colonial regime often responded to the war with adroit measures despite the inability of the Spanish monarch to interpret what needed to be done in order to save the fortunes of the Mexican viceroyalty.

One reason that Spanish military forces temporarily gained the upper hand against insurgents in Mexico resulted from the valuable tactical lessons they had learned from fighting the French invaders in Spain. After leading veteran forces from Germany on an effective campaign throughout Spain, Napoleon left the Iberian peninsula in Jan-

uary 1809 to prepare for war in Austria. The emperor's departure meant that overall supervision of French forces declined. Spanish guerrillas inflicted serious losses upon the French army. The Spanish partisans fought hard because French commanders attempted to prepare areas such as Aragon for annexation to France. Offering reforms, amnesties, and intimidation but using brute force did not succeed. In August 1812, Wellington's Anglo-Portuguese army liberated Madrid; Napoleon's decision to divert French reinforcements for the Russian campaign allowed Spanish partisans to gain the initiative. The formidable guerrillas learned to take advantage of the inability of French generals to cooperate with one another. Many guerrilla leaders had been regular Spanish army officers; later, they applied their skills as partisans in a counterinsurgency role in Mexico.

Domestic cleavages appeared in Spain that resembled as well as affected Mexico. Many Spanish priests participated in the war against the French and claimed that killing French soldiers opened the gates of heaven to Spanish rebels. Meanwhile, the basically liberal Spanish parliament attempted to neutralize the Spanish military as a factor in domestic politics. In Spain, as well as in Mexico, independence struggles became ideological conflicts against traditional privileges. The Spanish legislators in Cádiz, for example, abolished previously rigid distinctions between soldiers and officers as part of an attempt to indoctrinate troops with liberal notions of civic virtue. In 1814, the Congress created a national guard wholly under the control of civil authorities, particularly *jefes políticos*, to whom the generals were subordinated. The liberals also attempted to mobilize the masses both within Spain as well as throughout the empire. In their desire to end restrictions upon individuals and groups, the deputies wrote the 1812 Constitution so that it abolished all distinctions based on race. Indians became citizens with the same rights as all other inhabitants of the empire. By allowing all citizens the right to sell land, the 1812 Constitution also ended the impregnable sovereignty of indigenous control of *ejido* land.

But this was not what the *criollo* representatives from Mexico in Cádiz wanted to hear. They appealed for economic aid, mlitary assistance against rampaging Indians, and appointments of bishops. A *criollo* from New Mexico, Don Pedro Baptista Pino, pointed out that no bishop had visited New Mexico for 50 years and the territory had witnessed no baptisms. Therefore, the poor lived in sin, since they could not afford to travel to Durango, where the nearest bishop resided, to whom they could apply for marriage. Pino also warned the deputies of the growing U. S. presence in New Mexico, but his views fell on deaf ears. The Spanish legislature consistently failed to understand or recognize the grievances articulated by the *criollos*, who did not want independence at this point but autonomy.

The return of the Spanish monarchy witnessed a switch from often radical reforms to a reactionary refusal to accept reality. Napoleon released Fernando VII in a desperate bid to end the Peninsular War by returning a ruler who would curtail the amazing mass mobilization often led by the liberals. Fernando received a rapturous welcome when he crossed the Catalonian frontier in March 1814. But he insisted upon absolute rights in an attempt to turn the clock back to a divine right monarchy. The Cortes refused to recognize Fernando as king until he would swear allegiance to the 1812 Constitution. Therefore, Fernando encouraged a reactionary faction of the army to overthrow the parliament. When Fernando entered Madrid, the masses cheered him while authorities arrested most of the liberal leaders by May 10, 1814.

The war in Mexico became a stalemate, much to the resentment of the generals as well as the conscripts. Spain might have been able to hang onto Mexico had it planned its expeditions and financial necessities better, but Fernando could not compromise with or even understand *criollo* resentments. He and his advisors dismissed serious consideration of Mexican *criollo* demands; the court became confident that a military solution to the insurrection was the best choice. Although Spain seemed to have restored its domination over most of Mexico by 1816, the politicians and court strategists never thought that they had defeated the insurgents completely. Yet Fernando and his advisors pursued the policy of retaining the empire more strongly than the liberal-dominated parliament. Meanwhile, Spanish merchants and manufacturers argued that their interests in Mexico had to be defended.

The royalist revival occurred partially as a result of flexible socioeconomic management of New Spain. Although many captured rebels faced immediate execution in the early years, gradually the royalists made extensive use of pardons to the point that pardoned insurgents often comprised 50 percent of Spanish units. The Cortes urged Viceroy Calleja and his successors to distribute vacant royal lands, particularly to defenders of the monarchy who did not possess property. To attract more *criollos* to actively defend the imperial interests, the Spanish announced the abolishment of monopolies on leather, alum, lead, tin, and tobacco. Many taxes on taverns were lifted while mezcal production was freed from all restrictions. In 1817, the Council of State granted freedom of agricultural, industrial, and manufacturing activities throughout the Americas.

The royalists also actively mobilized female supporters. Thousands of women migrated to Mexico City to escape the fighting. Poor women often migrated on their own in search of employment in the capital's industries and service sector, particularly as servants and nursemaids. The Patriotas Marianas became the first known female organization in Mexico after the widow of an *audiencia* judge put them together. They published pamphlets and raised funds to support needy families of royal soldiers.

The viceroyalty also abolished the African slave trade on December 19, 1817. In reality, Mexico's slave traffic had been suspended for several years, but ending the African slave trade gave royal officials credibility with reformers. Finally, the Inquisition ended in 1820. Although Fernando knew that it would be difficult to convince the most determined rebel leaders to quit, he believed it possible and practical to weaken support for the insurgents by offering reforms in various aspects of colonial life.

The independence movement deteriorated into a series of local insurgencies that strengthened regional leaders whom no one controlled. Although persistent regional rebellions constituted the insurgency's strength, they could not coordinate or articulate a campaign for national power. Mexicans joined the insurgency for a variety of reasons. When the first wave of Spaniards began leaving Mexico in 1814, just as Spain began to enjoy peace, they closed their businesses and left Mexico with much wealth, thus angering many Mexicans in the process. On the other hand, Spanish merchants in rural areas invested in local landowners. Eager to cast off their debts, many Mexicans attacked Spanish merchants. Of course, different regions had specific motivations for hating Spaniards. In Zacatecas, for example, mine workers resented food shortages. Mayan peasants seized the initiative in Yucatán to organize politically, reject taxes, refuse forced labor, and stop payments to the Church. In fact, independence was of little or no importance to many rural people who fought instead over land and water. Fighting was fierce and people changed sides with alarming frequency. The insurgency spread through a network of contacts among priests, muleteers, and bandits. The priests remained unhappy. Of the 678 Jesuits expelled from Mexico, over 500 were *criollos*. The 1812 decree authorizing military trial and execution of captured rebel priests drove many clerics into the rebel ranks. Although *criollos* controlled only one bishopric, their domination of cathedral chapters provided a powerful dose of religious ideology which the regional leaders used to rally mass support. The decline of living standards expanded political consciousness among the peasantry.

After the collapse of the Morelos movement, Vicente Guerrero became the most prominent insurgent leader. A rural southerner from Tixtla, Guerrero had *mestizo* and African bloodlines. His country rhetoric often produced ridicule but

Guerrero was also conversant in the dialects of central Mexico. Shrewd and persuasive, Guerrero became committed to ending racially defined social distinctions. He spent his life as a laborer and muleteer before enlisting in Morelos's army in December 1810.

Guerrero quickly proved to be a resourceful and brave leader. In 1812, he participated in the capture of Oaxaca and commanded forces raiding the western borders of Tehuantepec, Puerto Escondido, and Santa Cruz. During the summer of 1814, a dispute over regional command left Guerrero with 500 troops armed with only three rifles. Showing his resourcefulness, Guerrero launched this force against a royalist detachment and routed them. By 1816, the insurgents were confused as to who should assume overall command of the movement. Guerrero did not attempt to assume supreme command; he merely stressed that he only sought to continue Morelos's cause for the underprivileged.

As the insurgency weakened, so did Guerrero. In 1816, he was nearly captured, and in March 1817 his fortress was overrun. Despite numerous appeals to surrender and accept a pardon—Guerrero's father delivered one appeal—he continued to resist. By 1818, Guerrero's small force had to avoid large royalist formations. But in September, Guerrero defeated several viceregal units and dominated the Balsas Valley. There he established his own civil government, modeled upon Morelos's previous government, led by a junta and a congress. Although it dispersed later in 1819 and Guerrero suffered a severe defeat at Aguazarca on November 5, 1819, Guerrero continued to attack. By 1820, the situation was a stalemate. The insurgents could no longer threaten important areas of New Spain but the royalists were unable to destroy the rebel bases.

The other insurgent leaders were a mixed bag. Nicolás Bravo came from a landowning family while Francisco Javier Mina was a Spaniard who became so fired up with concepts of freedom and equality that he undertook to liberate Mexico. After disembarking on the Gulf coast, Mina marched to the Bajío but was captured and shot.

Guadalupe Victoria studied law in Mexico City before joining the Morelos campaign. Magnificently successful with Morelos, Victoria became the principal insurgent leader in Veracruz and once commanded 2,000 soldiers before falling on hard times. Refusing to accept a pardon, Victoria wandered in mountain forests between Puebla and Veracruz until the collapse of Spanish power. Thus the insurgency gradually fragmented into rebel redoubts incapable of winning national power.

In addition to reforms and concessions from Madrid and Mexico City, the viceroyalty held off the insurgents by means of fairly effective military decisions. From 1811 to 1820, Spain dispatched seven expeditions to Mexico with 9,685 troops. To pay for the dispatch of these forces, taxes on many items, including bullfighting tickets, provided necessary revenues. Forced loans were also crucial. Within Mexico, Calleja virtually converted royal rule to military rule. Calleja ordered the conscription of all males over the age of 16. Military discipline was harsh; authorities arrested many for making insulting remarks about the viceregal government. *Crillo* landowners were obligated to raise militia and defend their land, freeing up Spanish regulars to attack beleagured rebels. After Calleja's departure in 1816, Viceroy Juan Ruiz de Apodaca endeavored to carry out a reconciliation between the colonial regime and the *criollos* that drew substantial support. For this reason, the royal army and militia grew to 39,000 by the end of the conflict. Both regular and militia garrisons utilized mobile detachments to suddenly sweep into suspected rebel areas.

The military supported successful commanders by allowing them to establish their own regional power structures when they secured vital areas. In other areas, royal officers distributed booty to their troops without reporting it to civil authorities and treasury officials. Perhaps the most hotly contested area was Veracruz. Between 1805 and 1820 the fragile structure of Mexican commerce wilted under the stress of Spanish demands for increased revenues and the viceroyalty's inability to provide a secure business environment. The arrival of

Spanish troops failed to dislodge the guerrillas. Scorched-earth tactics employed by both sides made agricultural production hopeless. Therefore, the Spanish commander implemented a policy of resettling amnestied guerrillas on properties where sympathetic landowners would charge no rent for five years.

At this time Antonio López de Santa Anna arrived on the scene and demonstrated the effectiveness of royalist counterinsurgency tactics. In 1818 Santa Anna commanded a militia unit in his native Veracruz near the port city. Frustrated with the timidity of the local governor in pursuing rebels, Santa Anna boldly confronted and captured guerrilla leaders, and also searched aggressively for insurgent bands. Santa Anna distributed land to people willing to fight for the crown and thus established four agricultural communities which made him a successful regional leader. As he carefully organized these hamlets into a fighting force, Santa Anna received the right to overrule judicial officials in military matters. At the same time he built churches in each community and raised living standards. The result was the area that Santa Anna controlled enjoyed peace and prosperity. Although not all royal commanders could rival Santa Anna's energy and skill, his success indicates that bold tactics and imaginative responses to suffering civilians could turn the tide against the guerrillas.

Profound cultural changes took place at this time. Certainly the upper class feared the masses more than ever. Many, such as the family of José Miguel Sánchez Navarro, had their comfortable pattern of shipping wool from their Coahuilan hacienda to merchant houses in exchange for finished goods ruined temporarily. The conflict affected nearly everyone. While many of the rich suffered, *castas* and Indians experienced upward mobility in Guadalajara as the old correlation between ethnicity and occupation began to break down. In the Bajío, insurgents seized estates and subdivided them into *rancheros*, which amounted to a regional social revolution until the 1830s. The capitalist mode of production discriminated less than medieval institutions that began to wear out. The arrival of British capital into the Guadalajara economy raised land values, eroded family networks, and increasingly gave way to impersonal, explicit contracts rather than traditional handshakes. In dynamic *criollo* strongholds such as Guadalajara, Spaniards found themselves working at nearly every kind of occupation rather than sitting firmly on top of the social pyramid. By 1820, Puebla merchants were more *criollo* and increasingly involved with regional activities. In fact, the urban population remained largely passive during the insurrection, which contrasts vividly with the violence in the countryside. Relations between males and females became more open. Also interesting is the shift in illegitimacy patterns. Out of wedlock births for Indians and *castas* increased during the years from 1811 to 1821, while such illicit spawning decreased for whites. Perhaps such a change can be attributed to the general fear that whites experienced as opposed to the more aggressive behavior of the *castas*. Yet social disruption appeared in many cities. Unemployment, vagabondage, prostitution, and crime shocked foreign visitors to Puebla.

Certain writings emphasize the clash of emotions and ideals. Freedom of the press, albeit temporary and usually short-lived, produced many magazines and pamphlets. Indigenous peasants did not produce significant proclamations during these years; village priests and urban intellectuals took up this challenge. Educated persons with degrees (*letrados*) found themselves in high demand. Mexico's premier intellectual, José Joaquín Fernández de Lizardi, reflects the skepticism with which the *criollos* viewed the insurgents as well as their disdain for the Spanish hegemony. His periodical, *El Pensador Mexicano*, criticized Hidalgo and refused to support Morelos. The absolutist rule of Fernando VII resulted in Lizardi being tossed into jail for his mild reformism. After Lizardi's release, he published *El Periquillo Sarmeinto* in 1816, which was the first novel published in Mexico as well as on the American continent. His criticism of the Spanish Church, social evils, and call for a reform of social services struck a tangible response.

In addition to domestic strife, the viceroyalty had to respond to various external pressures in the northeast as well as northwest. Florida was particularly vulnerable to aggression from the United States. In 1811, a number of U.S. "patriots" in Baton Rouge had organized an "independence movement" and requested the United States to intervene on their behalf. Staged U.S. forces moved in quickly and seized a slice of West Florida. Eager for reelection, President James Madison believed that a similar scheme, on a larger scale, would succeed in East Florida. Southerners had long resented the Spanish policy of accepting runaway slaves with the result that Florida had become a natural sanctuary for slaves escaping from plantations in Georgia and the Carolinas. Moreover, Spanish citizenship provided protection for Africans and Indians, which made Florida an effective buffer zone. The Spanish governor armed the free blacks who routed a covert U.S. attempt to capture St. Augustine in September 1812. Seminole Indians furnished most of the Spanish defense when the Seminole War began in earnest in November 1817. Spain finally lost Florida in 1819.

The purchase of Louisiana led to difficulties in Texas which the viceroyalty surmounted. Spain made the mistake of allowing U.S. colonizers into Texas, assuming they would assimilate peacefully. Filibusters entered Texas in 1812 from Louisiana as Comanches revolted. The Gutierrez-Magee filibusters seized San Antonio in 1813 but slaughtered hundreds of Spanish residents. Rebel excesses angered the local population as the Republican Army of the North captured Nacogdoches, Trinidad de Salcedo, and the south Texas fortress of la Bahia. The royalist commander Joaquín de Arredondo marched an army of 1,830 troops from Laredo to quell the rebellion and triumphed at the battle of Medina on August 18, 1813. Santa Anna participated in the battle and observed the execution of the republicans, concluding that they lacked courage but that harsh measures were the best alternative. Under James Long, another group of filibusters seized Nacogdoches and declared Texas independent until Spanish troops once again restored order. But

Arredondo unwisely gave a colonization project to Moses Austin in 1821.

Further west, New Mexico's representative to the Cortes warned that the Crown's neglect of the colony might lead to greater tensions between indigenous groups and Spaniards. The presidios, he advised, had to be restructured in order to deal with hostile Indians. Pino also pointed out the growing U.S. presence in New Mexico and opined that the Santa Fe trade would soon dominate the older Taos fair. New Mexico soon traded with Kansas City and St. Louis where mules and stock found customers. New Mexico, he concluded, faced total ruin as well as possible loss.

The future of Alta, California, also became uncertain. The independence struggle disrupted mission economies because viceregal aid to California friars ceased after the Hidalgo insurrection. The war increased pressure on the Franciscans, nevertheless, to supply military garrisons now cut off from their traditional sources of local goods and intensified illegal trade with foreign merchants. The growth in production forced the Franciscans to recruit additional workers to replace indigenous converts, who continued to die at alarming rates.

Even more alarming to royal officials was the arrival of Russians in California. In March 1812, a Russian ship sailed into a small cove near Bodega Bay. In command was Ivan A. Kuskov, chief deputy of the Russian American Company, chartered by Czar Paul I to control all Russian exploration, trade, and colonization in North America. Kuskov and his colony of 25 Russians and 80 native Alaskans built Fort Ross, which resembled Siberian fortresses. Fortunately for the viceroyalty, the sea otter herds began to decline by 1816, and by 1820 the settlement was more a food base than an otter-hunting station.

Although the far North became threatened, royal officials beat off what appeared to be serious challenges early in the insurrection, losing only Florida in the process. King Fernando also resisted efforts by Britain to mediate the bloody struggle, confident that Spanish forces would inevitably crush the insurgents.

ITURBIDE AND THE *CRIOLLO* CONSENSUS

Political changes in Spain finally established the conditions for breaking the stalemate that had existed in Mexico since 1815. Restoration of the 1812 Constitution appealed to the *criollos*, who still sought to establish autonomy and keep the insurgents out of power. But the Spanish legislators once again alienated the *criollos* who shifted their support to Agustín Iturbide when he proposed a stunningly successful solution to the impasse by means of his Plan de Iguala.

Discontent in Mexico. The insurgency strained the resources of the royal government. By 1820, the viceroyalty had run up a staggering debt of 50 million pesos. Once the traditional tribute system collapsed and funds from indigenous villages could no longer be collected, taxes were borne disproportionately by the *criollos* and *mestizo* masses alike. The disintegration of many large estates motivated landowners to sell their haciendas or divide them into smaller plots and rent them. Taxes to support the royal army increased the costs of food, business transactions, industrial goods, and mine production. Aggressive tax collectors sometimes stripped males and females of their ragged clothes if they lacked the money to pay. Some committed suicide to avoid the nightmare of tax officials confronting them. Stores that catered to everyday needs were heavily taxed, but Spanish cloth dealers enjoyed exemption from municipal taxes in Puebla. Corn and meat supplies fell dramatically and became very expensive for the poor. Both sides requisitioned carriages and mules while imposing a new system of road tolls. Church loans shifted away from hard-hit ranchers and farmers and into the hands of industrialists.

Restoration of the 1812 Constitution. A Spanish military revolt led to the restoration of the 1812 Constitution in both Spain and Mexico. As a large expeditionary army began to concentrate in southern Spain for eventual embarkation to the Americas, the troops became disenchanted. The government attempted to censor news from Mexico but rumors of savage fighting, disease, and an unhealthy climate soon became rampant. By 1819, few Spaniards believed that force could achieve peace in Mexico. Therefore, when Major Rafael Riego issued a liberal *pronunciamiento* (a call for political support issued by a military leader), demanding that the king reinstitute the1812 Constitution, the soldiers supported him mainly in order to avoid what they believed to be certain death. With the backing of rebellions in other Spanish cities, the king gave way and the constitutional system returned with the Spanish liberals.

The revival of a constitutional regime in Madrid encouraged the *criollos* to work within the system to secure home rule while remaining subject to imperial tutelage. More flexible than Calleja, Apodaca implemented the restoration of the constitution in 1820 withour fear or malice. The years of insurgency gave *criollos* opportunities in civil and military institutions in large numbers. Their new status had solidified their opposition to the kind of revolution led by Hidalgo and Morelos. Now the *criollo* autonomists sought political control through elections. Hundreds of city councils appeared as a result of the constitution's 1,000-person qualification that entitled formerly unrepresented towns to receive recognition as legal municipalities. In addition, Apodaca scheduled elections for new provincial legislatures in 1820 so that six newly elected deputations soon functioned. These elections politicized Mexican society because more than a thousand towns and cities carried out elections for municipal government, the provincial legislature, and deputies to represent Mexico in the Spanish Parliament. No literacy or property qualifications existed because all Mexicans were citizens as well as Spaniards.

The results weakened the royalist forces. Newly elected municipalities quickly stopped many of the unpleasant war taxes. Moreover, defiant authorities often took issue with authoritarian military officers, occasionally threatening to prosecute the more abusive royal officials. The constitution also abolished the existing militia structure and necessitated a new national system that would mandate municipal control over locally raised military forces. Faced with a denial of tax revenue and a future cutoff of new conscripts as well as defiant *ayuntamientos*, the military leadership strove to maintain the continuity of colonial life.

Gradually, however, the *criollo* autonomists realized that the Cortes would never grant autonomy to Mexico. The Mexican autonomists gained control of most municipalities and provincial legislatures. The deputies representing Mexico in the Spanish Parliament also called for home rule. Led by Mariano Michelena, José Miguel Ramos Arizpe, and Lucas Alamán, they urged that Mexico be recognized as a separate kingdom with its own legislature while promising to help pay off Spain's debts. The Spanish liberals still grasped at maintaining imperial rule and rejected pleas for autonomy. They reflected general Spanish opinion, which maintained that granting concessions or reforms in Mexico should be considered treacherous and tantamount to conceding impotence. On matters of trade and equality of representation in the Cortes, Spanish liberals also disappointed Mexican autonomists. Various Mexican regions pleaded for more local legislatures, but the Cortes agreed to only one. Mexican liberals were aghast when Fernando VII, at one point, considered fleeing to Mexico in December 1820, so he could rule as an absolute monarch.

Perhaps most antagonistic to many Mexicans was the anticlerical nature of Spanish liberals within the Cortes. Priests once again lost their *fueros* and came under civil jurisdiction. In addition, the Cortes abolished land entailments maintained by clerics. The Church and its various convents, monasteries, and teaching institutions were not allowed to establish mortgages on private properties. Since the Mexican upper and middle class often depended on Church credit for land and business transactions, this legislation struck them as unusually restrictive. Many of the more radical Spanish liberals began to seize lands from the Church and carry out public sales of monastic properties. Soon several priests in Spain were murdered in cold blood. Thus Mexican Catholics realized that the king of Spain could not protect them from liberal anticlericals.

Other issues troubled the *criollos*. The autonomists became nervous when many Spanish liberals naively assumed that the reintroduction of the 1812 Constitution could produce a reconciliation with the insurgents. Many *criollos* often assumed that the anticlerical policies of the new Spanish liberal regime emerged from a Spanish desire to attract the insurgents and ignore proponents of home rule. The reality, of course, is that the Spanish liberals were so badly out of touch with reality that they did not understand that the insurgents were more religious than the *criollos* and that, since 1813, most regional revolutionaries wanted little or no ties to Spain or the rest of Europe. Spanish liberals also blundered by urging that communal lands be taken from villages in order to increase production once it came under the ownership of more energetic Europeanized farmers. Although the foolish law was never implemented, it only strengthened the insurgent cause. Finally, in September 1820, the Cortes passed legislation subjecting militia forces to civil jurisdiction in all offenses except those of a military nature. Seven months later, the law deprived the regular army of its *fueros*. Once royal officers were prohibited from imposing taxes in order to support military operations, officers considered this decree as fatal to their future.

Iturbide's Background. Agustín de Iturbide represents the critical transition between the final year of the colonial regime and full independence from Spain. He reflects the traditional views of upper class *criollos* determined to preserve Hispanic continuity into the future. From a respected Basque family that emigrated to Michaocán in the middle of the eighteenth century, Iturbide was an inattentive student who preferred managing his father's hacienda. Like many other *criollos*, Iturbide also enlisted as an officer in a viceregal regiment at the age of 14. After his 1805 marriage to

an upper-class *criolla*, Iturbide supported the Mexico City revolt that dumped Iturrigaray in favor of the Spanish hardliner Pedro Garibay. The Iturbide family sent funds to the new Spanish junta and Iturbide himself purchased a hacienda worth 93,000 pesos.

The Hidalgo insurrection mobilized Iturbide quickly. Hidalgo's followers sacked Iturbide's property as well as his father's hacienda. Not surprisingly, Iturbide fought at the battle of Las Cruces and received promotion to captain. The viceroyalty was very pleased when Iturbide stopped rebel momentum in the Bajío by fortifying cities and towns with regular troops. Calleja made Iturbide overall regional commander by the end of 1813.

But Iturbide soon clashed with Spanish authorities. His frustration resulted from personal ambitions. Obviously a gifted military leader, Iturbide became angry when Spaniards blocked further promotion because of his *criollo* status. The royalists had also received many complaints about Iturbide, who forced Bajío hacendados to garrison their own estates. Apparently Iturbide decided that women and children should receive the same harsh treatment as captured rebels. Spain had employed tough counterinsurgency tactics throughout Mexico but rejected various cruelties allegedly proposed by Iturbide. Others accused Iturbide of being an agnostic, jailing women, torturing prisoners, and seizing properties as well as reselling their produce for personal profit. This last charge, although unproven, resulted in Calleja removing Iturbide from command of troops.

At this point, Iturbide would not consider joining the rebels. Instead, he dreamed of knighthood and traveling to Spain. He sulked in Mexico City, often spending large sums on gambling and prostitutes. Beginning in 1816, Iturbide attended the salon of Maria Ignacia Rodríguez de Velasco, where many discussions about independence took place. Bitter about his inability to clear his name and his demotion, Iturbide gravitated toward the autonomy group and once considered forcing Apodaca to recognize a new *criollo* regime.

Iturbide's fortunes changed when Apodaca appointed him royal commander of 2,500 veteran troops to pacify Guerrero by offering him a pardon. Iturbide departed Mexico City on November 16, 1820 with great enthusiasm. But Guerrero defeated Iturbide's royalists twice in January 1821. Stunned by his first military setback, Iturbide contemplated a political solution. Guerrero urged Iturbide to support independence and offered to place himself under Iturbide's command in return for such a pledge. Iturbide agreed to resolve his differences with Guerrero, interpreting such a decision as compatible with Apodaca's desire to end the Guerrero revolt bloodlessly. As Guerrero subordinated himself, Iturbide quickly began negotiating with various generals, bishops, autonomists, and other influential *criollos* so that he secured independence by means of a brilliant compromise.

The Plan de Iguala. Iturbide announced the Plan de Iguala from his Cocula headquarters on February 23, 1821. It is the most effective political document ever pieced together in Mexican history and a truly national *pronunciamiento* because most political pronouncements were regional or local during the nineteenth century.

The Plan of Iguala brought together liberals and conservatives, rebels and royalists, *criollos* and Spaniards under broad provisions. Of the 26 articles in the Plan de Iguala, its Three Guarantees were it's most important assurances. First, Catholicism would remain the national religion and other faiths would not be tolerated; the second guarantee proclaimed that Mexico would be independent as a constitutional monarchy; finally, equal treatment for all Spaniards and Mexicans would establish a policy of ethnic equality. This was Iturbide's major innovation. Iturbide had asked Africans and Asians to join his movement. Socially inclusive and not a threat to the economic system, the Plan de Iguala struck many as a solid reform. Indians had little concern with forming a nation-state but thought in terms of a monarchy, which aided Iturbide's success.

Whites stood to gain more than anyone else. Iturbide and most *criollos* felt that only a monarchy could preserve order. The thought of fighting mass unrest worried the autonomists sufficiently to finally realize that independence had become the only method to retain home rule under the 1812 Constitution. Therefore, representative government would still be tied to Spain. Following Spanish tradition, a junta would rule until a newly elected legislature would elaborate a constitutional system. Not by coincidence, autonomist *criollos* made up the overwhelming majority of the junta. Unlike Hidalgo and Morelos, Iturbide was less bitter against Spanish rule. He interpreted Mexico as having developed to the point that it could separate from Spain as a child eventually departs from its parents. Spaniards approved Iturbide's promise to return to the clergy all its property and privileges. Iturbide promised to never tolerate the anticlericalism that now appeared in Spain. In addition, Spanish officeholders could continue in their positions provided they accepted the Plan de Iguala. Even the titled nobility willingly discarded their titles and entailed lands because their strength lay in extended family connections and mixed investments. For the upper class, the end of Spanish rule reflected not only prudent self-preservation but also the loss of legitimacy that Spain had suffered since 1804.

Particularly striking is the rapid consensus that Iturbide's masterful agreement established. Although Guerrero objected to some of the Plan de Iguala's details, he accepted it on March 9, 1820, and merely hoped for improvements. As first chief of the southern forces of the Army of Three Guarantees, Guerrero rejoiced that the colonial caste system had been abolished. Although none of the 38 members in the junta that Iturbide appointed came from the insurrectionists, Guadalupe Victoria and Nicolás Bravo joined Iturbide that summer. Upset that Apodaca could not prevent information about the Plan de Iguala from arriving in Mexico City or stopping demonstrations in favor of it, a hard-line faction of the royal army forced Apodaca to resign on July 5. The clumsy Field Marshall Francisco Novello tried to block the final phase of independence but could do little as the Army of Three Guarantees controlled all of Mexico except the port of Veracruz and Mexico City. Iturbide treated surrendered royalists kindly, which added to his momentum.

The unprepared Spanish monarchy responded prudently. News of Iturbide's revolt astonished Spain. The liberal Cortes insisted that once Mexicans began to appreciate the benefits which they would enjoy from the 1812 Constitution, their revolt would end. The Cortes then referred the Iturbide problem to a committee which eventually produced an inconclusive report. Mexican deputies in the Cortes had already set the stage for the climax of colonial rule by persuading the Cortes to replace Apodoca with Juan O'Donojú in January 1821. Since the provincial deputations had suspended relations with the viceroyalty, the Cortes had abolished the viceroy title and, therefore, O'Donojú arrived as the Political Chief of the Provincial Deputation of Mexico. In addition to having had a great career in the army and cabinet, O'Donojú was a liberal who had come to arrange autonomy for Mexico. Spain's weak position in Europe contributed to the attainment of independence. Iturbide accepted O'Donojú's offer to negotiate and they both met in Córdoba.

O'Donojú accepted quickly Iturbide's conditions, known as the Treaty of Córdoba, on August 23, 1821. O'Donojú committed Spain to recognize the new Mexican empire as an independent, constitutional monarchy. Furthermore, the Treaty of Córdoba stipulated that Mexico would be ruled by Fernando VII, one of his sons, or someone designated by the Cortes. The treaty also ratified Iturbide's junta with the understanding that it would select a regency. The next day, O'Donojú signed a peace treaty, resigned his position, and accepted Iturbide's invitation to join the junta. Iturbide and the principal insurgents entered Mexico City triumphantly on September 27, 1821.

With the Spanish capitulation completed, Iturbide finally assumed a specific role in the new government. The junta, consisting almost entirely of autonomists with few conservatives, signed a declaration of independence on September 28. That evening, they selected the regency, a body of three people to serve as the executive authority. The regency, in turn, decided that Iturbide would be its president. Sovereignty resided in the legislature, however, in accordance with Spanish tradition.

To a certain extent, independence came about because localized concerns became transformed into a national bargain. But the cost was high—600,000 lost their lives, which amounted to about half the work force. Most who died came from indigenous communities. In essense, the royal army freed Mexico, unlike Spanish South America, where patriot forces won independence on bloody battlefields. Brazil resembles Mexico in terms of the pacific nature of its emancipation, partially on the basis of an elite decision to establish a monarchy. None of this would have happened had not Iturbide developed so rapidly into an effective leader. He understood that the continuity of Spanish colonialism could not be altered excessively, unlike Hidalgo and Morelos, who stressed liberty more than independence. Iturbide, on the other hand, stressed independence without overemphasizing the dimensions of liberty. While liberty and independence walked hand-in-hand within the United States, the two concepts parted company somewhat in Mexico because of the sectarian violence unleashed by Hidalgo and Morelos, as well as the brutal counter-insurgency tactics adopted by the Crown. Nevertheless, independence from Spain created the foundation for a unique and distinct Mexican culture and meant freedom for repressed *mestizos*. The transatlantic relationship had been altered but not destroyed. Mexico achieved political sovereignty while its economic ties to the rest of Europe now reached out on a direct basis.

SUGGESTED READING

Aarom, Sylvia M. *The Women of Mexico City, 1790–1857*. Stanford, CA: Stanford University Press, 1985.

Anna, Timothy. *The Fall of the Royal Government in Mexico City*. Lincoln: University of Nebraska Press, 1978.

————. *Spain and the Loss of America*. Lincoln: University of Nebraska Press, 1983.

————. *The Mexican Empire of Iturbide*. Lincoln: University of Nebraska Press, 1990.

Archer, Christon I. "The Army of New Spain and the Wars of Independence." *Hispanic American Historical Review* 61:4 (November 1981), 705–714.

————. "The Young Antonio López de Santa Anna: Veracruz Counterinsurgent and Incipient Caudillo." In Judith Ewell and William H. Beezley, eds., *The Human Tradition in Latin America*, Wilmington, DE: Scholarly Resources, 1989, pp. 3–16.

————. "La Causa Buena: The Counterinsurgency Army of New Spain and the Ten Year's War." In Jaime E. Rodríguez, ed., *The Independence of Mexico and the Creation of the New Nation* (Los Angeles: UCLA Latin American Center and Mexican/Chicano Program, 1989, pp. 85–108.

Castillo Ledôn, Luis. *Hidalgo, la vida del heroe*. 2 vols. Mexico City: Talleres Graficos de la Nacion, 1948–1949.

Costeloe, Michael. *Response to Revolution: Imperial Spain and the Spanish American Revolutions, 1810–1840*. Cambridge: Cambridge University Press, 1986.

Flores Caballero, Romeo. *Counterrevolution: The Role of the Spaniards in the Independence of Mexico, 1804–1838*. Lincoln: University of Nebraska Press, 1974.

Florescano, Enrique. *Memory, Myth and Time in Mexico*. Austin: University of Texas Press, 1994.

Guedea, Virginia. *En busca de un gobierno alterno: Los guadalupes de Mexico*. Mexico City: UNAM Press, 1992.

Hamill, Hugh. *The Hidalgo Revolt: Prelude to Mexican Independence*. Gainesville: University of Florida Press, 1966.

Hamnett, Brian R. *Roots of Insurgency: Mexican Regions, 1750–1824*. New York: Cambridge University Press, 1986.

Ladd, Doris. *The Mexican Nobility at Independence, 1780–1826*. Austin: University of Texas Press, 1976.

Lemoine Villicaña, Ernesto. *Morelos, su vida revolucionaria a través de sus escritos*. Mexico City: UNAM Press, 1965.

Lynch, John, ed. *Latin American Revolutions, 1808–1826: Old and New World Origins*. Norman: University of Oklahoma Press, 1994.

Robertson, William S. *Iturbide of Mexico*. Westport, CT: Greenwood, 1968.

Rodríguiz, Jaime E. O. "The Transition from Colony to Nation: New Spain, 1820–1821." In Jaime E. Rodríguez, ed. *Mexico in the Age of Democratic Revolutions, 1750–1850* Boulder, CO: Lynne Rienner, 1994, pp. 97–132.

Sprague, William. *Vicente Guerrero, Mexican Liberator: A Study in Patriotism*. Chicago: R. R. Donelly and Sons, 1939.

Taylor, William B. "Banditry and Insurrection: Rural Unrest in Central Jalisco." In Friedrich Katz, ed., *Riot, Rebellion and Revolution*. Princeton, NJ: 1988, 205–246.

Teja Zabre, Alfonso. *Vida de Morelos*. Mexico City: Andres Botas, 1916.

Thomson, Guy. *Puebla de los Angeles: Industry and Society in a Mexican City, 1700–1850*. El Paso: Texas Western College Press, 1963.

Tutino, John. "The Revolution in Mexican Independence: Insurgency and the Renegotiation of Property, 1800–1855." *Hispanic American Historical Review* 78:3 (August 1998), 367–418.

Van Young, Eric. "Moving Toward Revolt: Agrarian Origins of the Hidalgo Rebellion in the Guadalajara Region." In Katz, *Riot, Rebellion, and Revolution*, pp. 176–204.

————. "Millennium on the Northern Marches: The Mad Messiah of Durango and Popular Rebellions in Mexico, 1800–1815." *Comparative Studies in Society and History*, 28:3 (July 1986), 385–413.

————. "The Raw and the Cooked: Elite and Popular Ideology in Mexico, 1800-1821." In Mark Szuchman, ed.,*The Middle Period in Latin America: Values and Attitudes in the 17th–19th Centuries* Boulder, CO: Lynn Rienner, 1989, 75–102.

Villoro, Luis. *El proceso ideológico de la revolución de independencia*. Mexico City: UNAM Press, 1967.

7

The Early Republic, 1821–1835

Independence may have brought freedom from Europe, but it did not confer stability. Iturbide's empire collapsed rapidly because the elites could not agree upon how Mexico should be governed. The sharp decline of the economy produced fiscal as well as financial problems that made living conditions difficult, particularly for the masses. As the elites fought one another and the church lost some of its privileges, caudillos emerged to fill the political vacuum. Political struggles between radicals, moderates, and centralists thwarted the formation of Mexican nationalism. Despite the common ground of antiforeign sentiment, regionalism exercised a vital role as Mexico's crisis became so severe that it often seemed on the verge of dissolving until the last quarter of the nineteenth century.

FAILURE OF ITURBIDE'S EMPIRE

The Liberator as Monarch, 1822–1823. The reluctance of the new junta to represent the insurgents became a serious mistake. Nearly all of them were upper-class residents of Mexico City who had previously served the colonial regime. Convinced that the autonomist movement had triumphed, the junta feared the racial and

rural insurgency of regional leaders who generally wanted a complete rupture with Spain. Although not representing national interests, the junta selected a regency which named Iturbide president of the junta and commander of the military. The civilian autonomists believed that they were now in charge, but in reality they had alienated most of the military insurgents.

Mexico seemed to be on the verge of a solid future. Now Latin America's most populous nation, Mexico, had seven million citizens as opposed to four million in Brazil. Mexico had also become the largest Latin American nation in terms of physical size—it covered more than one-third of the entire North American continent. An explosion of joy, optimism, and confidence in the future became manifest in ceremonies where citizens pledged oaths to a seemingly prosperous opportunity to interact with the rest of the world. Iturbide abolished racial definitions for citizenship and enjoyed popular festivities and sermons which eulogized him as a hero. This unreal expectation crashed within a few months.

The junta disappointed many Mexicans eager to participate in new changes. Clearly the junta had little interest in social reforms and did nothing in that area. Instead, it concerned itself with commercial adjustments that the *criollos* favored. For example, the junta reduced maritime tariff charges to 25 percent, decreed free trade, and reduced the alcabala sales tax to 8 percent. The junta also limited the amount of money Spanish citizens could take out of Mexico once many Hispanics began to leave for Iberia. Concerned about tradition and order, the regency finally responded to growing unrest by outlining regulations for the election of deputies to a new Congress. Iturbide based the new constituent assembly upon a corporate model so that clergy and hacendados received the largest properties of seats for deputies. Both the junta and regency stressed that newly elected deputies should concern themselves primarily with writing the new constitution.

As soon as Congress assembled, it quickly asserted itself. In February 1822, 100 deputies arrived in Mexico City to be sworn in. The Congress sought public support by reducing the prices of tobacco and pulque at a time when it needed revenues to pay for a large army and an expanded bureaucracy. Therefore, Congress approved questionable emissions of paper currency and forced loans upon the church. But Congress also suspended another forced loan against large, generally Spanish mercantile firms that the junta had decreed earlier because larger amounts of capital had begun leaving Mexico. The question of executive rule quickly became a burning issue. When Fernando VII rejected a Mexican throne and Spain disavowed the Treaty of Córdoba, most deputies favored another candidate from a European dynasty. Because deputies from the periphery outnumbered those from central Mexico, the desire for regional autonomy appeared quickly. Also, the deputies suddenly insisted that sovereignty belonged to the nation as vested in the legislature. Opposition to Iturbide and the junta had been minimal until Servando Teresa de Mier and Manuel Torres began to speak out.

Congressional ambitions motivated Iturbide to seize power. Not only did Congress dissolve the junta, but it also demanded an oath to it by all government officials. As pressure for a republic mounted, Iturbide gave in to popular demands that he resign as president of the defunct junta. But when Iturbide resigned as commander of the army, the military would not accept his resignation. Emboldened by this stance, Iturbide pressured Congress into building a stronger army and giving them pay raises. As he began to plot his takeover, Iturbide believed that he represented the national will. On the evening of May 18, 1822, army sergeants began walking throughout Mexico City calling for Iturbide to become emperor. Crowds took up the cry as paid shouters joined them in a march to Iturbide's residence. There they stood under Iturbide's balcony and continued shouting for him to accept their plea. Although Iturbide declined, more army units came over to join in, shouting "Viva Emperor Iturbide!" Of course, Iturbide gave in and asked the crowd to accept him as emperor. Soldiers then summoned 87 deputies from their beds and escorted them into the legislature at six o'clock in the morning. Surrounded by an excited crowd, they voted Iturbide in as emperor by a vote of 87 to 15. Many deputies preferred Iturbide rather than a Spanish monarch because the legislature hoped to dictate the terms of the emperor's oath of office. With Church support, the army claimed that Spanish rejection of the Mexican throne, as well as Madrid's disavowal of the Treaty of Córdoba, made this procedure necessary.

Determined to maintain the tradition of loyalty to a crowned monarch during the colonial era, Iturbide and the legislature agreed on the elaborate coronation that took place in July. The deputies even hired a French baroness to duplicate her earlier efforts for Napoleon Bonaparte. As cannon roared and military bands played, the empress passed below an awning suspended from the emperor's mansion to the national cathedral, conducted and seated on her throne by two uniformed gentlemen and five maids of honor, who held the trail of the empress's dress. Accompanying her were Iturbide's sister and her three small daughters dressed in white and crimson silk velvet robes trimmed with gold lace. Iturbide followed, accompanied by his son, designated earlier as "Prince Imperial." The thrones for the emperor and empress sat on the altar of the cathedral with cushions of crimson velvet trimmed with gold lace and tassels on which to place their feet. Vicente Guerrero carried the imperial insignia during the coronation ceremony. As Captain General of the South, he received promotion to field marshall. Nicolás Bravio also supported Iturbide's coronation. Congress had an important role in the ceremony as well. In addition to installing a throne for the congressional president on the altar across from the emperor and empress, the legislative leader placed the crown on Iturbide's head with the utmost seriousness. Thus, Iturbide tried to combine continuity with the Hispanic past as well as an effort to include his legislative and military peers. In attempting to identify the new empire with himself during a ceremony that impressed commoners as well as the upper class, Iturbide seemed to have a fine future as Mexico's first emperor.

Iturbide's Foreign Policy. Iturbide made foreign policy decisions which greatly affected the future. Certainly Iturbide was ambitious; at one point, he considered taking over Cuba. In January 1822, Nicaragua, Honduras, Guatamala, and Costa Rica pledged their loyalty to Iturbide. Iturbide incorporated Chiapas even though it belonged to the Captaincy General of Central America. But when the six provinces of Central America elected to join the Mexican empire, Mexico's borders stretched from Oregon to Panama. Difficulties arose when El Salvador's Congress proclaimed its desire to become part of the United States. When El Salvador sent a five-member delegation to apply for U. S. statehood, Iturbide sent troops to Central America in a failed effort to regain their loyalty.

Iturbide promulgated an Imperial Colonization Law in January 1823, so that foreigners could colonize the north in return for a pledge of allegiance to Mexico and conversion to Catholicism. The procedure was somewhat chaotic because a new committee was appointed each month. Applicants such as Robert Leftwich of Tennessee sat in on the sessions of the Colonization Committee as they deliberated on the law. Iturbide himself plotted secretly to set aside one-third of Texas as

the "Province of Iturbide" with himself as commandant general. Stephen F. Austin became the first colonizer to obtain a contract to establish a settlement in Texas.

The new empire established lukewarm relations with the United States. President James Monroe disliked emperors and monarchies but authorized Joel Poinsett, a rich South Carolina planter who had lived in Chile and spoke fluent Spanish, to visit Mexico as an agent. Poinsett interviewed Iturbide in the fall of 1822 and formed a negative impression, which has colored interpretations of the emperor for decades. Nevertheless, Iturbide dispatched José Manuel Zozaya to Washington, D.C., as minister plenipotentiary in order to obtain a loan, clarify the U. S. boundary, and to encourage prospective settlers to colonize in northern Mexico. Hardly able to snub Mexico's first diplomatic representative, Monroe authorized a reluctant U. S. recognition of the empire in December 1822. Despite this triumph, Iturbide did not inspire confidence in Spain, where stubborn authorities named a new viceroy to manage Mexico. But the unrealistic Spanish attitude only made independence more acceptable to Mexicans.

Iturbide's Fall. Economic, financial, and political problems soon brought the empire down. The crisis of funding became severe. The euphoria of independence from Spain encouraged early leaders to reduce or eliminate taxes at a time when they needed revenues badly. The mining industry had been devastated by marauding armies during the independence struggle and now produced very little. Agriculture remained weak after the death of so many laborers and demands of armed groups hungry for food. Most of those who died were from indigenous communities and had come from villages to toil on estates. Independence brought Mexico much closer to the international economy by means of direct trade, but the empire had little to exchange for imported goods. Iturbide raised tariffs higher than the junta, but not enough to protect regional economies from foreign competition. An example of Iturbide's failure to accommodate regional interests was his first tariff, which placed only a modest 25 percent ad valorem duty on cotton imports—so that Puebla merchants could not compete against finer British goods. Worse, Puebla's weavers could not afford raw cotton and cotton yarn that had to be imported.

Of the major points in the Plan de Iguala, only one became honored—independence and monarch—but protection of clerical privileges and Spaniards broke down when the imperial government imposed forced loans upon both groups. Amid steadily mounting debts and worsening economic conditions, Iturbide established a poll tax on adults as well as a 40 percent property tax. Reports circulated that the treasury minister was going door to door asking for tax payments.

Congress and the emperor could not work together. The first issue between them was a free press, which Iturbide opposed. Unable to withstand criticism, the emperor closed several liberal newspapers that espoused republican ideals and even a conservative journal that favored a European prince rather than Iturbide. Opposition deputies soon began to plot until a government spy revealed them, and they were arrested. The legislators also opposed Iturbide's handpicking of the supreme court until both parties agreed on a compromise. Insisting upon an absolute veto of all proposed legislation led to more arrests of angry deputies who clashed with the emperor. Becoming impatient with the whole process, Iturbide finally dissolved Congress and appointed a Junta Nacional Instituyente to replace it. At that point, Iturbide had lost much of his early popularity and sentiment for a republic increased. Iturbide had ignored the movement for provincial power too much even though federalism had become highly popular.

By concentrating excessively on the center of his empire rather than the periphery, Iturbide sowed the seeds of his destruction. The regional elites and municipalities wanted autonomy more than ever and demanded a constituent congress to write a new constitution. Sixteen provincial deputations backed such sentiments and withdrew support of the empire. Santa Anna, who had many personal differences with Iturbide, revolted in Veracruz and obtained the support of Guadalupe Victoria, as well as Guerrero. They agreed upon the Plan de Casa Mata in February 1823. By granting the Veracruz legislature vested authority over its own affairs, the Plan de Casa Mata also demanded the restoration of congress and assured each state that its deputies to the national Congress would have administrative control over their domain. The Plan de Casa Mata did not call for a republic but insisted that sovereignty resided in the Congress. Although the emperor promised to reconvene the legislature, the urge to implement regional control had become national. As Iturbide scrambled to obtain a loan from the British, the United States favored the rebels. By the end of February, Iturbide controlled little beyond Mexico City and decided to abdicate in March, hoping that his offer to resign would be refused. In this decision, Iturbide lacked his previous shrewd judgment.

Several factors led to the failure of Mexico's first empire. Iturbide had promised a limited monarchy, but his rule turned out to be authoritarian. The emperor's power base appears to have been built upon unwarranted hopes rather than real benefits. Moreover, the monarchy became too expensive—a court emulating those in Europe and an expensive palace remodeling—during a period of fiscal crisis. The belief that a republic would bring about faster economic growth became pervasive. To his credit, Iturbide withdrew from further conflict rather than try to defend his crown.

Demise and Death. Exile to Europe did not prevent a fatal return. Iturbide departed Mexico in May 1823, after accepting a handsome chunk of money in exchange for a promise never to reappear. Insecure after the government did not send his pension, Iturbide also believed that his life was in danger. The ultraconservative Holy Alliance of European governments considered Iturbide a threat. Therefore, Iturbide took up residence in London, partially because Britain opposed the Holy Alliance's hostility to constitutional rule. Iturbide began to assume that only he

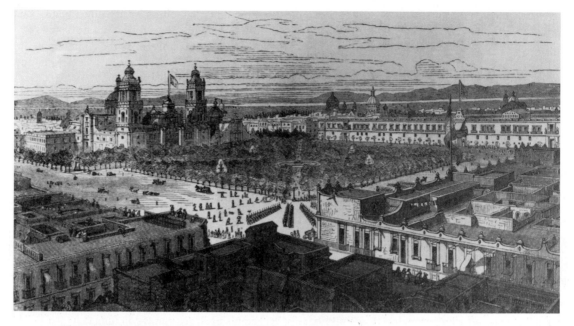

Plaza Mayor of Mexico City. *Courtesy of Special Collections Division, the University of Texas at Arlington Libraries, Arlington, Texas.*

could prevent the difficulties facing the early republic. Despite the attempts of Argentine exile José de San Martín to persuade him not to return to Mexico, Iturbide claimed that the masses wanted him back and imagined that only he could halt a feared invasion of Mexico by the Holy Alliance powers.

Iturbide's end was tragic. After he sailed from Southhampton in May 1824, six days passed before anyone noticed that Iturbide had left. On board his ship, Iturbide wrote pamphlets stating that he came not as an emperor but as a soldier who could defend as well as unify Mexico. What he did not know was that the Mexican Congress had already declared that should Iturbide reenter, he would be condemned as a traitor. Nevertheless, Iturbide landed in Tamaulipas wearing a disguise. But a local soldier recognized Iturbide's style in mounting a horse and reported him to local authorities. By almost unanimous vote, the Tamaulipas state legislature condemned Iturbide to death. Shot at the age of 41, Iturbide's compelling significance faded quickly away. Later, in 1838, the

government brought his remains to Mexico City and provided his relatives with financial security.

Iturbide experienced a strange fate for a leader who finally brought about Mexico's independence. The Plan de Iguala was a brilliant solution to the racial and political problems that plagued Mexico during the independence struggle, but Iturbide's interpretation of the monarchy was too centralizing when most regions favored autonomy. Iturbide supported a strong Church but provoked distrust among Catholics as well as resident Spaniards with forced loans. The economic and fiscal difficulties that the empire inherited could not be resolved. Iturbide took a keen interest in international affairs but weakened the north with colonization schemes that would eventually result in revolt. After Central America learned that Iturbide had quit, a loosely knit Central American federation was formed in July 1823. Although the masses supported his appeal for equality, Iturbide did little in terms of social reform. Cruel as a general, Iturbide became magnanimous to enemies later on. Although he was a great soldier and a skilled leader in his early days, Iturbide demonstrated that *criollos* could be vain as well as inexperienced. By ending a bloody insurrection with an imaginative compromise acceptable to nearly all, Iturbide merits a better legacy than the relative obscurity that he has endured.

BREAKDOWN OF THE SOCIOECONOMIC ORDER

After the collapse of Iturbide's empire, Mexico's early republic experienced one crisis after another. A severe economic slump as well as an acute fiscal crisis hampered national development. Society changed less than other categories of Mexican life, although it became clear that reforms were needed. The appearance of anticlerical policies, however, disrupted the national culture and became a devisive political issue. Caudillos serving as representatives of various regions filled the political vacuum created by the departure of the colonial and short-lived imperial apparatus. However, political clashes among the ruling class weakened Mexico because the *criollos* could not agree on how Mexico should be governed despite the new 1824 Constitution.

Economic Decline. The continual departure of Spaniards certainly weakened economic stability. Capital flight accelerated because Spaniards took many of the nation's assets. Worse, the Spaniards for centuries had served as experienced managers, technicians, and administrators; once they left, it became difficult to replace them. By 1827, Spaniards became convenient scapegoats for Mexico's difficulties and in that year they were ordered out of the country, thus violating a major provision of the Plan de Iguala. But because of exemptions that many Spaniards claimed, only about 1,000 actually migrated to Iberia on a permanent basis. The 1820s was a period when the labor supply became generally disrupted. The abolishment of slavery in 1829 resulted in difficulties throughout Veracruz and many of the tropical plantations. However, the economic downturn soon created employment scarcities with the result that landowners enforced debt peonage traditions.

Particularly ominous was the deterioration of the mining sector. Ransacked by royalist as well as insurgent forces earlier, many of the mines also decayed from disuse. Discouraging entrepreneurs was the enormous expense of putting flooded mines back into full operation. Moreover, the price of mercury rose sharply in the 1830s. British investors gradually initiated a mild recovery of the Zacatecas silver mines. Only by 1855 would mining production roughly equal eighteenth-century levels; even by 1868 the total would not approximate the 1808 boom days. Although the early half of the nineteenth century represents a difficult period for mining activity, the mines had become more important than ever; mining accounted for 92 percent of all Mexican exports by 1842.

The prominence of mining is explained by the low productivity of the rest of the Mexican economy. Sugar, for example, which attained an export value of 1.5 million pesos in 1800, that nearly disappeared 25 years later. Mexico City's largest manufacturing industry was the cigarette factory, followed by the mint. Although tobacco production survived at respectable levels, the output of the mint was less than six million pesos by 1821 and not much more thereafter. In general, manufacturing production experienced an overall reduction to half its previous levels. Free trade formulas soon revealed that *laissez-faire* ideas were a luxury for more advanced capitalist countries. Mexican industry continued to be artisan in nature throughout the countryside as well as within cities. Mexico could not compete with the price or quality of goods arriving from Europe and the United States. For these reasons, many artisans quickly found themselves out of work. In Oaxaca, for example, there had once been 500 looms producing local cotton products; by 1827 barely 50 remained. Manufacturing languished in the 1820s largely because the traditional merchant involvement in industry could no longer deal with the new free trade policies of the 1820s. Foreigners continued to dominate retailing in general.

The French monopolized retail drapery, the Germans hardware, and the Spanish dominated foodstuffs. Not surprisingly, hard-hit cities such as Puebla became firm protectionists as they were forced to diversify by the 1830s. The social effects became obvious; while Mexico City grew continually, Puebla experienced a net decline in the number of its inhabitants. In general, Mexican national production declined by 3 or 4 percent from 1810 to 1845.

The United States competed strongly with Great Britain for the Mexican market as well as imports of Mexican silver, either in specie or bullion. To encourage trade from Mexico, the U. S. Congress admitted Mexican silver and gold on a duty-free basis. In return, Mexico imported large quantities of U. S. finished cottons, wheat flour, and raw cotton. The British, meanwhile, concentrated on the Veracruz trade, while the United States moved into northern Mexico and the Santa Fe trade.

By encouraging agriculture and ranching by means of expanding haciendas, several regions began to prosper by the 1830s. To motivate hacendados to expand production, many state governments began abolishing communal ownership of land: Chihuahua, Jalisco, and Zacatecas in 1825; Chiapas and Veracruz in 1826; Puebla, Sonora, and Sinaloa in 1828; and the state of Mexico in 1833. These large estates accounted for the bulk of agricultural production. Hides became the primary export item followed by henequen, cochineal, lumber, dye woods, and coffee. Owning land was a wise choice. Most hacendados enjoyed a constant rate of profits while the sale price of estates generally rose throughout the nineteenth century. Hacendados were primarily businessmen who invested in irrigation works, diversified crops, mastered animal breeding, and purchased urban real estate. Successful proprietors owned more than one hacienda and managed them carefully from city offices as vital parts of their business interests.

Clearly the most successful hacendado that embodies these traits is the Sánchez Navarro family of Coahuila. Their latifundia of 17 haciendas covered an area of 16.5 million acres within the present borders of Coahuila, Durango, Zacatecas, and Nuevo León. José Miguel Sánchez Navarro used a Church office to establish himself and then a store to underwrite new land holdings with a network of commerce to ensure supplies. Steady food production, debt peonage systems for his laborers, and good communication with regional and national leaders ensured success. Uninterested in prestige, the Sánchez Navarros sought financial liquidity. Family ties achieved loyalty based on education as well as successful litigation.

Financial Crisis. Almost immediately, the early republic suffered from a lack of revenues. The major tax which the national government collected was the customs tax. Yet overall foreign trade declined from 21.5 million pesos in 1800 to 6.5 million pesos in 1825. To make matters worse, an 1824 federalist law mandated that proceeds from the sale of tobacco products were to be shared with the state governments. The *criollos*, in a burst of euphoria, eliminated many of the previous colonial taxes. The result was that whereas the 1802 colonial government had an income of 22 million pesos a year, by 1828 the republican regime had revenues of only 8 million. Not until 1875 did government income reach the colonial level.

Feeble banking facilities contributed to the financial ruin of the early republic. Convents, monasteries, and the archdiocese of Mexico were continual sources of capital, as well as export-import firms, guilds, and merchants. Pawn shops served the needs of ordinary Mexicans with the more prosperous citizens availing themselves of the government-sponsored monte de piedad. The government did not set up a bank until the Banco de Avío appeared in 1830, primarily to loan funds to industrialists.

Fiscal problems resulted mainly from the fear of European intervention. The Holy Alliance detested the liberalism which permeated the independence movement and many believed, correctly as it turned out, that a Spanish invasion was inevitable. For that reason, military spending dominated budgets. The 1824 federal budget called for expenditures of 15 million pesos. Of that total, the army received 9 million pesos, the navy 1.5 million pesos. Colonial military expenditures never exceeded 4 million pesos, but republican budgets would eventually reach 31 million pesos for an army claiming to total 50,000 soldiers. The 1824 budget also earmarked 2 million pesos for the foreign debt. To make matters worse, the cost of collecting taxes amounted to another 2.5 million pesos, since Mexico's early republic depended on an antiquated system of tax farmers. Graft and corruption, pushed on by the insecurity of the times, cost the government even more in terms of lost funds which it should have received.

Because the budget produced obvious deficits, the early republic quickly got sucked into a series of foreign loans with dire consequences for the future. In 1823 two quick loans for 32 million pesos with British bankers netted the government 17.5 million pesos. With high interest rates and questionable military supplies and various commissions attached to the loans, these funds turned out to be quite costly. Toward the end of 1827, Mexico defaulted on the interest payments. U. S. financiers refused to get involved in Mexican fiscal affairs; in fact, foreign banks hesitated to loan money to Mexico until the 1860s. Things got worse. When the government assumed claims and obligations resulting from the independence struggle amounting to another 45 million pesos, it soon had a total debt of 73 million pesos. Unable to pay such crushing obligations, regimes had to borrow from various *agiotistas* financiers and other domestic capitalists at enormously high interest rates. The result was that by 1850 Mexico's foreign debt had grown to over 56 million pesos and domestic debt amounted to about 61 million pesos. With income that did not exceed 20 million pesos, the early republic found itself in an extremely difficult financial situation that was never resolved satisfactorily until the end of the century.

Social Structure. Independence did not significantly change Mexico's social order. As in the colonial period, very little social mobility existed.

Stagnation in Mexican society retarded the sense of nationality that had developed at the end of the eighteenth century. From 1821 to 1871, the population grew considerably less than during the latter part of Spanish rule. The inability of the early republic to maintain political order, promote economic growth, and reform social problems served to fragment society rather than unite it.

The upper class enjoyed traditional privileges but had very little concern for the masses. Neither uneducated nor foolish, many in the upper class were intelligent, although several made unfortunate mistakes. Their intellect compares favorably with the founding fathers of the United States; their sophistication continued unhindered as a result of the prosperity of the eighteenth century. *Criollos* considered themselves to be *gente de razón* (people who reasoned) and believed that they were superior to the *mestizo* and indigenous groups. The colonial caste system ideology did not die away after independence.

Political exclusion widened the gap between upper and lower classes whenever the privileged elite controlled the national government. After giving up their titles, most of the nobility recovered their fortunes and maintained control over the means of production well into the middle of the nineteenth century. The old aristocracy often served in key cabinet positions. Virtually all the upper class supported the centralist faction, which decided that only respected, educated, and moneyed males—known as *hombres de bien*—should exercise the full rights of citizenship. Therefore, conservatives devised electoral laws that excluded the vast majority.

The upper class also resisted anticlericalism and patronized the Church as well as a national military. Conservatives supported the army and Church as a means of maintaining the status quo because the military and clericals both opposed public intervention into landholdings, wealth, or supervision of privileges that remained after independence. Able to place their sons into the army as officers and establish wealthy chapels which served as trust funds secure from confiscation until 1859, powerful landowners and merchants also supported convents and monasteries, which allowed their offspring to live quite comfortably above the level of the sweaty masses.

The upper class remained urbane and discriminatory. Forced to flee to the cities during the struggle for independence, Spaniards liquidated their rural investments and often became financiers. Those Spaniards who left Mexico came from the lower echelons of Mexican society. An aristocracy still made its presence felt in Mexico City after the creation of a republic. Another reason for upper-class urbanization was that many were merchants. A major difference between the lower and upper classes was that the upper class took great pride in its Hispanic roots and resented efforts by Vicente Guerrero's regime to exile Spaniards. Even white reformers such as Lorenzo de Zavala could not shed their racist views; like many other Hispanics, de Zavala referred to the indigenous population as a nuisance. Conservative whites were more critical of the masses throughout the nineteenth century.

Naturally, the middle class was more numerous than the upper class; but the middle class lacked wealth and connections and thus settled into a life of financial uncertainty. The army offered the major avenue of social mobility, and by 1836, the military was basically republican, although many of its leading officers continued to be conservatives. Many insecure males sought leadership in the national guard or militia units on the regional and local level. When financial conditions permitted, the middle class expanded by serving in the national as well as regional bureaucracies. Many middle class Mexicans established themselves as physicians, educators, lawyers, and notaries. Entrepreneurs operated dozens of textile factories while a rural middle class developed hundreds of ranches. Several family enterprises preferred speculation rather than commercial transactions.

The masses comprised the overwhelming majorty. Most lived miserably because the earnings of most workers were so low they could barely support their families. Hacendados continued to pay in scrip redeemable only at company stores. Major factors that prevented acute suffering were

that wages were stable and corn production doubled during the early republic. But a sack of corn, nevertheless, required four to five days of work. Often hungry, shabbily dressed, and illiterate, the masses became increasingly desperate. Most laborers also amassed high debts which employers encouraged. Landowners traditionally loaned sums to field hands which could rarely be repaid because their wages were usually less than the standard of living. In practice, this resulted in peons being bought and sold for the price of their debts. A young U. S. army officer recorded these practices in 1846:

> … I received a letter today from my friend the mother-in-law of the Sr. Alcalda (sic) at Matamoros, Señora Doña Anna Domingo Garcia de Chapa. She has sent her servant to ketch (sic) a run away servant. Such are the laws of Mexico that the Alcalda of Matamoros gives a warrant which being received by the Alcalda here will carry back the peon to Matamoros if he does not pay his debt. (Samuel Ryan Curtis, *Mexico under Fire*. Fort Worth: Texas Christian University Press, 1994, p. 127.)

The working class became increasingly anticlerical. Most Mexicans supported liberal legislation in 1833 which made payment of the tithe voluntary. But the high fees charged by parish priests for weddings, baptisms, and funerals were often beyond the means of workers and peasants. Commoners often paid about five months of wages for a baptism, marriage, or burial. Some estate owners filed suit on behalf of their workers to reduce these costs. The same U. S. officer who observed alcaldes apprehending fleeing workers in Matamoros calculated the cost of marriage at $32.50—which meant debt peonage for most males.

The class structure also had a strong racial connotation that weakened national unity. The indigenous population, which comprised one-third of Mexican society, often lived in a state of legalized servitude like many *mestizos* in the north. Few Indians spoke Spanish. Suffering the loss of their communal lands to hostile legislators, the indigenous population had little reason to support the Mexican government. Payment of head taxes was a hated remainder of the colonial system. Forced labor practices, known as *fagina* in the Yucatán, was a particularly resented custom as well as the sale of orphans as servants by municipal officials. Harsh punishments and vagrancy laws also angered indigenous societies. Some were sold as slaves to Cuban buyers. Efforts by elites in the state of Guerrero to alter the political status of villages and to intervene in their internal political apparatus triggered revolts which spread to other regions.

President Vicente Guerrero modified the social order more than anyone else by emancipating all African slaves in the Mexican federation. It is no coincidence that Guerrero accepted a $10 million loan from the antislavery British and then abolished slavery on September 15, 1829. His proclamation also sought to stem the tide of U. S. emigrants crossing the Sabine River into Texas. U. S. colonists already established in Texas often panicked when they learned of the law. Therefore, San Antonio officials kept the law from publication and forwarded a memorial to Mexico City asking for relief. On December 2, Guerrero exempted Texas, stating "that no change must be made as respects the slaves that legally exist in that part of your state."

Cultural Patterns. Independence enabled cultural changes to play an increasingly vital role in forging national identity. Mexico's national cuisine took shape in the nineteenth century; the consumption of chicken, ducks, pork, and beans with hot sauce crossed ethnic and class boundaries throughout Mexico. *Mole poblano*—turkey in a deep brown sauce of Europeans seasonings and Mexican chile peppers—and tacos made with corn tortillas and pork sausage became recognized as fixtures of Mexican meals. The country's first cookbook, *El cocinero mexicano*, appeared in 1831. Authored by an anonymous author who used only words with Mexican origins, the nationalistic flavored bestseller passed through several editions. Fifteen other cookbooks came out

during the nineteenth century and tended to avoid regional variations.

Gambling became one of many national diversions. Simple dice games, roulette, and the lottery, as well as cockfighting, consumed people's interests. Theater provided comedy, tragedy, and religious representations, particularly in the cities. To attend the theater after a promenade in the local plaza was an accepted routine for many urban dwellers. Patriotic festivals and the habit of referring to one another as "citizen" became staples of nineteenth-century life. Encouraged by traveling companies from Europe, opera became popular in Mexico City as well as regional cities. Students such as the brilliant Angela Peralta studied in Europe as operatic and orchestral societies established themselves. The music that Mexicans listened to also utilized more instruments from the various regions. Formal art suffered somewhat, partially because governmental inability to pay salaries and rent forced the renamed National Academy of the Three Arts of San Carlos to close its doors. But Mexican devotional *retablos*, oil paintings on tin, used indigenous elements to express gratitude to Christ, the Virgin of Guadalupe, and one of the saints for recovery from illness, accident, or natural disaster. Many Mexicans placed *retablos* that depicted the sacred person who had intervened on behalf of the petitioner on the walls of a church or a shrine near the altar. Others placed *retabos* in the privacy of their homes.

Educational campaigns became part of a liberal *criollo* attempt to insist that indigenous communities shed their traditional lifestyles and adopt European culture. Reforms emphasized the Lancasterian teaching method, founded by Joseph Lancaster in Britain, which became popular. Mexicans accepted it because of the emphasis upon rewards and punishments. Older students conveyed instructions from a master teacher. Surveillance monitors enforced discipline. In certain situations, disobedient children could have a sign placed around their necks which said "pig," "naughty," "gossiper," or "unruly." Whipping could be used against serious offenders. Such authority resulted because youngsters participated actively in the educational process while the teacher tended to guide learning procedures. The system worked best with advanced students in small group, but a lack of trained educators hampered the implementation of such innovations. Regional governments often had difficulty in repairing the damage caused by the insurgency struggles.

Families and Females. Most Spanish law carried over almost unchanged from colonial hegemony to the postindependence era. Particularly notable in this transition was the extraordinary protection that Mexican law provided for a family's property. Nowhere was the Hispanic preoccupation for social order so well revealed as in its concern for the conservation of the family, the social organ that faithfully maintained traditions and status. Families tended to be broader and more complex in the early nineteenth century than later on in the Gilded Age. Illegitimate children often lived in the same household with a father's legitimate offspring and sometimes received preferential treatment. The choice of a mate was central to the family's maintenance of a decent standard of living. And individuals could and often did fall into bankruptcy; but their wives and children and the larger, extended family did not. All property acquired during a marriage belonged jointly to both spouses. Neither could enter into contracts that risked this joint property without explicit permission or license from the other. Contracts requiring a husband's permission for his wife to engage in business suggest that the institutional framework was rigged to restrict women's participation in business. In a general sense, a husband also had to obtain his wife's consent to enter into certain kinds of transactions. If he did not, creditors might not be able to seize the wife's share of a property offered as collateral.

Wives enjoyed a special status as preferential creditors of their husbands regarding property, such as the dowries that they brought into a marriage. They could and did sue their spouses to obtain control of assets after a business disaster. To take advantage of this shelter, businessmen some-

times deliberately assigned property to their family to keep it safe from creditors. Specific legislation existed to protect children's property, not only from creditors, but also from parents who had second thoughts. Property transfers to minors were simple matters; land awards away from minors required a lengthy and complicated court procedure.

After independence, women became more active despite a restrictive legacy. Mexico's new rulers still considered females mentally deficient and therefore ineligible to govern others. Authorities considered males more decisive, physically robust; therefore, early republic officials gave men more family rights as well as authority. Although women could own property, men usually controlled its income. Women enjoyed more freedom on the northern and southern frontiers. Mexico City officials reporting on Laredo in 1828 concluded that the city consisted of "…carefree spirits who are fond of dancing and little inclined to work. The women are ardently fond of luxury and leisure; they have rather loose ideas of morality." Fear of a wife's infidelity irritated many husbands, who often resorted to physical violence against women. Jurists, however, viewed the husband's right to kill an adulterous wife as too extreme. The weakening of the Church had unpleasant repercussions because secular law more clearly legitimized the double standard in its greater tolerance of male adultery. Individualism tended to reward males, widows, children, and single females more than it did wives, whose subordination to husbands continued to dominate a collective view of social harmony.

Working did not improve women's rights or their place in society until several decades later. Upper-class women did not work in order to maintain their status. Middle-class females often worked as schoolteachers and shopkeepers. Vocational training intended for poor females did not materialize and their opportunities for gainful employment shrunk. *Casta* women continued to be concentrated in domestic service as maids or in food as well as apparel industries. Economic recession and political unrest restricted employment opportunities. Nevertheless, one-fourth of the women in Mexico City worked during the early republic, since women frequently needed to support themselves.

Working conditions were often unpleasant; therefore, many women chose to place themselves under a husband's supervision. *Casta* women were often pressured to marry because their offspring served as insurance for old age or bad health. Mexico City women married at the age of 22 and most became widowed after they turned 40. One-sixth never married at all; spinsterhood, however, carried little stigma. In rural areas women married at younger ages and those who worked devoted themselves to agricultural tasks. Throughout Mexico, women owned 25 percent of all properties.

The Church. After 1821 various governments began to remove the strong ties which formerly bound Church and state together. Furthermore, strained relations between Spain and Mexico limited the continuity of Catholicism after colonial rule. During the early republic, Mexico's new governments, reflecting the anti-Spanish trends in the population, attempted to replace Spanish friars with Mexican priests as much as possible. Mass resentment against Spanish clerics often arose out of disputes over Catholic theology. Spaniards stressed the divinity of Christ rather than his humanity. But the masses identified themselves with the suffering of Jesus, which enabled a certain resignation to their plights. In addition, such antagonism limited the ability of the Franciscans to enlist new recruits to serve in the Mexican frontiers. The shortage of friars in Mexico became critical as Mexican xenophobia heightened.

In 1833 a short-lived liberal Congress in Mexico legislated the secularization of the Alta California missions. The Bourbons had considered turning mission properties over to Indians earlier but lacked available secular priests. But the 1833 congressional bill made no mention of how mission land was to be distributed. The California legislature, however, decided to administer the missions for their own benefit. Therefore, more than 800 grants of large land tracts went to prominent politicians and settlers. The recipients of such grants stocked their estates with livestock from mission herds and increased their export of hides and tallows. The legislators blocked Indians, Mexican immigrants, foreigners, and lower-class Californios from obtaining land grants.

Events in the north also affected the church adversely. During the independence struggle, hacendados and ranchers avoided paying tithes in a number of ways. With peace restored, landowners wanted the tithe to be made voluntary or eliminated officially. Landowners who employed significant numbers of indigenous laborers particularly resented having to pay religious taxes for those who toiled under their supervision. A reformist priest in New Mexico, who objected to mandatory tithes on agricultural products and livestock to clerics, wrote a treatise against the practice and presented it to the territorial assembly of New Mexico. Father Antonio José Martínez enjoyed unusual stature and the local legislature approved his appeal and sent it to the national Congress. In Mexico City, newspapers discussed the measure excitedly and, in a special session in 1833, the Mexican Congress removed compulsory tithes.

Liberals considered the Church greedy and wasteful. Critics attacked those nuns who had servants fussing over them in lavish quarters. Few could afford such attentions; it cost 5,000 pesos to send most females to a convent. Pressures against such practices soon reduced the number of women in cloistered nunneries by 40 percent in 1850. Service-oriented orders with more social responsibilities grew.

Church wealth also received hostile attention from anticlericals. By 1850, Church capital amounted to roughly 100 million pesos with another 50 million in investments which earned additional income. This amounted to perhaps one-fourth of all Mexico's wealth by mid-century. In addition to rural landholdings, which were considerable in Yucatán and other regions, the Church owned many urban properties. By 1850, the Church owned half the real estate in Mexico

City and 72.5 percent of all property in the city of Oaxaca. High rents motivated many liberals to lash out as anticlericals.

Finally, the Church opposed public education but did not do enough to promote education itself. By 1838, only one-sixth of Mexico City women attended primary school. Schools entailed high costs, and sufficient numbers of schools simply did not exist. Moreover, middle-class Mexicans often sought modern curriculums which emphasized science, languages, and civic instruction. The removal of the Jesuits had created a vacuum to some extent since they were the best educators, and it was difficult for the church to replace them.

THE 1824 CONSTITUTION

After the collapse of Iturbide's empire, a three-member junta governed Mexico on a provisional basis. But the authority of the Congress restored by the junta, after having been deposed earlier by Iturbide, now faced new challenges. Jalisco and other states demanded that a new Congress, chosen on the basis of proportional representation and fully committed to regional autonomy, replace the older group. Several state governments had polled their municipalities and found that local followers strongly favored federalism. Radical liberals and federalists viewed the new republic as a pact of states. They were so determined to fight for their beliefs that in 1823, 10 of the 19 states had broken formally from junta control. The central government invaded Puebla and Oaxaca in order to crush the autonomist sentiment, but the demand for a federalist constitution enabled regional leaders to defeat the junta so that each state could have administrative control over their domain. Therefore, it did not take long for the new Congress to proclaim a federalist republic after elections took place.

The problem of attempting to create an independent republic from colonial and monarchical traditions would be difficult to surmount. Conservatives continued to argue for a strong central state and moderates feared the rise of the masses.

Liberal federalists prevailed until 1834 and the new constitution reflected their views. Produced mostly by federalists during the constituent congress that met in November 1823, the 1824 Constitution enabled regional governments to enjoy a great deal of autonomy. Each state had sovereign powers within its jurisdiction as a federation of equals. The drafted preamble simply stated that "The Mexican Nation is composed of the provinces." State legislatures would elect the president, vice-president, and senators. These offices were to be awarded to candidates from any party after being endorsed by a majority of the 19 state congresses. The federal legislature represented national authority, with a chamber of deputies making up the lower house. The landed elites throughout the region exercised real power through their control of local legislatures. Two senators represented each state and one deputy spoke for every 80,000 inhabitants. The president had little actual power. He was given the title of commander-in-chief, but the armed forces consisted of 24 regional commanders for each state and the four territories. The absence of national supervision allowed regional military leaders to exceed their prerogatives throughout the early republic.

The 1824 Constitution generally reflected colonial desires for local representation by means of the 1812 Spanish Constitution with some influence from the United States. The chief protagonist of the federalists, Miguel Ramos Arizpe, presented the Congress with a working document modeled upon the U. S. Constitution. The main U. S. contribution to the new Estatos Unidos Mexicanos was the adoption of a bicameral system. The separation of powers clause defining the authority of execuive, legislative, and judicial branches also reflects U. S. influence.

The parallelism of the Spanish and Mexican constitutions can be found, however, in clause after clause where not only Hispanic concepts became adopted but also even the exact words. Although the United States allowed a second term for its president, Mexico, following Spanish tradition, did not. The 1824 Constitution was exactly the same as the Spanish regarding its procedure for amending the constitution. A period of six years had to pass before any amendment could be introduced.

The 1824 Constitution also conceded several guidelines that are strongly Hispanic in terms of continuity from the colonial era. These compromises to centralist demands were crucial issues. The conservatives persuaded Congress to have Catholicism mandated as the only religion so that Church and state were not separated. In fact, the 1824 Constitution states that the clergy would continue to be subject to their existing authorities in judicial disputes. The military also enjoyed legal immunities from civil courts. The 1824 Constitution confirmed King Fernando's restoration of military jurisdiction over soldiers. Wives, children, and various individuals living with military personnel, such as servants, came within the jurisdiction of military courts. As a reflection of elite desires to control the masses, the 1824 Constitution said nothing about equality before the law. Furthermore, the president could assume extraordinary powers similar to a state of siege during national emergencies. Thus, the 1824 Constitution provided a traditional institutional continuity in terms of religion and the armed forces while maximizing regional autonomy.

The Guadalupe Victoria Regime, 1824–1828.

Not only did Victoria become the only president to serve out his constitutional term during the early republic, but also most of the problems of this era emerged at the same time. In June 1824, a national election took place in which the three members of the former junta opposed each other. Guadalupe Victoria was elected president, Nicolás Bravo became vice-president, and Vicente Guerrero received the lowest number of votes. Guerrero retreated from public life to try to improve his health.

Revered for his refusal to surrender and accept a pardon from the Spanish, Victoria seemed well suited for the presidency. The new ruler maintained an open-house policy for all citizens from 1:00 to 2:30 in the afternoon. Tall, homely,

and modest, Victoria attempted to work amicably with his opponents. Although a federalist, he invited conservatives such as Lucas Alamán into his cabinet.

Eager to have an experienced officer in charge of his new navy because of Spain's refusal to recognize Mexico's independence, Victoria appointed David Porter, a hero of the War of 1812, to take command in 1826. A British officer had drowned en route to take command of the Mexican navy earlier. The president correctly guessed that Spain would soon invade Mexico and therefore planned to take the initiative by attacking Cuba and harassing Spanish commerce in the Caribbean. Colombia even prepared troops to attack Cuba on a joint basis, but both countries backed off when the United States, as well as Britain, opposed the plan; they preferred to see the island controlled by Spain. Angered by Porter's failure to get along with Mexican officers and treasury officials, Victoria sought to restrict U. S. adventurers flowing into Texas.

But Victoria's regime suffered from a worsening financial situation. Victoria cooperated with the British, particularly in tariff policies, by lowering customs rates. Alamán realized that increasing tariff rates actually diminished government revenues yet Victoria found himself in an insoluble situation because to raise internal taxes invited domestic revolt. On the other hand, if the government failed to service the foreign debt, European intervention would be a threat. All of Mexico's early republic conflicts had, to some degree, the issue of unpaid debt in the background. In 1827, Mexico defaulted on its British loans. The only solution seemed to be producing more currency. With silver in short supply, the government flooded the country with copper coins.

Although attempting a policy of goodwill, Victoria was indecisive and simply lacked talent. Physical impairments affected his mental capacity. Contemporaries attributed health problems to Victoria's epilepsy. It would be more accurate to consider a brain tumor and hypoglycemia as the actual culprits. Many noticed Victoria's swollen eyes, convulsions, and intense vomiting. Fond of speeches, the vain Victoria gave in to flattery. He tended to rely on old army friends who enriched themselves.

The morose and gradually withdrawn Victoria could not deal with increasingly bitter political strife between centralists and federalists. A particularly devisive issue was the procedure whereby journalists, lawyers, and priests were generally those who met qualifications for serving in public offices. Federalists preferred a more open system. No political parties existed but many secret societies, particularly Masonic lodges, became the arenas for political intrigue. A particularly glaring weakness of the 1824 Constitution was that an elected vice-president could be a political opponent of the president. This problem bedeviled Victoria because Vice-President Nicolás Bravo joined a revolt by other conservative generals, who attempted to dismiss federalists within the Victoria regime with the help of Scotch Rite Masons. Despite his weak health, Guerrero became supreme military commander, and on January 7, 1828, he killed or captured the entire rebel force at Tulancingo. Guerrero returned a hero but the rebellion heightened tensions as the 1828 presidential elections approached.

A major consequence of the Bravo revolt was the division of the liberals into radicals and moderates. The issue was whether to defend the Victoria regime or not. Moderates rallied behind the government's minister of war, General Manuel Gómez Pedraza, who had served in the royalist forces before backing Iturbide. Radicals supported Guerrero, a hero of the independence movement. How can the differences among the three different political factions be summarized?

More than anything else, the radicals considered federalism an attempt to allow the popular will to reach its truest and most popular expression. Federalism became the doctrine of popular sovereignty carried to its maximum level. Strongly opposed to taxes and regulations, landowners in the periphery supported federalism because they could control local legislatures and not have to worry about regulations from a central government. The federalist movement also sought to

expel Spaniards from Mexico. In order to tap into foreign markets, federalists tended to favor free trade, particularly in the north and south. Yet state of Guerrero cotton growers and Mexico City artisans opposed free trade in order to avoid competition with lower-priced imports. Many radical ideologues, such as José Luis Mora, considered the Church to be the chief obstacle to socioeconomic change. Mora particularly wanted to replace the Catholic *colegios* with secular institutions. Thus, the radicals sought to free individuals from the Hispanic legacy by guaranteeing civil liberties while eliminating the privileges which the army, church, university, and Indians had enjoyed in the past. The radicals planned to establish a volunteer civic militia in order to limit the national army's political influence. In addition, the radicals wanted to continue mobilizing the urban masses and install a populistic agenda.

The most energetic radical activist was Lorenzo de Zavala. Like many other radicals, Zavala originated from the south. Elected to the Mérida city council at the age of 23, Zavala served in the constituent congress until his election to the senate; afterwards he received an appointment to be governor of Mexico state. A federalist and populist, he belonged to the York Rite Masonic Lodge founded by Poinsett. A reformer striving to empower the middle class, de Zavala pushed his ideas as a journalist.

General Manuel Gómez Pedraza became the first leader of the moderate faction when the conservatives attempted to revolt against Victoria. Disenchanted with the prospects of democracy in Mexico, moderates like Gómez Pedraza favored a conservative republic that would not cater to the interests of the masses. Tending to emerge from the north, moderates enjoyed support from bureaucrats, modest property owners, military officers, and lawyers. The moderates also distrusted the national army and favored militia forces restricted to property-owning citizens. Suspicious of the Church for its role in the independence movement, moderates scorned the insurgency for its clerical leadership. Moderates were convinced that privileged protection of communal properties for indigenous communities was an anachronism. Eager to reform but not weaken the Church, the moderates believed in competition and individualism. Proud of their "clean blood," moderates viewed themselves as a class apart from the indigenous peoples. Somewhat suspicious of municipal assertiveness, moderates felt that municipal governments should sell off communal lands and pay their own way in order to develop politically. Convinced that ownership of property by the "progressive" class would improve Mexico, moderates wanted small property holders to be their political base. Moderates sought restricted free trade and favored a peaceful resolution of differences with Europe and the United States.

Centralists sought a strong national state by allying with the Church and the regular army. In the early nineteenth century, this often meant advocating a monarchy. Conservatives restricted social mobility by denying full citizenship to the lower class out of their fear that the urban masses would overturn the existing socioeconomic order. Centralists, therefore, endeavored to maintain the colonial social system. In general, conservatives favored a Hispanic tradition of internal production behind high tariff protection and distrusted Britain as well as the United States. Tending to occupy the central region of Mexico and Mexico City in particular, centralists were the well-to-do, high clergy, wealthy landowners, senior military officers, bankers, rich merchants, Spaniards, and a few European-oriented *criollos*. In central Mexico, the elites had become wealthy through commerce and mining. Eager to promote industrialization, conservatives sought to keep foreigners and immigrants out of Mexico. Conservatives justified industrialization as the best means to stabilize urban society and restore public order.

The great conservative statesman was Lucas Alamán. Oriented to Europe and committed to establishing a constitutional monarchy, Alamán was a delegate to the Spanish Cortes during the independence struggle. A member of the Scottish Rite Masonic order, Alamán considered liberalism "the most powerful and destructive device imaginable" and believed that its policies would

result in enslavement to foreign commerce. Democracy, he concluded, was a "foreign doctrine without roots in the Spanish or Aztec past." Alamán considered the policy of colonizing Texas with U. S. settlers catastrophic. Alamán also upheld the privileges of the Church and the army. Toleration of other religions, he argued, would weaken traditional values.

Guerrero's decision to run for president in 1828 resulted in a major revolt. Guerrero seemed certain to win as Victoria's regime approached bankruptcy and could not pay public employees. A symbol of resistance to Spanish colonial rule, Guerrero became the fiery leader of the radicals. However, conservative centralists joined moderates in backing Gómez Pedraza. The campaign became bitter as newspapers from both sides smeared opposing candidates. Immensely popular because of his military accomplishments and rabid speaking style, Guerrero also appealed to the majority because of his African-*mestizo* background. He lashed out at low tariffs, which had much to do with the unemployment of so many artisans, and called for the expulsion of Spaniards. Demonstrations against Spaniards took place in many regional cities throughout 1828 as Mexico sensed that Madrid would invade.

As so many of his successors would do in the future, Victoria attempted to rig the presidential elections so that his favorite, Gómez Pedraza, would win. Particularly ominous was Victoria's failure to request Gómez Pedraza to resign from the war ministry after announcing his candidacy. Victoria's decision was critical because the secretary of war was supposed to certify ballots counted by the state legislatures, thus putting the war ministry in a position to alter or destroy ballots. To the anger of most, Gomez Pedraza "won" with 11 states to Guerrero's 9. Guerrero partisans refused to accept the election results and accused Victoria of presiding over a fraud. Sentiment for rebellion spread when Guerrero, Santa Anna, and de Zavala began to plan their revolt.

The Victoria government collapsed as a mass revolt jolted Mexico City. Gómez Pedraza soon realized that his cause was hopeless and prepared for exile while federal troops began to desert to Guerrero's movement. De Zavala encouraged the urban masses to seize the downtown area. After three days of street fighting, Guerrero's supporters prepared to celebrate at the central plaza in front of the national palace. Although his government had capitulated, Victoria doggedly negotiated with de Zavala over final details. Suddenly on December 4, 1828, a mob of 5,000 looted the Parián building on the other side of the main plaza. For more than a week, the streets of Mexico City belonged to the rioting masses and defiant soldiers. It took several weeks for authorities to restore order. The Parián had become a convenient target because it housed wealthy Spanish merchants who sold coveted import goods that competed with items produced by local artisans. The upper class concluded that mass mobilization would have to be repressed more than ever. Mexico's descent into political chaos began with the failure of the Victoria regime. Military leaders, the Mexico City elite, and provincial as well as urban masses now began to struggle for control of the affairs of government. In many ways it was a continuation of the independence conflict. Mexico was not unique in this sense; many other Latin American countries experienced similar disorder. In Portugal, 40 governments ruled in the 31 years from 1820 to 1851.

RISE OF THE CAUDILLOS

As in Spain and other Latin American countries, caudillos became a vital feature of nineteenth-century politics. Charismatic, normally flaunting the masculine characteristic of machismo, the caudillos of Mexico operated in an arbitrary manner as part of a quest for personal power. Often large landholders, caudillos could become successful military leaders by using peons as the foundation for a personalized army. Actual governmental power for those who controlled regions or even the national capital became based on clans and kinship ties. Many caudillos wore fancy uniforms and medals to impress those lacking in

political conscience. A successful caudillo also had a gift for theatrics and impassioned oratory. Demagogic caudillos frequently indicated that they were willing to die for their cause or the nation. Thus, they could construct a network of loyalties in regions where the locus of power now rested. From 1821 to 1855, the average life of a Mexican national government was nine months, although 20 of the 44 changes during this period of government involved four caudillos.

Guerrero as President. When Guerrero became president on April 1, 1829, he faced immense problems and his populist approach angered the elites. He inherited a bankrupt treasury, an economy in shambles, and few sources for further revenue. Many bureaucrats lost their jobs and their replacements were political dependents instead of the old core of career professionals. Furthermore, the end of African slavery, which Guerrero supported and legalized in 1829, angered Anglo settlers in Texas. Meanwhile, the United States attempted to purchase Texas outright. Guerrero's enforcement of the second Spanish expulsion law on March 20, 1829, further alienated the Spanish community as well as Madrid. Yet Guerrero's leniency in issuing exemptions upset radical nativists.

Guerrero attempted to reverse traditional financial policies. He particularly wanted to use tariff protection to increase industrial production and employment. Pressure from textile mills in Puebla and Querétaro added to the attempt of this fiscally weak regime to move away from free trade. Guerrero also supported Treasury Secretary Lorenzo de Zavala's efforts to gain revenue—including a graduated income tax and property taxes.

Guerrero survived a clumsy Spanish invasion of Mexico. After the Spanish Council of State recommended to King Fernando in 1828 that he stop exploring efforts to attract international support for retaking Mexico, the monarch decided that revenues from Cuba would enable him to seize Mexico by himself. Then Mexican revenues would supposedly enable Spain to reconquer the rest of its former empire. The Mexican navy offered no resistance as 4,000 Spanish soldiers burst into Tampico, hoping to attract supporters. But Santa Anna arrived and attacked them on August 20, 1829, until he arranged a truce. After Santa Anna's forces increased to 5,000, he began a final attack on September 9. Spanish general Isidro Barradas lost 900 troops, forcing him to request a surrender.

During the invasion, Guerrero responded firmly. Despite bitter resistance from Congress, he obtained special war powers. This was the first of many occasions when presidents would receive such authority. De Zavala came under criticism when he enacted forced loans, reductions in pensions and salaries, wide-ranging new taxes, and property seizures in order to fund the war effort.

The Spanish invasion had temporarily breathed new life into Guerrero's regime, but the added burdens of war proved to be Guerrero's demise. In August the Jalisco legislature called for a northern confederation. Their main grievances included accusations that de Zavala's new taxes encroached upon provincial domains. A tax on absentee ownership of land particularly irked state governments, which viewed this type of taxation as an intrusion into local decisions. Several states complained that Guerrero had abused his emergency powers. In order to appease this opposition, de Zavala agreed to resign in October, but more of Guerrero's opponents forced many of his additional supporters out of the federal government. In December, officers in charge of a reserve army—created to fight the Spanish invaders—drew up an insurrectionary plan at Jalapa. Vice-president Anastasio Bustamante joined the rebels, indicating support from conservatives for the regional revolt. Guerrero voluntarily resigned his war powers and attempted to gain congressional support. When this failed, he personally led an army to quell the revolt. But within a week, the capital fell to the rebel militias. Guerrero's army deserted him and on Christmas Day 1829, Guerrero promised to obey the new regime.

The Bustamante Administration, 1830-1832. Anastasio Bustamante was another cau-

dillo who dominated the early republic. Although not as well known as his rivals, Bustamante nonetheless served as president three times and actually ruled Mexico longer than Santa Anna. Bustamante relied primarily upon the army as his power base. More than any other caudillo, Bustamante employed his personal influence over other officers to unite with him for peace and order. Bustamante believed in a centralized republic within a nationalistic and Catholic context. The Church approved Bustamante because he fervently believed in the appearance of the virgin as the Virgin of Guadalupe. Both centralist and moderate landowners supported him for attacking Guerrero when Guerrero and de Zavala incited indigenous leaders to seize lands belonging to hacendados. Nevertheless, Bustamante offered up rhetorical appeals to respect the indigenous past.

Bustamante gained power by calling for peace and stability. He planned to make sure Mexico would enjoy centralized order when he assumed the position of chief of state. Alamán became the most powerful person in his cabinet. Alamán's policies limited mass elections, freedom of the press, and Masonic political activities. Any attempt to disturb peace would be met with harsh punishment. Alamán and Bustamante preserved the rhetoric of a federalist state but deposed federalists they disliked and purged hostile state legislatures.

Bustamante also revived the Church. Alamán had suggested a plan, initially contemplated by the Guerrero regime, that would send a list of acceptable bishops to the pope for his approval. The government would request the pope to select whomever he saw fit from the list, which restored some of the Church's power. The new plan would allow Church and state to be equal partners in patronage. Bustamante also permitted the Church to once again impose moral codes upon society. The administration attempted to offset fears of excessive clerical influence by allowing citizens to report any injustices committed by the Church.

Guerrero decided to revolt because of the persecution of his indigenous allies and his suspicion that Bustamante intended to kill him. But in January 1831, Bravo decisively defeated Guerrero's rebels near Chilpancingo. Guerrero fled to Acapulco to take refuge on a ship owned by a supposed friend, but the Italian captain betrayed him for 50,000 pesos. The government court-martialed and executed Guerrero near Oaxaca on February 14, 1831. This event shocked many because surrendering officers were normally treated with leniency. It is more than likely that centralists wanted Guerrero shot as a warning to those of mixed blood who aspired to mobilize the masses against the traditional order.

The Bustamante regime began to repair previous economic damage. Lucas Alamán once again dominated the government and centered his efforts on national economic recovery and restoring the government's credit. First, he sold the debt-ridden tobacco monopoly to private merchants. With Bustamante, Alamán also reduced the size of the army. Deficit reduction allowed Alamán to renegotiate Mexico's foreign debt with British

banks. Impressed with Alamán's fiscal measures, the British extended new credits.

The establishment of the Banco de Avío in 1830 clearly cast the conservatives on the side of protectionism. Alamán had argued in favor of promoting infant industries in his *Memoria de Relaciones de 1823*. The Banco de Avío loaned money to joint stock companies and industries and also purchased machinery which it normally gave to glass, iron, paper, and fifty textile factories. With capital of one million pesos obtained from a 20 percent tax on imported cotton goods, a three-member board and Alamán dominated policy. Despite a few careless loans and unrest throughout the country, the Banco de Avío financed 31 projects, only a few of which were total failures, until the bank closed in 1842.

Santa Anna created the spark for rebellion in Veracruz. Textile importers and Veracruz tobacco growers joined recently discharged soldiers who demanded new policies. When his friend and ally Pedro Landero lost his position as Veracruz port

Veracruz. *Courtesy of Special Collections Division, the University of Texas at Arlington Libraries, Arlington, Texas.*

commander, Santa Anna claimed that federalism and civil rights had been violated. He demanded new ministers and, when no answer arrived, Santa Anna revolted. The government beseiged Veracruz but failed to take it. Such defiance provoked additional revolts throughout the interior, partially because army officers resented Alamán's attempt to centralize control of the armed forces. Therefore, military caudillos worked out a deal according to their desires; civilians had little to say. Bustamante, Gómez Pedraza, and Santa Anna entered the capital after having decided that Gómez Pedraza would rule as interim executive until new elections could be held.

Santa Anna. The caudillo system of individuals frequently shifting positions suited Santa Anna, who was a crafty opportunist. President 11 times, Santa Anna was a great horseman, expert shot, and handsome demagogue as well as a superb organizer. Santa Anna did not always want to be a dictator, even when others insisted that he do so. Sensing the federalist mood at the time, Santa Anna forged an agreement with the principal radical leader, Valentin Gómez Farías, so that they could rule Mexico. Santa Anna realized that the radicals were a majority and, without an alliance with Gómez Farías, the state legislatures would not elect him to become president. As he hoped, regional deputies voted Santa Anna into power with Gómez Farías as vice-president.

At this point, the radicals seized the opportunity to legislate their ideology. Unable to support this program, Santa Anna retired to his half-million-acre estate at Manga de Clavo, claiming that his health prevented him from ruling as chief executive. The radical legislation alienated many because of its effort to encourage monks and nuns to renounce their vows and enter secular life. In addition to making the tithe voluntary, Gómez Farías stopped the transfer of property to religious orders and ended *fueros* for the military as well as the Church. Gómez Farías also closed the university and the National Ministry for Public Instruction in the federal district, as well as the territories. In general, the radicals shifted the re-

sponsibilities of education to the municipalities. The radicals weakened the army by pruning veteran units and debated whether or not to replace the army with regional militia. Not surprisingly, military officers revolted.

The second half of 1833 was very confusing until Santa Anna finally became a clear-cut conservative. At first, Santa Anna alternated between ruling as president and delegating the position to Gómez Farías while defending the government. His life long friend José María Tornel y Mendívil served Santa Anna capably. As 1834 began, he joined the conservatives to become their leader while promising to protect their interests. Assuming absolute power in April 1834, he ousted Gómez Farías, revoked the radical legislation, dissolved Congress, and fought with dissident governors.

Santa Anna Confronts the Radicals. Instability in the capital allowed federalism to take root throughout the regions. The army could not be counted on to maintain order as centralists in Mexico City desired. Preoccupied with regional autonomy, army officers refused attempts to place them under a central command. Prior to Santa Anna's 1834 regime, regional authority was vested in commandants-general whose decentralized commands became largely autonomous fiefdoms. State governments wrote their own constitutions and claimed the same patronage rights as the republic. Mexico state, for example, bickered with Mexico City over the right to nominate candidates for ecclesiastical offices, control of tithes, and confiscation of properties owned by religious orders. During the early republic, factional activity in the countryside and municipalities often reflected deep divisions linked to family rivalries and class interests rather than ideological differences. Personal security became a large issue in the north and south. No stable system for dispensing justice or defending against hostile Indian attacks protected Mexican frontier societies.

Regional economic patterns played an important role as a motivating factor for federalism. By 1830, economies in several regions had recovered, but the national government still struggled to generate revenue. Efforts from Mexico City to tax provincial wealth only generated suspicion in those states. Not surprisingly, those regions that prospered became the most ardent federalists. The north began to experience a lucrative trade with St. Louis, Missouri. Zacatecas, San Luis Potosí, and Jalisco revived their mines. Yucatán thrived from trade with New Orleans and Havana.

Zacatecas reflects the federalist sentiments that became so powerful. In Zacatecas, Governor Francisco García Salinas established the Fresnillo Company in 1831 to operate mines north of the state capital. Silver arrived at the Zacatecas mint in 1832 which by 1834 produced over two million pesos worth of coins. With its other mines, Zacatecas emerged as Mexico's leading silver producer. Wealthy upper-class leaders, no doubt, benefited personally from this prosperity and sought to protect their wealth from centralists in Mexico City. Certainly there was cause for optimism behind federalist supporters. Travelers passing through Zacatecas could see silver veins on the surface while approaching the capital.

Establishing a strong militia in 1829 became García's most notable achievement. García responded to an 1827 federal law which intended for militias to provide civil order, serve as a reserve against Spanish invaders, and fight Indian raiders. Although the Zacatecas militia participated in defeating the Spanish forces in 1829, it became a potent tool for García to expand his ambitions. Zacatecas supported Jalisco federalists who sought to move their government from Guadalajara and escape from Bustamante's military governor. In December 1831, the Zacatecan congress invited the Jalisco government to locate anywhere within Zacatecas. García also opened a munitions factory which made his militia the strongest of any state; with an active force of 5,000, it rivaled the national army. These militia fought outside the state and turned the tide in favor of Santa Anna during his 1832 revolt against Bustamante. Only after Santa Anna amended his initial proclamation to call for the return of Gómez Pedraza did Zacatecas mobilize its militia.

García attracted supporters with unusual programs. After abolishing communal properties, García called for the redistribution of large landed estates in general. In December 1829, the Zacatecas congress established a bank to purchase large estates, often Church owned, and rented them to landless families. When Bustamante came to power that same month, the national courts declared the Zacatecas law unconstitutional. Not to be outdone, the *zacatecanos* established a bank to purchase private lands for redistribution and it actually bought several haciendas.

Although it was not apparent earlier, Santa Anna represented the most lethal enemy to Zacatecas and federalism. On May 25, 1834, Santa Anna issued the Plan de Cuernavaca, which denounced anticlerical legislation, declared all Gómez Farías laws null and void, promised to enforce the constitution, called for the resignation of all senators and deputies who supported the radicals, and declared that the military would support Santa Anna. This exhortation represented the first real threat to the 1824 Constitution. Soon a group of skillful conservatives cleverly outmaneuvered their opponents and took advantage of the constant unrest to establish centralism as national policy.

Santa Anna promised that he would not tamper with the constitution. This may have been a trick to relieve himself of the responsibility, for Santa Anna knew that the now-centralist congress would do it for him. Nevertheless, Santa Anna reassured García that he had no intention of dismantling the federalist system. But during the summer of 1834, Santa Anna replaced many radicals in the national bureaucracy and discharged federalist governors. In response, Jalisco, San Luis Potosí, and Puebla openly rebelled. Santa Anna sent troops to quell these states, particularly a long siege of the city of Puebla that did not end until August.

These events forced a split in Zacatecas. On June 10, the Zacatecas legislature informed Santa Anna that they would defend their rights, but García and other *hombres de bien* agreed nominally with Santa Anna that the Gómez Farías laws were too radical and they decided to side with Santa Anna. García, therefore, resigned and Manual Gonzáles Cosío, a federalist, replaced García as governor.

In January 1835, a crisis emerged when the centralist congress in Mexico City began deliberations to weaken state militias. Eventually, the new legislature limited all militia to one solider per 500 inhabitants. This would have the effect of reducing the Zacatecas militia to 600 troops. The centralist measure became law on March 31, 1835.

Zacatecanos reacted with alarm. Not only were they concerned for their proud militia, but they also foresaw this step as the first to dismantle the federalist system and the 1824 Constitution. The Zacatecas legislature met in secret session and invoked Article 88 of the state constitution, which empowered the governor to use the militia to resist any external aggression.

Mexico City responded strongly. The conservative press denounced Zacatecas for its militia, calling it "the worst plague upon society." Members of Santa Anna's administration denounced *zacatecanos* as self-interested anarchists. Santa Anna agreed to command troops against Zacatecas at the request of Congress. The lack of national unity concerned the legislature because Juan Alvarez, caudillo of Guerrero state, led a revolt at the same time that the Zacatecas crisis emerged.

Unfortunately for Zacatecas, García was designated to command the militia after the capture of its former general. Soon many militia members deserted and public confidence wilted. García stupidly moved his troops from the mountain positions onto an open plain. Cut off and surrounded, the *zacatecanos* surrendered after being betrayed. Santa Anna's troops then plundered the homes of foreigners when they seized the capital.

Antiforeign resentment had been present as early as 1831, when Zacatecas and other states closed foreign-owned retail businesses because their cheap imports displaced local artisans. Other states also prohibited or discouraged foreign immigrants. Even the national Congress, on March 24, 1835, regulated foreigners; it stated that for-

eigners guilty of crimes of any category, or who participated in political revolts, would be punished by Mexican law.

Santa Anna chastized Zacatecas sternly. He appointed a military governor and seized the Fresnillo silver mines. When Santa Anna departed the city on May 27, he and his soldiers took two million pesos in plunder. To weaken Zacatecas, Santa Anna decreed Aquascalientes a federal territory since it supported Mexico City during the confrontation. Aquascalientes returned to Zacatecas in December 1836 but eventually achieved separate statehood in February 1857.

Zacatecas was not the only state to fight Santa Anna, but these struggles represented little more than the climax of federalism, which would gradually weaken before disappearing during the 1850s.

SUGGESTED READING

Aarom, Sylvia M. *The Women of Mexico City, 1790–1857*. Stanford, CA: Stanford University Press, 1985.

———. "Popular Politics in Mexico City: The Parián Riot, 1828." *Hispanic American Historical Review* 68:2 (May 1988), 245–268.

Anna, Timothy. *Forging Mexico, 1821–1835*. Lincoln: University of Nebraska Press, 1998.

———. *The Mexican Empire of Iturbide*. Lincoln: University of Nebraska Press, 1990.

Armstrong, George M. *Law and Market Society in Mexico*. New York: Praeger, 1989.

Benson, Nettie Lee. *The Procincial Deputation in Mexico*. Austin: University of Texas Press, 1992.

Brading, David. *The First America: The Spanish Monarchy, Creole Patriots, and the Liberal State, 1492-1866*. Cambridge: Cambridge University Press, 1991.

Brister, Louis E. *In Mexican Prisons: The Journal of Eduard Harkort, 1832–1834*. College Station: Texas A&M University Press, 1986.

Calderón de la Baca, Frances. *Life in Mexico*. Garden City, NY: Doubleday, 1970.

Chance, Joseph E. *Mexico Under Fire*. Fort Worth, TX: TCU Press, 1994.

Costeloe, Michael P. *The Central Republic in Mexico, 1835-1846: Hombres de Bien in the Age of Santa*

Anna. Cambridge: Cambridge University Press, 1993.

DePalo, William A. *The Mexican National Army, 1822–1852*. College Station: Texas A&M University Press, 1997.

Di Tella, Torcuato S. *National Popular Politics in Early Independent Mexico, 1820–1847*. Albuquerque: University of New Mexico Press, 1996.

Flaccus, Elmer. "Guadalupe Victoria: His Personality as a Cause of His Failure." *The Americas* 23:3 (January 1967) 297–311.

———. "Commodore David Porter and the Mexican Navy" *Hispanic American Historical Review* 34:3 (Aug.ust 1954), 365–373.

Flores Caballero, Romeo. *Counterrevolution: The Role of the Spaniards in the Independence of Mexico, 1804–1838*. Lincoln: University of Nebraska Press, 1974.

Fowler, Will. *Tornel and Santa Anna. The Writer and the Caupillo, Mexico 1795–1853*. Westport, CT: Greenwood Press, 2000.

Garza Villarreal, Gustavo. *El proceso, de la industrializacíon en la cuidad de Mexico (1821–1970)*. Mexico City: El colegio de Mexico, 1985.

Green, Stanley. *The Mexican Republic: The First Decade, 1823–1832*. Pittsburgh, PA: University of Pittsburgh Press, 1986.

Guardino, Peter. *Peasants, Politics, and the Formation of Mexico's National State: Guerrero, 1800–1857*. Stanford, CA: Stanford University Press, 1996.

Hale, Charles. *Mexican Liberalism in the Age of Mora, 1821-1853*. New Haven, CT: Yale University Press, 1968.

Harris, Charles. *A Mexican Family Empire: The Latifundia of the Sánchez Navarros, 1767–1867*. Austin: University of Texas Press, 1975.

Henson, Margaret. *Lorenzo de Zavala: The Pragmatic Idealist*. Fort Worth: Texas Christian University Press, 1997.

Macume, Charles W. "The Impact of Federalism on Mexican Church-State Relations, 1824–1835. The Case of the State of Mexico." *The Americas*, 40: 4 (April 1984), 505–529.

McLean, Malcolm, ed. *Robert Leftwiche's Mexico Diary and Letterbook, 1822–1824*. Arlington, TX: UTA Press, 1986.

Olivera, Ruth, and Lilliane Crete. *Life in Mexico Under Santa Anna, 1822–1855*. Albuquerque: University of New Mexico Press, 1991.

Pilcher, Jeffrey. *Que vivan los tamales!: Food and the Making of Mexican Identity*. Albuquerque: University of New Mexico Press, 1998.

Potash, Robert A. *Mexican Government and Industrial Development in the Early Republic: The Banco de Avío*. Amherst: University of Massachusetts Press, 1983.

Robertson, William S. *Iturbide of Mexico*. Durham, NC: Duke University Press, 1952.

Rodriguez, Jaime E., ed. *Mexico in the Age of Democratic Revolutions, 1750-1850*. Boulder, CO: Lynn Reinner, 1994.

———, ed. *The Independence of Mexico and the Creation of the New Nation*. Los Angeles: UCLA Latin American Center, 1989.

Rugeley, Terry. *Yucatán's Maoya Peasantry and the Origins of the Caste War*. Austin: University of Texas Press, 1996.

Salvucci, Richard. "The Origins and Progress of U.S.–Mexican Trade, 1825–1884. Hoc opus, hic labor est." *Hispanic American Historical Review* 7l:4 (November 1991), 697–735.

Stevens, Donald. *Origins of Instability in Early Republican Mexico*. Durham, NC: Duke University Press, 1991.

Tenenbaum, Barbara. *The Politics of Penury: Debt and Taxes in Mexico, 1821–1856*. Albuquerque: University of New Mexico Press, 1986.

Ward, Henry George. *Mexico in 1827*. London: H. Colburn, 1828.

Walker, David W. *Kinship, Business, and Politics: The Martínez del Río Family in Mexico, 1823–1867*. Austin: University of Texas Press, 1986.

Weber, David. *The Mexican Frontier, 1821–1846: The American Southwest Under Mexico*. Albuquerque: University of New Mexico Press, 1982.

Zoraida Vasquez, Josefina, ed. *La fundación del estado mexicano*. Mexico City: Nueva Imagen, 1994.

———. "Political Plans and Collaboration Between Civilians and the Military, 1821–1846." *Bulletin of Latin American Research* 15:1 (January 1996), 19–38.

8

War with the United States,
1835–1854

Conflict with its northern neighbor resulted in catastrophe for Mexico. U. S. migration to Texas triggered social conflict and defeat in 1836. Two years later, Santa Anna halted a French invasion and established an imposing authoritarian regime which improved social and financial conditions. But Mexican control over its northern territories and the southern periphery continued to decline. Once U.S. President James Polk decided that the United States had to acquire California and other Mexican lands, war became inevitable. The loss of half its national territory and the failure of Mexico's basic institutions created deep wounds. Given the role that the United States played, it is not surprising that Mexicans would remain suspicious of the United States for many years.

THE TEXAS REVOLT

The Texas Tinderbox Explodes. The United States had a strong interest in Texas. Despite Spanish assistance to the 13 colonies in achieving independence, the young republic claimed that Texas formed part of the Louisiana Territory purchased from France. Reviving an old claim, the United States insisted that the Rio Grande was the boundary between New Spain and the United States. In Mexico, the independence struggle

against Spain encouraged several filibusters to attack Texas, hoping to precipitate the annexation of Texas to the United States. Nevertheless, Spain eventually crushed the Texas rebels and defeated private expeditions from Louisiana. Only after the sale of Florida did Spain check U. S. expansionism toward Texas by means of official recognition of the Sabine River as the boundary between East Texas and Louisiana in 1819. New U. S. Minister to Mexico Joel Poinsett and various secretaries of state urged Mexico to sell the area from Louisiana to the Rio Grande.

The ideal community that Mexico desired in Texas could not develop. Medieval Spain and colonial Mexico were peculiar in that all citizens had definite rights within a hierarchical society. The unifying factors for this perfect society were the Spanish language, Catholicism, and land ownership. Although the Mexican state had the obligation to defend all social groups in this context, the formula did not work in Texas. U. S. nationalism and the pioneering individualism of Anglo settlers doomed such an ideal. The Texas revolt resulted from the failure to achieve a pluralistic society in Texas itself.

Land speculators unquestionably played an important role in fomenting the Texas revolt. Like the Spanish Bourbons, the early Mexican government decided that colonization by nationals as well as

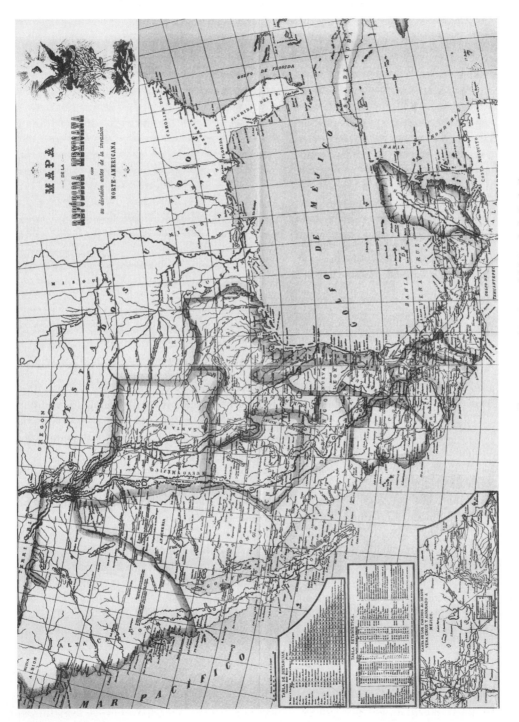

Mexico Before the U.S. Conflict. *Source: Archivo General del Estado de Coahuila*

foreigners was the best way to populate the thinly held frontier and defend it from raiding Indians. Emperor Iturbide promulgated the Imperial Colonization Law in January 1823 which allowed for colonization by foreigners who would pledge allegiance to the national government and convert to Catholicism. After Iturbide's abdication, Congress voided the law. But because the Imperial Junta had struck a deal with Stephen F. Austin under the Iturbide code and granted a contract, Austin became the only North American able to attempt establishing a colony in Texas under that particular law. It was not until August 1824 that Congress reenacted legislation for general colonization. The National Colonization Law gave individual states the power to administer public lands. In May 1824, Coahuila and Texas united into one large state; the new government in Saltillo then passed the liberal Coahuila y Texas Colonization Law.

The nature of land transfers and colonization worked directly against the cohesiveness of the Mexican confederation. The Saltillo law merely required that immigrants be of good character and present evidence of Catholic faith. Immigrants could receive land titles individually or through an *empresario* leader. Colonization policy entitled *empresarios* to vast amounts of land in return for the number of families they brought in. The law also exempted colonists from taxation for ten years. Eventually, Saltillo awarded 41 *empresario* contracts to various individuals. A great deal of speculation rapidly took place.

Land speculators tarnished by scandal became some of the most honored Texas leaders. After obtaining Mexican citizenship, Jim Bowie purchased inexpensive land certificates and resold them for a profit. Samuel May Williams, first a secretary and then a partner to Austin, became the most despicable speculator of all. Perhaps one reason for Sam Houston's arrival in Texas was to purchase stock in existing colonies while acting for brokers on Wall Street. Austin speculated in land and purchased grants from Mexican landowners for less than one cent an acre.

Mexico continued to encourage immigration and agriculture through generous land policies in order to populate the Texas wilderness. One of the most significant colonies was the enormous Leftwich Grant of 1825, which occupied an area 100 miles wide and 200 miles long. Under the leadership of *empresario* Sterling Robertson, nearly 600 families eventually resided in what came to be known as Robertson's Colony. In the course of the decade preceding the Texas revolt, almost 4,000 grants were issued in eastern, central, and coastal bend Texas. Land had developed as a major commodity of exchange because of the scarcity of money and credit. Because of their access to greater quantities of investment capital, U. S. speculators bought more land than Mexicans. The social structure changed as a result. By 1835, there were 30,000 U. S. colonists who brought 5,000 African slaves, but only 7,800 Mexicans in Texas.

At the urging of Lucas Alamán, the federal government finally attempted to regain control over Texas. The Law of April 6, 1830, suspended most *empresario* contracts and banned the introduction of additional slaves. It drastically reduced U. S. immigration to Texas, and Mexico attempted to colonize Texas with nationals. In the fall of 1830, authorities built a fort named Tenoxtitlan on the Brazos River to keep Anglo-Americans out of Texas and to protect settlers from hostile Indians. Despite attempts to repeal previous land policies, speculation by foreigners continued unabated, largely because the state of Coahuila y Texas continued to sell land as a revenue measure. At that point, conflict became increasingly probable.

By at least 1829, Anglo-Americans had become the majority in Texas and they resented Mexican rule. Imbued with aggressive entrepreneurial attitudes and a strident egalitarianism, the newer Anglo settlers did not fit into Mexican cultural norms. Many were southern slaveowners who disliked Mexico's attempt to abolish slavery as well as prostitution. Austin and others became particularly critical of the judicial system. Colonists objected to using Spanish as the official language, as well as the long journey to Saltillo in order to deal with the superior court. Authoritarian control of the *ayuntamientos* by the governor struck many as excessively rigid. Too often the Anglos did not understand the differences between their rights under Mexican law and those they relinquished when they left the United States.

Outright conflict finally began. Shots rang out when federal officials attempted to arrest William Barret Travis for raising illegal militias. Speculation on Mexican land grants and Texas real estate continued in the United States. Williams and Austin allowed nonresident landowners to claim land in their colony but failed to introduce any actual settlers. Austin was imprisoned in Mexico City in 1834 for writing an uncharacteristically frank letter urging Texans to organize themselves as a state separate from Coahuila. Mexican officials were so angry when Williams and others obtained an illegal land grant in May 1835 that they sent an army into Texas to arrest the offending land speculators. Colonel Domingo de Ugartechea ordered the apprehension of the malefactors in August 1835, but the citizens of Columbia would not surrender them. This incident led to the battle of Gonzales in October when angry colonists drove out 100 Mexican dragoons.

Santa Anna's new conservative regime had also precipitated conflict in Texas. Santa Anna increased the powers of national authorities enormously after he overthrew Gómez Farías in June 1834. The government disbanded state legislatures and dismissed governors who opposed the conservative drift. Santa Anna also scrapped the anticlerical legislation, attempted to halt the secularization of Franciscan missions, and restored the *fueros* privileges. In October 1835, the national legislature decided that all governors should hold office only at the will of the supreme government. The end of the federal republic became reality with the promulgation of the Siete Leyes legislation and the 1836 Constitution. Written by Lucas Alamán and Francisco Manuel Sanchez de Tagle, the new constitution stipulated that state legislatures were to be replaced by five-member councils to aid the governors. State governments became military departments while Mexico City

appointed local bosses. The bicameral legislature in the capital required members to own property and maintain minimal incomes. The president was to be elected by the chamber of deputies for an eight-year term and be eligible for reelection. Although modeled upon Napoleonic administration in Europe, the centralist changes sparked revolts in the northern and southeastern regions.

Texas was one of several federalist states on the periphery that reacted angrily by calling for restoration of the 1824 Constitution. In the southeast, the Campeche upper class suffered as shipping declined due to higher tariffs imposed by the new government. Yucatecan sugar growers became unhappy as their traditional demands for free trade and a powerful local oligarchy went unanswered. Similar unrest against centralism swept through the northern borderlands. Sonora and Sinaloa also objected to high tariff duties. In Texas, insurgents captured Goliad on October 10 while the revolt's leaders in Nacogdoches pushed for independence from Mexico. On December 20, at Goliad, rebels signed a stronger, formal declaration. They sent the manifesto to the provincial council at San Felipe which hoped to secure cooperation from dissidents in northern Mexico.

Santa Anna's harsh response to the Texas revolt led to open warfare. Alarmed by threats of rebellion from San Antonio, Santa Anna dispatched his brother-in-law, General Martín Perfecto de Cos, to reinforce the garrison. After a four-day battle, 300 U. S. volunteers and colonists forced Cos to surrender and retreat. This defeat was more than a military setback for Santa Anna; it became a national disgrace and a personal affront. Santa Anna's abilities as an organizer and leader enabled him to force loans from the Church and various lenders to rebuild the depleted army. Veteran units had been disbanded by federalist opponents. On February 12, 1836, a Mexican army of 6,000 crossed the Rio Grande. Maya recruits, unaccustomed to the rainy, cold northern conditions, suffered pitiably. The poorly equipped, badly dressed troops had little enthusiasm. Rebel scouts burned sparse grassland that had been counted on for forage. Many died of disease or deserted, but

Santa Anna relentlessly drove his army forward until he arrived at San Antonio and forced the startled defenders to take refuge in an old mission known as the Alamo.

The capture of the Alamo provided no strategic value and led to Santa Anna's doom. Santa Anna postured as the "Napoleon of the West" but disregarded the battlefield wisdom of his hero. Santa Anna could have bypassed the mission and attacked the disorganized Houston forces, destroying the main Texan army in the field. But Santa Anna quickly revealed his intentions. As soon as Mexican troops entered San Antonio, they raised blood-red flags, the symbol of no-quarter battle. The end came suddenly for the rebels in the chilly, predawn hours of March 6, 1836, as 2,500 Mexican soldiers attacked from each direction. In the final assault, the marksmanship of the 188 defenders could not halt the surge of muskets and bayonets.

The Alamo battle produced many results. For the rebels, it attracted hundreds of additional volunteers and provided Houston with desperately needed time to mold a semblance of an army out of his group. Santa Anna further blundered by ordering the execution of Davy Crockett and several rebels who were captured. Santa Anna's treatment of the six survivors and his obvious quest for glory provoked dissension among his army. In addition, the Alamo bloodshed encouraged many *tejanos*—Mexicans born in Texas—to join the independence cause. Previously, *tejanos* preferred working toward independence through legal channels, while Anglos had independence and U. S. annexation as their central concerns. At least 155 *tejanos* fought against Santa Anna. Finally, the Alamo episode settled the nagging question: Should Texas become an independent nation or fight to restore the 1824 Constitution? In a ramshackle hall at Washington-on-the-Brazos, 59 delegates signed an independence declaration formulated by land speculator George Childress.

U. S. involvement became critical to the outcome of the Texas revolt. As the insurgents struggled for independence, Austin and other Texans traveled to the United States seeking aid and recognition. Various Texas agents had toured the United States, raising $125,000 in pledges and cash. President Jackson, a friend of Houston, presided over a large buildup of troops which eventually crossed into Nacogdoches, 50 miles beyond the U. S. border. The newly arrived volunteers strengthened the *tejanos* and established Anglo colonists. In fact, only ten signers of the independence declaration had lived in Texas for as long as six years.

Santa Anna failed to capitalize on his subsequent victories. The provisional Texas government sent a column of troops to San Patricio in order to seize Matamoros as part of a scheme to encourage Mexican liberals to rise to Texas' support. Meanwhile, 100 miles southeast of the Alamo at Goliad, James Fannin could not decide what to do with his troops. Fannin finally left his fortress on February 28 to reinforce the Alamo but returned the next day when oxen pulling his supply carts wandered during the night. To the south, General José Urrea crushed the San Patricio forces in late February. Urrea then confronted Fannin's group, which surrendered after a short battle. The prisoners assumed they would be repatriated unharmed to the United States, but Santa Anna ordered the 360 prisoners to be shot, the same fate suffered by the ill-fated expedition which had captured Matamoros earlier.

Santa Anna continued to commit strategic blunders that led to his decisive defeat at San Jacinto. Splitting his forces and overextending his supply lines, Santa Anna courted disaster as he marched eastward. On April 17, Texan scouts captured three Mexican soliders who carried vital documents. The prisoners and their dispatches revealed the location, size, and plans of the Mexican army. Until then, the Texans believed that Santa Anna had returned to Mexico City after his Alamo victory.

Houston also learned that Santa Anna had separated himself from the main force and had rested the troops under his command at San Jacinto. Houston, therefore, ordered his small army to attack. The revenge-crazed Texans showed no mercy; they killed and scalped many who surrendered. Houston's troops captured Santa Anna, but he managed to save his life by promising to withdraw all Mexican forces below the Rio Grande. Several Mexican officers, such as Urrea and Pedro de Ampudia, wanted to regroup and fight. Even though the Mexican forces still outnumbered Texan troops seveal times over, General Vicente Filisola reluctantly obeyed Santa Anna's order to withdraw.

Texas was now lost forever and opened her land to even more rapid U. S. settlement. Many Texans desired to join the United States, but Jackson, fearing war with Mexico and domestic controversy, delayed annexation. Most Mexicans had little desire to join in a new Texas campaign that came to be viewed as meaningless. The federalist governors on the periphery would not contribute scarce resources to rebuild a federal army that might instead be utilized to extinguish their autonomy.

THE SANTA ANNA REVIVAL

The Pastry War. Conflict with France soon rescued Santa Anna from what appeared to be a certain end to his political fortunes. Houston sent Santa Anna to Washington, D.C., where he promised Jackson that Mexico would respect the independence of Texas. In return, a U. S. naval officer escorted Santa Anna to his plantation in Veracruz. There he waited for another opportunity to seize power. His anticipation was short-lived. The French government, under aggressive Louis Philippe, demanded that Mexico pay France 600,000 pesos. The "bourgeois king" insisted on this sum in order to satisfy the claims of French citizens in Mexico, including the owner of a pastry shop in Veracruz ransacked by Mexican soldiers. Paris also clamored for the removal of various public officials and most-favored-nation trade status. President Anastasio Bustamante ignored these demands, claiming that the actual damage to the bakery probably amounted to no more than 1,000 pesos. A French fleet, however,

appeared in March 1838 and blockaded Veracruz's port as the French minister demanded money and protection of foreigners.

Sloppy diplomacy and misunderstandings that normally characterized French–Mexican relations played to Santa Anna's advantage. In October, Bustamante agreed to pay the claims, but he learned that France had added the cost of the blockade to its original demands. When the French insisted upon payment of 800,000 pesos, negotiations ceased. French marines landed and seized the critical fortress of San Juan de Ulúa. Santa Anna had arrived earlier and urged the Mexican commander to surrender. This incident caused Bustamante to declare war on France. Santa Anna then rallied Mexican forces to attack the 3,000 French soldiers. Santa Anna counterattacked successfully but lost his leg, an event that he would use to his advantage. The French accepted the original 600,000 pesos that they had earlier demanded and departed after British mediation.

Once again, Santa Anna took advantage of a critical situation to become a national hero. He began by sending off a highly exaggerated account of the confrontation, suggesting that he was dying as he wrote it. The self-proclaimed hero then witnessed the decline of Bustamante, who fell victim to federalist revolts, financial difficulties, and a military which went unpaid for many months. A truce with loyal forces resulted in the permanent ouster of Bustamante. Santa Anna selected an Assembly of Notables to replace Congress, which in turn appointed him as president.

The new regime was uncompromisingly authoritarian and favored the upper class. Conservatives were convinced that only respected, educated, and moneyed males—*hombres de bien*—should exercise the complete rights of citizenship and, therefore, devised electoral laws that excluded most Mexican males. These *hombres de bien* supported Santa Anna because they enjoyed extravagant receptions, galas, military uniforms, as well as favoritism in contracts, land sales, and appointments. To pay for his expensive new dictatorship and build a political base, Santa Anna encouraged the Church to give his government

200,000 pesos in return for the end of liberal legislation. Santa Anna lowered real estate taxes to please his upper-class supporters, but general taxes increased enormously. The government maintained the colonial head tax on Indians. In a gesture toward nationalism, the new regime announced that foreigners could purchase land in Mexico as long as they obeyed Mexican law.

Santa Anna refused to recognize the independence of Texas. In retaliation for a Texas attempt to seize eastern New Mexico, Santa Anna sent army units across the border and occupied San Antonio in March and September 1842. The Texas attempt at retaliation failed when an unauthorized expedition to Mier collapsed. After entering Mexico, 11 of the 14 militia captains recklessly voted to dispute Alexander Somervell's order to retreat. The Texans were forced to surrender; Mexican forces then executed 17 Texans and imprisoned the remainder in Perote.

Now at the height of his power, Santa Anna gloried in bashing the Texans as his ego began to fly out of control. Santa Anna accepted an armistice offer from Houston but could not quite bring himself to approve a British–French guarantee of Mexico's northern border in exchange for Mexican recognition of an independent Texas. He sometimes treated prominent ministers as lackeys; Santa Anna once ordered Alamán to fetch his hat. The army increased greatly as Santa Anna's friends became officers. At one point, Santa Anna ordered his leg dug up from his hacienda and reburied in a pompous monument. Military units and cadets from El Colegio Militar escorted the leg to its ridiculous crypt as ministers and foreign diplomats observed the procession.

The Assembly of Notables finally produced the 1843 Constitution, which again committed the mistake of subordinating local governments to Mexico City. Free elections in 1842 had resulted in a federalistic Congress that disputed notions of despotism favored by Santa Anna. Therefore, the Assembly of Notables asserted itself and overruled the deputies. Like the 1836 Constitution, the 1843 document stipulated minimum incomes necessary in order to serve as deputies and sena-

tors or to even vote. Moreover, it maintained *fueros* for the church and army. To highlight his authoritarianism, Santa Anna rigged the 1844 election to become president again.

Santa Anna behaved foolishly, unconcerned with public reaction. When his wife died in August 1844, a supposedly grief-stricken Santa Anna requested the skeptical legislature's approval to mourn in Veracruz. But during his return, Santa Anna planned a new wedding with a 15-year-old beauty; the lavish ceremony that later took place disgusted Mexican society. When regional revolts flared, civic militia supported them. Both the national legislature and General José Joaquín Herrera united moderate as well as radical factions of the federalist movement to defeat Santa Anna. Mobs tore down statues of Santa Anna and urinated on his portraits. Santa Anna was captured while he attempted to escape, and the new government prepared to exile him in early 1845.

Society and the Economy. The social policies carried out by Santa Anna's ministers attempted to invoke the tenets of conservative nationalism characteristic of Santa Anna's general strategy. Although it is not surprising that Santa Anna's key supporters reformed the army more than other political factions, the *santanistas* also strongly promoted eductation. Their populism helped make the Santa Anna regime of 1841 to 1844 one of the most stable in nineteenth-century Mexico. The regime centralized education on all levels. The new Dirección General de Instrucción Pública agency began to carry out this task; it required stricter licensing of teachers and inspected private as well as religious schools. But the fear of U. S. invasion and regional revolts undoubtedly prompted the regime to promulgate a form of national unity by means of central control. Throughout Mexico, the primary curriculum now consisted of religious and political indoctrination, reading, writing, and arithmetic. Schools demanded discipline and order. Learning usually required rote memorization and recitation.

Given the difficulties faced by Mexico in the first half of the nineteenth century, educational progress became difficult to achieve. Military emergencies constantly drained off needed funds on the local level from both municipalities and state governments. Moreover, declining attendance at clerical schools in Puebla and Mexico City indicated that Santa Anna's demands caused the Church to lose revenue. Larger cities and towns fared better in promoting education than did rural areas. Normally one-third to one-half of eligible children attended urban schools and, by 1842, as many as 53 percent did in Guadalajara. Tornel succeeded in promoting the Lancasterian educational system throughout Mexico.

Mexico operated far more schools at this time than previously thought. Growth in private school enrollments actually outstripped those in state and religious schools. Religious motives often characterized the quest for education, but the desire for literacy became more tangible. In addition, the national government required more literacy in order to encourage urban economies. Therefore, in 1842 education became obligatory for males and females between the ages of 7 to 15. Tuition often became free to talented students who could not pay; secular and religious authorities often instructed pupils regardless of race or class. Greater use of the written word, however, did not result in a society that would support Santa Anna with gratitude.

Santa Anna's efforts to influence social trends also extended to cultural institutions. Particularly notable was the new national theater, the Teatro Nacional. Santa Anna placed its cornerstone in February 1842, and the building opened its doors two years later at a cost of 35,000 pesos. Magnificent chandeliers lit the eight tiers of seats which accommodated an audience of 8,000 within its elegant confines. Beautification of the Zócalo made it one of the favorite paseos (walks) in Mexico City by 1843. Santa Anna's government also rescued the Academy of San Carlos from the neglect it had suffered during the early republic. The academy remained traditional yet imparted a pluralistic concept of art that emphasized indigenous as well as European customs. The regime undoubtedly considered the academy as a means to channel artistic trends within a hierarchy of orderly, unified goals.

As a conservative, Santa Anna approved the revival of the church in order to reestablish a decidedly traditional society. The number of clergy increased from 3,463 in 1825 to 4,615 by 1850. The governor appointed to California attempted to restore church management of 12 missions. With great amounts of fixed assets, however, the Church did not do enough to provide for social needs. Thousands died without sacraments and more went without religious weddings due to the scarcity of priests and the high fees charged for basic services. Although the quantity of convents and monasteries declined, those wealthy enough to live within these cloistered confines enjoyed servants, diamonds, pearls, sumptuous meals, and regal settings, that, according to the wife of the Spanish ambassador, "might have served for a pope under a holy family." With its privileges intact, the Church retained the powerful religious sentiments of the masses. Religious festivals continued to be the most widely attended public festivities. Church lotteries provided extra revenues for hospitals, schools, and the maintenance of ten bishops and other ecclesiastics.

The steady growth of urban areas seems to indicate a period of recovery from the immediate postindependence decline. New palaces, promenades, and exclusive stores which sold costly imports gave Mexico City an elegant tone. European and North American attire tended to dominate among upper-class inhabitants of the larger cities. In the interior, a colonial rhythm predominated. Although a gala social life and colorful public fiestas seem to indicate content within the cities, social problems manifested themselves continually. Beggars and thieves jostled respectable citizens in churches and public events. After dark the streets became unsafe. Murder was a common crime.

The government relied upon social traditions to combat threats to health. Outbreaks of cholera and other epidemic diseases were particularly dreaded events. Earthquakes, such as the 1845 tremor that knocked down entire churches, caused innumerable deaths and illustrated the dearth of competent physicians. Bleeding and bathing continued to be favored remedies, but most families possessed a basic knowledge of medicine based on Mexico's long reliance upon herbs. Markets sold an enormous variety of herbal medicines. Eventually, the Santa Anna regime attempted to regulate physicians by establishing fees, demanding proof of certificates, and insisting upon minimal periods of residency in any given community.

Women enjoyed increased prominence as society searched for approaches to strengthen nationality during a period of international conflict. Women comprised 59 percent of the capital's population by 1848, largely because of continued female migrants searching for work as servants and nursemaids. War deaths also account for the increasing proportion of females in Mexico City and elsewhere. Widows became more active in businesses. Male fatalities are another reason that 37 percent of the labor force in Mexico became female. White and *mestiza* females served as teachers and physicians in increasing numbers. Although women could not enter universities, literacy among females clearly increased and stimulated a more heightened public role. Women, more than men, contributed to the nation's graceful cordiality, amiability, and warmth of manner for which Mexico is famous.

The stature of women went up as the prestige of motherhood rose. The spread of *marianismo*, a belief that women possessed a stronger ethical instinct and should therefore exercise more authority in family life, became acceptable. Mothers assumed legal responsibility for their children. The number of divorces increased once separation became less difficult to obtain. Beatings of wives became less tolerated.

Class differences in marriage patterns widened while urban tendencies diverged from country traditions. Upper-class women, who remained generally in urban environments, married later and worked more frequently than in the past. Only about one-half of all women were married during these troubled years, mainly because of the shorter lives of men. By 1848, however, lowerclass women married earlier. Twenty-two or twenty-three became the normal marriage age in cities while women in the interior continued to wed at earlier ages. Two to five children characterized the usual number of infants raised in Mexican families.

Despite a number of social improvements for women, the Church and men delineated women's spheres of influence. A male *novio* (sweetheart) could have an upper class woman placed in a convent before marriage in order to ensure virginity upon marriage. Females could still not dress like men. Women also required the approval of spouses in order to adopt children. The opportunity to be formally alone with men rarely existed. Although *marianismo* emphasized feminine spiritual strength, defeat in war with the United States reinforced a domesticated role for women. This conservative doctrine idealized women as domestic guardians and mothers, but it denigrated their civic roles as well as individual accomplishments.

A notable achievement of Santa Anna's regime were improved economic and financial conditions. Economic activity picked up considerably, particularly for those who had the foresight to purchase land after 1816. Healthy commercial life enabled the nation to avoid a trade deficit; the commercial balance from 1840 to 1844 was the best for any other period in the first half of the nineteenth century. Import taxes reached an all-time high as the government made a maximum effort to protect industry from manufactured imports as well as foreign liquors. In this sense, Santa Anna resembles Juan Manuel Rosas' nationalistic efforts in Argentina to encourage industry and to avoid foreign dependency.

The regime attempted to institutionalize its support for economic growth several times. The Banco de Avío sought to improve agricultural and industrial output by providing loans for technical innovations. Unfortunately, the bank did not analyze many of these loans thoroughly, and it closed its doors in September 1842. The regime also established a short-lived Escuela de Agricultura in 1842 and added an Escuela de Veterinaria in 1853. The critical oversights at both institutions were a lack of practical application and an excessively theoretical orientation. In December 1842, Santa Anna created a Junta General Directiva de la Industria Nacional, which intended to encourage industry and reduce contraband. Before its demise in 1845, this agency aided industry and created 64 juntas. In 1842, the government also established a Junta de Fomento y Administración de Minería in order to encourage mining. The regime also created chambers of commerce in all commercial centers larger than 15,000 persons. The rapid revival of groups representing commercial interests demonstrated the continuity of colonial tendencies.

Tariff protection and governmental concern often stimulated industry. Mining continued as the critical growth component of the economy. The mining revival in the 1840s helped stimulate development in Michoacán and many other states. Guanajuato began producing silver in quantities that nearly matched the late colonial boom. Mining remained a privileged activity, but decades of postindependence conflict restrained its recovery. The textile industry grew suddenly after 1830, particularly in Querétaro, reaching a peak in 1843 with 59 textile factories in operation. Six paper factories functioned by 1845. High tariff protection for agriculture continued until 1856, assuring Mexican landowners a guaranteed market. Artisan workers were the major group that suffered; their products could not compete with the many foreign goods that continued to reach the national market.

In general, heavy taxes at the state and local levels became the primary reason for the unspectacular growth of industry, agriculture, and commerce by the mid-1840s. If the tax policies of this period had not been so negative, the improved economic situation would have been much better. In 1843, mercury miners received various tax exemptions. Other miners, however, had to pay enormous taxes to state, municipal, and federal agencies, including a 3 percent rate for production and circulation rights. Sales taxes and ad valorem taxes on goods entering states plagued the interior. The internal customs barriers were chaotic, arbitrary, and unproductive. In states such as Michoacán, Querétaro, and Aquascalientes, local authorities imposed ad valorem taxes of 12 to 15 percent on items in return for entry and sales rights. High taxes became a hot issue that worked against Santa Anna's ability to unite the country around a theme of social stability and economic growth.

Monetary and fiscal measures are somewhat impressive. Santa Anna's outstanding finance minister stabilized the currency by ridding the system of copper coins and replacing them with bullion currency. The government also attempted to end abuses committed by pawnships that charged exaggerated interest rates for loans. Revenues for the 1843 and 1844 years became the highest since independence. Although the Santa Anna regime recorded high expenditures, it balanced the budget. The internal debt hardly increased during the early 1840s and the foreign debt actually declined. In 1842, Francisco Garay received permission from the government to establish a commercial bank. Mexican capitalism seemed to have an optimistic future. A year later, the regime allowed its Junta de Fomento y Administración de Minería to take charge of capitalizing and providing mercury to the mines. Economic and fiscal improvements as well as prudent administration no doubt encouraged Santa Anna and other Mexican leaders to believe that they could constrain their aggressive northern neighbor.

MANIFEST DESTINY AND THE RAPE OF MEXICO

Weaknesses along the Periphery. Mexico's inability to cement relations with the states farthest from Mexico City was a critical factor in the war with the United States. Political uncertainty, shaky financial conditions, and the flow of U. S. emigrants prevented Mexico from maintaining healthy ties to the frontier societies. External intervention also ruptured the possibility of forging a national identity. The upper-class in the periphery profited from U. S. trade while continuing to yearn for federalism.

California enjoyed a tranquil autonomy while New Mexico became sullen and divided. In California, the key event was the secularization of the missions in 1834. This created a large class of rancher-farmers and provided economic stability as well as godparent relationships within a less rigid class structure. Rancho life and strong family values dominated California society. Once California found that trade with New Mexico and Sonora could not develop, it formed commercial ties with U. S. merchants. This meant that, unlike Texas, the U. S. settlers in California never had to accept forced religion or taxes. New Mexico, on the other hand, was predominantly Hispanic rather than Mexican, and actively traded with U. S. merchants. But New Mexico governor Albino Pérez, an unappealing outsider, attempted to assert the centralization favored by Santa Anna. Most *nuevomexicanos* wanted municipal control of village life in the tradition of the indigenous culture. Pérez's moral and financial excesses, as well as his imposition of the authoritorian 1836 Constitution, motivated Hispanics and Indians in northern New Mexico to revolt in August 1837. The rebels killed Pérez and 16 of his officials. After the bloody uprising, Manuel Armijo defeated the rebels by means of inspired generalship and succeeded Pérez as governor.

Northern Mexico gradually felt estranged from the conservative regime in Mexico City. Long a center of federalist sentiments, the northern periphery had established a lifestyle that left its inhabitants outside the national life of Mexico. Merchants in northern and coastal areas profited from free trade rather than protectionism. Smuggling made Monterrey and Pacific coastal regions lucrative commercial areas. But the northerners had been accustomed to receiving assistance in fighting Indians, which was not forthcoming from the central government after independence. The absence of economic integration and decent roads, as well as the neglect of colonization projects, led to an eventual lapse of allegiance to the national government.

Yucatán resisted centralist rule more intensively. The white minority seized indigenous lands and water rights in order to produce sugar and henequen. Santa Anna's centralist regime angered the white elite as the national government's authoritarianism infringed upon their ability to usurp land and prosper from free trade. Higher tariffs, the stationing of federal troops, and local conscription provoked a successful revolt in Valladolid by 1839. In June 1840, the Yucatecans defeated an army sent by Santa Anna.

Yucatán determinedly asserted its autonomy. In direct defiance of Santa Anna, the legislature created an ultraliberal constitution in 1841. When Santa Anna closed off Yucatecan trade with Mexican ports, the Yucatecans hired a fleet of warships from the Texas navy while the governor hoisted a new flag for the "sovereign nation" of Yucatán. In late 1842, the Yucatecans defeated yet another Mexican army sent by Santa Anna. The compromise agreed to in Mexico City whereby Yucatán enjoyed autonomy was the *convenios* agreement of December 1843, but in February 1844, Santa Anna suddenly decreed that major Yucatecan products could not be exported dutyfree. As Santa Anna was a gulf-coast hacendado, he undoubtedly restricted Yucatecan products so that he and other coastal landowners could prosper. After Santa Anna's exile, the national government and Yucatán could not resolve the autonomy dispute. Yucatán declared its independence two weeks after the national Congress formally repudiated the *convenios* in December 1845.

Manifest Destiny and James Polk. By the 1840s, many U. S. citizens came to believe that God had preordained their expansionism across the continent. The rationale behind U. S. diplomacy was Manifest Destiny, which defended expansionism on three points. First, God had blessed the United States, allowing it to grow stronger while punishing Mexico for clinging to Catholicism; second, as U. S. pioneers spilled across the Mississippi River, they converted British and Mexican land into free, democratic areas; third, the United States was growing so rapidly that the republic needed more land. The only questions were how far the United States would expand and whether it would use diplomacy or war to do so. Fear of British interference against U. S. strategy also fueled Manifest Destiny.

James Polk strongly favored annexing Texas where two of his cousins had participated in the Texas war for independence. He triumphed in the 1844 presidential election by articulating Manifest Destiny to a boisterous public that boasted of its freedom from European tradition. Polk interpreted his victory as a mandate for expansion. Concerned that the union was shaky, Polk decided that expansionism would unify the republic. He was one of many Democrats who wanted to consolidate the union by moving westward, partially as an attempt to maintain a Jefferson-styled agricultural society because many southerners disliked an urban, industrial nation with a new working class of European immigrants. As if to underline Polk's views, Congress annexed Texas shortly before Polk's inauguration.

Origins of the U. S.–Mexican War. Both the United States and Mexico must bear responsibility for the war because they made mistakes and misunderstood the intentions of the other. Polk was determined to acquire territory by peaceful means but was not adverse to using the threat of war to accelerate the process. Mexico eventually chose to fight rather than accept the annexation of Texas or cede more territory.

Various U. S. factions supported expansion. Agrarian cupidity, desire for trade, racial prejudice, and insecurity made Manifest Destiny palatable in every region of the United States. New England merchants demanded deep-water ports in California as a link to Asian markets. The South fretted over the possibility of new states becoming free of slavery while the West was full of land speculators and feared that Europeans would seize western territories. A joint Mexican–U.S. claims commission could not satisfy the largely western claimants who demanded payment from the Mexican government. Pressure on California became acute. John Stockton attempted to provoke war during an 1845 California revolt in

which the Polk administration instructed various U. S. diplomats to obtain California.

Polk sent John Slidell, a New Orleans lawyer, to obtain agreement on the Rio Grande border, as well as to purchase California and New Mexico. Tensions increased dramatically when Mexico would not recognize Slidell's credentials. Mexico agreed to receive Slidell as a special commissioner to settle disputes but not as a resident minister. After U. S. Consul Larkin reported that the British were not really interested in obtaining California from Mexico, Polk modified his instructions to Slidell in December 1845. Now President Joaquín Herrera was to be informed that if Mexico showed no interest in selling California, then this issue should not upset the chances for normalizing relations between Mexico and the United States.

But the damage to Herrera had already been done for any Mexican leader to negotiate the surrender of national territory was tantamount to political suicide. Added to these difficulties was the small but influential Mexico City press, which, beginning in early 1845, repeatedly demanded war to resolve the Texas issue. When President Herrera appeared ready to receive Slidell, a monarchist group in Mexico adopted a belligerent tone as the Spanish strongman in Madrid, Ramón Narváez, used General Mariano Paredes as part of a complex plot to place a Spanish prince upon a Mexican throne. As Herrera tried to avoid war by discussing with his supporters whether he should receive Slidell, Paredes overthrew Herrera with the support of the monarchists. Finally, Gómez Farías led a federalist campaign which insisted upon Mexico reconquering Texas.

At this point, Polk took the initiative. First, he sent General Zachary Taylor to Corpus Christi, Texas, as part of his continued effort to claim the Rio Grande boundary. Taylor's occupation of Corpus Christi became a serious move since Corpus Christi is at the mouth of the Nueces—the southern boundary of Texas as claimed by Mexico. In an obvious attempt to intimidate Paredes, Taylor followed orders and moved his volunteer force toward the Rio Grande. U. S. warships also dropped anchor off the Mexican coast. Mexico still counted on European support, but Britain was about to peacefully settle the dispute over Oregon. At one point, Polk considered sacrificing Oregon if Britain could convince Mexico to sell California, but the aggressive Polk now found himself in a position to triumph on both fronts. The U.S.–British treaty of mid-1846 doomed Mexico to fight without European allies. Finally provoked into fighting, Mexican forces attacked a U. S. scouting party in April 1846. Polk called for war, claiming that "American blood has been shed on American soil," even though it had happened in a disputed area with virtually no U. S. citizens.

Santa Anna Leads Mexico to Defeat. Taking advantage of his charisma and the early failures of the war, Santa Anna once again appeared as Mexico's leader. Paredes' government lost prestige immediately after military disasters in Texas at Resaca de la Palma and Palo Alto. From Cuba, Santa Anna managed to conclude a secret agreement with Polk to sell Mexican territory north of the Rio Grande and end hostilities in return for U. S. aid in sending him into Mexico. The ambitious strongman also promised to reimpose the federalist 1824 Constitution, which Congress reinstated on May 18, 1847. Santa Anna increased his public appeal by opposing a monarchy. After Gómez Farías and General José Mariano Salas deposed Paredes in August 1846, they invited Santa Anna to command all of Mexico's armies. Federalism once again seemed to capture the allegiance of most. Santa Anna left Havana and met with Yucatecan leaders in Sisal where he promised to support the *convenios*. Rather than independence, Yucatán now accepted autonomy with tacit recognition of a limited role in the war with the United States.

The course of the war deteriorated sharply. Despite Santa Anna's opportunistic commitment to federalism and his cynical alliance with federalist leader Gómez Farías, Mexico was in crisis. The radical federalists, who in 1846 took the name of *puros*, could not develop alliances with senior of-

ficers, who ditched *puro* attempts to mobilize a civic militia. Santa Anna encouraged Gómez Farías to nationalize Church property up to a value of nearly 15 million pesos in order to fill the nearly empty treasury. The army had more officers than troops, but Santa Anna was at his energetic best in forming a new army. The 23,000 untrained and poorly equipped troops marched 250 miles from San Luis Potosí until Santa Anna led them to the hacienda of Buena Vista, near Saltillo. The approaching battle was crucial because Taylor had recently occupied Monterrey after three days of street-by-street fighting. Mexico took the offensive and Santa Anna fought the battle to a draw on the first evening. Santa Anna had force-marched his soldiers through desert containing little food or water. The next day, February 23, U. S. artillery proved too much for the advancing Mexican forces. These guns enabled

General Mariano Arista who was defeated at the battles of Palo Alto and Resaca de Palma. *Courtesy of Special Collections Division, The University of Texas at Arlington Libraries, Arlington, Texas.*

Taylor to maintain possession of the battlefield. As typhus killed many of his exhausted troops, Santa Anna felt compelled to retreat.

At this point, Santa Anna had lost momentum, but hard fighting continued for seven months. Mexico confronted an exalted generation of U. S. army officers. Colonel Stephen Kearney's forces overran New Mexico easily and Alexander Doniphan seized Chihuahua. In fact, El Paso fell after only a minor battle and New Mexico, as well as Tampico, capitulated without a shot. The only Mexican victory took place at San Pascual, 35 miles north of San Diego. During his retreat, Santa Anna learned that General Winfield Scott had successfully landed 5,500 U. S. troops at Veracruz against scant resistance. Many civilians died as a result of deadly fire from heavy naval guns installed behind Veracruz. After gunboats and schooners brutally hammered the hapless

General Pedro de Ampudia, who lost the battle of Monterrey. *Courtesy of Special Collections Division, The University of Texas at Arlington Libraries, Arlington, Texas.*

port, foreign consuls convinced the Mexican commander to surrender on March 27, 1847. Appalled by the rapid U. S. occupation of Veracruz, the national legislature decreed military service for all Mexican males capable of bearing arms. But a church-sponsored *polkos* militia uprising days after the Buena Vista battle also troubled Santa Anna. He responded by overthrowing Gómez Farías and obtaining a Church loan of two million pesos in return for ending anticlerical legislation. Santa Anna then departed for Cerro Gordo to confront Scott, but U. S. troops outflanked and defeated the Mexicans. As Scott approached Mexico City, U. S. casualties began to increase. But it is also obvious that Mexican support for the war was often weak.

Clearly a certain amount of collaboration took place. Although guerrilla warfare harassed U. S. advances in California and northern Mexico, many Mexicans were impressed with the ability of U. S. forces to either intimidate or pacify indigenous tribes. The upper class often believed that it had too much to lose if fighting continued. In Coahuila, the dominant Sánchez Navarro family provided supplies and equipment to U. S. forces. Saltillo, Matamoros, and Veracruz seemed to prosper under U. S. occupation. Hacendados startled many U. S. soldiers when they refused to provide Santa Anna with money. Several states did not provide national guard units because they were more concerned about preserving internal order. Other northerners prospered from sales of goods to U. S. units as well as gaining employment. Mexican women frequently nursed U. S. soldiers, foraged for food, sought water and ground corn for them. The invading troops had little difficulty in obtaining sexual liasons with Mexican females. U. S. soldiers described Mexican women as selfless and humane, although in reality, profit and survival were more realistic motivations.

More indicative of the weak ties that debilitated the war effort are the serious revolts that shook Mexico at this time. The Sierra Gorda rebellion of 1847–1850 affected the area around Guanajuato, Querétaro, and San Luis Potosí. Conscription

U.S. Army forces crossing a Mexican mountain.
Courtesy of Special Collections Division, The University of Texas at Arlington Libraries, Arlington, Texas.

and increased taxes provoked widespread discontent. And the sale of communal lands, particularly in Querétaro, Mexico state, and Puebla, mobilized indigenous communi-ties against the Mexican authorities. Furthermore, selling Querétaro clerical property provoked uprisings by January 1847. Before long, indigenous revolts spread throughout the state of Veracruz. Some rebels, as at the mine of Xichú, Guanajuato, actually proclaimed their support for the U. S. invaders.

The caste war in Yucatán became the most serious episode of national disunity. After Yucatán declared its reincorporation into Mexico during the autumn of 1846, the local elite imposed high taxes, forced labor, and expanded haciendas at the expense of village lands. Despite Mérida's constant clamor for decentralization, the Yucatecan legislature's penchant for authoritarian rule provoked nearby Campeche to revolt successfully. Fearful that U. S. naval forces would destroy their merchant fleet, Mérida's new rulers proclaimed neutrality for Yucatán. Troubled by the U. S. occupation of Carmen and Laguna, Yucatán attempted to gain U. S. recognition of its sovereignty. In February 1847, however, the Maya revolted with the intention of killing all the whites. The Maya succeeded in besieging Mérida and managed to control 80 percent of the peninsula. Eventually, 300,000 died, nearly half of Yucatán's population. As the whites contemplated disaster in early 1848, Yucatán's governor dramatically offered to accept annexation in return for foreign assistance in crushing the indigenous revolt. Not surprisingly, Polk urged the U. S. Congress to accept Yucatán's offer. Yucatán's experience during the war with the United States points out the tragic lack of social unity in Mexico. Chiapas and Tabasco considered uniting with Guatamala. Yucatán, however, became unique in that it courted the United States and Europe more blatantly than others.

The contrast in nationalistic attitudes within both countries is striking. In the United States, some states offered tax extensions or large awards as volunteers aroused adulation. National music, poetry, and enthusiasm encouraged many communities to contribute food, clothing, and money to the poor families who provided volunteers. In Mexico, unenthusiastic conscripts from Morelos, Guerrero, and Oaxaca returned to find their lands seized by local governments.

After Scott approached Mexico City, the battles became bloodier. After bitter fighting at Molino del Rey, Mexican defenders killed U. S. troops who had been wounded earlier. At Churubusco, Scott's forces encountered several hundred U. S. deserters, mostly Irish Catholics earlier formed into the San Patricio group who fought hard; all

General Antonio León, commander of the Oaxaca Brigade at the battle of Molino Rey, where he was killed in action. *Courtesy of Special Collections Division, The University of Texas at Arlington Libraries, Arlington, Texas.*

but the rest remained. The cadets resisted furiously when it became apparent that Scott's troops intended to kill all the defenders. Most of the cadets died or were taken prisoner. According to Mexican legend, although no proof exists, one cadet hauled the flag down, wrapped it around his shoulders, and hurled himself to death from the castle's walls. The *niños heróes* (boy heroes) thus became a symbol of nationalistic patriotism. The real heroes of Chapultepec were 400 soldiers of the San Blas Batallion, who attempted to halt the U. S. units on the eastern sloope of the hill. Only one officer and a handful of soldiers survived while the rest died on the battlefield. After U. S. forces captured the city's gates, General William J. Worth accepted the capital's surrender. Santa Anna and 10,000 troops proceeded to flee, triggering a wave of robbery and crime. A new government of moderates relieved Santa Anna of his command while both sides contemplated a peace agreement.

but 71 were killed or taken prisoner during the Contreras battle. U. S. forces subsequently tried and executed 50; they whipped and branded the remainder. Of the 1,300 troops facing U. S. forces at Churubusco on August 20, 700 were civic militia who fought hard until running out of ammunition. But the most emotional scene followed.

A vital topographic position, Chapultepec castle was the last major barrier standing between U. S. forces and the capital. Defended by 100 Colegio Militar cadets and about 1,000 troops, Chapultepec appeared to hold a formidable position. Scott feigned an attack on one of the Mexico City causeways that successfully fooled Santa Anna, who retreated into the capital. Heavy artillery bombardment demoralized the defenders; then three U. S. divisions attacked on September 12, 1847. After the cadets were ordered to withdraw, because they were too young for combat, 50 retired

General Gabriel Valencia, overwhelmed at Pedregal near Mexico City. *Courtesy of Special Collections Division, The University of Texas at Arlington Libraries, Arlington, Texas.*

The Treaty of Guadalupe Hidalgo. The peace agreement that ended the war achieved most of Polk's strategic goals but created enormous problems for Mexico. This loss of land and wealth also provided the environment for the economic and social disenfranchisement of Mexican descendants in the southwest.

Negotiations for terminating the conflict nearly failed because of Polk's and Santa Anna's unrealistic ambitions. Discussions actually began when Scott and Nicholas Trist, Polk's emissary, agreed to Santa Anna's overtures for a bribe in return for a favorable peace agreement. Santa Anna pocketed the $10,000 advance, but after the fall of Chapultepec, Santa Anna agreed to an armistice and appointed commissioners to negotiate. During the inconclusive discussions, however, Santa Anna used the truce to fortify Mexico City. Meanwhile, Polk contemplated annexing all of Mexico and recalled Trist. Polk also began forcing Mexico to pay for the costs of an unlimited occupation by means of forced indemnities. Scott demanded that state governments forward their customary tax revenue to him as if the occupation forces were a new nation-state.

At this point, Trist asserted himself. Santa Anna resigned and the head of the supreme court, Manuel de la Peña y Peña, became interim president. A moderate, Peña y Peña represented the upper-class fear that protracted warfare and unlimited occupation might erase Mexico from the map. Pressed by both Scott and Peña y Peña to remain, Trist disobeyed Polk's recall in order to continue peace discussions. Scott received an additional 1,400 troops in January 1848 and seized Toluca while threatening to capture Querétaro if results were not forthcoming.

A harsh treaty emerged from the village of Guadalupe Hidalgo. Sadly, the midday signing took place at a cathedral which was a shrine of the Virgin of Guadalupe. Here the virgin had supposedly appeared. Trist had threatened to break off negotiations earlier but persuaded British diplomats to pressure the three Mexican commissioners to finally agree to his terms. The United States gained California, New Mexico, Arizona, and parts of Colorado, as well as Wyoming, at the cost of $15 million and the assumption of $3.25 million in new claims by U. S. citizens against Mexico, and pledged protection of the Mexicans who decided to remain in the southwest. Although ratified in Mexico, the U. S. Congress attempted to weaken the clauses that protected the rights of former Mexican citizens.

The war and its resulting treaty created a distrust of the United States that still remains. Native Americans discovered that, although the treaty confirmed 35 Spanish land grants, local courts would not protect these holdings. As a class, Mexican Americans became economically inferior and politically impotent. After arbitrary state governments dispossessed much of their land, Mexican Ameicans sank into poverty and faced discrimination. Indian raids into Mexico from the southwest continued unabated. The gold boom in California heightened animosities. Just as the Santa Anna regime began to develop an economic, fiscal, and financial revival in the early 1840s, military defeat led to the loss of vast, rich resources to the United States. Most Mexicans continued to believe that the war was an invasion that allowed the United States to steal their northern frontier. This conviction encouraged migration into the southwest throughout the twentieth century. Finally, it became clear that in political terms, Mexico was still not a nation.

Domestic turmoil continued after the war. Many of the Sierra Gorda rebels fought on after the conflict because as army deserters, they did not qualify for amnesty. In order to consolidate power, the postwar regimes reduced taxes for hacendados and established military colonies. Filibustering, smuggling, and cattle rustlers plagued the northern frontier. The national government also dispatched arms and cash to the Yucatán. By now, Yucatecan *ayuntamientos* made it clear that reincorporation was paramount. Reunion occurred on August 17, 1848, when Mexico recognized Yucatán as sovereign in terms of internal administration yet subject to the national constitution. Yucatán lost its autonomy but preserved its socioeconomic system as a result.

The moderate Herrera was elected in 1848 for a two-year term and served his mandate despite *puro* and conservative opposition. When Paredes attempted but failed to throw Herrera out in 1848, conservatives formed a political party—Mexico's first—and swept the 1849 elections in Mexico City. But moderates retained control of most state legislatures, which chose Mariano Arista as president for the 1850–1854 term.

But when Arista cut military expenditures, conservatives persuaded army officers to revolt, which they did successfully. Conservative envoys scoured Europe for a suitable monarch but did not find anyone to their liking. Santa Anna agreed to return.

Santa Anna made one final appearance on the Mexican political scene. In order to stabilize the country, the respected Alamán convinced the legislature to request Santa Anna to serve as president for one year while a suitable monarch could be found. Unfortunately, Alamán died, leaving Santa Anna free to impose a national unity regime that revealed his usual characteristics in April 1853.

In the 1830s, Bustamante created a Dirección General de la Industria Nacional, which inaugurated a policy that encouraged collaboration among producers of the same commodity. This policy flourished well into the late twentieth century. By pooling their capital to create larger factories, producers increased efficiency. In 1853, the government reorganized the Dirección General as the Secretario de Fomente upon the recommendation of Miguel Lerdo de Tejada. The Fomente ministry endeavored to attract European immigrants. An 1854 federal commercial code standardized and secularized the procedures in the chambers of commerce. In addition to Church, military, and commercial courts, Mexico had tribunals for miners and vagrants. One panel tried infractions of laws concerning censorship and libel.

Authoritarian attempts to rule failed. After the Gadsden Treaty, Santa Anna once again restricted trade with the United States and attempted to make Mexico as self-sufficient as possible. The support given by the newly increased army was an important means by which Santa Anna could remain at the head of his authoritarian state. Agitation against his dictatorship increased, particularly when the government required citizens to obtain internal passports for domestic travel, as in Uruguay and Argentina. To please a lavish court and restless army officers, Santa Anna sold more national territory.

The United States was eager to acquire additional territory in the southwest. Mistakes committed in measuring the new post-1848 boundary, as well as claims presented by both sides for various violations, increased pressure upon Mexico to cede more land. U. S. railroad interests demanded a new route that would pass through the Mesilla Valley, an area west of El Paso occupied by many U. S. citizens who refused to recognize the governor of Chihuahua. In fact, the governor of New Mexico loudly demanded U. S. occupation of the area. To settle this problem, as well as disputes arising from attempts by U. S. builders to construct a railroad through Tehuantepec, James Gadsden arrived in Mexico as a special negotiator. A railroad builder himself, the aggressive Gadsden adopted an uncompromising attitude that, combined with the threat of military action, persuaded Santa Anna to part with more territory. In exchange for $10 million, Mexico lost 30,000 square miles along the Gila River by means of the Gadsden Treaty.

Santa Anna could not survive the resulting outcry over the Gadsden purchase of 1853. U. S. miners discovered great mineral wealth in the fertile Mesilla Valley. Mexico had now lost half its territory within six years. The conservatives had now discredited themselves, and it became apparent that Mexico needed sweeping institutional changes. In 1855, the liberals would respond to the desire for change by overthrowing Santa Anna and embarking upon a new interpretation of national identity. Ironically, the U. S.–Mexican War would indirectly trigger civil wars in both the United States and Mexico by 1861.

SUGGESTED READING

Bauer, Jack. *The Mexican War*. Lincoln: University of Nebraska Press, 1974.

Benjamin, Thomas. "Recent Historiography of the Origins of the Mexican War." *New Mexico Historical Review* 54:3 (1979), 169–181.

Calderon de la Barca, Frances. *Life in Mexico*. London: Dent, 1973.

Camarillo, Albert. *Chicanos in a Changing Society*. Cambridge, MA: Harvard University Press, 1979.

Chamberlain, Samuel. *My Confession: The Recollections of a Rogue*. Lincoln: University of Nebraska Press, 1987.

Connor, Seymor and Odie Faulk. *North America Divided: The Mexican War, 1846–1848*. New York: Oxford University Press, 1971.

Costeloe, Michael P. *The Central Republic in Mexico, 1835–1846*. New York: Cambridge University Press, 1993.

Curtis, Samuel Ryan. *Mexico under Fire*. Forth Worth: Texas Christian University Press, 1994.

de la Peña, José Enrique. *With Santa Anna in Texas*. College Station: Texas A&M University Press, 1974.

Eisenhower, John. *So Far From God: The U. S. War with Mexico, 1846–1848*. New York: Random House, 1989.

Fowler, Will. *Tornel and Santa Anna: The Writer and the Caudillo, Mexico 1795–1853*. Westport, Ct: Greenwood Press, 2000.

Francaviglia, Richard G. and Douglas W. Richmond, eds. *Dueling Eagles: Reinterpreting the U.S.–Mexican War, 1846-1848*. Forth Worth: Texas Christian University Press, 2000.

Griswold del Castillo, Richard. *The Treaty of Guadalupe Hidalgo: A Legacy of Conflict*. Norman: University of Oklahoma Press, 1990.

Haynes, Samuel. *Soldiers of Misfortune: The Somervell and Mier Expeditions*. Austin: University of Texas Press, 1990.

———. *James K. Polk and the Expansionist Impulse*. New York: Harper Collins, 1996.

Henson, Margaret S. *Juan Davis Bradburn*. College Station: Texas A&M University Press, 1982.

———. *Samuel May Williams: Early Texas Entrepreneur*. College Station: Texas A&M University Press, 1976.

Herrera Serna, Laura, ed. *Mexico en guerra*. Mexico City: Consejo Nacional Para La Cultura y los Artes, 1996.

Johannsen, Robert W. *To the Halls of the Montezuma*. New York: Oxford University Press, 1985.

Lack, Paul. *The Texas Revolutionary Experience: A Political and Social History*. College Station: Texas A&M University Press, 1992.

Lecompte, Janet. *Rebellion in Rio Arriba, 1837*. Albuquerque: University of New Mexico Press, 1985.

López Rosado, Diego G. *Historia y pensamiento economico de Mexico*, 5 vols. Mexico City: UNAM, 1968-1972.

Miller, Robert Ryal. *Shamrock and Sword: Saint Patrick's Batallion in the U. S.–Mexican War*. Norman: University of Oklahoma Press, 1989.

McLean, Malcolm D. *Papers Concerning Robertson's Colony in Texas*. 16 vols. Arlington, TX: The UTA Press, 1977–1989.

McDonald, Archie P. *William Barret Travis: Commander of the Alamo*. Austin, TX: Eakin Press, 1988.

Pitt, Leonard. *The Decline of the Californios*. Berkeley: University of California Press, 1971.

Pletcher, David. *The Diplomacy of Annexation: Texas, Oregon, and the Mexican War*. Columbia: University of Missouri Press, 1973.

Price, Glenn W. *Origins of the War with Mexico: The Polk-Stockton Intrigue*. Austin: University of Texas Press, 1967.

Reed, Nelson. *The Caste War of Yucatán*. Stanford, CA: Stanford University Press, 1964.

Reina, Leticia. "The Sierra Gorda Peasant Rebellion, 1847–50." In Friedrich Katz, *Riot, Rebellion, and Revolution*. Princeton,NJ: Princeton University Press, 1988, pp. 269–294.

Richmond, Douglas W. "Yucatán's Struggle for Sovereignty during the Mexican-U.S. Conflict, 1836–1848." In Richard Sanchez, Eric Van Young, and Gisela Von Wobeser, eds., *La ciudad y el campo en la historia de México*. Mexico City: Instituto de Investigaciones Históricas, Universidad Autonoma de México, 1992, pp. 173–183.

———, ed. *Essays on the Mexican War*. College Station: Texas A&M University Press, 1986.

Santoni, Pedro. "A Fear of the People: The Civic Militia of Mexico in 1845." *Hispanic American Historical Review* 65:2 (May 1988) pp. 269–288.

———. *Mexicans at Arms: Puro Federalists and the Politics of War, 1845-1848*. Fort Worth: Texas Christian University Press, 1996.

———. "The Failure of Mobilization: The Civic Militia of Mexico in 1846." *Mexican Studies/Estudios Mexicanos* 12:2 (Summer 1996), 169–194.

Sellers, Charles. *James K. Polk, Continentalist: 1843–1846*. Princeton, NJ: Princeton University Press, 1966.

Vaughan, Mary Kay. "Primary Education and Literacy

in Nineteenth Century Mexico." *Latin American Research Review* 25:1 (1990), 36–66.

Velasco, Márquez, Jesús. *La guerra del 47 y la opinión pública (1845–1848)*. Mexico City: Secretaría de Educatión Pública, 1975.

Weber, David. *The Mexican Frontier, 1821–1846: The American Southwest Under Mexico*. Albuquerque: University of New Mexico Press, 1982.

Winders, Richard Bruce. *Mr. Polk's Army: The American Military Experience in the Mexican War*. College Station: Texas A&M University Press, 1997.

Zoraida Vásquez, Josefina and Lorenzo Meyer. *The United States and Mexico*. Chicago: University of New Mexico Press, 1985.

Zoraida Vásquez, Josefina, ed. *De la rebelión de Texas a la guerra del 47*. Mexico City: Nueva Imagen, 1994.

———, ed. *La fundación del estado mexicano (1821–1855)*. Mexico City: Nueva Imagen, 1994.

———, ed. *México al tiempo de su guerra con Estados Unidos (1846–1848)*. Mexico City: Fondo de Cultura Económica, 1997.

9

Civil War and French Intervention, 1855–1876

Both liberals and monarchists could not interpret Mexican society in order to unite the country. The liberals brandished doctrinaire ideological solutions to the task of nation building without considering their ramifications. La Reforma, as liberals defined their policy, attacked the church and village communities but never replaced them with functional alternatives. Unrest resulted. The economy remained weak; liberal policy shifted from idealism to authoritarianism. Determined to maintain Hispanic continuity but unwilling to yield outmoded privileges, the conservatives committed costly mistakes before and during Maximilian's rule. The steadfast resistance of Juárez, the refusal of many liberals to compromise and U.S.pressure in conjunction with adverse changes in Europe doomed French imperialism. Modernization accelerated during the restored republic, but the destruction of indigenous and religious institutions continued unabated.

BENITO JUÁREZ AND THE LIBERAL TRIUMPH

Background of Juárez. The complex, ambitious Juárez emerged from humble origins. At the age of three, Juárez went to live with his grandparents after his Zapotec parents died. Hearing of opportunities in Oaxaca city, Juárez left the mountains to work for a bookbinder until he studied in a local seminary. Devout in his youth, Juárez, nevertheless had two illegitimate children. In 1827, the liberals established an Institute of Arts and Science in Oaxaca where Juárez studied political economy, experimental science, and law. As a student, Juárez became an alderman in the Oaxaca municipality; he moved on to the state congress in 1833 while teaching physics.

In 1834, Juárez attracted attention as an anticlerical. He defended villages against priests who demanded payment for expensive parish fees. Juárez now considered *fueros* the means by which privileged groups exploited society. When civil authorities jailed him and his clients at the request of ecclesiastical officials, an appalled Juárez concluded that the *fueros* also infringed upon national sovereignty.

Juárez soon became pragmatic in his quest for power. A full-time politician by 1843, Juárez married a woman of Italian origin. A year later, he became the governor's secretary and sat on the Oaxaca supreme court. Even though he accepted middle-class status, Juárez continued to oppose prosecution of those unable to pay tithes. Although quiet in the legislature, Juárez eventually gained respect for his leadership. Appointed provisional governor in 1847, Juárez was one of the few governors to support the national government during the war with the United States. Juárez also added 50 new schools after his 1848 reelection as governor and encouraged the education of women. His public works program resulted in new ports and roads. A conciliatory policy with the Church reveals his realism; subordinates aided the Church in collecting fees and handled touchy complaints concerning the church, but Juárez never did so directly.

Santa Anna's decline led directly to Juárez's ascendancy. Recalling that Juárez had denied him access through Oaxaca earlier, Santa Anna exiled Juárez once the "perpetual dictator" resumed control in 1853. Juárez used his banishment to New Orleans to read constitutional law and learn from Melchor Ocampo and other exiles. Ocampo advocated a mass-based Spanish *purismo* while Juárez embraced an elitist *modernismo* variation. The Gadsden Purchase fiasco encouraged serious rebellion. Regional caudillos and caciques would not tolerate further interference in their areas after Santa Anna broke his earlier promise to leave them alone. A rich Guerrero hacendado, Juan Alvarez, advocated popular demands and led liberal forces during his Ayutla revolt. After Alvarez's forces occupied Mexico City in 1855, Juárez became minister of justice and public education in the new government.

The unity of the victors was short-lived. Alvarez and the liberals agreed on federalism but little else. Alvarez advocated Guerrero villagers' land aspirations. Alvarez had dominated Guerrero for 30 years in a traditional style. Purely regional, Alvarez had no well-defined ideology. In addition to liberal ideologues such as Juárez and Ocampo, Alvarez turned administration over to Ignacio Comonfort, who had managed Acapulco for Alvarez prior to Santa Anna's collapse.

Liberal Ideology. War with the United States convinced liberals that anticlericalism, free trade, secular education, and civil liberties would establish a modern state. However, the contradiction between a self-serving elite and the liberal ideal of individual freedom resulted in an inability to articulate common goals. Juárez did not always represent mass needs. Class interests and social prejudices made the liberals hostile toward rural Mexicans. The rise of the liberals also represents fundamental social changes. About two-thirds of liberal leaders came from the numerically superior *mestizo* group. Many represented the periphery, which resented the traditional core center.

Liberal ideology underwent a transformation by the mid-1850s. Calls to free the individual from the Hispanic past and guarantees for civil as well as regional freedoms persisted. Reducing the central government's power appealed particularly to northerners and southerners. More than ever, a reduction in corporate privilege seemed to ensure a commitment to represent society more completely. Therefore, the liberals planned to reduce the *fueros* of the army, Church, university, and indigenous communities.

Attacks upon the church mounted. Specifically, the liberals decided to reduce clerical control of land, capital, vital statistics, and education. By now, the Church owned one-fifth of all Mexican land. Clerical control of much more land increased because the Church continued to demand land as security for mortgages. The liberals believed that clerical privileges limited economic growth and restricted individual freedom, but most Mexicans continued to give their loyalty to the Church. Popular songs and verse still reflected basic religious beliefs. Yet the liberals hoped to establish a modern state that would make the *patria* (fatherland) Mexico's basic source of loyalty.

The new state proclaimed a reduction of privilege but fostered racial inequality. The army and Church would now have to respect a national judicial system. The liberals also yearned to overhaul the educational system in order to produce citizens concerned with research, debate, social sciences, language skills, and the aura of science. Unfortunately, the liberal state became frankly elitist because liberals continued to view themselves as a class apart from Indians. Never interested in the pre-Hispanic past, liberals decided to seize indigenous communal lands on the rationale that municipal governments and ambitious individuals could develop such land more rationally. Indians were 3.5 million of Mexico's 8 million inhabitants, but scarcely a word about them appears in Juárez's massive correspondence.

At the core of liberal beliefs was the concept that ownership of property by a "progressive" class would provide more security. Naturally, small landowners would be the new political base, a situation which actually occurred in Spain under similar conditions at the same time. Liberals considered obstacles to obtaining wealth the weakness of Mexican development. Therefore, they assumed that free trade would provide benefits to a country that continued to depend upon mining and agriculture. Firm believers in the virtues of science and capital, many liberals accepted the notion that Mexico should become a U.S.protectorate. Not surprisingly, the 1856 tariff lowered the duties on U.S.finished cotton goods by 70 percent; general protection against U.S.goods was a tariff charge of only 30 percent.

The Liberals in Power, 1855–1858. After formally electing Alvarez as president, the liberals subverted their principles without establishing a viable social program. Eager to protect hacendados, the liberals became insensitive to the masses. The liberals failed to execute their legislative agenda and placed excessive faith in their characteristic individualism. The liberals also misunderstood the Church's capacity to resist, which led to increased conflict.

In November 1855, Juárez implemented his Ley Juárez. This mild legislation limited the *fueros* of the military and the clergy. The law restricted their courts; military and ecclesiastical courts could no longer hear civil cases. The Ley Juárez also annulled the *leva* draft, since military conscription had become highly unpopular and liberals hoped for a national guard to become more prominent. Bland compared to future decrees, the Ley Juárez provoked conservative protests, which motivated Alvarez to resign in December 1855. Ignacio Comonfort, a moderate liberal, became the new chief executive.

In June 1856, Treasury Minister Miguel Lerdo de Tejada ordered all corporate institutions to sell or disamortize their property. His Ley Lerdo was a momentous nineteenth-century event that would have a direct bearing on property relations throughout the twentieth century. The Church and its institutions now had to surrender all land not used for religious purposes. The law not only abolished mortmain, the perpetual ownership of church land, but also forced the sale of municipal and village land. Tenants and lessees were to receive the land in return for paying interest to the Church on the purchase price, an amount roughly equivalent to rents previously paid. The Ley Lerdo intended to create tax revenue by making property subject to market demands. The government collected a 5 percent tax on all land transactions. Proclaimed as a measure to create a nation of small farmers. the law achieved exactly the opposite: Hacendados, politicians, and merchants purchased the bulk of disentailed lands.

The Ley Lerdo reflects the self-serving nature of the liberals. Lerdo himself had been a consistent supporter of Mexican annexation to the United States and served both the pro-U.S. Mexico City *ayuntamiento* in 1847 as well as Santa Anna shortly thereafter. Lerdo cynically supported the Reforma when he realized that Veracruz and Mexico City merchants could profit. Lerdo, Comonfort, Juárez, José Maria Iglesias, and José Maria Lafragua all acquired Church property. Speculators used liberal legislation to acquire clerical land at bargain prices while indigenous communities suffered more than ever because they lost *ejido* lands as well as religious expression. Created during an economic depression, the Ley Lerdo did little to stimulate economic growth.

Prominent landowners profited most from the Ley Lerdo. Foreign control of the post-1821 Mexican economy actually seeded its early roots in the Reforma rather than the Porfiriato because textile manufacturers sold factories to French investors in order to enjoy the status of landed estates. The liberal regime gained little income from land transactions because the liberals overestimated Church wealth and placed too much land on the market in a short period. The Tabascan Church owned virtually no land while confiscated Church land in Yucatán consisted of one or two small plots adjacent to village churches. The Ley Lerdo declared civil jurispendence on all property, but the law became a parody of liberal ideals for small landowners. Now spared from the burden of clerical tithes, annuity payments, and interest accruing on large mortgages, the hacendados raised levels of profitability. Moreover, the gradual decline of indigenous communities provided hacendados with cheap labor and extra land. Nunneries began to disappear.

In early 1857, the Ley Iglesias became the most beneficial feature of the Reforma. This controversial law required the Church to provide free religious services to the poor. Others would pay modest fees. Because some priests invested fees from marriage, burial, and the sacraments into personal farms, ranches, and stores, these charges became high after the 1830s. In fact, several priests demanded more money than the Church authorized, to the point that corpses often went unburied in certain areas.

Melchor Ocampo became involved in a sinister incident which illustrates the vulnerability of clerics to liberal attacks upon their privileges. In 1851, a Michoacán priest refused to bury a widow's husband because she could not pay. When the widow asked what to do, the priest reportedly told her to salt and eat the body. After a polemical battle with the priest, Ocampo responded by calling for reduced fees charged for performance of the sacraments. Although Indians tended to trust the clergy, *mestizos* and professionals accepted Comonfort's 1857 decision to have civil authorities register births, marriages, adoptions, and deaths. The stigma of illegitimacy for failure to pay ecclesiastical fees had been extremely painful for poor Mexicans.

Not all Indians opposed Juárez. The effect of doing away with personal services in the 1850s enabled liberals such as Porfirio Díaz in Oaxaca and Juan Mendez in Puebla to attract large numbers of indigenous supporters. Wealthy families,

clergy, and local governments benefited from compulsory, unrenumerated services. When Juárez banned personal services, many Indians enrolled in national guard units. Liberal promises of autonomy also appealed to some indigenous communities.

The 1857 Constitution codified previous liberal legislation and outlined their vision of Mexico. In order to retain the republican flavor of early Mexican liberalism, the new constitution became somewhat federalistic. The delegates who wrote the document believed that constitutions anchored the success of U.S.and British societies; therefore, they studied the U.S.Constitution uncritically as a backlash against Santa Anna's nationalism. Moreover, the attack upon rural and clerical Mexico continued. Article 27 declared that indigenous and civil communities could not own *ejidos*. Catholicism was no longer the national religion. Encouragement of lay education angered the church. The state acquired more power than under the 1824 Constitution. Congress had the right to remove governors and a strengthened judiciary presided over an elaborate bill of rights. The 1857 Constitution abolished *fueros*, provided the right to *habeas corpus*, and ruled that indebtedness could not be grounds for jail sentences. Conservatives protested and the papacy refused to accept the 1857 Constitution as the clerical issue became more inflammatory than ever.

Villagers and indigenous communities suffered greatly from the liberal program. Comonfort established a vagrancy law in 1857 that seemed designed to make Indians serve as peons for the hacendados. Resentful of their landless status, many Indians succumbed to disease, malnutrition, and alcoholism. The expropriation of their communal lands helped precipitate a deadly destruction of forests because Indians did not want to become hacienda laborers or tenant farmers; they preferred living on a subsistence level. Despite this threat to the forests, the liberals considered conservation a hindrance to their illusory economic plans. Persecution of Indians became more savage than that of the gauchos by contemporary Argentine and Uruguayan governments, who also used vagrancy laws to repress rural inhabitants. Enforcing the law was a key feature of liberal attempts to decide justice within the context of a stronger state. On April 19, 1862, the Yucatecan legislature withdrew legal recognition of *compradrazgo*, a basic feature of Hispanic tradition that had united families for centuries. The liberals arrogantly assumed that they could supervise intimate personal relationships better than their own citizens. Indians preferred living on communal lands, but the liberals hoped that foreigners would develop rural areas because they had no confidence in their own people. Unlike Brazil and Argentina, however, few immigrants arrived. In 1857, Comonfort ordered all citizens to register with the government and removed civil rights from those who refused. Requiring a loyalty oath to the new constitution also disturbed many. Meanwhile, municipal governments lost power to state legislatures throughout the mid-to-late 1850s as elitism rather than the liberal rhetoric of equality blossomed.

Women gained little during the liberal period. The double sexual standard remained on an unchallenged basis. A married woman's legal status continued largely unchanged. Widows, however, received the right to govern their children. Ecclesiastical divorce remained the only form of legal separation until the liberals introduced civil separation in 1870. Wife abuse existed at all levels of Mexican society, but it became less tolerable in extreme manifestations, particularly in regard to violence and drunkenness. Compared to the late colonial period, mobilization of women declined.

Civil War, 1858–1860. Mexican society became so polarized over ideological issues by 1857 that civil war resulted. Aware that the enforcement of liberal legislation was incendiary, Comonfort resigned when clerical protests in Puebla indicated that major violence would break out. Juárez succeeded Comonfort since Juárez was next in the line of succession; Congress had elected Juárez to be president of the supreme court in 1855.

Juárez immediately confronted his adversaries. Austere and self-righteous, Juárez became stubborn. He resented the Church for having more income than the federal government. Conflict became inevitable because the Church decided that the Reforma had to be stopped at all costs; clerics could not envision compromise. General Félix Zuloaga revolted with the aid of virtually the entire army and clergy.

Meanwhile, Juárez obtained support from the periphery. Ignacio Pesquiera, who persecuted Mayo and Yaqui Indians in Sonora from 1856 to 1876, is a fine example of liberal caudillos who supported Juárez. Like Juárez, many hacendados in positions of power believed that peasants were obstacles to progress as long as they were Indians. Liberals consistently sought to gain control of community lands. Veracruz provided the most critical support. Its strong liberal tradition evolved from firm desires for laissez-faire doctrine, anticlericalism, and education as pivotal forces that should guide Mexico. Well-known *veracruzanos* such as Lerdo, Ignacio de la Llave, José María Mata, and Manuel Gutiérrez Zamora became key leaders during the struggle against Zuloaga. For three critical years, Governor Gutiérrez Zamora and the merchants provided financial support to Juaristas in return for valuable land concessions. Land sales enabled Juárez to purchase weapons and form an army.

Another reason for Juárez's success was his harmonious relationship with the United States. Desperate for funds, the liberals realized that Europe would not provide aid because of Mexico's indebtedness and unpaid European claims. On each of three attempts to establish formal economic relations with the United States, the liberals considered making Mexico into a U.S. satellite. Washington's consistent strategy was to demand Mexican territory. Nevertheless, the liberals preserved sovereignty without sacrificing territory but granted notable U.S. influence over Mexico's economic future.

The McLane-Ocampo Treaty in 1859 illustrates why U.S. relations were friendly. For only $4 million, the United States obtained access rights across Tehuantepec for 99 years. In addition, the United States received exclusive rights to develop northern Mexico and could send its troops to "protect" these areas. Fortunately, the U.S.Senate did not ratify such an onerous treaty; but Juárez gave serious thought to selling Baja California for $15 million.

The conservatives committed worse blunders. After they captured Juárez, the conservatives allowed him to flee. Zuloaga then returned Church property to clerics. Therefore, many landowners became uneasy or even reluctant to support Zuloaga. The Jecker bonds scandal became Zuloaga's most critical error. A Swiss banker, Jean Jecker, loaned 750,000 pesos to Zuloaga in return for bonds worth 15 million pesos. The conservatives lost their early military advantage partially because of their inability to reform the Church. Only a minority of Mexicans aided the Church in central Mexico. More became indifferent because of scandals committed by the Church hierarchy. Nonpayment of debts, seducing girls, and robbing religious ornaments from churches offended many, with the result that liberal forces became twice as large as conservative units.

Juárez became a tenacious leader who understood the political aspects of military struggle better than Zuloaga. The Juaristas enlisted the aid of bandits assuming that they could quell the disorder once liberal forces regained Mexico City. Juárez also decreed that all properties restored by Zuloaga's regime had to be returned to the original buyers. Even in conservative areas, such land became very attractive because Juárez sold or returned these properties for a fraction of their actual value. Export merchants, such as José Limantour, obtained 500,000 pesos worth of Church property in Mexico City in return for 25,000 rifles. Other Veracruz merchants received title to lands occupied by conservatives for merely a 5 percent tax.

Juárez continued to attack the Church fiercely. A series of decrees in July 1859 separated Church from state, nationalized Church land, suppressed orders, prohibited habits, and closed convents. In 1860, Juárez decreed religious toleration and abolished many religious holidays. Organizational skill rather than clerical xenophobia also enabled Juárez to prevail. After the death of 15,000, the liberals entered Mexico City in January 1861. Juárez presided over an exhausted Mexico and a subservient military. The conservatives appeared doomed until foreign intervention once again renewed civil war.

MAXIMILIAN AND FRENCH INTERVENTION, 1861–1867

Napoleon III and French Imperialism. Juárez could not stave off European intervention. He announced that all claims would be considered and offered assurances to investors. The government continued to sell nationalized property, but lack of capital meant that such properties could not be converted into cash to pay debts and compensate former tenants. With bankruptcy approaching, the regime suspended payment on the foreign debt in July 1861. France responded by summoning Spain and Britain to a London conference where they decided to force Mexico to pay by sending a joint fleet. Civil war in the United States facilitated their intervention. Once European navies arrived in Veracruz, Juárez promised to resume payment on the foreign debt as soon as possible; Spain and Britain agreed and prepared to leave, but France decided to seize control of Mexico.

French imperialism rested upon poorly conceived, greedy motives. After Juárez defeated Zuloaga, Jecker approached the Duke de Morny, Napoleon III's illegitimate half-brother, and offered him 30 percent of the Jecker bonds. Constantly in debt but influential at the royal court, Morny accepted the deal with the unsurprising result that Jecker's claim became a pretext for French intervention. Morny also made Jecker a French citizen. In order to obtain payment of the Jecker bonds, Morny installed his clone, the unscrupulous Count Alphonse de Saligny, as French minister to Mexico.

The ambitious Napoleon III attempted to bolster his reputation as a force to be reckoned with. Napoleon and his Spanish wife, Queen Eugénie, viewed French intervention as an opportunity to rebuild a French empire in the Americas. In addition, they hoped to gain Catholic support in France by smashing the anticlerical Juárez. Determined to acquire economic wealth in Mexico, Napoleon shared Eugénie's conviction that they had a duty to check the decline of Catholics throughout the world and reduce Anglo-American influence. Since 1830, French diplomats in Mexico had consistently believed that monarchy would be the best method to rebuild Mexico. Napoleon III assumed that a majority of the Mexican upper class would support a monarchy, thus making his undertaking relatively simple. French belief in Mexican inferiority convinced Napoleon that any resistance could be brushed aside easily.

Conservative Mexican exiles also paved the way for French intervention. José Gutiérrez de Estrada became the leading royalist. As a handsome young diplomat in Madrid, Gutiérrez de Estrada encouraged a Santa Anna scheme to have a European prince installed upon a Mexican throne so that Santa Anna could manipulate him. José Manuel Hidalgo was another monarchist who became intimate with the Countess of Montijo, mother of Eugénie. Hidalgo, who became involved with Eugénie as early as 1857, broached the subject of a French protectorate in Mexico with Napoleon and Eugénie while sailing in the Bay of Biscay. Much of Napoleon's superficial knowledge about Mexico came from unscrupulous Mexican exiles, who had rarely lived in Mexico and preferred Europe.

Largely because no one else wanted the task, the French decided upon the Archduke Ferdinand Maximilian to represent their scheme. Maximilian became the pawn for countless maneuvers. Probably the son of Napoleon II and the queen of Austria, he became the favorite in the Austrian court and next in the line of succession behind his brother, Franz Josef. Since Franz Josef resented Maximilian's popularity, he became willing to approve Napoleon III's venture. Commander of the Austri-

an navy from 1850 to 1854, Maximilian married the Belgian Princess Charlotte. The newly wedded couple governed Austrian possessions in Venice and Milan as somewhat popular rulers. When France defeated Austria in a war over northern Italy, Maximilian and Charlotte became unemployed monarchs. At his newly constructed castle along the Adriatic Sea, Maximilian enjoyed gardening, but Charlotte became bored and restless. When Napoleon presented his plan for a Mexican monarchy under French tutelege, Charlotte begged Maximilian to accept. Mexican monarchists finally persuaded Maximilian to take a Mexican throne when the French held a rigged referendum that convinced Maximilian to plan his monarchy.

But the French experienced difficulties in Mexico that Maximilian should have considered. On May 5, 1862, a greatly outnumbered Mexican army of regular soldiers and Zacapoastla Indians defeated 6,000 French troops decisively at the battle of Puebla. General Ignacio Zaragoza provided heroic inspiration during an event that subsequently became a national holiday, the Cinco de Mayo. The euphoria produced by this battle allowed Mexicans to regain confidence. The French had assumed that they could march up to Texas and supply Confederate forces. Napoleon responded by sending in a new force from Algeria under General Francois-Achilee Bazaine. The 300,000 French troops eventually occupied Mexico City and convoked a hastily formed Assembly of Notables, which repeated the monarchist invitation for Maximilian to become emperor of Mexico. In Yucatán conservative eastern elements revolted at Izamal on March 29, 1863 under the leadership Felipe Navarrete. In July, Navarrete occupied Mérida and pledged his allegiance to Maximilian.

During a gala March 1864 visit to Paris, the blond Hapsburg and his eager wife accepted Napoleon's crass terms: Mexico would have to pay the greater part of the French expeditionary force's costs, which amounted to 260 million francs. After July 1, 1864, Maximilian would be obligated to pay 1,000 francs a year for every French soldier in Mexico. Napoleon also included 25 million francs for various "wrongs" committed against French citizens as well as the Jecker loan. At the stroke of a pen, Maximilian signed documents which tripled Mexico's foreign debt. To pay these obligations, which covered part of his personal debts, Maximilian consented to a 200 million franc loan floated by Napoleon but paid for by unfortunate French shareholders. The French mollified Maximilian by assigning him a salary of 1.7 million pesos, which amounted to one-seventh of the Mexican treasury's annual receipts. Napoleon always assumed that he could squeeze enough money from Mexico to pay for his Mexican folly. But Maximilian had the good sense to refuse Saligny's attempt to place Sonora under direct French control, which would have given France prospecting rights.

Maximilian began to realize the full consequences of his actions when Franz Josef demanded that Maximilian sign away his hereditary Austrian rights. Despite his claim to desire a Mexican image, Maximilian did not renounce his Hapsburg origins. The Mexican envoys, who expected an unequivocal acceptance of their crown, found Maximilian too depressed to receive them. But by appealing to Maximilian's overdeveloped sense of chivalry, Napoleon jolted Maximilian out of his melancholy, and Franz Josef cajoled him into giving up his Austrian claims. For good measure, Napoleon promised that France would always protect Maximilian's empire.

Maximilian and Carlotta Confront Juárez.
After their drab arrival into a sullen Veracruz in May 1864, Maximilian and Carlotta (her Hispanized name) offended the Church. Encouraged by priests, many Indians greeted Maximilian as a religious savior. But before accepting his crown, Maximilian made it clear that he would not tolerate the pre-Reforma status of Church property. Because the seizures of clerical lands since 1789 were now part of the status quo in Napoleon's regime, the French opposed the Mexican regency's hope of returning Church lands sold earlier by Juárez. Therefore, France supported Maximilian's opposition to clerical land de-

mands. Moreover, many Mexicans supported Maximilian because they hoped that he would not merely defend the Church but reform it, as he had promised to do. Lack of celibacy on the part of countless priests, nonpayment of debts, political intrigues, neglect of religious duties, and exploitation of several parishes angered many.

Maximilian resembled Juárez in terms of Church policy. Once the papacy outlined its demands for the revised concordat desired by Maximilian, the new monarch insisted that the masses would receive sacraments without payment. Just as Napoleon had done and probably expected, Maximilian decreed the elimination of separate courts, encouraged public education, instituted civil registration of births, deaths, and marriages, and secularized cemeteries. When Maximilian proclaimed religious freedom, the papal nuncio withdrew from negotiations, which never succeeded anyway. Unlike France and Spain, the Church had limited opportunities in Mexico to acquire new wealth.

Maximilian's clerical land policy illustrates the basic thrust of his administration. Maximilian approached the issue of Church property as a liberal but altered his strategy in order to obtain revenue as the financial exigencies of the empire became pressing. After French authorities upheld Juarista land transactions, Maximilian decreed in February 1865 that the Church must be under state jurisdiction and that it had no right to possess property. In response to clerical protests, Maximilian appointed an imperial council to review all land transfers on an irrevocable basis. Those who had obtained land illegally would pay a 25 percent fine. But the difficulty in finding records, often destroyed, retarded the process of validating land transactions. Moreover, the empire encouraged denunciations, which slowed legalization even more. Because Juárez refused to recognize the council's decisions, ownership of nationalized property became tentative when Maximilian needed hacendado support.

Maximilian's land policy failed. Very few landowners paid fines. When the council discovered invalid land purchases, the sympathetic ad-

On n'a jamais pu savoir au juste le maximum du poids que peut porter un mulet d'infanterie.

Le mulet des Sapeurs. Tout son corps est couvert de pointes menaçantes.

Les cantinières. Donnent un démenti au proverbe: pierre qui roule n'amasse pas mousse.

Tous les bourriquots ne sont pas des quadrupèdes. Go cartouches, 4 jours de vivres, de l'eau et du bois pour la grand'halte, la marmite de l'escouade, armes, capote, couverture, tente-abri; voilà, avec quelques autres bijoux le fidèle "et aussi" de qui se compose le bagage d'un fantassin français.

Costume des Officiers. — Auraient un succès-bœuf, le mardi gras, sur le boulevard.

Various scenes of French soldiers in Mexico (Petit Jean, Accession No. 93.R.3).
Reproduced with the permission of The J. Paul Getty Trust/The Getty Research Institute.

ministrators often required guilty landowners to pay as little as 2.5 percent. Hacendados, liberals, and capitalists did not suffer during the French occupation and they consistently opposed any revision of land transactions. In the face of such strong resistance, Maximilian finally repealed the revision decree and ratified all present and past land transactions in return for a 15 percent validation tax on legalized properties not yet submitted for revision. Paying twice for their properties angered many landowners.

In many respects, Maximilian attempted to aid the less fortunate far more than the liberals. Maximilian initially ordered the division of rural property prior to its disposal and mandated that such land could only be sold to landless persons, hence the intense pressure against the revision policy by hacendados as well as clerics. Unlike the liberals, Maximilian sought to give villagers ownership of communal lands. In many cases, Maximilian canceled mortgages owed by schools and other charitable organizations.

Maximilian's social reforms enabled the empire to enjoy a substantial base of support. Empress Carlotta revived women's philanthropic groups. On November 1, 1865, Maximilian outlawed debt peonage, which the liberals never implemented, despite Article 5 of the 1857 Constitution. Specifically, Maximilian annulled all debts over 10 pesos, limited working hours as well as child labor, and gave workers the right to labor where they chose. To limit external control, the government required all foreign landowners to accept Mexican nationality. As part of an effort to Europeanize Mexican culture, an amazing variety of theatrical fare became available to the lower class while the well-to-do enjoyed the best European performers.

The emperor began to identify with Mexican culture. Maximilian brought Angela Peralta back to Mexico in triumph and appointed the 20-year-old diva as court singer and presented her with diamond jewelry after a particularly stunning performance on January 29, 1866. The emperor also cultivated operas by other Mexican composers.

Because colorfully-dressed rural horsemen known as *charros* were prominent in the struggle for independence from Spain, the big-hatted rider became a national symbol. But it was Maximilian who was largely responsible for the costumes that *charros* still wear today. He enjoyed the style of prosperous hacendados and ranchers and took the style up himself, making it popular throughout Mexico.

As Maximilian became increasingly interested in Indian culture, he encouraged indigenous artistic themes at the Academy of San Carlos. Maximilian established a Comité Protector de las Clases Menestrosas, which was unprecedented. Indians could appeal to this agency with some hope of obtaining justice, although war prevented Maximilian from comprehensive protection of indigenous lands. In 1865, Indian villages obtained the right to own property; a year later, several communities received *ejidos*.

Maximilian could also be generous. When he realized that aiding the city of Oaxaca exceeded the abilities of local officials, Maximilian contributed personal funds to aid reconstruction and ordered that meat be distributed to the city's poor. Those who needed work found employment by building municipal roads. Thus Maximilian won over many local adherents and Oaxaca became an early imperial stronghold. Not by coincidence, French cooking styles gradually displaced colonial Hispanic items temporarily. This trend began during the early republic and now reached its zenith.

Maximilian's financial and economic policies were uneven. The empire obtained three French loans which increased Mexico's debt to 182 million pesos. Indebtedness to France virtually assured monetary and deficit weaknesses. On the other hand, Maximilian raised taxes for merchants and retailers. In general, fiscal reform attempted to tax those with wealth.

The economy indicated that better days lay ahead. Trade with Europe tripled within a short time. Agriculture and stock raising maintained steady output. Henequen production in Yucatán increased greatly. Huge textile factories in Europe led to a demand for the fiber exceeding its production with the result that henequen prices quadrupled by the early 1860s. Not surprisingly, the U.S. presence diminished notably; trade between both Mexico and the United States was a mere $7 million by 1867, and total U.S investment amounted to only a few million dollars.

Maximilian also encouraged construction of the Veracruz-Mexico City railroad. Only a few miles had actually been laid before the arrival of Maximilian. Little progress had taken place before 1864 when Antonio Escandón formed a British company to complete the project. Steady construction soon followed, with most of the funds coming from the Escandón family and Maximilian's government. Later, Juárez received much of the credit for completing the line when Maximilian actually encouraged and established the railroad's foundation.

But far too often, the empire lacked coherent administration. After Maximilian arrived, the ayuntamientos fell under control of appointed alcaldes, who answered to a chain of political prefects. Maximilian tended to be indecisive or even foolish. He began by naively appointing liberals to his government in a vain attempt to weaken Juárez. To appease the upper class, Maximilian and Carlotta renovated Chapultepec castle for their living quarters and invited wealthy guests to lavish parties on a frequent basis. Maximilian traveled excessively and literally chased butterflies. As he became anxious about his future, Maximilian lived in nearby Cuernavaca for several months. Carlotta actually performed much of the day-to-day administration. French authorities considered Carlotta to be far more intelligent than Maximilian. During her visit to Mérida and Campeche at the end of 1865, Carlotta won over the local elites.

Maximilian declined partially because of the poor quality of his advisors, who often took advantage of him. The most notable of the self-centered individuals who gained Maximilian's trust was Agustín Fischer, a German emigrant to the United States who converted to Catholicism hastily in a California gold field. Fischer came to live under the protection of the Sánchez Navarro family. Fischer entered the court as a Jesuit confessor and wormed his way into Maximilian's

confidence. Carlos Sánchez Navarro and Fischer persuaded Maximilian to decree that the daughter and grandsons of Iturbide were Mexican princes. Maximilian obviously intended to make them adopted heirs. But Carlotta became depressed when Maximilian did not bother to discuss the matter with her before making his poorly received announcement. Maximilian initiated numerous love affairs and reportedly gave Carlotta syphilis. The subject of unflattering songs about her inability to produce an heir, Carlotta became morose and detached at a critical time.

Maximilian's surprising attempts to forge an independent foreign policy became prone to error. When the caste war in Yucatán spilled over to Belize, Britain threatened that its forces might pursue the Maya raiders into Mexico. Maximilian responded by claiming Mexican sovereignty over most of British Honduras. Such a nationalistic claim made the empire popular in Yucatán, but Maximilian's attempts to gain a concordat failed. Father Fischer offered concessions in Rome, but his seedy background appalled papal officials. Maximilian did obtain foreign troops in addition to the French corps. About 6,000 Austrians arrived as well as 1,500 Belgians and 500 Egyptians. However, U.S. Secretary of State William H. Seward outwitted Maximilian by pretending to consider extending U.S. recognition to the empire when he had no such intention. Maximilian foolishly rejected an alliance with the Confederacy out of the faint hope that Seward would establish formal relations with the monarchy. If Maximilian had allied with the South, the French army could have marched north and shoved Juárez out of Mexico. As Maximilian became increasingly unrealistic, he planned for an imperial navy to dominate the Caribbean, which would enable Mexico to control Central America.

The beginning of the end occurred when the French became frustrated with guerrilla warfare and began to withdraw from smaller towns in the autumn of 1865. Bazaine convinced the normally humane Maximilian to sign an October 1865 decree which allowed military forces to execute civilians who aided Juárez. Many previously neutral Mexicans decided to oppose Maximilian as a result of this brutal measure. Also in 1865, Maximilian responded harshly to a major strike that broke out in San Ildefonso. After workers sent word to him of their plight, the emperor ordered his troops to shoot them. The French became increasingly unpopular because they often behaved as nobles who disdained Mexicans. According to historian Charles Berry, disputes between Mexican administrators and European military officers were the key reason for the empire's failure. All of Maximilian's civilian representatives were Mexicans with imperial rank. Bazaine also made the mistake of reducing the Mexican imperial forces to a mere two regiments. Had the French allowed indigenous troops to serve in foreign legion units, Maximilian might have been able to fight victoriously against Juárez.

The U.S. Role and European Problems.

Juárez gradually reasserted himself in tandem with Seward's policy of establishing a harmonious atmosphere for U.S. investors in Mexico. During the earlier Three Years' War, Miguel Lerdo de Tejada overshadowed Juárez. But in the war against French occupation, Juárez emerged as the leader of national unity. As the U.S. Civil War came to a close, Seward asked Napoleon to enact a timetable for French withdrawal from Mexico. The French presence and Confederate veterans in Orizaba angered U.S. generals. As a large U.S. army assembled on the Texas border, Juárez became more confident of victory. Despite a French attack on Chihuahua in August 1865, Juárez wisely declined an offer from the mayor of El Paso to cross into Texas. Despite French accusations that he had fled Mexico, Juárez continued to resist. He also offered more land to his allies. By means of his July 20, 1863, public land law, Juárez established a Public Land Claims Commission that would lead to widescale land distribution a decade later. The massive land transfers that took place in the Porfiriato actually had their legitimacy established during the Reforma.

Juárez enjoyed U.S. support partly because of the sophisticated efforts of Matías Romero, his minister in Washington. Romero befriended Republican congressmen and became one of Ulysses Grant's best friends. Republicans appreciated Juárez's decrees which had removed most customs rates along the border and remained in force until 1916. Eager for free trade, Romero and Seward signed a postal convent and extradition treaty in 1862. In their determination to encourage U.S. intervention, Romero and his agents promoted U.S. economic interests in Mexico. Romero considered parting with certain states in northern Mexico in exchange for U.S. troops driving the French out. But Seward preferred developing new Mexican markets. Juárez would not yield land to the United States but offered mineral and trading rights. Juárez also offered foreign volunteers regular Mexican army pay and land, with no necessity of Mexican citizenship. Many U.S. volunteers responded and formed an American Legion of Honor with their own officers and banners.

The changing situation in Europe also weakened the empire. The death of King Leopold shocked Carlotta and resulted in the new Belgian king not sending more troops to Mexico. Concerned about Seward's bellicose opposition to French forces, Napoleon also became preoccupied with Prussia's determination to unify Germany. At this point, Bazaine quietly planned the departure of his troops and broke off fighting. In April 1866, Napoleon informed a stunned Maximilian that the French army would soon depart. Prussia and Italy carried out a dramatic war against Austria in June 1866. Defeated decisively, Franz Josef also decided not to send troops to Mexico. Aware that his empire would collapse, Maximilian yearned to return to Vienna but Franz Josef denied him refuge.

Clearly Maximilian should have departed. Armed revolts against the empire broke out early in the summer of 1866. An anxious Napoleon suggested that Maximilian leave as soon as possible. As Maximilian considered abdication, Carlotta teetered on the verge of mental collapse. She unwisely urged that he remain while she sought aid in Europe. Unable to comprehend the changing realities of European power struggles, Carlotta failed to obtain support for the Mexican crown in Paris and the Vatican. By now psychotic, Carlotta retired to Belgium.

Querétaro and the Final Days. Indecisive as ever, Maximilian succumbed to his tragic sense of romanticized honor. Cognizant that Carlotta was insane, Maximilian decided to abdicate and left for Orizaba. But Fischer organized a paid mob to shout for Maximilian to remain. The Council of State and conservative intriguers pledged money as well as troops. A letter from his mother sealed Maximilian's fate. Queen Sophia took it upon herself to congratulate Maximilian for deciding to remain. Knowing that Maximilian could not handle a demented Carlotta, and believing reports that Carlotta had become pregnant by a Belgian officer, Sophia sent off her ill-timed advice. In January 1867, Maximilian returned to Mexico City but failed to prepare for action.

The end became imminent when French troops completed their evacuation in February. Surrounded in the capital, Maximilian decided to make a heroic gesture by departing for Querétaro. There 8,000 imperial troops came under his command. But Maximilian had committed a foolish mistake; he could neither be reinforced nor supplied and 40,000 Juaristas cut him off. Captured after deserters betrayed him, Maximilian refused to attend his trial. A military court found him guilty of revolting against the republic. Despite numerous appeals to save his life, Juárez asserted that the public will necessitated Maximilian's execution. Shot on June 19, 1867, Maximilian's death served as a warning against further foreign intervention. It was the last time that Europeans used armed force against Mexico.

JUÁREZ AND THE RESTORED REPUBLIC

The restored republic was a crucial period in Mexican history. As Daniel Cosío Villegas insists, the restored republic represents the origins of modern Mexico. Educational progress, working

class mobilization, and a free press represent a definite maturity. The conservative defeat encouraged an overconfident Juárez to equate liberalism with nationalism. An ideological banner such as the 1857 Constitution failed to become a unifying myth under the liberals. Economic stagnation caused many to lose faith in traditional liberalism.

Often an unscrupulous politician, Juárez would not tolerate genuine opposition. Juárez reentered Mexico City on July 17, 1867, as a hero, but his faction began to experience difficulties with the 1857 Constitution. Regional oligarchies controlled Congress, eager to defend speculation, contraband, and commercial monopolies now threatened by a stronger liberal state. To centralize his regime, Juárez attached a set of restrictive referendums to the ballot during elections that Juárez ordered only a month after his return to the capital. The referendum called for veto authority, an upper house, and allowing federal employees to become congressional deputies. Juárez demanded this legislation because he claimed that the executive required more authority. Voters rejected these changes, but Juárez stubbornly sent the measures to Congress, where deputies refused to enact them.

These events triggered a major struggle between Juárez and the caudillo governors, who appointed deputies through sham elections in order to protect federalism. Therefore, Juárez used public funds to set up a political machine in order to impose loyal *jefes políticos*, deputies, and governors. From 1867 to 1872, Juárez replaced representatives of local regimes with party loyalists. By the time Juárez held a majority, Congress granted him extraordinary powers in finance and war and sanctioned the use of federal troops in the interior. Because governors loyal to Juárez monopolized power, revolts broke out. The political system established by Juárez later became perfected by Porfirio Díaz, indicating the continuity between the restored republic and the twentieth century. Constitutional dictatorship in future decades became a logical extension of the Reforma past.

His authoritarian tendencies alienated many of Juárez's key followers. Because the machine existed to maintain incumbents with little concern for public sentiments, liberalism became fractured and weak. Some of the traditional liberal ideologues protested the Juarista drift to centralization of power. Ignacio Ramírez, for example, felt that municipalities should be the focus of civic liberty so that property owners could lead communities. When Juárez sacrificed classical republican ideals in the construction of a more authoritarian state, Ignacio Altamirano also broke with the president. Juárez's aloof personality manifested itself when he humiliated Porfirio Díaz. During his entry into Mexico City, Juárez had Díaz ride behind him, even though Díaz had captured the capital earlier and spent 20,000 pesos out of his own pocket for an elaborate reception. Popular because of his excellent military record, Díaz decided to challenge Juárez for the presidency during the 1867 presidential elections. But caciques used national guard units to enable Juarista control of national as well as local elections. Despite liberal promises, the tyrany of small town autocrats did not end, thus preserving the long continuity of political manipulation at the local level.

Juárez began his new term of office by promising to obey the constitution. He provided stable internal administration but little else. The release of 60,000 troops became a particularly serious error. These embittered veterans received neither pensions nor a dignified ceremony before beginning an often unsuccessful search for work. A similar mistake in Brazil eventually cost Dom Pedro II his throne after the Paraguayan War. Throughout the interior, many soldiers became bandits. The Golden Age of bandits was 1857-1867, when former army troops, disgruntled peons, opportunists, escaped convicts, and adventurers became marauding brigands. At first polite to their victims, bandits became bolder and more violent. They terrorized towns, travelers and merchants. Juárez retaliated by increasing the number of federal police, known as rurales. Created in 1861 by José Maria Lafragua, the brutal Spanish Guardia Civil became the model for the restored republic's attempt to control an often rebellious citizenry.

Juárez's appeal declined. Detractors claimed he was an intellectual puppet of Sebastian Lerdo de Tejada, head of the supreme court. Juárez also took 200,000 pesos in back pay, which represents a sharp contrast to 1861 when Juárez cut his salary. Meanwhile, treasury officials suspended salaries of public employees. Always a conscientious agnostic, Juárez alienated more Mexicans by beginning the tradition of Mexican presidents who never went to church. Juárez also enacted legislation to permanently disenfranchise the Church and abolished many religious holidays. As Juaristas fought over churches, marriage fees, and cemeteries, the funds from seized clerical mortgages and other formerly religious endeavors fueled unusually violent political infighting from 1867–1871.

Spanish law continued to dominate the Mexican legal system until the promulgation of a Civil Code in 1870. The Civil Code became the most significant liberal innovation because it removed all legal limitations upon free commerce. Although the Civil Code facilitated market exchange by simplifying the rules of contracts, it permitted either party to sue for rescission if experts determined that the purchaser had paid twice the fair price or the seller had received less than two-thirds the real worth of the item in question. The law also required masters to compensate their apprentices and that education could be a component of their wage. Although the code subordinated custom to contract as a source of payment to rural workers, bargaining between workers and landowners rarely occurred.

During the nineteenth century, most Mexican women assumed that their laws were reasonable by the international standards of the time. In some respects, Mexican women had more legal protection than foreign counterparts. In both Britain and the United States, property was transmitted through the male line, avoiding daughters. In contrast, a Mexican wife maintained an independence that enabled her to own property, bequeath it without permission, retain custody of children in most separations, and maintain her maiden surname. As the liberals expanded the role of the central government in deciding justice and enforcing law, state governments accepted the Civil Code with few variations.

The liberals failed to nurture economic growth because they had little to offer other than making private investments safe. Only in the periphery did regional economies grow. The northern textile industry, for example, superceded antiquated mills in Puebla and Tlaxcala. Generally, industrial growth sputtered, which reflected lack of direction from Mexico City. Impoverished indigenous communities and small internal markets also restricted the economy. Commercial growth was nil. Mexico continued to export raw materials and import manufactured goods as well as luxury items. The role of money was minimal beyond towns and cities. Internal tariffs between each state burdened trade. Regressive taxes reduced potential investment funds while free trade did little to promote true development. A modest road construction project attempted to improve the rickety infrastructure. Juárez also contracted a British railroad company to finish building the line from Veracruz to Mexico City. But critics attacked the subsidies paid to the builders, which amounted to a million pesos annually for 13 years—10 percent of the national budget.

Juárez's refusal to recognize external debts and the poor image created by Maximilian's execution resulted in isolation. Mexico's only friend was the United States, which Juárez mistrusted. At least both countries finally processed claims dating back to 1848. Prussia's defeat of Napoleon III and the execution of Jecker, shot during the Paris commune revolt, became the only bright lights on the gloomy international horizon.

Rural Unrest and Agrarian Revolt. Serious revolts, usually caused by anticlerical abuses and the expansion of latifundia, broke out after 1869. Unlike many South American liberals in the second half of the nineteenth century, Juárez prolonged unnecessary religious conflict by enforcing anticlerical legislation. At a time when reconciliation should have been considered, Juárez appointed Ignacio Ramírez as Minister of Justice and Public Instruction. Ramírez made no

secret of his atheism or his desire for European migrants. Particularly acrimonious was the regime's decision to ban regional and local religious processions. Angry Indians protested quickly and revolted. Rebels seized Pachuca temporarily with the cry "death to Protestants" and "long live religion." Aided by a messianic religious leader, Maya rebels continued to control eastern Yucatán. The cult of the Virgin of Guadalupe retained such patriotic fervor that Juárez exempted the sanctuary from Reforma laws. The liberals simply refused to recognize that religion continued to be Mexico's major cultural thread. Like the Spanish Bourbons, Juárez would not accept the fact that religion had often been the dominant concept binding Mexico together. Although the Bourbons attacked the church as an institution, they never questioned religion as many liberals did.

Agrarian revolts persisted because the liberals opposed village control of land. Ramírez and Altamirano typified liberal elitists who considered indigenous villages as obstacles to national integration. An August 1867 decree instructed local councils to apply the Ley Lerdo in order to sell municipal, clerical, and indigenous properties and to transfer all *ejidos* to individuals already in possession of them. Indigenous communities fought back, often allied with bandits. Despite resistance to land occupation and defense of communal lands, three-fifths of the land seized by the liberals eventually came from *ejidos*. Too often white entrepreneurs harvested nonagricultural cash crops, such as coffee, henequen, and sugar, or emphasized ranching, all of which Indians disliked. The liberals insisted that Indians had no capacity for material progress. Reforma land procedures clearly widened the socioeconomic distance between whites, *mestizos*, and Indians. Since disentailment often encouraged denunciations, the rapid seizure of communal lands during the 1860s meant that whites frequently displaced Indians.

Liberal land policies favored the small minority of 13,000 landowners who controlled 58 percent of the land. Despite unprecedented conflict, hacendados generally continued to prosper. Profits remained constant, estate sale prices rose, and irrigation investments continued. Rural *mestizos* as well as Indians detested the hacendado habit of expelling sharecroppers and seizing their goods. Class as well as racial distinctions sharpened during the Reforma. Owners of ranchos sparked many revolts because of their rapid increase at the expense of village lands. Liberal land policies precipitated a nasty caste war in Chiapas from 1868 to 1870.

Partisanship often determined who received land and who lost it. Colonel Jesús Carranza obtained land in Coahuila in return for his timely aid to Juárez when France invaded the north. Because Carlos Sánchez Navarro had served Maximilian as grand chamberlain, the liberals confiscated his enormous latifundia. Luis Terrazas in Chihuahua also profited from eventual loyalty to Juárez. Only in Chihuahua did the local patron survive the turmoil of the Reforma where one elite family combined entrepreneurship and domination of the local economy. Changes in land ownership therefore facilitated the construction of Juárez's political machine. In order to consolidate the new state and hasten the destruction of the *ejidos*, villagers who adhered to Juárez received land grants.

In 1869, a terrible drought caused the liberals to reevaluate their rural fiscal policies, but little resulted. Congress rejected executive proposals for taxing unused land and did nothing to establish a fair fiscal policy. Miners and hacendados paid almost no taxes—those earning over 20,000 pesos usually paid a mere 20 pesos. Taxes became particularly regressive in the countryside. State governments often received 80 percent of their revenue from the poor—by means of sales taxes which often equaled the price of taxed goods. Head taxes on Indians continued to be collected. Therefore, skilled workers and local industries could not develop. The custom of local governments to spend lavishly for the construction of gaudy buildings while providing little funding for education became particularly galling to rural inhabitants. Constant revolts in opposition to land tenure patterns as well as unequal fiscal policies resulted in a period of almost uninterrupted internal warfare.

Juárez's Final Years. Juárez could have departed office as a patriot, but his ambition besmirched his reputation. The death of his wife in 1871 provided temporary sympathy. These sentiments vanished when Juárez decided to seek his fourth presidential term that year. Such authoritarianism obviously violated the republican legacy and the 1857 Constitution. Despite the advice of friends to the contrary, an overconfident Juárez had become accustomed to ruling and considered himself indispensable. Revolts flared up even before voters cast their ballots because the election became a rigged farce. An uprising in Mexico City resulted in the rebels taking possession of the Cuidadela for several days. In October 1871, Congress compliantly ratified Juárez's vain triumph. By now the restored republic had become so unpopular that Indians maimed themselves rather than be conscripted into the army. Díaz now called for revolt with the theme of no reelection, but his movement fizzled out. Other uprisings, particularly in the north, cost Mexico thousands of lives. In July 1871, Juárez finally died of a massive heart attack.

Lerdo de Tejada, 1872–1876. Sebastián Lerdo de Tejada, the head of the supreme court, quickly imposed himself as president. A former Jalapa school teacher, Lerdo was a *criollo* bourgeois who fled with Juárez during the French invasion. Lerdo built a power base in the bureaucracy as a Juarista minister. By the time of Juárez's death, various governors and deputies supported Lerdo. Lerdo may have been Mexico's most intellectual president, but he never understood how to rule the country. He was a good orator, but lazy, arrogant, and overconfident. Lerdo pacified Congress by means of phony elections and reduced the army to 15,000 after proclaiming an amnesty. But his budget was a mere 17 million pesos—still less than the late colonial era. Nevertheless, Lerdo built more railroads, telegraph lines, and schools than Juárez. The construction of La Reforma Boulevard in Mexico City signifies the city's beautification. Unfortunately, Lerdo committed the mistake of surrounding himself with virtually the same officials that Juárez had used, with the result that Mexico City continued to be distrusted by most of the rest of the nation.

Social Change and Positivism.

The liberals failed to respond to critical social and cultural transformations. Powerful religious sentiments dominated the lives of the masses. Gambling and drinking continued to be pronounced male activities. Much to the annoyance of liberals, bullfighting dominated popular culture while uncensored newspapers criticized the country's social and drift. In response to the demand for urban laborers and the decline of artisan industries, a proletariat grew. The increasing number of those without land meant that a significant working-class movement became a reality in the form of mutualism, cooperativeness, and the arrival of socialist as well as anarchist ideas. Radical ideals were bought by immigrants from Spain and other European countries with them where such ideologies had already become well established. Not surprisingly, 20 strikes occurred during the restored republic.

Anarchism promised liberty and justice in the countryside. Displaced artisans and craftsmen from developing urban areas often became the initial anarchist leaders. The liberal free trade policies thus created new centers of resistance to the liberal regimes, particularly when industrial methods replaced handcrafted modes of production. European immigrants such as Plotino Rhodakanaty encouraged peasants to preserve their traditional patterns of life and to identify with local villages rather than a distant national government. After his arrival in 1861, Rhodakanaty began organizing cooperatives based on the principal that humans were basically good, but that private property corrupted society. During the 1860s, the anarchist movement also began to acquire an increasingly socialist viewpoint. Rhodakanaty eventually believed that democracy would fail unless socialism nurtured a transformation of society.

In 1869, one of the rural followers educated by Rhodakanaty's program, Julio Chávez López, issued a manifesto calling people to arms in order to establish a new agricultural order, resist the upper class, and overthrow the government. Chávez López favored the creation of peasant utopias where a free village could operate without the state's influence. An indigenous leader from Chalco, López assumed that peasants were natural anarchists. After López had seized a few haciendas, federal forces finally placed him against a wall and shot him.

Positivism became the dominant intellectual trend. It succeeded because positivism finally began to unify the upper class. August Comte formulated the new ideology in France during the 1840s. Comte believed that "scientific" laws governed human behavior and that such laws could be formulated from economics and sociology. Thus, Comte presented a theory of behavioral control for governments to use. Comte suggested that the state's role must be to promote such laws with the implication that dictatorship could be more rational. Comte's theory of history held that society passed through three stages. In the first, theology predominates; religious thinkers explain phenomena that humans cannot understand. Then follows the metaphysical stage, characterized by abstract, humane values to guide society toward social justice. The final historical stage is the attainment of a scientific society. Here the use of law based upon scientific experiments attains the utmost social development. Many of Professor Comte's students were Latin Americans tired of disorder and disappointing economic conditions. Such students often concluded that positivism was the solution to bring about progress. Positivism influenced Latin America far more than Europe. Mexico became one of many New World examples.

Positivism had great appeal to elite Mexicans. It emphasized demonstrable, empirical science as the basis for all truth. All freedom became geared toward altruism. Unlike the total individual freedom espoused by classical liberals such as Ocampo, freedom was redefined by the positivists as following impulses within a legal structure, which guaranteed that framework, the harmony of agreement within verifiable science. While positivism proclaimed separation of church and state, it also rejected the church's spiritual basis, since that authority based itself upon faith, not on demonstrable reality. Positivists claimed that their creed did not threaten freedom because education would be its basis. Interested in order and economic growth, conservatives accepted the new ideology willingly. Many liberals applauded positivism's scientific, secular approach as well as a means to justify foreign capital and immigration. Both groups despised Indians and desired to build an economic infrastructure while laying aside their fear of Europe and the United States.

Gabino Barreda became the ambitious student of Comte who instituted positivism as the ruling dogma. Barreda returned to Mexico City as a physician at the national university but retained his interest in positivism and education. Like many others of his generation, Barreda became disillusioned with classical liberalism; egalitarianism and democracy seemed unattainable. Barreda became one of Juárez's advisors and began to impose a positivist educational system upon Mexico in 1867. In his famous civic oration that year, Barreda proclaimed that the liberal triumph signified Comte's transition to the scientific age.

As traditional liberals and Catholics protested, the new Ministry of Justice and Public Instruction controlled a uniform curriculum based on Comte's scientific approach. The law mandated free, obligatory primary education. Municipalities had to provide schools and funds; hacendados and plantation owners became obligated to finance school construction. In public schools, the metric system, physics, chemistry, national history, geography, and civic instruction replaced religion and classical, humanistic studies. Females began to study sewing and hygiene.

Most Mexicans placed high hopes upon education. Catholics gradually accepted increased science and patriotism in the classroom despite their insistence upon religion. Artisans assumed education would end oppression, and liberals considered education a means of discipline. But the new schools often alienated rural Mexicans in terms of teacher absenteeism, cruelty to children, and an insistence upon speaking Spanish.

The restored republic encouraged education as well as the arts and letters. It is surprising that no great novel emerged to glorify the struggle against France. Although the defeat of French imperialism should have accelerated the growth of nationalism, the liberals alienated too many social groups. Nevertheless, censorship vanished. A free exchange of ideas encouraged the diffusion of learning. After 1861, Juárez decreed schools for deaf mutes, law, medicine, mining, and the arts. The Escuela Nacional Prepatoria became a crucial vehicle for higher educational standards as well as positivist indoctrination. Admission was based on merit and the school sought exceptional students who were expected to become the new elite with an egalitarian learning environment. Throughout Mexico, the number of schools tripled. By 1874, 8,000 schools existed with 350,000 students. Juárez and Lerdo lacked the funds to fully implement the positivist system, but Porfirio Díaz did so later.

Success and Failure of the Reforma. The liberals achieved some notable triumphs. Juárez and Lerdo broke up Church property and reduced ecclesiastical power for the first time since the eighteenth century. The liberals abolished privilege in theory and established civil rights. Promoting education and encouraging intellectual expression became notable byproducts of the optimistic tendency of many liberals. In defeating France, the regime preserved Mexican independence and La Reforma championed patriotism as well as self-confidence.

Unfortunately, the liberals failed to build the strong nation they desired. French intervention required unpleasant concessions to the United States in order to win. Poor agrarian policies precipitated constant revolts. The liberals despised the indigenous communities and attacked religious traditions foolishly. By 1876, Mexico remained unintegrated socially. Perhaps the greatest weakness of the Reforma was its inability to promote economic growth.

SUGGESTED READING

Barker, Nancy M. *The French Experience in Mexico, 1821–1861: A History of Constant Misunderstanding*. Chapel Hill: University of North Carolina Press, 1979.

Bazant, Jan. *Alienation of Church Wealth in Mexico: Social and Economic Aspects of the Liberal Revolution, 1856-1875*. Cambridge: Cambridge University Press, 1971.

Berry, Charles R. *The Reform in Oaxaca, 1856–1876: A Microhistory of the Liberal Revolution*. Lincoln: University of Nebraska Press, 1981.

Blázquez, Dominguez, Carmen. *Miguel Lerdo de Tejada: Un liberal veracruzano en la política nacional*. Mexico City: El Colegio de México, 1978.

———. *Veracruz liberal, 1858-1860*. Mexico City: El Colegio de México, 1986.

Blumberg, Arnold. *The Diplomacy of the Mexican Empire, 1863–1867*. Malobar, FL: Krieger, 1987.

Brading, David A. "Liberal Patriotism and the Mexican Reforma." *Journal of Latin American Studies* 20 (May 1988), 27–48.

Chapman, John. *La construccíon del ferrocarril mexicano (1837–1880)*. Mexico City: Sepsetentas, 1975.

Coatsworth, John H. "Obstacles to Growth in Nineteenth Century Mexico." *The American Historical Review*, 83:1 (February, 1978), 80–100.

Cosío Villegas, Daniel. *La Constitucíon de 1857 y sus críticos*. Mexico City: Sepsetentas,1973.

Dabbs, Jack. *The French Army in Mexico, 1861–1867: A Study in Military Government*. The Hague: Mouton, 1963.

Díaz y Díaz, Fernando. *Caudillos y caciques*. Mexico City: El Colegio de México, 1972.

Dolkart, Ronard. "Angela Peralta: A Mexican Diva." In Judith Ewell and William H. Beecley, eds. *The Human Tradition in Latin America*. Wilmington, DE: Scholarly Resources, 1989, pp. 161–174.

Fraser, Donald J. "La politica de desamortizacíon en las comunidades indíenas, 1856–1872." *Historia Mexicana* 21:4 (April–June 1972), 615–652.

Fuentes Mares, José. *La emperatriz Eugenia y su aventura mexicana*. Mexico City: El Colegio de México, 1976.

Hale, Charles. *The Transformation of Liberalism in Late Nineteenth Century Mexico*. Princeton, NJ: Princeton University Press, 1990.

Hamnett, Brian. *Juárez*. New York: Longman, 1994.

Hart, John M. *Anarchism and the Mexican Working Class, 1860–1931*. Austin: University of Texas Press, 1978.

Haslip, Joan. *The Crown of Mexico: Maximilian and his Empress Carlotta*. New York: Holt, Rinehart and Winston, 1971.

Knowlton, Robert J. *Church Property and the Mexican Reforma, 1856–1910*. DeKalb: Northern Illinois University Press, 1967.

López Cámara, Francisco. *La estructura económica y social de Mexico en la epoca de la reforma*. Mexico City: Siglo Vientiuno, 1967.

O'Connor, Richard. *The Cactus Throne*. New York: Avon Books, 1976.

Olliff, Donathon C. *Reforma Mexico and the United States: A Search for Alternatives to Annexation, 1854-1861*. Tuscaloosa: University of Alabama Press, 1981.

Perry, Laurens Ballard. *Juárez and Díaz. Machine Politics in Mexico*. DeKalb: Northern Illinois University Press, 1978.

Powell, T. G. *El liberalismo y el campesinado en el centro de México (1850–1876)*. Mexico City: Sepsetentas, 1974.

———. "Priests and Peasants in Central Mexico: Social Conflict During La Reforma." *Hispanic American Historical Review* 57:2 (May 1977), 296–313.

Roeder, Ralph, *Juárez and His Mexico*. 2 vols. New York: Viking Press, 1947.

Rugeley, Terry. "The Liberal Reform in Southeast Mexico, 1855–1876." Paper presented at the 34th Conference of the Southwest Council of Latin American Studies in Santa Fe, New Mexico on March 23, 2001.

Schoonover, Thomas. *Dollars Over Dominion: The Triumph of Liberalism in Mexican-American Relations, 1861–1867*. Baton Rouge: Louisiana State University Press, 1978.

———. *Mexican Lobby: Matías Romero in Washington, 1861–1867*. Lexington: University of Kentucky Press, 1986.

Simonian, Lane. *Defending the Land of the Jaguar: A History of Conservation in Mexico*. Austin: University of Texas Press, 1995.

Sinkin, Richard N. *The Mexican Reform, 1855-1876: A Study in Liberal Nation-Building*. Austin, TX: Institute of Latin American Studies, 1979.

Tamayo, Jorge. *Juárez en Chihuahua*. Mexico City: Libros de Mexico, 1970.

———. *Antología de Benito Juárez*. Mexico City: UNAM, 1971.

Thompson, Guy P.D. "Bulwarks of Patriotic Liberalism: The National Guard, Philharmonic Corps and Patriotic Juntas." *Journal of Latin American Studies* 22:1 (February 1990), 40–48.

Zea, Leopoldo. *Positivism in Mexico*. Trans. Josephine H. Schulte. Austin: University of Texas Press, 1974.

10

The Era of Porfirio Díaz, 1876–1910

Porfirio Díaz became the most successful leader in nineteenth-century Latin America. Under his control, Mexico started to become a modern nation as Díaz consolidated the power of the central government. A master politician with a pragmatic approach, Díaz understood Mexico better than anyone else. Juárez had constructed a political machine, but Díaz transformed it into a legitimate regime. Díaz shared power with a new oligarchy of bankers, industrialists, and exporters as well as the traditional hacendados, foreign merchants, and intelligencia. Although Porfirian rule successfully directed solid economic growth, its final result was mass insurrection.

POLITICAL AND IDEOLOGICAL FOUNDATIONS

The Rise of Porfirio Díaz. Díaz was a warrior who fought his way into leadership of the nation. A Mixtec Indian from Oaxaca, Díaz had little Spanish blood. After quitting his legal studies to fight for the liberals, Díaz became an outstanding soldier. During the struggle against French intervention, Díaz demonstrated that he was perhaps the best general in Latin America. Although he gained polish in middle age, Díaz always retained the tough mannerism of a guerrilla chief. Eventu-

ally, Juárez allowed Díaz to strengthen his Oaxacan militia into a national guard. With obvious ambition, Díaz became the inevitable successor to Juárez when it became clear that liberalism had failed.

Díaz was also a classic *caudillo*. Over six feet tall, Díaz knew how to deal with indigenous as well as *mestizo* and white groups. A great horseman, a good shot, and personally honest, Díaz had demonstrated his bravery more than once. In many ways, he was the incarnation of machismo. After his *mestiza* wife died in 1880, Díaz married into the upper class when the pious doña Carmen Rubio accepted his hand. With a wife from the cream of society, Díaz reinforced his popular appeal. His father-in-law, Manuel Romero Rubio, directed the national *camarilla* (a political group loyal to one individual) in Mexico City. As Díaz became more powerful, he preserved kinship ties by placing his supporters into the army and bureaucracy. As a prominent hacendado in Oaxaca, Díaz shared similar concerns with the Mexican upper class.

Díaz carried out an uncomplicated seizure of power. Only about 30,000 citizens could vote in the 1876 elections, but the increasingly unpopular Lerdo intervened in the interior to try and reinstall himself. Díaz revolted and proclaimed the Plan de Tuxtepec, which promised effective suffrage and no reelection, along with a pledge to restore liberalism to its earlier, purest form. In reality, his personal qualities rallied supporters to his cause rather than an ideological rationale. Once Díaz's forces defeated federal troops in Tlaxcala on November 16, he occupied the capital five days later.

During his first presidential term, Díaz demonstrated his nationalist tendencies as well as administrative skills. Díaz reduced graft and cut governmental salaries, including his own. Determined to establish domestic order, Díaz provided concessions to those who would obey but harshly cut down most who revolted. As peace returned, trade and agriculture revived. Although Germany extended diplomatic recognition to Díaz, the United States position became increasingly critical once it became clear that both Ulysses Grant and Rutherford Hayes wanted large claims payments, as well as the right to send U.S. troops into northern Mexico without first securing Mexican permission. Díaz gained great support by placing Mexican troops along the border with orders to resist if U.S. soldiers crossed the border. At the same time, Díaz and his advisors wooed U.S. investors by means of a very clever public relations campaign. Once Grant himself and other U.S. investors received lucrative concessions, Hayes gave in. Unable to secure reparations from France, Díaz finally reestablished relations with Paris in 1880. With his popularity rising, Díaz stepped aside so that his old friend Manuel González could be elected president.

The interim rule of González reveals Díaz's adroitness. Díaz had a policy of letting subordinates take the blame for various injustices. When González continued Diaz's practice of encouraging foreign investment, the government spent excessive amounts for subsidies to railroad builders, as well as concessions for cable service and port inprovements. González suspended payment to the bureaucracy and criticism began. González seems to have enriched himself, but Díaz and his allies exaggerated the corruption of the González regime. As rumors suggested that the new president had turned the national palace into a saloon and a brothel, González's wife even attacked his morals. Díaz served briefly in the government but never controlled González as a puppet. Since Díaz rarely identified himself with González, their distance worked to Díaz's advantage. This was particularly true when González recognized a British debt of 91 million pesos. Assuming a debt contracted by Zuloaga and other conservatives triggered rioting in the streets, although Britain reopened diplomatic ties to Mexico. Later, Díaz reduced the interest charges and benefited politically. When González passed unpopular legislation that favored foreigners, Díaz preserved it quietly when he returned to power in 1888.

Díaz's Political Centralization. Reinstalled as chief executive, Díaz became the first Mexican leader to control all the interior. With his military prestige undisputed, the army became a personal tool. Zone commanders consolidated Porfirian rule in key regions. Díaz purged the officer corps and replaced them with loyal followers. Graft, plunder, and estates cemented ties to Díaz among his cronies. Unreliable officers served abroad as military attachés while the uncooperative faced execution. To ensure obedience, Díaz split the army into smaller units and scattered them throughout the countryside on a rotating basis. Although reduced to 9,000 officers and 18,000 troops, Díaz also modernized the army. New equipment from Germany and France as well as enhanced technical training satisfied the generals. Díaz also reformed the Colegio Militar and began a modest arms industry. The army contributed to social stability by using the draft to pick off malcontents.

As if to underline the Porfirian drive for centralized power, the army conducted ruthless military campaigns against Yaqui and Maya resistance. Sonora Yaquis revolted when the ruling clique pushed indigenous groups out of the Yaqui Valley in order to seize their land. The army defeated Cajeme and 3,000 of his troops and deported Yaquis to other parts of Mexico. In Yucatán, General Ignacio Bravo defeated the remnants of the Maya who had resisted the encroachments of white settlers. By building a railroad to Chan Santa Cruz and occupying eastern Yucatán, the army finally beat the Maya into general submission by 1901. Diaz spent 55 percent of the budget on military and police services.

The *rurales* represented Diaz's effort to keep the countryside quiet. Reorganized and increased from a thousand in 1875 to roughly 2,400, the famous *rurales* received good pay and wonderful uniforms. Many were former bandits.Patterned after Spain's Guardia Civil, the heavily armed *rurales* did not hesitate before shooting. At least ten thousand cases of *ley fuga*—a police report that claimed arrested victims had been shot while supposedly trying to escape—enabled Mexico to become a reasonably orderly country. In addition to serving as an effective counterbalance to the army, the *rurales* obeyed Díaz's orders directly. After 1840, the *rurales* were composed primarily of campesinos and artisans as well as former brigands. Although weakened by high rates of desertion, alcoholism, and corruption, the *rurales* enjoyed an image of reliability. Foreign investors appreciated having a detachment of *rurales* garrisoned nearby. Banditry declined and the *rurales* became the elite of the armed forces.

Díaz also benefited from a clever arrangement with the Catholic church. Ending the sectarian and wasteful strife between Church and state enabled the Porfirians to pursue more meaningful tasks other than religious conflict. Carmen Romero Rubio de Díaz served the regime well by arranging a meeting between don Porfirio and the archbishop, which resulted in a secret arrangement: Anticlerical legislation would remain but not be enforced. Clerical appointments had to have Díaz's approval. Education became a sensitive issue because clerical schools lost students to public institutions that charged no fees. Díaz kept clerical influence out of state schools but allowed the Church to maintain its own classrooms. In addition, Díaz quieted those who wanted to restrict the Church and permitted religious institutions to accumulate property. With its wealth growing, the Church preached obedience to Díaz and his government.

To reassure Catholics that anticlericalism would not threaten social stability, Díaz supported a campaign to crown the Virgin of Guadalupe. The Bourbons and liberals had frustrated such a drive after it began in 1740, but doña Carmen publicly urged the raising of funds to have the dazzling crown made in France. In a profoundly nationalistic ceremony, the 1895 coronation drew upon the sympathies of the lower classes throughout Mexico. Such common sense would rarely be duplicated in the twentieth century.

By means of shrewd manipulation of politicians from his cabinet down to local *presidentes municipales*, Díaz took control of Mexico and assured his continued succession to the presidency. Díaz understood the needs of the regional elites, who sought stability and retained control of local taxes. Díaz made sure that most governors became close friends so they could both control state legislatures. In turn, regional representatives and Díaz decided who went to the national Congress, which became little more than a rubber stamp for Porfirian decisions. The process consisted basically of Díaz and members of the regional upper class drawing up a list of those persons whom they wanted to reward. A key event occurred in 1891 when governors received the right to appoint *jefes políticos*. A few hundred *jefes políticos* made sure that the system worked

The chapel Guillermo Purcell in San Lorenzo, Coahuila. *Personal collection of the author.*

by controlling key districts. As time went on, *jefes políticos* usurped the power of locally elected officials and their municipalities. The national legislature also chose the judiciary, who became easily manipulated. Finally, Díaz federalized water rights in 1890; local control vanished. Foreigners and the wealthy could obtain water rights by means of contacts in the federal district.

Mexico maintained only the outlines of a true republic. Elections became so fraudulent that officials sometimes forced prisoners in jail to mark ballots. Rigged voting results always conformed to earlier decisions. Blatant ballot box stuffing removed any doubts concerning the outcome of elections. Thugs known as *bravi* cowed the press into submission when necessary. Often subsidized to write flattery, newspapers rarely criticized Díaz.

Díaz controlled the political system tightly, but not inflexibly. The elite often fought among themselves for land, concessions, and public office. Díaz permitted regional oligarchies a certain amount of autonomy as long as trouble did not become visible. In this manner, Olegario Molina and Avelino Montes dominated Yucatán and made it into the richest state in Mexico. But in Coahuila, Díaz committed a mistake when he imposed José Maria Garza Galán in 1886. A personal favorite of Romero Rubio and the *científico camarilla* in Mexico City, Garza Galán became more unpopular after another imposition in 1889. During the 1890s, resentment against foreign control of the Laguna and other areas of Coahuila made powerful landowners such as Venustiano Carranza and Francisco Madero conclude that municipal liberty would be Mexico's salvation. When the Carranza family revolted in 1893, they represented the frustration of ranchers and the middle class to install a government more sensitive to their needs. Taxes hit the middle and lower classes hardest. Eventually, Díaz allowed the Carranzas to select an alcoholic interim governor under the custody of Bernardo Reyes, the strongman of neighboring Nuevo León state.

Díaz's policy with the middle class generally succeeded. It consisted mainly of giving them jobs to keep them quiet. Before long, 50 percent of the bureaucracy became middle class. To provide increasing public employment, the federal payroll increased ninefold from 1876 to 1910. Faithful friends predominated in public offices, but the possibility of obtaining such status made Díaz popular among whites and *mestizos* for many years. The Hispanic ideal of not working with one's hands remained a powerful factor in determining who was respectable in Mexican society. Education was the other critical factor in determining the difference between the *gente baja* (low people) and the middle class. Therefore, Díaz spent a high proportion of educational funds on higher education. The Porfiriato made excellent progress in fostering medicine and engineering. The allocation for primary education was comparatively meager, but Justo Sierra and his group had partially succeeded in providing mass education. Although the regime failed to reach its goal of mass literacy, the government provided more technical training. The Porfiriato contemplated mass education carefully but built most of the new schools in urban areas to aid the middle class. An effort was made to train teachers, who increasingly took part in fostering upward social mobility. During this period, Mexico City became beautified with statues, parks, and efficient public transportation. The palace of fine arts thrilled middle-class audiences with its opulence and theatrical performances. The western half of Mexico City became upscale when the elite vacated colonial homes east of the Zócalo to live on former church land seized during the Juarez period. In 1900, Miguel Angel Quevedo completed draining the lakes around Mexico City, the largest and most successful drainage project ever conducted in Mexico.

Although an accelerated exploitation of the land took place during the Porfiriato, public concern about ecological land use resulted in the establishment of conservation policies. Because many of the middle class had become avid mountain climbers, the railroad's consumption of forests alarmed public officials. In 1898, concern about deforestation prompted Díaz to create the country's first national forest at Mineral del Chico in the state of Hidalgo. Other decisions led to the precedent for a forest reserve system being established throughout Mexico. The Porfiriato also mandated the first laws for protection of wildlife, except for "dangerous" ones.

Científico Policies. Once he entrenched himself as the undisputed ruler of Mexico, Díaz became open to suggestions about which ideology to pursue. Classic liberalism obviously no longer provided answers to Mexico's problems. Díaz mitigated the traditional antagonism between conservatives and liberals in order to establish a pragmatic coalition. Gradually, supporters of positivism known as *científicos* (advocates of science) gained power in the Díaz regime. Gabino Barreda and his *científico* ideologues published their ideas in *La Libertad*, a newspaper which argued for an authoritarian government with Díaz in charge. The *científicos* claimed that liberalism, with its emphasis upon civil rights and individualism, merely brought on disorder and economic stagnation. They urged Díaz to promote foreign capital, which they assumed to be the key to economic success. Positivism elaborated the concepts of order, progress, and privilege. The *científicos* maintained that Mexico's indigenous heritage was generally negative. Therefore, the Indians should have their lands seized and given to "capable" citizens for development. But most positivists considered indigenous peoples as redeemable through the adoption of education and European culture.

Once Herbert Spencer vulgarized Darwin's theories on natural evolution, Spencerian racism became popular among the upper and middle classes. The *científicos* stressed the struggle for existence in order to claim that certain races and groups of people possessed a mandate to rule. Spencerian racism held that innately inferior races were doomed to extinction; therefore, it served no good to attempt mitigating harsh social conditions. Justo Sierra became Mexico's best-known intellectual. Like many others of the elite, Sierra admired Spencer as well as Comte. A his-

torian who succeeded Barreda in educational policy formation, Sierra wrote that the masses must respect the bourgeoisie for the fruits of their victory. To avoid the problem of Díaz being a *mestizo*, Sierra and other *científicos* insisted that *mestizos* could progress but that Indians were decidedly inferior. Sierra stimulated *mestizo* nationalism when he and others concurred that Mexico's future lay in an educated Europeanized bourgeoisie of mixed blood. Meanwhile, Díaz whitened his skin and insisted upon Caucasian servants.

The *científicos* became an influential although unpopular clique. Their National Liberal Union party lacked popularity because many Mexicans resented the wealth which *científicos* accumulated. The masses also detested *científico* efforts to attract foreign immigrants. Like the liberals, the *científicos* believed that white immigrants could advance Mexico economically and politically while "improving" its racial composition. The government encouraged 68,000 European and U.S. immigrants to enter Mexico from 1895 to 1910.

It was obvious that positivism elaborated concepts involving progress yet emphasized cultural deviations for the powerful while minimizing equality. The masses often took exception to the influence of U.S. and European sports. The elite now participated in activities such as roller skating, bicycling, and baseball. The middle class viewed boredom, idle time, and vice as interrelated. Popular religious traditions that ridiculed Porfirian figures irked many officials. Behavior on the job and in public had to be orderly so that the class relationships would be preserved. Therefore, the regime moved Saturday Judas burning festivities into back streets. The poor, in particular, held on to traditions involving fairs and holy days such as the Judas burning. The upper-class Jockey Club continued Judas burning after many elites lost interest, particularly when humble citizens made unflattering images of local officials. The main event featured exploding effigies with pesos inside. The poor who had come to witness the event groveled for the coins while the Jockey

Club members sat back and laughed at them. What had once been a shared event had now become a means for the well-heeled to humiliate the downtrodden. Middle class morality continued to insist that family development was the woman's most important duty. Moreover, the 1884 Civil Code removed many social, political, and legal rights previously granted to women.

Although the government responded belatedly to social changes, it never assumed a reactionary stance toward women. Thousands of middle-class women worked as teachers; 1,785 served in the federal bureaucracy. It is significant that schools of medicine, law, and commerce accepted the first female students for such careers. Women entered office work and joined the growing industrial labor force. Several feminist journalists and activists began to demand greater educational opportunities, decent wages, and an end to the sexual double standard.

The Porfiriato also achieved modest educational progress. Public officials strongly criticized families which kept children out of school during religious pilgrimages and critical harvest and planting periods.

The number of public primary schools doubled from 5,000 in 1878 to about 10,000 in 1907. Enrollments tripled during the same period. For purposes of comparison, it should not be forgotten that the United States possessed only 10,000 high schools at the same time. By 1907, 31 percent of Mexico's children attended either a religious or public school. The number of teachers went up from 13,000 in 1890 to 21,000 in 1910. Literacy increased from 17 percent in 1895 to 29 percent by 1910. The demand by intellectuals for a national education system resulted in state rather than municipal control over the schools. Justo Sierra created the Ministry of Public Instruction and Fine Arts in 1905; five years later, he reopened the national university.

While urban residents enjoyed their new schools, those in rural areas suffered not only from lack of educational facilities but also few social services in general. Insufficient numbers of rural schools indicate a denigration of indigenous

culture since the cities had higher proportions of whites. The centralization of finances often left local authorities without funds for education. Because of poor health programs in the interior, an already high mortality rate actually increased. Life expectancy was barely 30 years while it was 50 in the United states. Half the country's inhabitants lived in wretched *chozas* (thatched roof huts); alcoholism and gambling increased sharply during the Porfiriato. Persistent poverty in the countryside appalled foreign observers consistently. Enraptured by the attitudes of Western nations and eager to pursue their pastimes, the Mexican elite obviously disregarded its rural inhabitants. Caste wars and regional revolts simply exemplified mass discontent, which the ruling class ignored or decided to suppress.

Undoubtedly the most tragic revolt took place in the village of Tomochic. Nestled in the mountains of western Chihuahua, the community became distressed with the end of collective landholdings and the secularization of religious traditions, particularly marriage and education. The villagers continued to embrace their faith in magic, saints, and witches much to the annoyance of local authorities. Because of a severe drought and the international financial crisis of 1890, their living standards declined sharply. They turned to an extraordinary teenage healer, Teresa Urrea, to struggle against the local tyrants. After ambushing and fighting off Mexican army units, the military savagely besieged Tomochic and wiped out its inhabitants.

THE CURSE OF NEWLY ACQUIRED WEALTH

Astonishing economic growth took place because Díaz and the oligarchy worked primarily toward moving the economy into greater export production. Díaz opened up Mexico to massive foreign investments and modern technology. Multinational corporations, international banks, and investors created an infrastructure and provided credit. The Mexican upper class comprised only 1.4 percent of the population but became flexible and enterprising. Those who understood trade and invested in diverse economic pursuits prospered.

Role of Foreign Capital. U.S. capital dominated foreign investments in Mexico, accounting for 60 percent of the 3.4 billion pesos invested by 1911. Although most U.S. investors failed in Mexico, the Porfiriato attracted $1.5 billion and became the largest source of U.S. external investments anywhere in the world.

Mexican mines and railroads accounted for 83 percent of U.S. capital. The Guggenheims dominated Mexican mining when they established foundaries in Monterrey, Aquascalientes, Sierra Mojada, Chihuahua, and Baja California. Because the Guggenheims monopolized silver prices, minting, and marketing, Mexican miners had to sell ores at prices and quantities dictated by the Guggenheim trust. After the discovery of the first oil fields, Díaz willingly granted generous concessions when President William Howard Taft requested them. A California oilman, Edward Doheny, soon prospered after his first land purchase at Cerro de la Paz. Díaz also permitted International Harvester to monopolize henequen production in Yucatán with little regulation. International Harvester received 99.8 percent of Yucatecan henequen in return for loans to the planters. Maya laborers and plantation owners fell into debt peonage. In 1882, the U.S.-owned Continental Telephone Company bought the first telephone concession from a Mexican citizen and created Mextelco, which absorbed smaller Mexican firms. In 1885, Díaz established a free trade zone along the northern border that stimulated U.S. commerce at the expense of Mexican mechants. By the end of the same year, the United States accounted for 40 percent of Mexican trade.

British investments enhanced the Mexican economy greatly, even though British investors rarely realized an equal return for their capital investments. After Mexico had restored diplomatic relations, British investments soon amounted to roughly £40 million by the early 1890s. The British controlled utilities, an important portion of railroads and oil fields, and about 46 percent of commercial agriculture. Streetcars, dams, and sewer systems also resulted from British investment.

But British interest declined after most of their mining enterprises ended in disaster by the end of

Irrigation works in the Laguna region of southern Coahuila. *Personal collection of the author.*

the 1890s. Too often, British investors purchased property and mines without exploring their true worth; they feared that others would profit from a missed opportunity. British financiers often spent more money developing products for a Mexican market than what actually was returned to Britain. Common stock issues for rail building showed meager returns because of the high rates that British railroads charged. Afterwards, U.S. investors bought up British ventures and controlled more rail lines. By 1900, there were no British firms in Veracruz nor a wholesale outlet in Mexico City. Other parts of the empire presented more opportunities and only two or three British export houses existed in all of Mexico by 1904. Sir Weetman Pearson's Eagle Oil Company, on the other hand, became Mexico's most productive oil operation. After the successful exploitation of his first refinery at Minatitlán, this international engineer efficiently built a fortune. Sir Weetman enjoyed the active support of Porfirian officials, who always desired a European balance to U.S. influence.

The British slump occurred partially because Germany attempted to achieve economic gains in Mexico. German businessmen sold textiles, hardware, and purchased Mexican state bonds. Although 13 percent of all Mexican imports came from Germany by 1910, the unwillingness of German investors to acquire raw materials limited total German investments to 6.5 percent of all foreign capital in Mexico by the end of the Porfiriato.

Díaz steadily encouraged foreign investments by passing laws that allowed landowners to control the subsoil wealth of the nation. In 1887, Díaz exempted iron, coal, sulpher, and mercury from taxation. He also reduced the tax rates on other minerals to 2 percent of their value. Additional legislation in 1892 and 1905 relaxed further government control on the mining industry. A 1901 law enabled state governments to offer concessions from public lands to foreign investors. Díaz's 1909 law granted property holders ownership of natural resources—a legal sanction for monopolization.

Fiscal and Economic Policy. A powerful *científico*, José Ives Limantour consolidated financial policies beginning in the 1880s. Limantour's outlook reflected his fondness for Comte and Spencer. He believed that by virtue of their race and culture, the oligarchy should enjoy needed credit. Therefore, Limantour improved banking services. The *científicos* permitted 24 banks to maintain low reserves in proportion to the currency they issued. Because they offered technological and financial assistance, foreigners controlled the banking structure. The new banks often denied credit to Mexican cattlemen, preferring foreign ventures instead. Mexico did not have a national bank.

Tax reforms stimulated the economy but privileges persisted. A notable improvement occurred after the regime ended the sales tax in 1896, as well as customs charges levied by state governments. Direct taxes on income, property, and capital took place as time went on, but in many regions, smaller merchants and professionals paid a disproportionate amount of municipal taxes. Hacendados in Coahuila and other states paid relatively low taxes. Merchants and industrialists enjoyed tax-exempt status in several areas. Saltillo was one of many city governments in chronically bad shape because the upper class refused to pay a fair share of taxes.

Fiscal policy raised exports and maintained credit abroad. Increased tax revenues enabled Mexico to enjoy a budget surplus by 1894. Prices for Mexican goods sold abroad went up faster than the cost of imports. But going on the gold standard in 1905 hurt economic growth. This decision devalued the currency so that two pesos equaled a dollar. Two staples of male *norteño* (northern) life, Winchester rifles and Stetson hats, soon cost twice as much. Inflation also permitted foreign goods to undersell domestic products. In addition, devaluation encouraged foreign capital because when it converted into pesos, its original value appreciated greatly. Investments increased, but continued reliance upon foreign loans reflected an excessively orthodox financial policy. Díaz sought credit and promised to pay external obligations. Limantour did not significantly reduce the foreign debt, which consumed about one-third of government income after 1893. Foreign debt payments prevented the regime from carrying out more public works. Given its high cost, Mexico renegotiated the external debt in 1899 but pledged customs revenue as collateral.

Although building the infrastructure became a task for foreigners, its construction was a durable legacy. Improved harbors, new docks, public buildings, telegraph and telephone lines generated unprecedented economic activity. To symbolize the Porfirian determination for economic growth, *rurales* hanged vandalizers of the communications system along its poles.

The railroad system grew rapidly, from only 400 miles of track at the beginning of Díaz's rule to 15,000 miles by 1910. Despite his fear of excessive North American influence, Díaz allowed a variety of Yankee entrepreneurs to build five major lines from the border. Mexico intially provided land as an incentive before shifting to a policy of paying subsidies of 6,000 to 15,000 pesos for every kilometer of railroad lines built. Eventually, Mexico granted $32 million in subsidies for 2,500 miles of a north-south railroad network. In May 1880, a train went from Chihuahua to Mexico City for the first time. Díaz adopted a nationalist policy after 1902 when he purchased majority blocks of stock in companies that operated two-thirds of the railroads. Díaz reduced U.S. influence by controlling 8,000 of the 13,000 miles of railroad track when he formed the Mexican National Railways in 1908. The desire for railroads manifested itself on the regional level as well. In Yucatán, the local oligarchy financed construction of a railroad for the entire state. As part of the Porfiriato's late nationalism, the regime decided to end Mextelco's telephone monopoly by granting a new concession to José Sitzenstatter, who created a joint venture with a Swedish investor. They formed Mexeric, which had close ties to the Mexican government.

Steel rails brought tangible results. Railroads established trade and population centers throughout Mexico. The railroads offered such low passenger fares that Indians and *mestizos* traveled to other regions in search of work or simply to change a lifestyle. Transportation costs decreased greatly, which was a significant factor in econom-

The Guadalupe dam near Torreón, Coahuila. *Personal collection of the author.*

ic growth. The cost of shipping textiles from Quarétaro to Mexico City dropped from $62 dollars a ton in 1877 to $3 dollars a ton by 1910. The very axis on which the economy turned—from the colonial east-west route running from Veracruz through Puebla and Mexico City to Guadalajara—now became a new north-south axis tying Mexico into the U.S. economy by means of trunk railroad lines linking Mexico City with Laredo, El Paso, and Nogales.

Díaz also encouraged the growth of Mexican industry. He consistently maintained high tariff duties upon foreign goods The 1880 tariff made Mexico's rates on finished cotton goods the highest in the world. Duties upon foreign goods increased again in 1905. Industries normally enjoyed tax-exempt status for up to 30 years. New commercial codes in 1884 and 1887 simplified requirements to form corporations and enabled shareholders to guide policy and management. Foreigners continued to control retailing areas such as draperies and foodstuffs, but foreign capital furnished only 29.9 percent of the capital in Mexican industry. The volume of manufactured goods actually doubled, particularly in light industries such as breweries, glass factories, or plants producing cigarettes and soap. Established in 1899 with ten million pesos, the Compañia Fundidora de Fierro y Acero de Monterrey began producing steel for the national market in 1903. This Monterrey steel plant became the only one in Latin American until World War II. Textiles became Mexico's major industry to the extent that the percentage of foreign textiles sold in Mexico dropped from 32 percent in 1889 to 3 percent in 1910.

The Monterrey region assumed leadership of the modernization process, a role the Grupo Monterrey would retain throughout the twentieth century. By 1902, Nuevo León became the most industrialized state, even outdistancing the federal district. A small number of elite families in the Grupo Monterrey controlled financing and interpreted their mission as the modernization of the entire region. Extensive family ties produced a unanimity of interests within the Grupo Monterrey while success provided unflagging confi-

dence. With the aid of cosmopolitan interests, the Grupo Monterrey turned the Laguna region of nearby southern Coahuila into a fast-growing cotton producer centered in the city of Torreón. The Grupo Monterrey held an overt political power, usually operating through regional strongman Bernardo Reyes. But the leading cotton farmer of the north, Francisco Madero, attempted to spread the vision of modernization throughout the remainder of Mexico.

During the Porfiriato, capitalism began to define itself through family enterprises within a continuity of Mexican values. The Gómez family, for example, became vital to the Mexican textile industry after they moved from Puebla to Mexico City. The Gómez business was the basis of the family income and each member protected the operation by assuming clearly defined positions. Their beliefs envisioned work to enhance social status rather than accumulate profits. All the Gómez males focused totally upon entrepreneurship by working in various family businesses. Early on, each male was expected to initiate his own company, utilizing the extensive Gómez resources. Daughters and wives functioned primarily as social agents. The family operated on a corporatist tradition in that the priority of the family over the individual never wavered. Hence, management became centralized and autocratic. The main purpose of their labor was taking care of other family members. Therefore some offspring were kept on the payroll even if they did little or nothing. Continuity was maintained by the family rituals of Christmas, weddings, religious festivities, and regional traditions.

The Porfiriato's balance sheet of rapid economic production is impressive. International trade quadrupled as exports increased sevenfold at an annual average rate of 6 percent. The value of gold exports increased twenty-five times. Silver mining tripled its value; two-thirds of world silver supplies came from Mexico. Copper exports went from a value of 260,000 pesos in 1880 to 32 million pesos in 1910. Lead, zinc, and sulpher production surged tremendously, and Mexico became the world's third leading oil producer by 1911. Moreover, agricultural exports grew. Yucatán enjoyed an international monopoly of insect resistant henequen, a critical binder twine for agricultural harvests. Henequen exports rose from 40,000 bales of fiber to more than 600,000 bales. Cotton harvests almost quadrupled from 1892 to 1910. Sugar, coffee, and rubber became important items on the world market. Although beans and beef accounted for only one-tenth of agricultural exports, their production increased by 10 percent.

Díaz came to understand that agriculture was the most important branch of national wealth and that the best way to increase the land's productivity was by providing additional water resources. Before anything was done for the small farmers, the Tlahualilo cotton company took as much water from th Rio Nazas while small, downstream farmers in Coahuila received very little. Although the large, rich, and politically valuable landowners were highly visible, Díaz slowly realized that the small farmer was where he should direct his concerns. Then the Porfirian legislature passed regulations that enabled the small landowners to obtain water first.

Land Policies. Porfirian land policies favored powerful supporters and discriminated against the masses. In its drive to increase economic growth, satisfy prominent landowners, and attract foreign investment, the government allowed its supporters to take direct control of much of Mexico's public lands. The Fomento ministry, charged with overseeing the expansion of infrastructure and using roughly a third of the national budget, required vast budget increases. Fomento reasoned that unused land would stimulate economic activity if placed on the market so that the regime's allies could prosper. As if to illustrate the continuity between the Porfiriato and the liberals, the *científicos* used the 1863 public land law issued by Juárez to justify selling public lands. In addition, an 1883 colonization law encouraged the survey of frontier areas where the need for security supposedly dictated the settlement of families near borders. Little colonization actually took place.

The 50 land companies which undertook the surveys indicate the relationship between state and society. Díaz used the land companies cleverly to avoid direct criticism. Usually partnerships or joint-stock companies received the concessions to survey public lands. To encourage quick work and to provide pleasant rewards, the state allowed the survey companies to keep one-third of the land which they measured. In the often uninhabited north, there was less resistance to the surveys than in central Mexico or during the 1890s. The surveys sometimes raised land values, but at least one-third of the measurements resulted in opposition. *Rurales* and courts experienced protests from country villages, some of which lost their *ejidos*. Much public land went to railroad companies. Sparks from the trains angered peasants and communities resented the noise when the landowners moved their produce from station to port. Hacendados purchased public land on easy terms. State governments encouraged this sharp change as eagerly as Fomento officials. In 1894, the Coahuila legislature ordered that all communal lands be converted into private ownership. Approximately 40 percent of public lands eventually went into private hands as a result of this bidding on the public domain. This huge transfer of land, the largest in Mexican history, cut off pastures, forests, and hunting areas traditionally accessible to villagers. Ambitious peasants were now denied the possibility of rising to the status of *rancheros*.

The privatization of land became a strange mixture of neofeudalism and modern capitalism. Rural inhabitants could usually protect their property by presenting titles to judges. As in the colonial period, individuals eager for indigenous lands claimed that such property was vacant. Gradually abandoning his patriarchal relationship with indigenous communities, Díaz allowed individual foreigners, such as William Randolph Hearst, to buy millions of acres. International companies also pursued Mexican land ownership. In 1888, the national Congress permitted the British-controlled Compañia Tlahualilo to purchase 44,000 hectares of rich agricultural land in

Mexico's northeastern cotton-growing zone. Soon to become a foreign enclave, the Laguna produced cotton at an impressive rate but featured more foreigners than any other area except Mexico City. The Compañia stirred resentment because it enjoyed preferential water rights, duty-free tariff privileges, and a ten-year exemption from all municipal taxes. Often in collaboration with foreign businesses such as the Guggenheims, small groups of elite families dominated San Luis Potosí and other regions. Allowing foreign investors to control perhaps 25 percent of Mexico's national territory, particularly the very choicest lands, became a major error.

Rancheros also profited from Porfirian land policies, although they resented a loss of regional political power. Because the ranchos also expanded at the expense of *ejidos*, they increased from 14,075 in 1877 to 48,663 in 1910. Most rancheros were *mestizos* who lived by means of subsistence farming. Díaz counted on them for support in the interior, but many *rancheros* wanted to return to the nineteenth-century concept of greater local autonomy. By the end of his term, Díaz allowed his various allies to obtain one-fourth of the national territory.

Not surprisingly, the hacienda system reached its zenith during the Porfiriato. At this time hacienda profits and production revived because landowners adapted to new markets, pursued efficiency, and enjoyed low labor costs. The 8,431 haciendas spread so quickly that they contained almost half the rural population. Peons lived in squalor while the highly capitalized hacendados enjoyed luxury. Hacendados often spent their time in the capital or traveling abroad, usually visiting their estates each year. A majority of Mexico's 1,500 millionaires were hacendados.

Luis Terrazas became the greatest hacendado. He eventually owned half a million cattle and seven million acres in Chihuahua. Terrazas and his son-in-law, Enrique Creel, served as governors of Chihuahua for 20 years; Creel eventually became a minister of foreign relations. No other family in any other state at any other time equaled the Terrazas' complete domination of a political

and economic infrastructure. The Terrazas-Creel group exercised absolute control over the non-mining sectors of the economy, which became the fruit of their control of Chihuahua. As with other elites, the interrelationship of economic and political machines gave Terrazas the ability to create advantageous business conditions—which generated even more wealth and political spoils. The Chihuahua oligarchy granted favors only to itself and well-established foreigners. They excluded the nascent middle class because it was difficult to obtain land without political influence. Although the Terrazas-Creel alliance had an ability to exploit the export economy by means of favorable treatment accorded to foreign interests, they never played the subservient role to foreign enterprise that other elites did, when Mexicans often acted as intermediaries.

Díaz seems to have had misgivings about Fomento land policies but could not always control rural oligarchs. In some cases, Díaz sided with rural protesters out of his fear of instability and new revolts. In 1901, Congress revised Article 27 of the constitution to legalize land ownership by indigenous villages. The following year, Díaz personally took control of land surveys and ruled that cash would replace land as compensation to the land survey companies. In 1909, Díaz suspended contract purchases indefinitely, and new land recipients had to cultivate their property or the government would return it to the original owners. Nevertheless, hacendados used cooperative *jefes políticos* to acquire land despite Díaz's eventual dislike for the expropriation of *ejidos*.

Mexico Compared with Argentina. At this time, oligarchies controlled other Latin American societies. The process of modernization became quite similar during this period. How does Mexico compare with Argentina, usually considered the best-developed nation in Latin America during the late nineteenth and early twentieth centuries? Although the Argentine oligarchy is the most impressive elite system, the economic accomplishments of the Porfiriato mitigated its harsh social features.

Bullfight in Torreón, Coahuila, 1907. *Personal collection of the author.*

Mexico diversified its economic growth far more than Argentina. Díaz also encouraged industry more consistently than the Argentine oligarchs. The increased entrepreneural activity is revealed by the fact that patents registered in Argentina by 1904 were only a third of those in Mexico. The Porfirian railroad policy is probably the best of all the Latin American oligarchies because Díaz did not grant guaranteed profit clauses to foreign investors. Therefore, antiforeign sentiment against the railroads never appeared in Mexico to the extent that it did in Argentina. But Díaz failed to develop a national market that rivaled Argentina, where the domestic market for imported goods was three times larger than in Mexico.

Despite these differences, Mexico and Argentina experienced similarities. Terms of trade did not improve, although both countries enjoyed a surplus in trade earnings every year except one after the early 1890s. Like the Argentine oligarchs, the Mexican elites invested in a variety of ventures but habitually overextended themselves.

Social change had better results in Argentina. One exception is that positivism instilled a measure of intellectual self-confidence in Mexican elites and even stimulated a certain Mexicanism. The rivival of Sor Juana Inés de la Cruz's reputation began before 1910. The paintings of José Maria Velasco, Mexico's greatest landscape artist, evoked a deep pride in the light and shadow of the countryside. After his appointment to the National School of Fine Arts in 1877, Velasco exhibited his work in Madrid and Chicago. Argentina's immigration experience succeeded far more than in Mexico. The Porfiriato resolved its lack of manpower by using landless Indians. Argentine living conditions unquestionably surpassed those in Mexico. Real wages went up in Argentina almost continually; in Mexico, they leveled off after 1900. Rural Mexicans earned an average of 19 cents U.S. a day. Mexico's middle class grew to only 8 percent of the population, while in Argentina the middle class was a third of Buenos Aires and became rooted deeply throughout provincial cities. Harsh working conditions characterized both countries, but they were less appealing in Mexico.

Foreign Relations. Mexico's international prestige had increased greatly by 1900. Once Japan adopted a policy of bilateral negotiations, Mexico concluded a significant treaty of amity and commerce with the Asian power in 1888. Mexico became the only country in the world whose citizens could reside and trade anywhere in Japan. Mexico gradually expanded trade with Japan by exchanging silver for porcelain, furniture, and other Japanese products. Although fraud and other abuses bothered Japanese contract laborers, Japanese investors became active in Mexico after 1900.

Mexico also enjoyed excellent relations with Europe. Growing concern over unregulated foreign enterprises in all areas of Mexican life concerned the elites, who did not necessarily desire U.S. economic domination. Therefore, the *científicos* granted additional favors to British, German, and French investors. Díaz also welcomed German advisors to manage military reorganization, plan compulsory military service, and sell armaments. These developments, however, did not weaken good relations with the United States.

Although State Department officials lauded Díaz continuously, they noticed a growing Mexican assertiveness on the world scene. During the 1898 conflict between the United States and Cuban rebels against Spain, Mexico favored Cuban independence yet feared the eventual U.S. military occupation. The Díaz regime decided to support continued Spanish control of Cuba after the landing of U.S. troops and adopted a pro-Spanish position, despite public protestations of strict neutrality. Díaz had to be careful because the United States backed Mexico's position in resolving the Chiapas boundary dispute with Guatemala. Nevertheless, Díaz supported Nicaraguan President José Santos Zelaya, who the United States attempted to overthrow. U.S. investments also created some animosity because many Mexicans believed that Díaz was turning

the country's resources over to the United States. Therefore, a 1909 mining law prohibited mining in Mexico near the border.

As a testimony to Mexico's heightened diplomatic stature, Díaz hosted the second meeting of the Pan American Conference. Mexico's foreign relations minister announced this Porfirian triumph on January 31, 1902, it was a proud moment. Porfirian progress impressed the participants who attended the gala meeting. But outside the capital, unrest began to appear.

DISCONTENT DURING THE PORFIRIATO, 1900-1910

Evolution of the Labor Movement. The isolation of social and ethnic groups, a strengthened Church, and bleak opportunities within the elitist educational system discouraged the class awareness of the working class. Of five million working citizens by 1910, agriculture employed 3,957,000. About 565,000 more worked in light industries, 97,000 served in the mines, while communications and transport workers numbered 54,000. Dependent upon personal relationships with their employers, workers expected little from the Porfirian policy of basing economic growth upon cheap, submissive laborers. Paid poorly and lacking effective political representatives, the workers often reacted strongly against specific grievances.

Workers became increasingly nationalistic as part of an overall quest for social justice. About 250 strikes during the Porfiriato reflect a determination to reject cultural changes often imposed by foreign employers. Mexican workers often resisted toiling on a daily basis and preferred departing mines and refineries when they pleased. Drinking liquor during leisure time and often a missing a Monday morning annoyed foreign overseers.

Perhaps more than any other issue, workers resented the unusual privileges that foreign workers enjoyed. Because Mexican workers had little access to managerial or technical positions, they resented discrimination. Mexicans usually received lower wages than U.S. or European employees. Foreign workers nearly always avoided speaking Spanish as did many company doctors who treated Mexican laborers. Aroused by radicals, the workers fervently backed the popular slogan, "Mexico for Mexicans." With few death and injury benefits, workers began to organize.

Mutualist societies nurtured the first buds of working-class solidarity. French thinker Pierre Joseph Proudhon urged workers to obtain just compensation for their labor by establishing agricultural and industrial communes. In Mexico, Proudhon's distaste for urbanization and fondness for rural values emerged in more conservative organizations. Mutualist leaders established societies of shoemakers, bakers, musicians, mechanics, and pulque workers. Generally apolitical, mutualism operated by means of small payments of 50 centavos each month in return for medical funds, burial fees, and emergency loans. After the first mutualist society appeared in a Mexico City neighborhood in 1853, a central organization of mutualist societies met for the first time in 1870.

A cooperative movement also stimulated class consciousness. Like the mutualists, cooperative organizers convinced villagers to set up independent production groups that exchanged their goods with other communities. The cooperatives stimulated cultural preparation, civil rights instruction, and literary reunions. As brotherhoods sprang up in the 1870s and 1880s, the press encouraged their activities.

Díaz and Labor. To pacify labor, Diaz provided peaceful worker organizations with printing presses, buildings, and night schools. Díaz also sponsored several cooperatives and allowed pliant labor leaders to win elections. The government tolerated some strikes if they responded to pay cuts or various abuses. Labor leaders often requested Díaz's intervention and he usually tried to mediate peaceful strikes. Moderate labor leaders were in a position to urge obedience to the government because real wages increased from 1877 to 1898.

Anarchism eventually became the dominant ideology of Mexican labor. Influenced by Rhodakanaty's extreme libertarian and socialist views, strikes and *campesino* revolts erupted. Advanced labor ideas continued to flow into Mexico and spur growing militancy. After the first national workers' congress took place in 1876, anarchism spread quickly by means of syndicate organizations. Syndicalism gradually replaced mutualism and cooperatives as Spanish exiles aided the organization of several unions. A steady stream of U.S. anarchist writings also encouraged syndicalist solidarity.

The most famous anarchist was Ricardo Flores Magón. He became influential by founding the newspaper *Regeneración* in 1900. Familiar with Bakunin and Kropotkin, Flores Magón wanted to destroy the capitalist state by means of an armed proletariat organized in cells. As an anarchocommunist, Flores Magón urged that village communes and small labor unions replace the Díaz regime. Hounded out of Mexico and harassed by U.S. police who facilitated the work of Mexican agents, Flores Magón spent virtually his entire life in jail or exile. But his prestige among miners and *campesinos* increased due to the influence of *Regeneración*, which argued that the land should be redistributed and the *ejidos* restored.

Labor Conditions. Mistreatment of Mexican workers was severe. Often forced to pay bribes to keep their jobs or buy gifts for their foremen, workers wanted respect. Lack of dignity arose from fines imposed upon those who danced, shouted, and behaved in any way that management considered unfit. Most workers received their pay in scrip that was redeemable only in company stores. Particularly resented was the quota system in which workers had to complete assigned tasks before leaving. Toxic chemicals and high humidity in the textile plants endangered many lives.

Labor conditions varied according to region. In the south, brutal treatment on plantations created a labor shortage. Unscrupulous officials sold prisoners who rarely lived more than a year as slavery predominated. Foreigners exploited southern workers more directly whether they were German coffee growers in Chiapas, Spanish and Cuban tobacco planters in Oaxaca and Veracruz, or U.S. rubber planters in Tehauntepec.

Central Mexico experienced a labor surplus because the haciendas grew at the expense of villages. Peasants competed to become sharecroppers in return for handing over 40 to 50 percent of their harvests. Sharecroppers usually worked on undesirable land and frequently fought each other as unemployment increased. In the north, haciendas paid good wages because of the competition for labor among miners, U.S. developers in the southwest, and the railroad builders.

Weaknesses of the Economy. Despite the impressive growth of exports, increased emphasis upon commercial items such as rubber, coffee, henequen, and sugar resulted in declining food production in terms of beans, corn, and chile peppers. Food became twice as expensive when it became less available. The country increased from 9 million to 15 million inhabitants and a high demand for food resulted. Mexican cattlemen shipped more stock across the border because it sold for higher prices in the United States. When real wages declined after 1898, the poor ate less and begging occurred on a greater scale. The diet suffered because the landowners also tripled the production of mescal and tequila, while pulque output quadrupled. Alcoholism and gambling among working people increased as part of their general desperation.

In addition to lack of food, the economy experienced a grim recession. After 1902, prices for imports went up faster than exports. The intense interdependence that evolved with the United States after the 1870s forced Mexico to accept the unpleasant ramifications of the 1907 crash north of the border. Unemployment suddenly increased in the north as well as the rest of Mexico. A major problem was that rural as well as urban laborers could not often find work in the growing cities. The peso began to lose value because of a fall in silver prices. The Díaz government began restricting foreign companies from transferring ownership to foreign nations. From 1900 to 1910, the regime also subjected many companies to national law. But criticism of U.S. control of the economy became so intense that Díaz shut down three newspapers from 1909 to 1910. The inability to halt the economic crisis cost Díaz his credibility.

Labor Opposition. Flores Magón organized the Partido Liberal Mexicano (PLM) in St. Louis, which would play a key role in the early years of the civil war. More police harassment motivated Magón to declare the Plan de 1906. Here the PLM called for a four-year presidential term with no reelection. The declaration demanded the emancipation of women, an eight-hour working day, minimum wages, and the end of child labor. In order to escape police arrest, Magón moved to Los Angeles and began sending raiders into Coahuila from Del Rio and El Paso by 1907. Although the PLM was still a nominally liberal group, Magón secretly committed the PLM to revolutionary anarchism in 1908. Under pressure from Enrique Creel, the Mexican ambassador, local authorities arrested Magón, who did not reemerge until August 1910. Followers such as Práxedis Guerrero continued to lash out at Díaz in three newspapers until Guerrero was killed in 1910 at Janos, Chihuahua. By then, Magón accepted class struggle and the necessity to destroy the state as well as crush capitalism in order to end poverty.

Increasingly militant syndicalism continued. The formation of a Grand Circle of Free Workers in the Orizaba textile zone led to the establishment of 80 more branches throughout Mexico. On June 1, 1906, workers voted to follow its tough syndicalism with the hope that widespread strikes would improve working conditions and topple Díaz. They went on strike in late 1906 and early 1907. At the same time, Díaz succumbed to the pressure of foreign capitalists when he came down hard on the textile workers. Locked out of their jobs at Rio Blanco, workers attacked the company store and rioted in a spontaneous revolt until army troops killed over 100 of them. In Cananea, Sonora, a bitter strike erupted in June 1906 when the U.S. owners refused to meet demands for better jobs and pay. To make matters worse, Porfirian authorities allowed Arizona state rangers to shoot down the strikers.

By 1910, Díaz and the *científicos* had aroused mass opposition. Once the value of their wages had sunk to 1877 levels, workers increasingly adapted new ideas of class conflict. Crushing the strikes at Cananea and Rio Blanco had also alienated moderate labor leaders who had previously supported Díaz.

Political Unrest. Publicly expressed dissent first came from the traditional sector of the upper class, the group usually considered the most privileged. Not all landowners were able to survive the 1908 credit crisis, which was accompanied by a severe drought. Limantour had endeavored to rescue the weakening banks by calling in mortgages and denying long-term credit to insolvent hacendados. These new credit restrictions elicited a storm of protest from many landowners. In addition to financial difficulties, hacendados could no longer draw upon as large a rural labor force as they had in the past. By offering better wages, cotton plantations, textile factories, and mines contributed to the shortage of field hands. The practice of directing federal expenditures to profitable areas resulted in regional imbalances that also angered landowners. *El Estandarte*, representative of the elite point of view, printed landowner attacks against the *científicos* on its front pages.

Overwhelmingly favorable to Díaz and his regime for many years, intellectuals increasingly attacked Porfirian policies after 1900. Some criticized Díaz's abuse of power while others, such as Andrés Molina Enríquez, lambasted the haciendas as economic fossils. Disturbed by the materialistic attitudes of the *científicos*, Catholic writers imbued with a social reform doctrine criticized rural labor conditions and alcoholism forced upon indigenous people. Moreover, U.S. intervention in Cuba shocked Mexican elites, who had considered the United States cured of its territorial appetite. As a consequence, nationalist intellectuals conceived of a Hispanic brotherhood against U.S. imperialism.

The problem of who would succeed the aging Díaz sparked widespread political mobilization. Events began in March 1908 when Díaz, by means of a newspaper interview with U.S. reporter James Creelman, announced that he would not seek reelection in the 1910 presidential election. A crafty politician who had no interest in yielding power, Díaz undoubtedly wanted to draw out his opponents by pitting them against one another.

The immediate result was that Bernardo Reyes seemed to be the probable winner. Many of the traditional elites, as well as the middle class, supported Reyes for his opposition to *científico* policies. These groups felt that favoritism frustrated their political and economic ambitions. Reyes articulated a growing nationalism by attacking dreadful labor conditions in the Guggenheim mines. Reyismo became stronger in the northeast when it became evident that the Tlahualilo company wasted an inordinate amount of its excessive water rights, defaulted on its payments, and embezzled funds.

Another challenger was Francisco I. Madero. An idealistic Coahuilan landowner worth $25 million and convinced that he could democratize Mexican political life, Madero established an antireelectionist party and opposed Díaz candidates during the 1905 elections. He also published a highly influential book, *La sucesión presidencial en 1910*, in which he called for an effective vice-president, a restoration of constitutional norms, and accused Díaz of abuses instigated for his personal benefit. A gradualist at this time, Madero also demanded new leadership from the municipalities as well as state governments. Popular after the publication of his book in early 1909, Madero yearned to defeat both Reyes and Díaz. Momentarily caught off guard, the *científicos* pushed the candidacy of Limantour, since he represented their interests better than anyone else.

Worried about the widespread political mobilization that had developed, Díaz allowed the *científicos* to name him as their candidate shortly afterwards. The wily despot seemed to leave open the choice of his vice-president as Reyes stepped forward to offer himself. Instead, Díaz imposed his choice of Ramón Corral, the current vice-president, who apparently suffered from syphilis contracted in one of his own Sonora brothels. The selection of Corral alienated many because he was an Indian slaver despite his reputation for educational reform. Almost immediately, *científico* newspapers attacked Díaz opponents as police initiated a rough crackdown upon Maderistas and Reyistas. The compliant Reyes accepted a military commission to Europe in order to repay past favors to Díaz. Díaz jailed Madero, and in June 1910 the government announced that Díaz had triumphed in the presidential elections. The issue of honest elections would dog Mexican governments well into the 1990s.

Although Dîaz had increased state control over the church, *ejidos*, and foreigners to a varying degree that future Mexican governments would follow, the socioeconomic discontent that intensified after 1900 served to isolate Díaz and his cronies. Corral was the only person in the upper echelons of the elite under the age of 65. Governors and bureaucrats roughly averaged 70 years old. They seemed out of touch with a newly assertive nationalism. During the centennial celebrations in 1910, Porfirian officials did not place Mexican items on menus for the constant banquets held at this time.

Díaz succeeded early in his career because he eschewed ideology, promised upward mobility, and possessed a sense of realism which enabled him to construct the modern Mexican state. Although he never lost his vision of a thriving nation, Díaz minimized the needs of average Mexicans. Díaz had also united the ruling oligarchical clique and incorporated it into the Porfirian state. But the 1907 economic crisis divided the elite to the point that Yucatecan planters plotted to defeat Olegario Molina's control of the henequen trade. Overall, the Porfiriato was a successful exercise in modernization, but the human cost limited its overall achievement. After 1900, the reconcentration of prosperity and an alienation of the national domain resulted in a Díazpotism which had widened the gap between rich and poor.

SUGGESTED READING

Alder Lomnitz, Larisa and Marisol Perez-Lizaur. *A Mexican Elite Family, 1820–1980. Kinship, Class, and Culture.* Princeton: Princeton University Press, 1987.

Albro, Ward S. *To Die on Your Feet: The Life, Times, and Writings of Praxedis Guerrero.* Fort Worth: Texas Christian University Press, 1995.

Anderson, Rodney D. *Outcasts in Their Own Land: Mexican Industrial Workers, 1906–1911.* DeKalb: Northern Illinois University Press, 1976.

Basurto, Jorge. *El proletariado industrial en México, 1850–1930.* Mexico City: UNAM Press, 1975.

Bazant, Mílada. *Historia de la educacíon durante el porfiriato.* Mexico City: El Colegio de Mexico, 1993.

Beezley, William H. *Judas at the Jockey Club and Other Episodes of Porfirian Mexico.* Lincoln: University of Nebraska Press, 1987.

Benjamin, Thomas, and William McNellie. *Other Mexicos: Essays on Regional Mexican History, 1876–1911.* Albuquerque: University of New Mexico Press, 1984. .

Benjamin, Thomas and Marcial Ocasio-Meléndez. "Organizing the Memory of Modern Mexico: Porfirian Historiography in Perspective, 1880s–1980s." *Hispanic American Historical Review* 64:2 (May 1984), 323–364.

Bernstein, Marvin D. *The Mexican Mining Industry, 1890–1950.* Albany: State University of New York Press, 1964.

Brown, Jonathan C. "Foreign and Native-Born Workers in Porfirian Mexico." *American Historical Review* 98:3 (June 1993), 786–818.

Buchenau, Jürgen. *In the Shadow of the Giant: The Making of Mexico's Central American Policy, 1876–1930.* Tuscaloosa:University of Alabama Press, 1996.

Ceceña, José Luis. *México en la orbita imperial.* Mexico City: Ediciones El Cabillito, 1970.

Cockcroft, James D. *Intellectual Precursors of the Mexican Revolution, 1900–1913.* Austin: University of Texas Press, 1968.

Coerver, Don M. *The Porfirian Interregnum: The Presidency of Manuel Gonzalez of Mexico, 1880–1884.* Fort Worth: Texas Christian University Press, 1979.

Cortés Conde, Roberto. *The First Stages of Modernization in Spanish America.* New York: Harper and Row, 1974.

Cosío Villegas, Daniel. *The United States Versus Porfirio Díaz.* Lincoln: University of Nebraska Press, 1963.

Flandrau, Charles M. ¡*Viva Mexico*! Urbana: University of Illinois Press, 1964.

French, William E. "Prostitution and Guardian Angels: Women, Work, and the Family in Porfirian Mexico." *Hispanic American Historical Review* 72:4 (November 1992), 529–553.

Hale, Charles. *The Transformation of Liberalism in Late Nineteenth Century Mexico.* Princeton, NJ: Princeton University Press, 1989.

Hart, John M. *Anarchism and the Mexican Working Class, 1860–1931.* Austin: University of Texas Press, 1978.

———. *Revolutionary Mexico: The Coming and Process of the Mexican Revolution.* Berkeley: University of California Press, 1987.

Holden, Robert H. *Mexico and the Survey of Public Lands: The Management of Modernization, 1876–1911.* DeKalb:Northern Illinois University Press, 1994.

Johns, Michael. *The City of Mexico in the Age of Díaz.* Austin: University of Texas Press, 1997.

Joseph, Gilbert M. *Revolution From Within: Yucatán, Mexico, and the United States, 1880-1924.* Durham: Duke University Press, 1980.

Katz, Friedrich. "Labor Conditions on Haciendas in Porfirian Mexico: Some Trends and Tendencies." *Hispanic American Historical Review* 54 (February 1974), 1–47.

Knight, Alan. *The Mexican Revolution.* Vol. 1: *Porfirians, Liberals, and Peasants.* New York: Cambridge University Press, 1986.

Kroeber, Clifton B. *Man, Land, and Water: Mexico's Farmlands Irrigation Policies, 1855-1911.* Berkeley: University of California Press, 1983.

MacLachlan, Colin M., and William H. Beezley. *El Gran Pueblo: A History of Greater Mexico.* Upper Saddle River, NJ: Prentice Hall, 1994.

Macias, Anna. *Against All Odds: The Feminist Movement in Mexico.* Westport, CT: Greenwood Press, 1982.

Martínez Jimenez, Alejandro. "La educacion elemental en el porfiriato." *Historia Mexicana* 22:4 (Jan.-Mar. 1973), 514–52.

Meyers, William K. *Forge of Progress, Crucible of Revolt: The origins of the Mexican Revolution in La Comarca Lagunera, 1890–1911.* Albuquerque: University of New Mexico Press, 1994.

Pletcher, David M. *Rails, Mines, and Progress: Seven American Promoters in Mexico, 1867–1911.* Ithaca,NY: Cornell University Press, 1958.

Raat, W. Dirk. *Revoltosos: Mexico's Rebels in the United States, 1903–1923.* College Station: Texas A&M University Press, 1981.

Randall, Laura. *A Comparative Economic History of Latin America, 1500–1914.* 4 vols. Ann Arbor, MI: University Microfilms International, 1977.

Richmond, Douglas W. *Carlos Pellegrini and the Crisis of the Argentine Elites, 1880–1916.* New York: Praeger, 1989.

———. "Comparative Economic and Financial Structures in Argentina and Mexico: A Study of Elitist Policies, 1880–1916." *Essays in Economic and Business History* 11 (1993), 38–48.

Stevens, Donald P. "Agrarian Policy and Instability in Porfirian Mexico." *The Americas* 39 (October 1982), 153–66.

Tischendorf, A. D. *Great Britain and Mexico in the Era of Porfirio Díaz.* Durham, NC: Duke University Press, 1961.

Vanderwood, Paul J. *Disorder and Progress: Bandits, Police and Mexican Development.* Lincoln: University of Nebraska Press, 1981.

———. *The Power of God against the Guns of Government: Religious Upheaval in Mexico at the Turn of the Nineteenth Century.* Stanford, CA:Stanford University Press, 1998.

Walker, David. "Porfirian Labor Policies: Working Class Organizations in Mexico City and Porfirio Diaz, 1876–1902." *The Americas* 37 (January 1981), 257–89.

Wasserman, Mark. *Capitalists, Caciques, and Revolution: The Native Elite and Foreign Enterprise in Chihuahua, Mexico.* Chapel Hill: University of North Carolina Press, 1984.

Wells, Alan. *Yucatán's Gilded Age: Haciendas, Henequen and International Harvester.* Albuquerque: University of New Mexico Press, 1985.

———. "All in the Family: Railroads and Henequen Monoculture in Porfirian Yucatan." *Hispanic American Historical Review* 72 (1992), 159–209.

Wells, Allen and Gilbert M. Joseph. *Summer of Discontent, Seasons of Upheavel: Politics and Rural Insurgency in Yucatan, 1876–1915.* Stanford: Stanford University Press, 1996.

Zea, Leopoldo. *The Latin American Mind.* Norman: University of Oklahoma Press, 1963.

11

The Revolution Begins, 1910–1914

The insurrection that began in November 1910 became the bloodiest confrontation ever fought in the Americas. The reformist and nationalistic tendencies of the Mexican Revolution made it similar to other international social movements, particularly in China and Turkey. A historic culmination of the Mexican search for identity as well as increased class conflict also characterized this conflict. Porfirian capitalism had ignited a rebellion that became dynamic where labor had mobilized, foreign capital dominated, and where industry as well as haciendas had a prominent presence. The conditions that provoked the Mexican Revolution depended on specific grievances in each region and state. Because the north reflected much of this discontent, first Francisco Madero and then Venustiano Carranza triumphed by 1915.

REFORMIST LEADERSHIP UNDER MADERO, 1910–1913

The Madero Campaign. Madero's wealthy family owned about 1.7 million acres of land and he was the biggest hacendado in Coahuila. Large cotton producers, the Madero family began losing money after the 1907 depression hit Mexico. The Maderos also enjoyed a nationalistic reputation because they owned the only Mexican smelter in the northeast and had joined the 1893 revolt with the Carranza family as well as having opposed the Tlahualilo company's water monopoly in the Laguna.

Madero exhibited strange oddities uncharacteristic of contemporary Mexico. Only 5 feet 2 inches tall, Madero spoke with a squeaky voice and perhaps weighed 140 pounds. A vegetarian who did not drink and a spiritualist who claimed he heard voices, Madero studied law in Paris. He also completed a semester at the University of California in Berkeley. Madero's studies abroad also exposed him to humanitarian ideals. After his 1896 return to Mexico, Madero provided respectable housing, decent wages, rudimentary educations, and physical examinations for his workers. Not only patriarchal, Madero also used new technology to increase production on his hacienda.

Madero strongly resembles the moralistic call for reforms voiced by the progressive movement in the United States. After the Creelman interview, Madero summarized his ideas in a book. He praised Díaz's economic progress but called for free courts, an open press, and honest elections. Although mediocre and lacking clarity, the book made Madero popular as he toured Mexico. Once Reyes departed, many former Reyistas joined

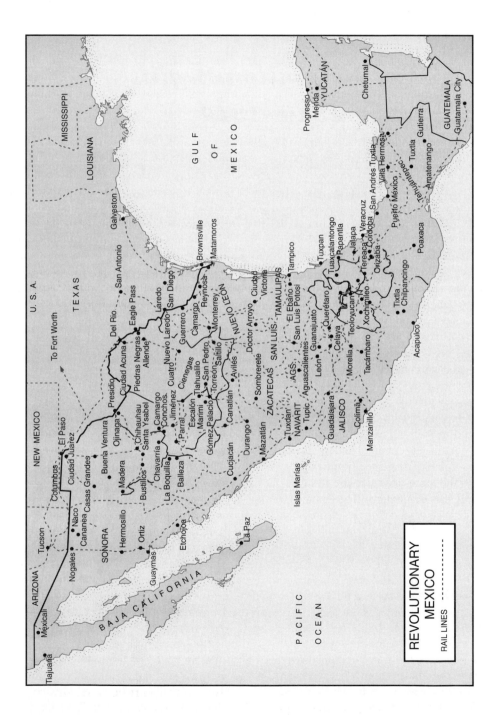

Mexico, 1910–1920

REVOLUTIONARY
MEXICO

RAIL LINES - - - - - - - - - -

Madero's antireelection party or its numerous clubs that sprang up in 1909. During an interview with Díaz, Madero explained that he sought to arouse society to take politics seriously. Díaz dismissed Madero as an eccentric until Madero attracted larger crowds. Now 80 years old, Díaz jailed Madero and celebrated the centennial anniversary of Mexican independence. The government spent 20 million pesos on fiestas, parades, and 20 carloads of champagne. As an indication of the closed nature of the political system, Madero received only 196 votes in the elections.

The 1910 Revolution. Freed on bail, Madero escaped from Mexico on October 7 and slipped into San Antonio, Texas. There he proclaimed his Plan de San Luis Potosí, backdating it to the last day Madero remained in the city. This call for revolt nullified the elections and named Madero provisional president. Madero emphasized parliamentary democracy as his goal and promised to limit foreign concessions. He said little about social problems but promised that lands seized unjustly would be returned. Madero declared that government should not improve labor conditions. He insisted that political freedom and the right to organize unions were what Mexican workers needed most.

Planned for November 20, 1910, Madero's revolt turned out to be an initial failure. Only 25 unarmed rebels greeted Madero when he crossed the border. A militant labor organizer, Aquiles Serdán, and his wife became the only real antireelectionist heroes. In Puebla, Porfirian forces besieged their home before killing them. Limited fighting erupted in Coahuila. While Maderistas attacked the Laguna region and seized Gómez Palacio, the Carranza brothers fomented other revolts in various Coahuilan towns and villages, but these efforts lacked direction and failed to triumph decisively.

Victories in Chihuahua occurred when leaders relatively unconnected with the Maderista campaign started winning as guerrillas. Quite discouraged, Madero unceremoniously began departing for New Orleans and Europe until Pascual Oroz-

co won some important victories. Porfirian restrictions had cut into Orozco's freight business which angered him greatly. The muleteer and a famous cattle rustler, Pancho Villa, agreed to fight for a revolt organized by Abraham González, a dissident member of the oligarchy who joined the Antireelectionist Party earlier. An encouraged Madero returned to Mexico again in February 1911 but proved to be an ineffective military leader. Therefore, he returned to San Antonio and organized a Junta Revolucionaria Mexicana to recruit troops and form a provisional government.

Madero's revolt soon forced Díaz to quit by May 1911. Only about 20 percent of the population actually participated in the struggle against the Porfiriato, but since few defended the Díaz system, small numbers of armed rebels eventually won. An extremely diverse group fought in the name of Madero. Several mountain peasants living in isolated areas resented their loss of political autonomy and supported Madero's calls for effective suffrage and municipal liberty. Diverse working-class groups felt that Madero would support a drive to improve their lives. Substantial leaders

Francisco I. Madero, President of Mexico, 1911 to 1913. *Courtesy of Centro de Estudios de Historia de México.*

Maderísta rebels seizing a passenger train in Coahuila.
Personal collection of the author.

rose to shape such social desires. Anxious to overthrow the local oligarchy, José M. Maytorena triumphed in Sonora by April, with the aid of Yaqui Indians. When the *científico* oligarchy in Hermosillo denied Guaymas merchants a railroad, Maytorena took up the cause of Sonora's major port. Offering volunteers 500 pesos to fight for Madero helped ensure victory. In the south, Emiliano Zapata organized a formidable campaign. The Porfirian land grab angered Zapata and other villagers because the *científicos* permitted wealthy Morelos sugar planters to take *ejido* lands from the rural population. After Flores Magón's forces succeeded in capturing Mexicali in January, the Maderistas planned to seize Ciudad Juárez. But Madero began arresting anarchosyndicalists who did not support him because the Magonistas offered a radical agenda that could not be co-opted. Nevertheless, Madero enjoyed widespread popularity at this point in his career.

Peace negotiations with Porfirian representatives ended the surprisingly brief struggle. Conferences between Maderistas and Díaz arbitrators began in Ciudad Juárez after they declared an armistice on April 22, 1911. Díaz agreed to the resignation of Vice-President Corral but little else. Madero did not make very ambitious demands and brushed aside objections from many rebels that the *científicos* should be kicked out of the government along with Díaz. Unable to decide, Madero broke off negotiations and ordered his supporters to withdraw from their positions near Juárez. But Orozco and Villa attacked the city anyway, and it capitulated on May 21. The resulting treaty forced Díaz to leave. But Madero accepted as interim president Francisco León de la Barra, a Porfirian official sympathetic to Maderistá goals. The bureaucracy and military remained intact with the same personnel. Madero only gained the promise of free elections, various cabinet seats, and a few new governors. Disenchanted rebels such as Venustiano Carranza prophetically opposed the settlement by claiming that a revolution which compromises only commits suicide. Madero quieted Carranza by naming him minister of war four days later and agreed that he should be the new governor of Coahuila. But Madero snubbed Orozco by giving him an unimportant position. The result would be prolonged factional conflict.

The Madero Government. After the defeat of Díaz, Mexico needed socioeconomic reforms badly but remained unprepared for democracy. Madero never solved this dilemma and, for that reason, his regime lasted only 14 months. De la Barra, Madero, and a number of intellectuals associated with the dictatorship agreed that a union movement should be permitted, limited land redistribution could take place, and that *campesinos* required more educational opportunities.

The interim presidency of de la Barra succeeded in establishing a National Agrarian Commission as well as a national labor agency. But the masses became impatient with legalistic reform and vented their anxieties through land seizures, strikes, and general violence. Yet the willingness of conservatives to consider social change in 1911 illustrates the continuity between the Porfiriato and twentieth-century Mexico. The masses expected significant changes from Madero, who was really a "silk hat revolutionary," in the words of William H. Beezley, who evoked enormous expectations despite his wealthy background.

During the first fair election in many years, Madero triumphed easily in October 1911. But the presence of *científicos* in charge of the bureaucracy and hostile military officers handicapped the degree to which Madero could carry out meaningful reforms. Tied to a superficial reformism, Madero assumed that a change of government would satisfy society. He continued to insist that Mexico would develop through clean elections. But with three-fourths of the citizens of Mexico illiterate, Madero's idea of reform was unrealistic. As a rich hacendado, Madero represented the bourgeoisie that wanted modifications to Porfirian policies but not major changes.

Madero did not attempt to curry favor with U.S. interests. His government encouraged foreign capital to invest but disapproved of legal privileges for U.S. trusts. Madero imposed a 20 centavo tax per barrel on all crude oil producers. He also forced them to adopt the metric system and dismissed several hundred U.S. employees from the national railway system because they would not speak Spanish. The Madero regime also refused to compensate the United States for loss of life and property during the early phase of the Mexican Revolution. Madero would not agree to a reciprocal treaty with the United States because such an agreement would reduce Mexican customs fees.

Continuing the policy of the recent Porfiriato, Madero seemed to favor increased European participation rather than U.S. control of the economy. Partially because of family ties to the Deutsch-Südamerikanische Bank and other German firms, Madero allowed the Germans to control a new Mexican mortgage bank. Trade with Germany reached its height during the 1911–1912 years. Madero rarely took any steps that British or French investors disliked.

Madero's social reforms became a major disappointment. The new president appointed a cousin to head a National Agrarian Commission, which had been created earlier by the de la Barra regime. After considering the land problem, the agency concluded that the government should purchase a few large properties and sell them to landless peasants. But with only 10 million pesos with which to operate, the commission could do little, and hacendado opposition blocked action. The government reluctantly agreed to return *ejido* land unjustly seized earlier, but few villages benefited.

Madero also continued the Díaz policy of attacking radical trade union activity and attempting to attract backers from new labor organizations. Guided by laissez-faire thinking, Madero's small Department of Labor did not sympathize with the needs of workers. When mediating a conflict between striking Puebla textile workers and the Spanish owners, Madero's officials favored the employers. The regime may have deplored the miserable living conditions of most working-class Mexicans, but it feared strikes and favored business interests consistently. Not surprisingly, Madero tried to weaken anarchosyndicalism by exiling its leaders and closing their organizations. Nevertheless, the Casa del Obrero Mundial (House of the World Worker) emerged in the summer of 1912 to organize skilled workers, service workers, and students. When they began preparing their adherents to carry out anarchosyndicalist strikes, Madero cracked down. Because the Casa del Obrero Mundial had weak links with industrial workers, Madero encouraged these laborers to organize into mutualist societies. Many unions emerged in the freer atmosphere of the Maderista period, but they did not enjoy great satisfaction from the government's attempt to win their support through federal arbitration.

Meager educational progress frustrated many. The government built 50 new schools and provided poor students with free lunches, but the budget for education remained virtually the same as during the Porfiriato. True educational improvements actually depended upon state and local entities, which came about in the north. But with *científico* ideas still intact within the federal education bureaucracy, the school system usually retained an excessive centralization. Many intellectuals and academics detested Madero.

Given the absence of desire for thorough reforms on the federal level, state governments had the responsibility for implementing deep reforms. Madero believed that social and economic reforms became the responsibility of fairly elected local rulers. He installed antireelectionist governors in each state, but most became ineffective. In Yucatán, for example, the ruling oligarchy co-opted the Maderistas and opposed the formation of a public henequen monopoly. Madero's weak political linkage to the interior occurred partially because governors had few guidelines other than to encourage free elections and discharge rebel troops.

Nevertheless, strong reformers enacted striking reforms in Sonora, Chihuahua, and Coahuila. In these states, popular governors supported strikers, improved education, and began regulating foreign investments. They also revised tax systems to provide public services on the municipal level while forcing hacendados and privileged indus-trialists to pay more. Somewhat moralistic, they also initiated a campaign against vice. Nearly all rejoiced when these states outlawed *jefes políticos*. Madero frequently argued with Governor Carranza of Coahuila and others concerning the size of state military forces. The reformers also demanded that Madero's government assume a wider responsibility for tighter federal regulation of major industries as well as improved labor reforms.

Political Opposition to Madero. Madero's early popularity declined quickly. The federal army attacked rebel groups who still refused to lay down their weapons. Madero also practiced blatant nepotism. Because Madero insisted upon loyalty as his major prerequisite for public office, his brother Gustavo and various uncles as well as cousins took over key posts. More disheartening was the crass corruption displayed by family members. Not surprisingly, several early Maderistas lost faith in the president and formed a Bloque Renovador in Congress. Led by Luis Cabrera, they called for land reforms by December 1912 and demanded hacienda expropriation and ejidal restoration. Madero attempted to compromise by demanding that agrarian reform would consist of having the land worked by those who could purchase it and make such property more productive.

Given the slow pace of Madero's reformism and the government's growing political isolation, major revolts soon broke out. Conservatives in the legislature, as well as hostile newspapers, took advantage of increased civil liberties to attack the regime unrelentingly. During the period of rebellions that erupted, Madero fought the revolutionaries more vociferously than the conservatives.

The first major confrontation concerned the anarchosyndicalists. Aided by I.W.W. radicals in the United States and activists like John Kenneth Turner, the Magonistas extended their influence in Baja California. The PLM seized Tijuana in May 1911. Initial attempts by Flores Magón to work with Madero ended when the anarchosyndicalists continued to articulate radical demands. Flores Magón wanted to create a new egalitarian society and continued to direct revolts throughout the summer of 1911. Although the Magonistas did not threaten U.S. property in Baja California, which continued to be quite extensive, the State Department permitted Madero's troops to cross the border on railroads and chase the Magonistas out in June 1912. A precedent existed because British marines had landed briefly in the small town of San Quintín on the Baja California coast in April 1911, at the request of Porfirian officials. Madero profited from Flores Magon's decision to write rather than lead his followers in the field. Although his army lacked food and ammunition,

Flores Magón would not leave Los Angeles. An effective propagandist, Magón never controlled his subordinates and lacked administrative ability. Arrested and jailed again in 1912, Magón never resumed a key role in either the Mexican civil war or U.S. labor activities.

Nevertheless, Madero could not reestablish peace when Zapata proclaimed his Plan de Ayala in Novermber 1911 and revolted. Zapata had pressed Madero for immediate land distribution when they had met in Mexico City. Zapata represented a heritage of agrarian revolt in Morelos and was unimpressed with Madero's assurances that legislative legal reforms had to be implemented. Unable to persuade Zapata to quit, Madero sent General Victoriano Huerta and federal troops into Morelos in a futile attempt to squelch a full-scale peasant revolt.

Meanwhile, conservatives counterattacked. At the moment that Zapata began fighting Madero, Bernardo Reyes crossed the Texas border and proclaimed his own revolt in Tamaulipas. Outdated and unable to attract supporters, Reyes failed; Madero jailed him quickly.

The Pascual Orozco insurrection became far more serious. It began when Emilio Vásquez Gómez revolted in late 1911 and early 1912. Orozco eventually elbowed Vásquez Gómez aside and proclaimed the Plan Orozquista in March 1912. Orozco called for improved working conditions, nationalization of the railroads, and land reform. After Ciudad Juárez, had been seized, another 2,000 Orozquistas led by José Inés Salazar stormed into Coahuila by April. A separate Orozquista army of 8,000 marched toward Mexico City and defeated a large federal force near the Chihuahua-Durango border. But support from hacendados, as well as weapons and money from U.S. companies, weakened Orozco's legitimacy as a true revolutionary. Shortly afterwards, Huerta stopped Orozco and restored order by concluding an agreement with Orozco for future cooperation.

The last major revolt occurred when a nephew of Porfirio Díaz, Feliz Díaz, attempted to seize power from Veracruz. Revolting in October 1912,

Vazquistas in February, 1912. *Personal collection of the author.*

the bumbling Díaz hoped to lead a counterrevolution by rallying the federal army against Madero. Skeptical generals, however, questioned Díaz's ability, and he became isolated despite the aid of U.S. diplomats and businessmen. Díaz neglected to post sentries, which allowed Maderista forces to capture him easily. But Madero committed a great mistake when he placed Díaz in jail with Reyes, where they both began to plot a new revolt.

The Fall of Madero. Madero's naive belief that the army would remain loyal eventually cost him his life. Madero had opposed militarism in favor of a parliamentary system. He had hoped that the introduction of national military service would tame the army, which did occur in other Latin American countries. Nevertheless, Reyes and Díaz started a military revolt on February 8 by ordering army cadets and the Tacubaya garrison to march on the national palace. Presidential guards killed Reyes, but the rebels holed up in an armory under the leadership of Díaz. The following day, Huerta pledged his loyalty to Madero and assumed command of loyal federal troops. But Huerta betrayed Madero by negotiating with the rebels almost immediately. In attempting to terrorize the capital to accept an agreement that would allow him or Díaz to replace Madero, Huerta bombarded Mexico City, except the positions held by dissident forces, for ten nightmarish days. Huerta also sent loyal units on suicide attacks but held back troops that supported his cause.

At this point, diplomatic intervention became critical. Increased democracy, labor activity, and regional revolts angered several foreign governments. The United States ambassador, the alcoholic Henry Lane Wilson, became Madero's foremost antagonist. A tool of Guggenheim interests and a fanatical defender of the Porfirian order, Wilson threatened Madero with armed intervention if he did not resign. Rebuffed by Madero, Wilson organized the Pact of the Embassy on February 18. The agreement proclaimed Huerta as provisional president with the understanding that Díaz would succeed him in subsequent elections. Arrested the same day by rebel officers, Madero and his vice-president resigned in return for promises that they would not be harmed. Congress overwhelmingly accepted these resignations that evening. But when Huerta asked Wilson for his opinion of what to do with them, Wilson made it clear that he would not oppose their executions. On the evening of February 21, the Huerta regime had Madero and the former vice-president murdered during a staged transfer to the federal district penitentiary.

Compared to other Progressive Era reformers throughout the hemisphere, Madero takes on a decidedly conservative hue. As governor of New Jersey and president, Woodrow Wilson passed legislation that established a national income tax, created regulatory agencies, and instituted a federal reserve banking system. In Argentina, Hipólito Yrigoyen supported some strikes, fomented education, and projected a magnetic populist appeal. Guillermo Billinghurst in Peru and Arturo Allessandri in Chile also radiated charisma and attacked oligarchs publicly. A failure as a reformist president, Madero now became a martyr as civil war and social revolution accelerated.

THE HUERTA DICTATORSHIP, 1913–1914

Victoriano Huerta's Background. Huerta was born in a small Jalisco village in 1854. His *mestizo* father and indigenous mother provided only a rudimentary education. Huerta attached himself to a federal general who stopped in his community. Huerta's fortunate selection as a personal secretary resulted in his patron getting him admitted into the Colegio Militar. Once the young cadet graduated in 1877, he supervised plans to create a new military map of Mexico. His cartographic work carried him to nearly every state, until he was recalled in 1890 and made a permanent member of the army general staff. Notable for his ruthlessness, Huerta flattened a revolt in Guerrero in 1893 and executed several rebels despite an amnesty. Then he fought Yaqui rebels in Sonora. Huerta participated in the final defeat of the Maya in Yucatán and received promotion to general in 1901. Huerta was a supporter of Reyes, and the *científicos* frustrated Huerta's ambitions. Therefore, he resigned and worked as an engineer in Monterrey.

Huerta's unrestrained personality is a significant aspect of his career. A brave but disciplined soldier, Huerta also fathered 11 children. Egotistical temper tantrums, stubborn impatience, and a deceitful tendency further characterized his personality. There is no question that Huerta had a pathological need for alcohol and seems to have enjoyed smoking marijuana. Also corrupt, he apparently stole 1.5 million pesos during the Orozco campaign. When he ousted Madero, Huerta stuffed his pockets with 500 peso notes given to him by conservative Mexican supporters as well as U.S. businesses. By enthusiastically attacking Orozco and Zapata while meddling with the reformist governor of Chihuahua, Huerta served notice that he had little in common with the insurrectionaries.

Huerta also made it plain that he would rule as a traditional dictator. Certainly the foreign diplomats expected this. The German and British ambassadors promoted him eagerly as a strongman while Henry Lane Wilson introduced Huerta to his colleagues as the "savior of Mexico." According to the 1857 Constitution, the minister of foreign relations, Pedro Lascurain, assumed the presidency. Lascurain performed only one act as chief executive: He appointed Huerta as minister of interior, next in line for the presidency, and resigned. By this maneuver, Huerta became interim president in a technically legal sense. Mindful of the presence of Huerta's troops,Congress accepted this charade as the Archbishop of Mexico offered a Te Deum. With solid support from the military, landowners, and foreign investors, Huerta set out to crush his opposition.

Carranza and the Constitutionalists. Huerta's seizure of power convinced Carranza to revolt. He became the first governor to reject Huerta's February 18 circular telegram. This message declared that the Senate had authorized Huerta to assume executive authority. Carranza disputed the legality of Huerta's status; from their green congressional building, 11 Coahuilan deputies granted Carranza authority to overthrow Huerta. On February 19, Carranza called upon all of Mexico to join him in armed revolt.

Its narrow political focus limited the early phase of Carranza's movement. His followers called themselves constitutionalists because their general concern became the defeat of Huerta and holding new elections. Despite Carranza's record as a proven reformer, his Plan de Guadalupe said nothing of social or economic reforms. Many rebels wanted to crush the clergy, distribute land, and destroy the economic system. Carranza wanted to provoke as little opposition from the oligarchy as possible and urged his followers to ratify socioeconomic reforms later. After his supporters accepted Carranza's cautious strategy, leaders in Sonora and Chihuahua recognized him as First Chief of the Constitutionalist movement. Carranza insisted upon unconditional victory, but the federal army soon forced him to retreat from Coahuila. After a 79-day horseback journey, a bedraggled Carranza arrived in Sonora while Pancho Villa, Al-

varo Obregón, Jesús Carranza, and Pablo González battled Huerta's offensive.

The Constitutionalists became stronger as they called for populistic reforms within a nationalist context. Carranza appealed for a new constitution that would provide social benefits. Carranza did not encourage legal legislative land distribution during the anti-Huerta struggle, but several of his followers seized land to give to supporters in various states. Because few hacendados supported Carranza, he persecuted several of them. Carrancista forces ransacked many haciendas for cash and food. Carranza also formed an agency to seize enemy land. Created as a war measure to secure supplies and revenue while denying them from Huerta, the Bienes Intervenidos (intervened lands) office seized property from the Church, foreigners, and wealthy citizens amid expectations of land reform. The First Chief obtained working-class support as he built armies from diverse social sectors.

With a military that possessed a general commitment to reform, the northern movement defeated the Huerta forces and expanded quickly. These forces grew as it became clear that the Constitutionalists intended to make major changes in national policy. A cohesive leader who satisfied many groups, Carranza did not alienate the elites completely. Despite the novelty of campaigning, the Constitutionalist leaders became fairly competent. Carranza's provisional government also contained capable intellectuals who provided efficiency and a high degree of organization.

Huerta's War Measures. War on two fronts weakened Huerta, who had to send troops to Morelos after Zapata rejected the dictator's offer to become governor. Zapata's peasant army proved to be a formidable opponent because the Zapatistas distributed land wherever they operated. Furthermore, revolts broke out in 13 other states as civil war coincided with increased social revolution. Huerta responded with generally military reflexes. He quickly cashiered the Maderista governors and convinced Pascual Orozco to serve in the *rurales*. As the war intensified, Huerta tried

Mounted rebel troops assembling outside Monclova in March, 1913. *Courtesy of Centro de Estudios de Historia de México.*

to militarize Mexican society. Following Huerta's command to obtain order at whatever cost, the army campaigned ruthlessly. Nearly everyone had to wear a uniform as the draft picked off thousands. Schools provided military instruction and war production increased. Although the army numbered perhaps 200,000, many of the troops deserted at the first opportunity. Defeats in Chihuahua by the fall of 1913 made Huerta's situation quite serious.

Diplomatic Intervention by Woodrow Wilson. To Woodrow Wilson, Huerta represented all that was evil in Latin America. The former Princeton president had little in common with Huerta. Wilson decided to revise the tradition of recognition after he had made up his mind about Huerta. Unlike Madero, Huerta offered to settle all disputes based upon the State Department's position. In harmony with his simplistic notions of democratic idealism, Wilson stated publicly that he would make moral judgments concerning the fitness of Latin American governments. In ad-

dition, Wilson would not tolerate limitations upon U.S. investments. But when U.S. economic interests clamored for recognition of Huerta, Wilson told friends that he would not deal with "butchers." Huerta and Wilson represented a battle of wits in which both parties were unarmed.

Determined to topple Huerta one way or the other, Wilson dismissed Henry Lane Wilson (no relation) and sent a series of presidential emissaries to obtain Huerta's resignation. John Lind, a Minnesota governor who spoke no Spanish and knew nothing about Mexico, became the first envoy. In August 1913, Lind demanded an armistice, free elections, and that Huerta not be a presidential candidate. Huerta objected and became angered when Lind offered him a loan to stay out of the voting. Once Huerta publicized the notes of the "peace" mission, Wilson backed the Catholic Party to succeed Huerta. Reginald del Valle, a Los Angeles resident, entered Mexico as the second envoy. His Hispanic heritage did not improve matters. Disdainful of the insurgents and contemptuous of the masses, del Valle failed clumsily.

Wilson's attempt to ally with the Constitutionalists collapsed. By clamping an arms embargo on the Huerta regime, Wilson sought sympathy from Carranza, but don Venustiano refused to back Wilson's proposal for armed U.S. intervention on a joint basis. Too nationalistic to become identified with North American meddling in domestic affairs, Carranza also refused to consider a Wilson proposal that northern Mexico separate itself from the rest of the country. Although lifting the embargo in February 1914 enabled the Constitutionalists to unleash a spring offensive, Carranza decided to win with minimal foreign aid.

Huerta's Policies. Basically, Huerta decided to maintain the Porfirian policy of supporting European capital against U.S. interests. In return for favored treatment, the Europeans quickly extended diplomatic relations. British investors in Mexico supported Huerta without reservation. In order to improve their position in Mexican oil production, the British opposed Wilson, partially because the Royal Navy had converted from coal to oil. Sir Lionel Carden, the British ambassador, became one of Huerta's closest advisors and won concessions for Lord Cowdray's oil operations. But when the British admiralty discovered that Cowdray's Mexican oil possessed too low a quality for the fleet, British backing of Huerta began to slacken. As World War I approached, the British needed U.S. support. The Germans initially backed Huerta as much as the British; but their determination to avoid war with the United States made them back off from outright alliance. Nevertheless, the Germans proposed a joint intervention by European powers to save Huerta and sent their fleet into Mexican waters. They enthusiastically supported any attempts to maintain Huerta while the German ambassador mediated various conflicts between Huerta and Wilson.

Huerta, meanwhile, became a ruthless dictator. The government shut down critical newspapers as a vast network of secret agents spied on the population. The Huerta regime was responsible for dozens of assassinations, including a courageous deputy, Serapio Rendón, and Senator Belisario Domínguez. Once legislators protested publicly, Huerta closed Congress and marched 83 of the lawmakers to jail between columns of soldiers with fixed bayonets.

To tighten his grip, Huerta sent Félix Díaz out of the country. Díaz represented the only legal opposition, so Huerta dispatched him to thank the emperor of Japan for Japanese participation during Mexico's 1910 centennial celebration. Even though Huerta did not carry out a campaign and had promised that he would not be a candidate during the October 1913 elections, the government declared that Huerta won the presidency. Hand-picked deputies and senators whom Huerta selected earlier also "won" during the elections.

Generally a conservative restoration, the Huerta regime lasted longer than Madero's, largely because the army and landowners knew that they faced the loss of their land and the end of a traditional military if the insurgents won. Not as reactionary as portrayed traditionally, Huerta tripled petroleum taxes and discussed nationalizing Mexican oil. Modest attempts to integrate Indians into the social order took place. Increasing educational opportunities in certain areas and the distribution of small amounts of land were somewhat positive signs, although such measures took place toward the end of Huerta's tenure when it had become too late. The Catholic party dominated Congress and the Church dedicated Mexico to the Sacred Heart of Jesus. Huerta allowed the Church to organize a Catholic Association of Mexican Youth, which had become concerned with the life of laborers. Never a captive of the church, however, Huerta purged the leadership of the Catholic Party. Huerta, like Díaz, also tried to secure labor support and allowed the Casa del Obrero Mundial to organize a large May Day festival in 1913. The Casa enjoyed its greatest membership drive. Once they criticized the government openly, however, Huerta repressed them and exiled several Casa leaders.

Ministerial instability is one of the reasons for Huerta's decline. Huerta's personality could only accept bootlickers to the extent that he used 32 different ministers during his 17 months in power.

The ministers usually formulated reforms, not Huerta. But by meeting with them in taverns or restaurants, Huerta disrupted any administrative continuity. Most of the reforms came too late to stop the rebels.

Collapse of Huerta's regime. When a German-led consortium of European bankers provided Huerta with £16 million in June 1913, Huerta committed himself deeply to foreign dependence. These banks controlled Mexican finances but became angered when Huerta seized customs revenue committed previously to payment of his loan. Printing excessive amounts of paper money that lost rapidly its value, the government operated with a deficit that amounted to six million pesos monthly. Fiscal crisis resulted when foreign governments called in the debts; the Huertistas added to Mexico's miseries by imposing forced loans. The economy did not really stagnate, but the Constitutionalists controlled key production centers, particularly when they inflicted a crushing defeat on the federal army in the middle of the cotton-producing region at Torreón on April 2, 1914. The same month, Carrancista troops probed Tampico's defenses in the oil-producing northeast.

In states such as Coahuila, Huertista rule alienated virtually every level of society. Heavy taxes upon cattlemen reduced the size of herds, while the Coahuila government seized horses and cattle in exchange for worthless promisory notes. Municipal taxes increased by as much as five times the original assessments. Huerta continually demanded more taxes and diverted these funds to Mexico City instead of for use by local authorities. An increase in vice, repression of civil liberties, and the reintroduction of the hated *jefes políticos* angered many. After centralizing the Coahuila school system rigidly and withdrawing funds, the state government closed all its schools by May 1914.

Huerta may have repressed most of his political opponents, but he could not stop U.S. intervention. The pretext that Wilson used against Huerta was the brief detention of a U.S. officer and six sailors by a federal garrison during Huerta's defense of Tampico on April 9, 1914. Unaware that the sailors had been released, Admiral Mayo lodged a strong protest and the Mexican commander apologized, ordering the arrest of the unfortunate officer involved. But the State Department claimed that the whale boat from which the shore party had arrived supposedly flew a U.S. flag. Wilson demanded that the flag be hoisted on the shoreline with the Mexicans obliged to fire a 21-gun salute to it. Huerta offered to fire a simultaneous salute and recommended that the international court at the Hague arbitrate the dispute. Wilson, however, obtained congressional approval to intervene in Mexico.

At this point, Wilson committed one of the ugliest deeds ever inflicted upon Mexico by the United States when he ordered an attack upon Veracruz. When Wilson learned that a large cargo of U.S. armaments purchased by British and French investors would arrive aboard a German vessel from Hamburg, U.S. forces invaded Veracruz on April 21. With no warning, the fleet shelled the port and inflicted many civilian casualties. The cynical Huerta withdrew federal troops but enraged inhabitants fought U.S. sailors and marines. Young Mexican naval cadets became some of the bravest defenders until literally blown out of their fortifications by point-blank shelling from U.S. naval guns. Many women died in the streets and U.S. troops executed those suspected of resistance.

Huerta, however, tried to use the tragedy at Veracruz to strengthen his position. Huerta falsely claimed that Spanish war vessels fought for him against the U.S. fleet in Veracruz. Huerta also attempted to induce Carranza to join him in defending the country, but the First Chief refused. Despite Carranza's protests, Huerta ordered his governors to convince the public that Villa and Zapata would march on Veracruz. The saddest aspect of Huerta's opportunism is that many citizens flocked to join the federal army in a burst of anti-U.S. patriotism, only to be sent north to battle the Constitutionalists. Meanwhile, the German vessel which had caught Wilson's attention quietly sailed from Veracruz with its deadly cargo and calmly unloaded the armaments at a southern port.

As domestic opposition to this fiasco mounted in the United States, Wilson agreed to mediation from Argentina, Brazil, and Chile. But Wilson once again failed when he attempted to use the peace table to impose a government to his liking in Mexico. Huerta, however, could no longer hold out. As the Constitutionalists marched toward Mexico City, they shattered federal units at Zacatecas in June 1914. Huerta resigned on July 15 and sailed to Spain on a German cruiser. There he plotted to return to Mexico with German aid in conjunction with Orozco. After arriving in the United States, Huerta was arrested by judicial agents and jailed in Fort Bliss, Texas. Although the El Paso city death certificate claims that Huerta died of cirrhosis of the liver in January 1916, Huerta actually passed away on the Fort Bliss operating table while in the hands of a U.S. doctor.

NATIONALISM AND CLASS CONFLICT

Mexico's Social Structure. Society had grown rapidly during the last quarter of the nineteenth century, but colonial attitudes persisted. Mexico remained overwhelmingly rural, since 79.1 percent of its labor force worked on ranches and haciendas. The small middle class often resented the oligarchy but depended upon them for employment. Banking and finance accounted for 5.2 percent while bureaucrats accounted for 1.4 percent. Thus, a huge number of rural workers and a growing proletariat supported the tiny elite. Antipathy by whites against the *mestizo* and indigenous majority had been a way of life that had changed little for many decades. Rigid barriers against upward mobility and the poverty of the masses increased class antagonisms in early twentieth-century Mexico.

Powerful groups of foreigners heightened the ethnic hostility that gradually erupted during the Mexican Revolution. By 1915, foreigners numbered 116,347. Spaniards, who numbered approximately 50,000, became by far the most influential group of non-Mexicans. Most Span-

iards had nothing but contempt for Mexican culture and folklore. As the owners of countless haciendas, the Spaniards pitifully exploited Mexican laborers and aligned themselves openly against the rebel movements. By operating many of the retail outlets, hotels, restaurants, and casinos, Spaniards, often arrogant, came into direct conflict with Mexican society on an everyday basis. After Spain had restored the monarchy in 1876 and enjoyed economic growth up to 1929, Spaniards often exaggerated the alleged superiority of their Hispanic roots.

During the struggles against Díaz and Huerta, rebel factions seized land belonging to Spanish landowners and priests. In many Mexican regions, Spaniards became exiled. Spanish merchants also suffered the confiscation of their goods and general looting. The tendency of Spanish merchants to speculate and raise prices when food prices increased after 1914 often resulted in such seizures. Refusal to pay taxes and accept Constitutionalist issues of paper currency added to the persecution of Spaniards. Carrancista attacks against Spanish merchants aroused an intense nationalism that added to Carranza's popularity.

Many Mexicans despised the Chinese. Ethnocentric and isolated, the Chinese resembled the Spaniards in terms of their tendency to advance materially as petty merchants and shopkeepers. Social reformers, as well as traditionalists, resented the Chinese because some Asians sold opium, operated brothels, and provided gambling outlets. Massive anti-Chinese resentment fueled class conflict in many areas of northwestern Mexico.

Westerners did not often come into contact with average Mexicans. Because U.S. and British residents often worked as technicians, only public officials and the upper strata dealt with them. But an insistence upon speaking English grated nerves. At least the French and Germans tended to mingle with Mexicans somewhat more and even took some interest in local culture. The privileges that North Americans and Europeans enjoyed with their own governments kindled many Mexican resentments.

Class Conflict Emerges. Mass violence threatened Mexico's social structure after 1911. Killings and executions became widespread, although the status quo did not break down completely. Certainly many revolutionaries wanted to restructure society entirely while others fought merely for personal gain or even simple survival.

The working class participated in the civil war because of food shortages; increased wages did not keep pace with inflation, which reached triple digits in 1916. It often required a week of toil to buy a pair of pants and a shirt for the typical worker. Because many of the poor could not purchase food, they died of hunger. The standard of living declined in urban areas even more than in the countryside. Angry workers burned the homes and warehouses of several wealthy merchants. Radical and populist governments in many cities instituted forced loans and ad hoc taxes upon previously comfortable citizens out of a desire to improve the lot of workers. Rob-

beries, rapes, and murders resulted from fighting inside numerous towns.

Class conflict also intensified in the countryside. Many peasants denounced the "filthy landowners" when they demanded land reform. Defiant *campesinos* squatted on land they considered their own and sharecroppers often refused to pay rent. Brute force replaced subservience to the upper class. Zapatistas often executed landowners who tried to use government currency. As a symptom of a drive for egalitarianism, oil workers no longer tipped their hats to white-skinned bosses in the oil region. Nor did peons on plantations bow their heads. A sense of dignity appeared among working people by 1920. Because the masses felt that they stood to gain an increase in their standard of living by attacking the upper class, many Mexicans usually had to decide which side to join.

The rebels flourished because they often persecuted privileged groups. As a symbol of the cru-

The First Chief receives a commission from the Casa del Obrero Mundial in Mexico City, August 1914. *Courtesy of Centro de Estudios de Historia de México.*

sade to eradicate Porfirian privileges, Carrancistas plundered the elite Jockey Club in Mexico City before turning it over to the Casa del Obrero Mundial. Carranza generally allowed his followers to ransack gambling casinos, haciendas, and businesses. Swept aside rhetorically, the upper class disdained Mexico's new rulers, whose crude notions of social justice forced a new definition of status as well as national harmony.

Class conflict also cut across gender lines. Prior to the extensive organizational drives to organize female workers, women had established unions of cigarette makers, tailors, and seamstresses. Strikes, such as the October 1914 tumult at the Palacio de Hierro in Mexico City, broke out over bad working conditions and arbitrary managers. The tradition of equality for females had manifested itself within the Casa del Obrero Mundial and served to mobilize women who worked in breweries, candy factories, flour mills, and hat shops. With desperate living conditions threatening many families, women often took on piece rate work in their homes, having to toil as long as 13 hours daily while minding children. A strike by seamstresses in Orizaba at a factory which produced army uniforms resulted in occupation of the textile mill by state authorities.

Although females had always participated to some extent in the Mexican military, women *soldaderas* in the thousands fought during the civil war. At least 53 served in red blouses and black skirts in their capacity as nurses for anarchosyndicalist formations. *Soldaderas* participated in most of the armed groups as actual fighters. During these wartime experiences, women demonstrated leadership abilities and attained levels of self-confidence as well as acceptance not previously known. Songs and legends concerning female participation in the social conflict became numerous.

Growth of Nationalism. More than other leaders of the Mexican Revolution, Carranza articulated a cohesive nationalist ideology. He and his supporters backed labor reforms and criticized the hacienda system. Carranza also benefited from antiforeign resentment by regulating the

Valentina Ramírez, a Carranoista soldadera serving in the forces of General Ramón Iturbe, September, 1913. *Courtesy of Centro de Estudios de Historia de México.*

economy to the increased benefit of the masses as well as the middle class. Tighter regulation of the mines and oil fields became a strong feature of the nationalism in Mexico that characterized much of Latin America in the twentieth century. As a statesman, Carranza also defended Mexican sovereignty consistently.

For the first time since Santa Anna, active hostility against the United States became the norm. Since Mexicans considered the United States their traditional antagonist, nearly half the 1,477 foreigners assassinated during this decade of violence were North Americans. Anti-U.S. demonstrations broke out constantly, whether because of the lynchings of Mexican citizens in the United States or the constant fear of U.S. military intervention. Unlike the 1846–1848 war, little collaboration took place with U.S. military forces, at least on a comparative basis.

For society in general, Mexican nationalism became a vibrant set of attitudes and emotions that responded to different regions and occupations quite flexibly. Social changes became positive in the sense that optimism began to replace the sense of inferiority that characterized much of the nineteenth century. A tremendous amount of internal migration, mainly by northerners traveling through the central plateau and the southeast, made many Mexicans appreciate the uniqueness of their country. Increased egalitarianism resulted in greater social unity by means of miscegenation. In isolated towns and villages, a younger generation previously frustrated by Porfirian privileges for the traditional elite now exercised power. The spoken Spanish acquired a more national dialect as regional peculiarities began to break down. A national resurgence that would be free of privileges appealed to the middle class as well as the masses. Artists reflected a new pride in the nation's majestic indigenous heritage by painting it in sympathetic tones. David Alfaro Siqueiros and José Clemente Orozco joined the Carrancistas and articulated a national reconstruction devoid of most European influences.

After coming into contact with *campesinos* and indigenous groups, many artists broke with the current artistic traditions which normally came from Europe. It became apparent to many artists that the revolution should be fought from the artistic front. This new type of art, Siqueiros and others believed, should reflect Mexican culture by portraying a modern society and allude to historical change as the basis for current realities. For Siqueiros and Orozco, this meant that art should be able to communicate with the masses—that it should be monumental.

Music also reflected the nationalist sentiment. When an army captain wrote "La Valentina," he had no idea that everyone would love singing it as the Constitutionalists' primary marching song. This and other personal *corrido* songs reflected the rise of common tastes. The trumpet mariachi also emerged from the Mexican Revolution. Popular music emphasized heroes, courage, and honor in a somewhat rebellious context. Field workers in dance halls, streets, and taverns rejoiced to hear their feelings echoed throughout Mexico.

The civil war even influenced drinking habits. Until the early 1900s, tequila's popularity remained limited. Middle-and upper-class Mexicans preferred French cognac over tequila, then considered the drink of commoners. During the revolution, tequila's popularity took off, thanks in part to gun-slinging revolutionaries who would gulp a few shots before returning to battle and to celebrate the end of combat.

SUGGESTED READING

Aguilar Camín, Héctor. *La frontera nómada: Sonora y la revolucíon mexicana.* Mexico City: Siglo Veintiuno, 1977.

Beezley, William H. *Insurgent Governor: Abraham Gonzáles and the Mexican Revolution in Chihuahua.* Lincoln: University of Nebraska Press, 1973.

———. "Governor Carranza and the Mexican Revolution in Coahuila." *The Americas* 33 (July 1976), 50–61.

Benjamin, Thomas, and Mark Wasserman, eds. *Provinces of the Revolution: Essays on Regional Mexican History, 1910–1929.* Albuquerque: University of New Mexico Press, 1990.

Cumberland, Charles C. *Mexican Revolution: Genesis Under Madero.* Austin: University of Texas Press, 1952.

Fabela, Isidro. *Mis memorias de la Revolucíon.* Mexico City: Editorial JUS, 1977.

Grieb, Kenneth. *The United States and Huerta.* Lincoln: University of Nebraska Press, 1969.

Henderson, Peter. *Felix Díaz: The Porfiriato, and the Mexican Revolution.* Lincoln: University of Nebraska Press, 1981.

———. "Woodrow Wilson, Victoriano Huerta, and the Recognition Issue in Mexico." *The Americas* 41:2 (October 1984),151–176.

———. *In the Absence of Don Porfirio: Francisco León de la Barra and the Mexican Revolution.* Wilmington, DE: Scholarly Resources, 2000.

Hill, Larry D. *Emissaries to a Revolution: Woodrow Wilson's Executive Agents in Mexico.* Baton Rouge: Louisiana State University Press, 1973.

Katz, Friedrich. *The Secret War in Mexico: Europe, the United States, and the Mexican Revolution.* Chicago: University of Chicago Press, 1981.

Knight, Alan. *The Mexican Revolution. Vol. 1: Porfirians, Liberals, and Peasants.* New York: Cambridge University Press, 1986.

Limones, Georgia. "Las mujeres en la Casa del Obrero Mundial." Paper presented at El Colegio de Mexico, Mexico City on March 11, 1987.

Meyer, Michael. *Pascual Orozco and the Mexican Revolution, 1910–1915.* Lincoln: University of Nebraska Press, 1967.

———. *Huerta: A Political Portrait.* Lincoln: University of Nebraska Press, 1972.

O'Shaughnessy, Edith. *A Diplomat's Wife in Mexico.* New York: Harper and Brothers, 1916.

Palomares, Justin N. *La invasión yanqui en 1914.* Mexico City: Editorial Costa-Amic, 1940.

Quirk, Robert E. *An Affair of Honor.* New York: Norton, 1967.

Richmond, Douglas W. *Venustiano Carranza's Nationalist Struggle, 1893–1920.* Lincoln: University of Nebraska Press, 1983.

———. "Factional Political Strife in Coahuila, 1910–1920." *Hispanic American Historical Review* 60 (February 1980), 49–68.

———. "Nationalism and Class Conflict in Mexico, 1910–1920." *The Americas* 43:3 (January 1987), 279–303.

Ross, Stanley R. *Francisco I. Madero, Apostle of Mexican Democracy.* New York: Columbia University Press, 1955.

Ruiz, Ramon. "Madero's Administration and Mexican Labor." In Wilkie, James, Michael C. Meyer, and Edna Monzon de Wilkie, eds., *Contemporary Mexico.* Berkeley: University of California Press, 1976, pp. 187–203.

Salas, Elizabeth. *Soldaderas in the Mexican Military: Myth and History.* Austin: University of Texas Press, 1990.

Taylor, Lawrence. "Gunboat Diplomacy's Last Fling in the New World: The British Seizure of San Quintin, 1911." *The Americas* 52:4 (April 1996), 521–543.

Turner, Frederick C. *The Dynamics of Mexican Nationalism.* Chapel Hill: University of North Carolina Press, 1968.

Wolfskill, George, and Douglas W. Richmond, eds. *Essays on the Mexican Revolution: Revisionist Views of the Leaders.* Austin: University of Texas Press, 1979.

Womack, John. "The Mexican Revolution, 1910–1920" In Leslie Bethell, ed., *Mexico Since Independence.* New York: Cambridge University Press, 1991, pp. 125–200.

12

Revolution and Civil War, 1914–1920

The Mexican Revolution did not end with Huerta's defeat. It became a civil war among the victors when Villa decided to oppose Carranza's leadership of the Constitutionalists. Partially because the revolution evolved as a series of regional revolts, each with certain marks of distinction and uniqueness, Zapata also fought Carranza. Villa and Zapata seemed to have forged an unbeatable combination. But Carranza possessed Díaz's administrative skill, as well as crucial support from urban labor, peasants, and the middle class. After Carranza broadened and clarified his nationalistic program, he provided direction and focus to many regional struggles when he instituted attractive socioeconomic reforms that enabled him to rule until 1920.

PANCHO VILLA: AN INCOMPLETE REVOLUTIONARY

Villa's Early Career. Born in the state of Durango in 1878 as Doroteo Arango, Francisco Villa became the best known Mexican ever. He grew up on a large hacienda with his peon family. Villa never received formal education, which limited his future as a revolutionary. An explosive personality became a major feature of his life. Bad tempered but true to his word, Villa was alert, quick,

and abrupt. As legend maintains, Villa killed a Spanish foreman who raped his sister. Then he took to the hills as a bandit and adopted the name Pancho Villa. He lived by rustling cattle from the Terrazas hacienda and acquired fame for his courage. Villa joined the Madero revolt by siding with Orozco against Díaz. A natural guerrilla, Villa gained the support of landless *campesinos* and cowboys. Estate dependents living on northern haciendas became particularly attracted to Villa. In general, many of the rural poor considered Villa a sort of Robin Hood who would alleviate their poverty. Many small ranchers, apprehensive about the acquisitive hacendados who controlled the northern governments, also backed Villa.

Villa remained loyal to Madero during the Orozco revolt; afterwards he seemed content. Madero had saved Villa's life. Shortly after the Rellano battle, Huerta attempted to execute Pancho Villa for the theft of an expensive Arabian mare, whose owner complained to Huerta. Only the intervention of Madero's brothers prevented Villa from being shot. Given 50,000 pesos as mustering out pay, Villa attempted to settle down as a tenant farmer and to sell beef in Chihuahua city. He imported refrigeration equipment with the help of U.S. technicians and had the city's first modern meat service. Nevertheless, he undoubtedly continued to steal cattle. Madero's murder soon returned Villa to action.

Villa quickly formed a powerful army, the Division of the North. It became the largest and best-known military organization during the revolution. At its height, this force increased to 50,000 soliders. Villa paid his soldiers two pure silver pesos a day, provided food, and as many as three sets of clothing. Concerned with the welfare of his troops, Villa left money for wounded soldiers whom he put up in hospitals and hotels. Led by a brilliant commander who utilized night attacks and reckless cavalry charges, Villistas became the cutting edge of the Constitutionalist forces. On November 15, 1913, Villa and 3,000 troops rode triumphantly into Ciudad Juárez after Villa had hijacked a train which had been traveling south, taking the *federales* by complete surprise. Battles which Villa won at Torreón and Zacatecas during the spring of 1914 became key events in Huerta's defeat. A famous writer, John Reed of the *New York World*, helped popularize Villa. After traveling with the Villista army and gaining Villa's trust, Reed published his famed *Insurgent Mexico* in 1914. The book portrayed Villa as a primitive but sincere and idealistic revolutionary. Although only a minority of North Americans sympathized with the revolution's ideals, Reed's image provided Villa with strong popularity in the United States for a short time. Ambitious and charismatic, Villa asserted himself against Carranza.

Civil War within the Revolution. Villa and Carranza gradually drifted apart. Carranza became apprehensive about the growing number of *federales* in the Villista army, particularly the opportunistic General Felipe Angeles, who wanted to maintain the federal army. When it became clear that Carranza wanted to destroy the Porfirian military, Angeles encouraged Villa to oppose Carranza. In addition, Villa's pro-U.S. sympathies alienated him from the more nationalistic groups. Villa and Angeles became the only leaders who supported the U.S. invasion of Veracruz. Villa's friendly relations with the State Department and

Pancho Villa. *Courtesy of Centro de Estudios de Historia de México.*

U.S. generals also caused further animosity. The influence of George C. Carothers, a U.S. mining engineer in northern Mexico with close ties to the State Department, also bothered Carranza. When remnants of the Madero family decided to back Villa, Carranza's concern rose. Finally, the murder of a British citizen, William Benton, angered Carranza, particularly when Villa refused to conduct an investigation. Once Villistas attacked the forces of Pastor Rouaix, a Carrancista reformist in Durango, Carranza decided to take action.

The break with Villa occurred when Carranza ordered the temporary stoppage of coal shipments to Villa's army, so that Obregón and Pablo González could capture Mexico City first. Villa resigned his army command briefly, until his generals convinced him to return. Villa promised not to interfere with civilian governments and, in return, Villa received more coal and cash as late as September 1914. Carranza, at that time, invited Villa and other insurrectionary leaders to Mexico

City in order to resolve differences so that agreements could be established. Villa, however, refused to come and withdrew recognition of Carranza as Mexico's interim chief executive. Although the Mexico City meeting took place and Carranza reiterated his commitment to several reforms, civil war within the revolution approached.

Villa's and Carranza's generals then called for their own meeting at Aguascalientes in late September 1914. Carranza offered to abdicate if Villa would do the same. But the convention's president, Eulalio Gutiérrez, appointed Villa as chief of the convention's armies. To avoid this deadlock, Villa proposed that he and Carranza commit suicide simultaneously. The Aguascalientes convention formed a separate government when Carranza refused to recognize it. Forced to choose sides, the generals proclaimed their loyalties and an even bloodier round of fighting began. Although Villa gained Zapata's support and met him near Mexico City in December, the convention government disintegrated. A reign of terror took place soon after Villa occupied Mexico City. The Zapatistas and Villistas failed to construct a common organization or develop an ideology which both could share. The Villista *camarilla* of old liberals and populists clashed with the anarchist Zapatista advisors. Instead of striking together for national power, Zapata retreated.

At this critical juncture, Carranza gained the initiative. He was bolstered by large amounts of military supplies that U.S. forces left at Veracruz when they pulled out in November 1914—it remains unclear whether this took place deliberately or because of convenience or ineptitude. These armaments, some of which arrived at the port before Huerta's collapse, aided Carranza greatly. Villa's regional outlook prevented him from understanding the need to attack Veracruz. Instead, the Villistas attacked Jalisco and took over Guadalajara briefly. Obregón occupied Puebla in January 1915, as the beginning of a general offensive. Near Tampico, Carranza forces won a decisive victory under Jacinto B. Treviño at El Ebano in March after 72 days of bitter fighting. The Celaya battle became the turning point. Villa un-

derestimated Obregón's ability and ignored the advice of Angeles not to attack Celaya. Knowing that he lacked ammunition, Villa went on the offensive anyway. In April, Villa divided his forces and attempted to assault Obregón's entrenched soldiers with disastrous results. This clash in Guanajuato became the largest battle fought in the Western Hemisphere since the U.S. Civil War. Raked by machine-gun fire, stumbling in irrigation ditches, and caught on barbed wire, the Villistas lost at least 12,000 troops. New defeats at León and Trinidad shortly afterwards forced Villa to retreat to the north. Thereafter, Villa reverted to becoming a dangerous guerrilla with a few thousand followers.

Failure to Consolidate Reforms. Villa lost to Carranza in part because of a failure to clarify his ideology and project a consistent set of reforms. Erratic and unable to accept criticisms, Villa served as governor of Chihuahua for only a few days in December 1913. Villa's administrative weaknesses cut into his mass support. Villa did not permit elections to take place and it became clear that democracy would not blossom in Villista regions. Yet there is no doubt that Villa enjoyed initial popularity. He loved children, and the subject of educating them would bring tears to his eyes. Promising schools and rationing meat at reduced cost for the needy demonstrated egalitarian tendencies. Like most other revolutionaries, Villa hated smoking and alcoholic beverages. To pay his forces, the Villistas rounded up cattle in Chihuahua during the summer of 1913 by offering $5 dollars a head to hacendados. But these transactions became tantamount to no payment at all once Villa sold the cattle through El Paso banks in order to obtain military supplies.

Villa's social reform policy focused on the redistribution of wealth in Chihuahua, Durango, and wherever else the Villistas arrived. It became standard practice to assemble the wealthy and demand that they hand over money for the cause. The expropriation of the Terrazas latifundia benefited nearly everyone. Particularly tangible was Villa's decision to provide inexpensive Terrazas beef so that the masses, including the unemployed, could eat well. Villa sold seized cattle and cotton from the Laguna to offer free medical care, boarding schools for children, and pensions for widows. Although there was not a political party to implement land distribution pledges, Villa did get rid of the hated *jefes politicos* and reestablished the municipal councils. Since humble rural citizens made up most of his army, Villa considered their domination of the ayuntamientos a form of the majority exercising its will. Although Villa detested priests, he tolerated religious practices and traditions much more than his *carrancista* rivals.

Villa lost a great opportunity to expand his image as an agrarian revolutionary after he decreed the expropriation of all haciendas. But only his generals controlled the land as well as the state bureaucracy. Administrators often managed the land poorly and pocketed profits. Only one case exists where landless peasants in Chihuahua received land outright. In addition, working conditions on expropriated property did not change significantly. Peasants and sharecroppers had to pay one-third to one-half of their crops to Villa as rent. Despite advice from his more revolutionary subordinates to distribute land, Villa rarely did so and promised that land would be given out only after his troops defeated Carranza. Villa did not decree a national land reform policy until May 1915. The decree granted great authority to local governments and, since Villa was losing at this point, it affected little land. But the decree also mandated that peasants would have to pay in installments for any land which they received.

Other problems caused Villa's popularity to decline after 1915. Villa never decreed thorough labor reforms and, therefore, labor groups hesitated to support him, particularly the Casa del Obrero Mundial. Villa did not oppose U.S. investments and often defended them in return for protection money. With the Guggenheims, Villa threatened to shoot anarchists if they struck the company. Gradually, Villista administration became chaotic. Villa trusted too many people who often cheated him, particularly on munitions purchases. Villa could never solve the problem of inflation once the paper bills that he issued became worthless. Many areas in northern Mexico under his control suffered from food shortages.

Villa could also become quite cruel. Many of his troops had to choose between joining him or being shot on the spot. Villa also killed unarmed Chinese, believing that they had no business in Mexico. Suspicious and unrealistic, he executed families who refused his orders or female *soldaderas* who slowed his campaign down. Thousands of families reacted with terror if they heard that Villa was approaching their homes. Parents hid young women or sent them across the border rather than allow daughters to fall into the hands of Villistas. It became common knowledge that Villa kidnapped those who would not give him money.

The Pershing Expedition. The United States enraged Villa when Wilson allowed Carranza forces to cross the border and reinforce their garrison at Aqua Prieta, Sonora. Villa lost this critical battle with high casualties. But Wilson's diplomatic recognition of Carranza in October 1915 made Villa thirst for revenge. In January 1916, Villista officers murdered 16 Guggenheim engineers. Villa's attack against the border town of Columbus, New Mexico, became very significant. At 4:00 A.M. on March 9, 1916, Villa and 485 of his raiders caught the garrison unprepared despite rumors which had predicted this bold action. Columbus suffered the deaths of 8 civilians and 10 soldiers. Because this was the first attack on U.S. soil since the British burned the capital in 1814, Wilson responded by sending General John Pershing into Mexico with orders to disperse the Villistas.

Why did the assault occur? There is little doubt that German agents who served Villa as a physician and arms agents goaded him to attack at the behest of the German espionage service. Germany obviously wanted to provoke U.S. intervention into Mexico rather than Europe. Because Columbus served as the point where Carranza troops passed through to reinforce Agua Prieta, Villa wanted to punish the town of 300. In addition, Villa discovered that Columbus merchants and bankers had cheated him. Also, Villa may have wanted to provoke U.S. intervention in order to weaken Carranza. To justify his actions, Villa claimed, mistakenly, that Carranza intended to sell Mexico out to the United States.

The Pershing expedition became a farce, but Villa never became a major factor in the civil war afterwards. Villa avoided capture from Pershing forces and actually built up his forces somewhat for carrying out such a macho deed against the United States. But Carranza strengthened his position more than anyone once his forces defeated U.S. units at Carrizal in June 1916. Many rallied to Carranza's defense during a series of demonstrations throughout the north. Afterwards, Carranza consolidated his regime and attacked the Villistas constantly.

But Villa managed to survive in Chihuahua, which was governed by a panicky former *jefe político* who had served the Porfiriato. The regime of Ignacio Enríquez in Chihuahua did little to attract mass support. In late 1916, Villistas captured the state capital twice; in 1917, Villa took the frontier settlement of Ojinaga on two occasions. Only after Francisco Murguía relieved the bumbling Jacinto B. Treviño as the main army commander in Chihuahua did the military situation against Villa improve. Villista attempts to capture Ciudad Juárez in 1919 ended in defeat only after two days of hard fighting.

EMILIANO ZAPATA: A SINCERE REVOLUTIONARY

Zapata's Background. A zealous agrarian leader who defended the village economy and its local culture, Zapata understood his people and learned how to fight for a way of life that had declined. Born in the small Morelos village of Anenecuilco in 1879, Zapata had a soft voice but a strong will. He respected nature, loved the land, and believed firmly in the dignity of hard agricultural labor. Although he could barely read and write, Zapata had learned Mexican history by lis-

tening to *corridos*. He was religious and rarely criticized the Church. Zapata's family had fought against the French intervention and became fairly prosperous peasants who owned cattle and sold various goods. A *mestizo* sharecropper who sold melons, Zapata acquired fame for breaking horses. But the sugar boom of the 1880s resulted in tremendous pressure upon village land. Zapata resented this change, particularly when Anenecuilco lost some of its land to sharecroppers in 1887.

Zapata began to oppose the Porfirian order during the gubernatorial campaign between the aristocratic, British-educated Pablo Escandón and a reformer, Patricio Leyva. Despite Díaz's promises of fair elections, Escandón won by use of force and implemented laws that favored plantations. By then, 30 hacendados controlled 62 percent of the cultivated land in Morelos, now Mexico's major sugar-producing area. In the midst of this crisis, Zapata's village elected him as their *presidente municipal* in 1909. The young Zapata enjoyed respect because he wanted little for himself. Despite Zapata's attempts to defend the village legally and peacefully, the authorities drafted him rather than confront a local revolt. Zapata became radicalized when a wealthy hacendado used his influence to obtain Zapata's release in return for having Zapata groom his horses. The experience nauseated Zapata when he saw horses receiving better care than people.

Zapata left in disgust and armed his villagers to regain their corn patches. District officials honored Zapata's refusal to pay taxes to hacendados for land that actually belonged to his village. But he wanted more than the right to avoid taxation. After obtaining an appointment with Díaz, Zapata demanded a definitive ruling to ensure that the disputed land would remain with his village. As the centennial celebrations ended in Mexico City, Zapata began to tear down hacienda fences that encroached upon other village lands. By now, friend and foe alike recognized him as a local leader.

Zapata's Agrarian Revolution. Morelos had experienced several agrarian revolts before 1911, but the Zapatista movement was unique in Mexi-

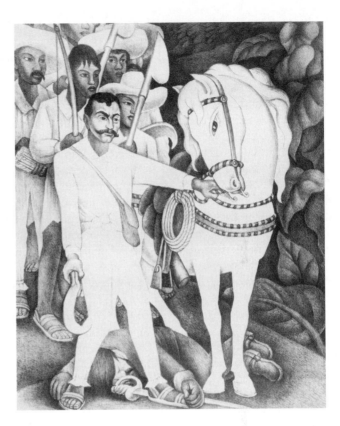

***Zapata* by Diego Rivera.**
Courtesy of the Gallery at UTA
(University of Texas at Arlington).

can history. Encouraged by the outbreak of Madero's revolt in the north, Zapata organized armed groups, appointed leaders,and patiently waited for the right moment to strike. Finally, in March 1911, Zapata declared his revolution in the village of Ayala. Hundreds of farmers joined his rebel army in the Puebla mountains. After his victory at Jojutla, Zapata informed Madero that he was taking charge of the Morelos revolt. In May, Zapata's bloody victory at Cuautla encouraged Díaz to quit two days later.

The agrarian issue gradually led to a falling out between Madero and Zapata. Four days after signing the Treaty of Juárez, Madero ordered Zapata not to attack haciendas. Concerned that Madero wanted to sell out the revolution, Zapata went to Mexico City in June to plead for a clarification of Madero's land policies. Madero gave Zapata an ambivalent response and allowed the Morelos planters to maneuver the new govern-

ment against Zapata. Despite Madero's pitiful attempts to promote peace in Morelos, Huerta and interim president Francisco León de la Barra tried their best to capture Zapata. But Zapata had a knack for combining military and political action. He humiliated Huerta by infiltrating past the potent but clumsy federal columns. In response to Madero's repeated demands that his forces turn in their weapons, Zapata promised to do so if Madero would pull Huerta's army out, distribute land, and recognize himself as the legitimate ruler in Morelos.

In reply to Madero's continued refusal to meet his demands, Zapata proclaimed the Plan de Ayala on November 28, 1911. Standing on a table, Zapata declared that Madero intended to establish a dictatorship "more terrible than that of Porfirio Díaz." He recognized Orozco as head of a new revolution and declared that village lands seized by past governments should be returned immediately. In addition, one-third of hacienda lands were to be distributed as soon as possible. Those hacendados who resisted would lose all their property.

Zapata demonstrated a commitment to true agrarian reform instead of simple land redistribution when he established a credit bank based upon funds from seized land and crops, so that farmers could have seed, tools, animals, and credit. Zapatistas encouraged peasants to establish cooperatives based on the Aztec tradition of communal landowning as a better way to market crops. Rather than producing for capitalistic markets, peasants used Zapata's agrarian reform to become subsistence farmers.

The Zapatista Military Campaign.

The agrarian revolution resulted in a clean break with tepid reformers in Mexico City. When Madero sent a negotiator to obtain a compromise, the angry Zapata threatened to hang Madero from a tree. Zapata also invited Flores Magón to establish his headquarters in Morelos. Zapata's successful guerrilla campaign began in January 1912. Although General Juvencio Robles had forces that outnumbered Zapata's 2,800 troops, his harsh tactics alienated the rural population. The ruthless Robles burned villages and took hostages until Madero replaced him with Felipe Angeles. Angeles and the new Maderista governor decided to negotiate. A stalemate developed when Zapata found it difficult to obtain war material. In addition, the election of a middle-class congress in Cuernavaca frustrated Zapata from seizing the initiative.

Fighting in Morelos intensified when Huerta seized power. On March 2, 1913, Zapata notified Huerta that he would continue his revolution. Huerta responded by reappointing Robles as commander in Morelos. But Zapata struck back by taking Jonacatepec in April. Zapata also revised the Plan de Ayala to denounce Huerta and Orozco, giving himself undisputed leadership of the Morelos revolution. Meanwhile, Zapata disciplined his followers as much as possible. These modest troops rarely looted and often wore a Virgin of Guadalupe icon upon their sombreros. Many joined Zapata out of conviction as well as

Zapatistas **by José Clemente Orozco.** *Courtesy of the Gallery at UTA (University of Texas at Arlington).*

necessity. Free peasants comprised the bulk of this army while hacienda peons remained only a minority. The Robles tactic of deporting civilians angered many peasants. Zapata soon controlled the country towns and even seized Chilpancingo in neighboring Guerrero. His efforts to centralize control over the movement sometimes irritated subordinate leaders. As Huerta collapsed in the spring of 1914, Zapata advanced toward Cuernavaca and Mexico City. But Carrancistas occupied the capital and received the surrender of the federal army at Teoloyucan when Zapata occupied Cuernavaca in August.

Zapata Joins Villa against Carranza. Zapata always distrusted Carranza but agreed reluctantly to negotiate with Carranza's emiss-aries in Morelos. But Zapata became inflexible and his *camarilla* demanded that Carranza accept every feature of the Plan de Ayala unconditionally. Zapata refused additional discussions when Carranza invited him to attend the October 1914 convention in Mexico City. Unable to deal with Carranza, Zapata shifted his sympathies to Villa. When the Aguascalientes convention did not accept the Plan de Ayala and merely promised to accept its principles, Zapata accepted. At that point, Zapata sent a delegation of 26 trusted followers to Aguascalientes after first discussing Zapatista ideals with Villa.

Zapata's alliance with Villa never became particularly harmonious. The tendency of Zapata's inner circle to sabatage diplomatic alliances appeared ominous. His principal adviser, Antonio Díaz Soto y Gama, crumpled the Mexican flag in his fists; in typical anarchist rhetoric, he called the flag a lie in front of the startled Aguascalientes delegates. Claiming that the Plan de Ayala possessed more importance than the flag indicates the stubborn regional focus of the Zapatistas. Eleven days after the last session of the Aguascalientes convention, the Zapatistas entered Mexico City on November 24.

Villa and Zapata enjoyed meeting each other in December, but their differences became pronounced. Zapata and his anarchist advisors envi-sioned a society built upon village democracies, while a national state would basically resolve regional and local interests. Villistas, however, preferred private property rather than village holdings. Villista officers enraged Zapata when they murdered Paulino Martínez, one of Zapata's most trusted ideologues. Partially because they never received promised amounts of war materiel that Villa had agreed to send, the Zapatistas withdrew to Morelos in early 1915. They loved their homeland and had tired of Mexico City. Internal quarrels in the capital and the thought of more warfare sapped their determination to continue fighting once it became time to tend crops.

As Zapata entered the ultimate phase of the revolution, he intensified his plan for a self-supporting agrarian revolution. In early 1915, Zapatistas distributed *ejidos* throughout Morelos, while land commissioners traveled to nearby states. Once the convention government transferred itself to Cuernavaca in January, Zapatistas took over the agricultural ministry as well as several other cabinet seats and began additional land surveys. In October 1915, Zapatistas enacted a comprehensive agrarian law which stated that everyone had the right to land. This somewhat moderate law provided for indemnities and placed fixed limits, determined by climate and quality, on the amounts of property that individuals could own. As Villa quarreled with Zapata and lost interest in reforms, the Zapatistas controlled the convention administration and wrote most of its progressive laws concerning rural labor, education, and land colonies.

Decline of Zapata, 1915–1919. Unable to assume the characteristics of a national leader, Zapata never attempted to articulate the form of a future Mexican government. Zapata wanted to continue a subsistence economy that had become unrealistic in the north or within urban areas. For these reasons, Zapata rejected the use of paper bills issued by the convention government in favor of crudely minted silver coins from Guerrero. He also opposed the idea of federal taxes. By continuing to attack the anticlericalism of the

Carrancistas, Zapata lost potential followers outside Morelos. As the political and military situation deteriorated, internal strife weakened the Zapatista movement. Conflicts between villages broke out frequently as did confrontations between headquarters and villages. Officers and troops deserted, cliques formed, and constant killings took place. Otilio Montaño and other members of the *camarilla* abandoned Zapata when he refused to compromise his ideals.

As his fortunes declined, Zapata became somewhat sophisticated in terms of his campaign strategy. Díaz Soto y Gama finally persuaded Zapata to appeal to the working class and project anti-imperialism. The Zapatistas also circulated a newspaper outside Morelos which attempted to acquire more village support in southern Mexico. Jenaro Amezcua went to Havana to obtain international support while Gildardo Magaña tried to link up with anti-Carranza exiles in Texas. But those who stressed local reforms, such as Manuel Palafox, broke with Zapata by 1918. Eventually, Zapata's advisors betrayed him at one point or another.

The Carrancista onslaught became too much for the Zapatistas. Pablo González began probing Morelos in November 1915, and unleashed a massive attack in 1916. The Zapatistas drove them out by the end of the year, but brutal fighting had weakened the village system seriously. Because Zapata had not partitioned the land legally, some villages affiliated with Carrancistas, whose policy had the sanctity of the state and favored agrarian reform by constitutional, documented means. As Zapata became surrounded by questionable leaders, such as ex-Hueristas Higinio Aguilar and Benjamin Argumedo, he also carried out joint campaigns with the conservative forces of Félix Díaz in 1917. The Zapatista army had the weaknesses of peasant groups because it depended upon small bands which rotated every three months between farming and soldiering. Effective as guerrillas, they could not organize sufficiently for offensive campaigns.

Zapata soon received fatal blows. Pablo González returned with stronger forces and captured large towns permanently. In February 1918, Zapata proposed discussions with Carranza so that Morelos could obtain a negotiated form of autonomy, but Carranza did not even reply. As the guerrillas tried to hold out in the towns and mountains, Zapata became moody and snappish as Morelos suffered. By either death or emigration, the state lost one-fourth of its population by 1918. Spanish flu killed thousands during the 1918–1919 winter, perhaps as many as 400,000 nationwide. Throwing aside his usual caution, Zapata was lured into a trap by Carrancistas and he was assassinated at the Chinameca hacienda on April 10, 1919.

VENUSTIANO CARRANZA'S NATIONALIST VICTORY

Carranza's Socioeconomic Reforms. A nationalistic program of reforms became the driving force behind Carranza's triumph over his rivals. As governor of Coahuila, Carranza implemented improved health services, expanded educational opportunities, legislated progressive taxation, and championed labor against foreign interests. Carranza was never a revolutionary, but his reformist background and his opposition to Díaz, and even Madero, indicate dissatisfaction with the oligarchy. Ambition and opportunism also motivated Carranza. He and many of his elite followers assumed that the Mexican state had to institutionalize revolutionary desires in populistic terms. After Carranza revolted against Huerta, he promised a new constitution, land and labor reforms, a national bank, and a stridently independent foreign policy. Therefore, Carranza possessed a multiclass following committed to changing the nation.

Carranza's economic reforms became critical for both the constitutionalist movement and his regime. To prevent hoarding, Carrancistas forced merchants to sell food at low prices. Banks had to maintain 100 percent bullion reserves in proportion to the amount of currency they could issue. Since few banks could meet this demand, domes-

Constitutionalist encampment at Ramos Arizpe, Coahuila in March 1913.
Courtesy of Centro de Estudios de Historia de México.

tic and foreign banks fell under tight government regulation for the first time. Carranza also nationalized the railroad and telegraph networks. The move toward nationalizing Mexico's telephone service began in 1915, with Carranza's order to nationalize Mextelco. Despite the chaos brought on by civil war and revolution, the Carrancistas administered the communications systems in surprisingly efficient fashion. Tariff protection for Mexican industry aided the growth of Mexican industries. Because the Carrancistas resorted to printing paper money rather than obligating themselves to a foreign loan, inflation plagued Mexico until the end of 1916. But the reintroduction of metal currency in 1917 brought about monetary stability relatively soon.

Carranza's regulation of foreign investments became highly critical to his nationalism. Mine owners and oil companies had to consider themselves Mexican citizens under the law and accept government policies without requesting diplomatic protection. Once Carranza declared the nation's legal ownership of its natural resources, he forced the largely foreign owners to pay greatly increased taxes. Oil taxes, for example, rose seven times from 1917 to 1920. Carranza's taxes on the Guggenheim mines were eight times higher than Villa's. More than any other leader of the revolution, Carranza articulated and implemented the grievances of Mexicans concerning external control of their economy. Despite United States and European resistance to Carranza's reforms, exports nearly doubled from 1916 to 1920. The economy recovered unexpectedly soon. Although agriculture faltered, henequen, oil, and silver production increased steadily, thanks to world demand.

Carranza finally realized that he could not compete against Villa or Zapata without an effective agrarian program. His moderate but crucial law of January 6, 1915, became a major event that won the support of many rural people. Although undoubtedly opportunistic, this decree returned all communal lands which had been despoiled by application of the 1856 Reforma legislation up to the late Porfiriato. Carranza's land law nullified titles to land expropriated on the basis of Reforma legislation and allowed villages to reclaim their lands through formal petition. Carranza also authorized temporary land seizures and allowed villagers to request land from a new national land commission. Emphasizing the return of *ejido* land in an orderly, legal framework, Carranza's land reform also reduced foreign control of the land and increased the federal domain. But a decline in food production, common to many countries that experience land reform for the first time, gradually limited the scope of Carranza's land reform. Ironically, Carranza probably distributed more land than any of his opponents.

Carranza supported the working class more consistently than his rivals. By distributing food to the masses in several areas, Carranza became popular in the cities. Abolishing company stores, outlawing debt peonage, and legalizing an eight-hour day, as well as mandating minimum wages, added crucial dimensions to his populism. Ending debt peonage enabled workers to become more mobile. As labor shortages affected several regions, laborers could barter for loans and better wages once market conditions began to dictate payments to workers.

The decision of the Casa del Obrero Mundial to ally with Carranza in February 1915 became a particularly notable event. The Casa furnished Carranza with six "red" battalions in return for the right to strike and organize, as well as the First Chief's support of these strikes. The anticlerical outlook of many Carrancistas also persuaded several working-class groups to support Carranza rather than Villa or Zapata. Carrancista subsidies allowed Casa del Obrero Mundial affiliations to establish themselves in at least 30 cities. But during a 1916 war threat with the United States, Carranza crushed the Casa's attempt to foment a general strike. The fact that few unions supported the general strike indicates that nationalism and populism had become tangible in attracting workers toward a policy of reform. Carranza never attacked Marxists but disliked radicals who opposed him publicly. He allowed unions to form a national labor organization, the Confederación Regional Obrera Mexicana, (CROM) in 1918 without trying to hamper the general growth of the working-class movement.

*** Politics and the Nationalist State.*** Carranza's political ideology departed from the past. Not a liberal, Carranza preferred to rule as an authoritarian leader of a stronger state and placed little emphasis upon political parties or legislatures. Although Carranza was not charismatic, Mexicans nevertheless respected him for his austere tastes and devotion to work. Implementing the 1917 Constitution became perhaps his greatest domestic accomplishment. At first, Carranza considered the document too radical but soon accepted most of it. Three key provisions are significant: Article 3 stated that education would be secular and free; the Church could no longer control schools. Article 123 provided labor with a host of benefits, particularly the right to strike and organize for collective bargaining, an eight-hour day, and minimum wages. Article 27 was the most fundamental provision because it mandated land reform, stating that land must have a useful social function. The concept of public utility allowed governments to nationalize property in order to benefit society, as well as general economic development. Subsoil rights now belonged to the state, not private concessionaires.

During the Carranza period, a limited amount of democracy existed because the president clearly influenced elections. A weak ruling party evolved by organizing political clubs to back its slates. State governments became somewhat unpredictable in that some enacted progressive changes while others behaved deplorably. In most cases, local rulers rigged elections but at least attempted to expand education, carry out tax reform, distribute small (if any) amounts of land, and restrict the Church. Governor Salvador Alvarado in Yucatán represents the most radical phase of Carrancista provincial rule when he mobilized workers, controlled henequen sales in the form of a profitable state monopoly, and built dozens of schools. His extreme anticlericalism, political ambitions, and land reforms nevertheless

Carranza departing from the Colegio Militar after reopening it in February 1920. *Courtesy of Centro de Estudios de Historia de México.*

resulted in Carranza's opposition. On the other hand, Oaxaca declared its independence in June 1915, and the insurgents did not give in until 1919. In general, Carrancista governors along the border and coastal areas succeeded more often than their peers farther inland. The periphery had more developed middle and upper classes as well as flourishing economies.

Carranza's army officers came from relatively undistinguished backgrounds and supported egalitarian tenents of Carrancismo. Composed of able ideologues, as well as dependable campaigners, the army appreciated Carranza's efforts to provide them with equipment and prestige. As an indication of revived military influence, 14 generals controlled various states in 1917 and 1918. Prone to corruption, the military yearned for increased political power, but Carranza favored civilian administration and reduced army influence as much as possible. His last great gesture to the army became the reopening of the Colegio Militar, which Huerta had closed.

Foreign Policy. Carranza was a solid statesman when he dealt with foreign affairs. Once Wilson realized that Carranza would challenge U.S. in-

vestments, his opposition to Carranza's nationalism became the central issue. Determined to defend his domestic reforms almost to the point of war, the idealistic, clever, and stubborn Carranza achieved most of his goals.

In order to receive U.S. recognition, Carranza provoked the Plan de San Diego revolt in Texas. Texas irrigation owners angered him greatly when they diverted the entire streamflow of the Rio Grande, although 70 percent of these waters originated in Mexico. Carranza backed Mexican Americans who called for an independent republic which would later be annexed to Mexico. This radical revolt called for the deaths of all Anglo-Americans and the return of all land taken from the Mexican community after 1848. With Carranza's support, over two dozen raids struck south Texas after October 1915. Once Wilson recognized Carranza, however, the revolt sputtered out temporarily.

U.S. recognition of Carranza encouraged Villa to attack Columbus, New Mexico. Against Carranza's opposition, Wilson sent General John Pershing and 10,000 troops to subdue Villa. But the result became a fiasco for Wilson, particularly when he unsuccessfully attempted to make withdrawal of the Pershing column conditional upon

Workers of Construcciónes Aeronauticas support Carranza's presidential campaign in September 1916. *Courtesy of Centro de Estudios de Historia de México.*

Carranza's nonenforcement of his reforms. Carranza refused, and with his sense of history, proclaimed the 1917 Constitution on the day that the last U.S. troops departed from Mexico.

War in Europe affected both countries. The Pershing expedition resulted in Carranza seeking support from Germany. Eager to distract the United States from the European conflict, Arthur Zimmermann, the Kaiser's foreign relations minister, secretly offered Carranza the southwestern territories lost by Mexico in 1848 in return for military alliance and financial aid. Tempted to accept the terms of this January 1917 telegram, Carranza also realized that Mexico had suffered destructive warfare. The Germans approached him later, but Carranza decided to remain neutral. Fortunately, he made the right decision, because U.S. entry into the war became virtually inevitable once the British decoded the German message and revealed its contents, thereby reducing U.S. pressure on Carranza.

During World War I, Carranza continued to succeed. He increased regulation and taxation of U.S. investments despite serious opposition from the State Department. When Carranza formulated his Carranza Doctrine, he challenged the Monroe Doctrine by asserting that the United States had no right to intervene in domestic affairs. Carranza also frustrated Britain and France from disrupting his regime. He also lined up El Salvador and Honduras against Guatemala, Mexico's traditional enemy in Central America. Even after the European war, Carranza cleverly obtained war materiel from Japan and Germany by means of secret transactions. Under Carranza, Mexico not only fashioned an aggressive foreign policy but also established itself as an independent power on the world scene.

Society during the Carranza Era. Carranza carried out some important social changes from 1915 to 1920. Mexico required serious social reforms since society had become disrupted. During the factional struggle, approximately 10 percent of the population—about 1.5 million people—either died or left Mexico. The average citizen had to struggle in order to survive, particularly during the critical 1915 to 1916 years.

Carranza's reforms attempted to eradicate vice as well as to provide opportunities for the masses to better their lives. The government restricted the drinking of alcoholic beverages, gambling, drug use, and bullfighting. Attempts to inculcate a new morality brought questionable results, but Carranza did establish day-care centers and orphanages to care for the working poor as well as abandoned children. Carranza also ordered the nefarious pawn shops to charge fair rates and suppressed the national lottery. Carranza became the first Mexican president to demand that migrant Mexican workers in the United States be treated fairly.

Within Mexico, Carranza instituted tangible improvements in the lives of many Mexicans. He supported a National Consumers Society to which he appropriated 150,000 pesos from the federal budget, although his government experienced early financial strain. The National Consumers Society enjoyed strong backing from workers and the middle class, because it alleviated hunger and helped ordinary citizens avoid food speculation, which resulted from hoarding and inflation. Carranza continued to subsidize a large number of cooperative and mutualist undertakings as Díaz had earlier.

Public sale of basic necessities at reduced prices continued after the factional struggle. The president reduced rents for urban dwellers and imposed tax reforms that benefited the needy while coming at the expense of the well-to-do. The government beautified Mexico City with parks, gardens, and walks, and the capital enjoyed clean drinking water as well as decent public transportation. Huerta had been very hostile to the conservation suggestions of Miguel Angel Quevedo, Mexico's premier environmentalist. But the Carranza regime pursued a much more positive policy. Quevedo and Pastor Rouaix convinced Carranza to establish the Desierto de los Leones as Mexico's first national park.

Carranza encouraged more opportunities for women and championed the right to divorce by legalizing absolute divorce in 1917. One of his

Carranza lays the first stone for the Escuela Normal of Saltillo, Coahuila, December 1915. *Courtesy of Centro de Estudios de Historia de México.*

former secretaries, Hermilia Galindo de Topete, became a fiery reformer who organized several feminist clubs. She also circulated the *Mujer moderna* magazine with executive support. President Carranza's Law of Family Relations diminished the control of husbands over wives. It guaranteed the right of married women to draw contracts, take part in legal suits, act as guardians, have equal rights as males to the custody of their children, the right to spend family incomes, permit paternity suits, as well as to acknowledge illegitimate children. An attempt to have women over 21 vote in municipal elections and hold public office failed when feminist leaders did not attend the Second Feminist Congress.

Carranza strolls through the Merced marketplace in Mexico City, August 1917.
Courtesy of Centro de Estudios de Historia de México.

The middle class gradually became Carranza's strongest supporters. Once he swept out the pre-1915 bureaucrats from public service, a large number of the middle class replaced them. The same tendency occurred in the military and local governments. Carranza also staffed newspapers with loyal supporters from the petty bourgeoisie. Tariff policies encouraged Mexican entrepreneurs to form businesses with adequate protection from foreign rivals while obtaining scarce materials at lowered cost.

Carranza's efforts to improve education did not particularly succeed. Because of the success of a decentralized school system in Coahuila, Carranza felt that local control of education would allow learning to flourish. The municipal and state governments did not often have the necessary revenues to support expanded school enroll-ments. The illiteracy rate did not drop substantially, and by 1919, the total number of students attending elementary schools may have actually declined. Meanwhile, critics lamented the lack of qualified teachers in the twilight of the Carranza regime. Nevertheless, institutions to care for the retarded, deaf, and blind appeared, as well as commercial, industrial, and night schools. Carranza also instituted curricular changes that

stipulated physical education, history, foreign languages, and science.

A rejuvenation of Mexican culture occurred in intellectual life. The regime trained archivists and in 1919 the Academia Mexicana de Historia established itself in Mexico City as a prestigious correspondent of the Real Academia in Madrid. *Gladios* and *La Nave* are examples of elite journals that conveyed important intellectual trends toward a nationalistic pluralism. Carranza upgraded the national university, which had only been reopened in 1910. The Escuela de Altos Estudios and the Universidad Popular grew in Mexico City because Carranza supported the generally popular open-air cultural format that had developed under its predecessors. Antonio Caso, Lombardo Vicente Toledano, and Daniel Cosío Villegas became famed members of the "generation of 1915" that favored an idealistic, indigenous interpretation of Mexican reality. Many intellectuals joined propaganda missions organized to politicize the masses in the interior. Poets such as Ramón López Velarde and novelists like Mariano Azuela championed the nationalist movement that sought to rediscover the essence of Mexican society. In music, Manuel Ponce established a new indigenous esthetic, while young

Carranza awarding kindergarten diplomas to Mexico City children in September 1914. *Courtesy of Centro de Estudios de Historia de México.*

Carlos Chávez experimented with indigenous rhythms. Federico Mariscal made the same connection in the field of architecture while egalitarian, anthropoligical concepts appeared in Manuel Gamio's influential *Forjando patria*, which anticipated his research at Teotihuacán. Beginning in 1917, large-scale excavations were carried out by the Mexican government along Teotihuacán's principal avenue.

During this period, officials and scholars debated the best approach to revive education and assimilate Indians. By 1920, they agreed that indigenous groups should be gradually reincorporated, with special attention given to preserving viable indigenous traditions within a Mexican as well as Hispanic context. José Vasconcelos championed a national public school system that would resolve a crippling strike that left state and local school systems in a shambles by the 1919–1920

period. Inadequate financing and decentralization had weakened mass education. Vasconcelos assumed that rural education could reach Indians, who still remained largely in the interior.

Much of the 1920s artistic renaissance appeared now, although in embryonic forms. Adolfo Best Maugard, as well as Saturino Herrán, became apostles of the new national art because they painted indigenous scenes and Mexican themes throughout the 1915 to 1920 period. Painters such as David Alfaro Siqueiros and José Clemente Orozco had served in Carrancista armies during their quest for social justice. Carranza approved the new art and commissioned shows as well as international tours. The president sent Siqueiros to Europe as chancellor to the Paris consulate. Both he and Alberto Pani convinced Diego Rivera to return to Mexico after paying for Rivera's crucial Italian trip. There Rivera decided to employ fresco techniques as part of his decision to emphasize the collective goals of the new art.

Because many of his lower-and middle-class followers favored a crackdown against the Church, Carranza rose to power partially as an anticlerical. But Carranza himself maintained a moderate attitude toward religious issues. He did not want to antagonize the Church once the conservative forces of Félix Díaz became his most dangerous opposition after 1916. Moreover, Carranza objected to the unrealistic restrictions placed upon the Church's role in education which the radicals had codified in Article 3 of the 1917 Constitution. Although Carranza insisted upon separation of Church and state and seized clerical properties, he eased the early anticlerical persecution that many regional governments promoted. Although angered by Carranza's friendly reception of Protestant missionaries, the Church worked out a modest compromise with Carranza toward the end of his regime.

Undeveloped or simply meager, many of Carranza's attempts to reform society enabled his successors to build upon the new attitudes and intellectual currents that developed during this important period.

The Fall of Carranza. The end of World War I meant that Carranza could no longer depend upon significant aid from Europe. Now he faced the United States alone. Nearly all of Carranza's exiled opponents agreed to topple his government; this attempt was led by Félix Díaz and supported by U.S. investors. Although the conservative exiles failed, stopping them became a major task. Moreover, domestic discontent surfaced in the form of falling real wages in rural areas and the decline of social reforms. As strikes broke out over falling demand for Mexican goods worldwide and employers took a hard line on wages and working conditions, workers searched for militant leaders. Carranza's only real overture to labor was his support of foreign leftists who focused upon attacking U.S. imperialism.

In 1919, Carranza committed a major error by sharply restricting the distribution of *ejido* land. The regime had become alarmed over declining food production. But the *campesinos* now had to pay taxes on land obtained through the legalistic land reform bureaucracy and indemnify the government for land awards. Returning land to hacenados, such as the Terrazas family, became Carranza policy. Meanwhile, Carranza prospered as a landowner whose estate totaled 50,000 hectares.

Fatal political miscalculations matched mass discontent. In August 1918, Carranza backed off from restrictions and taxes placed upon oil companies and even raised the possibility of framing Article 27 into a law that both sides could live with. Obregón deserved to be the next president, but Carranza refused to permit the popular general to succeed him. Fearful that Obregón would sell out to the United States and determined to control events by imposing a colorless successor, Carranza foolishly decided to back the candidacy of the relatively unknown Ignacio Bonillas. News of this mistake increased opposition to the regime by the summer of 1920, particularly when Carranza clumsily attempted to repress Obregón's campaign.

By violating the principle of no reelection, Carranza faced imminent revolt from the army. In Sonora, Plutarco E. Calles and the state governor issued the Plan de Agua Prieta, which called for Carranza's overthrow. Within a few weeks, Carranza had to flee the capital in a vain attempt to reestablish himself in Veracruz. But rebel forces halted the presidential train in the Puebla mountains and assassinated Carranza in the tiny hamlet of Tlaxcalontongo.

Carranza's early social reforms, political nationalism, and statist economic policies generally proved a winning formula and set the outlines of official policy throughout the twentieth century. Despite the strength of his convictions and determination to set a fresh, independent course for Mexico, Carranza failed to form a solid political foundation for his nationalist ideology, which left his program somewhat rudderless at times. Still, one cannot separate the unifying impulse of socioeconomic reform from Carranza's insistent nationalism and the concept of a strong Mexico. Carranza was one of several contemporary nationalist leaders whose struggle with state building in a hostile environment moved in spurts and formed institutions that could deliver only part of what he promised, an outcome not dissimilar to the result of most revolutions.

SUGGESTED READING

Brunk, Samuel. *Emiliano Zapata: Revolution and Betrayal in Mexico.* Albuquerque: University of New Mexico Press, 1995.

Coerver, Don M., and Linda Hall. *Texas and the Mexican Revolution: A Study in State and National Border Policy, 1910–1920.* San Antonio, TX: Trinity University Press, 1984.

Cumberland, Charles C. *Mexican Revolution: The Constitutionalist Years.* Austin: University of Texas Press, 1972.

Henderson, Peter. "Modernization and Change in Mexico: La Zacualpa Rubber Plantation, 1890–1920." *Hispanic American Historical Review* 73:2 (May 1993), 235–260.

Joseph, Gilbert M. *Revolution from Without: Yucatán, Mexico, and the United States.* Durham, NC: Duke University Press, 1988.

Katz, Friedrich. *The Life and Times of Pancho Villa.* Stanford, CA: Stanford University Press, 1998.

———. "Villa: Reform Governor of Chihuahua." In George Wolfskill and Douglas W. Richmond, eds. *Essays on the Mexican Revolution.* Austin: University of Texas Press, 1979, pp. 27–45.

———. *The Secret War in Mexico.* Chicago: University of Chicago Press, 1981.

Martínez, Oscar J. *Fragments of the Mexican Revolution.* Albuquerque: University of New Mexico Press, 1983.

Moguel Flores, Josefina. *Venustiano Carranza: Primer Jefe y Presidente.* Saltillo: Gobierno del Estado de Coahuila, 1995.

Niemeyer, Victor E. *Revolution at Querétaro: The Mexican Constitutional Convention of 1916–1917.* Austin: University of Texas Press, 1974.

Parkinson, Roger. *Zapata.* New York: Stein and Day, 1975.

Peterson, Jessie, and Thelma Cox, eds. *Pancho Villa: Intimate Recollections by People Who Knew Him.* New York: Hastings House, 1977.

Reed, John. *Insurgent Mexico.* New York: International Publishers, 1969.

Richmond, Douglas W. *Venustiano Carranza's Nationalist Struggle, 1893–1920.* Lincoln: University of Nebraska Press, 1983.

———.*La Frontera México-Estados Unidos Durante la Eposa Revolucionaria.* Saltillo: Gobierno del Estado de Coahuila, 1996.

———. "Mexican Immigration and Border Strategy During the Revolution, 1919–1920." *New Mexico Historical Review* 57 (July 1982), 268–269.

———. "La guerra de Texas se renova: Mexican insurrection and Carrancista Ambitions, 1900–1920." *Aztlán* 11 (Spring 1980), 1–32.

———. "Intentos externos para derrocar al regimen de Carranza, 1915–1920." *Historia Mexicana* 32 (July-September 1982), 106–132.

Sandos, James A. "German Involvement in Northern Mexico, 1915–1916: A New Look at the Columbus Raid." *Hispanic American Historical Review* 50 (February 1970), 70–89.

———. "Pancho Villa and American Security: Woodrow Wilson's Mexican Diplomacy Reconsidered." *Journal of Latin American Studies* 13 (November 1981), 293–311.

———. *Rebellion in the Borderlands: Anarchism and the Plan of San Diego, 1904–1923.* Norman: University of Oklahoma Press, 1992.

Schmidt, Henry C. *The Roots of Lo Mexicano: Self and Society in Mexican Thought, 1900–1934.* College Station: Texas A&M University Press, 1978.

Smith, Michael M. "Carrancista Propaganda and the Print Media in the United States: An Overview of Institutions. *The Americas* 11 52:2 (October 1995), 155–174.

Smith, Robert Freeman. *The United States and Revolutionary Nationalism in Mexico, 1916–1932.* Chicago: University of Chicago Press, 1972.

Stout, Joseph A. *Border Conflict: Villistas, Carrancistas, and the Punitive Expedition, 1915–1920.* Fort Worth: Texas Christian University Press, 1999.

Womack, John. *Zapata and the Mexican Revolution.* New York: Alfred A. Knopf, 1969.

———. "The Mexican Economy during the Revolution, 1910–1920. Historiography and Analysis." *Marxist Perspectives* 1 (Winter 1978), 80–123.

13

Obregón, Calles, and the Maximato, 1920–1934

The 1920 to 1934 period featured efforts to institutionalize a policy of authoritarian populism which would endure throughout the twentieth century. The Sonorans attempted to subordinate religious sentiments, the military, foreign investors, and regional leaders to their interpretation of anticlericalism, unionization, and land reform. The national leaders in Mexico City did not always have the power to attain their goals nor did Mexicans always agree with their policies. Sputtering economic growth and the Great Depression further limited the reach of the nation state. Obregón and Calles gave northern Mexico a prominent position. Nevertheless, a successful revival of the artistic and intellectual scene provided self-confidence and a measure of cultural unity.

ALVARO OBREGÓN: AN ACCOMMODATING PRESIDENT

Rise to Power. Alvaro Obregón Salido was born in 1880 as the youngest of 18 children on the Siquisiva hacienda in the northwestern state of Sonora. Perhaps because he grew up without a father, Obregón did not speak for five years. Gifted with a perfect memory and hardworking by nature, he excelled at farming, mechanics, music,

and photography. Obregón also grew up with Mayo Indians and spoke their language. A likeable person of great intelligence, Obregón invented a chickpea harvester that enabled him to afford to attend the 1910 centenary fiesta in Mexico City.

Obregón's military skill undoubtedly became his greatest accomplishment. His sympathy for Porfirio Díaz caused him to shun the Madero insurrection, but in 1912 he put together a battalion of 300 troops to battle Pascual Orozco. Often disobeying the orders of superiors, Obregón displayed imaginative tactical skills which enabled him to ambush, assault, and encircle enemy forces. This resulted in rapid promotion. In 1913, he joined the Constitutionalist struggle against Huerta and captured the port of Guaymas, gaining a major victory at Santa Rosa in May 1913 by means of a clever encirclement. Therefore, Carranza promoted Obregón to command the Army of the Northwest, which depended on Yaqui as well as Mayo fighters. After arriving in Mexico City, Obregón was a major general who accepted the federal army's surrender on August 11, 1914.

Obregón became recognized as the preeminent general during the struggle against Villa and Zapata. At the beginning of 1915, Obregón flattened a Zapatista army at Puebla. But the real danger to the Carranza regime was Villa. In Guanajuato, Obregón defeated Villa's troops although the *Vil-*

listas outnumbered Obregón. Obregón neutralized Villa's cavalry by hiding his men in foxholes and trenches shielded by stone fences as well as barbed wire. Defeated at Celaya, Villa regrouped again to attack at León. There at the Santana del Conde hacienda, Obregón lost his right arm in a blast from one of Villa's cannons.

The loss of his arm overwhelmed Obregón. He whipped out a pistol to kill himself, but an aide took it away, put a tourniquet on his ruptured arm, and carried the general on a stretcher through plowed fields to a railroad car. There, before surgery, Obregón dictated a telegram to Carranza explaining that he expected to die and requested that Benjamin Hill lead his troops. "I die blessing the revolution," the telegram declared. Although reputed to be corrupt, Obregón subsequently joked that he was less of a thief than other leaders because he had only one arm with which to steal.

Obregón and fellow Sonorans seized power in 1920. Earlier, on June 1, 1919, Obregón urged voters to elect him president. Although Obregón had the backing of Sonoran businesses, Sonora governor Adolfo de la Huerta, the state's military commander, Plutarcho Elías Calles, and numerous U.S. companies, Carranza suspected that Obregón would favor U.S. interests. In fact, Obregón owed W. R. Grace and Company no less than $1.8 million. When Carranza would not recognize the inevitable, Obregón issued his Plan de Agua Prieta in April 1920. Obregón proceeded to gather overwhelming support from almost all major groups with the exception of Carranza's diehard supporters. Governor Bill Hobby of Texas convened a meeting of the seven southwestern governors who had endorsed Obregón's revolt. The last successful *golpe* against a twentieth-century Mexican government, the Plan de Agua Prieta promised electoral integrity but ushered in two decades of unquestioned authoritarianism.

Attempts at Centralization. Obregón and Calles agreed to allow de la Huerta to serve as provisional president until formal presidential elections would be held in September 1920. A smooth politician, de la Huerta conciliated sup-

Obregón with a child. *Courtesy of Centro de Estudios de Historia de México.*

port for the government in his charge and attempted total pacification of Mexican regions. No true political parties existed at the time; personalism usually dictated the outcome of political differences. Vital to this process was de la Huerta's amnesty declaration. This enabled the participants in the Tlaxcalontongo murder of Carranza to be set free. More importantly, the regime bought Pancho Villa a big hacienda that cost 800,000 pesos and covered 80,000 hectares. This deal enraged Obregón, but de la Huerta thought of his political future with Villa and realized that no one could relax until Villa gave in. After his capture, Félix Díaz agreed to leave the country and Pablo González was set free after revolting. Fifteen provisional governors began to take over in other states where loyalty to Obregón was dubious. Perhaps de la Huerta's best decision was appointing José Vasconcelos to become the rector of the national university.

Obregón, meanwhile, campaigned for the presidency. A military hero and down-to-earth nonideologue, Obregón used his excellent sense of humor to great effect. He also promised to respect the rights of both citizens and foreigners. Obregón went out of his way not to utter false promises or radical solutions. Like don Porfirio, whom he resembled in so many ways, Obregón offered wise administration. His weak opposition consisted of a virtually unknown former Carranza agent whose only real support came from the Catholic party. Finally, Obregón received 1.3 million votes and his opponent a mere 47,000. As an indication of how the Sonora dynasty had already established accommodations with other regional caudillos and camarillas, states such as Tamaulipas and Tabasco recorded no votes for Obregón's challenger.

A major problem to solve was the army. There were still 500 or so generals in the country who were often just as ambitious as Obregón himself. The most popular were brought into Mexico City and removed from their troops. In the bustling capital, opportunities for making money abounded. Obregón offered "silver cannon balls" of 50,000 pesos to those who took their time in deciding whether or not to support the regime. Many generals were soon rich businessmen and hacendados. Army officers were not allowed to campaign for civilian politicians who disagreed

with the regime. Obregón also rotated officers out of regions where they could develop a strong following. Some generals, such as Obregón favorite Francisco Serrano, had their gambling debts paid off while others enjoyed European vacations. Those who refused to cooperate were cashiered out of the army. When a military revolt did occur in 1921, the major participants, such as General Francisco Murguía, were shot. Obregón also reduced the number of military officers in the cabinet, although they still controlled most state and local governments.

Obregón also gained control of the country's only political party, the weak Partido Liberal Constitucionalista (PLC). Calles, who also served as interior minister, soon experienced disagreements with PLC leaders Benjamin Hill and José Inés Novelo. When Obregón ignored the PLC political platform and became closer to Calles and labor leader Luis Morones, the PLC tried to restrict executive authority and name cabinet ministers. The PLC still controlled the legislature, which was basically independent of the president, as under Carranza. After Obregón invited Hill and Inés Novelo to dine with him, both became poisoned and died. Calles followed up by forming a new political party, which he forged out of four smaller ones with money given to those who

Obregón with cabinet members. *Courtesy of Centro de Estudios de Historia de México.*

would cooperate. The PLC soon collapsed. Real debates in the Chamber of Deputies began to fade away once harassment and control of the legislators began. Press censorship also reappeared, but Obregón and subsequent presidents failed to create a professional police force.

Obregón decided to accommodate regional leaders as a realistic assessment of the limits of his power. He had become president of a country that did not want to be governed by the federal district. Therefore, he tolerated regional caudillos and independent-minded state governors. Obregón also wanted to ally the national regime with reformist governors rather than depend on military chiefs. Several young leaders had taken over their states when they backed the Agua Prieta rebellion. Colonel Adalberto Tejada became governor of Veracruz with Obregón's consent in 1920. Because General Guadalupe Sánchez controlled military and landowner support in the Veracruz region, Tejada mobilized workers, campesinos, and Marxist parties. In the southeast, Felipe Carrillo Puerto rose to prominence as an agrarian organizer under Salvador Alvarado. In 1919, he became the first regional leader to declare for Obregón; thus Obregón rewarded him with the governorship in 1922. Tomás Garrido Canabal had served as provisional governor of Yucatán and had been influenced profoundly by Carrillo Puerto's socialism. Following the model of his Yucatecan mentor as well as Tejada, Garrido established a regional labor-campesino federation in order to establish cooperatives and increase agricultural wages.

In Tamaulipas, Emilio Portes Gil illustrates how becoming too aggressive a reformer could result in failure. He had supported oil workers in a general strike. This brought him into conflict with the powerful caudillo of the region, Manuel Peláez. Thus his provisional administration collapsed under Obregón's disinterest. Francisco Múgica, elected governor of Michoacán in 1920, was a zealous reformer but too independent for Obregón because Múgica would not abide with the tiniest federal meddling in Michoacán. The final straw came when Múgica objected to federal troops disarming local campesino civil defense units. Obregón attempted to apply the *ley fuga* to Múgica, who survived only when Lázaro Cárdenas, the military zone commander, ignored Obregón's order.

In general, the reformist governors of the early 1920s did not radically reshape society in their domains. Hacendados, military leaders, the Church, and disinterest in Mexico City limited what they could achieve. Nevertheless, a minimal amount of mobilization did occur and the appeal of reformers would leave a lasting mark upon political leaders and their constituents. Local governments often played a more significant role than the federal government, by blocking or implementing socioeconomic reforms and in creating the bureaucracies which the central state would eventually take over. Likewise, the development of a national bourgeoisie and the formation of many capitalist institutions also occurred. Like Carranza, Obregón also understood that he needed old as well as new elites in order to survive politically and create new wealth. The old elite still possessed considerable economic power, and intermarriage provided status and continuity for the new, largely urban elites who emerged during the civil war.

Land and Labor Policies. During the stressful years of his government, Obregón emerged as an emphatic compromiser. Nationalism slowed down considerably as the establishment of a system that prevailed throughout twentieth-century Mexico became consolidated. Carranza had earlier told the elite that they had to cooperate with the government for the national good. When most refused, a standoff resulted until reconciliation. Obregón had observed this and now persuaded opponents of the new Sonoran order that they had much to gain by accepting a populist state. To the public, Obregón portrayed himself as a friend of the masses.

Obregón's labor policy exemplified the contradiction between official populism as well as the continuity of past efforts to increase economic growth with foreign investors, provide stability, and restore confidence. Therefore, serious reform did not work in this equation. Although he favored industrial workers over campesinos, Obregón tended to allow governors to make final decisions regarding industrial disputes. Unless strikes became a serious threat to national goals, Obregón avoided a direct role. To enhance a populist image, CROM labor leaders received several appointments in the government. Henceforth, they recruited a larger membership, which increased from 50,000 to 1,200,000. But unions had to obey the CROM as well as the regime. When Obregón did become involved in labor disputes, he urged workers to obey the law and respect governmental decisions. Strikes broke out and workers sought unionization as well as an improved standard of living. Nevertheless, Obregón became very concerned about inflation and favored consumers. Obregón also eased the anxieties of businesses by emphasizing the need for productivity rather than the redistribution of wealth: "We gain nothing by giving felt hats and shoes to those who wear straw hats," he observed.

In strikes involving foreign ownership or important domestic sectors of the economy—oil, minerals, fishing, and the railroads—Obregón favored capital. For example, when Puebla textile workers struck in order to gain recognition of their union, Obregón did little and authorized the deployment of troops against them. The exhaustion of the oil fields and the postwar decline in oil prices late in 1921 had made labor in the foreign-controlled oil fields quite insecure. Activists from the Industrial Workers of the World had played a crucial role in establishing the first oil workers' unions in Mexico. Thus, tension developed between the companies and the workers, who sought union autonomy, a concept long-rooted in Mexican labor's anarchosyndicalist traditions. Worse, the companies lowered wages and fired workers without giving severance pay while relying upon temporary labor for renewed operations. Obregón did nothing, leaving unemployed strikers to fend for themselves. Obviously, he was more concerned about government revenues, which depended greatly upon oil tax receipts.

When the crisis stabilized, striking El Aguila workers occupied the refinery until management promised an eight-hour day, higher wages, and severance pay. When these concessions vanished, scabs moved in to take the jobs of strikers. Obregón refused to back up the workers, stating that property could not be seized by strikers.

Another example of ideals turning into opportunism was the land reform issue. The land reform process rested upon connections with Obregón and regional mobilization. Obregón understood the significance of land rewards to those who had fought for him earlier and he utilized a moderate agrarian policy to solidify his political following.

After assuming power, Obregón decided to maintain the Comisión Nacional Agraria to deal with petitions for land grants. Formed by Carranza's decree of January 1915, the commission subsequently passed a Law of Unused Lands in June 1920 in order to produce food supplies. This ruling enabled municipal leaders to award unproductive private holdings to those willing to work them. In addition, Obregón broadened the definition of who was entitled to receive land grants and restitutions. Because of the legalistic bureaucratic procedures, peasants became dependent upon the national government when Obregón assumed direct control of the land distribution process. This served as a vital mechanism to enforce loyalty on those who accepted land awards. Once in legal possession of hacienda land, ejidatarios had to pay the corresponding land tax. Within a few years, many ejido committees fell behind on tax payments and became liable to crop embargoes. Gradually, Obregón condoned tax debts in exchange for pledges of efficiency and political loyalty. Obregón also responded to genuine mobilization among campesinos eager for land. One factor that contributed to land requests was that the Comisión Nacional had been composed of enthusiastic employees who encouraged many villagers to assemble data and file claims during the Carranza period. Thus Obregón found himself in a position to carry out quick presidential decisions on land grants, usually on a provisional basis. Since Obregón had allowed campesinos to solicit him directly for land awards, his popularity was enhanced. Therefore, he greatly increased the number of employees within the Comisión Nacional. During Obregón's presidency, strong *agrarista* leaders began to mobilize supporters for agrarian reform and dominate significant portions of rural Mexico. Backed up by their armed guards, many *agrarista* leaders enjoyed virtual autonomy in some areas, particularly where the civil war had generated strong peasant participation. In Michoacán, Primo Tapia and Francisco Múgica organized the League of Agrarian Communities of Michoacán in December 1923. In 1924 and 1925, additional agrarian leagues appeared in Tabasco, Puebla, Tamaulipas, San Luis Potosí, and Chiapas. Recent migrants to the United States often sparked the drive for land reform in northern Mexico.

Virtually all land reform took place in regions that were potential sources of rebellions or were part of Obregón's attempts to reward powerful leaders. One-fourth of Morelos was turned over to villages as part of governmental efforts to enshrine Zapata's legacy and create peace. In addition to serving in many governmental positions, former *zapatistas* such as Genovevo de la O served as chief of military operations in the state of Tlaxcala. Chihuahua and Durango recorded large amounts of land redistribution in order to keep Villa isolated and unable to stir up a revolt. In San Luis Potosí, Saturino Cedillo and his brothers had organized a grass-roots agrarian movement of rancheros and indebted peons into a guerrilla movement. Obregón permitted Cedillo to keep his *agraristas* armed so that he could use them against rebels elsewhere. Much like a warlord, Cedillo acted as a power broker between the central government and the local population. This differed from Portes Gil, Tejada, and Garrido Canabal, who utilized political machines they had organized on the state level but whose fate became tied to favorable relationships with Obregón.

Obregón initiated the change whereby the agrarian bureaucracy administering land reform gradually began to replace the patronage systems developed by individual military commanders as well as state governors. Thus the central government promised land to armed *agraristas* in return for military service. During his first two years in power, Obregón favored gulf states for their assistance to the Carrancista cause. However, the sierra states of Puebla, Tlaxcala, and Hidalgo also received large numbers of land awards because of their local agrarian uprisings.

Yucatán, however, was the state where Obregón distributed the most land, about 715,000 hectares. Felipe Carrillo Puerto, once a train conductor, took over Yucatán in 1922 and embarked upon serious reforms. His Partido Socialista enrolled 80,000 members in its organization and affiliated 400 *ligas de resistencia* to pressure for unionized labor contracts, better schools, new rights for women, and even to paint public buildings as well as churches red. Led by local power brokers, the *ligas* focused upon land reform. Carrillo Puerto had little interest in urban labor unions. Able to speak in Mayan and genuinely concerned about far-reaching changes, Carrillo Puerto established a new university.

Thus land reform became an orderly procedure that was essentially a political tool. Foreigners, for example, never had to worry about seizure of their land. Obregón publicly predicted that starvation would occur if Congress adopted a bill making ownership of properties more than 50 hectares illegal. The only area where he agreed with idealistic revolutionaries was that there was no question that the villages needed ejidal lands. Obregón himself personally benefited because he established a large latifundia complex. By the time Obregón left office, 624 villagers had received 1.2 million hectares, about 3 million acres.

EDUCATIONAL REVIVAL AND ARTISTIC RENEWAL

As Obregón sought to develop patriotism, loyalty, and social control over peasants and workers, a cultural renaissance unequaled in Mexican history took place. Within the framework of nationalism and populist emphasis upon indigenous pride, Obregón sought to unify Mexico with the aid of educators and artists.

Obregón realized that unions and mobilized agrarian communities were trying to control schools. Therefore, he created the Education Secretariat in 1921, which aimed to establish rural primary schools for all Mexicans through a homogenous curriculum in federal classrooms. The tireless José Vasconcelos continued serving as the minister of education after earlier leading the national university. A philosopher from the Ateneo group of the late Porfiriato, Vasconcelos directed a popular mass literacy campaign which benefited at least 100,000 people. Very honest and idealistic, Vasconcelos was one of the few nonpolitical appointees in Obregón's cabinet. Obregón and the national legislature supported his efforts by approving larger amounts of funding for education than anything else except military spending. Often Congress voted more money than what the government asked for, but as Vasconcelos once noted, what was actually spent became another question altogether. Perhaps his greatest achievements were a reorganization of teacher colleges, as well as improvements in elementary, secondary, and technical education.

Many communities had high expectations of what schools could accomplish other than the Yaqui and Tarahumara regions, which viewed federal education programs as symbols of intrusion into their constant attempt to maintain autonomy. There can be no doubt that education increased as a result of federal stimulation. Gaining the ability to read and write added greatly to the self-confidence of small communities. The government built about a thousand schools in the countryside, where locals often took great interest in the curriculum. Villagers frequently drove unpopular, incompetent instructors out of their towns. Certainly the *maestro* (teacher) now emerged as the most important person in many villages. They doubled as ayuntamiento secretaries, dealt with the bureaucracy, managed record keeping, drafted contracts, mediated labor

disputes, and directed patriotic festivals. Most *maestro*s taught the basics of reading and writing, in addition to new tasks such as how to improve diet and hygiene, be more sensitive to children, and reduce drinking. Vasconcelos also viewed education as a defense of Hispanic culture and the Iberian connection to Europe. In addition to two million standard textbooks, many learned Spanish classics such as *Don Quijote*. Vasconcelos believed indigenous features were minimal aspects of Mexican culture.

Moisés Sáenz, one of the architects of the rural school program, disagreed. Unlike Vasconcelos, he keenly appreciated the indigenous legacy which he valued greatly. In educational terms, Sáenz wanted to incorporate Indians into a civilization which would merge the European and indigenous contributions. Like Franz Boas, the dominant anthropologist in the 1920s, Sáenz saw culture as relativistic, with the indigenous peoples as being equally cultured. Therefore, the Education Secretariat trained bilingual instructors to deal with the problem of poverty in indigenous communities.

Thus, *indigenismo*, the incorporation of indigenous peoples into the mainstream of Mexican society, became a major feature of education. Once Indians participated fully in the culture, a *raza cosmica* (cosmic race) would appear. Such an outlook symbolized the new self-confidence that appeared as part of rediscovering and recovering Mexico by Mexicans. Therefore, educators attempted to minimize foreign influence and glorify the Olmec, Mayan, and Aztec foundations of Mexico. Despite the logic of the proposals of Obregón and Vasconcelos, education overlooked the obvious fact that without economic growth, the poor would remain unemployed and despondent. Nevertheless, educational administrators blamed the poor for having the wrong attitude.

Vasconcelos also considered art an expression of universal as well as Mexican sentiments. Therefore, he took a direct role in developing the famous mural painters. In 1920, Vasconcelos discussed with Alfredo Ramos Martínez, a popular impressionist excited by fresh painting techniques observed during his travels in Europe, a new method of artistic instruction which came to be known as the open air school of art. Ramos Martínez encouraged the use of naturalistic observation in an abstract form. Stylistic devices contributed to the general mood of immediacy—vigorous lines, earthy colors, sharp black-and-white contrasts, strongly modeled figures. A tendency toward exaggeration, whether the subject was an elaborately-costumed folk dancer or a gaunt child suffering from starvation, became part of a glorious and formative artistic period that seduced the imaginations of painters and printmakers in Paris, Madrid, and New York.

Mexico City's murals are regarded as the best of a genre that flourished in the United States and Europe. Though they carried some of the same ideological content as the populist murals found in the Depression-era museums and post offices in the United States, Mexican murals contained a passion and populism considered a major departure in modern art. Born as an art movement in 1922, these celebrations of the working masses first brought artistic attention to Mexico's pre-Hispanic past. Mexican artists felt that art should speak to everyday experiences to demonstrate that art should not be a stranger to working-class lives.

Diego Rivera was one of the great innovators of twentieth-century art. A fanciful, creative egotist, the amoral Rivera grew up in Guanajuato. Possibly because they were in danger from conservative forces in the region, the liberal Riveras fled to Mexico City in 1893. There, at the age of ten, Diego gained admission to the prestigious San Carlos Academy. His most valuable training came from José Guadalupe Posada, who illustrated broadsheets for ballads which carried the latest news. Posada taught Rivera about artistic movement, emotion, and human feeling. Not always believable, Rivera described in his memoirs how he and other students ate human meat obtained from the city morgue. Disillusioned with the academic training he received in Mexico, Rivera received funding for travel to Europe from Veracruz Governor Teodoro Dehesa. He left at the age of

21 and spent the next 14 years traveling between Spain, Brussels, Paris, and Italy, hobnobbing with the European avant-garde.

In 1907, Rivera went to Spain to continue his training. He studied at the Eduardo Chicharro studio and drew sketches of Goya paintings in the Prado. He became so skilled at copying composites of Goya items that several, believed to be original Goyas, later hung in private collections. At this time, however, Diego was searching for himself, uncertain how to express his feelings on canvas. He spent a lot of time in cafés, heatedly debating art and politics. Rivera first read Karl Marx and other socialistic works during his time in Spain. Observing poverty, assassinations, and a confused imperial monarchy, Rivera became a socialist until his life ended. But Rivera became disappointed with the few paintings he produced and left Madrid in the spring of 1909.

Once Rivera arrived in Paris, he embraced modernism with a vengeance, trying his hand at everything from Mondrians, Monets, Seurats, to Picasso. He had hoped to study with Cezanne, but the master had already died. By now art had become his first love; others around him were of secondary importance. Rivera enjoyed sexual orgies, drinking binges, avant-garde discussions with other artists, but he did not overindulge.

In 1910, Rivera returned briefly to Mexico for a show of his Spanish works. The exhibition, held at San Carlos Academy, was a critical and financial success. Carmen Romero Rubio de Díaz, wife of President Porfirio Díaz, purchased 6 of the 40 paintings. Ironically, the exhibit opened on November 20, 1910, the same day that the Mexican revolution began. Rivera's work already reflected his deep feelings for the painful sufferings of common people. He tried to infuse his passion for local roots in his paintings. He also designed a poster which encouraged peasants to seize land. Rivera even spoke at underground meetings, encouraging revolution. He fled Mexico City and returned to Europe in 1912 when he heard that the authorities wanted to execute him.

Back in Europe, Rivera entered his cubist phase. He befriended Braque, Picasso, and Juan

Gris. His lifelong friend Picasso helped establish Rivera as a cubist in the European art community. Cubism provided Rivera with an outlet for his virtuoso painting techniques and also gave him a means of adopting abstract techniques to Mexican culture. His cubist masterpiece, the 1915 *Zapatista Landscape,* is a collage of shapes, textures, and colors that highlight the guerrilla leader's serape, sombrero, and rifle framed by angular forms representing the mountains outside Mexico City. By the end of 1918, 200 of Rivera's paintings had been sold in Europe and the United States. Practically none found their way to Mexico. However, other cubists objected to the Mexican texture of Rivera's paintings. His paintings were not severely distorted and portrayed human activities which academicians considered vulgar. Picasso and Braque dominated cubism to the extent that there was almost no room for Rivera.

Friction with Picasso and art critics led Rivera to the muralist epoch. Perhaps influenced by his relationship with Mexican and Russian revolu-

Zapatista Landscape by Diego Rivera. *Museum del Palacio del Bellas Artes, Mexico.*

tionaries, Rivera announced that cubism was elitist and had to be replaced by art accessible to mass tastes. Rivera believed that World War I would do away with the bourgeoisie, leaving the working class in power. Because the masses knew little about art, he proposed taking it to them. The Russian revolution also heightened Rivera's enthusiasm for participating in the social changes going on in Mexico. To articulate a truly popular art that would reform mass tastes excited him. The new art, he concluded, would have to hold the attention of the masses by means of exciting subject matter rather than subtleties of style, and it would have to be visible in public places rather than cloistered within museum walls. Through this thinking, Rivera arrived at mural painting—a new field, if done according to his criteria. All this coincided with a pledge by Vasconcelos to educate illiterates by means of using murals as texts. Emotional frescoes would be painted directly on wet plaster before it dried. Therefore, Vasconcelos financed a trip for Rivera to study Italian medieval and renaissance frescoes. When he learned that his father was dying, the homesick Rivera left his Russian wife in Europe and returned to Mexico in 1921.

Rivera became the most prominent painter of the vast program of commissioned art for public buildings that Vasconcelos began. Rivera's murals were to become his greatest achievement. He developed a social realism style that was accessible to the masses and sophisticated in its fusion of European and indigenous Mexican traditions. A huge, genial, and controversial figure, Rivera with his 300 pound frame and large stetson hat created a lasting image. Strangely enough, Rivera's first mural, *Creation*, was a failure. Painted in the National Preparatory School in 1923, this fresco was dated classicism intended to impress the traditionalist views of Vasconcelos. Rivera painted human figures symbolizing wisdom and strength around a large pipe organ; it stated little about Mexican humanity. Rivera then found his niche by traveling to Yucatán and Tehuantepec, where his indigenista mode was triggered. Rivera began to emphasize the dignity of traditional labor, folk customs, and the pleasures of family life. In 1922, he began to amass his impressive collection of pre-Hispanic art.

In 1923, the Obregón regime commissioned Rivera to paint 124 panels of frescoes at the courtyard of the Education Secretariat. He created boldly contoured images that reflected a synthesis of art and science, people and nature, past and present. Scenes of peasants and laborers struggling to improve their lives, meetings of the proletariat contrasted with fancy dinners of capitalists, revolutionary martyrs, heroes, and soldiers resulted. The project took four years to complete and covered 5,000 square feet. One mural contained controversial political images, a Rivera trademark. He painted a poem encouraging miners to seize a mine for themselves. Vasconcelos pleaded with Rivera to remove these inflammatory words. The Painters Union encouraged him to leave the fresco as it was. In the end, Rivera agreed to remove the words, and Vasconcelos allowed Rivera to showcase a less offensive poem on another fresco.

Earlier, in 1921, Rivera had joined the Mexican Communist Party and had begun writing for their newspaper. More a populist than a communist, Rivera did not actually call for an overthrow of the elite. The Red Army Club asked him to paint a mural in Moscow where he traveled in September 1927, as a member of a Mexican delegation of workers and peasants. Bureaucratic delays hindered his getting started on the mural, and in the spring of 1928, his hosts asked Rivera to return to Mexico. Rivera believed that Russian artists resented his painting a mural honoring Russian peasants because he was a Mexican. This only increased his pride in being a *mexicano*.

Upon his return, Rivera began work on the National Palace stairway mural. He considered this his finest work because it illustrated his new medium well. His space was the large stairway which branched left and right at the second level. To the right, he portrayed Mexico before the Spanish invasion: A paradise lost in which the Aztecs did not lord over other peoples nor practice human sacrifice; social harmony prevailed.

To the left was the future revolutionary Mexico marching under Marxist banners to equality and technology. On the six-arched central wall was the colonial era: bloodshed, torture, lusting priests, murderous conquistadors, sadistic plantation owners, and money-grubbing capitalists. With the mural, Rivera followed the architectural movement of the stairway itself and related it to the upward movement of the Mexican Revolution. Each figure in the mural is connected with his neighbors in agreement with historical roles. The mural became a beacon to Rivera and he continued returning to it, making changes until 1955.

Rivera had several interesting commissions in the United States. Like most other government jobs, the post of mural painter did not pay well. Rivera earned about $2 a day, but he had an entree to a world where he could profit from private undertakings. Perhaps the most controversial of Rivera's murals was one commissioned by John D. Rockefeller for Rockefeller Center in New York in 1933. An ardent fan of Rivera's work, Rockefeller followed the development of the mural enthusiastically until it was brought to his attention that Rivera had depicted Lenin in one panel. Rockefeller contended that this image would be too controversial for a public mural, particularly one in this location. The debate over the inclusion of Lenin developed into a power struggle between Rivera and his patron. Ultimately, Rockefeller refused to accept Lenin and had it smashed to pieces.

While Rivera seemed content to glorify the indigenous peoples and Mexican folk traditions, José Clemente Orozco and David Alfaro Siqueinos cut deep below the surface. Their passionate paintings portray the heart and soul, the blood and guts of the overburdened working class in whose hands they felt Mexico's future lay. Orozco's purely Hispanic background and privileged education contrasted sharply with his artistic techniques and subject matter—exploiters, poor, prostitutes—which define a true artistic sense of social responsibility that became awakened after 1913. In the positivist tradition, Orozco portrayed Mexican society as a living entity composed of different segments. Orozco's ability to visualize social problems and interpret reality is another sign of greatness. In emphasizing the dehumanizing power of machines and technology in U.S. society, where he visited in 1917, Orozco's message of humanity communicated across ethnic and national boundaries. Orozco created images of alternative, socialistic societies. He painted the indigenous people of Mexico and their history, incorporating geometric Christ figures and creation scenes inspired by the great murals and frescoes of the Renaissance, always implying hope for a brighter future. Very much opposed to war, apolitical, antiracist, and a leftist who never lost his idealism, Orozco enjoyed the respect of many throughout the world.

José David Alfaro Siqueiros was the Mexican muralist par excellence; he made it an art form that is at once monumental and personal. He began his artistic career with a political objective. At the age of 15, Siqueiros participated in protests, student strikes, and political conspiracies. While studying in Europe, he met Rivera, who, along with several European artists, significantly influenced the development of his style. Although Siqueiros and Rivera disagreed politically, both chose to return to Mexico to re-create Mexico's past and present in their murals.

Though Siqueiros adopted much Aztec and Olmec imagery in his work, he warned artists not to simply reconstruct traditional art but instead draw upon its energy and style to generate a new artistic form. He considered *indigenismo* somewhat counterproductive; Siqueiros maintained that Mexican society should not be divided into Spaniards, *mestizos,* or Indians, but people. There was no dichotomy for Siqueiros between art and politics. Combining his inner artistic passion with an outward revolutionary fervor, he created some of the most powerful social art of the twentieth century. The technical mastery and the profound aesthetics of his murals are a match for the greatest masters of the Renaissance.

Siqueiros promoted an art form called the "plastic exercise," which refers to art that is painted on the interior as well as exterior of buildings.

It is plastic in the sense that it has to conform to the architectonics of the structures on which it is painted. Siqueiros emphasized that it required collective effort because the size of public projects are such that one person could not attain the artistic perspective necessary to complete such tasks. It was revolutionary, he insisted, because it appealed to the masses rather than a select few because of its ideological objective to fulfill the needs of peasants and workers.

Obregón and the Church. Obregón was not a Catholic, but he refused to persecute the Church. Like Díaz and Carranza, Obregón preferred respecting the Church's traditional rights and privileges. In a 1923 address to the archbishops and bishops, Obregón declared

> The present social program of the government is essentially Christian, and it is complementary to the fundamental program of the Catholic Church. (Robert E. Quirk, *The Mexican Revolution and the Catholic Church*, 1910–1929 (Bloomington: Indiana Press, 1973) pp. 134–35.)

Part of Obregón's motive to make peace with the Church was his desire to utilize the Church's educational system while the public schools were being expanded. When questioned about the legality of his position in relation to the anticlerical tone of the 1917 Constitution, Obregón replied

> Yes, it is illegal, and we are not unaware of the menace of these Catholic schools, whose aim is to inculcate antigovernment and antirevolutionary propaganda. But at the present, there is not money enough nor facilities for the government to teach all Mexican children. It is preferable that they receive any instruction, rather than grow up illiterate. (Robert E. Quirk, *The Mexican Revolution and the Catholic Church*, 1910–1929. Bloomington: Indiana Press, 1973, p. 120)

Obregón's most striking constitutional violation was his consent for a public ceremony to erect a monument to Christ near León. When the

1923 ceremony took place, thousands of Catholics attended to recognize Christ as the supreme sovereign. The symbolism of this ceremony contrasted starkly with the populist aims of many anticlerical regional governments. But Obregón was a realist above all.

In order to encourage agricultural production, Obregón granted Mennonites a 50-year lease on more than 100,000 acres of land for $8.25 per acre. Members of a Protestant denomination that originated in Europe during the eighteenth century, the Mennonites emphasized a simple lifestyle, believing that the Bible forbids them from going to war or holding offices that require the use of force. The Mennonites arrived in Mexico in March 1922, after the Canadian government threatened to draft them into the army and incorporate them into Canada's educational system. About 5,000 arrived in Chihuahua in three separate trains, along with their personal belongings, including buggies and horses. Although the desert, heat, and lack of rain bothered many of them, the Mennonites persisted and became prosperous. Obregón always respected successful capitalism and sought friendly ties with Canada. Catholics objected, but Obregón was preoccupied with obtaining friendly ties with his northern neighbor.

Economic Relations with the United States.
Obregón decided to end Carranza's confrontational anti-imperialist policy so he could obtain U.S. loans and diplomatic recognition at almost any cost. The problem was the U.S. oil, banking, and commercial interests which dominated the corrupt Warren G. Harding government. Obregón's definition of foreign investment in Mexico established the model for Mexico's relations with the world economy.

Mexico's economic future did not look particularly good when Obregón began his presidency. Northern states, where the country's wealth lay, had suffered during the civil war. Transportation and communications were ruined in many regions. Livestock, agriculture, commerce, and mining had been disrupted. More than a million

head of cattle had grazed throughout Chihuahua in 1910, for example, but only a tenth of that number remained in 1920. To make matters worse, severe drought struck Chihuahua in 1920, 1921, and 1922. The retail trade never recovered its pre-1910 vitality.

Key sectors of the economy gradually declined. In the northeast, total oil production shot up to 193 million barrels—60 percent of Mexico's external trade and 25 percent of world production—but production began to fall thereafter. In the northwest, as well as in Chihuahua in particular, more ore was extracted and treated in 1921 than at any other time in its history. But mineral production stagnated the next year and began a sharp rise the following year. Notwithstanding occasional production increases, a decline of silver and copper prices became problems in the 1920s. Meanwhile, the henequen industry began to collapse in the Yucatán.

As the traditional sectors of the economy faltered, newer and more informal activities increased. Tourism to Mexico from the United States increased greatly. Many U.S. citizens traveled across the border for quick divorces. Although Yucatán required a six-month residence to obtain divorce papers, local officials would sail out to a boat and take care of a divorce in return for a negotiated price. Sonora required only three days residence for divorce, but one Mexican lawyer handled over 100 cases a year by mail. Drug smuggling became a multimillion dollar business during the early twentieth century. During Prohibition, many U.S. citizens found an outlet in opiates and cocaine by crossing into Mexico border towns. Saloons, downtown honky-tonks, brothels, and open gambling attracted more tourists. The click of dice, riffle of cards, and excitement of roulette tables proved irresistible. Nude dancing, red-light districts, and cabarets provided sexual thrills. By the end of the decade, gambling revenues accounted for the bulk of Chihuahua's revenues.

Oil became the key issue between Obregón and the United States since it dominated the national economy. Although there was a sharp drop in direct foreign investment during the 1920s, the oil sector was an exception. Edward L. Doheny had made the first oil discovery in 1901. Obregón continued Carranza's policy of taxing oil and prevented companies from drilling wells not registered in Mexico City. Yet Obregôn was very eager to negotiate as he badly needed a loan as well as increased revenues. At the same time, oil had been recognized as a strategic resource throughout the world. Moreover, the Russian revolution and U.S. control over Cuba were important factors. Mexico feared that Harding might try to attack Mexico and make it into a virtual protectorate. On the other hand, Washington, D.C. disliked Carranza's insistence upon upholding the national sovereignty features of Article 27 and feared that the Russian decision to nationalize their oil fields in 1920 might become an unhealthy precedent. Many business people in the United States with powerful connections publicly linked Russia's and Mexico's governments. Senator Albert Fall of New Mexico conducted public investigations concerning Mexico's policies before moving up to become Harding's secretary of the interior.

At first, Obregón publicly continued Carranza's policy of taxing oil and sought to prevent companies from drilling wells not registered in Mexico City. But he backed off quickly when U.S. companies boycotted Mexican oil exports in 1921 as a protest against *carrancista* oil taxes. The British El Aguila Company paid the taxes but continued to drill while five U.S. producers finally agreed to negotiate with Obregón. In the meantime, Obregón sent Harding two letters reiterating that he would not apply Article 27 retroactively, in other words, drilling conducted before May 1, 1917, when the constitution had gone into effect. Clearly, both sides wanted accommodation. Therefore, Obregón instructed the Mexican Supreme Court to rule that Article 27 could not be applied retroactively against foreign oil companies if they had performed some "positive act" which would indicate drilling or some other activity prior to May 1917. In this way, he protected all leases and agreements made up to that date by

ruling that the 1917 Constitution did not apply to such titles. Moreover, Obregón agreed to lower the export tax and discuss Mexico's foreign debt.

Obregón's desire for a loan was paramount because the infrastructure had to be rebuilt, malnutrition was serious, unemployment rampant, and a central bank was needed for agrarian reform and other new policies. A successful discussion with bankers, Obregón assumed, would help him with the oil companies. He selected de la Huerta to negotiate for Mexico, but this became a mistake. De la Huerta did not clearly understand the issues and was too easily impressed by Thomas Lamont and other U.S. negotiators. De la Huerta even began to rely on Lamont and the oil companies for advice, which resulted in his giving up Obregón's request for a loan and money to rebuild agriculture. Increasingly suspicious that nothing good was happening, Obregón ordered de la Huerta home with the agreement so they could go over it point by point. The resulting 1922 debt agreement was not good; it set the total public debt at $1,451,737,587. Worse, the agreement bound Mexico to make a $40,000,000 payment on interest during 1923, and an annual payment which increased by $5,000,000 each year until 1928, when the yearly payment would become $50,000,000. At least the United States government realized that Obregón was serious about accommodation.

Meanwhile, Obregón was left with a financial commitment that would be very difficult to fulfill, except through concessions to the foreign oil industry. Establishment of a central bank was postponed. Mexico also had to give back railroads nationalized by Carranza and make necessary repairs. Moreover, railroad, as well as oil revenues, were now pledged to pay off the debt. This was a major reason why economic recovery was slow.

Obregón took a direct hand in getting a loan. The Juan Felipe fields in Veracruz soon became the tool that Obregón used. The most productive oil producing region in the world by 1921–1922, Juan Felipe became the scene of fierce competition among the oil companies. By playing one company off against another, Obregón allowed

Doheny's Huasteca Company to drill Juan Felipe in return for financial assistance. In return, Doheny promised to undertake conservation measures. The 1923 loan was critical because military and administrative officials could not have been paid otherwise.

The Bucareli Agreement. Obregón could still not obtain U.S. diplomatic recognition because the United States wanted the 1921 Supreme Court ruling made into a diplomatic agreement as a means to protect investments from expropriation. Obregón, therefore, agreed to informal talks with Harding representatives and even offered to discuss domestic legislation.

The Mexican negotiators were Fernando González Roa, a brilliant lawyer for Pierce Oil Company, and Ramón Ross, a close personal friend of Obregón. The first meeting in May 1923 got off to a shaky start when Ross passed out on the negotiating table after having too many drinks on the way over. He woke up when he heard Panama referred to and then launched into a wild tirade against the U.S. role there. He insisted that no possible comparison existed between Panama and Mexico. When U.S. representatives questioned his ability to speak English, Ross called them "sons of bitches." The U.S. delegation prepared to leave at that point. Obregón avoided disaster by promising that Ross would not drink and that Roa would speak less.

The Bucareli conference finally concluded in August 1923. Obregón assured the public that nothing was being agreed upon and that Mexican representatives were only explaining the law. The truth is that agreements were made in the form of carefully recorded minutes with nods of approval at key points. There were four vital understandings. First, Obregón agreed to protect U.S. investments on a retroactive basis and that anyone could drill for oil despite Article 27. Mexico now allowed the United States to represent any U.S. investors affected by expropriation and that those holdings which exceeded 1750 hectares would receive cash payments. Petroleum lands were immune to expropriation. Also, a claims commis-

sion composed of one Mexican, one U.S. representative, and a neutral participant would decide upon claims which the Mexican government would have to pay to U.S. investors for losses suffered during the revolutionary period. Finally, oil production taxes would be paid to an Anglo–U.S. Banker's Committee on Mexican debts.

The agreement is considered a stunning triumph for the State Department, a violation of the 1917 Constitution, and a sellout by Obregón. When a Mexican senator complained in public about the one-sided nature of the agreement, he was murdered. As late as the 1970s, the Mexican foreign relations archive maintained that the original documentation was missing. Meanwhile, the secretary of state told the Senate that U.S. property in Mexico was now "safeguarded." After Harding read the minutes and agreements, he announced recognition of the Obregón regime on August 31, 1923. De la Huerta, however, got hold of a secret copy of the Bucareli agreement and saw that the commissioners had signed the minutes. He declared that Obregón had betrayed Mexico.

The De la Huerta Revolt. Already outraged by the Bucareli talks, de la Huerta had heard many urge him to seek the presidency in 1924. Thus he was excited when Obregón asked him to take a drive to Chapultepec Park in late 1923. Unfortunately for de la Huerta, Calles also came along, and Obregón picked his fellow Sonoran to be the next president. Not by coincidence, Villa was assassinated, mainly because Villa was a friend of de la Huerta and had promised him military support in case of a squabble. Calles undoubtedly arranged this murder in Parral.

Drawing upon a wide base of supporters which included conservatives, Church leaders, nationalists, labor leaders, and *agraristas*, this group united at the prospect of Calles taking over. Several union leaders also decided to join de la Huerta, particularly railroad workers. Even CROM officials considered backing the revolt. They urged de la Huerta to revolt, which he agreed to do after resigning from Obregón's government. Meanwhile, *Obregonistas* claimed that de la Huerta had stolen public funds.

The revolt became a serious threat until its demise. After issuing a Plan de Veracruz in December 1923, which called for more ejido distribution, the de la Huerta movement began in Veracruz as most army units sided with it. The *Delahuertistas* captured Puebla and quickly overran Yucatán, where they executed Carrillo Puerto when landowners paid off de la Huerta generals to kill the governor. But the tide turned against them when Obregón, still the country's best military commander, took to the field with loyal army officers as well as CROM militia. Ejido farmers proved particularly helpful. Tejeda and Galván mobilized agrarista guerrillas who assisted in the recapture of Veracruz. Former Zapatista generals helped retake Puebla. The United States also supported Obregón by furnishing him with arms and munitions.

Obregón decided to put the revolt down firmly. When lawyers and other civilians surrendered thinking that they could not have the *ley fuga* applied to them, they were "commissioned" into the army as officers and shot quickly, by War Department orders. Juan Escudero, who founded the shipworkers union in Guerrero, was executed. In Michoacán, Primo Tapia switched sides several times during the revolt, angering Calles considerably. Therefore, he was brutally tortured and killed. *Agraristas* in Tlaxcala and other regions who supported de la Huerta were murdered shortly afterwards. Calles emerged in a stronger position because hostile military officers had been eliminated.

CALLES AND THE MAXIMATO, 1924–1934

Background of Calles. Plutarco Elías Calles would always be troubled by his illegitimate birth. Although his alcoholic father came from a respected family, his mother died when Calles was three. Raised by an uncle, Callas enjoyed a lower-middle-class background in Sonora. In 1888, he studied at an impressive new teacher's academy which had been set up by the Porfirian governor, Ramón Corral. As much as he enjoyed the thrill of educating others, Calles did not attain professional success as a young man. He was dismissed from his teaching position when parents complained of personal misconduct and anticlerical rantings. Often lapsing into heavy drinking, Calles read *Regeneración* and became a determined reformer. His uncle got him a job as city treasurer in Guaymas, but he was fired when shortages appeared in his department. Then he worked as a bartender until managing hotels, milling, and farming. He failed to achieve middle-class respectability until the Maderistas named him justice of the peace in Agua Prieta. Tough and authoritarian, he made a career of politics. Careful to obey his superiors and never tolerating dissent, Calles once had a worker hanged from a bridge by barbed wire for shouting "down with Madero" in public.

Soon he became a regional leader whom Obregón promoted to the presidency. Calles joined the Constitutionalist forces and rose to be a division general after producing a good military record against Huerta as well as Villa. Carranza named him interim governor of Sonora in August 1915. Always assuming the role of an unsmiling teacher who rarely laughed, Calles outlawed the sale of alcoholic drinks in 1916 and prohibited gambling as well as speculation. An atheist since childhood, he ordered all priests out of Sonora. On the positive side, he encouraged unionization, land reform, and built 127 new schools. Under Obregón, he joined the cabinet as secretary of the interior. Here his iron will, inexhaustible drive, and distrust of everyone manifested themselves. As a shrewd but blunt president, he never ceased showing his vulgar temperament.

Socioeconomic Policies. At the onset of his presidency, the Church, foreign investors, and conservatives believed that Calles was an extremist who would hurt their interests. Actually, Calles did much to aid the interests of business people and stabilized the economy as much as possible.

Fiscal and financial policies were prudent. Calles reduced the budget deficit from 58 million pesos to 40 million pesos at the end of 1924 to none at all in 1925. The regime also introduced the first standard income tax as well as a National Banking Commission. On September 1, 1925, the long-awaited dream of a national bank came true when the Banco de México, the country's sole bank to issue currency, became a reality. With reserves of 100 million pesos, it prudently issued banknotes at a two-to-one ratio in proportion to its reserves. Manual Gómez Morín, the conservative and brilliant president of the Banco de México, served well. Morín also founded the National Bank of Agricultural Credit as part of Calles's desire to increase agricultural production. However, the bank often gave loans to generals, and the largest borrower was none other than Obregón.

The Calles regime was much more emphatic than its predecessors in attempting to build an infrastructure. Dams and canals accounted for 6.5 percent of the budget from 1925 to 1928. Not surprisingly, most irrigation works appeared in the northwest. Calles's 1926 Irrigation Law utilized Porfirian guidelines in attempting to allocate water to large farmers and colonization projects rather than ejidos. Even after Calles departed from the scene, irrigation boundaries would not coincide with ejido land. Responding to outside pressure, the government sold Mextelco phone company to a U.S. company, International Telephone and Telegraph. This sale indicated a privatization trend. Calles returned the railroads to private owners. Moreover, he initiated a public works campaign to build new all-weather highways, particularly on the west coast.

The optimism behind these plans rested upon a short-lived prosperity which soon faded into a recession. Initially, silver production in the early 1920s reached a higher point than even in the colonial period. Mexican industries, particularly textile production, remained in the regionalized corridor between Veracruz and Mexico City. They had escaped relatively unaffected from the violence of the civil war. Direct U.S. foreign investment into the manufacturing sector was only 1 percent; nonetheless, Ford, Siemens, Colgate, and Palmolive soon established themselves in Mexico prior to 1928. Because of Mexico's increasing ties to the U.S. market, export sales dropped when the demand for Mexican products declined by 1926. When oil prices fell in 1926, the petroleum companies sought out more permissive working conditions in Venezuela. Eventually, 50,000 Mexican oil workers lost their jobs in the 1920s.

Other problems manifested themselves. Sisal, although a fiber indigenous to Yucatán, did not grow well there. But after German growers introduced it to German East Africa in 1892 and similar experiments flourished in Java, sisal passed henequen by because it was stronger and adapted itself well to defibering machinery. By 1927, Asia and Africa accounted for about half of the world's hard fiber production. The invention of the combine, which did not use twine, hurt the Mexican henequen industry badly, with the result that production collapsed. Although undamaged, the textile industry used outdated machinery and became wracked by constant disputes between management and workers; about 72 percent of the strikes during the Calles presidency occurred in the textile industries. The decline of silver and copper prices also became a severe problem in the mid-1920s. Not by coincidence, government revenues fell 15 percent from 1925 to 1928.

Calles responded with debt renegotiations. Alberto Pani, the treasury minister of Obregón and now Calles, canceled the Bucareli agreements and succeeded in obtaining a downward adjustment in both principal and interest. Thus, the foreign debt fell from 1.5 billion pesos to only 850 million pesos. The October 1925 revision of the 1922 agreement opened the way for more cordial relations between Mexico and the industrial nations. Both settlements illustrate the Mexican elite's reliance upon debt renegotiation to avoid the hostility of foreign bankers, aggressive governments, and domestic unrest. Unlike Brazil and Argentina, debt in Mexico remained a small fraction of direct foreign investment until the Great Depression. The only criticism of Pani's visit came when a New York newspaper accused him of seducing a local celebrity. When asked about the incident at a news conference, Calles snapped that he did not want "a cabinet of eunuchs."

Like Obregón, Calles sought to reclaim survey-company land grants as efforts to strengthen state authority in the countryside. Calles did not want to destroy the latifundia but to create a balance between it and the ejido, often at the expense of the ejido. Local caudillos or landowners often resisted *agrarista* pressures by means of hired thugs, injunctions, and personal mobilization of supporters. Nevertheless, the early Calles government evolved from simple land distribution to agrarian reform whereby access to water, credit, resources, and markets became a larger step forward. By 1926, the Liga Nacional Campesina emerged by integrating 11 state locals representing over 300,000 campesinos. The energetic Marte Gómez, mastermind of agrarian reform in Tamaulipas, became subdirector of the National Bank of Agricultural Credit in 1926. Eventually, Calles gave out three times more land than Obregón. He also emphasized rural education so that 2,000 federally funded agricultural schools appeared in various Mexican regions. Like Carranza and Obregón, however, he began to fear that food production would drop at a time of economic uncertainty and thus began to curtail land distribution before his term ended.

The labor policies reflected Calles' authoritarian populism as well as his attempts to modernize. The most influential cabinet member in the Calles government was Luis Morones, secretary general of the CROM and minister of labor, industry, and commerce. In addition to being the best friend of Calles, Morones became the most powerful cabinet member. He assumed many roles with great energy. As head of the CROM, he claimed to have two million workers unionized by 1928 although the actual number was probably about 100,000. The CROM enjoyed great power because it sent members to the legislature as deputies and senators; occasionally, the CROM even controlled state governments. Despite his crude display of wealth—a bombproof Cadillac and diamond rings—the former electrician was a tremendous

orator and a nationalist ideologue in his own right. Morones realized that wealth had to be produced instead of merely seized and therefore encouraged industrialization. Moreover, he sought to modernize industries and encouraged consumers to buy Mexican-produced goods.

Did the workers improve their lot? Undoubtedly, real wages increased although the fear of unemployment became rampant as the 1920s wore on. As in other Latin American countries, the labor ministry controlled strikes carefully. As the pace of modernization wore on, industries reduced workers and they clamored for protection by communists, anarchists, and traditional unions, such as the railroad workers' affiliation, when things got tough. Of course, strikes not coordinated with Morones or independent of the CROM had little chance of being sanctioned by the federal government. The number of strikes decreased from nearly 10,000 in 1921 to barely a thousand by 1927. The CROM fought hard against competing unions, particularly those organized by the Catholic Church.

The Cristero War, 1926–1929.
Both Church and state wanted control of the Mexican people and neither was willing to share its claims. The Cristero War became a struggle between two mutually exclusive ideologies rather than a political conflict. The *Cristeros* were a peasant society facing class grievances similar to those of the Zapatistas—shrinking access to land and a shift to insecure combinations of sharecropping and seasonal labor. Therefore, they organized their communities around private property and the Catholic Church and rose in revolt.

An acute problem between Church and state was the creation of Catholic unions. Father Méndez Medina formed the first Catholic union, a construction workers' syndicate, in 1913. Interestingly, this union called for social reforms before the 1917 Constitution proclaimed the same changes. Other priests called for rural reforms intended to aid agrarian workers. Catholic reforms enjoyed support from the Vatican after Pope Leo XIII's *Rerum Novarum* manifesto in which he encouraged the

Church to be an "agent of progress." In light of this proclamation, Catholic self-help organizations that promoted solutions to social problems began to spring up. Although this represents a new direction for Catholicism, after 1910 increasingly aggressive bishops and lay organizations came into conflict with government efforts to unionize. Much as in the Juárez period, the populist state labeled Catholic activists counterrevolutionaries. The priests resented their lack of full citizenship while popular religion continued to produce a host of local saints, prophets, and healers.

The direct cause of the Cristero War began in 1925. At that time Morones attempted to do away with the Roman Catholic Church and replace it with a Mexican Catholic Church. The CROM leadership was concerned about the emergence of various Catholic unions that competed with CROM unions for membership among the rural workers. Due to the pressure of Calles and government agencies, the Liga Nacional de Defensa Religiosa emerged in 1925. Then Calles waited for the state governments to enforce the anticlerical provisions of the 1917 Constitution. When their efforts did not meet his goals, Calles announced in January 1926 that Articles 3 and 130 would be enforced. This was not an idle boast. During the next month, the Education Secretariat attempted to incorporate religious schools, seizing or closing many. This prompted Archbishop José Mora y del Rio to attack the offensive constitutional norms in a newspaper interview. He and other clerics were concerned that the 1917 Constitution would allow national and state governments to seriously restrict religious life. Calles also announced in June 1926 that any Church official criticizing the government or its laws would be jailed. Furthermore, Calles forbade religious education in primary schools and the control of schools by a religious body. He outlawed monastic orders and nunneries. Calles also warned the clergy not to participate in political activity or permit political meetings inside Churches. It also became illegal for any political organization to bear a name related to a religious creed. Suddenly, the regime deported large numbers of priests.

Open defiance began when Calles allowed governors to enforce constitutional regulations which permitted them to register priests and to establish the number who could perform religious services. The more extreme Callista rulers made ridiculous rulings: Durango, 25 priests, Tamaulipas, 12, Yucatan, 12, and Tabasco, only 3. When the bishops urged Calles to moderate, he told them to take their complaints to Congress, which brushed aside their protests. Therefore, the clergy withheld mass and declared a religious strike. The Liga initiated an economic boycott. This attempt to weaken Calles included a refusal to buy goods except those absolutely necessary. Liga followers would not purchase clothing, fruits, candy, ice cream, soft drinks, or lottery tickets; they refused to drive automobiles or attend movies, dances, and parties. The Liga also requested parents to withdraw their children from public schools. When those actions failed, the Liga decided upon armed rebellion. As the Church hierarchy faded into the background, the movement against the government became more revolutionary. Insurrectionary Catholics embraced the banner of Christ and the battle cry "Viva Cristo Rey" (long live Christ the King).

The Cristero rebellion became the bloodiest religious war fought in the American hemisphere during the twentieth century. The first fighting broke out in October 1926 as René Capistrán Garza began the actual revolt that soon drew in 50,000 *cristeros* in 17 states from southern Sinaloa to Oaxaca. Most of the fighting took place in Jalisco and the center-west region. Before long, the Liga recruited Enrique Gorostieta to lead the *cristeros*. A cadet at the Colegio Militar who was an inspiring leader and a fine tactician, Gorostieta defied government troops skillfully. The *cristeros* controlled Jalisco's interior and contemplated seizing Guadalajara or even Mexico City. The *cristeros* were often frustrated, but martyrdom kept them going.

In many ways the heirs of the agrarian, rural Catholic world that the Zapatistas had fought for in the 1910s overestimated the allegiance and support of fellow Catholics. The *cristeros* never

***Equilibrio* by Jesús Escobedo.**
*Courtesy of the Gallery at UTA
(University of Texas at Arlington).*

obtained substantial financial aid from wealthy Mexicans, U.S. Catholics, or the Vatican. Without this support, the *cristeros* had to survive with little ammunition. Even worse than physical deprivations, the lack of material support signaled that many Catholics did not see religion as a holy crusade for which one should give one's life. More importantly, the Catholic hierarchy in Mexico and in Rome never seemed to fully condone the rebellion. Instead, they withheld their approval, contingent on its success. Many *cristeros* were property holders and somewhat older. Attempts by the Sonora dynasty to establish *agrarista* supporters often resulted in Catholic *ejiditarios* opposing land reform. Nevertheless, *agrarista* campesinos often opposed *cristeros* although they remained Catholics. Particularly effective against the *cristeros* were *agrarista* fighters, perhaps as many as 25,000, whom Calles brought in from other states to contain the revolt. Prominent among these forces were the Cedillo *agraristas*. Although Cedillo himself did not share the same anticlericalism of Calles, the real issue was that his *agraristas* received land by means of the third largest agrarian reform program in Mexico. In addition, the *cristeros* enjoyed little support in urban areas, other than among females. They could not work out an alliance with Yaquis, who were revolting at the same time because of broken promises regarding land reforms. Other Mexicans

objected to the burning of schools and the killing of teachers. Catholics in rural areas often objected to Mexico City's commitment to secular education and the fact that the *maestro* often usurped the place of the priest as the most important person in Mexican villages.

The most peculiar episode of the rebellion came with the move toward peace. The army could control key cities in the disputed regions but not the countryside. Despite the burning of villages, mass executions, and shooting of nearly 100 priests, Calles could not break the stalemate. The death of Calles's wife in June 1927 did weaken some of his resolve to the extent that he freed some jailed *cristeros*. The death of Gorostieta, during a government ambush in June 1927, was a grave blow to the *cristeros*. But peace largely came about by means of U.S. Ambassador, Dwight B. Morrow, who arrived in Mexico City in late 1927. Morrow quickly became a trusted friend of Calles and convinced him that resolving the religious controversy would improve Mexico's international standing. As the end of his term neared, Calles moderated. Afterwards, the despised registration law for priests was reinterpreted to mean that governments could not appoint or assign priests who had not been designated by their superiors. In addition, religious instruction could take place in clerical institutions but religious instruction would not be permitted in public schools. Finally, both sides agreed to an amnesty. Amazingly, Morrow even composed the actual agreement. Most of the Vatican's demands were not accepted. But when the Churches reopened after almost three years of silence, Mexicans flocked into them joyously. But the Church had regained only a fraction of its former power. While it retained a powerful spiritual hold over Mexican society, the Church had lost its legal authority.

Cultural Currents. Under Calles, the renaissance in artistic creativity as well as Mexican society continued. The expansion of education spurred the continuation of a dialectic pursuit of national identity. Modern science helped dispel the myth that Mexicans were inferior; interaction with foreigners who lived in Mexico confirmed the growing confidence in *lo mexicano*, a reassuring concept that the essence of being Mexican was worth celebrating.

The painters continued to dominate the cultural scene during the remainder of the 1920s. By the mid-1920s, the artists had founded the Syndicate of Revolutionary Mexican Painters, Sculptors, and Engravers. Siqueiros, the dominant member, claimed that the syndicate's goal was to socialize artistic expression and do away with bourgeois individualism. He claimed that capitalist countries had exported to Mexico their music and art which promoted bourgeois attitudes. Such artistic forms had contaminated the middle class as well as the masses. Siqueiros held that only the peasants still maintained traditional good taste. Because of this past corruption of the culture, Siqueiros maintained that artists could not be neutral in the political context; artists would have to choose between art that served the bourgeois or the proletariat. In choosing to aid the masses, Siqueiros believed that he had chosen a path toward "pure art."

Although Frida Kahlo was a lifelong Marxist, her art is inseparably intertwined with her physical anguish. Beneath the self-dramatization, Kahlo was really a very great artist. Born in 1907 in the Coyoacán suburb of Mexico City, Kahlo was the daughter of a German-Jewish immigrant father who was a prominent photographer, and a Mexican mother of Hispanic-indigenous descent. She survived an attack of polio at age six that left her right leg slightly shorter than her left, a defect she disguised most of her life by wearing long skirts. Kahlo's outspokenness set her apart from most females. As one of the first women admitted to the National Preparatory School, Frida became a rabble-rouser. She was part of an intellectual student group and eventually joined the Young Communist League.

When she was 18, a near-fatal accident changed her life forever. A trolley car struck the bus she was riding home from school; a handrail smashed her spinal column in three places, crushed her pelvis and foot, and broke several ribs. As a result of the accident, she was unable to bear children and suffered physical and psychological pain all her life. Kahlo underwent dozens of operations and at least three therapeutic abortions. While recuperating, Kahlo painted a self-portrait for her boyfriend in an attempt to keep him from forgetting her. Although her efforts to maintain the interest of her lover failed, Kahlo unwittingly embarked upon her career as an artist in 1925.

Kahlo's physical suffering was exacerbated by her tumultuous marriage to Diego Rivera in 1929. During her lifetime, Kahlo's work was overshadowed by that of her world-famous husband. As a woman in the male-dominated art world, Kahlo never received the attention she deserved until later. Rivera quickly recognized Kahlo's artistic abilities and urged her to continue painting. Rivera often claimed that Frida painted better than he. Frida, on the other hand, recognized that her husband's work was more successful and lucrative. Kahlo emphasized her various illnesses and mental aberrations to draw the viewer into her art, just as she used them to bind Rivera to her as much as possible. As a young bride, Kahlo adored Rivera and anguished over her inability to bear him a child. Kahlo's need to immerse herself in a spouse who functioned as both father figure and artistic mentor is reflected in a small portrait in which Rivera's head and hers are merged.

The Two Fridas **by Frida Kahlo, 1939.** *Museo Nacional de Arte Moderno, Instituto Nacional de Bellas Artes, Mexico City, Mexico.*

The marriage was a stormy relationship of mutual admiration and antagonism. Rivera, a notorious womanizer, had countless affairs which caused Kahlo much grief. When she discovered that Rivera was having an affair with her younger sister, Kahlo painted a picture entitled *A Few Small Nips*, which shows Rivera wielding a knife above Kahlo's dead body, which is bleeding from multiple stab wounds. In turn, Kahlo retaliated by having numerous affairs with both men and women, including notables such as Leon Trotsky. In spite of numerous separations and a 1939 divorce, Kahlo and Rivera gravitated constantly toward each other.

Kahlo always maintained her unique and at times eccentric personality. She wore almost exclusively the colorful, flowing clothes of the Tehuanas of Oaxaca. Kahlo was a striking woman with long, dark hair which she loved to braid and weave with flowers and ribbons. Although she spent a great deal of time in braces, surgical corsets, and wheelchairs, Kahlo moved in a circle of intellectual bohemians. She and Rivera were active in the Communist party and also associated with other artists such as Pablo Picasso and Andre Breton.

With a great deal of raw talent but no substantial formal training, Kahlo developed her own unique style which focused on her physical and emotional pain. Her haunting self-portraits with cameo images revealing her innermost thoughts and fears are startling. Frequently, she represented the unique pain of women—miscarriages, infidelity, and loneliness. An impressive colorist and meticulous technician, Kahlo, like many other Mexican artists of the 1920 to 1940 period, incorporated elements of folk art into her compositions. An observer cannot help but appreciate the exquisite detail with which she describes the elaborate floral motif of a native indigenous costume or the colorful cross pattern with which she adorns a frame. There were only two exhibitions of Kahlo's work during her lifetime: in New York City in 1938 and in Mexico City shortly before her death in 1954.

The populistic aspect of Mexico's cultural nationalism attracted U.S. and European artists and intellects. Coincident with the contemporary belief that European civilization had become a failure, figures such as D. H. Lawrence considered Mexico a culture of extraordinary depth. Inexpensive housing, food, and drink contributed to creativity so that cultural interaction stimulated great writers such as Katherine Anne Porter. During her residency in Mexico from 1920 to 1931, Porter played an active role in Mexican political life, but her mood swings between depression and elation influenced her alternating visions of Mexico. Porter considered Mexico as an earthly Eden where hopes for a better society could be realized or as a place of hopeless oppression for the masses.

The foreign visitors often assumed a bohemian lifestyle in Mexico which resulted in short stories, novels, poems, and essays. Among the most notable U.S. writers were Hart Crane, John Dos Passos, Waldo Frank, George Biddle, Stuart Chase, Susan Smith, Alma Reed, and Archibald McLeish. Notable Europeans were Jean Charlot, D. H. Lawrence, and Somerset Maugham. McLeish insisted upon traveling in Córtes's footsteps, the result being one of his best poems. Biddle, who witnessed the movement well, wrote in his *An American Artist's Story* (1939) that Mexican muralism was the most significant movement since the Renaissance because it tied together artistic concepts and social justice. His Mexican experience eventually enabled Biddle to convince U.S. President Franklin D. Roosevelt to establish a public works program similar to Mexico's.

The artistic renewal also attracted anthropologists, archaeologists, historians, and other social scientists. Books which resulted from Mexican experiences, such as Carleton Beal's *Mexico: An Interpretation* (1923), Frank Tannenbaum's *The Mexican Agrarian Revolution* (1929), and Robert Redfield's *Tepoztlan: A Mexican Village* (1930) revived U.S. interest in Mexico, especially in academic circles. Professor Tannenbaum, for example, engaged his classes directly in Mexican studies, thus training a whole generation of excellent Latin Americanists.

Even in the field of education, U.S. influence became far-reaching. John Dewey had a compelling impact upon Mexican politics by means of his disciple Moisés Sáenz, as well as through his books and conferences. Linguists William Cameron Townsend and Mauricio Swadesh were fundamental in training experts from both countries engaged in the study of 183 languages and dialects spoken in Mexico. Although innovative, the Summer Institute of Linquistics aroused the suspicion of Mexican nationalist because of its political and religious undertones.

Mexico also lured U.S. and European photographers. Paul Strand made poignant portraits of rural subjects such as strong-jawed men from Michoacan. Laura Gilpin captured the grandeur of the newly restored site at Chichen Itza. Others addressed harsh reality. Henri Cartier-Bresson aimed his camera at heavily made-up prostitutes staring brazenly at passers-by. Manuel Alvarez Bravo zeroed in on an assassinated worker with blood from a head wound streaming onto the pavement.

Tina Modotti became the most compelling photographer of this era. Born in Italy to a working-class family that emigrated to the United States, Modotti utilized her great beauty to act in Hollywood. Her husband, poet and painter Roubaix de l'Abrie Richey, died during a 1922 Mexican visit before Modotti could join him. Modotti arrived the next year with her lover, the photographer Edward Weston. It was from Weston that Modotti learned photography, particularly the direct representation of the subject in pursuit of pure formal values. But Modotti's approach drew her toward an overtly political subject matter. When Modotti photographed hands, it was vital that they be hands at work, those of washerwomen or puppeteer, because she was a Marxist. Modotti also portrayed revolutionary symbols; a guitar, a sickle, and a bandolier of bullets arranged on a mat became attributes of peasant revolutionaries. The tension between content and contrived form was one of the reasons why she abandoned photography after her 1930 expulsion from Mexico.

Mexican peasants reading El Macete, 1932. Photo by Tina Modotti. *National Archives.*

The Mexican film industry stagnated during the 1920s and only four films emerged in 1923. Theater and vaudeville still commanded more attention. Failure to emphasize regional diversities also handicapped cinema despite an emphasis upon patriotism and folklore. Moreover, the role of Hollywood increased in the 1920s, by means of aggressive distribution chains. The pressure to make pictures with sound revealed the difficulties in attempting to compete with foreigners.

Mexican artists, writers, and technicians also traveled abroad. Orozco, Rivera, and Siqueiros enjoyed successful visits to the United States, as did musicians such as Carlos Chávez, who studied in New York during the 1920s, as well as Blas Galindo and Pablo Moncayo, who matured under Aaron Copeland a bit later. Alfonso Reyes transmitted French culture to Mexico by means of journals and discussion forums on both sides of the Atlantic. Orozco perhaps encountered his most vivid experiences in California, New York, and Dartmouth. But at Laredo, a customs official destroyed all his sketches because he considered them pornographic. Texas as well as New York patrons at least became major supporters of Mexican talents.

Like Porfirian thinkers, Calles had high hopes for education in a clear continuity of educational policies. Calles agreed with those of the Vasconcelos era who considered education a panacea, but with a distinct difference. He did not try to educate the masses on the basis of idealistic humanism; making sure that education contributed to economic development and social reform appealed to him much more. Calles wanted campesinos who could make the soil productive and workers who could utilize technical improvements to bring order out of economic confusion. Many newly trained teachers taught all over Mexico's regions as never before. The Secretaría de Educación Pública expanded and organized itself on a large scale.

Calles also enacted a forestry law in 1926 whereby all individuals had to submit plans for their forest activities to agricultural officials for review. The same law pledged that public employees would manage public lands as well, particularly in terms of restricting timber concessions. Calles also created forest zones, in which only marked trees could be cut down. Campesinos, who normally considered trees as sources of fuel, now received instruction about their long-term value. Enforcement of these codes yielded a mixed record and Calles never created national parks.

The Political Panorama. When Calles assumed power in December 1924, the central government was stronger than when Obregón had taken office in 1920. Calles demanded loyalty from the governors and, when that was not forthcoming, he either initiated or permitted the ousting of over 25 governors in 15 different states. Because of the need for federal support of local regimes, opportunistic regional allies offered themselves to Calles, partially so that they could pursue reform or become wealthy. Abelardo Rodríguez, for example, acquired nine companies in Baja, California, where he governed from 1923 to 1929.

Populist techniques of political control spread into many regions. In Tlaxcala state, Ignacio Mendoza, an *agrarista* governor elected in 1925, copied the example of Tomás Garrido Canabal in Tabasco and organized a Partido Socialista party which landowners in some districts supported. Only 12 villages received ejidos from 1925 to 1929. Thus incorporation rather than mobilization often characterized the relationship between governors and union leaders as well as agrarian leagues. This was particularly true in Guanajuato, Yucatán, Campeche, and Chiapas. This was less the case in Tamaulipas, Tabasco, Veracruz, Querétaro, and San Luis Potosí.

An example of self-serving populist rhetoric is that of José Guadalupe Zuno, "elected" governor of Jalisco in November 1922. A ruthless opportunist who enriched himself and friends by means of shady deals, Zuno also established ties with radical labor and campesino organizations. But he made the mistake of attempting to channel worker groups away from Calles and Morones. Although Zuno did distribute a respectable amount of land and threw his support to communist labor leaders who aggressively unionized industrial workers and miners, Calles became angry, forcing Zuno to resign in March 1926.

Another regional leader who tried to distance himself from Mexico City also failed in Chi-

huahua. Jesús Antonio Almeida ruled the state from 1924 until ousted by a coup in 1927. Almeida simply set out to build an empire for himself and his family. He used the state's agrarian code to force U.S.-managed lumber companies to sell the properties. Little land redistribution took place while he was governor. As during the Carranza period, the Terrazas family continued to repurchase their old holdings. More in sympathy with Porfirian goals than peasants and workers, Almeida lost popularity by imposing his brother and brother-in-law upon key municipalities. Thus Calles did not mind when the last independent government in Chihuahua collapsed in 1927.

The kind of governor that Calles preferred was Emilio Portes Gil in Tamaulipas. During the three years of his administration, Portes Gil implemented anticlerical and antisaloon legislation, encouraged workers' cooperatives, established a respectable land reform program, and earned a reputation as incredibly energetic. Portes Gil made it clear that he was loyal to Calles numerous times and enjoyed populistic ceremonies involving land awards before carefully assembled journalists. With his influence in Tamaulipas secure, Portes Gil took the critical post of secretary of government in the Calles cabinet.

The most crucial decision Calles made was naming his successor. He undoubtedly preferred his close friend Morones to anyone else, but when Obregón made it known that he wanted to be president once again, Calles gave in and ordered Congress to amend the constitution to permit one nonconsecutive presidential reelection. Obregón had chosen exactly the same method as Porfirio Díaz in getting reelected. Obregón either wanted more future terms or may have considered alternating in power with Calles. In January 1928, Congress enacted a measure extending the presidential term to six years, just as Díaz had requested in 1904.

Calles certainly intended to keep his end of the bargain. When General Francisco Serrano attempted to contest Obregón's candidacy and revolted, he and other military opponents were executed. Another to die was General Carlos

Vidal, who directed Serrano's presidential campaign and joined Serrano's rebellion. Because Vidal had been governor of Chiapas, Calles wanted to take no chances with the possibility of regional unrest. Therefore, the federal garrison in Tuxtla Gutiérrez seized control of the Chiapas government, rounded up the leading state officials, and shot them.

The new elite who controlled politics became less haughty, more urban, and were frequently middle class. The desire to enrich themselves permeated ambitions. Many had survived military service. Success as intermediaries with Mexico City depended upon their ability to consolidate the dependent nature of populist labor and peasant organizations. The degree of control was a function of the competition for intermediary power and the initiative of mass leaders to co-opt the mobilized constituency. Since Juárez and other border cities survived by means of gambling, vice, and entertainment—activities regulated closely by regional and federal officials—it became critical for business people to participate directly in politics. Elements of the old social hierarchy joined the fray in maneuvering for influence. Though their hegemony had been broken, notable families retained considerable advantages in attempting to maintain their positions.

International Relations. Relationships with the United States were generally bad until reconciliation arrived. When Calles tried to return to the Carranza position of defending Article 27, U.S. Ambassador James Sheffield and Secretary of State Frank Kellog accused Calles of behaving like a Bolshevik. They had become angry when the Mexican Congress initiated a new petroleum code in 1925 which limited foreign ownership to 50 years. In addition to 50-year concessions, the oil companies would have to accept the Carranza Doctrine, whereby they would renounce diplomatic protection and agree to respect Mexican law. Calles also denounced the Bucareli agreements, asserting that the minutes could not be considered diplomatic treaties, nor could they infringe upon the 1917 Constitution, which, of

course, they did. Not surprisingly, Doheny and Fall, as well as the Hearst newspapers, called for intervention. President Coolidge considered intervention, but the Teapot Dome scandal exposed corrupt dealings between U.S. officials and oil companies.

New Ambassador Dwight Morrow resolved this and other disputes with Calles. Morrow was a superb diplomat. Although he had worked for J. P. Morgan on Wall Street, who had many bonds in Mexico, Morrow arrived with an attitude of attempting to understand the situation. He impressed Mexicans with his objectivity and casual dress. Morrow astonished Calles by calling him directly on the phone to invite the Mexican president out for lunch. To indicate trust, Morrow even used Calles's interpreter during their discussions. Calles felt relaxed enough to have drinks and eat his favorite meal of popcorn and chocolate. It became clear that Mexico captivated Morrow and he pleased Calles by bringing celebrities, such as Will Rogers and Charles Lindbergh, to Mexico. Gradually, Calles softened his position on oil company ownership and issued new drilling permits that would not expire after 50 years. Morrow responded by advocating that disputes concerning oil holdings in Mexico would be settled in Mexican courts. Although the oil companies believed that Morrow had conceded too much, the agreement held up until 1938. Morrow also conceded Mexico's right to tax the companies and Calles recognized the oil companies' pre-1917 property rights in 1929. Morrow used his influence with the National Catholic Welfare Conference to help end the Cristero War. Morrow and Calles even reached an understanding in which the two agreed that their countries would support each other in time of need.

With the rest of the world, Calles pursued a much more aggressive diplomacy than Obregón. Whereas Obregón had eliminated the Mexican secret service, claiming that its cost of 100,000 pesos a year was excessive, Calles became somewhat daring. He persuaded the British to become more flexible than even Morrow. Mexico and the Soviet Union established diplomatic relations in

1924. Mexico saw itself as resembling the Soviets in their struggle to utilize a five-year plan when Calles set up a six-year plan. Calles, however, repudiated the Soviet system for its excessive central control. Rivera and Siqueiros visited the Soviet Union and praised its accomplishments.

Calles also challenged the U.S. Pax Americana in Central America. Backed up by Spain, Mexico supported Central American criticism of U.S. interventionist policies at inter-American conferences and supported attempts to form a Central American union. In 1926, Mexico also provided arms and ammunition to Nicaraguan liberals who revolted against the conservatives, who were U.S. clients. Calles even promoted revolutionaries August César Sandino of Nicaragua and Farabundo Martí, who posed proudly in Mérida for photographs. Behind the scenes, however, Calles maintained friendly ties with Central American rulers and used real revolutionaries as propaganda props. Mexico backed off from its support of Nicaraguan insurrectionaries when Washington reinforced its marine contingent in Nicaragua. Calles also learned that Central Americans were unenthusiastic about the possibility of Mexico becoming the new dominant power in their region.

The Maximato, 1928–1934. Calles continued to dominate Mexico during the Maximato years. The formation of the Partido Nacional Revolucionario (PNR) filled the political vacuum created by the death of Obregón. Through brilliant maneuvering, Calles established the PNR's all-embracing ideology. He received the informal title of "jefe máximo" because of his deft monitoring of various generals and local caudillos within their respective regions while manipulating three chosen presidents who could not maintain their autonomy. Meanwhile, the economic depression reduced Calles's options. He felt that he had to curb labor, the military, the Church, and unions in order for the nation's institutions to succeed.

In 1928, Obregón had won reelection with the support of Calles, Congress, and the army. But Obregón's assassination only two weeks later on July 17, 1928, required the intervention of Calles. José de León Toral, a Liga leader in his Mexico City suburb, had been talked into carrying out the deed by the nun Madre Conchita. An aspiring artist, Toral drank a Carta Blanca beer and then calmly walked into la Bombilla restaurant, requested to paint a relaxed Obregón, and then began poured bullets from his .38 caliber pistol into Obregón's face and body. The entire country was shocked to the core as Mexicans purchased tens of thousands of newspapers to try to understand what had happened and how Calles would respond. Because many believed that Calles and Morones were behind the murder, Calles's authority became greatly weakened. Calles had to proceed very skillfully because an attempt to remain in power would surely provoke a revolt by Obregón's partisans.

The crisis revealed Calles's statesmanlike qualities. He permitted *obregonistas* to vent their wrath unchecked. To cap the desperate political situation, Calles called on Congress to name an interim president. Maneuvering behind the scenes, Calles arranged for Portes Gil to take over since he was partial to the *obregonistas* and hated Morones. Thus Calles had bought himself time to outthink ambitious generals who supported Obregón. During his last presidential address in September 1928, Calles had promised that he would leave the presidency at the end of his term in December and never seek reelection. More importantly, he urged his country to abandon the rule of caudillos and establish the rule of institutions and legal procedures. Calles made it clear that an active military leader should not succeed him during the presidential campaign planned for 1929. This political masterstroke temporarily neutralized generals plotting to take over.

Emilio Portes Gil, 1928–1930. Primarily a politician rather than a social reformer, Portes Gil focused on economic recovery and controlling political unrest. Virtually every policy he backed had political objectives designed to advance him personally. For example, he supported the re-creation of the ejido but viewed it as a temporary measure to be eventually replaced by private property. He preferred promoting small family properties but not at the expense of the large estates. Within the collective spirit of the 1917 Constitution, the government issued a new Civil Code in 1928, which contained many limitations on freedom of contract in a paternalistic attempt to protect the weak from abuses. Therefore, for example, hoarding became illegal. The 1929 Depression struck Mexico with the result that commercial and export economies were hardest hit. Thus the Depression weakened the elites who controlled on commercial and export production. Not surprisingly, they had helped block land distribution but Portes Gil actually increased it more than Calles had. The CROM had collapsed with the demise of Morones, and unions stepped into a fluid situation in terms of negotiating for strikes with the labor ministry and local businesses. But when the oil companies resumed layoffs once again in 1930 after prices fell, unions found themselves in a weaker position than during the 1920s.

Portes Gil did not try to block social reforms that had little effect on the political situation. The tremendous loss of life during the 1910–1929 period motivated the government to abolish the death penalty in 1929. The 1930 census, far more accurate than the flawed 1921 count, provided grim statistics. Life expectancy at birth was well under 30 years while one-fifth to one-quarter of babies died in the first year of life. Since the beginning of the 1910 Revolution, 2.5 million Mexicans had disappeared, 1.6 million of whom were mortalities from 1921 to 1930. Emigration was significant, but not a major factor in the sharp fall of the population. To atone for this loss of life, Mexico permitted a large influx of Jews during the 1920s, which continued in the early 1930s. Often their parents sent them, in response to pograms, poverty, and discrimination. Or Jews came in search of adventure and economic opportunity. Many began as peddlers who eventually opened their own stores and businesses. Selling what they could on the streets of Mexico City or door-to-door, they made themselves understood

in sign language before they learned the words for their goods.

Women continued to mobilize. In 1921, Sofia Villa de Buentello was the upper-class author of *Women and the Law*, which was one of the few books that pondered the civil status of females. Feminists continued attempting to do away with prostitution as well as conventional restrictions which maintained that single women should live at home until 30. In 1923, the first birth control clinics appeared in Mérida after Margaret Sanger's pamphlets circulated throughout Yucatán. Fewer women worked in textile factories as several feminists demanded better working conditions as well as equal treatment.

The Church opposed even the most conservative feminist format. Several priests denounced the women's movement in the 1920s and early 1930s. José Castillo y Pina and José Cantu Corro, two of the most political priests, argued that the women's movement would destroy traditional values. In 1925, Archbishop José Mora y del Rio disapproved of women working for a wage, claiming it was a "North American custom." The Church position caused many pious Catholic females to avoid the feminist movement. Church opposition resulted in many feminist leaders emerging from Protestant, agnostic, atheist, and Marxist backgrounds.

A high turnover in leadership weakened the women's movement considerably. Much of this resulted from disagreements over issues, tactics, and programs. Lack of financial support was also a severe problem, forcing many women back into domestic life. Very few leaders lasted more than a decade. Elvia Carrillo Puerto and Maria Rios Cárdenas became active in the 1920s and continued their work into the 1930s. Only the teacher and writer Julia Nava de Ruisanchez worked in the movement from its beginnings into the 1940s.

Mexican feminists had little support from the press. Many newspapers were strongly antifeminist. Poverty made it extremely difficult for the masses to read or do more than survive. Rios Cárdenas founded the monthly journal *Mujer*, but feminism was not a particularly large consideration in the lives of most women. Moreover, the government always feared that women would back the Church if they could vote. At least the revision of the civic code made women better off. Sometimes, however, women took matters into their own hands. Miss Mexico killed her abusive husband in 1929. A sensational trial resulted in no charges being presented against her. Such a ruling would have been unthinkable decades before.

Another group that received attention were students. In 1929, the national university won autonomy. Much of this occurred as a result of the transformation brought on by the 1910 revolution. Portes Gil also decided to grant autonomy in response to student demands. The students had gone on strike in May 1929 against the university's rector, Antonio Castro Leal, who required law students and other professional aspirants to take written exams. Traditionally, oral exams had been the norm. Actually, many students simply wanted a forum where they could speak and recommend changes. When the government balked, a strike committee organized debates and collected a petition from hundreds of students indicating that they would not attend class until their demands were met. Finally, Portes Gil gave in so that a circumscribed autonomy resulted.

Political issues drew in students and others who wanted Vasconcelos as the next president. Many students viewed Vasconcelos as honest and creative, a pioneer in education and culture. Former antireelectionists considered Vasconcelos far more democratic than the authoritarian Calles. Moreover, Vasconcelos was becoming Catholic and conservative in his positions. The *Jefe Máximo* feared that Vasconcelos would garner in the support of many *cristeros,* particularly when contact between both groups became known. During his call for liberty and constant attacks against Morrow's U.S. diplomatic victories, Vasconcelos assumed a moral authority often lacking in the corrupt practices of the Sonora dynasty. Although he urged that *agrarista* activists be purged from the agrarian reform practices, Vasconcelos promised more land to a somewhat unconvinced rural population. He appealed more to the middle class

and city dwellers. By now General Gonzalo Escobar had attempted to revolt in March 1929 and had failed within a matter of weeks. With only Vasconcelos to challenge his designated successor, Calles rigged the presidential election so that Vasconcelos officially lost by a large margin in November 1929. Actually, he could have won a fair contest.

The most significant Calles contribution was the establishment of a national political party. Late in the fall of 1928, Calles conceived the notion of a party which would unify the "revolutionary elite" to consolidate the ideological, regional, and factional political groups. Portes Gil influenced Calles by stressing the need for a populistic structure that would manifest mass support for government policies. On the day that Portes Gil took office, the PNR Organizing Committee announced its formation and invited all those of a "revolutionary tendency" to participate in talks with Organizing Committee chair Calles to officially establish the party, approve its statutes, and select a presidential candidate. Thus a new political age developed. In proclaiming the PNR as the guardian angel of the revolution, as the focus for the structuring and development of a populist link between the masses and national leadership, Calles provided his successors with the vehicle with which to take power. Thus the Juárez/Díaz machinery of the nineteenth century mended regional regimes to the national government through federal patronage and programs. A bureaucratic apparatus tied to labor and peasants now monopolized political power. Calles did not want presidents elected by temporary coalitions that would splinter after tasting the fruits of victory. Calles designed the PNR in order to alleviate tensions between Obregón's close followers and *callista* associates. In addition to solving the headache of presidential succession, the PNR also advanced Calles's power.

Calles's institutionalization of the PNR also represents the continuity of the Porfirian solution to a multiparty platform that could dissolve into insurrection. The PNR attempted to confederate the various regional and local factions into a national party. Calles encouraged the process by forbidding the confederated regional parties, thus establishing the PNR as a party that transcended the Díaz technique of loyal cliques directed by Mexico City. A certain amount of legitimacy annointed Calles's efforts because of the desire for education which Calles, like Díaz, sought to satisfy by means of a hierarchical political party.

Calles had taken a Carranza approach in emphasizing civilian presidents by tasking Joaquín Amaro with creating a loyal military. The army would no longer concern itself with politics but devote its attention to preserving internal order. Thus the size of the army declined and Amaro designed a regulatory code that specified promotion standards, discipline, retirement, and benefits. The PNR weakened the military more. A new curriculum at the Colegio Militar emphasized professionalism. Skills tests eliminated substandard officers as well as unwanted enlisted personnel.

Pascual Ortiz Rubio, 1930–1932. Ortiz Rubio fit Calles's plans nicely. The PNR leaders sharply debated who should succeed Portes Gil until Calles threw his support to Ortiz Rubio at the last moment. Without any large political following because he had been ambassador to Brazil, Ortiz Rubio was not charismatic and had little hope of winning against Vasconcelos unless the PNR arranged the election so that he could "win."

With the *Jefe Máximo* formulating strategy in the background, the Ortiz Rubio regime became notable for its repression. An assassin nearly killed the newly inaugurated Ortiz Rubio, hitting him in the jaw with bullets while striking his wife's ear. A nasty crackdown resulted because the assailant was considered a Vasconcelos supporter. About 60 of a group of interrogated and tortured Vasconcelos adherents died when the federal district military garrison forced them to dig their own graves, hanged them, and then buried the bodies near Mexico City in March 1930.

Perhaps the worst mistake committed was a brainless revival of Jacobinist anticlericalism in 1931. The "defanaticization" program directed against religion involved the banning of religious

processions and open air services. Worse, many Maximato regional governments burned local relics, images, and even Churches, while changing street and place names from religious to secular designations. Teachers insisted that students celebrate Day of the Mother, Day of the Race, and even Corn Day rather than Catholic festivals. Some anticlericals even stopped the ringing of church bells or stole them. Resistance, of course, was massive and wise regional rulers ignored Maximato urgings to harass Catholics. At the same time, the Ortiz Rubio regime attacked Cristero veterans throughout 1931 despite the 1929 accord. Five thousand died as a result of this renewed conflict.

The Chinese population also fell victim to governmental persecution in 1931. Here the authorities played upon grass-roots animosities because the Chinese had become successful shopkeepers, traders, and business people in the north. Because the Chinese lacked powerful diplomatic protection, Calles allowed mass expulsions to take place in 1931.

As the economy bottomed out from 1931 to 1932, support for peasant and labor programs declined. Ortiz Rubio and Calles decided to defend existing landholding patterns as the demand for Mexican agricultural products withered. Although the agrarian leagues' movement reached its height in Veracruz during the early 1930s, the PNR removed Tejeda's radical *agrarista* faction from control of several municipalities and the legislature. Land reform came to an abrupt end in Tlaxcala and other states because of the increasingly restrictive Maximato agrarian policies. The government feared that the bleak, hopeless situations of many desperate, insecure, working-class people would be worse if land reform decreased food production. Ortiz Rubio did enact a 1931 Labor Code, which made employers justify their actions, provide a three-month severance pay, and prohibit lockouts. But enforcement was sporadic at best and no strong national labor union replaced the defunct CROM.

As the Maximato shifted to conservative positions, the regime became less tolerant of leftists.

Mexico had broken relations with the Soviet Union when the Mexican Communist Party attempted to direct its fighters to precipitate a peasant uprising. Many Marxists believed a true revolution was imminent; therefore, Calles declared a virtual war against them. Its leaders wound up with Madre Conchita on the Tres Marías penal colony island. Anticommunism reached its peak in 1930 and 1931, years that witnessed the appearance of the Gold Shirts, a fascist-inspired organization of those whose self-appointed task was to terrorize communists and Jews.

Ortiz Rubio did not support all these policies as he was basically a moderate. When he attempted to challenge Calles, who with Portes Gil expelled his supporters from the party and the government, Ortiz Rubio had no recourse but to resign. He had become the butt of innumerable jokes, particularly the legend that he learned of his resignation only by reading about it in the newspaper.

Abelardo Rodríguez, 1932–1934. The self-styled "friend of the workers" became the last Maximato president. Perhaps the most compliant of the *Jefe Máximo's* subordinates, Rodríguez had gained great wealth in Baja, California, from owning gambling casinos and smuggling liquor into the United States. With little desire to actually run the country, Calles and his subordinates continued to set policy. In 1933, for example, Governor Victórico Grajales closed all the Churches in Chiapas while public bonfires destroyed parish records and religious artifacts. Shortly afterwards, he expelled all the priests.

In this depressing atmosphere, the expansion of intellect and education created an earnest pursuit of national identity. Samuel Ramos served as one of the architects of the new ethos. Ramos espoused reason as an equilibrium between intuition and positivism, not to mention cosmopolitanism and nationalism. Now, he asserted, Mexico could concentrate on entering the world on equal terms, inviting foreign influence only where it could embellish and improve its unique

identity. Ramos particularly sought to minimize U.S. influence and hardly mentioned it in his classic *Profile of Man and Culture in Mexico* (1934). Ramos viewed Mexican history as transcending future conflict by reaffirming Mexican humanity in a universal context. Unlike Maximato politicians, he believed that a "religious sense of life" is the foundation of every culture, particularly in Mexico.

Also during the early 1930s, *indigenismo* reached its height. At this time Gregorio López y Fuentes became its most noted practicioner. In *El Indio* (1935) the incredible harshness of a Maya village grasps the reader. The outsiders who control them are patently exploitative and indifferent to indigenous suffering. In *Tierra* (1932), López y Fuentes describes a segment of the Zapatista revolution, emphasizing his sincere goals as well as his betrayal. The novel has a sense of reality by using years as chapter titles and citing Zapata's actual words. This novel parallels failed attempts by the Maximato to move Zapata's remains to Mexico City from Cuautla.

Also notable was the emergence of Carlos Chávez as Mexico's first international figure in music. He led Mexico to musical maturity by composing, conducting, and teaching. His most significant forms were for orchestra, the first of which emerged in 1933. He began as a nationalist who found more stimulation in Mexico's artistic ferment than in older European standards. Chávez felt his heritage forcefully and with pride, compellingly evoking folk melodies. Manuel Maria Ponce achieved much the same for the guitar. Foreign music became much less popular during the period of artistic nationalism.

Thus, *lo mexicano* attempts to isolate Mexico from external trends reached the end by 1934. Antiforeign movements were not enough to unite Mexico while it attempted to understand itself and articulate a new continuity with the past. Musicians and novelists tended to reflect the realities of Mexico; philosophers were often elitist and abstract. Thus, the artists' union broke up in 1934 when Siqueiros lamented that painters who catered to tourists and politicians had reduced the group during what he termed a decline into "cerebral masturbation." Foreigners succeeded when they tapped into genuine cultural beliefs. Therefore, Russian filmmaker Sergei Eisenstein produced a masterpiece when he arrived in 1932 to incorporate religious metaphors into his powerful film *Que Viva Mexico*, which glorified indigenous life.

The economic and political situation appeared bleak as the Maximato considered its future. At the end of the summer of 1933, Rodríguez glumly declared that Mexico could not even begin to think of restructuring its debt in the continuing crisis. In 1932, Mexico did not have diplomatic relations with Venezuela and Peru. Its relations with Guatemala had deteriorated because Mexicans had killed Guatemalans. The Maximato's attempt to control genuine mass participation, combined with the accumulating effects of the Depression, resulted in rising discontent. A popular movement for reform among the leftist wing of the PNR focused upon Lázaro Cárdenas. The PNR gradually came to believe that mass incorporation was necessary for the survival of the PNR and the revolution it claimed to lead. In this context, Rodríguez instituted the minimum wage in 1934.

SUGGESTED READING

Ankerson, Dudley. *Agrarian Warlord: Saturino Cedillo and the Mexican Revolution in San Luis Potosí.* Dekalb: Northern Illinois University Press, 1984.

Bailey, David C. *!Viva Cristo Rey!* Austin: University of Texas Press, 1974.

Becker, Marjorie. *Setting the Virgin on Fire.* Berkeley: University of California Press, 1995.

Benjamin, Thomas. *A Rich Land, A Poor People: Politics and Society in Modern Chiapas.* Albuquerque: University of New Mexico Press, 1989.

Benjamin, Thomas, and Mark Wasserman, eds. *Provinces of the Revolution: Essays on Regional Mexican History, 1910–1925.* Albuquerque: University of New Mexico Press, 1990.

Carr, Barry. *Marxism and Communism in Twentieth Century Mexico.* Lincoln: University of Nebraska Press, 1992.

Centro de Estudios de Historia de México. *Los Cristeros.* Mexico City: Condumex, 1996.

Charlot, Jean. *The Mexican Mural Renaissance, 1920–1925.* New Haven, CT: Yale University Press, 1967.

Dulles, John F. *Yesterday in Mexico: A Chronicle of the Revolution, 1919–1930.* Austin: University of Texas Press, 1961.

Fell, Claude. *José Vasconcelos: Los años del águila.* Mexico City: Universidad Nacional Autónoma de México, 1989.

Fowler Salamini, Heather. *Agrarian Radicalism in Veracruz, 1920–1938.* Lincoln: University of Nebraska Press, 1978.

Haber, Steven. *Industry and Under Development: The Industrialization of Mexico, 1880–1940.* Stanford, CA: Stanford University Press, 1989.

Hall, Linda B. *Oil, Banks, and Politcs: The United States and Revolutionary Mexico, 1917-1924.* Austin: University of Texas Press, 1995.

———. "Alvaro Obregón and the Politics of Mexican Land Reform." *Hispanic American Historical Review* 60 (May 1980), 213–238.

———, *Alvaro Obregón, Power and Revolution in Mexico, 1911–1920.* College Station: Texas A&M University Press, 1981.

Hart, John. *Revolutionary Mexico.* Berkeley: University of California Press, 1987.

Herrera, Hayden. *Frida: A Biography of Frida Kahlo.* New York: Harper and Row, 1983.

Hershfield, Joanne and David R. Maciel, eds. *Mexico's Cinema: A Century of Film and Filmakers.* Wilmington, DE: Scholarly Resources, 1999.

Joseph, Gilbert M. *Revolution from Without: Yucatán, Mexico, and the United States, 1880–1924.* New York: Cambridge University Press, 1982.

Knight, Alan. "Racism, Revolution, and Indigenismo: Mexico, 1910–1940." In Richard Graham, ed., *The Idea of Race in Latin America, 1870–1940.* Austin: University of Texas Press, 1990, pp.71–113.

———. "Popular Culture and the Revolutionary State in Mexico." *Hispanic American Historical Review* 74:3 (August 1994), 393–444.

Krauze, Erique. *Mexico: Biolgraphy of Power.* New York: Harper Collins, 1997.

López y Fuentes, Gregorio. *El Indio.* New York: Unger, 1961.

Macías, Anna. *Against All Odds: The Feminist Movement in Mexico to 1940.* Westport, CT: Greenwood Press, 1982.

Marnham, Patrick. *Dreaming with His Eyes Open: The Life of Diego Rivera.* New York: Knopf, 1998.

Meyer, Jean. *The Christero Rebellion: The Mexican People Between Church and State, 1926–1929.* Cambridge: Cambridge University Press, 1990.

Meyer, Lorenzo. *Mexico and the United States in the Oil Controversy, 1917–1942.* Austin: University of Texas Press, 1977.

Mora, Carl J. *Mexican Cinema: Reflections of a Society, 1896–1980.* Berkeley: University of California Press, 1982.

Purnell, Jenne. *Popular Movements and State Formation in Revolutionary Mexico.* Durham, NC: Duke University Press, 1999.

Reed, Alma. *Orozco.* New York: Oxford University Press, 1956.

Romanell, Patrick. *Making of the Mexican Mind: A Study of Recent Mexican Thought.* Notre Dame, IN: University of Notre Dame Press, 1971.

Ruiz, Ramón Eduardo. *Labor and the Ambivalent Revolutionaries:Mexico, 1911–1923.* Baltimore, MD: Johns Hopkins University Press, 1976.

Salisbury, Richard W. *Anti-Imperialism and Competition in Central America, 1920–1929.* Wilmington, DE: Scholarly Resources, 1989.

Tuck, Jim. *The Holy War in Los Altos.* Tucson: University of Arizona Press, 1982.

Vaughn, Mary K. *Cultural Politics in Revolution: Teachers, Peasants and Schools in Mexico, 1930–1940.* Tucson: University of Arizona Press, 1997.

Walsh, Thomas F. *Katherine Anne Porter and Mexico.* Austin: University of Texas Press, 1992.

Wasserman, Mark. *Persistent Oligarchs: Elites and Policies in Chihuahua, Mexico, 1910–1940.* Durham, NC: Duke University Press, 1993.

Wolfe, Bertram D. *The Fabulous Life of Diego Rivera.* New York: Stein and Day, 1969.

Zoraida Vázquez, Josefina. *La educación en la historia de México.* Mexico City: El Colegío de México, 1995.

14

Lázaro Cárdenas Redefines the State, 1934–1940

Many supported the Cárdenas effort to mobilize workers and peasants through the expansion of federal authority but the leftist direction of *Cardenista* policies resulted in disappointment. Eventually, Cárdenas redefined his priorities toward economic growth and improved U.S. relations. Undoubtedly the most controversial twentieth-century Mexican president, Cárdenas maintained the populist agenda but reinterpreted it so that Mexico could survive during a period of international tensions.

Rise to Power from Michoacán. Born in 1895 as the eldest of five sons in a family of eight children, Cárdenas had to leave school at the age of 12 when his father's health and grocery store began to fail. He worked at the local tax office and toiled each night in a small print shop until 1913, when he joined the revolt against Huerta. Cárdenas participated in the early period of the civil war with two small rebel bands, but military defeats forced the teenaged junior officer to flee to Guadalajara, where he labored in a brewery before returning to the revolution in 1914 as a *convencionista*. When ordered to report with his cavalry regiment to Sonora, Cárdenas switched sides to Carranza, joining Calles at Agua Prieta and fighting to defeat Villa's attack on the border town. This new alignment made Cárdenas a

colonel at the age of 20, and he forged a strong relationship with the Sonora dynasty. He aided Obregón and Calles greatly by helping to crush the de la Huerta revolt.

At this point, Cárdenas began to formulate his ideology. Lacking a broad education and not well read, Cárdenas came under the influence of family friend Francisco J. Múgica. Múgica had helped the Cárdenas family during their difficulties and Cárdenas listened to his radical views about drinking, smoking (which Múgica sought to prohibit), rabid anticlericalism, land reform, and unionization. Both of them were appalled by the highhanded treatment they received while garrisoned in the Veracruz oil district. The oil companies closed access roads at their whim, even detaining a military zone commander when the mood struck them. Such an affront shocked Cárdenas and he became determined to right such arrogance thereafter. An association with Múgica clarified Cardenas's leftist tendencies and ensured self-confidence as well as poise. About 1926, Cárdenas began reading Karl Marx for the first time.

Gradually, Cárdenas became an influential leader who wanted to accelerate the changes outlined in the 1917 Constitution. Many responded to him because Cárdenas was humble, worked hard, and was tough. During the 1926–1927 Yaqui wars, Cárdenas volunteered to crush them, urging that the Yaquis be expelled after their defeat, much in the Porfirian style. After rising to the rank of *divisionario* general, Cárdenas became governor of his native Michoacán where he established a powerful organization, the Michoacán Revolutionary Confederation of Labor. Largely dependent upon *agraristas* and teachers, these activitists could count upon weapons and funds from the state government in their drive to force businesses and schools to open up their own schools or encourage the creation of new ejidos. Even though Calles considered the ejidos a failure, Cárdenas gave land grants to 181 villages. As in the rest of Mexico, they also burned religious artifacts and uged abstinence from alcohol. During this intense period of his career, Cárdenas also served as head of the PNR from November 1930 to August 1931 and secretary of interior for two months in 1931 under Ortiz Rubio. He managed to avoid offending both Calles and the embattled president but found himself in limbo as the military commander of Puebla.

As the Depression continued to ravage Mexico and the popularity of the Maximato faded, Calles decided to have Cárdenas replace him on the basis of a Six-Year Plan. The Depression seemed to indicate that traditional economic concepts were not working. By 1932, half of Mexico's 90,000 mine workers were unemployed; from 1934 to 1940, 559 of the 879 mine companies eventually closed down. Mining was important since it provided 28 percent of all federal revenues, more than any other source. Therefore, leftist ideas began to gain the upper hand within the PRN. In May 1933, Calles responded by calling for the creation of a Six-Year Plan. When Portes Gil and others within the inner circle began to float the idea of Cárdenas becoming president, Calles withdrew his own favorite and decided upon a very surprised Cárdenas in June 1933. As a result he Six-Year Plan became crucial in order to legitimize Cárdenas as the new president. It had five main elements: (1) construction of 12,000 new rural schools within the context of socialist ideas, (2) collective bargaining as the norm for unionized workers, (3) stimulation of agricul-

Lazaro Cárdenas, President of Mexico, 1934–1940. *Courtesy of Centro de Estudios de Historia de México.*

tural and industrial cooperatives, (4) simplification and acceleration of land reform, and (5) more public works projects in the form of roads, railways, and highways in order to rejuvenate the economy and provide work. When the delegates met in Querétaro in December 1933 to present their project, radicals took control of the meeting when Cárdenas accepted the plan as well as the PNR nomination. Although the Six-Year Plan was a patchwork of compromises, contradictions, and utopian affirmations, it emphasized administrative approaches to provide land and credits for new owners. The radical wing of the PNR now believed that the incorporation of the masses was absolutely necessary for the survival of the party they aspired to lead and manage. Regional reformers joined them to arrest the centralizing aspects of the *Jefe Máximo*.

POLITICAL PERSPECTIVES

Early Cardenismo. Cárdenas envisioned a mass mobilization designed to carry out an unprecedented level of reforms. Only 39 years old, Cárdenas took his presidential campaign seriously, even though he could not really lose. Traveling 18,000 miles throughout Mexico, Cárdenas often visited small villages on the back of a burro. He impressed many because he listened with genuine sincerity and obviously represented a change. Cárdenas went to great lengths to build as well as reconstruct linkages to agrarian and union organizations. Even though Cárdenas had disarmed radical forces in Veracruz and other regions when he served Calles, he replaced them with *Cardenistas* who understood that he would rejuvenate reform at the right moment, which now had come. Although it became increasingly clear that Cárdenas would retain control of these organizations as the new president, many regional leaders overlooked Cardenas's endorsement of the PNR's effort to centralize power. Out of the four presidential candidates, Cárdenas received 2.2 million votes while the others recorded a combined total of 40,000 votes.

Reinterpretation of the Populist State. Although Calles assumed that he could manipulate Cárdenas after the "election," Cárdenas immediately let it be known that the increasingly moderate direction of the Maximato had become a thing of the past. In his inauguration speech, Cárdenas promised an acceleration of socioeconomic reforms. An idealistic leftist who lived simply, Cárdenas, like Carranza, moved his personal residence out of Chapultepec Castle, which eventually became a wonderful museum. Cárdenas lived more modestly at nearby Los Pinos. More fundamentally, Cárdenas endeavored to set a puritanical example. Not corrupt, he avoided the discredited Maximato politicians. He shut down gambling casinos throughout Mexico, including a particularly fancy bar at the Bellas Artes theater. He even cut his salary in half as police arrested hundreds of loiterers, thieves, criminals, drunkards, and prostitutes. Cárdenas intrigued many Mexicans very early in his presidency by allowing anyone to send him, free of charge, a telegram about their problems and complaints.

Land, Labor, and Religious Policies. After his inauguration, Cárdenas decided to mobilize

the masses for better working conditions in factories as well as agricultural fields. The agrarian reform consisted of distributing 45 million acres of land (17.9 million hectares) to 750,000 rural families in 12,000 villages. Campesinos also began receiving decent quality land. The all-abiding passion of Cárdenas was his fervent belief that agrarian reform would result in a great success. To the end of his life, he believed that, although the outcome was much different. During his regime, a great change occurred in the possession of cultivated land; ejido farmers owned almost as much land (17.5 million acres) as the small and large landowners (19.5 million acres) by 1940. Whether tilled or not, hacendados would continue to own three times more total land than ejido owners. Cárdenas also attempted to make many ejidos into large-scale cooperatives capable of producing food for the national market as well as foreign export. Profit-sharing, he assumed, would motivate campesinos to work hard. Out of 18,000 ejidos, about 500 cooperatives were established.

But the National Bank of Ejido Credit became rigid, corrupt, and inefficient with the result that credit and technology did not often reach those in need. Certainly the living standards of some campesinos did rise, but not in terms of agricultural yield per acre of land. Agrarian reform thus became a success in social and political terms but an economic flop. After Cárdenas expropriated the cotton growing haciendas of the Laguna region in late 1936, production declined and critics complained that the area had become a dust bowl. In the Yucatán, Cárdenas nationalized nearly two-thirds of the henequen plantations in August 1937. The overwhelming majority of the new ejidos eventually failed, largely because of the heavy-handed, unresponsive land reform bureaucrats. In general, the parcels of land given out were frequently too small to support families. The result was that subsistence farming became the norm on many ejidos with fewer food supplies reaching the cities and villages.

On the other hand, Cárdenas expropriated large amounts of foreign holdings right up to the end of his term. He had not forgotten the earlier period he had witnessed when U.S. and European owners could do as they wanted on Mexican soil. Cárdenas not only wanted to right the wrongs when foreigners acquired Mexican land by suspicious techniques, but he was also concerned about the future. In 1939–1940, for example, Cárdenas expropriated six million hectares of land in Tabasco when it was suspected that sizable oil deposits lay under the jungle canopy.

The labor policy of Cárdenas envisioned everyone working at jobs with decent pay and improved working conditions. Cárdenas assumed power as labor unions competed with one another for the allegiance of often desperate workers. Cárdenas decided to support a wave of strikes as a means for workers to gain wage increases and as an indication that he would attack traditional capitalism. The recognized policy became checking the assets of any company, particularly foreign enterprises, to determine if they could pay higher wages. Although the first oil workers' labor union had formed in late 1933 and 15,000 oil workers had lost their jobs in the early 1930s, the CROM had allowed only 13 strikes in 1933. Under Cárdenas, the number of strikes increased from 202 in 1934 to 645 in 1935. Eventually, 2,800 strikes took place during the Cárdenas

years, more than under any other president. Soon the Confederación de Trabajadores Mexicanos (CTM), under the leadership of Marxist Vicente Lombardo Toledano, became the dominant national labor organization. Although Cárdenas sympathized with socialist ideology, he never considered Marxism a realistic solution for Mexico's problems, but he did what he could for workers all over the country. Mine workers, for example, gained a closed shop and collective contracts. The minister of education even announced that Mexico was moving closer to a dictatorship of the proletariat. Such rhetoric was often intended to impress those on the left and intimidate rightist opponents. But Cárdenas did favor worker control of industry. Therefore, he turned the operation of the railroads over to labor union leaders. Because of their inexperience, a high increase in the number of accidents, poor management, and deterioration of rolling stock as well as equipment occurred. But there were limits to labor's power. Cárdenas thwarted Toledano's ambition to unionize campesinos, who were directed to a new organization, the Confederación Nacional de Campesinos (CNC). This provided a political base for the new regime to ward off an inevitable counterattack by Callistas.

Stevedores
by Pablo O'Higgins.
Courtesy of the Gallery at UTA (University of Texas at Arlington).

Cárdenas also maintained the policy of religious persecution. The president wanted to re-shape citizens by means of civic festivals and secular education. But expelling priests, destroying religious symbols, and burning as well as closing churches alienated many. In February 1935, Cardenas signed a law forbidding religious materials to be sent through the postal system. Garrido's Red Shirt fanatics came from Tabasco to Mexico City and shot five people in the Coyoacán suburb. To the outrage of many, Garrido freed the Red Shirts that police had arrested. Meanwhile, a section of the unionized left as well as Toledano had been campaigning for "socialist education" and finally got their wish. The government announced that it would destroy God and inaugurate the First Congress of the Proletariat Child. Although doomed from the start, proponents of socialist education claimed that scientific, health, and civil programs would be the norm. Cárdenas and his advisors were simply responding to the ideological circumstances of the decade, which made socialism useful as rhetoric but not as an underlying goal. Ill-defined and the subject of endless speeches which did little more than inflame the passions of those who feared sex education, the blatant anticlericalism of socialist education provoked large protests. Women mounted fierce campaigns against religious persecution throughout Mexico, often reopening churches by sheer force. Cárdenas began to back down from anticlericalism.

POLITICAL CONSOLIDATION

Confrontation with Calles. Cárdenas had observed the Maximato with some discomfort, and once in office, he determined to free himself of Calles's influence. He was aware that Calles's control over Portes Gil, Ortiz Rubio, and Rodríguez had rested heavily upon army support and he began to assiduously cultivate promising junior officers. Not only did Cárdenas raise salaries and benefits, but he also supported an improved system of education within the army and backed

a far reaching internal review of the entire military structure. The navy and army were separated into two different ministries. Officers who had opposed the Sonora dynasty, even Villistas, Carrancistas, and Zapatistas, received command positions throughout the countryside. To control the 350 generals who played a vital role in politics, Cárdenas transferred them without their troops if he suspected them of disloyalty.

When Calles realized that he could not manipulate Cárdenas as he had the previous three presidents, he began speaking out vociferously, which weakened his prestige. In June 1935, Calles began to publicly criticize Toledano, strike activity, and "personalism." Cárdenas responded by asking his largely Callista cabinet to resign. Portes Gil assumed control of the PNR. As Calles and Morones dashed to Calles's palace in Cuernavaca, Cárdenas began cashiering 14 Callista governors. The government tightened its control over the judiciary and legislature. Not by coincidence, worker and peasant groups began demanding that Calles be evicted. Calles soon discovered that newspapers would not print his "defense" of past regimes during the Maximato. Through the foreign press, Calles claimed that Cárdenas was taking Mexico toward communism. Finally, in April 1936, Calles, Morones, and a few of their supporters were rounded up and deported to California. When police apprehended Calles, he was reading Adolf Hitler's *Mein Kampf.*

But the crisis with Calles resulted in the establishment of conservative governors who were Cardenistas but in reality opponents of the president's mass mobilization. Sensitive to Callista accusations that Mexico was becoming Marxist and eager for U.S. support, Cárdenas allowed open gubernatorial elections. To oust the Callista governor in Sonora, Cárdenas sided with Obregonista General Ramón Yocupicio and his coalition of Maya Indians, Catholics, landowners, and business interests in 1935. But the following year, Yocupicio easily defeated his Cardenista rivals by setting up his own corporatist organization. Labor supported the governor simply because he provided the most benefits. Mine workers organized independently of the CTM out of a desire for democratic unions. Using Porfirian strategies of the past, Yocupicio manipulated peasant organizations to minimize class conflict by giving in to many local demands while building up a successful political machine.

Similar regimes led by regional caudillos maintained a personalist grip over various states. In San Luis Potosí, Cedillo continued to utilize patronage as the means to control peasants and workers while enjoying strong ties with the landed and financial upper class. Cárdenas viewed Cedillo as a threat to the consolidation of the postrevolutionary state and, therefore, brought Cedillo into the cabinet in 1938 to keep an eye on him. Two brothers, Maximino Avila Camacho and Manuel Avila Camacho, firmly controlled the state of Puebla. While Manuel served Cárdenas in the war ministry, Maximino became the autocratic boss of Puebla, even though he was a conservative. To the detriment of historians, Maximino sold or destroyed the executive branch papers of the Puebla state archives in the late 1930s. Thus the populist national governments reverted to the Porfirian formula in working out political relations between Mexico City and the regions.

Cárdenas could not control every region that he desired, but he sought the ears and emotions of average citizens. One item was the creation of a national broadcasting system. Cárdenas distributed a radio receiver to nearly every agricultural and workers' community in the nation so people could listen to educational and political programs broadcast on stations operated by the national educational department and the official political party. Cárdenas also sponsored public monuments. He inaugurated the Obregón Monument in 1935, which contained the general's arm in a three-story obelisk with oversized pewter doors on the site of the La Bombilla restaurant where Obregón died. During the same year, Cárdenas arranged to have the remains of the independence heroes (except Iturbide) moved to the new Monument to Independence on the Paseo de la Reforma. As the basic elements of the official history of the Mexican Revolution began to appear, the

The Monument to the Revolution, Mexico City, where the remains of Villa, Madero, Carranza, Calles, and Cárdenas are interred. *Courtesy of Centro de Estudios de Historia de México.*

effort to create the Monument to the Revolution finally culminated in 1938 with a "Revolution Day" ceremony on November 20. Cárdenas also urged Mexicans to exercise and participate in sporting events, sometimes setting an example by swimming publicly.

A severe financial crisis in 1937 began to alter the political landscape. Mexico nearly went bankrupt as spending continued to accelerate and deficits soon tripled. Agrarian reform had reduced food production and fearful landowners hesitated to expand operations out of their fear of expropriation. The dwindling supplies of food resulted in a frightening wave of inflation.

Cárdenas found himself dealing with a severe crisis. At the beginning of his regime, Cárdenas employed antibusiness rhetoric as part of a process to redirect the anger of the population toward entrepreneurs. The Garza-Sada families emerged as the most prominent Monterrey elites and began to oppose Cárdenas strongly. Now strongly entrenched in the emerging industrial center of the north, the Grupo Monterrey utilized paternalistic family connections to establish successful joint ventures in beer, steel, and textiles. Rejecting corrupt, unreliable politicians at the local level and not dependent upon local landowners, these home-grown nationalists on the regional level became a formidable force. Not surprisingly, capital flight and food imports increased as overdrafts at the Banco de México appeared.

Former law professor Eduardo Suárez served Cárdenas heroically during the 1937 crisis when he and other officials at his treasury secretariat actually took the lead in fashioning financial policy. As much as Cárdenas believed in land and labor reforms, he was pragmatic enough to approve Suárez's steps. One of them was a 3 percent income tax followed by the reinstitution of corporate

***The Orator* by Pablo O'Higgins.** *Courtesy of the Gallery at UTA (University of Texas at Arlington)*

taxes. Suárez also issued bonds to finance public works projects by using sugar and cotton harvests as collateral. As a Keynsian ideologue who had ties to U.S. policymakers with similar beliefs, Suárez persuaded the sympathetic Franklin Delano Roosevelt administration to buy 35 million pesos of Mexican silver and gold for U.S. reserves.

Political conflict intensified in 1937. Cárdenas decided to resume a strongly populist course of action to mobilize workers and campesinos. Spearheaded by CTM activists, they attracted a mass following, thousands of whom received weapons and military training. Opposing Cárdenas was a new rightist movement which used the media, literature, and spontaneous grass-roots organizations to convince many that "fat lips" Cárdenas, as they termed the president, was leading Mexico to disaster. Women demanded the vote and continued in their struggles to reopen churches. In 1937, the Unión Nacional Sinarquista appeared, which was a mass-based Catholic movement spreading out from Guanajuato. Appealing to campesinos eager for inculcating the values of property, family, hierarchy, and religion while opposing U.S. influence, the Sinarquistas soon claimed a million followers. Fascist-style Gold Shirts also began to organize in imitation of similar movements that had begun in central Europe. As formidable opposition appeared in Hidalgo, Tabasco, San Luis Potosí, and Sonora, a nationwide Catholic campaign forced Cárdenas to allow religious tolerance.

In order to consolidate his control of the federal government, Cárdenas redesigned the government's political party. To establish a more balanced equality among all the major sectors of the Mexican polity, Cárdenas proposed in his 1938 New Year's Address the formation of a "workers' party." In most of Latin America, the Depression had destroyed civilian regimes but not in Mexico and Chile. Chile had elected a popular front government in 1938, when Marxists took their cue from the seventh congress of the Soviet Comintern, whereby the left would join with reformers to stop the advance of fascism. Toledano pressed Cárdenas to accept this concept so that the CTM would lead it. Cárdenas and his advisors, however, preferred that the state lead this drive rather than the CTM. Shortly after the New Year's speech, Cárdenas proposed to a PNR commission that a new party include only workers, peasants, and the military. Commission members, nevertheless, convinced the embattled president that professions should be included to avoid pushing the middle class into opposition parties. Delegates to the special convention persuaded Cárdenas and the PNR commission to accept a new name, the Party of the Mexican Revolution (PRM) instead of the Mexican Socialist Party, which Cárdenas had favored.

The PRM represented an important change. Its 1938 program was substantially more radical than the PNR version from 1934. The earlier manifesto had called for only "the betterment of the masses," whereas the PRM stressed the theme of class conflict and considered the creation of a "worker democracy" as the first step toward socialism. What emerged was a corporatist framework with the principle that organized groups would be the sole representatives of each social sector. The state would mediate all conflicts and intervene in the economy to promote the common interest. The final arbiter would be the president. In this sense, the new state resembled similar structures in Spain, Italy, and Portugal during the 1920s.

Cárdenas divided the organized labor movement into three separate entities, each under a different government agency. Juan Perón emulated the same sort of organization a decade later in Argentina. Industrial workers remained inside the CTM. Cárdenas placed campesinos in the newly created CNC in 1938, so that Toledano could not control them. Cárdenas also initiated the formation of government employees into a union called the Federation of Workers in Service to the State. This union included all public employees except for the top 10 percent of the government bureaucracy, based on the premise that this exclusion would give the organization a working-class orientation. Here Cárdenas began to establish a distinct middle-class "popular sector," because this

union as well as the National Confederation of Small Agricultural Property could not join the CTM. Cárdenas also brought the armed forces into the corporate structure as a separate group. He wanted more complete control of the military and to establish a counterveiling force to the organized workers and peasants. The officers complied without protesting.

The corporatist system was based upon organized labor at the center of power, but it was derived from a continuity that had deep roots in Mexican history. The 1917 Constitution had distinct corporatist features that had their origins in the colonial era. Cárdenas agreed with the corporatist views of 1930s intellectuals in Mexico that pure democracy was inappropriate for Mexico because of extreme social and economic inequalities; therefore, they argued that proportional representation should be favored. Cárdenas envisioned a direct link with the general population, bypassing the traditional regional organizations. The subsystems of Mexico were being stripped away, making possible a degree of national integration and centralized power nonexistent since the pre-Hispanic era. The increasing unpopularity of Cardenista policies did not make this possible as the 1930s came to a close, but they would become a firm part of the political landscape for the next half century.

CULTURAL HORIZONS

As part of the Cardenista attempt to reform society, the government intensified its efforts to purify daily living and to raise educational standards. Cultural trends took on an even stronger ideological emphasis among scholars as well as artists. Cárdenas also sought to improve the lives of women, particularly toward the end of his tenure.

Rivera and the other painters continued their leftist emphasis. Rivera, however, emphasized cultural aspects of *indigenismo* by striving to forge a new multiracial and cross-cultural national identity. Rivera created images connecting the nation's ancient civilizations to modern society.

Although he began to paint canvases that were surrealist, Rivera never lost his adulation of the Soviet Union. Siqueiros at one time became the general secretary of the Communist Party of Mexico and was a colonel in the Spanish Republican Army fighting against the conservative forces of Francisco Franco during the Spanish Civil War.

Marxism attracted poets and scholars as well. After publishing his first poem at the age of 17 in Mexico City's *El Nacional* newspaper, Octavio Paz studied law at the National Autonomous University of Mexico (UNAM) where he joined a Marxist student group. His early works caught the attention of Pablo Neruda, a famous Chilean poet. In 1937, the two attended the Second International Anti-Fascist Congress in Spain at the height of the civil war. Entranced by the leftist cause, Paz traveled to the battlefront and joined a regiment commanded by Siqueiros. Commanders nevertheless denied Paz a rifle and sent him home because his commitment to Marxism was not deep enough.

Marxist history flourished during the Cárdenas presidency. Scholars such as Rafael Ramos Pedrueza, Alfonso Teja Zabre, and Luis Chávez Orozco analyzed the class structure and economy very skillfully. The Marxists also concluded that the resulting policies from the revolutionary civil war of 1910–1920 had laid the foundation for the completion of social justice programs to aid the working class. The government, of course, was delighted that their attempts to extol the revolutionary line coincided with the views of the leftist historians. More importantly, these historians began to ask innovative questions about regionalism, land, labor, indigenous peoples, imperialism, and *mexicanidad*. Although the answers to these questions never created any consensus, the new exchange of ideas was unquestionably stimulating.

Cárdenas also created several significant cultural institutions that would dominate the remainder of the twentieth century. One of the most important was the establishment of a first rate publisher, Fondo de Cultura Económica in 1934. Soon Mexico's largest and best publisher of high-quality studies, Fondo de Cultura Económica be-

came an invaluable landmark of Mexican culture. Another important innovation which helped professionalize the study of history was the Escuela Nacional de Antropología e Historia in 1935. After Cárdenas left Chapultepec and turned it into a fine museum, the renamed Instituto Nacional de Antropología e Historia moved into the castle in 1939.

Cárdenas finally worked out a compromise with the UNAM, which resisted the imposition of a socialist curriculum and the centralization of control over its affairs by the Education Secretariat. Rector Manuel Gómez Marín fought back with the result that the government cut the UNAM budget and threatened to close it. Cardenistas considered the faculty elitist and reactionary. The faculty, however, continued to teach on reduced salaries while Gómez Marín secured private funding. The most exciting debate on campus took place between philosopher Antonio Caso, who defended critical anaylsis and research, and Toledano who advocated socialism as what he considered the foundation of scientific truth. Toledano lost out, and in 1937 Cárdenas agreed to a compromise whereby, in return for decent funding and academic freedom, the UNAM would accept as its primary obligation that of serving the nation with a sense of national mission through scientific research and training Mexico's future leaders.

A commitment to Mexico, national unity, and overall development became the primary focus of Cárdenas's educational policy. He viewed a new educational program as a primary means to dismantle the old hierarchical order and their hold on the masses. Therefore, special attention was given to urban education. Technical and mass secondary schooling was viewed as the means to battle traditional values among workers and to support national control of the economy through greater productivity as well as a platform to improve living conditions. There was much to accomplish because less than one-third of rural children enrolled in schools from 1920 to 1930 and all but 2 percent dropped out, usually in the first two years.

Under Cárdenas, tensions developed between officials of the Secretaría de Educación Pública and teachers in rural areas familiar with local needs. The new government teachers attempted to Mexicanize regional inhabitants by means of civic rituals, public works programs, and nationalist rhetoric. Many villagers resented anticlerical rantings and simultaneously opposed coeducation for males and females. In their determined efforts to stop the consumption of alcoholic beverages, teachers often butted into the homes of their students to lecture them on proper cooking and food preparation. Some instructors organized "toilet days" for the construction of latrines. Much conflict ensued because many villagers wanted the increased access to education and school supplies but not the strident political centralization that Cardenistas demanded. Although the educational secretariat did incorporate some constituencies on their terms, the Cárdenas agenda generally failed because towns and states negotiated or rejected socialist education yet received the tools to fight illiteracy. Male literacy rose from 23 percent in 1910 to 38 percent by 1940. Female literacy increased from 18 percent to 22 percent for the same years.

More Protestant evangelicals also entered at this time. Under the auspices of Cárdenas, Wycliffe Bible translators arrived in Mexico. The Summer Institute of Linguistics taught indigenous people to read Spanish and assisted them in integrating into Mexican life. Although translators were not officially allowed to establish churches, they quietly prepared others to do so. The first indigenous Protestant community was founded in Oxchuc, Chiapas.

Particularly in Chiapas, indigenous ties with Cárdenas became very close, partially because the government distrusted traditional regional sentiments there. In 1936, the Cardenistas established the Department of Indigenous Affairs, whose goal was to promote, unify, and supervise the activities of federal and state governments on behalf of indigenous peoples. Soon the department declared that conditions of virtual slavery existed in Chiapas. Wages for Indians averaged 30 centavos a day, although the minimum wage for *mestizos* was one peso and 30 centavos. To atone for the lack of property ownership among indigenous people, Cárdenas divided the large estates in the central highlands into 53 ejidos comprised of more than 500,000 hectares so that 60,000 families had access to communal land. Unhappy about this loss of land, large landowners frequently retaliated. Educational efforts also antagonized Chiapas landowners. If a ranch had more than five families, the landowner was obligated to provide a school and a teacher. Efforts to force payment of a minimum wage also irritated landowners, who claimed that the laborers were not worth it and would use the money to get drunk. Unfortunately, PRM caciques began to control municipal governments and ejido organizations.

A major shortcoming of the Cárdenas era was its refusal to understand why campesinos and urban workers held so stringently to Catholicism. Religion permeated all aspects of their lives, particularly for women, but the Cardenistas viewed such behavior as "fanaticism." In reality, the Church was still the mortar that held everyday life together. Women found solace in the social aspects of church ritual and ceremonies. Catholicism allowed males who held little control over their economic futures to control their households.

The tragedy is that many Cardenistas were Catholics themselves; those who composed the anticlerical sector were not necessarily the majority; they were simply more vocal. Like the sixteenth-century missionaries, Cardenistas sought to nationalize rural life. In Chiapas as elsewhere, they closed churches, tore down altars, burned statues of the saints in the streets, shut down religious schools, and forbade priests to wear clerical collars. Nuns could not dress in their habits. Instead, the Cardenistas encouraged boys to participate in sports on Sundays, while females were invited to sew. Unfortunately, the Cardenistas often lacked the social perspective to involve themselves *realistically* in the campesino culture.

Cárdenas was not particularly interested in the feminist cause at first but then devoted himself more to it toward the end. Several women were attracted to the problem of male alcoholism as was the president. Women often detested male drinking because it impacted their family budgets. Cardenistas, however, expected female activists to spy on their neighbors and report women who were "backsliders" and even recommend punishments. Nevertheless, most leftists and government supporters feared that women could be manipulated by the Church. Eventually, Cárdenas concluded that female voting rights would help Mexico more than hurt it. This decision was bolstered by the fact that feminists had become much more unified in their desire for the vote than they had been previously and were willing to act upon that desire with marches and protests. In 1937, Cárdenas responded by declaring that women should have the right to vote. On November 23 of that year, the minister of the interior announced that men and women should have full rights by means of a constitutional amendment. As women became elected to run Chilpancingo, the Guerrero state capital, 16 other states gave women the right to vote. In 1939, the Mexican Congress came very close to passing a constitutional amendment that would officially give females complete voting rights. However, the firmly implanted notion that women were not ready to vote caused the ratification of the amendment to be stalled and finally abandoned for nearly 20 years.

INDEPENDENT FOREIGN POLICY

International relations intensified considerably during the Cárdenas era. Undoubtedly, the most stunning diplomatic event was the 1938 oil expropriation of U.S. and European holdings. Cárdenas also responded to European events adroitly. Supporting the Spanish Republic and bringing its exiles to Mexico demonstrated a true sense of statesmanship.

The Petroleum Nationalization. Militant labor organization, oil company greed, and his

declining popularity forced Cárdenas to nationalize the foreign oil companies in March 1938. The organization of an aggressive oil workers' union precipitated the crisis. When the national labor leadership had supported Cárdenas against Calles in 1935, oil unions won the right to organize the entire industry. About 20 oil unions joined to form the Union of Oil Workers of the Mexican Republic in 1935 and offered a collective contract to the oil companies. They demanded a 40 hour week, paid vacations, salaries of one dollar and a half each day, pension plans, union control over hiring and firing, and better opportunities for Mexicans in managerial and technical jobs. Both British and U.S. companies considered the union's appeals excessive. In order to avoid worker walkouts, Cárdenas began labor talks between the union and oil companies. After the union began to strike in 1937, Cárdenas agreed to a union suggestion that a government arbitration board research company finances in order to decide whether or not they could pay for the contract. The government experts then filed a report in August 1937 which supported most, but not all, of the union demands. Enormous oil company profits, which were higher than in the United States; justified the report's conclusions. Nevertheless, the oil companies complained that paying more than $1.00 a day to their workers would put them out of business.

Everyone was eager for the clash to be resolved because Mexico had become dependent upon gasoline for trucks and automobiles. Mexicans were now consuming more than half the country's oil production. Moreover, bad weather and inflation became critical issues as the economy seemed ready to crash. Panic purchasing and hoarding ensued as the Laguna cotton district collapsed. The nationalization of the railroads did not excite the country, because workers were not being paid, the rural banks had no funding, and unemployment became rampant.

The oil companies then protested the arbitration board's recommendations and took their case to the Mexican Supreme Court. In February 1938, the court ruled against oil company demands for an injunction and backed the arbitration committee unanimously. The court gave them a deadline to comply, but the companies refused. Cárdenas urged the oil magnates to comply and even promised them various assurances if they would obey the law. But events began to move beyond Cárdenas's plan to simply seek higher taxes. Unions began to force the issue by threatening a nationwide strike when the oil union workers called for expropriation. When the oil workers began to seize oil installations and disrupt deliveries, Cárdenas recalled that Bolivia had nationalized oil companies a year earlier. The high-handed attitude of the oil companies became apparent when they questioned the president's integrity, asserting that his word was not sufficient. Because the oil companies refused to obey national law and insulted him, Cárdenas decided to expropriate on March 7. When he announced this on March 18, 1938, Cárdenas saved himself politically and delighted most Mexicans. By reasserting Mexico's dignity, Cárdenas reflected the widespread belief that foreign oil companies had no interest in the country's welfare.

The Good Neighbor Policy. Herbert Hoover first used the "good neighbor" phrase during the ten-country tour of Latin America between his 1928 election and the 1929 inauguration. But when Franklin Delano Roosevelt mentioned the need for a Good Neighbor policy during his brief inaugural address on March 4, 1933, the term became associated with Roosevelt. Mexico became the key country affected by Roosevelt's attempt to improve relations with Latin America as war clouds darkened over Europe and Asia.

Josephus Daniels, the U.S. ambassador to Mexico, typified the New Deal spirit. An old hand at Democratic politics in North Carolina, Daniels was rewarded with a cabinet post as secretary of the navy, where his chief assistant was Roosevelt, now the president 20 years later. The two became strong friends and Daniels worked hard for Roosevelt during the 1932 presidential campaign. After turning down one appointment, Daniels asked for and received the ambassadorship to

Mexico though he could not speak one word of Spanish, and Daniels was the one who had passed the order to invade Veracruz in 1914. At least he had questioned the ultimatum of Admiral Mayo in ordering the Huerta government to salute the U.S. flag. He also opposed vested U.S. interests, particularly oil companies who constantly clamored for naval protection and other privileges in Mexico. Like many other New Dealers, Daniels felt that foreign trade could be expanded by means of friendship.

Daniels won over critics and made friends in Mexico. Protests broke out in Mexico because of the Tampico incident when the Daniels' appointment became public. The train taking him from Fort Worth, Texas, to Mexico City nearly became derailed when rioters tore up the train tracks. He was not convinced when Mexican officials claimed that the rails had twisted due to overheating. After arriving in the Mexican capital, Daniels won over the press by giving a sincere newspaper interview praising New Deal goals. His natural charm, political skill, and experience—he was 70 years old—soon paid off. Daniels often drove around Mexico City out of curiosity, dismissed the embassy guards, and wore Mexican clothes.

The problem for the Good Neighbor policy in Mexico was how much the United States would intervene when the Cárdenas policies affected U.S. interests and investments. Daniels believed that Cárdenas should be supported because his program seemed to resemble the New Deal. Therefore, the ambassador refused to help bankers collect debts when he knew the Mexican treasury was broke. Daniels simply believed that businessmen operating abroad could not expect the State Department to secure special advantages for them and that they must obey the laws of host countries. Thus the oil issue became a case where the national U.S. interests—a stable, friendly Mexico—outweighed private interests. The State Department had always maintained that Mexico had no right to expropriate land owned by U.S. citizens when land reform began, except when quick compensation would be awarded. But because Daniels had sympathized with small landowners in North Carolina, he supported land reform in Mexico as a means of social justice.

Daniels became a critical player in the oil crisis. Because Daniels insisted on understanding the Mexican point of view and not giving in to the oil companies, the Good Neighbor Policy became strengthened in the long run. Daniels warned that a get-tough attitude by the Treasury Department or State Department would result in a strong outburst of anti-U.S. feelings at a time when World War II was nearing. Cárdenas promised to compensate the oil companies four days after Daniels stalled, delayed, and watered down State Department protests in order to avoid a complete break with Mexico. The resulting *rapproachement* with Mexico became critical to U.S. strategic interests on the eve of World War II. His failure to learn Spanish limited Daniels. Despite Daniels's astuteness, professionals in the State Department actually negotiated the final settlement once the greed of the oil companies became apparent to all.

Cárdenas at a reception with U.S. Ambassador Josephus Daniels. *Courtesy of Centro de Estudios de Historia de México.*

At first, Roosevelt took a hard line against the expropriation. In retaliation for the oil nationalization, Roosevelt blocked much-needed loans to Mexico from the Export-Import Banks, as well as private New York banks, lowered the world price of silver, and established low import quotas on Mexican oil. Cárdenas responded as a statesman when Roosevelt threatened him to hurry up and agree on a compromise for compensation. Cárdenas interpreted the nationalization as an issue of national sovereignty upon which Mexico would not budge.

Roosevelt finally acquiesced to Cárdenas's expropriation for two reasons. First, Daniel's dispatches made clear that Mexican popular opinion so strongly favored expropriation that Roosevelt could do little to alter the situation without provoking a diplomatic break. That result clearly would be contrary to the broader goals the Good Neighbor policy had been designed to achieve. Secondly, in line with his empathy for Cárdenas and his cognizance of the nature of Cárdenas's overall program, Roosevelt was no doubt more willing to cooperate with an action that in a different context might have seemed entirely antagonistic to the capitalist system.

One must keep in mind that Cárdenas's action was selective and directed only at the oil industry. He emphasized that the oil companies were a special case, stressing that Mexico still actively sought foreign investment. His main condition was that foreign firms obey Mexican law for Cárdenas objected not to the mere presence of foreign firms but to their unpleasant behavior within Mexico.

Cárdenas correctly assumed that the British would be too concerned with the approach of war in Europe to resist expropriation. Britain actually suffered greater losses than the United States but decided to yield in order to protect other investments. Stunned by the nationalization decree, British oil companies begged the unsympathetic Foreign Office for aid. But the British leaders had become too worried about Hitler's annexation of Austria to deal with Mexican problems. The British, however, blundered by calling into question Mexico's ability to compensate the oil companies and published their notes to Cárdenas in Mexican newspapers. The Foreign Relations Secretariat angrily recalled its diplomat from London. In May 1938 Mexico proudly paid off British claims resulting from the 1910–1920 civil war, while a humiliated Britain recalled its ambassador from Mexico City. Worse, the United States refused to represent British interests in Mexico; instead the Danish government had to do it. Roosevelt did not get along with the pompous British Prime Minister Neville Chamberlain and his ill-fated appeasement policy with Hitler. Therefore, Mexico scored a great triumph because the British/Dutch oil companies now had no diplomatic representation.

The oil expropriation took place just as Saturino Cedillo finally decided to revolt. Plotting against Cárdenas since 1937 despite tight surveillance, Cedillo objected to socialist education and considered the ejido collectives a Soviet limitation. Like other conservatives, he opposed the government's support of strikes and, above all, fought Cárdenas's attempt to take over his peasant organization in San Luis Potosí. Ousted from the agricultural secretariat, he sought support from the oil companies, Germany, the United States, Britain, and other regional leaders. But only his peasant leagues backed the ill-fated revolt which Cedillo could have avoided when Cárdenas ordered him to the military command in Michoacán and traveled personally to San Luis Potosí to convince Cedillo to yield. Instead, he revolted, fled to the mountains when his support melted away before being hunted down and killed in January 1939. It was the last military revolt in twentieth-century Mexico.

Another repercussion was a spark of national unity. Cárdenas now faced external as well as internal opposition in mid-1938. Thus, the PRM founding convention took place only a week after Cárdenas issued the oil expropriation declaration. Women became particularly active in supporting the 1938 nationalization. On April 12, 1938, tens of thousands of women went to the national plaza, parks, and the Palace of Fine Arts to take off wedding rings, bacelets, earrings, and other valuables to place them into receptacles as part of a national campaign to pay off the oil companies.

Relations with Europe. Cárdenas also became very active in dealing with Europe. One of the most sensational events was the decision by Cárdenas to allow Soviet exile Leon Trotsky into Mexico. An outspoken critic of the Soviet Union's emerging totalitarian bureaucracy, Trotsky called for socialism run by workers, not by a new ruling class. As Josef Stalin's reign of terror accelerated, Trotsky's writings were banned, his life threatened, and he was finally expelled by Stalin. Cárdenas allowed Trotsky, his wife, and son to embark at Tampico on January 9, 1937, so that people would not accuse his government of being authoritarian or sympathetic to Stalin. By now the Mexican Communist Party (PCM) reached its pinnacle of membership. A sympathetic Cárdenas and powerful bastions in the railroad unions and newly formed cotton ejidos within the Laguna seemed to augur relative success for the PCM.

But Trotsky split the communists as well as the left in general. Diego Rivera was instrumental in gaining entry for Trotsky, whose family lived in the Rivera home, but differing political views severed that friendship. Meanwhile, the PCM followed the Moscow ideological line to the letter, which was embarrassing because the line shifted at least six times, often contradicting itself. Meanwhile, Cárdenas became irritated when the iconoclastic Trotsky began assailing state capitalism and claimed that the authoritarianism of Mexico's PCM prepared the country for fascism. It was not long before retaliation from the Kremlin was felt. On the night of May 23–24, 1940, twenty heavily-armed assailants attacked Trotsky's home. Soon the house became a fortress with gun turrets on the roof, explosion-proof iron shutters, and mostly North American bodyguards. The final straw for Mexican citizens was the assassination of Trotsky. On August 20, 1940, Ramón Mercader, a Spaniard working for Stalin, entered Trotsky's study posing as a sympathizer. As Trotsky read an article, Mercader stood behind Trotsky, slipped a pickax out of his coat and killed him. Cárdenas blamed the PCM for participating in the conspiracy and virtually fired all communists from his government. Internal purges weakened the PCM further when the leadership removed all those who had supported Trotsky or objected to his execution.

Cárdenas and Spain. Cárdenas, because of his leftist ideological affinity and fear of fascism, decided to support the Spanish Republic against the Francisco Franco revolt. Spain had enjoyed friendly relations with the Maximato, even before its epic civil war broke out in 1936. During the Maximato, Calles had established a Mexican coast guard with a loan from the fledging Second Republic to build gunboats and transport vessels. The *Jefe Máximo* wanted to end any U.S. illusions about invading Mexico by constructing port facilities for the Mexican navy along various Pacific locations. Calles assumed that the Spanish Republican ideals would dissipate conservative ideology among Spaniards in Mexico.

During the Spanish Civil War, Mexico played a unique and lonely role. Mexicans were generally apathetic to the conflict or opposed to the increasingly leftist Spanish Republic. Moderates felt that aid sent abroad during a fiscal economic depression was not fair to the suffering that most Mexicans endured. However, Cárdenas' foreign relations officials, army officers, union leaders, and key individuals such as Isidro Fabela, Adalberto Tejada, and Alfonso Reyes worked particularly hard on behalf of the Republic. Cárdenas appealed to the League of Nations and sought support throughout Latin America to aid the Republic. When Cárdenas shouted the traditional independence *grito* on September 15, 1936, in the main plaza of Mexico City, he surprised many by crying out "Long live the Spanish Republic!"

When the conflict started, Cárdenas rejected U.S., British, and French appeasement policies and committed Mexico to becoming the only country in the world to publicly aid the Republic. Mexico's support of the Republic demonstrated a certain amount of sentimental loyalty to the Hispanic motherland, which exasperated Western powers. Cárdenas sought to persuade the West that the Spanish Civil War was another episode of external aggression against a weakened country that would endanger world peace. Therefore, he permitted the Republic to recruit volunteers in Mexico, of whom 300 fought for the loyalists. Most served as officers but only 20 percent survived. Moreover, Cárdenas shipped 20,000 rifles and several million cartridges to Republican forces.

Cárdenas's incessant arms shipments frequently brought the world press down on Mexico. Perhaps most of Cárdenas's condemnation came from Portugal, which backed Franco. One item featured a hydrophobic-looking Spanish "red" murdering several noncombatants with a rifle marked "made in Mexico." Adverse radio and newspaper criticism caused Chile to break relations with Mexico before a popular front regime took over in 1938. Cárdenas also incurred the displeasure of the United States. He supplemented weapons shipments by purchasing airplanes and engines from the United States, declaring that the aircraft would be used for the Mexican air force or to transport mine workers. Eventually, 60 airplanes arrived in Spain, but U.S. newspapers produced a sensational story about Mexico shipping U.S. planes to the "Spanish communist forces." Roosevelt asked Cárdenas to stop and the State Department canceled future shipments. Cárdenas remorsefully announced that Mexico would not ship weaponry to Spain without U.S. permission.

But Mexico had also turned to European markets for weapons. In August 1936, Mexican agents in Paris contracted to purchase 50,000 bombs and 200,000 hand grenades from a Brussels company, which were billed to a third-party, allowing the company not to violate international agreements or compromise local governments. That same month, Mexican officials made the "third party" military purchases from Switzerland and Poland in such a way as not to compromise those governments.

In many respects, Cárdenas was retaliating against Franco who began to send secret agents and provacateurs to Mexico in order to weaken

Cárdenas. Also, Franco attempted to organize all Spanish descendants in Mexico to support him in Spain. In Mexico City, a Franco office organized pro-Franco social functions and the local Falange movement, the political arm of the Franco movement, began to attack Cárdenas openly. After the collapse of Cedillo, the Falange recruited thousands of Spaniards in Mexico to join its ranks. But the Hitler-Stalin nonaggression pact in August 1939 weakened the credibility of rightists.

Cárdenas became a humane statesman when he decided to bring at least 30,000 and perhaps as many as 50,000 Spanish refugees into Mexico. As the Republic began to lose the civil war, Mexico adopted a policy of protecting helpless refugees from the mass executions characteristic of Franco forces. About 800 Spaniards received protection in Mexican diplomatic compounds in Madrid, Valencia, and Barcelona. As the end neared in early 1939, Cárdenas began to accept desperate Republicans. Cárdenas considered the fears of many Mexicans who suspected that the Spanish would engage in radical political unrest. Cárdenas, therefore, made it clear that politics was off limits to refugees. Few Spanish farmers arrived, but Mexican officials attempted to locate refugees in the countryside. Many of these Spaniards were educated and even intellectuals; therefore, many drifted back into Mexican cities.

The Republic exiles provided many benefits. They were never a drag on the Mexican economy since they used Republican funds or paid their own way. Spanish physicians eradicated several diseases while other refugees filled important diplomatic posts. There is no doubt that Spanish exiles raised the country's intellectual standards. Many became excellent teachers and also revitalized the publishing industry. One of the greatest decisions of Cárdenas was the establishment of La Casa de España in July 1938, a cultural endeavor which provided Mexico with tremendous benefits. Although five of its first six professors were Spaniards, La Casa de España established the policy of inviting international scholars and providing a sophisticated learning environment that stimulated students. Shortly afterwards, it

was renamed El Colegio de México on October 9, 1940.

The biggest disappointment for the average Republican exiles was their isolation. Their social and political organizations served to isolate them from life in Mexico, partially because most expected to return to Iberia. When they did visit Spain later on, they were startled at how quickly the polemical issues of the Republic and the civil war had begun to fade. Moreover, the children of Spanish immigrants quickly became assimilated into Mexican society and lost interest in their parents' political ideals.

The last diplomatic initiative by Cárdenas was an attempt to rescue 100,000 Republicans in Nazi-occupied France. The Mexican ambassador in Paris reached a quick agreement so that Mexico would grant all Spanish refugees immigrant status and provide them with diplomatic protection as well as Mexican residence. The real problem was transporting them because Mexico had few ships and the Germans controlled the French merchant marine. Therefore, Mexico's minister in Berlin requested the use of the French merchant marine directly from Alfred von Ribbentrop, Hitler's foreign relations minister, with the Mexican concession that the Nazis could select who could leave. Von Ribbentrop considered the Spanish Republicans potential troublemakers who would create instability in Mexico that would tie up precious U.S. resources and preoccupy Roosevelt. In response to von Ribbentrop's query, Franco approved the idea. But the German army refused the Mexican request, so that the approximately 123,000 Spaniards became stranded and often suffered a dismal fate. Mexican diplomats did succeed in rescuing many Jews and antifascist Spaniards anyway, until the Germans closed their pipeline to Veracruz.

THE 1938 TRANSITION

The year 1938 became the turning point from Cardenista leftist mobilization to the moderation that dominated the rest of the twentieth century.

Cárdenas had enough integrity to realize that his early agenda of social justice could not create new wealth because redistribution worked against economic independence.

A primary cause for Cárdenas to scuttle his populist emphasis was a new economic crisis in 1938. This became a serious problem because Mexican exports, oil and agricultural production, ejido credit, private bank loans, foreign exchange holdings, and government revenue all declined until 1940. Part of the reason for this downturn was the devaluation of the peso, which occurred during the oil nationalization. Devaluation immediately raised prices by 20 percent, but it did not receive serious attention amid the tremendous excitement of nationalizing the oil fields. The overwhelming need to export natural resources from Mexico made it imperative for Cárdenas to somehow integrate the country into the world economy as international conflict began. Thus, moderation became imperative on the global scene as well as within Mexico.

One result was that centralized planning emerged as a key feature of the 1938 transition. Here Cárdenas assumed a position similar to the U.S. New Deal—the more nationalistic concept of a nation working together rather than fomenting class conflict. Cárdenas concluded that national planning would solve the problem of regional weaknesses, incompetent local administration, sloppy use of raw materials, and depressed incomes. Thus, the corporatist ideal of classifying labor groups as well as economic interests began to fade.

Cárdenas also sought consensus on the political scene. When his all-out populist campaign failed in 1938, Cárdenas began to consult conservative governors and various elites who still held positions of regional leadership as well as economic power. Gradually, a tendency toward compromise rather than confrontation took shape. Although the regime would never allow fascist, religious, and *sinarquista* groups to organize legally, Cárdenas did permit a new political party, the Partido de Acción Nacional (PAN) to establish itself in 1939. With the PAN under the leadership of the conservative Gómez Marín, who had helped fashion the economic and financial program of the Calles era, Cárdenas had little to fear since Morín frequently praised the patriotism of Cárdenas. The PAN, however, lambasted agrarian reform and the overly politicized labor organizations. To Marín, the Cárdenas regime had been confused and disorganized. Therefore, the PAN appealed to Catholics, business people, and traditional values.

As Cárdenas began to understand that economic growth had to take place before any additional serious redistribution of wealth could take place, he began to discourage strikes and land reform. In May 1938, for example, Cárdenas established an Office of Small Property Holders to protect peasant landowners from squatters and *agrarista* diehards. Certificates of exemption from land seizures also became available to landowners. Like Carranza, Obregón, and Calles, Cárdenas also realized that land reform was a form of social justice that did not produce economic dividends. Unlike the earlier period of his government, Cárdenas warned workers not to protest or make excessive demands. In March 1939, Cárdenas specifically demanded that mine workers not go on strike. When railroad workers asked for a raise in 1940, Cárdenas accused them of lacking discipline as well as undermining national goals. By consolidating the state's control over rural and urban labor, Cárdenas also handed his successors a valuable tool for the maintenance of a system of glaring social and economic inequality.

A decisive achievement of Cardenismo was the great impetus it gave to the development of Mexican businesses. Administrators within his government began to urge Cárdenas to industrialize three months after World War II began in Europe with the German invasion of Poland on September 1, 1939. The rest of Latin America was taking advantage of the war to industrialize, and Cárdenas agreed that Mexico should not miss this opportunity. Massive investments in infrastructure and public works stimulated industrialization while juicy public contracts provided safe and easy profits for incipient Mexican entrepreneurs. When Cárdenas established the Comisión Federal de Electricidad in 1935, he envisioned state control of Mexico's electric power system, much of it owned by foreigners. Afterwards, the Comisión began to harness Mexico's natural resources to achieve electrical independence while meeting the country's increasing energy demands. With the establishment of Nacional Financiera in 1935, Monterrey and Guadalajara became more industrialized than ever. Nacional Financiera provided low-cost loans for industrialists by means of bond sales. Perhaps even more important was the sale of cheap fuel from PEMEX, the new national oil organization. A cadre of sympathetic public officials, often people of modest origins, instituted a series of government measures in 1938 to assist businesses throughout Mexico. Cárdenas and many others began to view small and medium producers as the vanguard of a nationalistic and reformed capitalism.

Regional elites in Monterrey pushed hard for a new emphasis on industrialization. Their fierce opposition to unionization and labor reforms, as well as open backing for political opponents of Cárdenas, finally forced the regime to give in. Represented by the conservative Juan Andrew Almazán, the local military zone commander, the *Grupo Monterrey* openly demanded more conservative policies. Because of their cohesive, stubborn leadership, Cárdenas decided that Monterrey's support was vital for the new transition. By 1938, the regime agreed to the Monterrey interpretation of the future and acted upon populism only as a political expedient. The nation itself was worn out from appeals to social justice which helped enable the *Grupo Monterrey* to play a major role in moving the national government toward a more traditional continuity in terms of religion and regional economic development along Porfirian lines. In 1939, the *Grupo Monterrey* took credit for moving the government to emphasize industrial growth rather than social reforms. In response, Cárdenas toured northern Mexico in 1939 and attacked communism while praising northwestern businesses.

During the latter half of the 1930s, Mexican manufacturers enjoyed growth and self-confidence. Although entrepreneurs distrusted the Sonoran presidents, they reacquired trust with the late Cárdenas regime so that investment increased during the final period of the Cárdenas regime. Certainly industrialists were pleased by the shake-up of the agrarian economy. And even when they opposed tighter federal controls, businesses such as radio station owners found ways to flourish. The Azcarraga family, for example, began to consolidate its influence over the media during this period. Encouraged by new tariff protection, Mexican businesses grew from 6,909 in 1935 to 13,510 by 1940.

The 1938 transition also involved a national emphasis on attracting foreign visitors. With the creation of the Tourism Secretariat in 1936, the Cárdenas regime sought to duplicate the success of governor Miguel Alemán in Veracruz. U.S. travelers could no longer afford the expense or danger of traveling in Europe and Asia, therefore, the new tourist officials made solid overtures for international visitors to come and enjoy Mexico. State and even local governments joined in the tourist campaign, which would pay excellent dividends in the future.

A badly needed corrective to past policies was the stabilization of education. With a compromise worked out between UNAM faculty and the Education Secretariat for agreed-upon goals, the middle class in urban areas slowly began to restrain some of their criticism of the Cardenismo. By 1938, the middle class was clearly the favored group in educational policy since most of the new schools became part of city rather than rural landscapes. Perhaps most importantly, references to socialist education faded away and teachers were told to concentrate on education rather than political mobilization.

Cárdenas also began a policy of reconciliation with past political enemies. Many of the Porfirian or other exiled dissidents living abroad were finally allowed to return to Mexico and live out the remainder of their lives. Had Francisco León de la Barra lived another few months, the Cárdenas regime would probably have included his name among those officially forgiven and allowed to return.

Of course, the biggest accommodation of all took place with the United States. Despite initial ill-will over the oil nationalization, the two sides agreed to gentlemanly negotiations over compensation. Cárdenas did not have to be reminded that U.S. mining investments provided most of Mexican tax income. Moreover, Suárez had obtained a desperately needed loan from the U.S. Treasury Department. Cárdenas appreciated Roosevelt's rejection of a joint Anglo-U.S. coalition against Mexico during the oil crisis, and the United States approved Mexico's aggressive anti-British policy under Cárdenas. Although Mexico emerged less politically dependent upon the United States after 1938, the nationalization of oil did usher in a technological dependence because Mexico lacked the means to fully take advantage of its newly reacquired oil. Also, the loss of the European oil market in 1940 pushed Mexico into closer United States relations. For the remainder of the century, the United States would not object to Mexican nationalism or its populistic agenda.

The beginning of World War II also tightened relations between Cárdenas and Roosevelt. Both presidents had spoken out earlier against the rise of fascism in Europe. Privately, Roosevelt was an advanced critic of the isolationist mood in the United States, but highly placed Mexicans knew that he could not become public in his condemnation of appeasement for fear of losing the 1940 election. This ideological affinity became much warmer during the 1938 transition. For that reason, the FBI began training Cárdenas's secret service in surveillance techniques. Moreover, the Mexican military, now an official sector of the PRM, began to make it clear that they wanted Mexico to actively participate in the war on the side of the Allies.

The final element in the 1938 transition toward moderation involved the selection of Manuel Avila Camacho as the next president. One factor that moved Cárdenas to favor Camacho was the victory of Franco in Spain by April 1939. Cárde-

nas began to argue that Camacho, then the defense secretary, needed to maintain control over the army in view of the growing strength of international fascism. Moreover, the newly powerful industrial as well as traditional landowning groups made it clear that they could work out some sort of accommodation with Camacho but that another leftist president was out of the question. Now that a much more dynamic, interactive regional relationship had been established with the president's office, Cárdenas could not really have anyone other than a moderate as the next president. Moreover, his attempts to convert labor and agrarian supporters in various regions had not always worked out because peasants and workers were just as likely to rally around local leaders and their patronage machines.

The religious issue also inclined Cárdenas toward moderation. In response to Cárdenas's moderating stance on anticlericalism, a tempered wing of the Church gained ascendancy by the end of the 1930s and reconciled themselves to compromises with Cárdenas. And Cárdenas appreciated clerical backing of the oil expropriation. Also, many urban Catholics were uncomfortable with the zealous rural base of the Sinarquistas and reflected a somewhat more accommodating stance as represented by the PAN.

Cárdenas encountered the deadliest challenge to the populist hegemony since 1923. He wanted to implement a succession that would preserve national unity and maintain economic growth. In addition, Cárdenas sought to solidify his social justice measures as well as the corporatist framework that he had instituted.

Of those who sought national leadership, only two mattered. Francisco Múgica seemed an obvious candidate in view of his long career as a populist leader. Moreover, he had been a close associate of Cárdenas since their youth. But Múgica remained a staunch anticlerical, and the Trotsky fiasco had weakened his credibility. Cárdenas was now striving to become a true nationalist toward the end of his term while Múgica continued to believe in class interests. Camacho, on the other hand, had few enemies. National leaders and officials within the administration clearly favored him over Múgica. And the military naturally felt more comfortable with one of their peers in charge. Camacho had a gentlemanly demeanor with no ideological heat. Anxious to avoid a split within the PRM and aware that the United States would not prefer Múgica, Cárdenas concluded that Camacho would preserve national unity.

Cárdenas decided to impose Camacho upon Mexico when he saw that too much opposition existed. Cárdenas even ignored PRM rules that would have allowed the labor and peasant sectors leading roles in selecting the PRM candidate to be their candidate. Party rules required the candidate to be nominated in an open convention. Instead, Cárdenas manipulated the CNC to back Camacho since Cárdenas considered the campesinos his personal power base. Cárdenas also persuaded Toledano to publicly support Camacho in return for a promise that Cárdenas would be personally responsible for Camacho's program. Thus, Cárdenas worked behind the scenes within the administration and must bear a good deal of responsibility for the failure of the PRM to dominate within democratic norms, thus robbing it of true legitimacy.

Almazán emerged as the most formidable challenger to the Camacho imposition. He enjoyed a good working relationship with Calles in crushing the Escobar revolt and became wealthy by building highways throughout Mexico. As far back as 1928, there had been speculation that Almazán would be a fine president based on his business ability and military past. Well dressed, smiling, energetic, and a hit with women, Almazán even enjoyed a favorable press in New York by 1938. In response to various promises from Cárdenas that he would respect the results of the 1940 presidential election, Almazán finally consented to becoming a presidential candidate in November 1938. Governors in Oaxaca and Nuevo León openly called for Almazán's election, as did bishops who approved of his strong support of the Church. As a candidate, Almazán normally closed his speeches with the ringing "Long Live the Virgin of Guadalupe!" Particularly vital to Almazán

was a Comité Revolucionario de Reconstrucción Nacional presided over by various artists, military officers, veterans, journalists, and professionals who insisted that the financial crisis of 1937 could only be surmounted by Almazán instead of the Cárdenas approach.

In addition, independent groups who could not affiliate with or tolerate the PRM policies threw their support to Almazán. Notable among them was the Partido Nacional Feminista, which failed to persuade the Cardenista legislature to give them the right to vote. University students also rallied to Almazán in another burst of idealism comparable to the Vasconcelos campaign. Moreover, large numbers of soldiers volunteered their services to Almazán even though the regime trotted out constitutional provisions making military obligations incompatible with political activity. Finally, Almazán founded his own party, the Partido Revolucionario de Unificación General in January 1940. Although head of a weak organization, Almazán himself was a charismatic speaker who evoked a mass movement with thundering rallies unseen since the days of Madero. Workers and peasants became attracted to Almazán's promise to eliminate waste, corruption, and foreign values. At a fiery meeting in Mexico City on June 30, 1940, Almazán even obtained the support of Sinarquistas, Gold Shirts, and the PAN. As mass popular support continued to grow, Cárdenas responded with a repressive manipulation of the election.

Convinced that Almazán's certain victory would disrupt the state, tarnish his reforms, and allow conservatives to undo all that he had toiled for, Cárdenas refused to allow fair elections. The turnout was enormous as both groups fought for control of the voting booths. Thirty people died amid violence in the capital. When the votes were announced, the PRM claimed that Camacho had beaten Almazán by 53,000 to 13,000 votes in the Almazán stronghold of Monterrey. Although the government conceded that Almazán had indeed carried Mexico City, the final totals for the entire nation were an unbelievable 2.26 million votes for Camacho to a mere 129,000 for Almazán.

Like Madero in 1910, Almazán retired to Alabama in the United States in August 1940; he considered rebellion but finally gave in and conceded defeat in November. By providing clean drinking water, vaccinations, and rural medicine, Cárdenas had performed many noble deeds for those in need. But the crass violation of a popular mandate for his opponent was shameful.

SUGGESTED READING

Ashby, Joe C. *Organized Labor and the Mexican Revolution Under Lázaro Cárdenas.* Chapel Hill: University of North Carolina Press, 1967.

Bantjes, Adrian. *As if Jesus Walked on Earth: Cardenismo, Sonora, and the Mexican Revolution.* Wilmington, DE: Scholarly Resources, 1998.

Becker, Marjorie. *Setting the Virgin on Fire: Lázaro Cárdenas, Michoacán Campesinos, and the Redemption of the Mexican Revolution.* Berkeley: University of California Press, 1995.

Benjamin, Thomas. *A. Rich Land, A Poor People: Politics and Society in Modern Chiapas.* Albuquerque: University of New Mexico Press, 1989.

Brown, Jonathan C., and Alan Knight, eds. *The Mexican Petroleum Industry in the Twentieth Century.* Austin: University of Texas Press, 1993.

Brown, Lyle C. "Cárdenas: Creating a Campesino Power Base for Presidential Policy." In George C. Wolfskill and Douglas W. Richmond, *Essays on the Mexican Revolution: Revisionist Views of the Leaders.* Austin: University of Texas Press, 1979, pp. 101–136.

Córdova, Arnaldo. *La política de masas del cardenismo.* Mexico City: ERA, 1974.

Cronon, E. David. *Josephus Daniels in Mexico.* Madison: University of Wisconsin Press, 1960.

Fagen, Patricia. *Exiles and Citizens: Spanish Republicans in Mexico.* Austin: University of Texas Press, 1973.

Gladhill, John. *Casi Nada: A Study of Agrarian Reform in the Homeland of Cardenismo.* Albany: State University of New York, 1991.

González, Luis. *Los artífices del cardenismo.* Mexico City: El Colegio de México, 1979.

———. *Los dias del presidente Cárdenas.* Mexico City: El Colegio de México, 1981.

Haber, Stephen. *Industry and Development: The Industrialization of Mexico, 1880–1940.* Stanford, CA: Stanford University Press, 1989.

Hamilton, Nora. *The Limits of State Autonomy: Post-Revolutionary Mexico.* Princeton, NJ: Princeton University Press, 1982.

Hernández, Alicia. *La mecánica cardenista.* Mexico City: El Colegio de México, 1979.

Knight, Alan. "The Rise and Fall of Cardenismo." In Leslie Bethell, ed., *Mexico Since Independence.* New York: Cambridge University Press, 1991, pp. 241–320.

———. "Popular Culture and the Revolutionary State in Mexico, 1910–1940." *Hispanic American Historical Review* 74:3 (August 1994), 393–444.

Lerner, Victoria. *La educación socialista.* Mexico City: El Colegio de México, 1982.

Macias, Anna. *Against All Odds: The Feminist Movement in Mexico to 1940.* Westport, CT: Greenwood Press, 1982.

Medin, Tzvi. *Idelogica y praxis política de Lázaro Cárdenas.* Mexico City: Siglo Vientiuno, 1971.

Meyer, Lorenzo. *Mexico and the United States in the Oil Controversy, 1917–1942.* Austin: University of Texas Press, 1977.

Moguel Flores, Josefina. "La ayuda mutua: Calles y Almazán." *Haciendo Historia* 1:1 (January 1999), 26–31.

———. "Porque surge candidato electoral el general de division Juan Andrew Almazán?" *Haciendo Historia* 1:3 (May-June 1999), 32–37.

Powell, T. G. *Mexico and the Spanish Civil War.* Albuquerque: University of New Mexico Press, 1981.

Saragoza, Alex M. *The Monterrey Elite and the Mexican State, 1880–1940.* Austin: University of Texas Press, 1988.

Schuler, Friedrich E. *Mexico between Hitler and Roosevelt: Mexican Foreign Relations in the Age of Lázaro Cárdenas.* Albuquerque: University of New Mexico Press, 1998.

Serrano Alvarez, Pablo. *La batalla del espíritu: El movimiento sinarquista en el bajío 1932–1951.* Mexico City: Consejo Nacional Para la Cultura y Las Artes, 1992.

Sherman, John. *The Mexican Right: The End of Revolutionary Reform, 1929–1940.* New York: Praeger, 1997.

Townsend, William C. *Lázaro Cárdenas: Mexican Democrat.* Ann Arbor, MI: George Wahr, 1952.

Vaughn, Mary K. *Cultural Politics in Revolution: Teachers, Peasants, and Schools in Mexico, 1930–1940.* Tucson: University of Arizona Press, 1997.

15

Political Stability and Industrialization, 1940–1970

Populism evolved into a more durable state in which the ruling elite maintained a strong base of general support while simultaneously imposing significant constraints on mass participation. Mexican leaders outmaneuvered their U.S. and European counterparts to increase political and economic sovereignty by taking advantage of opportunities which became available during the Second World War. As during the Porfiriato, the economic leaders and political elite fashioned a policy of confidence and stability.

WORLD WAR II

Camacho Takes Command. The Mexican citizenry knew little about Avila Camacho before the 1940 presidential election. In fact, Camacho became nicknamed "the unknown soldier." His reputation in the army was that of a compromiser rather than a forceful leader. On the day that Congress declared him president in September 1940, Camacho declared to a magazine writer that he was a *creyente* (believer in God). This candid response impressed the public and presaged changes to come. The remark meant that anticlericalism would not be part of his administration, but more generally, it indicated that overall policy was about to change fundamentally.

Although the candidate for the presidency surprised the Mexican people by confessing his faith so openly, PRM leaders were not surprised. The politicians who gave Camacho the nomination knew that he was more conservative than Cárdenas. In his inaugural address, Camacho suggested that the civil war was over, that its populistic goals had been completed, and that Mexico was moving from a revolutionary period into an evolutionary era. Four days later, the Mexican ambassador to the United States received assurances that Roosevelt recognized the 1940 presidential elections. Shortly afterwards, Camacho stated that Mexico would fight Germany if it attacked the United States.

Almazán attempted to have fascist groups support a revolt which would have placed him in the president's office. Almazán, with the backing of Calles, asked the Spanish Falange to organize weapons purchases in the United States for his revolt. Their hopes centered on a northern insurrection. Mexican troops searched for arms in Chihuahua throughout September 1940. Military commanders offered land or jobs to Almazanistas if they would surrender. Meanwhile, Franco agreed to support Almazán's bid in October but wanted the Germans to move the necessary munitions through Japan across the Pacific. But Hitler considered Almazán too pro-U.S. and hoped to do

295

business with Camacho. Above all, the Third Reich did not want to provoke a U.S. declaration of war once it became clear in the fall that Britain would not capitulate. This was the final blow to Almazán's hopes since Franco was not in a position to provide substantial aid given the destruction caused by the Spanish Civil War. Therefore, Almazán returned to Mexico City in November and conceded defeat.

Camacho also inherited a significant Axis presence in Mexico that had become public during the Cárdenas era. From 1934 to 1936, Mexico had sold large quantities of rice and cotton to Germany in exchange for machinery and chemical products. The Nazis attempted to obtain secret drilling rights to oil reserves on the Coahuilan border. Nothing came from this attempt, but eventually 48 percent of all Mexican oil exports went to the Third Reich from 1938 to December 1941. In 1936, a German submarine practiced firing torpedoes in a Mexican bay. Two years later, ME-109 fighter planes carried out demonstrations in Mexico City. Meanwhile, German pilots flew over Mexican territory and mapped the coastline. Hitler's agents used microscopic dots to send secret messages to Berlin. Mexican security was not very tight either. A German spy had an affair with the sister of a Mexican diplomat. Even before World War II started, Mexico allowed the export of strategic raw materials such as mercury, lead, zinc, copper, graphite, and wood to Germany, Italy, and Japan.

The turning point came in 1938 when an independent oil merchant, William Davis of New York, began to buy Mexican oil for sale to Axis powers. The British blockade of 1939 destroyed European markets because Mexico had no shipping fleet, whereas Davis could provide his own tankers as well as a refinery. Although Cárdenas did not want to sell to the Axis and made his reservations clear to Roosevelt, he nonetheless resented the oil company boycott of Mexican petroleum. Most of Davis's oil sales went to Germany, but he also sold at least two million barrels to Japan and supplied enough fuel to Mussolini to keep the Italian navy afloat for six months in

1939. More importantly, the Davis deals broke the oil company blockade against Mexico.

Camacho observed the thorny disputes which prevented settling the compensation issue with the oil companies. It was not easy to do. When the State Department reprimanded Mexico for supplying oil to the Axis, Cárdenas pointed out quickly that the U.S. companies had sharply increased oil sales to the three Axis nations during the same period. Roosevelt had stood firmly against those in the State Department who supported the oil company boycott of Mexican -produced oil and who otherwise sought to punish Mexico in hopes of overturning the nationalization. In their desire to retain ownership and avoid a compensation settlement, the oil companies persuaded manufacturers not to use Mexican oil or sell drilling equipment to PEMEX. Through their gas stations, oil companies tried to discourage tourism to Mexico and made false claims that Mexican gas was inferior. Public relations executives sent malicious material to be printed in newspapers about Mexico. However, another breakthrough occurred in 1940 when one company decided to accept a Mexican offer of several million barrels of oil as compensation. At that point, Vice-President Henry Wallace attended the Camacho inauguration ceremony which paid off handsomely because the Mexican congress applauded Wallace and Daniels for several minutes.

About that time, a Mexican suggestion for an overall settlement of all problems between the United States and Mexico enabled Camacho to preside over a successful resolution of the oil company dispute. The State Department had now become impatient with the oil companies, which still felt they should be compensated for the value of all their lost properties. But the State Department had also tended to support the oil companies' claim that they deserved $400 million in compensation, an absurdly high figure. Therefore, Roosevelt had the Interior Department and the Treasury Department check the oil company figures. It came as quite a shock to the State Department that their two sister secretariats agreed with the Mexican conclusions, namely that minus the oil, oil company property in Mexico was worth about $13 million. Treasury and Interior experts were particularly critical of the miles of corroded pipelines and useless equipment claimed as assets even though many of these items were 25 years old.

As the German panzers began tearing their way through Russia in June 1941, Mexico and the United States began to realize the strategic importance of cooperation. Camacho let it be known that he was willing to entertain the possibility of joint ventures between U.S. firms and PEMEX, an idea that Roosevelt accepted. PEMEX no doubt would have benefited from an influx of investment capital, as long as Mexican sovereignty on its operations would remain unquestioned. Camacho also began restricting Mexican imports to the Western Hemisphere. Nevertheless, the oil companies continued to balk until Roosevelt forced Secretary of State Cordell Hull to sign agreements with Mexico just as Daniels retired from his post.

The comprehensive plan agreed to by both sides called for Mexico to pay $40 million over the next 14 years for all land seized from U.S. citizens. The United States agreed to build the Pan American Highway through Mexico and keep up with purchases of Mexican silver. Each government agreed to appoint experts to determine the amount owed the oil companies. Mexico gave a down payment of $9 million. Eventually, both experts agreed on a value of $23 million for oil company properties and reiterated what Daniels and Roosevelt had conceded from the start: that oil companies could expect to recover their investments only—not future profits in the ground. The date of this agreement is most compelling— November 18, 1941—only 18 days before the Japanese assault on Pearl Harbor.

The U. S–Mexican Alliance. During World War II, Camacho realized that Hitler had begun to direct his attention toward Mexico in an effort to weaken it as well as the United States. Because of Mexico's proximity to the United States, Germany had targeted Mexico for espionage. Nazi

agents entered to learn what they could about weapons development, ship movements, military recruitment, and political events in the United States. Hitler sought to shape resident Germans in Mexico into a Nazi mold. Therefore, German agents encouraged local Germans to join the Nazi party or the Hitler Youth. Agents succeeded with local German merchants more than others, partially because Hitler's interest in Mexico was basically economic. In 1939, Germany proposed the construction of an airplane factory that would be large enough for Mexico to sell aircraft throughout Latin America. Cárdenas refused the offer with the result that Germany made Mexico the center for sabotage against the United States, as well as Canada. The Germans envisioned using the Irish Republican Army against Canada and the United States and set up ammunition depots along the U.S.–Mexican border. Von Ribbentrop even proposed blowing up Mexican oil installations to weaken Allied petroleum supplies. Hitler by now, however, had become too preoccupied with his extermination plans for occupied Europe to be interested in Mexican opportunities.

Eager to strengthen itself with the aid of an anxious United States, the Mexican military cooperated with the United States on a level unseen since the days of French intervention under Maximilian. News of the German aircraft offer encouraged the United States to offer warplanes to Mexico. Hitler's invasion of Poland motivated Roosevelt to lift the arms embargo against Mexico and offer credit to enable Mexico to purchase surplus U.S. weapons. But when Roosevelt backed off this offer, Cárdenas responded by declaring Mexican neutrality. The War Department, fearing that Mexico would be uncooperative, considered the possibility of seizing Mexican ports with or without Mexican consent—identical to the situation when the United States was unsure if Brazil would allow bases to patrol the South Atlantic and supply North Africa. But the fall of France to Hitler's army in only five weeks shocked both the United States and Mexico into the realization that the war had become very critical by May 1940.

Thus, the first wartime talks between Mexican and U.S. military officials took place in June 1940. The North Americans pressed Mexico for bases and an alliance against a feared Axis invasion. Mexico responded by pointing out that excessively strong commitments to Mexico's old anatagonist would weaken the Camacho campaign. Anyway, Cárdenas favored a Latin American alliance to protect Mexico from U.S. aggression. Mexican representatives also pointed out that its military lacked training and modern weapons. Therefore, they requested immediate U.S. aid. Disturbed that Cárdenas opposed bilateral U.S.–Mexican military cooperation, Roosevelt requested that Henry Wallace discuss with Avila Camacho the possibility of creating a joint U.S.–Mexican defense committee during the December 1940 inauguration. Of course, Camacho could do little in the face of Cárdenas's criticism of closer U.S. relations, but the Japanese attack upon Pearl Harbor changed that.

Almost immediately after the December 7, 1941 disaster in Hawaii, Camacho became more emphatically aligned with Roosevelt. He broke off all diplomatic and consular relations with the Axis powers and granted permission for naval ships of any American country to drop anchor in Mexican ports, as long as they provided prior notice. Although these decisions had Cárdenas-style overtones of hemispheric solidarity, Camacho feared nationalists would overthrow him if he came under fire for compromising national sovereignty. Therefore, Camacho appointed Cárdenas commander of the Pacific military region so that critics could not complain that U.S. troops would occupy Mexican soil. Nevertheless, the United States gained permission from Mexico to increase flying rights over Mexico. Moreover, Mexico extended special port rights for the U.S. Navy and permitted the United States to purchase oil for naval use against German U- boats and the Japanese fleet. On New Year's Day 1942, Camacho declared that Mexico's war would be waged in the factories and fields on behalf of the Allies. He made rubber grown in Mexico, as well as other resources, available to the United States. Also in

January 1942, Mexico was most eloquent in its endeavor to win backing for of a U.S.-supported recommendation that all Latin American governments sever relations with the Axis. In many respects, unity within the Americas depended upon Mexico more than any other Latin American nation during the depressing period of early 1942. Castillo Najera, the Mexican ambassador to the United States, became a profound link in building up Pan American relations during the war.

Military cooperation accelerated in 1942. The U.S.–Mexico Military Commission became the forum for military planning as well as assistance. Lend Lease arrangements were put in place so that considerable amounts of military hardware flowed into Mexico by March 1942. During World War II, Mexico obtained over 100 ships of various kinds, including 2 small aircraft carriers. Destroyer escorts were generally the biggest items sent to Mexico, but civilian cargo ships performed vital tasks. Mexico also received enough Sherman tanks and other armored vehicles to outfit three mechanized units. Aircraft included P-35 planes that the United States no longer wanted. P-41 and P-43 fighter aircraft, predecessors of the better known P-47, also arrived along with transport planes. Eventually, Mexico obtained about 76 P-47s for its growing air force. To calm the fears of those who resented the closer U.S. ties that these weapons of war brought, Camacho named Cárdenas defense minister in 1942. Cárdenas had earlier proven to be a tough bargainer in terms of U.S. desires for radar stations, landing rights, and naval patrols. Therefore, Cárdenas became somewhat neutralized in Mexico City where the wartime alliance could not be as seriously threatened.

All-out war finally arrived in the spring of 1942. Shortly before midnight on May 13, 1942, the 6,132-ton Mexican oil tanker *Portrero del Llano* neared the Florida coast with its cargo of 37,358 barrels of crude oil for the U.S. war effort. But German U-boat 564 sank the ship, killing 14 of its 35 sailors. Mexico protested bitterly, claiming that it was a neutral country, and the ship had its lights illuminated with the Mexican flag spotlighted. On May 21, slightly more than a week after this attack, another of Hitler's submarines torpedoed the Mexican oil tanker *Faja de Oro*, despite its blazing lights and Mexican flag prominently in view. The empty ship exploded immediately because fumes trapped in the storage tanks had become highly combustible. Twenty-eight crewmen died while six more suffered serious wounds.

The sinking of the two tankers, previously confiscated from Italy for Mussolini's nonpayment of debts to PEMEX, provoked an angry response from many Mexicans as well as a strong protest from the Camacho regime. Hitler did not respond to the Mexican objection because of Camacho's support for the Allies. The day after the assault on the second tanker, angry Mexican students hurled rocks through the windows of the German Club and screamed that the Nazis must leave. Nevertheless, the vast majority of Mexicans had little interest in seeing Mexico enter the war against the Axis powers. Polls taken after the sinking of the *Portrero de Llano* indicated that most respondents wanted to avoid participation in World War II.

Camacho now believed that Mexico was compelled to join the Allies in their battle against the Axis powers. Because of the bitter public sentiment against the United States, Mexico did not officially declare war against the Axis powers but announced on May 28 that a state of war existed, somewhat like the response to the United States in 1846. Moreover, the Camacho government made their declaration retroactive to May 22. By this move, Camacho suggested that Mexico was in a defensive struggle whose hesitant population was now forced to oppose an aggressor. In June, Mexico signed the United Nations Pact to officially join the Allies. This was the first time Mexico had become involved in a war beyond the hemisphere. As patriotic support slowly began to rise, despite the initial shock of such a monumental event, the Mexican military paraded its new Lend Lease equipment on September 16, 1942. Six former presidents joined the ceremony as part of a display of national unity. It was difficult to

accept the reality that Mexico had now become an ally of the United States. Shortly after U.S. troops landed in North Africa, the pro-Nazi Vichy regime of France broke ties with the United States. Only then did Mexico break with the Vichy collaborators, even though Jacques Soustelle and 6,000 other French citizens resident in Mexico had urged Mexico to end relations with the shameful Pétain government since 1941. De Gaulle's Free French movement had been much more popular in Mexico than with U.S. officials, who sought to discredit him.

Relations between Mexico and the United States continued to warm up. During Christmas of 1942, Mexican officials honored Dallas, Texas Mayor Woodall Rodgers, animator Walt Disney, and actress Ann Sheridan at a fiesta in Mexico

A World War II poster encouraged Mexican-Americans to join the war effort. *The Dallas Morning News.*

City. Roosevelt himself made a secret trip to Monterrey to meet with Camacho on April 20, 1943. There Roosevelt promised that the ideals of the Good Neighbor policy would be upheld in the future. Not by coincidence, the Altos Hornos Steel Mill received military orders to make liberty ship plates for the U.S. Maritime Commission. By now the tide had turned against the Axis once the Japanese had been crushed at Guadalcanal in December 1942, and the German disaster at Stalingrad had climaxed with a shocking surrender in January 1943. Now Camacho wanted to be part of the postwar peace settlement which could favor Mexico. Therefore, a Mexican physicist, José Rafael Bejarano, helped the U.S. Manhattan Project work on the atomic bomb. A reciprocal agreement that made citizens of one country who were living in the other nation eligible for the draft in their country of residence was also unprecedented. Thus, U.S. citizens living in Mexico could be drafted by Mexico and vice versa. Camacho even allowed the United States to set up recruiting stations in Mexico. It is difficult to estimate how many Mexican nationals served with the U.S. military during World War II, because many were categorized among the 300,000 Mexican Americans who were in U.S. military units. But at least 14,000 Mexicans found themselves in combat, often motivated by wartime U.S. legislation that promised U.S. citizenship to Mexicans who enlisted.

Enboldened by the excellent reputation of Mexican soldiers and encouraged by his own military, Camacho approved of Mexican aviators serving with the Army Air Corps in the Pacific. Unofficially, Camacho offered Mexican troops to join the U.S. war effort. In the spring of 1944, Roosevelt responded with an offer for U.S. aviators to fight with the Mexican Air Force. Mexico established the Fuerza Aérea Expedicionaria Mexicana, which later became known as Squadron 201.

In July 1944, the first of 300 Mexican aviators came to the United States to train in P-40 and P-47 fighter planes. Initially stationed at Foster Field in Victoria, Texas, they also trained at Pocatello Air Base in Idaho and Majors Field in Greenville, Texas. Accidents took the lives of two pilots in Texas. On March 18, 1945, they shipped out of Majors Field for the Philippine Islands, arriving on the island of Luzon on April 30. From there, Squadron 201 flew 59 combat missions against Japanese positions under U.S. as well as Mexican flags and insignia. Five Mexican pilots died in the Philippines. Japanese anti-aircraft fire killed one, another died in a crash, and three others ran out of fuel, crashed, and perished at sea after becoming lost in bad weather. The war enabled Squadron 201 also to assault Japanese targets on the Chinese Island of Formosa before Japanese surrender ceremonies took place on September 2, 1945.

Squadron 201 returned to Mexico City on November 18, 1945. Camacho and a proud nation gave them a tumultuous welcome. Thirteen days later, Camacho terminated and mustered out the Fuerza Aérea Expedicionaira Mexicana. Other than Brazil, no other Latin American country had stood with the Allies and fought the Axis threat to humanity. Members of Squadron 201 are the only Mexican veterans of foreign wars. Although large numbers of Mexican citizens fought with the U.S. military as well as French and British armies, those soldiers were U.S., French, and British veterans. Members of Squadron 201 became celebrities and movies exploited their feats. Colonel Carlos Garduño Nuñez was a Squadron 201 veteran who developed the Aviation Department of the Mexican government after the war. From 1958 to 1964, he was the personal pilot for President Adolfo López Mateos.

Life on the Home Front. During the war years, Camacho not only accelerated improved U.S. relations but also sought to establish domestic order. From 1940 and up to 1982, the presidency became increasingly powerful in its relation to regional governments, political organization, the military, and the official party.

Once the war in Europe began, Mexican authorities feared that Axis sabotage, particularly on the west coast as well as the U.S. border, could be a serious problem. When Miguel Alemán assumed control of the Gobernación (Interior) Secretariat, serious investigations of people with Axis backgrounds began. He worked with FBI and other U.S. intelligence agents to identify covert Axis activities in Mexico. By 1941, Gobernación acted more forcefully as a result of information compiled by U.S. operatives, often expelling Germans involved in propaganda activities considered a violation of Mexican sovereignty. On August 8, 1941, Mexico ordered all German consultates closed because of threats to Mexican neutrality. After Pearl Harbor, Gobernación placed 24-hour surveillance upon Axis legation buildings and advised Axis officials that they could not leave Mexico City without permission from the Foreign Relations Secretariat.

Mexican and U.S. officials also worried about the potential of Japanese espionage in Baja, California. Even before Mexico entered the war, the Mexican navy forced a Japanese fishing boat to land at Acapulco for supposedly making depth soundings near various ports. Moreover, Gobernación became alarmed when the Japanese government encouraged the Federation of Japanese Associations to organize more efficiently and maintain contact with Japanese diplomatic personnel in Mexico. By mid-1941, Gobernación agents began watching Japanese carefully, if only because few of them were naturalized Mexicans.

In response to the fear of Axis espionage, many Mexicans urged their government to restrict individuals of German, Japanese, and Italian descent. The fear of sabotage against oil installations or an invasion of the Pacific coast motivated many ordinary citizens to urge that highly restrictive measures be carried out. The governor of Veracruz even rounded up all Axis residents and ultimately sent them to Mexico City. In response, Mexican officials began to force people of Axis descent to move away from the U.S. border and the coastal areas by mid-1942. As a further precaution to limit Axis activity in Mexico, authorities suspended letters of naturalization for citizens of Germany, Japan, and Italy. In addition, officials revoked the citizenship of any person from Axis countries who had been naturalized

after January 1, 1939. This included citizens of Romania, Hungary, and Bulgaria, other lesser-known Axis allies. Camacho also established a Comité Consultivo de Emergencia Para la Defensa Política to restrain suspiciou activities and establish an internment policy for dangerous Axis foreigners. By July 1942, Germans, Japanese, and Italians considered security threats were concentrated at Castillo de Perote in Veracruz state and also at other locations throughout the republic. Japanese in Baja, California, had to report to Guadalajara or Mexico City. There Gobernación agents registered them to monitor their movements.

As was the case with Japanese interned in the United States, the 2,000 Japanese in Baja, California, suffered extensive property losses. Before leaving, Japanese had to turn over administration of their property and assets until the end of the war. Many sold off businesses at substantial losses. Having to live in Mexico City deprived Japanese of any means to support themselves. Because of wartime measures, the Japanese could not work and they were completely dependent on Mexican officials. Mexico did not end its concentration policy until October 1, 1945. About 4,000 Japanese had been concentrated by then.

Mexico also subjected Germans to financial difficulties. Gobernación often pressured companies to fire German employees. The policy of freezing the funds of anyone suspected of being Axis-related hurt many Germans. People of influence or with the means to buy their way out of Perote confinement often had to surrender cash to Mexican officials to live more comfortably, albeit under constant surveillance. Certainly the property losses of Germans were more substantial than those of the Japanese. Eventually, officials seized control of Boker y Cía, a large hardware company that had dominated Mexico City since the Porfiriato. The Junta de Administración y Vigilancia de la Propiedad de Extranjera, which administered Axis properties, refused to return German properties to their owners.

Although the army enjoyed more weapons and the prestige of participating in World War II, Camacho decided to reduce their political presence. It began when Camacho removed the army as one of the four sectors of the PRM in December 1940. Now that the oil crisis had become a negotiated process, the military would not have to advise civilians, whom Camacho preferred. The portion of the budget allocated for military spending declined to only 14 percent. Few officers served in the cabinet and it became clear that they were not to meddle in politics. In return, the military received a central hospital, headquarters, and new schools for medicine and engineering. To make sure that officers would not be tempted to back conservative or religious groups, Camacho decreed in November 1943 that uniformed military personnel could not attend religious services. This decision backfired, however, when an artillery lieutenant, Antonio de la Lama, attempted to shoot Camacho as he entered the National Palace in April 1944. The former seminary student missed his target as the president subdued him personally. Later, de la Lama had the *ley fuga* applied to him, probably on brother Maximinio's orders.

The threat from the religious conservatives was not an illusion. About 500,000 followers backed the Sinarquistas. Not everyone favored the Allies, and there is no doubt that many preferred the Axis powers. The Sinarquistas continued to oppose Marxism in any form and particularly resented the activity of Cárdenas in defense issues. Their armed presence was such that Sinarquistas temporarily took control of Morelia and Guadalajara in 1941; they also fought in the streets of Puebla for control of that city. Because the Sinarquistas were openly pro-Nazi and espoused retaking the southwest from the United States if Germany won the war, the United States encouraged Camacho to crack down on the Sinarquistas. By disbanding them in 1944, Camacho gave the Sinarquistas a formal end because by that year the leadership began to moderate. Ardent Catholics strongly supported Camacho's decision to rewrite Article 3 of the Constitution so that inflammatory references to socialist education were removed. Moreover,

openly Marxist teachers were expelled from the school system.

The policy toward land reform and labor also moderated. Camacho distributed only five million hectares to campesinos but the quality of the land was so poor that recipients often refused to take it. Distraught by treasury losses from investments into the ejido banks, Camacho emphasized irrigation much like don Porfirio and the Sonoran presidents. Thirty-five major irrigation projects indicated the new direction that favored medium as well as large landowners. The 1942 Agrarian Code emphasized more protection for landowners from the possibility of expropriation. Labor had to accept a policy of fewer strikes as part of a wartime pledge to give its total support to the government. As part of the shift to industrialization, the CTM signed off on a pact to cooperate in the creation of more factories and businesses. Toledano, obviously out of favor in this climate, resigned leadership of the CTM in 1943, supposedly to struggle against foreign imperialism. Fidel Velázquez, the pliant labor moderate with few ideological bearings, proceeded to keep labor quiet under his firm hand.

Clearly the new mass base of the Camacho government was the middle class. The new Confederation of Popular Organizations in 1943 effectively represented the rise of the middle class and various business elements. This organization received 56 of the 144 congressional candidacies in the year 1943. The PAN was also allowed to put up candidates for the thirty-ninth legislature. But fears of religious insurrection and disorder resulted in none of the PAN aspirants being allowed to take seats in the thirty-ninth legislature.

Of course, the big question was who would obtain Camacho's approval to become the next president. In another novelty, Secretary of Foreign Relations Ezequiel Padilla openly campaigned for the official PRM candidacy. But he was doomed by the dogged ambition and energy of Miguel Alemán. A close friend of the president, Alemán impressed everyone with his university background and promises of prosperity. Padilla was a gentleman and respected statesman, but many considered him too close to the United States.

Another surprise awaited the voters in July 1946. The PRM was renamed the Partido Institucional Revolucionario (PRI). The change of names represented the moderation of the late Cárdenas years as well as the totality of the Camacho regime. By calling for the replacement of class struggle with social harmony, Camacho had offered the church, private property, and foreign capital a place within a more tolerant but centralized state.

Mexico was very active in postwar activities. Camacho appointed the able Luis Fernández Guachalla to the Intergovernmental Committee for relocating refugees. Under Mexican pressure, Cuba agreed to find homes for European refugees and to use Havana as an intermediate station for refugees to other nations. After the creation of the United Nations in June 1945, Mexico successfuly proposed that Spain not be allowed to participate because of Axis aid that assisted Franco during and after the Spanish Civil War. Republican exiles in Mexico had a hand in drafting the Mexican proposal.

PRI PRESIDENTS, 1946–1970

Increasing political professionalization, bureaucratization, and centralization have been noticeable PRI trends since 1946. Rather than the fairly young PRN veterans under the age of 40, PRI leaders have normally been between 40 and 59 years old. In some ways, the PRI reinstituted the essence of the Porfiriato while institutionalizing the rhetoric that revolutionary changes continued. As in the days of don Porfirio, an urban, highly educated elite of politicians called the tune. Unlike the Porfiriato, however, the link between political leaders and the economic elites has not been that tight. Since part of the populistic tradition insisted on a nationalistic defense of Mexican sovereignty, the entrepreneurs could not directly be included in the political process because nearly half of them had foreign back-

grounds. In order to satisfy the business sector within its corporate structure while at the same time maintaining a revolutionary mystique, the PRI established a duality whereby the conservative wing would establish economic policies while the leftists would frequently articulate foreign policy. The PRI favored the accumulation of capital for economic growth as well as improved infrastructure. The tendency to support leftist revolutions in Central and South America also arose from the need to have Mexico assert its independence from the United States as a nonaligned nation during the Cold War.

The PRI presidents brought in a new generation of educated civilians to manage the country, thus avoiding the Porfirian mistake that allowed one generation to remain in power far too long. As in earlier times, continuity also asserted itself in terms of family networks continuing to exert important influence upon the composition of various regimes, national as well as regional. The PRI leaders usually shed a military background, much preferring a university education, particularly legal studies at UNAM, or some other kind of professional background. Unlike virtually the rest of Latin America, Mexico kept the military at a distance.

But institutional stability came with a cost. Although Mexico enjoyed economic growth, PRI leadership shifted to Mexico City, leaving national leaders gradually less in touch with regional populations. As in the past, individual loyalty rather than ideological ideals or patriotic service became an overwhelming defect. The authoritarian tendencies of earlier centuries remained intact. Therefore, bills sponsored by PRI executives passed almost unanimously while those from deputies in the national legislature became law only a third of the time. The rapid turnover in public office led to continued corruption because the realization of their short-lived opportunity tempted officeholders to steal what they could at various times.

Miguel Alemán Valdés, 1946–1952. The first civilian president since Carranza, Alemán began in the populist tradition. He was born in Sayula, Veracruz. Alemán's father fought for Carranza with Cándido Aguilar and participated at the battle of Celaya, but he committed suicide when surrounded by government troops for supporting the illfated Escobar revolt in 1929. His son Miguel had already entered the UNAM to study law. There Alemán made many friends and entered politics by backing Generals Gómez and Serrano against Obregón. But he distanced himself from Vasconcelos, obtaining his law degree, writing his thesis about unhealthy working conditions in the Real del Monte mine. As a young lawyer, he worked for the oil workers' union as a specialist in labor law. Maintaining contacts with his father's friends and developing new ties with labor leaders, Alemán made money on the side in real estate ventures. After cofounding the Socialists of Veracruz group, Alemán was selected by Cárdenas to manage his campaign in Veracruz. Cárdenas rewarded him with an appointment as an appeals court judge, but this was not what Alemán really sought.

Alemán received national attention as governor of Veracruz. Cárdenas had earlier favored Manilo Fabio Altamirano to run the state, but his suspicious murder paved the way for Alemán. At the age of only 36, Alemán ended many years of religious persecution by allowing the churches to reopen. Alemán promoted tourism and the Mexican film industry while calming the constant agitation of *agraristas*. Prison reform and the opening of several schools while aiding the formation of numerous businesses added to his list of accomplishments. With an eye to the future, he not only endorsed the 1938 oil nationalization, but he also traveled throughout Mexico to insist that the oil companies depart so that PEMEX could develop energy resources to industrialize. His energy caught the attention of Camacho and the two struck up a pleasant relationship. In 1940, Alemán resigned as governor to run the successful presidential campaign of Camacho, which clearly needed the work of an able assistant to facilitate an unpopular imposition. Due to Alemán's zeal, Camacho appointed him to be Secretary of Gobernación.

During World War II, Alemán nourished his presidential ambitions. When Secretary of Foreign Relations Padilla began to position himself to be a candidate, Alemán had supporters of Padilla and even family members arrested when they attempted to distribute literature and pamphlets advocating a Padilla presidency. An old Callista, Padilla became the rightist alternative enabling Alemán to garner labor support from the CTM when it became clear that Camacho did not want either of two leftists, Javier Rojo Gómez and Miguel Henrìquez Guzmán. By the autumn of 1945, the middle class sector, the CNC, and even the Mexican communists had endorsed Alemán. Alemán pledged to democratize the ruling party and promised a glowing future to business leaders. Alemán also smeared Padilla as being pro-United States so that the mantle of nationalism could be claimed by him. Toledano thus gave his blessing to Alemán, even though Alemán had assured U.S. officials that the left would have no place in his government and that Mexico would industrialize with U.S. funding while ties to the Soviet Union and Britain would be minimal. The mysterious but opportune death of Maximino Camacho removed the last barrier to presidential ambitions when the president's brother died at a banquet.

The new presidential style inaugurated by Alemán was energetic and contagious. Always smiling, speaking from flatbed trucks beside beautiful ladies, Alemán traveled tirelessly and promised a new era of economic prosperity. The PRI no longer represented the hegemony of labor activities, Marxist intellectuals, and *agraristas*. Many of Alemán's closest friends worked in the cabinet with him. The president's business instincts continued unabated so that he acquired ownership of vast numbers of enterprises. It soon became apparent that he owned much of Acapulco and Alemán often acted as the unofficial head of national tourism. He dallied with actresses, often leaving his wife alone. Alemán seemed to be everywhere as he inaugurated countless airports, highways, and even the newly constructed university city in its new location to the south, where a statue of Alemán briefly presided. The problem was that Alemán's friends and appointees imitated him by enriching themselves while serving as public officials. When he retired, Alemán was one of the wealthiest men in Mexico.

The presidency became more powerful than ever. Extensive press censorship and control of the media reached new levels. The military received only 7 percent of the budget as well as less than 10 percent of political offices. But beginning with Alemán, the Mexican government used the military to enforce internal order. One of Alemán's first acts as president was to insist that strikes threatened national policy. When oil workers rejected a 10 percent raise and threatened to strike for more, Alemán ordered troops to take over gas stations and the Atzcapotzalco refinery. New CTM boss Velázquez declared that CTM workers had to support the PRI. When Toledano formed a rival left wing party, the Partido Popular, Alemán had it subsidized with government money so that Toledano became little more than a loyal opposition. Leftist labor leaders fell by the wayside as Alemán and Velázquez installed *charro* leaders who favored restraining strikes and selling out their followers. They received the name *charro* from the cowboy outfits favored by railroad union leader Jesús Díaz de León, who ousted a reformist leader subsequently jailed on trumped up charges of theft from union funds.

Alemán's centralization of presidential power extended to political practices. The Mexican Communist Party by now felt secure in its collaboration with Toledano and the CTM. But Alemán suddenly turned against them, expelling many Marxists from union activity and government positions. Within the PRI, Alemán diminished the influence of its sectors so that presidential authority became unquestioned. Alemán abandoned the practice of adopting a party platform. By means of the 1946 electoral law, federal authorities took complete control over voting procedures so that authorities in control of polling places assumed the task of stealing ballot boxes. The result was a compliant legislature which approved nearly everything the executive wanted, frequently by unanimous vote. The young Adolfo López Ma-

teos became the smooth legislative liason between the president and the legislators. López Mateos made sure that internal dissent within congressional halls disappeared. He encouraged deputies to enjoy the benefits of PRI patronage. The Supreme Court, weakened by Cárdenas earlier, became equally submissive, rarely questioning executive desires.

Relations with the United States remained harmonious. President Harry Truman traveled to Mexico City in March 1947, where he laid a floral wreath at the monument to the Niños Héroes at Chapultepec. Alemán reciprocated, becoming the first Mexican president since Santa Anna to visit Washington, D.C., where he addressed the U.S. Congress in May 1947. Mexico had become a close friend during the Cold War but never had to sign a military alliance as most other U.S. partners had to do. Later, both countries exchanged war trophies from the U.S–Mexican War one hundred years earlier, which dissipated some of the bitterness that had remained in Mexico since 1848.

Adolfo Ruiz Cortines. Alemán made it known that he wanted another presidential term. That, of course, was out of the question with the PRI leadership, particularly Cárdenas. When Alemán attempted to impose his friend Fernando Casas Alemán, who happened to be the supine regent of Mexico City, he ran into solid opposition. Finally, there was a compromise whereby another *veracruzano*, Ruiz Cortines, satisfied PRI leaders enough to make him the new president.

Ruiz Cortines wanted to rekindle confidence in the integrity of the PRI. He had to repudiate the bad reputation of the Alemán administration by means of his reputation for honesty and his down-to-earth background. Sixty-two-year-old Ruiz Cortines embodied these qualifications well. A person who enjoyed a drink, was a good baseball player in his younger days, and was fond of dominoes, Ruiz Cortines had many characteristics of the average person. Although his education did not extend beyond the secondary-school level, Ruiz Cortines became renowned as a person who understood numbers. By the age of 15, he was a junior accountant before serving the Carrancista army and fighting at El Ebano. Thereafter, he became a paymaster and made clear his other attribute, his honesty. Ruiz Cortines received the honor of escorting Carranza's train with the national treasury back to Mexico City shortly after the First Chief's murder in 1920. After he left the army, Ruiz Cortines served in the Department of Statistics from 1926 to 1935.

Ruiz Cortines began his political career during the Maximato. His first major position was chief administrative officer of the federal district. Here he cemented his reputation for efficiency and integrity. By managing the finances of the Camacho campaign, he came into contact with Miguel Alemán. In 1944, Ruiz Cortines became the governor of Veracruz where he enjoyed fame for never hiring his friends. In addition to having a reputation for party loyalty, Ruiz Cortines also became known for his integrity. As governor, he established commissions which investigated fraud as well as waste. The state treasury bulged with revenues twice as high as the earlier administration. Such frugality impressed Camacho who recommended to Alemán that Ruiz Cortines's talents not be wasted. Thus, he became Secretary of Gobernación under Alemán, where he managed affairs firmly despite an atmosphere of corruption, free spending, and extravagance. After his "unveiling" as the new PRI candidate, Ruiz Cortines promised to return to the values of sacrifice and devotion to the ideals of reform. He was one of several new Mexican leaders who offered bizarre and often impossible promises. Ruiz Cortines campaigned under the slogan of a "march to the sea" and encouraged Mexicans to fish. The hardworking but unspectacular president did not disappoint those who had urged a cleansing of bureaucratic corruption. In his inaugural speech, Ruiz Cortines insisted that he would demand strict honesty and ordered all 250,000 public officials to make public their financial holdings.

Behind his modest facade, Ruiz Cortines ruled firmly. He fired a number of notorious grafters and scrutinized requests for spending projects with great care. As a symbol of his rise to power, he traveled throughout Mexico in the railroad car that Carranza had used to flee from Mexico City in 1920. The new president made sure that virtually all the governors were directly under his control when his six-year *sexenio* term came to an end. The army received less money than under Alemán and fewer governmental appointments. The Supreme Court and legislature remained intimidated by the power of the president. Within Gobernación, a tough official, Gustavo Díaz Ordaz, became well known for making sure that governors, members of the press, and dissidents stayed in line. Adolfo López Mateos arbitrated hundreds of strikes firmly. The number of *charro* leaders who sold out their working-class subordinates increased dramatically during this period. Teachers and railroad workers considered Ruiz Cortines stingy with counteroffers to improve their threadbare living standards, but the president would not tolerate massive demonstrations or earnest strikes. Like his predecessors, Ruiz Cortines had little faith in agrarian reform, handing out a mere 3.2 million hectares of land.

In many ways, this was a remarkably easygoing period compared to what had happened before or after. Impeccably honest in his private life, Ruiz Cortines often seemed as if he were an honorable father figure at the head of a family. The *Hora Nacional* (National Hour) expanded greatly during this period after its creation in 1942. This government radio program dominated the airwaves each evening at ten o'clock with dramatic re-creations of historical events or discussions of various projects and accomplishments. Crime declined and *granaderos* (grenadiers) symbolized the regime's determination to crack down on those who would disrupt order. Political murders and assassinations seemed to fade away. A notable expansion of the IMSS (social security) offered free hospital services as well as basic care for many indigents and those in need. Opposition parties, particularly the PAN, drew the president's scorn but at least campaigned and took their seats in the legislature as the official but nonthreatening rivals.

Foreign relations reflected the calm waters of this epoch. After Fidel Castro, Ernesto "Che" Guevara, and other members of the Cuban revolutionary movement took up residence in the Chalco area of Mexico City, Intelligence Chief Fernando Gutiérrez Barrios interrogated the young Castro and gave him the freedom to train his group to return to Cuba in their eventually successful effort to topple dictator Fulgencio Batista. Although Guevara noted in his memoirs that Castro's organizing in Mexico City experienced surveillance, arrest, and harassment from FBI agents, the president's desire to have them expulsed from Mexico never materialized because Cárdenas, after a spirited discussion with Castro, interceded and obtained permission to have them finish their preparations before departing from Tampico in 1956.

With the United States, Ruiz Cortines maintained the World War II partnership but asserted Mexico's independence enough to reaffirm its traditional concern for national sovereignty. As an unmistakable sign of approval of the moderate position Ruiz Cortines had staked out in his presidential campaign, U.S. President Eisenhower dispatched Vice-President Richard Nixon to the inauguration ceremonies. But when Nixon later began to lecture Ruiz Cortines about the threat of communism, the new Mexican president instead took Nixon on a tour of various slums and described the endemic poverty within the hastily constructed shacks as the real concern that Mexico faced. Although Mexican diplomats tended to support Eisenhower on most international issues related to the Cold War, Mexico differed with Washington when its Central Intelligence Agency brought down the leftist regime of Jacobo Arbenz in Guatemala. When U.S. Secretary of State John Foster Dulles attempted to obtain an inter-American condemnation of the Arbenz government, Mexico joined Argentina in opposing the proposal. When Eisenhower visited Mexico to inaugurate a new hydroelectric project, Ruiz Cortines made it a point to lecture him publicly on the need for nonintervention within the American hemisphere. Finally, Ruiz Cortines nationalized several U.S.-owned properties along the border on July 31, 1958, so that Mexican nationals could control an important commercial zone.

Ruiz Cortines's last message to Congress departed from twentieth century PRI leaders. He had begun to consider critical voices and, rather than exalt PRI success, Ruiz Cortines took the occasion to emphasize some of the shortcomings of the system. The social flaws troubled him more than the deficiencies of one-party rule or executive dominance. The Mexican masses had not benefited from economic growth as much as he had hoped. Populistic promises had yet to be fulfilled. Ruiz Cortines confided that the desired equation between economic development and social justice favored of the former.

PRI officials agreed. The pace of social development had slowed and, since 1940, had almost ground to a halt in the minds of many. Perhaps a moderate shift to the left would mute critics of the PRI and reinstill some faith in "evolutionary" ideals. They decided to give it a try with a younger, more dynamic candidate.

Adolfo López Mateos, 1958–1964.

The presidency of López Mateos represents the climax of an unusual period of stability and confidence that had begun in 1940. Although he ruled with a firm hand, López Mateos was the most popular president in twentieth century Mexico. The handsome president presided over six years of political order, skillful diplomacy, and improved living conditions. Compared to future regimes, this period was an island of tranquility and rising expectations.

Background. Born to a dentist and a teacher near Mexico City, López Mateos lost his father at an early age, like many other Mexican presidents, but obtained a fine education. His skill at public speaking won him great admiration, particularly when he campaigned for Vasconcelos to be president. After receiving his degree in economics from the UNAM in 1930, López Mateos began working in the government of his native state of Mexico. There he came under the tutelage of an old Carrancista, Isidro Fabela, who after hearing a particularly moving López Mateos oration-managed to have López Mateos appointed to the national Senate. Because of López Mateos's skill at containing the labor movement, Ruiz Cortines decided on López Mateos to invigorate the presidency. After an energetic campaign in which the opposition candidates except the PAN endorsed him, López Mateos could claim to have won about 90 percent of the votes cast. Only 47 at the time of his election, López was the last twentieth-century president to attract youth. More intellectual than other recent presidents, López Mateos indicated during his campaign that he planned to accelerate social reforms. Two days before his inauguration, López Mateos suffered a particularly debilitating migraine headache. When taking the presidential oath, he could barely raise his arm to be sworn in. Therefore, the actual burden of attending to day-to-day government machinery fell into the hands of hardworking Gustavo Díaz Ordaz, the newly appointed Secretary of Gobernación.

Domestic Policies. Only a day after making himself comfortable in the presidential office, López Mateos had to confront a serious regional crisis in the state of San Luis Potosí. An opthalmologist by the name of Dr. Salvador Nava had formed a broad-based movement to protest the continuation of a corrupt governor controlled by local cacique Gonzálo Natividad Santos, who had had the state under his thumb for decades. Nava sought to become municipal president of San Luis Potosí, the state capital, and demanded honest elections. To make his demands felt, Nava organized a strike that had massive support and forced the current governor to flee for his safety to Mexico City. On December 2, 1958, Díaz Ordaz assured Nava that the elections would be honest and that a new governor would replace the lackey of Santos. Nava took office and ran a popular government in the state capital until he attempted an ill-fated campaign to become governor in 1961.

In general, López Mateos enjoyed good relations with his governors so that for the first time since the Porfiriato, little domestic agitation occurred on the regional level. Díaz Ordaz was quite effective in persuading dissident governors to resign, particularly those who had been in power far too long. More importantly, the national government spread out greatly improved social security benefits, federal education programs, and health measures that virtually eliminated malaria while reducing polio and tuberculosis. Education had now become the largest item in the federal budget. Eva Sámano, the first lady, assumed an active role by directing a government institute for the protection of children and traveled extensively throughout the regions to listen to problems of the poor. She once spent two weeks in a remote, tropical region helping hurricane victims. Healthy drinking water, better roads, and a belief that the future held hopes for a higher living standard contented many. The creation of CONASUPO provided inexpensive food by means of government outlets throughout Mexico.

The labor movement, as well as the tradition of leftist activism, also reached their climax during the López Mateos presidency. The watershed event that damaged the left and precipitated the decline of the labor movement was the railroad workers' strike in March 1959. Initially, railroad workers seemed to be in a strong position. Under independent, aggressive Demetrio Vallejo Martínez, they had a leader who sought a badly needed wage increase and who confidently set a strike date for February 25, 1959. Although CTM leader Velázquez attacked the large number of communists on the railroad worker's executive committee, Vallejo enjoyed support from independent unions free of *charrismo* as well as favorable public support. The government offered and the workers accepted a 16 percent wage increase. The problem was that two semiprivate railroads were not part of the contract. When they hesitated to endorse the February contract, which included housing and health provisions for railroad workers, Valentín Campa and other communists on the executive board called on all railroad workers to go on strike in March.

The government found itself in a major crisis and took firm measures. López Mateos offered to discuss the matter with Vallejo. Overly concerned that the executive committee be informed of his negotiations, Vallejo insisted on bringing a tape recorder during his discussions with the president. That, as well as the fear of a general strike, the creation of independent unions free of government control, and a violation of the normally secretive nature of governmental deliberations, motivated López Mateos to crush the strike by jailing its leaders and arresting thousands of workers who refused to operate the railroads. Because the strike occurred during the Easter holidays, when Mexicans normally travel throughout the country, public support for the strike waned considerably. Two days after Easter, Díaz Ordaz convinced more compliant union leaders to break the strike. For good measure, police arrested muralist Siqueiros for harsh criticism of the president, citing the law against "social dissolution." López Mateos did not set Siqueiros free until July 1964.

The railroad confrontation had many consequences. The 1958 strike was to be the last major labor confrontation for the duration of the twentieth century. Independent unions began to disappear as Velázquez tightened his grip on the labor movement. From this point on, the communists could not respond creatively to independent social movements of teachers, doctors, slum dwellers, and campesinos. Bickering among themselves, leftist leaders seemed to lack the imagination to understand women, indigenous communities, and students, who themselves formulated organizations and new frameworks with which to challenge the PRI hegemony.

In addition to weakening labor militants, López Mateos discouraged any challenges from agrarian outbursts. Rubén Jaramillo, who had demanded agrarian reform in Morelos, became the last major agrarian leader in Mexico. An incredibly humble as well as devoted leader, Jaramillo would not sell out his followers and engaged in constant confrontations with local caciques. Particularly troublesome to authorities was his role as a Methodist reformer, urging his followers away from alcoholic beverages and tobacco. Be-

cause Jaramillo could not be bought out, orders came down to murder him and his family on March 23, 1962. Peasants who seized or squatted on land belonging to others received similar treatment. To mitigate the negative publicity from this killing, López Mateos posed as the friend of agrarian reform, publicly ordering the distribution of 11.4 million hectares of land, which would have placed him second only to Cárdenas in terms of land awards. In actuality, he distributed only 3.2 million hectares of land, usually in rocky, poor quality southern areas.

Although the president enjoyed good relations with the general public, the PRI came under more criticism. Alienation was broadly based, cutting across class lines and most ideological persuasions. The desire for true democracy, in spite of all the governmental obstacles, became a crucial goal. Properly conceived and channeled skillfully, it could lead to not merely an increase of the gross national product but also a major redistribution of wealth. Cárdenas became the chief challenger of López Mateos when he praised the new regime of Fidel Castro in Cuba and nagged López Mateos to free political prisoners. In August 1961, Cárdenas formed a new leftist organization, the Movement for National Liberation. He particularly sought the attention of growing numbers of Marxist intellectuals, who were impressed by the success of Castro in educational expansion, dramatic improvements in health services, and his triumphant defiance of the United States. Not until López Mateos appointed Cárdenas to head the Balsas River Committee, a hydroelectric project which affected Cárdenas's native Michoacán, did the old general back off.

López Mateos took notice of attacks against the political system and had the foresight to push through a 1963 constitutional amendment that changed voting practices in the Chamber of Deputies. As a means to establish a more inclusive group of parties other than the PRI in the lower house of Congress, this amendment mandated that any party which could win 2.5 percent of the vote could have five deputies in the Chamber of Deputies, even if their candidates did not win their political contests. For every half percent of the vote that opposition parties won, they now received additional deputies, up to a maximum of 20, each of whom could occupy a new seat but not replace an incumbent deputy. This reform enabled the PAN to obtain 20 congressional seats in the 1964 elections while the Partido Popular got 10 seats.

Cuba dominated international relations. As relations worsened between the United States and Cuba, the Eisenhower government attempted to pressure López Mateos into backing an Organization of American States resolution isolating Cuba. Mexico, of course, had long insisted on nonintervention and now fell under increasing criticism of the many who had become enraptured with the early Castro regime. In the midst of delicate discussions with Washington, D.C., López Mateos invited Cuban president Osvaldo Dorticós to visit Mexico in June 1960, where López Mateos compared the Mexican Revolution to the Cuban Revolution in glowing terms. With Kennedy, relations improved despite the Bay of Pigs fiasco, when a U.S.-sponsored invasion by Cuban exiles failed. But when Castro declared Cuba a Marxist state in December 1961 and began planning liberation movements throughout Latin America, López Mateos became apprehensive.

Perhaps the most exciting diplomatic exchange occurred when John and Jackie Kennedy visited Mexico City in June 1962. Huge crowds greeted them or waited to catch a glimpse of their motorcade. A joke originated which related that Kennedy admired a gold and diamond-encrusted wristwatch on the wrist of López Mateos. In keeping with Mexican custom, López Mateos offered it to the U.S. president. Then he placed his arm around Jackie and admired her in hopeful anticipation of a similar offer. On a more serious note, Kennedy prayed at the Basilica of the Virgin of Guadalupe. He also announced that the aims of the Mexican Revolution coincided with his Alliance for Progress program. Mexicans were much more impressed by Jackie, who spoke perfect Spanish. Four weeks after Kennedy's assassination in Dallas, new President Lyndon Johnson got the idea of appointing Mrs. Kennedy as ambassador to Mexico. "God almighty," he blurted to an aide, "all she would have to do would be to just walk out on her balcony once a week."

Another result of the Kennedy visit was the beginning of the Chamizal negotiations. The unfirm soil in and around El Paso could be easily shifted by the Río Grande currents. After the river suddenly shifted the boundary southward in 1864, Mexico had lost yet more territory to the United

John F. Kennedy waves to the crowds during a visit to Mexico in June 1962. *Corbis.*

States. Naturally Mexico demanded that this land be returned, but nothing was done until the matter was brought to Kennedy's attention in Mexico City. Kennedy responded by having the U.S. ambassador resolve the issue so that in 1963 the disputed area reverted to Mexico. It was a great triumph for López Mateos to sign the accord with Johnson a year later.

López Mateos often asserted that Mexico was not an inert neutral country during these years but an active, independent player on the diplomatic scene. In accord with this stance, López Mateos traveled tirelessly throughout the world, giving Mexico its highest profile since the Porfiriato. Mexico also received world statesmen like Charles de Gaulle and India's Jawaharlal Nehru. When the Olympics Committee designated Mexico as the site of the 1968 Olympics, it seemed as though the rest of the world had raised its judgment of Mexico considerably.

Gustavo Díaz Ordaz, 1964–1970. The pleasant period of growing confidence which had evolved since the Camacho presidency came to an abrupt end in 1968. President Díaz Ordaz became a very authoritarian ruler whose violent repression of the 1968 student movement plunged Mexico into a political crisis that never faded away for the remainder of the twentieth century.

Antecedents. The son of a Porfirian *jefe político* in Oaxaca and Puebla, Díaz Ordaz was not blessed with good looks. His mother ridiculed his protruding teeth, skinny body, and unpleasant appearance. As a strict school teacher, she should have understood the impact of her negative comments. Not by coincidence, the young Díaz Ordaz developed a habit of prolonged work and reading. Defensive about his ugliness, Díaz Ordaz studied hard at the Institute of Arts and Science in Oaxaca which Juárez and Díaz had attended earlier. Here Díaz developed a remarkable memory and even became a good basketball player. After the family moved to Puebla when an earthquake demolished their Oaxaca home, Díaz Ordaz began his legal studies at the Universidad de Puebla. His

rise to power began when he worked as an office boy at the Puebla state Ministry of Interior in 1932. After becoming an effective court agent, he caught the eye of Governor Maximinio Camacho, who put him to work arbitrating labor disputes. Intelligent and honest, Díaz Ordaz diverted himself with jigsaw puzzles as he developed a reputation for competence. New promotions pushed him up to be vice-rector of the Universidad de Puebla and president of the state supreme court. He became a full-time politician as a federal deputy and senator. It was in the national legislature that he befriended López Mateos. Since he had shouldered the burden of running the details of government under López Mateos in Gobernación, it seemed natural that Díaz Ordaz finally become president.

Since Díaz Ordaz had little interest in foreign affairs, he turned diplomacy over to a remarkable subordinate, Alfonso García Robles. As subsecretary of foreign relations from 1964 to 1970, Robles's major accomplishment was the 1967 Treaty for the Denuclearization of Latin America, known as the Treaty of Tlatelolco. It was a great diplomatic victory because the agreement embraced the much publicized disarmament issue without assuming any political risk. The treaty, which included many protocols to be signed by the nuclear powers and by European states with colonies in the Americas, attempted to keep nuclear weapons out of Latin America. It was never ratified by Argentina and Brazil, the only Latin American nations suspected of having nuclear ambitions. But it permitted Mexico to emphasize the need for nuclear disarmament. Later, the treaty earned García Robles a share of the 1982 Nobel Peace Prize, along with Sweden's disarmament advocate, Alva Myrdal.

García Robles's strategy was to brandish occasional banners on the international and regional diplomatic stage and then withdraw to the reality of Mexico's internal development and its close relationship with the United States. This fit the tastes of Díaz Ordaz, who exhibited no interest in traveling to Europe. Instead, he met many times with U.S. Presidents Johnson and Nixon. In Latin

America, Mexico's profile was low. Not surprisingly, South American nations felt little identification with Mexico. Contrary to past *sexenios*, Mexico paid little attention to the rest of the world.

Díaz Ordaz established a very repressive regime. Although spectacular projects arose, such as the impressive new subway system for Mexico City, first-rate museums, and well-planned Olympics events, Díaz Ordaz ruled with an excessively firm hand. He became particularly bothered by PAN victories in major cities such as Hermosillo and Mérida. Therefore, he took steps to see that his eager-to-please Secretary of Gobernación regained these defiant capitals by forceful means. When the PAN won in Tijuana and Mexicali, Díaz Ordaz simply annulled the elections. As the PAN succeeded in getting 11 percent of the votes, he became even more agitated. Always convinced that iron rule would preserve order, Díaz Ordaz crushed a strike initiated by physicians by making them unionize into a government union which was a CTM affiliate. Particularly notable was the government's use of pliable newspapers, paid off with *embute* (cash stuffed envelopes) inducements which attacked the physicians and printed untrue stories of dying children and other false allegations. Demonstrating his intolerance of critical analysis, Díaz Ordaz hounded the Argentine-born Arnaldo Orfila Reynal out of Fondo de Cultura Económica for publishing *The Children of Sanchez* a controversial study of family life by a U.S. anthropologist.

Perhaps the most damaging decision regarding the PRI was the dismissal of Carlos A. Madrazo, an ardent reformer. Madrazo had become president of the National Executive Committee of the PRI during the first two years of Díaz Ordaz's administration. He also represented the first of a series of failed attempts by progressive politicians to democratize Mexican politics from within the PRI. As was typical of many reformers, Madrazo rose to power on the basis of mass electoral organizations, whereas the *tecnicos*, who were university graduates who never won political office by means of campaigning, tended to oppose opening up the system. Madrazo wanted to modify the PRI selection process of leaders and bring youthful, more inclusive cadres into the PRI. Madrazo's call for primary elections on the local level particularly disturbed entrenched PRI leaders who appealed to Díaz Ordaz for their backing. Unfortunately, Díaz Ordaz supported the entrenched rulers and dismissed Madrazo when he attempted to involve students with PRI policy making as well as establish commissions to ferret out graft. After his 1965 removal from PRI leadership, Madrazo began to criticize the regime until he died in a very suspicious plane crash near Monterrey in 1969. Thus, a badly needed impetus for reform became crushed.

Unpopular and the butt of constant jokes, Díaz Ordaz isolated himself from serious problems. He curried favor with the Church by lashing out at communism and taking mass in the presidential estate. Obsessed with presenting himself well, Díaz Ordaz wore expensive clothes with a closet full of innumerable shoes. But gastrointestinal ailments worsened and he began to experience foot problems. Although he presented himself as a traditional family man, he took a lover, the actress Irma Serrano.

The Tlatelolco Massacre. Students decided to challenge Díaz Ordaz directly as part of an international trend when youth created new changes in politics and culture. A common belief, particularly among university students, emerged that government and PRI politicians were insensitive to the suffering of the poor and indigenous groups. Many students concluded that society was living in ignorance and exploitation. Moreover, Marxism became increasingly popular in the 1960s as a means to analyze the problems of racism, war, and poverty.

The 1968 student movement grew into a unified force. Students from technical and academic schools, provincial and Mexico City schools, as well as teachers and administrators, joined to make straightforward but dramatic demands, particularly recognition of constitutional guarantees and protection of civil liberties. The underlying cause was outrage at the priorities set by the Mexican government, symbolized by the lavish preparations for the 1968 Olympics in Mexico City. Since co-optation, harassment, and attacks against leading figures of the movement were useless, the government reacted with brute force.

Student unrest and government repression began in Michoacán. There students demonstrated against an increase in bus fares when one of them was shot by an undercover police officer in October 1966. Angry demonstrators then called for the resignation of the governor. An outraged Díaz Ordaz then ordered Gobernación head Luis Echeverría to organize an occupation of the university with paratroopers. In 1967 Díaz Ordaz also crushed protests at the University of Sonora.

The crisis in Mexico City, which triggered the eventual massacre, began on July 22, 1968. A brawl between vocational and preparatory students in the federal district resulted in harsh treatment by the *granaderos*. After chasing and clubbing the students who had been fighting each other, the *granaderos* brutalized many innocent bystanders. Therefore, student protesters marched toward the Zócalo with Marxist students commemorating Castro's July 26 revolution before police forced them back. After the arrest of several students, their friends began to occupy various preparatory schools and call for a strike. In response, soldiers seized the San Ildefonso Preparatory School after blowing its centuries old gate apart with a bazooka. Because the school was affiliated with the UNAM, its rector, Javier Barros Sierra, led UNAM students on a protest march a short way into the city until confronted by more *granaderos*. Díaz Ordaz at least offered an "extended hand" to the protesters, but their response was to form a national strike committee.

The student protest movement had begun in earnest. Thrilled by news of similar student activities in Paris, where students nearly overturned the de Gaulle government, the protesters decided it was time to organize for change. Meetings were held almost hourly in which representatives of every school and college of UNAM, the Politécnico, the Universidad de Chapingo, and most of the preparatory schools were given duties by the strike

committee. Contrary to the claims of the government, it was a very democratic and largely spontaneous effort without direct Cuban influence and minimal PCM members. The students divided themselves into brigades which held small meetings in popular public places, such as markets, subway stations, or neighborhood corners. In this way, they reached the very core of the population and gained growing mass support. The students called these meetings *relampago* (thunder) encounters because they had to be fast to avoid arrest by police or undercover agents. Students passed out flyers, explained the principles of the movement, and collected money to pay for paper and ink.

Now that the students had organized themselves, they presented their demands and offered to negotiate with the government. Formulated on August 4, 1968, the demands articulated by the students consisted of (1) freedom for all political prisoners, (2) revocation of the "social dissolution" article in the federal penal code, (3) disbandment of the *granaderos* and other repressive security forces, (4) dismissal of two police officials, (5) payment of indemnities to the families of all those killed and injured since the beginning of the conflict, (6) determination the responsibility of individual government officials involved in the bloodshed, and (7) respect for the autonomy of UNAM. To test their strength as well as probe the resilience of the government, one hundred thousand students marched into the Zócalo nine days later. On August 22, the government agreed to a public dialogue but became apprehensive when student leaders insisted that newspaper reporters and television crews capture the moment for public consumption.

The movement started to attract more national support, not only from the Mexican press, but also from the rest of the world. Many of the correspondents in Mexico who were sent to cover the Olympics became interested in student viewpoints and the issues they were fighting for. Journalists attended the universities and reported on the meetings and marches to gauge the feeling of the movement. Several newspaper writers who seemed to favor the students lost their jobs. Students were not the only ones marching. People in the streets joined them when they realized the students meant well. But as the marches increased, violence and altercations with the government became more serious. During one of the last marches on the Zócalo, international media highlighted students using profane language against Diaz Ordaz, draping the lampposts with red and black flags, posting pictures of Ché Guevara, and demanding a dialogue with the government shortly before Díaz Ordaz's state of the union address.

At this point, Díaz Ordaz gave the orders to crack down. He cleared the students from the Zócalo, claiming that a foreign conspiracy threatened Mexico. The students fought the soldiers and police throughout downtown Mexico City. In his presidential address, Díaz Ordaz claimed that the demonstrators were conspirators. The usually pliant Senate authorized him to use the armed forces in the name of national security. When Professor Heberto Castillo presided over a casual, lighthearted independence day celebration on the UNAM campus, Díaz Ordaz became incensed with what he considered a usurpation of traditional symbols and rituals. Therefore, ten thousand army troops seized control of the UNAM complex. Many of the students were beaten with batons and suffered from tear gas inhalation, while many others were categorized as "missing," meaning that the person died; because the government did not want to be responsible for a civilian death, they simply "lost" the body and any evidence that the family of the missing individual could use against the government. The rector resigned in protest but then withdrew his resignation on September 30, which prompted the government to withdraw the soldiers from both the Politécnico and UNAM.

The Tlatelolco slaughter capped more than two months of antigovernment demonstrations before the Olympic Games in Mexico City. The government clearly planned to end the student protests once and for all. Díaz Ordaz's belief that foreign communists were leading the student movement and his determination to enforce security led to the tragedy. Tourists eager to attend the Olympic games began to cancel their plans, infuriating the president even more. The weakened student organizations agreed to hold a general meeting in the Plaza de Tres Culturas in Tlatelolco on October 2, 1968. A crowd of ten thousand, mainly students, but also housewives with children, attended. They listened to speakers discuss national problems and measures that should be taken to change the government. Tanks and soldiers had already surrounded the plaza while members of the Presidential Guard had rented nearby apartments that surrounded the pre-Hispanic ruins, colonial cathedral, and the ministry of foreign relations.

The shooting began shortly after a speaker finished at about 5:38 in the evening. From the sky, a couple of assault helicopters emerged and dropped flares. A special unit from the Presidential Guard known as the Olympia Battalion began to pour fire into the crowd. Later the government would belatedly attempt to insist that soldiers received fire from student snipers. Tanks and soldiers replied by shooting into the crowd. At least 15,000 rounds were fired. Meanwhile, military buses positioned soldiers to intercept those who attempted to flee and to prevent anyone from entering. Electrical and phone service ceased immediately. The shooting lasted at least five hours as ambulances were turned away. Some demonstrators were bayoneted. At least 2,000 were taken away to be interrogated and tortured. Hundreds died immediately and many more were never seen alive again. The coordination between the army and the Presidential guard seems to have been confused or deliberately camouflaged. Perhaps defense minister General Marcelino García Barragán, angered at the Olympia Battalion firing at his troops, simply unleashed his forces in anger. This would partially explain why some students were taken to the soccer stadium and executed summarily. Dozens of blood-soaked shoes were the only remaining evidence of the massacre. Many of those killed were hauled away and burned. Thus, the Templo Mayor symbolized the continuity of national leadership taking a bloody toll upon dissidents nearly 500 years later.

ECONOMIC GROWTH

From 1940 to 1970, Mexico enjoyed a period of stable economic development. The investment policies initiated during the 1938 transition and solidified under Camacho finally yielded fruit during the 1950s in the form of improved living standards. Mexico benefited enormously from export-led growth during World War II. Afterwards, commercial protectionism took root in 1947 in response to high external demand.

Beginning with Cárdenas, the Mexican governments from 1938 to 1970 established the goal of Mexico becoming more self-sufficient in heavy industry and increasing its exports of manufactured items. The economy had grown at a rate of only 1.6 percent a year from 1920 to 1940. Obviously, that did not bode well for the future. However, the PRI became successful in establishing a "Mexican miracle" as outsiders lauded the fact that from 1940 to 1970, the economy grew at a rate of over 6 percent a year, a rate superior to all other Latin American countries except Brazil. Perhaps even more remarkable is that productivity went up by 200 percent from 1940 to 1970. Meanwhile, agricultural production exceeded the high birth rate during this period. Unlike the Porfiriato, when two-thirds of the investment capital for new projects came from foreign sources, 90 percent of all fixed investment was financed by Mexican capital. Each president faced certain pressures and responded to different priorities. Most of them had responsible subordinates who made sober decisions.

The World War II alliance provided unusual economic benefits for Mexico. Particularly vital was the enormous reduction of Mexico's foreign debt. Camacho wisely decided to retain Eduardo Suárez in the government as his finance minister. Suárez signed an accord with Thomas Lamont in November 1942. Not by coincidence this date represents the turning point of the war in Europe because of the U.S.–British landings in Morocco and Algeria, while the Germans became encircled at Stalingrad. At the stroke of a pen, Mexico swept out virtually all its interest charges. In order to avoid having funds wind up in the hands of the Axis powers and because the value of the bonds which financed past debts had fallen so low, the total foreign debt of $509.5 million dropped sharply to a mere $49.5 million—less than 10 percent of the original amount. The result was that Mexican credit increased sharply and the Banco de México suddenly piled up significant reserves. Never before had Mexico had such a notable financial triumph.

The economic linkage between Mexico and the United States accelerated throughout the remainder of the twentieth century once wartime policies drew both countries together. Camacho created a Supreme Defense Council to help mobilize once it was decided that Mexico would function in the war mainly as a source of raw materials. Not only were strategic metals, rubber, and lumber sent north but also agricultural crops such as tomatoes and coffee. To obtain funding to stimulate wartime production, the government passed a law in 1944 that allowed foreigners to invest in Mexican businesses as long as Mexican capital controlled majority stock. *Prestanombres*, those who loaned their names to qualify as Mexican participants in U.S. companies, flourished anyway. The 1944 law enabled large-scale U.S. investments to enter the manufacturing sector. The advantage to Mexico, compared to other Latin American countries, was that U.S. technological changes entered Mexico faster than in the rest of the American hemisphere. After World War II, Mexico became the largest single recipient of U.S. capital. After 1940, 75 percent of Mexican commodities would arrive in the United States as a result of wartime markets being developed.

One of the greatest benefits to Mexican agriculture occurred when the Rockefeller Foundation became involved in improving Mexican farming techniques. The introduction of a systemized agricultural improvement program in Mexico emerged from a suggestion made by Vice-President Henry Wallace to the Rockefeller Foundation president. Wallace theorized that a broad scientific approach to food crop improvement would be beneficial, not only to Mexico but also to other developing nations as well. The new venture became formalized when Rockefeller representatives signed a 1943 agreement with Mexico. The program had two major objectives: a qualitative and quantitative improvement of Mexico's basic food crops and the creation of a parallel teaching and outreach program designed to improve both local and national agricultural education and enhance public application of the scientific advances attained by Rockefeller and government scientific personnel.

Working with the Mexican agricultural ministry, scientists analyzed germ plasm, cross-pollinization methods, resistance to diseases and insects, and statistical methods to produce hybrid crops. Because of wartime shortages in both Mexico and the United States, it was imperative to increase food production since many areas within Mexico teetered on the brink of starvation during the war. Mexico's yield per acre was already extremely low until the new "green revolution" techniques raised production enormously in subsequent years. As in the United States, the new technology benefited large growers rather than small ones. The benefits in Mexico went primarily to the wheat-producing sector utilizing large, privately held land in less densely populated states. The ejidal lands, devoted largely to corn cultivation by Mexico's rural poor, did not really benefit because they were rain dependent rather than irrigated. A big change was that the Mexican diet shifted toward wheat, milk, and beef. Eventually, more food was grown, but it did not always reach the tables of commoners during the 1940s.

Another step forward was a 1944 treaty which defined how the Río Grande is to be shared so that water loans between the two countries can pass the boundary when the lending nation has an abundant supply. This treaty accomplished two objectives. It assures Mexico of water from the upper Río Grande north of El Paso, and it allots the United States water from the Mexican tributaries that feed the river from below that point. This agreement allows the United States to keep one-third of the water from Mexican river basins, such as the Rio Conchos and the Rio Salado. The United States also keeps the water from the few small Texas streams. Specifically, the pact guarantees the United States an average of 113.8 billion gallons of Mexican water each year. For his part, Camacho began to plan large irrigation projects for the north that, coupled with the Rockefeller innovations, enabled a transformation of Mexican agriculture. Now the federal government could use the water agreements to manage the traditional problem of droughts much more effectively.

The international circumstances generated by the war intensified the government's intervention into the economy. The drastic reduction in imports, demands for strategic minerals such as uranium and mercury, and the necessity for self-sufficiency in basic commodities and consumer goods put a premium on an enlarged and more efficient productive capacity. The Camacho government used Nacional Financiera to direct capital toward industrial expansion. By now industrialists had become a powerful lobby with the establishment of the Cámara Nacional de la Industria de Transformación Nacional in 1942. Using their clout, industrialists received tax exemptions for as long as five to ten years. The government gradually adopted a policy of paying them rebates for the purchase of raw materials. With a ceiling on interest rates from domestic sources and no longer having to worry about the anxiety of foreign loans, industrialists began to realize that domestic political order lay in the future. Public employees changed their attitudes to aid entrepreneurs. Having discovered that their political careers no longer depended upon the implementation of Cardenista populist reforms and that bureaucratic management of mass organizations was all that was necessary, these officials began fusing their ambitions with those of domestic and foreign business people.

Forced to create new industries, a boom resulted when Mexican entrepreneurs worked with U.S. companies to establish national production centers. A good example of local industries replacing foreign sources is a Jalisco textile plant. Initially, textile mills had imported rayon from Italy and Germany, until the war cut off supplies.

Mexican industry had no domestic source for such fibers other than a minor rayon operation run by Italians. Mexican officials decided to recruit a large U.S. company, Celanese of New York, whose synthetic fiber had a wide open and eager market, but only if the company established a Mexican plant. The government stood eager to assist; Celanese Mexicana was soon incorporated and Ocotlán, Jalisco, became the site of the new Celanese chemical plant. The company hired 12 chemistry students from UNAM and sent them to the United States for additional training. Celanese Mexicana constituted a near-perfect import substitution model. It attracted new capital, introduced modern technology, trained national citizens in advanced techniques, provided well-paying jobs to a poor town, and supplied an eager market. The managers and technicians were Mexican, with only a handful of foreigners involved in any operations.

Camacho had paid particular attention to the role of UNAM in economic development. Working with, rather than against, UNAM faculty and administrators, Alémán enacted new statutory regulations in 1945 that would endure for the remainder of the century. By means of a slow but gradual process, the institutes of astronomy, geology, and biology became attached to the UNAM in the 1940s. Thus, the foundation was established for a coherent institutional promotion of scientific research that would cater to the increasing demand from entrepreneurs for technical expertise.

Alemán solidified and extended the Camacho administration's shift from Cardenismo. Cárdenas had set aside populist mobilization out of necessity in 1938 and the war years had prompted Camacho to initiate their reduction. Alemán reduced social spending and significantly increased expenditures for economic growth. In fact, public investment in agriculture and industry increased as a percentage of total investment more than ever under Alcmán.

Alemán encouraged industrialization and private-sector investment in part because he established high tariff protection. Since the creation of

import controls in 1947, Mexico had one of the highest levels of tariffs in Latin America. Alemán introduced quotas and licenses in 1947 to protect local industries, which were often inefficient and technologically limited. Industrial production nearly doubled during the Alemán *sexenio*, growing at an annual average of 7.2 percent. Perhaps even more dramatic is that the number of industrial establishments shot up from 13,000 in 1940 to 73,000 by 1950. Particularly notable industries appeared at this time, such as Condumex, a producer of electric wire, ICA, Mexico's dominant construction firm, and Tubos de Acero, a major producer of steel pipe. Alemán also demonstrated a certain nationalism by forcing Mexeric telephone company to sell its majority ownership to a group of Mexican investors, who then renamed the company Teléfonos de México, or Telmex. Alemán also ordered Mextelco to integrate its web with Telmex. Nevertheless, U.S. chains such as Sears and Woolworth appeared in Mexico City. And Alemán contributed greatly to economic growth by constructing the first modern highways which connected regional cities by means of 11,000 miles of concrete and multilaned thoroughfares. In addition, modern airports appeared in the major cities while new railroads transported goods and travelers to heretofore remote destinations. With new pipelines and refineries, PEMEX doubled its production.

In the agricultural sector of the economy, Alemán favored larger, established interests. This is particularly true of the cattle industry. When an outbreak of foot and mouth disease struck Mexico in December 1946, the government took decisive steps to constrain the threat posed by this dread disease. Alemán established a joint commission with the United States to provide machinery, personnel, and medication to combat the viral malady. Canneries relieved the glut of cattle on northern ranges while markets for northern Mexican cattle appeared in central and southern Mexico. Thus, the foot and mouth disease forced Mexico to approach her livestock industry more systematically, for the slaughter of affected livestock in Mexico necessitated the introduction of clean, higher-quality stock in order to rebuild the industry in infected regions. Mexican laboratories worked hard to develop a control vaccine that became effective in the field.

Modern regional development began in the 1940s and 1950s with federal investment focused on the great river basins around the rivers Mayo, Lerma, Papaloapan, and Balsas. The Papaloapan project in the states of Veracruz, Puebla, and Oaxaca added tens of thousands of acres for agricultural production. In addition, it added a series of hydroelectric stations that contributed to a tripling of Mexican electrical output capacity by 1952.

The river projects were complemented by the construction of huge irrigation works in the northeast as well as in states like Chiapas, Guerrero, and Michoacán. By the late 1940s, massive public investments underwrote latifunda in the northern area, particularly northwestern Mexico. With certificates of "inaffectibility" in their hands, crop producers knew that their land could not be expropriated. The result was that bananas, grapes, cotton, coffee, sugar, and henequen increased notably. Irrigated land produced three to four times as much as nonirrigated fields.

Mexican policy continued to undermine the self-sufficiency of peasants and *ejidatarios*. For example, the Banco Ejidal would not loan money to villages that raised crops for local consumption. Instead, the Banco Ejidal loaned only to municipalities which promised to grow crops intended for cash exports. Eventually, 85 percent of the ejidos became subsistence oriented since they did not enjoy the luxury of irrigation and often had to pray for rain. Land distribution came to a halt under Alemán while federal expenditures for agricultural credit to the ejidos decreased.

During the Ruiz Cortines regime, the government emphasized austerity and careful financial management. Ruiz Cortines began on a populist note by insisting that the price of basic foods, particularly beans and corn, be lowered. The purchasing power of most consumers had declined since 1937 because of inflation or scarcities. The Korean War had encouraged agricultural interests to export abroad for healthier profits rather than consider the Mexican market. Therefore, Ruiz Cortines threatened that speculation, hoarding, and overpriced food would result in fines against big monopolies. Business interests objected and a wave of capital flight out of Mexico resulted. To increase investment, discourage purchases of foreign-produced imports, and pay for Alemán's deficit-funded outlays, Ruiz Cortines had to devalue the peso in 1953. It was an unpleasant but necessary move. The peso remained at 12.50 to the dollar well into the 1970s. The cautious president also initiated a reduction of inflation, which from 1955 to 1970 averaged only 3 percent in Mexico, a rate lower than in the United States. Ruiz Cortines maintained the healthy policy of avoiding foreign debt with the pleasant result that Mexico's national debt amounted to a mere $64 million when he left office in 1958.

López Mateos initiated a much more active role in the economy, as many claimed that Ruiz Cortines had done little to raise the standard of living among peasants or increase the economic power of the state. More seriously, it seemed to many that the pragmatic Ruiz Cortines had tied Mexico's economic future to the United States. The new economic policies adopted by López Mateos increased the role of the public sector. The fear of Marxist Cuba provided favorable terms for international credit which stimulated industrial growth and federal social welfare policies. The brilliant Antonio Ortiz Mena became the finance minister at this time. During his 12 years in power, the buying power of wage earners went up 6.4 percent per year. Although the government nationalized the motion picture and electric industries while extending Mexican ownership of Telmex, steel, fertilizer, aviation, newsprint, chemicals, and the railroads, Ortiz Mena balanced the budget and minimized the country's foreign debt. Only 2.2 percent of the budget went for defense and military spending, a record exceeded only by Panama and Costa Rica. Meanwhile, the quantity of mined iron doubled between 1958 and 1962. Private companies that had received generous concessions to produce lumber and paper from Mexican forests but with no attention to conservation lost their concessions in the 1950s. Publicly owned sawmills and paper factories began to reduce the ravages of deforestation, particularly in the upland temperate zones of southern Oaxaca, Chiapas, and the Yucatán. In 1957, López Mateos established a nuclear energy commission.

As his regime came to a close, López Mateos established CONASUPO, a government program to provide basic goods, particularly food, to working-class people. CONASUPO operated by purchasing grains and other agricultural products from cultivators at guaranteed prices before selling the same items to marginal consumers. When it emerged in 1961, CONASUPO could buy only corn, beans, and other basic agricultural commodities for distribution in urban areas.

Díaz Ordaz tied Mexico closer than ever to the United States economy while extending privileges to Mexican entrepreneurs. The Border Industrialization Program became the most important innovation during the 1960s. The end of the World War II labor contracting system in 1964 had contributed to unemployment rates of 40 to 50 percent in some Mexican border cities. At the same time, rising competition from European and Japanese industry inspired many U.S. electronics and garment industries to seek new areas of cheap labor in underdeveloped countries. Confronted by massive unemployment in a region with a small industrial base, the Díaz Ordaz government created the Border Industrialization Program in 1965. It allowed entirely foreign-owned corporations to set up labor-intensive assembly shops within a 12.5 mile strip south of the Mexican border, pay Mexican workers a fraction of the U.S. wage rate, and pay virtually no taxes or import duties to the Mexican government. The *maquiladora* plants were required to export all their production in order to protect Mexican industry.

U.S. companies such as Motorola, Levi Strauss, Fairchild, and Hughes aircraft soon stormed into the border area. Beginning with 72 authorized U.S. *maquiladoras* in 1967, the number grew to 273 by 1972 and reached 665 by late 1974. In a few short years, Mexico became the largest assembler of U.S. components processed abroad and re-exported to the United States.

For the men and women hired by the *maquiladoras*, their new place of work meant an improvement over the long tedious hours bent over an assembly line. The assembly shops had expanded the size of the available work force by hiring young females—many of whom were not previously job seekers—and by attracting even greater numbers of migrants from Mexico's interior. Some 70,000 workers came into the work force of the *maquiladoras*, a process which has changed their lives. The contrast between the environment of the shiny new factories and the young women's former lives as housewives, fieldhands, or domestics often created attitudes of loyalty and conformity. The companies worked hard to foster these attitudes through the organization of company soccer teams and beauty contests. But the companies resisted unionization when workers found that their wages could not always support families.

Meanwhile, tourist expenditures became vital. As more U.S. and European visitors flocked to sunny beaches and warm climates throughout Mexico, the government's excellent promotion of tourism paid off to the extent that by 1968, the country was earning more from tourism than from the sale of goods. Posted prices in hotel rooms assured visitors to Mexico that they could pay an established price which was normally quite affordable. Well-informed tourists learned that merely mentioning a desire to speak with tourism officials would straighten out difficulties with inattentive hotel employees.

On the surface, Mexico seemed to be enjoying good times. The gross national product grew by 8 percent in 1968. Although autocratic, Díaz Ordaz was also honest and not one to waste money. Therefore, the peso remained stable and Ortiz Mena could balance the budget. Moreover, Díaz Ordaz enjoyed excellent relations with the business community, partially because of the regressive nature of the tax system, which provided generous loopholes for entrepreneurs as well as owners of stocks and bonds. In 1965, the tariff wall that protected Mexican industries assumed monumental proportions when the government increased tariff charges by 6 percent. Nearly 13,000 new import quotas became enacted by the end of Díaz Ordaz's term.

Only a few troubling signs appeared. Because the economy had experienced considerable growth, the demand on electrical energy surpassed previous estimates. At the same time, oil prices climbed steadily in the late 1960s, and Mexico was forced to import oil by 1970. Therefore, the growing number of Mexican scientists and engineers trained in the United States to develop nuclear electric energy began to urge the nuclear commission to establish reactors in Mexico. By 1970, the government agreed to build a reactor at Laguna Verde on a fresh water lagoon adjacent to the sea about 50 miles north of Veracruz port. Meanwhile, the government's lack of interest in agriculture manifested itself when in 1966, corn production began to decline.

SUGGESTED READING

Camp, Roderic. *Generals in the Palacio: The Military in Modern Mexico*. New York: Oxford University Press, 1992.

Cárdenas, Enrique. *La hacienda pública y la política económia.*Mexico City: El Colegio de México, 1994.

Ceceña, José Luis. *México en la órbita imperial: las empresas transnacionales*. Mexico City: El Caballito, 1970.

Cline, Howard F. *The United States and Mexico*. New York: Atheneum, 1963.

————. *Mexico: Revolution to Evolution*. New York: Oxford University Press, 1963.

Cole, William E. *Steel and Economic Growth in Mexico*. Austin: University of Texas Press, 1967.

Esteva, Gustavo. *La batalla en Mexico rural*. Mexico City: SigloVeintiuno, 1980.

Fuentes, Carlos. *Tiempo Mexicano*. Mexico City: Cuadernos deJoaquin Mortiz, 1975.

Gonzáles Casanova, Pablo. *Democracy in Mexico*. New York:Oxford University Press, 1970.

Hansen, Roger D. *The Politics of Mexican Development*. Baltimore, MD: Johns Hopkins University Press, 1971.

Hellman, Judith. *Mexico in Crisis*. New York: Holmes and Meir, 1978.

Hernandez Rodríguez, Rogelio. *La formación del político mexicano: El caso de Carlos A. Madrazo*. Mexico City: El Colegio de México, 1991.

Johnson, Kenneth F. *Mexican Democracy: A Critical View*. 3d ed. New York: Praeger, 1984.

Kirk, Betty. *Covering the Mexican Front*. Norman: University of Oklahoma Press, 1942.

Kuntz Ficker, Sandra. *Empresa extranjera y mercado interior*. Mexico City: El Colegio de México, 1995.

Liss, Sheldon. *A Century of Disagreement: The Chamizal Conflict, 1864–1964*. Washington, DC: University Press of Washington, DC, 1965.

Medin, Tzvi. *El sexenio alemanista: Ideología y praxis política de Miguel Alemán*. Mexico City: Ediciones Era, 1990.

Medina, Luis. *Civilismo y modernización del autoritarismo*. Mexico City: El Colegio de México, 1979.

Middlebrook, Kevin. *The Paradox of Revolution: Labor, the State, and Authoritarianism in Mexico*. Baltimore, MD: Johns Hopkins University Press, 1995.

Niblo, Stephen R. *Mexico in the 1940s: Modernity, Politics, and Corruption*. Wilmington, DE: Scholarly Resources, 1999.

————. *War, Diplomacy, and Development: The United States and Mexico, 1938–1954*. Wilmington, DE: Scholarly Resources, 1995.

Paz, Emilia María. *Strategy, Security, and Spies: Mexico and the U.S. as Allies in World War II*. University Park: Pennsylvania State University Press, 1997.

Pellicer de Brody, Olga. *México y la revolución Cubana*. Mexico City: El Colegio de México, 1972.

Pellicer de Brody, Olga, and José Luis Reyna. *El afianzamiento la estabilidad política*. Mexico City: El Colegio de México, 1981.

Poniatowska, Elena. *Massacre in Mexico*. Columbia: University of Missouri Press, 1991.

Sepúlveda Amor, Bernardo, Olga Pellicer de Brody, and Lorenzo Meyer. *Las empresas transnacionales en México*. Mexico City: El Colegio de México, 1974.

Smith, Peter H. *Labyrinths of Power: Political Recruitment in Twentieth Century Mexico*. Princeton, NJ: Princeton University Press, 1979.

Story, Dale. *The Mexican Ruling Party: Stability and Authority*. New York: Praeger, 1978.

————. *Industry, the State, and Public Policy in Mexico*. Austin: University of Texas Press, 1986.

Torres Ramírez, Blanca. *Mexico en la Segunda Guerra Mundial*. Mexico City: El Colegio de México, 1979.

Wilkie, James W. *The Mexican Revolution: Federal Expenditure and Social Change Since 1910*. Berkeley: University of California Press, 1967.

16

Social Change and Migration, 1940–1970

An emerging confidence characterized much of Mexican society from 1940 to 1970. In the intellectual realm, Mexican literature entered a new tradition of emphasizing Mexican issues in universal terms. In contrast to the nineteenth century, which produced no great novel, brilliant works of fiction appeared beginning in 1947. Society enjoyed better schooling, particularly in terms of higher education. Nevertheless, many Mexicans grappled with poverty and for that reason, millions sought employment in the United States throughout virtually every decade of the twentieth century.

CULTURAL AND INTELLECTUAL TRENDS

Preserving the National Fabric. Mexican artists continued to receive public support and international acclaim. Mid-twentieth-century Mexican art reveals a growing diversity in artistic styles and purposes. Painters made a conscious effort to develop themes of humor, caricature, allegories of Mexican legends, and surrealist themes. Some continued to make an effort to establish continuity between indigenous tradition and twentieth century Mexican life. In the 1940s, Diego Rivera enjoyed a wealth of private com-

missions and had many patrons for his easel paintings. Portraiture, often of friends and lovers, became a central aspect of his art. His work in the 1950s, although painted during the Cold War, expressed hope for world unity and peace. At the time of his death, Rivera was among the best known and most admired artists in the world. A sophisticate who employed international modernist styles as well as ancient indigenous motifs, Rivera was a painter of epic historical mythology.

The new artists continued a nationalistic tradition but also reflected the cosmopolitan tendencies of Rivera. Juan O'Gorman painted wonderful historical panoramas but became best known for his design of the Central Library at UNAM. A fabulous mosaic of 10,000 stones explains the history of Mexico by means of a striking mural. Rufino Tamayo was even more of an international figure. Born in Oaxaca, he lived in New York for ten years. He rejected the explicitly political muralism of Rivera and Orozco in favor of a more intimate, personal style. Nevertheless, he fused elements of pre-Hispanic art with modern currents such as impressionism and surrealism. Tamayo, however, never maintained a consistent level of creativity. The abstractions of other artists during the 1950s were often mediocre and superficial.

The last of the important muralists, Siqueiros, experienced a transition from determined Marxist to the posh life of a government supporter. Sigueiros had earlier been an enemy of López Mateos when he openly labeled his presidency as "neo-Porfirian" and suggested that don Porfirio would highly approve of the direction that the PRI was taking Mexico. These words found Siqueiros serving a four-year prison term on trumped up charges. Although Siqueiros was able to sell paintings for $2,000 to $5,000 apiece while behind bars, the experience of prison ended Siqueiros's criticism of the government. Upon his release in 1964, Siqueiros was commissioned to paint the largest mural in the world—50,000 square feet—in a new Siqueiros Cultural Polyforum—a compound especially erected to house the mural. He was paid $800 per week to complete the mural in time for the 1968 Olympics. The project was an obvious ploy to attract tourists. Although criticized by several for selling out to the PRI, Siqueiros eagerly went to work, although neither the building nor the mural were ready in time for the games.

The Nueva Presencia movement of the early 1960s capped trends in painting. It began during a confrontation between socially conscious artists and the "pure painters." Newer painters had become increasingly critical of the great masters, particularly Rivera, who had become over productive. Rivera's tourist pictures, portraits of wealthy patrons, and sentimental canvases of big-eyed children weakened his reputation among modernists. United by their belief in the importance of the human image in art, artists such as Arnold Belkin, Francisco Icaza, and José Luis Cuevas distanced themselves from the social realism of their predecessors as well as the pure abstractions of many contemporaries.

At this time, Mexico established a reputation for innovative architectural accomplishments. The UNAM campus was a particularly breathtaking creation. Constructed as if it were an Aztec metropolis, it featured large structures as well as broad gardens and grassy promenades. Although it cost $25 million, the UNAM project became Alemán's monument and was well worth it. Meanwhile, the first high-rise apartments sprang

up in 1949 as the creation of architect Mario Pani. Another architect, Luis Barragán, designed the famous Pedregal suburb in the San Angel district of Mexico City. Here he turned formerly volcanic rock formations into flowered gardens where future presidents and wealthy business tycoons would live. The greatest Mexican architect of the twentieth century, Barragán embraced European modernism but developed a style that connected with pre-Hispanic traditions in a new, vital medium.

A particularly compelling legacy of this confident period were the high-quality museums that embraced the historical continuity of the Mexican past. López Mateos inaugurated the Museum of Natural History, another detailing the history of Mexico City, and a permanent exhibition of the colonial period. The magnificent Museum of Anthropology and History is the hallmark of the López Mateos presidency. One of the greatest museums in the world, it became an instant success with its intelligent presentation of pre-Hispanic artifacts on the lower level and current re-creations of indigenous life above. Parallel to the construction of museums was an ongoing attempt to restore and renovate historical buildings and landmarks.

Mexican music fortified traditional concepts while embracing new tunes. The phenomenally popular dance music, *banda*, had originated over a century earlier but continued to grow and eventually swept into Los Angeles. Mariachi music never lost its charm nor did *ranchero* ballads in the north. Mambo and cha cha cha music from Cuba became the rage of the 1950s. Carlos Chávez established Mexico's two national symphony orchestras and transposed European ballet and opera into Mexican mediums by synthesizing classical music concepts with Mexican folklore, rhythms, and modalities. In the late 1950s, jazz orchestras introduced rock music to Mexico. Bill Haley and Jim Morrison and the Doors performed in Mexico City despite the efforts of authorities to limit rock concerts. Expatriates such as Ricardo Valenzuela (who had his named changed to Richie Valens) and Carlos Santana, who emigrated from his native Jalisco to Tijuana and then to San Francisco, provided a sense of participation. Rock music appealed to Mexicans largely for its sense of rhythm which could easily stimulate dancing.

The government also invested into promoting the indigenous culture. The new Instituto Nacional Indigenista gained grudging acceptance from indigenous peoples as well as the population at large. It represented an official PRI commitment to improve living conditions. A basic literacy campaign was launched since the majority of Indians were monolingual in indigenous languages. Tourists were encouraged to buy handicrafts whose techniques were carefully preserved so that they would not die out. Radio broadcasts of indigenous music were tastefully managed by the early 1970s. The first regional development program in 1951 aided indigenous peoples by offering more schools, health services, and legal aid.

A Writing Boom.

Mexican fiction took its place in the mainstream of world literature. Four great writers insisted that Mexican problems were valid themes for fiction only if viewed in universal terms. Although the nineteenth century failed to produce a significant novel, the latter half of the twentieth century yielded several. The first of these was *Al filo del agua* (*The Edge of the Storm*) by Agustin Yañez in 1947. For many years a professor at UNAM, Yañez eventually became governor of his native Jalisco from 1953 to 1959 as well as secretary of education under Díaz Ordaz. Set in a rural village, the tense dialogue describes an isolated community in the context of the 1910 civil war. Yañez became the first Mexican to utilize Freudian techniques in a novel, introducing dreams within the narrative as well as sexual needs. Some of his characters even become psychotic. He also establishes Catholicism as the vital element within the community, continually interacting with the consciousness of the villagers. Despite the author's anticlerical tone, he does not attack religion.

Octavio Paz firmly believed that poetry constituted "the secret religion of the modern age." A

remarkable prose stylist, Paz wrote essays on art, literature, and politics. A moralist concerned with universal truths, he refused to compromise principle. Upon his return to Mexico from the Spanish Civil War, Paz began a career in Mexico's foreign service. Named ambassador to India in 1962, Paz resigned in protest of the government's massacre of students at Tlatelolco. He once sympathized with Castro's revolution but became disenchanted when the Cuban government became Marxist. He rarely left his Mexico City apartment in the 1970s but remained in the public eye with his political opinions, which often managed to annoy both leftist intellectuals as well as the PRI. In 1990, Paz became the first Mexican to win the Nobel Prize, boosting his international profile and cementing his legacy in Mexico.

His best known work is *The Labyrinth of Solitude* (1950) in which Paz explores Mexican character and history. Paz maintains that many Mexicans wear modern masks over ancient souls. The inner tensions of being *mestizo* has not been resolved because terms such as *chingar* (screw) refer to the rape of Mexican women by Spanish conquistadores. The violation of one's mother motivates many Mexicans, he concluded, to reject their indigenous and Hispanic past, creating isolation and an uneasy solitude. The natural response is machismo. In order for males to uphold the macho cultural standard of toughness, they must never back down. To do so demonstrates weakness just as opening up to those nearby lessens the defenses which maintain manliness. As Paz put it, "manliness is judged according to one's invulnerability to enemy arms or the impact of the outside world." This further enhances the solitude within Mexican culture, especially when the tenets of machismo are compared to women.

According to Paz, Mexican culture equates females to a dark, secret, and passive presence, even though it can be argued effectively that these passive cultural attributes, while providing the source for the high public respect for women, are merely hypocritical means of subjecting them and limiting their expression. The reality of this sex typing is what Paz refers to as the "masking" of truly intimate feelings, thus furthering the solitude that Paz concerned himself with.

Paz also surveyed the major periods in Mexican history and found that for most of the past, Mexicans have wandered through life without a cultural heritage that fits their historical reality. Hence the Mexican propensity for hiding themselves, for not revealing a true inner self. To relieve the tension of having to keep themselves in constant isolation, Mexicans celebrate myriad fiestas. Paz describes the fiesta as an explosion of self, a time when each Mexican breaks out of his solitude. The community comes away from the fiesta strengthened by contact between individuals.

The humble Juan Rulfo preferred avoiding publicity. His tragic childhood occurred during the Cristero revolt when his family experienced financial ruin, his parents died, and he lived in a Guadalajara orphanage. Although his education ended at the age of fifteen, Rulfo became a voracious reader. An exponent of magical realism, Rulfo developed into a magnificent writer who gained fame with *El llano en llamas* (*The Burning Plain*), in 1953, which depicts a powerful, corrupt, and heartless government which distributes worthless plots of land to ignorant peasants. It is a cruel, inhospitable, rural region where people struggle for survival. The main characters are poor campesinos whose existence is impaired by hard work, poverty, violence, and handicapped by erratic weather which often damages or destroys their crops. Physical and spiritual needs are frequently in open conflict for they are existential beings, true victims of circumstance. Thus, the fortunes of individual Mexicans show little indication of progress or some sort of "Mexican miracle."

Rulfo was very surprised by the success of his great novel *Pedro Páramo* in 1955. It is one of the few Latin American novels of this period to articulate the inner lives of campesinos. The novel is set in his rural Jalisco and Rulfo describes people associated with a wealthy landowner, the cacique Pedro Páramo. Rulfo has negated chronological sequence, causing the reader to never be sure whether the context is present, past, or even real.

It is clear that the landowners are not sharing revolutionary goals, but only manipulating the masses to defend their wealth and land. Rural speech, brief dialogues, and simple images provide a strong visual effect. In the final paragraph, Pedro Páramo dies, but he has actually been dead throughout the novel. Thus, the bitter evaluation of the outcome of the Mexican revolution provides little hope for the future, a major characteristic of most mid-twentieth century novelists.

Carlos Fuentes represents the nationalistic tradition of Mexican writers. Endowed with a solid sense of the country's history, Fuentes created a sense of Mexicanness that practically leaps from the pages of his brilliant novels. One of the few writers who could live solely on his income, Fuentes took center stage in Mexico during the Latin American "boom" in novels from 1956 to 1962. Fuentes, along with other illustrious Latin American authors such as Julio Cortázar, Gabriel García Márquez, and Mario Vargas Llosa comprised this "boom." The characteristics that these authors shared were belonging to an international literary circle, extensive travel, living in other countries, and finding inspiration from their cultural heritage. At that time, Fuentes was the most active of the four.

In *La región más transparente (Where the Air Is Clear)*, Fuentes emphasizes the loss of populistic energy after 1940. This 1958 novel is a complex and multilayered account of Mexico in the 1950s which Fuentes characterizes as a nation out of touch with itself; proud and dignified, but still seeking acceptance and approval. Fuentes presents the 1910–1920 revolutionary struggle as forging clear goals with a positive future but failing because of leaders who lost their idealism and became stagnant. Thus, the central figure is Federico Robles, an old revolutionary who enriches himself by applying capitalistic rules at the expense of others. Nevertheless, like all the other characters, he suffers an identity crisis. Intellectuals are disillusioned, finding no purpose. Hangovers from the Porfiriato merge into the new elite but are transparent and superficial. The title of the book, which is set in Mexico City, implies that

Fuentes could not find a place where he could breathe the clear air of a reformed Mexico—that Mexico City had become suffocating and fatal.

Fuentes's best novel is *La muerte de Artemio Cruz (The Death of Artemio Cruz)*, which appeared in 1962. This is the story of an illegitimate boy who fights successfully in the revolution only to betray it, becomes wealthy, but dies an embittered old man. The book is basically concerned with choice and survival. Cruz is presented with many options which enable him to acquire wealth by sharp deals made after 1920 involving short term loans and the acquisition of land courtesy of friendly Mexican presidents. Cruz is a master powerbroker, supremely skilled at utilizing Mexico's changing political scene, capitalizing on the weaknesses of others while he himself seems devoid of loyalty to anyone but himself. To Fuentes, this deceit symbolized the conduct of the PRI after 1940. Cold U.S. investors, bureaucrats, the middle class, and the educational system are also blamed for the falsehoods of Cruz, which sent the nation's wealth abroad.

Perhaps the most interesting stylistic aspects are the unique writing techniques. Interspersed with and balancing the flashbacks are scenes from the present where the dying Cruz describes his death agony in a vivid stream of consciousness. The words are dynamic and powerful. Internal monologues describe crucial events in Cruz's life. His machismo explodes constantly. Thus the novel serves to exemplify the Mexican character. It is also an extremely sensual novel. The reader tastes, touches, feels, smells, hears, and sees as Cruz does. It contains remarkable descriptions of regions such as lush tropical settings in Veracruz, the dry north, and the sensuality of Mexico City.

The novellete *Aura* (1962) is the most distinctive literature written by Fuentes. Here he demonstrates versatility in themes, structure, the fusing of past and present, and the use of surrealism. Particularly notable is an unrestrained imagination while Fuentes clothes his thoughts in sharp satire. He denounces the oppression of the weak and the ignorant, the pseudointellectuals for their superficiality, Mexico's subordinate relation with the United States, and the commercialization of the modern world. He rejects moral codes and social rules. A couple makes love while a crucified Jesus Christ hangs on the wall. The woman, opening her body is compared to Jesus Christ. Fuentes blames society for tolerating injustice and letting inequity flourish. He sees love as a source for providing meaning to life.

Academic Advances. After 1940, the government continued to invest a great deal in higher education. The UNAM remained largely autonomous from the state despite constant strikes and factional squabbling amid political factions. Marxism maintained a high profile among the largely part-time faculty. Retaining the European model inherited from the colonial period, the UNAM gradually became an open-admission university. Beginning in 1948, the tuition was merely 200 pesos a year for the rest of the century. In return, graduates had to provide a year of free national service. A particularly creative innovation was the establishment of the Instituto de Investigaciones Históricas in 1945.

The greatest success in the intellectual realm was the training of many great social scientists. In 1943, Leopoldo Zea published *El positivismo en Mexico*, the first major historiographical view of Mexican history. A phenomenal piece of intellectual history, Zea's study of positivism possesses tremendous meaning, context, and reality. Anthropology became a particularly active discipline. In his 1961 *Los antiguos mexicanos a través de sus crónicas y cantares*, Miguel León Portillo succeeded in persuading Mexicans to understand and take pride in their pre-Hispanic legacy. His gracefully written study rests upon zealous field work and deep thought. Between 1962 and 1964, Ignacio Bernal directed the restoration of Teotihuacan so that visitors could gain at least some impression of the city's former grandeur. Many scholars became secure enough to become openly critical of the national government. Pablo González Casanova, a political sociologist at the UNAM, published a devastating critique of the political system, *La democracia en México* (1965), which described its lack of democracy, dependent economic development, and called for independent social science research based on the needs of developing nations.

El Colegio de México expanded enormously from 1940 to 1970. It faced serious problems after the conservative secretary of education under Camacho stopped channeling funds to the institution because of the leftist affiliation of many of its Spanish faculty. The Rockefeller Foundation stepped in to continue its earlier support of Hispanic refugees as part of the foundation's broader policy to assist several areas of higher education in Mexico. Mexican intellectuals, led by historian Daniel Cosío Villegas, obtained permanent Rockefeller support for resident teachers, fellowships for full-time students, and funds for a library. As other institutions absorbed Spanish refugee scholars and the work of Mexican intellectuals gained increased recognition, the Mexican government replaced the Rockefeller Foundation in supporting El Colegio de México.

Cosío Villegas continued to guide El Colegio de Mexico to well-deserved prominence. He designed the institute after outstanding U.S. graduate schools so that full-time faculty emphasized seminars for students who obtained sufficient financial support to study effectively. The faculty utilized the latest methodologies while emphasizing social sciences rather than literature or law. Perhaps because its serious middle-class and upper-middle-class students rarely demonstrated or protested, El Colegio de México soon began receiving as much financial support as UNAM. A particularly notable accomplishment was the creation of the Centro de Estudios Históricos, directed by Silvio Zavala. Ten years later, in 1951, Cosío Villegas founded a first-rate journal, *Historia Mexicana*, which became the best historical journal in all of Latin America. During his tenure as director of El Colegio de México, Cosío Villegas established the Centro de Estudios Internacionales, reinforcing the cosmopolitan atmosphere at El Colegio de México. Finally, he resigned to complete his monumental *Historia*

Moderna de Mexico project, a nine-volume history of the restored republic and the Porfiriato. This 23-year project is undoubtedly the outstanding piece of Mexican scholarship the twentieth century.

While individual academics achieved distinction, most of society grappled with an intellectual atmosphere that still required attention. Most intellectuals served the national government out of necessity, often rationalizing that serving the state was their primary role. About 28 percent of the intellectuals became permanent government officials, usually in Mexico City, while the majority did political work of one kind or another. At this time, Mexican universities did not hire full-time professors and most faculty could not survive on their small salaries. Therefore, public service attracted many to the PRI. Compared to other nations, Mexico had a scarcity of books, libraries, bookstores, and active readers. By 1980, only 300 permanent libraries existed. Few private foundations provided for inquiring minds while the limited size of the Mexican publishing industry cramped the possibilities of offering academic insights. The limits of intellectual activity beyond what the government provided were also anchored in Mexico's social development at that time.

THE SOCIAL FABRIC

From 1940 to 1970, Mexican society experienced overall improvement. The position of women, an end to religious persecution, and better social services raised expectations for improved living standards. Critics, however, decried the persistence of poverty as well as increased cultural influence from the United States.

Social Changes. Tangible social shifts began during the World War II era. Obligatory military service for all males between the ages of 18 and 45 met with enthusiasm by some. But the draft also represented a violation of guarantees that constituted freedom of peasant life and the ability

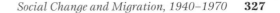

to provic / for families. Several peasant uprisings
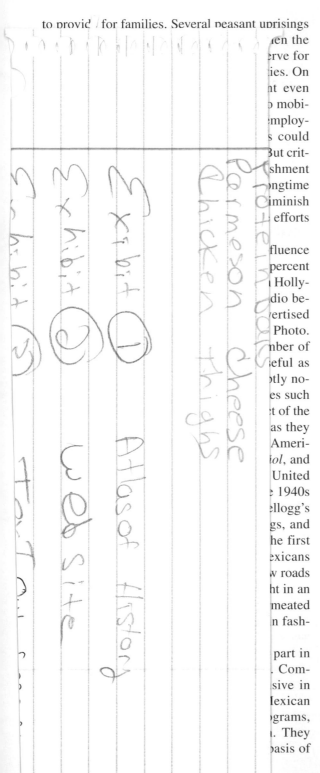
...en the
...erve for
...ies. On
...nt even
...o mobi-
...mploy-
...s could
...But crit-
...shment
...ongtime
...iminish
...efforts

...fluence
...percent
...Holly-
...dio be-
...vertised
...Photo.
...nber of
...seful as
...otly no-
...es such
...t of the
...as they
...Ameri-
...iol, and
...United
...e 1940s
...ellogg's
...gs, and
...he first
...exicans
...w roads
...ht in an
...meated
...n fash-

...part in
...Com-
...sive in
...lexican
...grams,
...They
...basis of

U.S. ratings. Telephone communications forced Mexico to adopt a faster rhythm of life. News agencies, such as United Press International and Associated Press, projected good and bad guy stereotypes according to U.S. interests. First, they condemned Japanese and Germans, later Russians, Chinese, North Koreans, and Cubans.

Comic books became extraordinarily popular. Perhaps 50 million were being published each month by the late 1970s. Some promoted the view that average citizens were powerless; others emphasized female escapism. Political satirist Eduardo del Rio attacked corruption. Comics were fairly free of foreign influence and even addressed regional humor and adventure.

The Culture of Poverty. A U.S. anthropologist articulated a culture of poverty that portrayed the poorest members of Mexican society in the 1950s. According to Oscar Lewis, the culture of poverty is a persistent condition, a remarkably stable lifestyle which is passed down from generation to generation among family members. Unemployment, low wages, unskilled work, child labor, absence of savings, shortage of cash, lack of food reserves, borrowing from local money lenders at high interest rates, and informal credit all characterize the constant struggle for survival. Lewis conducted his work by allowing the family of Santos Hernández, patriarch of the family described in Lewis's best-selling *The Children of Sanchez* (1961), to speak into tape recorders.

These first-person oral histories presented a nonsentimentalized account of urban Mexican poverty that was unprecedented among anthropologists. Lewis uncovered a pervasive lack of self-esteem among the poor. Frustrated fathers responded by drinking, wasting time and money, and engaging in casual extramarital affairs. Women seemed to accept philandering spouses. Shocking to many readers was the collapse of family units when fathers often disappeared, reverting to the worst aspects of machismo. The poor suffered from housing shortages and overcrowding to the extent that as many as 20 people lived in one-room homes. Because of low food supplies, children were expected to sell gum, matches, and even bandaids to help provide family incomes. Thus, the cycle of poverty perpetuated itself because little hope for entering the university or preparing a career seemed possible.

The Children of Sanchez and other books published by Lewis produced controversy. Other academics questioned his objectivity by seemingly selecting the lowest common denominator of Mexican society. Traditional values seemed absent among his figures who had little respect for neighbors while children questioned the authority of parents. Village life seemed to be disappearing and replaced with a new city outlook. Participants in the 1910–1920 civil war considered the revolution a failure since they had received no appreciable improvement in their living standards; although by 1959, Mexicans enjoyed several conveniences and services that earlier generations had yearned for. To many readers, the figures that Lewis interviewed seemed unwilling or unable to defer gratification for the sake of a planned future.

Living Standards. The PRI provided improved services to the majority which reflected a higher quality of life than before. But the government also allowed the business community to save and increase its profits with the unpleasant result that a highly inequitable pattern of income distribution resulted. The distance between rich and poor in Mexico became one of the worst in Latin America. Thus, a lack of tax reform became evident. Only 10.4 percent of Mexico's gross national product came from tax collection by 1965, the lowest figure for all of Latin America. Politicians rarely paid any taxes and 80 percent of businesses avoided taxes as well.

The public health services expanded periodically between 1940 and 1970. The Centro Médico in Mexico City was one of many clinics that provided free health services. Despite the claims of Porfirian elites that wheat was nutritionally superior to corn, research in the 1940s demonstrated that diets of beans, tortillas, and chiles were more than satisfactory. As *indigenismo* became

the basis for nationalism, tamales and enchiladas gained acceptance in the 1940s. Partially because of political order, life expectancy increased from between 33 and 38 years for the 1925–1940 years to 62 by 1970.

Mexico's commitment to education is illustrated by its employment of 360,000 teachers by 1970 with far fewer soldiers. Many other Latin American countries could not say the same. Although Alemán held teacher salaries so low that it became difficult to staff schools with certified instructors, primary grade enrollment increased 147 percent from 1950 to 1965; for secondary schools, attendance shot up by 552 percent. The growth in school attendance occurred primarily in urban areas. Most encouraging was the decline in illiteracy, which fell from 41 percent in 1950 to 16 percent by 1970. Nevertheless, only 3 percent entered higher education by 1969 and only 6 percent of the population purchased and read books.

Although the rich were better off than ever, real wages fell during the 1940s before improving during the last two decades of the century, averaging about 16 percent overall. And what can be said about the distribution of income compared to other countries? By 1963, the poorest half of the population received only 15.6 percent of national income. In the United States, the poorest half got 23 percent; in the United Kingdom, they received 25 percent. By 1963, 43 percent of Mexican families earned $48 a month or less. That is a sobering figure which calls into question any rhapsody about a Mexican miracle taking place.

The real crisis of Mexican society occurred in the rural regions. In 1960, slightly over 1 percent of the farming population owned more than 50 percent of total farmland. At the same time, 77 percent of farmers owned only 11 percent of private croplands. Much of the agrarian problem occurred because the ejido system had become an economic drain, usually supporting subsistence farmers. A million ejido residents had plots incapable of supporting a single family, largely because the government had given them inferior land. Lacking credit, irrigation, and technology by 1970, only 1.2 million of Mexico's 2.6 million ejidatarios had "agrarian certificates" which entitled them to benefits the others lacked. Competition for land had become intense. By 1960, the number of farm laborers without land had gone up from 2.3 million in 1950 to 3.3 million in 1960. In towns such as San José de Gracia, Michoacán, the poor could not support themselves and had to migrate to find a better life.

Urbanization. The decline of life in the countryside resulted in a substantial growth of cities. Most notable is the rapid population increase in Mexico City, which shot up from 4 million in 1950 to 12 million by 1975. Even though the pressure of newcomers flocking in served to keep wages low within the capital, the federal district offered more jobs and higher wages than their rural homelands. This transformation weakened the interior because the rural people who moved to Mexico City were younger, better educated, and more skilled in their jobs than the average person in their rural communities. Most who came had few regrets and vowed never to return. Because of the lack of housing in the core of Mexico City, most migrants settled on marginal land within the city's outskirts or in surrounding municipalities.

Strangely enough, many migrants became landowners for the first time in their lives, albeit by taking part in squatter invasions. After acquiring a plot of land, the migrants had a great incentive to obtain title to their land and to urbanize the communities through the extension of municipal services, such as water and electricity. In this atmosphere of mutual acquisition, many urban migrants learned to cooperate with each other by petitioning the government to address their needs. Since the size of many *colonias* expanded enormously—Ciudad Nezahualcóyotl grew from 10,000 to 2 million during this period—political opportunities also presented themselves.

The PRI learned to use migrant issues as a means of garnering publicity and political support from the lower classes. Most *colonias* relied upon a community leader who developed contacts with the government. These caciques as-

sumed the responsibility of taking on squatter petitions to PRI authorities. At the same time, ambitious community leaders would often hinder the completion of a street or school in order to maintain their position of power within the community. Caciques often required payoffs from residents or forced recalcitrant inhabitants to participate in community actions by threatening to throw them off their land. Meanwhile, the PRI co-opted community leaders by allowing them to succeed as caciques in return for the caciques lining up votes and public demonstrations for the PRI. Thus, *colonia* residents became politicized when they had needs to be filled, and they readily chose the path of political participation within proper government channels.

Although many predicted that poor migrants to the cities would become radicalized, the newcomers to Mexico City supported the government more strongly than those native-born. They believed that they could achieve more for their communities by manipulating rather than attempting to overturn the government. Much the same occurred in other cities. The PRI could maintain its tradition of populist rhetoric about supporting the needs of the poor in the name of social justice.

Women. World War II raised the position of women in Mexico considerably. During the conflict, women were employed in factories or other types of jobs normally reserved for men. Organizations like the Servicio Civil Femenino de Defensa performed social obligations such as blood drives. In 1945, women received the right to vote in municipal elections. A prominent movement soon began to campaign for the right of women to vote in national elections.

Amalia de Castillo Ledon was a talented playwright, educator, and social reformer who achieved that goal. She became one of the founders of the U. N. Commission on the Status of Women and was president of the Organization of American States' Committee on Women in Washington, D.C. by 1953. Ledon embarrassed Mexico for remaining as one of the few countries in the Americas to deny suffrage to women—the others being Colombia, Haiti, Honduras, Nicaragua, and Paraguay. Shortly after his presidential inauguration, Cortines discussed the issue with Ledon. In the interview, Ruiz Cortines promised to give women suffrage; and within a few weeks after taking office, Cortines sent an amendment to Congress giving women full citizenship and voting rights. It was the first piece of legislation that he sent to the legislature. The suffrage bill finally passed in September 1953; the Senate approved it by a 31 to 1 vote with a communist senator casting the dissenting vote.

In the 1958 elections, women took advantage of their voting power. A year later, nine women sat in congress. Significant numbers of women moved into government positions. Three were federal judges, 60 served as assistant prosecutors, 1 female headed the Federal Board of Conciliation, and another led the federal prison and parole board. Other females made their presence known throughout Mexico: two-hundred twenty-five were lawyers, another 100 were chemists. At UNAM, 30 percent of the faculty in the economics department were women while the majority in the veterinary department were females.

When López Mateos became president, he declared that "A woman is a citizen who works for Mexico. We must not treat her differently from the men, except to honor her more." Women were taken more seriously on the intellectual level as well. During the 1950s, an edition of the complete works of Sor Juana appeared.

It was also during this period that Mother's Day became a hallowed tradition in Mexico. During the early colonial period, the Spanish were surprised to see that motherhood, not marriage, constituted the major link between males and females. Thus Mother's Day constituted a major connection to indigenous continuity. Newspapers began to run stories praising maternal sacrifices. Even the Mexican stock exchange experienced lighter trading volumes when May 10 fell in midweek. Sons spent the day with mothers because they were viewed to the point of veneration. For centuries, the central role of a Mexican woman was to be a mother. Children still had more contact with mothers than with fathers. The mother-child relationship continued to be more intimate and more complex. Pregnancy was viewed as a suffering mothers underwent to give birth to their children. The rise of single mothers served to strengthen the role of a mother protector. And some mothers used their children as an escape for everything that they could not do, forgetting their own lives and living vicariously through their children, suffocating them with their need.

Some of the biggest changes have affected working women. After winning the right to vote on a fully franchised basis, more women began to work outside the home. But many traditional companies required newly hired females to sign a form in which they agreed to resign before getting married or having a child. Such practices became illegal in the public sector, although they continued to exist in the private domain. In northern Mexico, twice as many women migrated in search of work from the 1940s to 1970s as men. They were the *maquiladora* workers between 17 and 25 years old. Their need to support children—either offspring or siblings—pushed them into the work force. Many of the fathers, brothers, and husbands who lived with *maquiladora* workers were jobless or earned meager incomes in petty service, commercial activities, or by crossing the border illegally to work in the United States. Most females stayed on their jobs less than three years, sometimes to get married or have children. Most quit because of wages averaging under a dollar an hour, numbing manual labor, and high production quotas. Working conditions were not good. Although job-related health problems abounded in the garment and electronics industries, public officials looked the other way. When workers temporarily left to recover from sickness, they lost their seniority.

Women also assumed a direct role in preserving the long history of Mexican dance. Amalia Hernández had to plead with her father to allow her to become a dancer, a profession not particularly well regarded in the 1920s. Although trained in classical traditions, Hernández became drawn to the varied regional dance styles. In 1952, she founded the Ballet Folklórico, which brought together regional styles ranging from the foot-stomping *jarabe tapatio* to the slow, graceful *danzon* of the Gulf Coast to the polka-based dances of northern Mexico. Hernández also incorporated some of the dances of Mexico's indigenous groups in performances at Mexico City's Palace of Fine Arts, as well as tours in the United States and throughout the world. Considered the pioneer of folk revival, she broke ground by combining classical dance technique with traditional and regional choreography, and by bringing dances once confined to local festivities to fine art venues.

Not by coincidence, dance became very important in the school curriculum. Female instructors emphasized the traditional posture, demeanor, and jewelry used in folk dances and costumes. Their students learned that the smallest details of dances help define the differences between one state and its temperament from another. Women from Chihuahua, for example, furl their skirts with more enthusiasm than those from Nuevo León. Dances from the coast tend to have more expression, those from the interior are more subdued. Different dances reflected contrasting attitudes and unique indigenous customs. Dances from Tehauntepec, for example are more ceremonial and less festive. Changing the smallest detail means trampling upon the sense of identity inherent within complex costumes.

The Golden Age of Mexican cinema began during the 1940s and 1950s when romantic stars such as Jorge Negrete, Pedro Infante, Dolores del Rio, María Félix, and the comic actor Cantinflas helped build Latin America's most successful film business. With the advent of sound pictures and well-developed dialogues, cinema became the dominant form of mass entertainment. Entirely new genres became very successful. Jorge Negrete and Pedro Infante became identified with *ranchera* themes. The popularity of Pedro Infante, perhaps Mexico's most revered actor, singer, and hearththrob, transcended generations. Even after his 1957 death in a fiery plane crash, Pedro Infante

Dance performance in a Mexico City school, 1958. *Personal collection of the author.*

remained a nearly mythical figure in Mexico. Another genre was melodrama. In 1941, *Cuando los hijos se van (When the Children Are Gone)* reflected the tensions of the times by strongly emphasizing traditional family values in an attempt to minimize the threat of the Axis powers.

Some of the romantic stars also enjoyed success in Hollywood. Lupe Vélez made her film debut in 1927 before returning to Mexico triumphantly in 1937, and returning the following year to mend her marriage to Johnny Weismuller. She came back to Mexico in 1943 to make more movies at Aztec Studios in Mexico City. Her second cousin, Dolores del Río, became legendary. She starred in *Maria Candelaria* (1946) which became the first Mexican film to impact the United States and Europe after World War II. When this film won the Grand Prize at the Cannes Film Festival in 1947, the Golden Age became consolidated. Maria Felix, perhaps the most famous beauty, solidified her status in *Rio Escondido* (1947) which was a nationalistic portrait of social programs featuring a cameo performance by Miguel Alemán. By then the Mexican cinema had become the country's third largest industry, employing 32,000 people.

Spanish filmmaker Luis Buñuel was one of the founders of surrealist cinema and represents the cosmopolitan nature of Mexican culture. In 1946, he moved to Mexico City and in 1950 produced the classic *Los Olvidados (Young and the Damned)*. With this astounding film, Buñuel presented an uncompromisingly honest view of the poverty and desperation of young toughs in the depressing barrios surrounding Mexico City. Basing films on true events and utilizing authentic people rather than professional actors, Buñuel brought to the screen actual trauma among the lives of teenagers.

In 1952, the government banned all Hollywood movies that contained offensive portrayals of Mexicans. Many U.S. films that featured Mexican roles had tended to denigrate their character. The strategy of containing such depictions forced Hollywood to rethink its relation with Mexico. It also had the effect of protecting and encouraging filmmakers in Mexico to compete with their giant rival to the north.

Cantinflas, actor Mario Moreno's film persona, soon became the most popular movie star. The fourth of 14 children from a postal worker, he left his family at age 15 to travel with a theater troupe, singing and dancing the Charleston for audiences in the shantytowns of the Gulf Coast. After this start, Moreno worked odd jobs as a boxer, barber, and a cobbler before returning to the stage and breaking into movies in 1936. In a career that spanned more than 50 years until his death in 1993, Moreno made 56 movies. He coined the stage name Cantinflas to keep his family from finding out he had gone into show business. He fashioned the name from the expression, *en la cantina tu infilas* (in the cantina you inflate with drink). It was an appropriate label for the drunks, *pelados*, and vagabonds Morenos specialized in portraying. His characters have been compared to Chaplin figures, but unlike Chaplin, whose films criticized the class system in the United States and dramatized the plight of the poor, Moreno was no social critic. Like Pedro Infantes', Moreno's characters were poor but happy, even when victimized by corrupt officials and stuffy upper-class exploiters.

Despite the success of Cantinflas, by the 1960s Mexican films did not reflect the changes which Mexican society had undergone. Conflict arose among filmmakers themselves as formula pictures lost favor and U.S. films once again became more popular. As the epics of the Golden Age seemed old fashioned, many of the films that took their place were either sophisticated art films or cheap items about violent truckers and other rough sorts.

Religion. The Church began to regain its wealth under Alemán and it renewed pastoral activities and educational programs. Prestigious Catholic schools attracted many, if not most, of the middle-class youth. In the federal district, the Church censored various films, magazines, and those manufacturers that were blatantly Protestant. Now that the government worried less about the possibility of Catholics supporting the Sinarquistas or even the PAN, virtually no harassment of Catholic church activities took place. Ninety percent of Mexicans remained Catholic.

Under Ruiz Cortines, rituals in homage of the Virgin of Guadalupe operated freely. New churches were rapidly built. More Catholics began to accept the PRI and the government counted on their votes. Nevertheless, Lewis reported a surprising number of Protestants among poor Mexicans. As the 1960s began, priests assumed greater political latitude than even before the civil war. Since the Church no longer had extensive lands to protect, speaking out would not result in great losses. Particularly in rural parishes, many priests began to embrace radical social and political concepts. During the López Mateos *sexenio*, many Mexican priests studying in Rome became attracted to the theme of helping the poor during the Second Vatican Council of Pope John XXIII. Liberation theology, which embraced the notion of priests actively mobilizing the poor, permanently entered Mexico for the rest of the twentieth century. In Cuernavaca, Bishop Sergio Méndez Arceo, known as the "red bishop," targeted the indigenous peoples of Chiapas. The hierarchy, however, liked the piety of Díaz Ordaz and in 1968 even proclaimed its support of the 1910 revolution.

Social Unrest. Labor unrest, student turmoil, and general social upheaval increasingly became the norm during this period. Specific public demands included the release of all political prisoners, repeal of the oppressive "social dissolution" feature of Article 145, and ending the heavy-handed tactics of the *granaderos*. Progressively greater numbers of citizens, of all ages and from all social levels, turned out for peaceful demonstrations organized by railroad workers, students, and doctors. Unfortunately, the government lacked flexibility and gradually refused to listen to workers' demands for reforms as well as student grievances and became intolerant of public protest. The system feared for its survival and stifled opposition forces, thus retarding the growth of a pluralistic society. Draconian techniques to defuse organized opposition ranged from removing dissident union leaders, arresting protesters, exiling opponents, job blacklisting, to violence as well as death.

All the protest movements became extinguished, largely through government repression. During the 1958–1959 railroad strikes, the leaders were jailed, although their demands were fairly modest and the strikers had mobilized legally. The press, controlled by the government, labeled the strikers as unpatriotic and even subversive. During the doctors' strike of 1964–1965, the physicians sought better pay, upgraded working conditions, and improved health services. After doctors agitated at the Zócalo in downtown Mexico City, Díaz Ordaz allowed elected leaders to speak for three minutes and then tore into them with a furious tongue-lashing. Many doctors soon lost their jobs after winning minor wage concessions. In both situations, the government depicted the protest leaders as communists, foreign agents, and Mexican traitors. Massive campaigns to discredit and divide them succeeded. Strikers lacked

broad popular support to combat the lack of information about their movements, aided by government media censorship.

Coupled with the student movement of the 1960s was a rising tide of cultural protest. The sudden impact of rock and roll music hit Mexico in the late 1950s. Slowly but surely opposition to parental authority, long hair, an interest in Marxist ideology, and a franker sexual lifestyle became fashionable among middle class Mexicans in particular. New legislation attempted to arrest this defiant mode, which resulted in a sanitized version of the U.S. counterculture. New language, casual dress, and open drug use resulted in the *La Onda* movement by the mid-1960s. Even a hippie movement occurred as some younger Mexicans contemplated dropping out of society altogether. Eventually, a large rock festival took place in the fall of 1971.

Mainline middle-class youth also displayed a blander form of discontent with prevailing norms. Many hung onto the status of being middle class by spending excessively on flashy clothing. Females often sought out foreign mates. Five radio stations in the federal district played only British or U.S. rock and roll music. Others maintained a slavish devotion to anything European, lashing out at many staples of Mexican society. The Zona Rosa area of Mexico City became a slick atmosphere of escapism that heightened class differences. Virtually all Mexicans, and particularly the middle class, lamented that in the 12 World Cup tournaments since competition had begun in 1930, Mexico had made it to the quarterfinals only once since 1970. Thus the massacre at Tlatelolco and the arrest, imprisonment, and torture of hundreds of young people were direct consequences of Díaz Ordaz's desperate attempt to maintain the status quo.

THE MEXICAN DIASPORA *AL NORTE*

Drawing Mexicans to the United States were jobs—the same lure that in the late nineteenth century brought waves of migrants north to build railroads, irrigation systems, and toil in the mines. This diaspora is without precedent for Mexico, which lost 11 million people to the United States during the twentieth century—a stunning exodus that eclipsed all other migrations in U.S. history, including Irish and Italian immigration.

Carranza and U.S. Migration Policy. During the nineteenth century, Mexicans had emigrated to the United States on a permanent basis. Nearly 40 percent of all Santa Barbara, California, households were made up of former immigrants by 1860. The same is true of Texas, where 30 to 40 percent of the Tejano communities had a foundation of Mexicans who became permanent residents. Fewer came to New Mexico because of the slower pace of economic activity and because the entrenched Hispanic majority tended to look down on Mexican migrants, whom they dubbed *surrumatos*. The vast expansion of the Texas cotton industry, as well as the huge increase of agriculture in California, resulted in great demand for Mexican workers. Mexican workers soon replaced Asians as the dominant field workers because they accepted lower pay, usually a dollar a day. U.S. labor contractors aggressively recruited Mexican workers below the border.

Throughout the nineteenth century, the U.S.–Mexican border was open to the free movement of laborers. The United States imposed the first border restrictions in 1903. These controls were limited and largely designed to keep anarchists out. Most Mexican immigrants who crossed into the United States did so with relative ease. Only 60 mounted officials guarded the 1,900-mile long border.

The movement of Mexicans to the United States increased rapidly after 1907. When the crash of 1907 took place, it affected northern Mexico adversely. Therefore, one-third to one-fourth of Mexican migrants stayed in the United States to become permanent residents. The figure increased when the violence of the revolution became widespread. Particularly hard hit was Gua-

najuato as well as Durango, Jalisco, Michoacán, San Luis Potosí, and Zacatecas. There the haciendas suffered widespread destruction and the six states became battlefields. Since the haciendas had been the sustaining workplace for many rural Mexicans, the workers gravitated to the labor-intensive fields of lettuce, spinach, carrots, and beans throughout the U.S. southwest where employers hired them. Perhaps a million crossed the border during the revolution. In the process, they changed the demographics of many southwestern cities. By 1916, for example, El Paso's population became 53 percent Mexican.

Carranza decided to oppose emigration from Mexico because economic recovery in Mexico from the civil war had been disrupted by labor shortages, particularly in farming regions. Carranza also sought to protect those migrants whom he could not keep within Mexico. By January 1917, the Mexican government would not permit its citizens to leave unless they could show a labor contract that specified work and pay. Carranza also used Mexican consuls to protect immigrants as well as Mexican Americans for the first time. A consul in Arizona intervened in the Clifton strike to the point that workers received a wage increase there in 1915.

The response from the U.S. Congress was the Immigration Act of February 5, 1917, which insisted that all migrants had to be literate and that they also had to pay an $8 head tax. Much of this hostility toward migrants was directed toward Europeans, but Congress was certainly no friend of Carranza. The legislation allowed authorities to deny naturalization to radicals and to deport suspicious aliens. The Legislators however, forgot that the wartime demand for conscripts would affect agricultural harvests. Miners, railroad owners, and southwestern growers demanded that this absurd legislation be relaxed. Herbert Hoover served as their lobbyist and soon obtained results.

In May 1917, Wilson responded by amending immigration procedures so that braceros, legally contracted Mexican workers, could work for up to six months in the United States. They also had to work only in agriculture, carry an identification card, and could not stop working for more than two weeks or they would be deported. The revised 1917 legislation also declared that state governments were supposed to establish housing and sanitation standards. Growers were allowed to withhold wages of migrants in banks in order to discourage them from staying permanently. Braceros were paid only when they crossed back to their Mexican place of departure. Eventually, 72,000 Mexicans worked in the United States during World War I. Finally, Hoover convinced Wilson to end all restrictions until the end of the war.

Carranza continued to object. He frustrated labor recruiters looking for braceros in Mexico. Carranza also publicized the terrible working conditions in the United States and revealed that U.S. growers did not always honor signed contracts. Therefore, Carranza insisted that the United States government regulate braceros more thoroughly. But the Wilson government, in another attempt to weaken the Carranza regime, refused to sign a proposed agreement with Mexico that would have provided uniform regulations and border crossing permits. Perhaps most annoying of all was that Mexican migrants were conscripted into the U.S. Army and sent off to Europe. Mexican consuls gave money to those who could not find work in the United States and transported them back to Mexico.

The migrants endured unpleasant social conditions. The pressure of living without families drove some insane. Braceros also had to put up with segregated facilities in Laredo and other cities. In Dallas, Mexicans could not see outdoor movies at Pike Park until the 1920s. Some migrants were shot down at the border by U.S. troops in 1917 and 1918 until the arrival of Mexican reinforcements ended the worst outrages. The smuggling of tequila and drugs across the border into the southwest added to tensions. Mexican border towns began to develop an earthy reputation for horse racing, cockfighting, gambling, prostitution, and narcotics. Ciudad Juárez became known as the Monte Carlo of the southwest. Meanwhile, U.S. unions demanded that all Mexicans be deported and not allowed to return. The AFL claimed that U.S. workers were being denied jobs and had their wages cut, although government studies of 25 cities found that wages rose during World War I.

By 1920, the immigrants had impacted southwestern towns substantially. Dallas had 2,800 Mexicans in its Little Mexico by 1920. Many migrants walked from the border to Dallas in order to work at the Trinity Portland Cement Company in West Oak Cliff as well as Trinity Farms, a vast commercial farm that employed many Mexicans from 1915 to 1946 and provided segregated schools as well as a cemetery. By 1920, San Antonio had the largest community of Mexican migrants in the United States—some 40,000. Many of them worked on military projects. San Antonio musicians initiated musical accomplishments that surpassed other Spanish-speaking U.S. regions. In Los Angeles, a cultural revival became particularly notable. Hollywood encouraged the participation of Latino performers, technicians, and directors beginning in 1911. Dolores del Río, Anthony Quinn (originally Quiñones), Antonio Navarro, and Lupe Vélez made lasting imprints as actors. Musicians, playwrights, and intellectuals also flocked to Los Angeles, which became a cultural magnet for immigrant Mexicans much as Harlem did for African Americans.

The Immigration Process of the 1920s. Although generally a period of prosperity and opportunity, the 1920s appeared grim at first because of the postwar depression which cut the demand for Mexican field workers. Many braceros found themselves out of work and sought employment in the cities where tensions increased dramatically. In Fort Worth, Texas, blacks and whites marched on city hall out of fear that Mexicans would take their jobs. They even threatened to blow up the city as a protest. Municipal authorities reacted by arresting Mexicans on vagrancy charges or putting them to work on chain gangs. Meanwhile the *Dallas Morning News* claimed that Mexicans were a hygiene problem. Night riders beat up Mexicans, many of whom fled in terror.

At this point, nativists in the United States pressured Congress to enact highly restrictive immigration policies. Fear of radicals during the Red Scare, combined with a backlash against immigration, resulted in a 1921 congressional bill that limited the number of immigrants each year to 3 percent of the foreign-born of each national group living in the United States. In 1924, President Calvin Coolidge, in a national message to Congress, urged them to do something to keep the United States "American." Earlier, he had written an article in *Good Housekeeping* magazine which claimed that Nordics deteriorated when they intermarried with other ethnic groups. In response, Congress passed even more drastic immigration legislation six weeks later. The National Origins Act limited the total number of immigrants entering the United States to only 150,000 a year. Only 2 percent of each national group living in the United States was permitted to enter as part of an attempt to shut out immigrants from southern and eastern Europe.

The nativists also wanted to keep Mexicans out of the United States but lost the debate. Their main argument was that Mexicans could not assimilate into U.S. society and would always remain a group apart, thus becoming a "race problem." Others feared that radical ideas from Mexico would cross the Río Grande and lead to socialism or anarchism. Small farmers wanted to keep braceros out because larger ranches had begun squeezing them with Mexican labor.

Those who successfully opposed the nativists were large growers, railroad companies, mining interests, and the U.S. Chamber of Commerce. They sent lobbyists to Washington, D.C., to push for an open border. The southwest was becoming a valuable part of U.S. agriculture because it furnished 40 percent of the fruits and vegetables eaten in the United States by 1929. This group claimed that only Mexican workers could serve the southwestern economy, but that if problems ever resulted, such as a depression or an extended period of unemployment, that Mexicans could be deported. The State Department finally decided the political battle by opposing restrictions on Mexican migrants in order to improve relations with Mexico and the rest of Latin America at a time when U.S. businesses had begun displacing European markets during a period of rising nationalism in Latin America. The State Department feared that if quotas were placed against Mexico, riots and reprisals would result. Therefore, when an East Texas senator presented a bill to restrict Mexican laborers to only 1,500 a year, Hoover, who traditionally represented growers, intervened to have Republican leaders stop it. It was good timing because Mexican newspapers had begun attacking this legislation.

The only victory for the nativists was the establishment of the Border Patrol in 1924. Growers considered the Border Patrol a nuisance which interfered with their harvests. They could protest to the Labor Department when deportations occurred and work out agreements so that the Border Patrol would not disrupt harvests while

A Mexican immigrant with her new husband in California during the 1920s. *Personal collection of the author.*

braceros would be admitted. Thus, a typical pattern developed so that Mexicans were welcomed by industry and government at times when they were needed for the bustling U.S. economy. And migrants were ignored and rejected when times got tough.

The tense situation in the United States ended in 1922 when the economy revived. The recruitment of Mexican workers renewed in earnest because the Quota Acts of 1921 and 1924 did not apply to Mexico. With European and Asian labor markets closed off as a result of this legislation, Mexican migration reached peak levels by 1925 as southwestern growers once again claimed that a serious labor shortage existed. Another result of the Quota Acts' restrictions was that jobs opened for Mexicans beyond the southwest.

By 1930, 135,000 of the half million Mexican migrants in the United States had become employed in the industrial sector of the U.S. economy. Most of these jobs were located in Chicago where steel mills, railroad yards, and slaughter houses employed *mexicanos*. It was not always a happy story. Many were utilized as strikebreakers. The transition from living in isolated Mexican villages to large U.S. cities was very difficult. Housing was such a serious problem that many lived in abandoned boxcars. Pool halls served as the main recreational outlet. The Catholic church was not welcoming or as supportive financially of Mexicans as it was of other groups and pressed them to worship as Irish Catholics did. Since migrants could not vote, machine politicians ignored Mexican laborers as well. Police and courts had little sympathy or concern for them.

Urban conditions were better than agricultural labor. The average field hand saved about $100 after six months of work. Most Mexicans toiled in this manner because of the labor-intensive nature of farm employment. Planting and harvesting lettuce, for example, required ten times as many hours of work as an acre of wheat. The nature of seasonal work disrupted family life tremendously. Many migrant families had to move five different times in a single year. When not stooping in the fields, they were looking for the next job.

The effect of not belonging to any particular community was that little opportunity existed to establish permanent roots. Problems such as racism and crude exploitation had to be dealt with in virtual isolation. Deplorable living conditions were the norm, especially in migrant camps, because growers wanted to maximize profits as much as possible. Severe health problems and the lack of educational opportunities held down migrant workers for years.

Resentment of these conditions led to deep alienation. Only 6 percent of Mexican immigrants who remained in the United States decided to go through the legal procedures to become U.S. citizens by 1930. There are many reasons for this. Migrants considered the United States a place to make money and improve their social status before eventually returning to Mexico. The fear of deportation became something resembling a psychosis which only served to heighten the isolation of the Mexican community. Mexican patriotism remained high. Women continued to have babies born in Mexico while most celebrated Mexican holidays.

Manuel Gamio began interviewing Mexican immigrants who came to the United States in the 1920s. Key trends emerged, many of which held true throughout the twentieth century. Repeatedly, immigrants demonstrated their powerful allegiance to Mexican culture. One stated that he would "rather have his eyes taken out than to change citizenship." Mexico became one of the few countries in the world that did not allow its residents living outside its territory to vote in elections. Immigrants often admired the U.S. work ethic and enjoyed working in an open society without rigid social structure dominated by a well-defined elite. At the same time, immigrants resented the humiliation and exploitation they suffered. The most divisive wedge was the strong U.S. quest for money and the immigrant emphasis upon personal happiness.

Catastrophe during the 1930s. The effect of the Wall Street crash in 1929 was a disastrous situation for Mexican migrants. As the Depression overwhelmed the United States, many U.S. citizens feared that Mexicans held jobs and public assistance benefits that they were not entitled to. Therefore, local, state, and federal authorities initiated extensive efforts to drive Mexicans out. Eventually, about a million Mexicans, as well as Mexican Americans, had to leave the United States because many U.S. citizens assumed that they were an expensive burden.

The first manifestation of this nightmare was an immediate loss of jobs. Many states passed legislation requiring that all laborers on public works projects be U.S. citizens, particularly for highway work and construction. The effect of the New Deal was almost null since the Works Progress Administration eliminated aliens from eligibility. Moreover, the Wagner Act and Social Security did not cover agricultural workers. The collapse of the railroad industry cost many their jobs once factory orders nosedived. The number of sharecroppers in Texas dropped from 205,000 in 1930 to 39,000 by 1940.

Salaries were systematically lowered. During the Depression, wages of $1.50 a week became common. Hourly wages for farm workers plummeted from 35 cents an hour to 14 cents. When *mexicanos* protested, they found that whites would eagerly take their places in the fields. The arrival of whites in agricultural work only created a larger and more desperate labor pool to draw upon. As discrimination increased, recent arrivals from Oklahoma or other dustbowls received employment preference. Before the Depression ended, 85 to 90 percent of the workers picking fruit and vegetables were Euro-Americans. Hardest hit of all were the California garment workers, three-fourths of whom were *mexicanas*. Pressured by scabs, many of them earned only 50 cents a week. Not surprisingly, only 28,000 Mexican immigrants entered the United States during this terrible decade.

Typical of this crisis was the agony of the San Antonio pecan shellers. The industry forced thousands of Mexican females to accept wages of 5 or 6 cents per bag of shelled pecans that weighed 1 pound. The average worker could only fill eight or nine bags a day with the result that they earned about 50 cents a day. About 20,000 families subsisted on this miserable wage, while the Southern Pecan Shelling Company raked in $3 million a year by the mid-1930s as they ignored New Deal labor legislation. When strikes broke out against this pitiful exploitation, the company began a mechanization program that required fewer workers.

Local governments, encouraged by President Herbert Hoover, soon began campaigns to repatriate undocumented Mexican residents. It began when many immigrants found themselves in such desperate circumstances that they sought relief payments. Therefore, Los Angeles and other municipalities initiated scare tactics to force voluntary return to Mexico. Prodded by offers of free train tickets to Mexico, Mexicans left Los Angeles at a rate of one train a month so that at least 130,000, including many Mexican Americans, eventually departed from 1931 to 1934. Over 100,000 *mexicanos* left Texas during the same period. As the factories of the midwest closed operations, about half the migrants there also left for Mexico.

To make the tragedy even worse, the Cárdenas regime did little to aid its refugees. Most wound up in badly located communities with inadequate funding. Even though many of the repatriated Mexicans were children in the United States, and thus not Mexican citizens, the Maximato governments cooperated with Hoover at the outset.

The Bracero Program, 1942–1964. The United States became threatened by a severe labor shortage after the Pearl Harbor attack made war official. Because many U.S. citizens left rural areas to work in defense industries, conscription produced fears that crops would not be harvested in 1942. Concern about the reality of food shortages induced Secretary of State Hull to send negotiators to Mexico City to work out a bracero program.

The final agreement reflected earlier Carranza demands that the United States government supervise and regulate any program involving the use of

Mexican labor. Roosevelt agreed and promised that migrants would not be conscripted into U.S. military service. Public Law 45 also maintained that braceros would not experience discrimination and would be guaranteed living expenses, as well as free round-trip transportation from the border to the agricultural camps. Migrants were to receive the "prevailing wage" where they worked, as well as a guaranteed minimum wage of 30 cents an hour. In addition to the wartime Victory tax, braceros would have 10 percent of their wages deducted each week; U.S. officials transferred the money to Mexican agricultural banks for repayment as part of an attempt to ensure their return. Both Mexico and the United States assumed that this measure would minimize the problem of illegal migration. Camacho particularly wanted to control or eliminate the movement of undocumented workers; for that reason braceros were to be recruited deep within Mexico and not on the border or anywhere near it.

In order to make the Bracero Program acceptable within the United States, the agreement stipulated that braceros could not displace local labor or reduce their wages. Mexican Americans and labor unions feared that local salaries would decline if braceros entered in large numbers. To mollify the fears of large numbers of foreigners moving into the United States, the Bracero Program maintained that migrants could not stay more than nine months. Furthermore, they had to carry a photo identification card. Without it, they would be deported immediately. The accord was signed in July 1942, and the Mexican government ratified it in Mexico City ten weeks later.

Although the accord produced mixed results, both governments reached their basic goals. About 250,000 workers earned approximately $205 million from 1943 to 1947, which aided the Mexican economy considerably. A bracero's earnings supported not only himself but also his Mexican family. Workers were certainly more worldly upon their return to Mexico. The braceros often carried a positive impression of life in the United States. The program also became a convenient path to get rid of actual or potential inter-

nal opposition to the PRI. The government awarded more than half its bracero allotments to the north and center-west regions because this was where suffering had occurred at the highest level during the revolution. Moreover, these regions encompassed former Cristero as well as Sinarquista partisans. The program closely resembled the rotational colonial labor systems the braceros represented the continuity of dispersing potentially rebellious young males.

The Bracero Program did not lack critics. The first contingent of agricultural workers reported discrimination, poor working conditions, and substandard housing as well as wretched food. The United States agreed to allow labor inspectors to enter the bracero camps and established grievance channels, both of which improved matters. But the Foreign Relations Secretariat wanted all labor recruitment stopped and the Agriculture Secretariat joined the opposition. But in January 1943, Camacho overruled them and a compromise was reached whereby braceros were no longer allowed to work in Idaho and Texas, because of discriminatory incidents in both states. Attacks on Los Angeles zoot suiters heightened tensions. Within Mexico, the Church opposed the program and feared that Catholicism would be weakened. Priests predicted that a moral decline would set in when braceros became separated from their families. Hacendados protested the loss of their best farmhands as well as skilled workers. Nationalists did not like the idea of their people performing tasks gringos would not do, which they considered an affront to Mexican dignity.

The need for Mexican workers also surfaced in the form of a railroad bracero program. At the behest of several railroads, the United States and Mexico agreed that Mexican laborers could work for 36 U.S. railroads beginning in 1943. Over 100,000 braceros journeyed to Querétaro where they paid *mordida* bribes to journey north, where they usually toiled in track maintenance. Like those working in agriculture, the railroad braceros were normally young, unskilled workers from small villages. The railroads provided the actual

The daughter of a Mexican immigrant with two of her children in Walla Walla, Washington in the late 1940s. *Personal collection of the author.*

management of the program. Although paid lower than U.S. workers performing the same tasks and enduring poor food and miserable living conditions, railroad braceros were paid time and a half after eight hours of work. Among them, 89 died, usually in an off-duty situation, such as drowning, suicide, and fighting. There is little doubt that railroad operations would have practically ground to a halt without Mexican labor. Nevertheless, U.S. unions successfully opposed renewal of the program after the war.

The agricultural bracero accord, however, continued until 1964. Southwestern growers were satisfied with it because they enjoyed an inexpensive, nonunion labor supply that was hardworking and efficient. The PRI was equally content because it could devote its resources to industrialization and not worry about rural conflicts or religious insurrections. Thus, the agricultural bracero

agreement was renewed in 1947. By then, the United States was eager to export more food during the Cold War and Mexico had became dependent upon the dollars that braceros furnished. The Bracero Program became permanent when President Harry Truman signed Public Law 78 in July 1951.

The postwar phase of the Bracero Program featured less federal regulation. From 1947 to 1950, undocumented workers formed the majority of migrant laborers. Because of the demand for goods and services made necessary by the Korean War, the new accord became a treaty. The Department of Labor managed the recruitment of Mexican laborers and arranged their transportation up to the border. The United States also removed penalties for hiring illegal workers to the extent that the Border Patrol could not search farms. Ruiz Cortines attempted to protest the increased power of the growers and respond to internal protests resulting from more news of abuses. When he sought higher wages for braceros and threatened to cut off their labor in the southwest, the United States responded in 1954 by permitting bracero recruitment on the border. Despite the attempts of border guards to restrain them, desperate migrants overpowered them, crashed through the fences, and began working whether the government liked it or not. Humiliated, Ruiz Cortines agreed to permanent bracero recruitment on the border in March 1954.

The end of the Bracero Program finally occurred in 1964 for a variety of reasons. Many growers had mechanized operations to the point that fewer agricultural workers were required. In addition, the Labor Department began to force growers to provide better housing conditions and higher wages. Public concern mounted as documentaries and newspaper stories laid bare the squalid life of migrant workers. *Harvest of Shame*, a hard-hitting documentary shown during Thanksgiving 1960, particularly galvanized mounting demands among humanitarians to stop the Bracero Program. Labor unions had become more influential with the election of Kennedy in 1960, and they did not hesitate to criticize the program. At one point, Kennedy informed López Mateos to expect termination of the program, but López Mateos insisted so strongly that braceros continue to be allowed north that Kennedy relented.

When Lyndon Johnson succeeded Kennedy, however, there was no turning back. By then Chicano activists such as César Chávez Estrada had become important in Democratic Party activities and many Mexican Americans by now opposed the Bracero Program. After U.S. congressional investigators detailed rampant abuses of low-cost braceros working in unsafe conditions—sometimes despite injuries—the Bracero Program ended in December 1964, as concern for civil rights reached a climax. In Mexico, former braceros found that the 10 percent taxed from their wages could not be given back. Authorities claimed that no bank records of their savings account existed, even though U.S. government documents indicated that between $7 and $30 million disappeared because of "cheating" and "delays." At the turn of the century, braceros planned to file a lawsuit to regain the millions of dollars withheld from their pay.

Reshaping the Face of the United States.
After 1965, migratory traditions became institutionalized between U.S. and Mexican regions. Unlike previous waves of Mexican immigrants, the newcomers were more determined than ever to set down permanent roots. In one of the most dramatic shifts in the history of U.S. immigration patterns, Mexican immigration tripled from 1970 to 2000.

With the end of the braceros, new categories of migrants arrived. Section H-2 of the 1952 McCarran-Walter Immigration and Nationality Act allowed tens of thousands to work on farms each year. Also prominent during the last half of the twentieth century were green carders, the permanent-visa Mexicans granted resident status as long as they worked consistently and did not leave the United States for more than a year. Commuters who had white identification cards earned the privilege of crossing into the United States on a daily basis. Hundreds of thousands of commuters worked as maids, gardeners, and restaurant employees in many rapidly growing border cities.

Undocumented workers came in greater numbers than ever before. Swimming across rivers and trekking through blazing hot deserts, illegal Mexican laborers became the largest category of migrants. Often they replaced Mexican American workers in the U.S. work force. Capital-intensive, irrigated, export-oriented agriculture in northern Mexico made employment in the United States inevitable for many rural Mexicans. In the southwest, agribusiness made ever greater quantities of acres of newly irrigated land ready for producing fruit and vegetables. Fewer U.S. citizens would compete with Mexican migrants for these backbreaking tasks. *Coyotes* arranged the movement of migrants from the booming northern border cities into the United States by means of complex transportation systems. From 1947 to 1953, about 4.3 million undocumented migrants were apprehended and returned to Mexico. Most of them continued to try crossing *la frontera* until they succeeded.

Attempts to stem the diaspora did not succeed. U.S. public policy continued to follow the business cycle, alternately encouraging migrant workers to cross the border in boom times and blaming them for the structural problems of U.S. capitalism during downswings. Operation Wetback, a massive 1954 deportation campaign, apprehended many illegal migrants. Because it also broke up many families, it had the effect of frightening many to leave voluntarily, as in the 1930s. When migration increased again in the mid-1960s, lawmakers attempted a legislative approach. The Hart-Cellar Immigration and Nationality Act went into effect in 1968 and ended the 1920s national origin basis of admitting immigrants so that family reunification became the guiding norm for 40,000 Mexicans who came in legally from 1968 to 1976. Later, President Gerald Ford signed the Western Hemisphere Act, which established a 20,000 per country limit to Mexico and other Latin American nations in 1976. An inevitable backlog of nearly 100,000 applicants made this legislation virtually meaningless in terms of the needs of both big business and Mexican migrants. The disastrous presidencies of Echeverría and López Portillo only added to the pressure to migrate to the United States.

The 1980s represent a significant turning point. Not only did Mexico suffer an economic downturn but also the United States entered into a severe recession and in 1982, unemployment soon reached nearly 10 percent. The result was the Simpson-Mazzoli bill of 1982, which mandated sanctions, fines, and other penalties for employers who hired non-U.S. citizens. Factory sweeps and roundups by the Border Patrol became commonplace. Nevertheless, migrants crossed into the United States five or six times a year to work and reunite with families. They could expect wages 8 to 18 times higher than what they would receive in Mexico. Most migrants were young men between the ages of 15 and 29. About half were married and supporting up to four persons at home. They worked in the United States to accumulate money, pay off debts, and upgrade job skills. Most intended to return home. Many came from the more prosperous Mexican villages and from families with a tradition of migrating to the United States. They filled unskilled and semiskilled jobs with an hourly wage of $2.55 and worked a 48-hour week. Working conditions were harsh. Some were expelled after contracting tuberculosis, the plague, and even leprosy. Many understood that they were not always welcome but concluded that they were reentering the northern frontier which Mexico had lost to the United States in 1848.

Finally, the 1986 Immigration Reform and Control Act (IRCA) aimed at controlling migration but instead pushed immigrants into nearly every corner of the United States by the end of the 1990s. IRCA granted amnesty to 3.1 million immigrants, 85 percent of whom were Mexican workers already in the United States. It also strengthened the Border Patrol, reemphasized employer sanctions, and promised to block the border to new waves of immigrants. The confu-

Mexican immigrants participating in school festivities in Fort Worth, Texas during autumn 1989. *Personal collection of the author.*

sion and contradictions within the amnesty provisions meant that few migrants left. The sanctions did not discourage businesses from employing illegal migrants who simply obtained fraudulent documents and continued to avoid the Border Patrol despite a heightened presence in San Diego and El Paso. Because it was tougher to cross the border, many undocumented immigrants decided that they would not alternate between the two countries anymore. They would make the United States home and move inland, away from the Border Patrol agents. Since 1986, illegal and legal migration to the United States has averaged 340,000 per year.

Striking changes characterized immigration in the 1990s. The number of women and children who immigrated increased notably. The movement of Mexicans no longer became a sprinkling of people here and there. In New York City, for example, the number of Mexicans shot up from 90,000 in 1990 to 320,000 by 2000. Many had grown tired of corruption and authoritarian policies in Mexico. Ciudad Juárez became the busiest

immigration post in the world, where U.S. officials processed 500 visa applications each day. This consulate was the only one in Mexico that issued visas with the result that Mexicans from as far south as Chiapas traveled there to get legal passage to the United States. The majority of applications came from relatives of legal permanent residents in the United States. Congress boosted H-2 visas for agricultural as well as technological workers. By the end of the 1990s, employers in the booming U.S. economy obtained H-2 visas for industrial and service workers once they demonstrated that they could not find employees locally. To fill the need for workers from quarries to kitchens, U.S. diplomats in Monterrey established a Zacatecas program with the governor of that state in May 2000. This was the first time the U.S. government had worked with a Mexican regional government to recruit guest workers.

Newly elected President Vicente Fox decried the difficulties migrants faced and proposed changes. His courtship of Mexicans living in the United States was not just for their benefit. The

George W. Bush, then governor of Texas, talking to Mexican immigrants. *The Dallas Morning News.*

money they wired home accounted for Mexico's third largest source of income, after oil and tourism. Fox said he would like to see a permanent labor agreement in place between both countries and eventually a common North American labor market. He lobbied U.S. officials to raise the number of H-2 visas to as many as 250,000. By highlighting migrants as true Mexicans in need of recognition, Fox increased his popularity. When he visited border facilities in December 2000 and asked migrants if they had experienced shakedowns or demands for *mordidas*, he personally demonstrated a compassion for migrants never before seen. The Mexicans in the United States by 2000 also represented a change since two-thirds of the booming Latino population—about 30 million at the end of the twentieth century—were of Mexican origin.

SUGGESTED READING

Balderrama, Francisco and Ray Rodríguez. *Decade of Betrayal*: *Mexican Repatriation in the 1930s*. Albuquerque: University of New Mexico Press, 1995.

Bernal, Ignacio. *The Olmec World*. Berkeley: University of California Press, 1969.

Bortz, Jeffrey C. *Industrial Wages in Mexico City, 1939–1975*. New York: Garland Publishing, 1987.

Camp, Roderic A. *Intellectuals and the State in Twentieth Century Mexico*. Austin: University of Texas Press, 1985.

Conner, Floyd. *Lupe Velez and Her Lovers*. New York: Barricade Books, 1993.

Cornelius, Wayne A. *Politics and the Migrant Poor in Mexico City*. Stanford, CA: Stanford University Press, 1975.

Craig, Richard B. *The Bracero Program: Interest Groups and Foreign Policy*. Austin: University of Texas Press, 1971.

Cross, Harry and James Sandos. *Across the Border: Rural Development and Recent Migration to the United States*. Berkeley: Institute of Governmental Studies of the University of California, 1981.

DeLeón, Arnoldo. *The Tejano Community, 1836–1900*. Albuquerque: University of New Mexico Press, 1982.

Driscoll, Barbara. *The Tracks North: The Railroad Bracero Program of World War II*. Austin, TX: Center for Mexican American Studies, 1999.

Folgarait, Leonard. *So Far From Heaven: David Alfaro Siqueiros The March of Humanity and Mexican Revolutionary Politics*. New York: Cambridge University Press, 1987.

Fuentes, Carlos. *Where the Air Is Clear*. New York: Farrar, Straus and Giroux, 1960.

———. *The Death of Artemio Cruz*. New York: Farrar, Straus and Giroux, 1964.

———. *Aura*. Mexico City: Ediciones Era, 1962.

Gamio, Manuel. *Mexican Immigration to the United States: A Study of Human Migration and Adaptation*. New York: Dover Press, 1971.

Goldman, Shifra M. *Contemporary Mexican Painting in a Time of Change*. Albuquerque: University of New Mexico Press, 1981.

Gonzáles, Luis. *San José de Gracia: Mexican Village in Transition*. Austin: University of Texas Press, 1974.

Hoffman, Abraham. *Unwanted Mexican Americans in the Great Depression: Repatriation Pressures, 1929–1939*. Tucson: University of Arizona Press, 1974.

León Portilla, Miguel. *Aztec Thought and Culture*. Norman: University of Oklahoma Press, 1963.

Lewis, Oscar. *The Children of Sanchez: Autobiography of a Mexican Family*. New York: Random House, 1961.

———. *Five Families: Mexican Case Studies in the Culture of Poverty*. New York: Basic Books, 1959.

———. *Pedro Martínez*. New York: Vintage Books, 1964.

Mabry, Donald. *The Mexican University and the State: Student Conflict, 1910–1971*. College Station: Texas A&M University Press, 1982.

Mazón, Mauricio. *The Zoot-Suit Riots: The Psychology of Symbolic Annihilation*. Austin: University of Texas Press, 1984.

Meier, Matt S., and Feliciano Ribera. *Mexican Americans/American Mexicans*. New York: Hill and Wang, 1993.

Paz, Octavio. *The Labyrinth of Solitude: Life and Thought in Mexixo*. New York: Grove Press, 1961.

Pilcher, Jeffrey. *Cantinflas and the Chaos of Mexican Modernity*. Wilmington, DE: Scholarly Resources, 2000.

Reisler, Mark. *By the Sweat of Their Brow: Mexican Immigrant Labor in the United States, 1900–1940*. Westport, CT: Greenwood Press, 1976.

Richmond, Douglas W. "Crisis in Mexico: Echeverría and López Portillo, 1970–1982" *Journal of Third World Studies*, 5: 1 (Spring 1988), 160-171.

Rulfo, Juan. *Pedro Páramo*. New York: Grove Press, 1959.

———. *The Burning Plain and Other Stories*. Austin: University of Texas Press, 1967.

Rus, Jan. The "Comunidad Revolucionaria Institucional: The Subversion of Native Government in Highland Chiapas, 1936-1968." In Gilbert Joseph and Daniel Nugent, eds., *Every Day Forms of State Formation: Revolution and the Negotiation of Rule in Modern Mexico*. Durham, NC: Duke University Press, 1994, pp. 265–300.

Sandos, James, and Harry E. Cross. "National Development and International Labour Migration, Mexico 1940–1965." *Journal of Contemporary History* 18 (1983), 43–60.

Sommers, Joseph. *After the Storm: Landmarks of the Modern Mexican Novel*. Albuquerque: University of New Mexico Press, 1968.

Stevens, Evelyn P. *Protest and Response in Mexico*. Cambridge, MA: MIT Press, 1974.

Zea, Leopoldo. *Positivism in Mexico*. Austin: Unversity of Texas Press, 1974.

Zolov, Eric. *Refried Elvis: The Rise of the Mexican Counterculture*. Berkeley: University of California Press, 1999.

17

A Crisis Emerges, 1970–1982

The crisis that dominated Mexico after 1970 was preponderantly economic and financial. Poor fiscal planning and administrative mistakes compounded the sudden deterioration of Mexican society. Luis Echeverría and José López Portillo did not provide effective leadership that could mitigate the country's political decline. Attempts to use the state as the dominant source of solutions to Mexico's problems generally failed. Mexico faced the staggering task of addressing financial disorder, social fragmentation, and political apathy when López Portillo relinquished power in 1982.

THE ECHEVERRÍA REGIME DECAYS

Unrest and Violence. Luis Echeverría took over at a time of unprecedented crisis. The Tlatelolco massacre angered students and shocked the country. Few believed government statements concerning the bloodshed as writers openly criticized the president for the first time. Even Cárdenas was about to launch a scathing attack of PRI leadership when he died in 1970.

Despite early attempts to present himself as a conscientious leader, Echeverría muffled genuine dissent. As the former secretary of Gobernación

during the Díaz Ordaz regime, Echeverría obviously played an important role in the Tlatelolco incident. His personal qualities limited Echeverría's ability to define the goals of his vague *arriba y adelante* (upward and forward) presidential campaign. The new president was not particularly well educated, possessed little imagination, lacked a sense of humor, and was indecisive; therefore, endless meetings and waste of time characterized his *sexenio*.

The government barely contained the tense political situation of the early 1970s. Although Echeverría attempted to co-opt leftist reformers by appointing students and intellectuals to positions in his government, serious unrest broke out. Paramilitary *halcones*, organized by the PRI in 1968, killed 30 students during an orderly demonstration in Mexico City on June 10, 1971. Echeverría did little other than promise an investigation that never materialized. Named after an abortive 1967 guerrilla attack on a Chihuahua army post, the Liga 23 de Septiembre launched a period of urban warfare. Particularly in the state of Jalisco, Marxist students dynamited factories and monuments while they robbed banks and businesses.

Particularly serious opposition arose in the state of Guerrero. There Genaro Vásquez Rojas founded the Asociación Cívico Guerrerense to contest PRI rule. An idealistic teacher who attempted reform but was jailed, Vásquez finally resorted to armed struggle in the Sierra Madre until his death on February 2, 1972. Another teacher from Guerrero, Lucio Cabañas, operated as head of a guerrilla group near Acapulco known as the Partido de los Pobres. Kidnapping landowners as well as a state senator, the Cabañas group seized land and ambushed army troops until Echeverría sent in 10,000 soldiers to kill Cabañas in December 1974.

Violence and urban terrorism continued to trouble Echeverría. Guerrillas kidnapped several industrialists and a U.S. consul general in Guadalajara. The seizure of José Guadalupe Zuno, the 83-year-old father-in-law of Echeverría, particularly embarassed the president. For Zuno's release, the Revolutionary Armed Forces of the People demanded $1.6 million as ransom and the release of leftist prisoners. After regaining freedom, the influential Zuno criticized the government. When the Armed Forces of National Liberation murdered Eugenio Garza Sada, a powerful Monterrey industrialist, his family blamed Echeverría. The president came to Monterrey but listened in painful silence as criticism of his policies rang out during Garza Sada's funeral oration. Meanwhile, student clashes continued. In June 1973, five students died at the Universidad Autónoma de Puebla. Strikes broke out at the UNAM where students pelted Echeverría with oranges and bottles when he attempted to speak.

In 1976, the *Excelsior* scandal indicated that Echeverría would not tolerate meaningful dissent or criticism. The affair began when a PRI press secretary informed editor Julio Scherer that he could retain his newspaper only by firing a critical writer, historian Gastón García Cantú. When Scherer asked finance minister José López Portillo for advice, the minister's response was to get a gun. The regime pressured Scherer to resign. To remove Scherer from *Excelsior*, Echeverria organized a campesino group to occupy property owned by *Excelsior* in the federal district. Scherer wanted to develop this land in order to expand the newspaper's financial portfolio. Then government agents pressured *Excelsior* employees to vote the editorial board out of power. Meanwhile, the Echeverría family began buying other newspapers with the result that Echeverria became the major shareholder of *El Universal*. The new *Excelsior* management initiated a more favorable policy toward Echeverría.

Corruption as well as nepotism became severe problems. Lowering the voting age to 18 did not reduce cynicism because Rodolfo Echeverría emptied the accounts of the national film industry, reportedly to buy a floor of the Waldorf Astoria Hotel in New York. Rumors claimed that a son died in the capital's fashionable María Isabel hotel of a heroin overdose. Echeverría himself purchased the area around Cancún and profited immensely when the tourist agency promoted Cancún. Kickbacks and bribes characterized public works as well as private development.

International Relations. Criticism of Mexican jails affected Echeverría's relations with the United States. Dallas business leader Ross Perot engineered a raid into Piedras Negras's jail that freed 14 U.S. prisoners. Reports of brutal treatment toward prisoners harmed the tourist industry and led to the signing of a prisoner exchange. Prisoners convicted of political offenses and violations of international law could not be eligible for exchange, but inmates could decide to remain or not in each country. Few Mexicans returned and U.S. victims later signed affidavits claiming that guards kicked them in the groin, shocked them with cattle prods, and forced them to pay bribes in order to avoid such work details as washing prisons with rags the size of handkerchiefs.

Relations between Echeverría and the United States became increasingly strained. Mexico joined the growing number of Third World Nations claiming their share of world resources by establishing a 200-mile fishing and mineral rights zone. The United States intensified pressure to eradicate Mexican brown heroin as the major source of the illicit drug. With the breakup of the French connection and decline of Turkish supplies, Mexican heroin accounted for two of every three pounds seized in the United States by 1976.

Diplomats are normally circumspect not to publicly criticize domestic affairs, but in March 1976, the U.S. ambassador attacked the Mexican political system as "monarchial." For his part, Echeverría rejected an accusation by 76 U.S. congressional representatives that Mexico leaned toward communism and would create a "cactus curtain." Echeverría reinforced his belligerent posture by snatching protest signs from Mexican American picketers in San Antonio, who demanded prisoner releases. "Fascists," shouted the 54-year-old Echeverría, who attempted to strike one demonstrator until bodyguards pushed him inside a hotel while San Antonio police separated Mexican secret service agents from the crowd.

Echeverría courted Third World leaders with mixed results. Mexico had particularly angered the State Department by supporting a UN resolution condemning Israel as racist. But after losing millions of tourist dollars, Echeverría had to repudiate his vote both in the United States and in Israel. Nevertheless, Echeverría befriended the Chilean government of Marxist Salvador Allende during Allende's triumphant visit to Mexico. Mexico accepted Chilean refugees after Allende's downfall and Echeverría severed ties with military dictator Augusto Pinochet. Echeverría also strengthened relations with Cuba and China. Once his domestic policies failed, a strident Third World diplomacy became virtually all that Echeverría could offer the left. In 1974, the United Nations ignored his proposal of a Charter of Economic Duties and Rights of States. Claiming that it would discourage colonialism and promote Third World sovereignty, Echeverría promoted this idea on his world travels to little avail. Eager to become the UN Secretary General, Echeverría did manage to enact the Treaty of Tlatelolco, which banned nuclear weapons in Latin America.

Results of Echeverría's Social Policies. Despite the populist and occasionally radical speeches that Echeverría used to alarm the rich, he did little to bring about the social reforms that he championed so eloquently. Policies that favored the upper and middle classes at the expense of the workers and campesinos produced increasing inequality. In 1975, the Swiss Banking Society ranked Mexico's standard of living as lower than Libya or Iran in terms of per capita gross national product. It also became clear that Mexico spent too little on primary education. In 1974, over one-fourth of the Mexican people could not read or write. The problem of illiteracy reflected the PRI's favoritism of urban areas over rural inhabitants; only 6 percent of children in the interior advanced beyond the sixth grade, whereas 41 percent of children in urban areas did. While patronizing the urban middle class, the government allowed indigenous areas to stagnate. In Chiapas, the illiteracy rate actually increased from 45.4 percent in 1970 to over 48 percent in 1973. Throughout Mexico, the number of Indians who could not speak Spanish went up from 2.4 million in 1940 to 3.1 million in 1974.

Social problems multiplied. With a 3.5 percent annual population growth, Mexico had grown from 25 million inhabitants to 58 million within a quarter of a century. But society contained 19 million undernourished people, who often died from malnutrition because they could afford to purchase only beans, tortillas, and chile peppers. Soft drinks began replacing fruit juices because of the lack of potable water in many regions. The infant mortality rate due to malnutrition increased by more than 10 percent from 1966 to 1974. Mexico also became the world leader in work-related accidents. Half a million of the 3.8 million industrial workers suffered injuries by 1977.

Unemployment also became a serious concern. In 1960, only 506,000 persons found themselves without work. But this figure quintupled to 2.5 million by 1970. Since the economy could employ only 15 million people, 7.5 percent had to seek employment in the United States each year. Another 5 million could only work seasonally. As conditions worsened, nearly 40 percent of the population lacked full-time jobs and many toiled for wages below the minimum wage in the 1970s. Not surprisingly, 7.2 million migrated to the United States by 1978. By 1974, 7.5 million searched for work each day.

The standard of living for inhabitants of Mexico City deteriorated alarmingly. Operating largely on unleaded gas, autos as well as 30,000 factories, most of which burned low-grade sulfurous fuel, emitted 11,000 tons of gaseous waste each day into the air. With water wells running dry, the city pumped water in and sewage out over surrounding mountains at great cost. During the 1970s, Mexico City nearly doubled its population from 8 million to 14 million. One out of five Mexicans lived in the metropolitan area. Many migrants settled in Ciudad Netzahualcóyotl, a rough slum that grew from 580,436 in 1970 to 2 million by 1980. Three-fourths of its newcomers were less than 24 years old and only half found work. An estimated two-thirds of Mexico City dwellers suffered from undernourishment while perhaps 90 percent had tooth decay. During the mid-1970s, portions of restaurant meals became skimpier as the price for eating a *comida corrida* (full meal) jumped from 12 to 20 pesos.

When the smog drifted away each day, the capital revealed more suffering. Choked traffic, unbearable noise, and inadequate housing produced rampant anxiety. Fifty percent of the country's industry, banks, and centers of higher education functioned in Mexico City, which accounted for half the nation's consumption of electricity, gasoline, and natural gas. As unemployed, homeless campesinos seized unoccupied land and built shacks of rock, cardboard, and tar paper, they often encountered fierce resistance. Arsonists used Molotov cocktails to destroy Campamento 2 de Octubre in January 1976. Four days later, police moved in and began searches that left one resident dead and many wounded. In order to make a living, 5,000 families known as *pepenadores* sifted through the 6,500 tons of rubbish thrown away each day in the Mexico City garbage dumps.

At least the government recognized that something had to be done about the explosive population growth. In 1965, Mexican women gave birth to 7.2 children, on average. But at the Latin American Congress held in June 1970, Mexico was the only nation to oppose a resolution favoring birth control. The Mexican delegate stated:

The demographic explosion is a challenge to development and we have accepted the challenge. Before making plans for family planning, we have to find formulas to prevent unemployment, distribute the wealth, and give better assistance to the existing population ... to favor birth control is to oppose man. (*Christian Century*, Nov. 25, 1970).

Mexican agencies like the National Population Council and the nonprofit Mexican Foundation for Family Planning initiated birth control programs that provided information and contraceptives. Media campaigns urged delay of marriage and pregnancy while emphasizing the advantages of spacing the births of children. Both the Church and family planning agencies worked together to keep antagonism to a minimum. Ads listed the advantage of a small family without direct mention of contraceptives. Sex education entered public elementary schools without serious opposition. Birth control policies eventually reduced population growth nationwide from 6.1 percent annually in 1945 to 1.5 percent at the end of the twentieth century.

The slogan "make love, not war" became popular with Mexican women. They began to seek out relationships that were different from their parents:. Specifically, women wanted friendship with male companions as well as love. The right to pleasure became a particular goal even though many considered it subversive in a culture that remained somewhat authoritarian. Mexican women wanted democracy in all aspects of their lives, not just in the government. Cognizant of these changes, the legislature passed a bill in 1974 guaranteeing equal rights for women in employment and education. It was done because illiteracy for women had exceeded the rate for males. Women were hindered in pursuing education because of traditional objections from parents that they should not leave home, normally considered a threat to sexual virtue. With limited domestic finances, males usually received money out of the expectation that they would work all their lives but that females would just be temporary workers. Women also suffered a higher drop-out rate after the fourth grade. Rural women had the fewest educational opportunities.

Working women also suffered discriminatory treatment. Many were left out of the census count if they were raising animals, fruits, and vegetables for sale in villages. Female vendors, artisans, and renters were also ignored. In addition, domestic workers were difficult to unionize and received no social security benefits. At the workplace, pregnant women were routinely fired in order to avoid payment of maternity benefits. Sexual harassment remained common in businesses as well as public service.

The Polyforum inauguration ceremonies in December 1971 for the Siqueiros mural, the *March*, revealed the gulf between government attitudes and social reality. Siqueiros embraced Echeverría, who had ordered attacks on protesting students. In the eyes of many, this was the ultimate sign that Siqueiros had lost his soul. To complicate matters, the press raised questions about the shallow, abstract attributes of the Polyforum (spelled with an Anglo "y" instead of a Hispanic "i") that seemed more geared to tourists. Critics felt the mural betrayed the classical muralism of Orozco and Rivera. The mural required viewers to stand immobile in one place, and accept a staged light and sound program. The PRI did the same with its control of nominations, elections, and administration—which the public could only stand and accept. Murals had once graced public buildings and encouraged the masses to reach the goals of the revolution. The *March* excluded the common Mexican by requiring a paid admission to enter a specially constructed arena which was hidden by walls and trees, thus restricting public observation, just like PRI activities.

The *March* emphasized international rather than Mexican themes and thus became more palatable to viewing tourists. And it was constructed as a complement to a new, world-class hotel. When asked to explain the social significance of the mural, Siqueiros could not provide an acceptable answer. Because he was suspected of abandoning nationalism, the PCM expelled Siqueiros. This episode illustrates how politics

can incorporate art and how artists accommodate themselves to government.

In his clumsy attempts to woo academics and intellectuals, Echeverría made some progress. He raised the salaries of university faculties and appointed icons such as Fuentes to high places. Fuentes became ambassador to France and never criticized Echeverría. He was not the only one to accept government benefits. In 1974, Echeverría invited a large number of intellects to join him on a state visit to Peronista Argentina. Within 36 hours, more than 100 agreed to be flown to Buenos Aires for a dinner given by Echeverría for local intellectuals. Despite the crassness of this maneuver, Mexico continued to allow dissident South American writers and academics to settle there by the thousands. As in the Cárdenas years, which Echeverria tried to imitate, the refugees helped staff many new regional universities in the 1970s, as well as metropolitan branches of the UNAM. Echeverría also relocated El Colegio de México to new surroundings at a cost of 300 million pesos.

The cost of these policies was a decline in cultural standards. Open enrollment policies at UNAM led to declining academic standards by the 1970s. In the early 1970s, Mexican cinema turned away from the profit-conscious private producers. With the support of Echeverría, independents, including many leftist intellectuals, explored controversial political and social themes in film. Each year the government picked up the bill for a handful of "quality" films that were almost always box office flops—even in Mexico.

ECONOMIC AND FINANCIAL CRISIS

Echeverría plunged Mexico into a severe economic crisis by means of ambitious but ill-fated development schemes. Attempting to present himself as another Cárdenas, Echeverría inaugurated a giant public works program that pushed the principle of a mixed economy; a combination of foreign, private, and state investments sought to expand aggregate demand as well as production. By 1973, government spending had increased its 1970 expenditures by two and a half times. The administration provided fiscal plans for industrial development, goods in transit, and the acquisition of materials required to manufacture export products. Subsidized exports, public works projects that failed to generate foreign exchange, costly subsidies for food and fuel, and many high-paying useless appointments for friends and retainers were the unexpected as well as unhappy results. Echeverría's strategy differed completely from Taiwan, Singapore, and Malaysia where leaders built infrastructure and productive capacity aimed at generating foreign exchange to pay off loans.

Echeverría's development plan seemed ambitious but laudatory in the early 1970s. Education improved somewhat and the highway system doubled. Tourist centers appeared in new locations as the government regulated foreign capital more by means of a rigorous 1973 law. The 1973 foreign investment law provided exceptions for new foreign investment that contributed to manufactured product exports, brought in new technology, generated substantial employment, or furthered the territorial decentralization of economic growth. Sugar production recorded its highest level while the petrochemicals, oil, and steel industries expanded. Steel production doubled to 9.9 million tons annually as Mexico became an oil exporter in 1974. Daily oil production increased from 450,000 barrels per day in 1970 to 885,000 by 1975. Tax reform in 1972 sought to achieve more equitable taxation, improve control of taxpayers, increase revenues of states and municipalities, and raise federal government income. An Energy Commission created by presidential decree in 1973 invested in oil drilling and the construction of the nuclear-electric plant at Laguna Verde.

Attempts to speed up economic growth by means of direct government management often failed. Almost from the start, obstacles prevented Laguna Verde from coming close to completion during Echeverría's *sexenio*, when three different directors took the helm at the federal electricity commission. Mexican-built equipment proved far more expansive and of inferior quality than the same items produced abroad. Mexico did not have the technological infrastructure or expertise to be in a position to equip the Laguna Verde plant. The Echeverría administration poured huge sums of credits, subsidies, and direct investments into henequen ejidos and Cordemex, the state monopoly. The result was massive corruption, not a revitalization of the henequen industry. Echeverría had overlooked the fact that world demand for henequen had decreased. The PAN victory for control of the Mérida city government in 1967 was probably the real reason for such concern about henequen. The crucial mistake, which a freer market would have avoided, was Echeverría's efforts to revitalize or at least preserve an industry condemned to marginality by changes in the world economy. The government also became interested in communications. Arguing the lack of interest among Mexican investors, the Echeverría administration nationalized Telmex, which soon monopolized telephone operations throughout Mexico.

A major problem was that heavy borrowing to pay for these projects, as well as the growth of foreign capital, created serious dependency upon the United States. The foreign debt was $3.7 billion in 1970 but increased to $13.4 billion in 1975 and doubled to $25 billion by the end of 1976. As Echeverría failed to take constructive measures, the financial and economic situation fell into disarray. In 1973, exports increased by 10 percent but imports of U.S. goods went up by 60 percent. To compound this imbalance, the government recorded a budget deficit of 75,000 million pesos in 1974—approximately $6 billion. Echeverría blamed the private sector for not reinvesting, but capital flight became quite serious. An estimated $2.2 billion left Mexico in 1976 and the number of foreign exchange accounts went up in Mexico by 63.3 percent during the same year. To make matters worse, the appropriate agencies never collected approximately 80 percent of legal tax revenue owed by private industry. In 1976, the economy registered its smallest growth rate since 1953—the GNP went up by only 2.2 percent.

Neglect of agriculture accentuated financial problems. Agricultural production actually suffered a 1 percent decline in 1972, particularly for corn, wheat, beans, and sorghum as well as meat and milk. Food production increased by only 1.7 percent in 1973 at a time when the population was growing by 3.5 percent a year. Echeverría attempted to use CONASUPO to attain self-sufficiency in distribution, but basic items, notably sugar and dairy products, became scarce by 1973 as suppliers connived to drive up prices. The result was that Mexico had to purchase 93,000 tons of food from the United States in 1973. The failure of agricultural policy is best illustrated by the fact that from 1971 to 1974, 47,000 *ejidatarios* lost their rights to farm on the country's 6,000 *ejidos* because they rented their plots out illegally.

The economic crisis continued to produce social distress. In late 1972, inflation began to hit Mexico hard for the first time in decades. Prices went up 20 percent in 1973 and accelerated beyond 30 percent thereafter. In the face of a threatened strike, Echeverría ordered industry to accept pay raises that nevertheless resulted in a loss of real income for workers. By the time Echeverría left, nearly half the work force was either unemployed or underemployed.

Despite Echeverría's loudly proclaimed intention to reduce U.S. dependence, adverse conditions above the border seriously affected Mexico. Repeated attempts to diversify Mexico's trading relations amounted to very little. The United States still controlled two-thirds of Mexican trade and 80 percent of foreign investment by 1976. When a recession hit the United States, Mexico suffered. The collapse of the *maquiladoras* in 1975 sharply increased unemployment. Within a year, more than 20,000 Mexican workers in the north found themselves without jobs as one U.S. plant after another shut down assembly lines.

Depending upon U.S. markets also eroded the commercial sector. In 1973, the balance of payments deficit went up 68.7 percent within a single year. The trade deficit jumped from $1 billion in 1970 to $3.7 billion in 1975 before declining to $3.0 billion in 1976. In the stark atmosphere that preceded his departure, Echeverría decided upon drastic measures that resulted in disaster.

After months of denying that he would devalue the peso, Echeverría allowed it to float on August 31, 1976; this was the beginning of an intense trauma. The devaluation was basically an attempt to improve the trade deficit by making exports from Mexico cheaper and foreign imports more expensive. Tourism, which had fallen by four percent in 1975, also needed stimulation. The peso soon fell to 20 for a dollar until labor and business convinced Echeverría to have the Banco de México peg the rate. This was a mistake because the government never raised wages sufficiently to keep up with inflation. Merchants raised prices enough to discourage foreign buyers. Morover, the cost of servicing the national debt doubled since most of the debt was obligated in foreign currencies. Devaluation raised the prices of already expensive U.S. components in Mexican-made products. Inflation meant that prices for goods and services could not remain low. Mexico City was already the twenty-second most expensive city in the world. Foreign brokers did not lower prices for Mexican produce and the cost of manufactured U.S. imports soared. Clearly, monetary and fiscal discipline were far more necessary than devaluation. But Echeverría dismissed the advice of Hugo Margain, his treasury minister, who warned him that Mexico had reached its debt limit. In 1973, new treasury secretary José López Portillo allowed the president to control financial matters at an unprecedented level.

To compound the devaluation mistake, the government floated the peso a second time in October 1976, as Echeverría negotiated three loans for a total of $2.6 billion. But massive capital flight had occurred as a result of the first devaluation and never ceased. On one Friday, panic-stricken citizens bought $150 million. In response, the government had to suspend virtually all sales and purchases of foreign currencies, as well as gold, because of widespread desperation to dump pesos. The suspension decree raised the exchange of pesos from 24 to 28.4 that day. This final devaluation upset many because it halted the transfer of profits out of the country by foreign firms while companies importing goods had to defer payment in foreign currencies. The banks had simply run out of dollars and the Banco de México had little foreign exchange. Instead of shoring up the peso, these three devaluations created a crisis of confidence and unleashed hyperinflation. Meanwhile, business transactions slowed ominously as rumors circulated of a military coup or massive nationalizations.

The final crisis of the Echeverría regime involved a series of land invasions in the north. In October 1975, Sonora state police massacred campesinos with the result that the corrupt governor had to be removed. The large landowners responded two months later by staging a stoppage of food deliveries in an effort to force the Echeverría government to take a stronger stand against Mexico's growing campesino movement. Poor farmers claimed that the landowners violated agrarian laws, which limited land ownership to 100 hectares; but the law did not exclude various members of the same family from possessing adjoining lands.

Illegal squatting in Sonora soon erupted into a massive land invasion on November 19, 1976. Only six and a half hours later, the Agrarian Reform secretariat announced the expropriation of about 243,100 acres of rich farm and ranch lands. Later, the government divided this valuable property into 30-acre plots and gave them to 8,037 campesino families. Fearing the loss of farm machinery on these lands, the 72 wealthy families that lost their property fought back by parking their tractors in the streets of Ciudad Obregón. A one-day strike involving five million businessmen, industrialists, and workers swept through 11 states to protest the Sonoro expropriation. This became a serious matter since Sonora produced approximately 60 percent of Mexican wheat and a major portion of its cattle.

As social tensions increased, 20,000 campesinos threatened to seize thousands of acres of additional land in Sinaloa a few days later. Split

into dozens of groups, the squatters began meeting with Echeverría, who yearned to do something notable. But 28,000 Sinaloa landowners went on strike, fearing more expropriations. Echeverría persuaded both groups to agree that Sinaloa landowners would redistribute 33,345 acres and defer action on the remaining land to the incoming president. But on November 27, landless campesinos began squatting on 100,000 acres in the Carizo valley. Eventually, the squatters agreed to suspend their invasion until a federal judge could rule on landowner petitions for a court order declaring the seizures illegal and preventing other squatters. With this in mind, Echeverría gave title to 1.1 million acres of land, earlier expropriated at various times, to 40,000 peasants. On his last day in office, Echeverría signed about 700 decrees creating 62 new ejidos and expanding 50 others. About 400,000 acres of this land came from Sinaloa in order to defuse that crisis. Unfortunately, Echeverría's dubious decision paralyzed the rich farm land of Sinaloa during its planting season. Replacing the prosperous farmers were about 9,000 squatters throughout the valley in 80 shanty camps.

Emboldened by events in Sonora and Sinaloa, thousands of additional squatters seized 20 acres of land each in Torreón's southeastern section, joining about 3,000 others who had been there for a year. Despite support from students, 400 policemen evicted the squatters, who proceeded to demonstrate in the streets. Another 1,000 campesinos invaded farmland in northern Durango but left afterwards in order to demonstrate their confidence in new president José López Portillo. Echeverría's departure produced uncertainty about the future and doubts concerning the populist approach to land problems.

THE RISE AND FALL OF LÓPEZ PORTILLO

López Portillo did little to prevent the erosion of the PRI's outdated slogans. Primarily chosen so that Echeverría could maintain his power, López

Portillo claimed that his experience in the treasury secretariat would enable him to repair the economy. Because his predecessor had organized López Portillo's campaign and advanced the PRI's internal elections so that *Echeverristas* eventually dominated Congress, it took longer than normal for López Portillo to exercise his authority. López Portillo had never held political office and understood that he was not Echeverría's first choice to lead the country. Nevertheless, López Portillo gained the customary endorsement of smaller parties while the divided PAN could not even put up a candidate. Amid widespread apathy, López Portillo received 17.5 million of the 18.5 million votes cast; the rest going to the write-in PCM candidate.

López Portillo's inauguration reflected the failure of Echeverría. Two days before López Portillo took the oath as Mexico's sixtieth president since 1824, five explosions ripped through banks, Mexico City's leading hotel, and various U.S. companies. Police with rifles patrolled Avenida Reforma as a grim Echeverría marched into the hall of the National Auditorium to place the presidential sash across the chest of López Portillo. When the new president attempted to embrace Echeverría, the ex-ruler fended him off and tried to avoid a subsequent *abrazo*. The calm tone of López Portillo's voice distinguished his inaugural speech. López Portillo sounded a somber note and rallied his people to face austerity. He attempted to please business by stating that he respected the right to earn a profit. In keeping with PRI tradition, he also called for greater commitment to social justice.

López Portillo's background and style seemed to suggest a positive change from the insular and polemical Echeverría. Born in 1920 to a middle-class Mexico City family of Basque origin, López Portillo began his career as a law professor for 12 years at the national university. The author of two novels and a government textbook, López Portillo began public service with the education secretariat before advancing to the presidential legal staff. In 1971, Echeverría named his boyhood friend to head the Federal Electricity Commission until

moving him over to the treasury. Outgoing, jocular, and uninterested in discussing his ideological preference, López Portillo enjoyed early popularity.

The new president adopted something of a law-and-order stance by stifling domestic dissent. Troops and state police began moving squatters off seized land when they did not leave. At the national university, club-swinging police attacked 2,000 striking university workers, students, and professors during a predawn assault on July 7, 1977. The attack resulted in the arrest of up to 1,000 people and corroded López Portillo's benevolent image. As if to demonstrate its determination to hold down inflation and wage raises, the regime muffled press reports about the confrontation. The strikers had requested a Church-sponsored newspaper organization to call a press conference the day after the occupation. But later that day, two busloads of tactical police raided its office. Meanwhile, the government crushed the urban guerrilla movement, particularly the Fuerzas Revolucionarios Armadas del Pueblo. Police and military death squads gunned down hundreds of dissidents, particularly drug traffickers, political opponents, and PRI insiders who knew too much.

In order to divide opposition groups and gain international legitimacy for the regime, López Portillo reformed the political system in 1977. A detailed electoral law assured competing parties of winning some seats in the lower house of the federal legislature by creating two types of deputies. The law provided for 300 representatives to be selected by a simple majority and set aside 100 additional seats for the other parties. When the first elections under the new law took effect in 1979, however, the PRI won 296 of the 300 simple-majority seats. When voters democratically disputed the PRI, the government reverted to its traditional impulses. In Juchitan, the second largest city in Oaxaca, state police assaulted and occupied the municipality to toss out 100 members of the Coalition of Workers, Peasants, and Students of the Isthmus, an electoral alliance with the PCM. López Portillo's political reform actually weakened the left by allowing the opposition to break down into nine registered parties instead of the previous four. A short-lived attempt of the five leftist parties to unite behind a single candidate collapsed after ten weeks of negotiations. Mexico's most prominent leftist, Heberto Castillo, of the Mexican Workers' Party, withdrew from the talks during the autumn of 1981.

To minimize discontent and maintain the rhetoric of land reform, the regime announced that two-thirds of the governors had agreed to break up *latifundios* and settle existing land claims by 1980. López Portillo surprised many by taking over the property of large cattle ranches and cattle breeders in return for unspecified compensation. Eager to expand the domestic market in the countryside by striking at landowners without political bargaining power, the López Portillo administration had no interest in disturbing productive land, no matter how large the holding. On January 7, 1978, official peasant organizations assembled to protest conditions in the countryside. López Portillo responded with a promise to place agricultural reform on a par with petroleum development. But in Oaxaca, the PRI installed as governor the general whose troops had tracked down and killed Lucio Cabañas. Rural Mexico bristled with *pistoleros,* soldiers, and agrarian revolutionaries.

International Relations. López Portillo enjoyed a fairly successful foreign policy despite clashes with the United States. The president visited Spain in 1977; King Juan Carlos and Queen Sofia reciprocated with a Mexican tour the year after. After Franco's death, Mexico finally reestablished full relations with Spain. A devout Catholic, López Portillo allowed Pope John Paul II to visit Mexico in 1979. López Portillo arranged to have the pope celebrate mass at the executive residence. Pope John Paul carried out a whirlwind visit, driving people into fits of ecstasy. He inaugurated a major conference of Latin-American bishops and advised priests to stay out of politics but urged the church to aid the poor. López Portillo also strengthened relations with Cuba more than any other regime. Castro visited

Mexico in 1979 as Mexico offered to assist Cuba with offshore oil explorations.

Since good relations with Cuba encouraged López Portillo to believe that Castro would not foment guerrilla activities in Mexico, "don Pepe" desired the same understanding with Nicaragua. Therefore, Mexico canceled the debts of the Sandinista government and provided them with free oil. López Portillo also supported Marxist rebels in El Salvador and criticized the United States for supporting the repressive junta. Not surprisingly, a conference on world solidarity took place in Mexico. With France, Mexico recognized the FDR and FMLN factions in El Salvador in September 1981. Mexico joined Venezuela, Costa Rica, and Panama to call for a political-diplomatic settlement of Central American problems rather than military solutions. Mexico asserted its opposition to the El Salvadoran junta, as well as the rightist Guatemalan regime by having the army carry out maneuvers on the southern border. The 99,000-strong Mexican army received new equipment and orders to stay 2 miles away from the border. In order to discourage guerrilla activities in Chiapas, however, Mexico allowed Guatemalan forces to attack refugees and their sympathizers as part of the friendship between both country's military leaders.

Despite a promising beginning, López Portillo soon maintained a stubborn posture with the United States. In February 1977, Mexico offered to sell 40 million cubic feet of gas a day to help the United States deal with its energy crisis. López Portillo also promised to provide 600,000 barrels of crude oil along with an additional 2 million barrels a day if ships could be found to transport it. After both countries signed a memo of intent in August 1977, Mexico began building a 685-mile pipeline from oil fields in southeast Mexico to the Texas border. This transaction was a gamble for López Portillo, because his leftist critics charged that the pipeline was a giveaway of Mexico's natural resources that would make her even more dependent upon the United States. López Portillo maintained that the gas would be burned off anyway and that gas and oil sales would pull Mexico out of a "financial pothole." Relations became tense when six U.S. companies agreed to buy 2.2 billion cubic feet of gas per day; but Energy Secretry James Schlesinger vetoed the project. Schlesinger objected to Mexico's desire for a short contract and claimed that the Mexican price was excessive since it was tied to the price of heating oil delivered at New York harbor. Because of Schlesinger's high-handed arrogance, Mexico angrily refused to sell her gas until President Jimmy Carter convinced López Portillo to renegotiate. Although the United States was buying ten times the amount of natural gas from Canada than Mexico offered and for a lower price, arduous negotiations finally resulted in a September 1979 agreement.

The bitter feelings caused by the unpleasant gas negotiations affected U.S.–Mexican relations seriously. López Portillo attacked the bumbling Carter during the U.S. leader's December 1979 visit to Mexico. Carter clumsily alluded to Moctezuma's revenge while López Portillo charged that the United States had been deceitful with Mexico. But López Portillo revealed that he could be devious. He promised the Shah of Iran that he could count on a secure exile in Mexico but later expelled him. Mexican refusal to readmit the Shah hurt Carter badly; the Shah's presence in New York became a major factor in the takeover of the U.S. embassy in Tehran. Mexico's position of minimizing the increasing numbers of illegal migrants to the United States also angered Carter. López Portillo's approach simply demanded more research on the subject or claimed that migration must merely be interpreted as a domestic U.S. matter.

Corruption. Profligacy and nepotism eventually destroyed López Portillo's short-lived popularity as he and prominent members of his administration pocketed huge amounts of the country's cash. López Portillo was vain and unable to handle criticism; insiders knew him to be corrupt even before he became president. Nepotism became staggering. López Portillo appointed his son undersecretary of Budget and Planning. Sister Margarita became director of the radio, tel-

evision, and film industry. Cousins took charge of the National Sports Institute, the National Fruit Commission, and undersecretary of an agency to improve the atmosphere. Nephews directed the national airline and the sugar commission. Brothers-in-law also controlled key agencies.

The symbol of López Portillo's self-gratification was a 32-acre, multicompound palace near Mexico City that cost roughly $85 million. This estate consisted of a house for each of his three children with enclosed swimming pools, tennis courts, a gymnasium, an observatory, and a library with space for four million volumes. Not only did the mansion have a refrigerator for furs, but it also had marble and gold bathrooms as well as jade floors. López Portillo also reportedly owned properties in Acapulco, Miami, Rome, and Seville. Estimates of his personal wealth ranged from $1 billion to a Central Intelligence Agency (CIA) estimate of $5 billion.

Corruption also characterized high subordinates of the regime. Arturo Durazo Moreno symbolized corrupt cronyism while he served as Mexico City police chief. In reality, he was a high-living thug eventually convicted of extortion and weapons smuggling. A boyhood friend of López Portillo, Durazo amassed millions of dollars and built flamboyant residences, including a columned pink palace known as "the Parthenon" at the beach resort of Zihuatenejo. Another estate on the outskirts of Mexico City featured a race track, a full-scale reproduction of New York City's Studio 54, and a collection of 50 vintage automobiles. Durazo appropriated federal property to build his mansion and engaged in fraud, homicide, and tax evasion. Police and other public officials often became ineffective parasites. The Mexico City detectives were thoroughly corrupt and maintained torture cells so they could extort money from prisoners.

Even to the end, López Portillo maintained a disconcerting refusal to admit wrongdoing among his policemen. When Durazo finally died in August 2000, López Portillo told reporters that "I had lost a friend and a great collaborator. I remember his courage, his bravery, his honesty."

PEMEX executives became particularly notorious. Kickbacks, fraud, and price fixing became routine and cost Mexico millions of dollars. Audits of PEMEX accounts revealed vast quantities of oil and natural gas unaccounted for. Even though they had argued for closing duty-free shops because they damaged the economy, deputies returning from the United States went unpunished when caught with contraband goods. Dignitaries used three or four cars despite the poverty around them. In Coahuila, Governor Oscar Flores Tapia illegally acquired property worth a billion pesos. Directors of state-owned banks and industries routinely embezzled public funds.

After Octavio Senties retired as mayor of the federal district in 1975, the tenure of Carlos Hank González became grotesque. Basking in public attention, Hank González allowed voters to freely elect 16 new city councils. He claimed that Mexico City's problems could be solved with more money and greater efficiency. Although the new mayor spoke out against corruption, he stole funds to purchase a million dollar estate in Connecticut, a yacht, and other luxuries. González reportedly sold municipal water supplies for profit while ejecting the poor from their land so that the wealthy could build housing complexes.

On a more uplifting note, feminists founded the Coalition of Women because of the problem of rape and women battering. Two 1978 rape cases initiated the organization. In the first case, a 22-year-old woman killed her would-be rapist. Authorities immediately arrested her. Feminists responded by setting up an around-the-clock watch at the Mexico City prison where the police held her, demanding that she had the right to defend herself. After three days, authorities gave in and freed the woman. The judge cited a "defense of sexual liberty" law. In the second case, three men raped a 32-year-old woman on the UNAM campus. Citing a woman's right to have "sexual self determination," the judge handed down maximum sentences. The Coalition of Women, initially established to push for legalized abortion, opened rape-crisis centers in Mexico City and sponsored self-defense classes for females.

From Boom to Bust. López Portillo led Mexico from prosperity to a severe economic crisis. With a deceptively straight-speaking style, the president charmed the nation by means of an oil boom. By the time of his third state of the nation address on September 1, 1979, López Portillo declared that Mexico's economic problems were over. As Mexico moved up from the fifteenth crude oil exporter in the world in 1976 to the fourth, the eerie red glow of gas being flared off in the Reforma fields near Villahermosa seemed to reflect López Portillo's growing ebullience. Mexico's proven reserves increased from 7 billion barrels in early 1976 to at least 60 billion barrels within a year, which was double the size of U.S. reserves. Prompted by the Organization of Petroleum Exporting Countries (OPEC) latest price increases, Mexico excitedly raised oil prices. PEMEX also announced a six-year, $15.5 billion investment plan to satisfy domestic and international consumption, particularly in the area of offshore drilling.

In order to attain rapid economic growth, López Portillo's essentially pro-business administration encouraged foreign investment. Representatives from 140 Mexican companies met with López Portillo in December 1976 to join the government in investing $8 billion and creating 300,000 jobs. In return, the regime promised unrestricted respect for private property and better cooperation than during the Echeverría years. López Portillo also hoped to solve the economic and fiscal problems of the mid-1970s by attracting more U.S. private investment. Total foreign investment in Mexico rose from $5.3 billion in 1976 to $10.8 billion in 1982. During the same period, the number of firms with foreign capitalization rose from 4,359 to 6,129. In 2,778 of those firms, foreign owners held controlling interest.

López Portillo temporarily pleased the United States when he made Mexican entry into the General Agreement on Tariffs and Trade (GATT) the topic of national debate. But academic, labor, and business opposition forced the president to back down when they claimed that membership in a multilateral agreement compromised Mexican sovereignty and would lead to massive bankrupt-cies of national industries, as was the case in Argentina and Chile once tariff barriers and protectionism had ceased. Even the PRI was neutral as many ministries voiced their skepticism. In March 1980, López Portillo reconsidered and announced that Mexico would not join. Nevertheless, he continued to push for free trade by replacing the burdensome system of import licenses with import tariffs among 70 percent of Mexico's imported items by the summer of 1980.

López Portillo established the first comprehensive agricultural policy of any Mexican government. He planned to use oil revenues to finance a systematic revival of agriculture so that Mexico could break out of food export patterns by offering subsidies, price supports, and crop insurance as well as educational nutrition programs. López Portillo sought to increase private investment in commercial agriculture as well as in ejidos to solve the problem of underproduction. López Portillo committed immense resources to this program because he felt that Mexico could no longer afford the political luxury of the ejido.

Perhaps López Portillo's greatest mistake was his goal of selling enough oil to pay for Mexico's increasing indebtedness. Oil earnings soared from $3 billion in 1975 to $14 billion in 1980, but the government wildly over estimated oil reserves. Although López Portillo promised a diversified economy, oil's share of total exports rose from 42.5 percent in 1979 to 64.5 percent by mid-1980. Moreover, the exploration debts of PEMEX became quite high and the 1979 blowout of Ixtox I revealed PEMEX's inefficiency. PEMEX director Jorge Díaz Serrano's units had drilled the well sloppily. Poor drilling procedures ruined fisheries, agriculture, and the environment of Tabasco and Chiapas. The economy temporarily grew at about 8 percent a year, but by the end of 1980 inflation began to average 30 percent. Chaos in the antiquated ports and railroads created economic bottlenecks. Meanwhile, the purchasing power of the legal minimum wage fell by 6.5 percent and perhaps 40 percent of the work force earned less than the required minimum.

A worldwide oil glut that appeared in the spring of 1981 marked the beginning of a disastrous fiscal crisis. Excessive international production caused Mexican oil revenues to plunge. At that point, López Portillo should have stopped borrowing money, but he refused. Adding to the fiscal problem was that high interest rates raised the U.S. prime rate to 17 percent in 1981. Thus Mexican interest obligations soared from $5.4 billion in 1980 to $8.2 billion in 1981. In addition, the price of commodities such as silver, coffee, and copper also declined. Dependence upon oil and gas became so great that they accounted for 75 percent of total exports in 1981. The government failed to convince a pessimistic public that it was cutting the budget. The deficit increased to 14.2 percent of the gross national product, up from 7.6 percent in 1980. Attempting to maintain the peso when it became seriously overvalued was a mistake, because extra borrowing increased the public debt by $20 billion in less than a year.

A financial crisis struck furiously when López Portillo devalued the peso three times in 1981. After a 43 percent devaluation in 1976, another series of devaluations was difficult to face. A few weeks after promising to defend the peso "like a dog," López Portillo authorized the first devaluation in February 1981. In less than six months, the peso slipped 160 percent against the dollar, demoralizing many. Then the government froze all dollar accounts and instituted exchange controls that prevented Mexicans and foreigners from taking money out of Mexico. Previously, López Portillo had denied reports that exchange controls would be introduced, but the president blamed foreign news media for the devaluation, insisting that pessimistic news reports caused mounting capital flight. Once López Portillo had picked Miguel de la Madrid, head of the Planning and Budget Secretariat, to succeed him as president in late 1981, deficits grew when de la Madrid began giving in to cabinet officials' requests to enhance his presidential prospects. The central bank had nearly run out of reserves and de la Madrid allowed the peso to float.

The devaluations produced severe results. The cost of imports increased and the 1982 consumer price index rose by almost 100 percent as opposed to 43 percent in 1977. When the scarcity of dollars made it almost impossible for firms to buy machinery that would allow them to switch to local materials, industries began to lay off employees. Moreover, the private sector relied upon foreign borrowing as much as the government. Within a year, the public and private debt became quite high in short-term obligations.

In August 1981, Finance Minister Jesús Silva Herzog went to the United States and warned that Mexico was on the verge of bankruptcy. He first requested a 90-day postponement of principal payments while a long-term restructuring plan could be formalized. At the time, Silva Herzog had $120 million in liquid reserves when interest payments on the debt were several times higher. Insufficient credit to purchase commodities worsened the situation. Eventually, Mexico postponed three debt payments because the government encountered delays in raising new loans.

The climax to the crisis came on September 1, 1982, when López Portillo nationalized the banks, blaming them for the disaster. The bankers simply had to pay the price for government waste and ineptitude. Nationalization of the banking system was a great shock to the financial community as the private sector feared government ownership. Nationalization subsequently gave the state control of many other companies in the private sector because the banks, particularly BANAMEX, owned majority interest in more than 300 businesses. The day after nationalization, banks closed and apprehensive employees uneasily milled outside. Government technocrats assumed top-management positions as bank lending declined, which damaged economic productivity. As bank profits fell, the government converted existing banking institutions into 29 national credit societies. All dollar accounts were automatically converted into Mexican pesos at an unfavorable rate. This angered both Mexicans and foreigners who kept their savings in dollars. Capital flight intensified, totaling at least $11 billion

until 1987. Financial trust in the government vanished because Mexico had seized $12 billion on deposit by foreigners.

The disasters of Echeverría and López Portillo had wide repercussions. Mexico had to submit to an International Monetary Fund plan in November 1982, in return for renewed credit. Once again Mexico was on the defensive. Criticism of foreign banks mounted because the peso had been devalued by over 600 percent by the time López Portillo left office. Within a few years, Mexico owed $250 million a week in interest payments alone. Indebtedness and economic collapse increased the appeal of the PAN. By demanding fair elections and honest government, the PAN linked up with many who sought immediate change. Mass unrest threatened to explode when health services, education, and real wages declined. As opposition to the PRI hardened in the north, it seemed as though the country was on the verge of revolt. The debt crisis that ensued brought with it a lost decade for economic development as Mexico struggled with inflation, recession, sky-high borrowing costs, and falling living standards.

SUGGESTED READING

Basurto, Jorge. "The Late Populism of Echeverría." In Michael Conniff, ed., *Latin American Populism in Comparative Perspective*. Albuquerque: University of New Mexico Press, 1982, pp. 93-111.

Bataillon, Claude, and Helene Riviere D'Arc. *La ciudad de México*. Mexico City: Secretaría de Educación Pública, 1973.

Blanco Moheno, Roberto. *Si Zapata y Villa levantaran la cabeza: Díaz Ordaz, Echeverría, López Portillo*. Mexico City: Bruguera Mexicana de Ediciones, 1982.

Bodayla, Stephen. "Bankers Versus Diplomats: The Debate Over Mexican Insolvency." *Journal of Inter-American Studies and World Affairs* 24:4 (1982), 461–482.

Cosío Villegas, Daniel. *La sucesión presidencial*. Mexico City: Cuadernos de Joaquin Mortiz, 1975.

Fuentes, Carlos. *Tiempo mexicano*. Mexico City: Cuadernos de Joaquín Mortiz, 1972.

Grayson, George. *The United States and Mexico: Patterns of Influence*. New York: Praeger, 1984.

González González, José. *Lo negro del negro Durazo*. 2d ed. Mexico City: Editorial Posada, 1983.

Granados Chapa, Miguel Angel. *La banca nuestra de cada dia;* 3d ed. Edition. Mexico City: Ediciones Océano, 1984.

Johnson, Kenneth F. *Mexican Democracy: A Critical View*. 3d ed. New York: Praeger, 1984.

Jones, Earl D. "Laguna Verde or 'Laguna Muerte': Issues in the Struggle Over Nuclear Power in Mexico, 1968–1990." Paper presented at the Southwest Historical Association in San Antonio, Texas, on April 1, 1999.

Lenero, Vicente. *Los periodistas*. 8th ed. Mexico City: Editorial Joaquín Mortiz, 1983.

Loret de Mola, Carlos. *Confesiones de un gobernado,* 8th ed. Mexico City: Editorial Grijalba, 1978.

Mora, Juan Miguel de. *Lucio Cabañas: su vida, su muerte*. 2d ed. Mexico City: Editores Asociados, 1975.

———. *Esto nos dió López Portillo*. 4th ed. Mexico City: Anaya Editores, 1985.

Perez Chowell, José. *Requierm para un ideal: La liga 23 de septiembre*. 3d. ed. Mexico City: Editorial V Siglos, 1977.

Poniatowska, Elena. *Fuerte es el silencio*. 5th ed. Mexico City: Ediciones Era, 1983.

Richmond, Douglas W. "Crisis in Mexico: Luis Echeverría and José López Portillo, 1970–1982," *Journal of Third World Studies*, 5:1 (Spring 1988), 160–171.

Riding, Alan. *Distant Neighbors*. New York: Alfred A. Knopf, 1984.

Schmidt, Samuel. *The Deterioration of the Mexican Presidency: The Years of Luis Echeverría*. Tucson: University of Arizona Press, 1991.

Story, Dale. *Industry, the State, and Public Policy in Mexico*. Austin: University of Texas Press, 1986.

18

Dismay and Drift, 1982–2000

From 1982 to 2000, presidential leadership generally declined, thus weakening the legitimacy of the Mexican state. Fiscal, economic, and financial stress further alienated citizens from the PRI, which could not resolve the dilemma of attempting to carry out peaceful presidential transitions while maintaining political continuity. Calls for honest government never ceased as the drug trade expanded. By sacrificing potential pluralism for too many years, the PRI finally lost power during the historical 2000 presidential campaign.

FISCAL CRASH UNDER DE LA MADRID

Picking Up the Pieces. Miguel de la Madrid Hurtado, like his two predecessors, had no political experience, but his sober and more forthcoming approach to economic disaster temporarily brought Mexico out of its financial nightmare. De la Madrid decided to swallow the bitter pill of an International Monetary Fund (IMF) bailout that called for the postponement and rescheduling of payments as well as an infusion of $5 billion in new loans. Under these terms, 46 percent of the $83 billion foreign debt had to be paid in no more than three years, with 27 percent falling due in 1983.

The price for this financial rescue was an austerity plan. When de la Madrid took office on December 1, 1982, he wasted no time in implementing severe measures. He cut government spending drastically and scrapped or delayed major construction projects. The value-added or sales tax jumped from 10 to 15 percent in his first year. PEMEX raised oil prices within Mexico to 80 percent of the world price, which shocked businesses and individual drivers. Two subsequent price increases resulted in a 14 percent decline in gasoline purchases by the end of 1983.

Cutting subsidies was another surprise. In the past, many items had received government subsidies, but now real prices began to be paid. Cuts in government supports of bread and tortillas followed. Although inflation shot up to 100 percent in 1982, workers received only a 20 percent pay raise. Import restrictions deprived some industries of raw materials and spare parts. At the same time, government officials hinted that they would modify restrictions on foreign investment. In many ways, the old subsidies for Mexican industries had to be chopped because of interest payments on the foreign debt. Foreign investment was the best way for Mexico to get hold of large amounts of money without getting on its knees and begging reluctant banks for another loan. Regaining international trust after the irresponsible López Portillo would take time.

One of the reasons for the failure of the economy to grow in 1982—for the first time since the Depression—was that the debt crisis also affected the private sector of the economy. Gone were the foreign goods made artificially cheap by an overvalued peso. The August 1982 peso devaluation cut off foreign credit lines. Suppliers who had routinely granted companies 90 to 100 days to pay began to demand cash on delivery. As a result, Mexican industries had to quickly substitute domestic raw materials, many of which were of questionable quality. Moreover, many Mexican companies had invested recklessly with dollars from abroad. Grupo Alfa in Monterrey symbolized this plight. It went on a borrowing and buying binge in 1979, which left Alfa the largest conglomerate in Mexico—and an estimated $3.8 billion in debt.

In sharp contrast to López Portillo's reckless spending, de la Madrid evaluated and streamlined government projects. He halted work on Laguna Verde and supervised a thorough evaluation. Although problems had surfaced, de la Madrid cautiously resumed work on the site; he wisely reduced the role of nuclear power in future electrical production. A Russian nuclear disaster at Chernobyl in 1986 underlined the wisdom of deemphasizing nuclear investments because protests in Mexico resulted in clashes with police. De la Madrid also reformed PEMEX in order to reduce the possibility of theft and kickbacks. New financial controls made PEMEX more efficient. Layoffs were above the norm in PEMEX compared to other government institutions. The goal was to utilize PEMEX as a source of revenue instead of a subsidy operation. PEMEX became a workhorse rather than a glamour exhibit by reducing its debt to foreign banks. Of course, the debt payments came from Mexican consumers, who had enjoyed low energy prices.

For a brief period, hopes of a modest recovery lifted spirits. Aided by a sharp fall in imports, Mexico's foreign trade swung to a $4.3 billion surplus during the first four months of 1983, thus wiping out the deficit of a year earlier. A significant growth in nonoil exports also took place as part of an economic diversification. Economic restructuring of the flagging industrial sector had to take place in order to reduce Mexican vulnerability to outside influences. Reducing the government's deficit eased inflation fears somewhat, from a horrendous 100 percent in 1982 to 81 percent in 1983, and 59 percent in 1984.

Perhaps the keys to financial and economic recovery were the production and price of oil. De la Madrid's regime suffered as a result of the uninterrupted slide of both. A crisis in oil revenue shortfalls began in late 1984 when Mexico decided on a cutback of 100,000 barrels a day, claiming it was a voluntary decision to defend world oil prices. Mexico had never been a member of OPEC, but it had worked in cooperation with OPEC to stabilize the world oil market. But overproduction by some oil-producing nations forced PEMEX to drop its price of heavy Mayan crude oil by $1.50 a barrel in June 1985. As the fourth largest crude producer, Mexico depended on oil sales to generate half its revenues. Moreover, oil sales were crucial in order to pay off the $96 billion foreign debt. As part of an economic recovery program, de la Madrid broke ranks with OPEC for the first time and set a price of $27.75 for its Isthmus light crude, 25 cents below the mark adopted by OPEC earlier in 1985. After having seen its exports drop seriously, Mexico issued another $2.00 price drop. In response, Saudi Arabia threatened to double its output. In December 1985, the price of Mexican oil dropped for the fourth time that year. Nevertheless, clients refused to buy Mexican oil, saying PEMEX prices were too high. In a desperate attempt to compensate for further losses, the government doubled the tax PEMEX paid on its sales from 6 to 12 percent. It also increased the price of gasoline, diesel, and related fuels by more than 50 percent. In addition, electrical rates, telephone costs, and water services went up at annual rates of 120 percent.

In February 1986, Mexico dropped oil prices by an average of $4.68 a barrel, placing the country dangerously close to an extreme financial crisis. This brought the average price of Mexican oil to only $15.07 a barrel. For every dollar drop in oil prices, the government lost about $540 million in annual revenue. PEMEX responded by cutting its budget and suspending payments to domestic creditors and suppliers. At that point, Mexico was paying $14 billion annually on a $96 billion foreign debt—$10 billion in interest and $4.5 billion in principal. Daily exports by PEMEX dropped in January 1986 by an average of 350,000 barrels a day because of contract cancellations by clients not satisfied with the pricing structure. Exports thus dropped by a third in a short period. After shifting to a spot-market formula for its oil prices, Mexico still lost customers to other oil exporters who offered cheaper and more flexible terms. By April 1986, Isthmus crude sold for only $12.65 a barrel while heavy Maya crude went for a mere $9.72 a barrel. Dissatisfied with OPEC, Mexico spurned their invitation to attend a meeting in Germany as an observer.

The collapse of oil prices caused grave financial problems. Mexico had already rescheduled debt payments the year before as part of a multiyear agreement. In March, Mexico won a second six-month extension on payment of $950 million in principal on its foreign debt. De la Madrid initiated negotiations with the IMF for new loans in May 1986. U.S. bankers wanted Mexico to reach an agreement with the IMF before they themselves began discussions on a fresh debt package. Both the IMF and the banks made it clear that de la Madrid had made major financial adjustments by cutting its budget deficits, opening its markets to more foreign trade, reducing inflation, and permitting greater external investment. By July 1986, Mexico obtained $12 billion in new loans, twice the amount under consideration earlier. De la Madrid fully realized that the Mexican public sector had become too large while the private sector had been neglected. That summer, the peso began to slide, creating genuine panic. New devaluations in July exacerbated an already high demand for dollars because of speculation and increased summer travel. In one day the peso lost 32 percent of its value.

The financial problems hit de la Madrid particularly hard at that point. Many considered him a weak leader who offered indeciveness rather than robust solutions. At the opening ceremonies of the World Cup soccer championship in Mexico City, the crowd of 100,000 booed the president's speech. During a meeting of private businessmen, the commerce secretary was heckled in the presence of de la Madrid.

The pace of reform accelerated after the IMF bank loan. At U.S. insistence, Mexico joined the GATT in order to open up Mexican markets to freer trade. In that direction, Mexico lowered import barriers considerably and promised not to subsidize exports. Import licenses and permits were removed. The central bank began restricting credit to private firms, and this forced them to bring back funds that had been sent abroad. This move reversed the problem of capital flight, as well as a decision to allow dollar accounts since López Portillo had prohibited them in 1982. In 1986, de la Madrid also announced plans to reduce high-level government personnel by 25 percent. He also cut the 1986 budget by $1 billion.

Perhaps more controversial than any other policy was the decision to increase foreign investment. It began slowly, with the creation of a position for the promotion of foreign investment in October 1983. What foreign investors wanted, however, was greater control of firms where they put their money. In March 1984, Mexicans began to bend the rule which restricted foreign investment to 49 percent of any company so that international capital could have dominant control of various machinery industries, pharmaceutical substances, and computer as well as telecommunications equipment. Particularly notable was a decision to allow International Business Machines to manufacture personal computers with 100 percent foreign capital in July 1985. A year later, the investment law was changed so that small-and medium-sized companies could invest in Mexico, either through joint ventures or by 100 percent ownership. Hewlett Packard joined IBM in Guadalajara in building mini- and microcomputers. Ford and Chrysler began exporting Mexican-made vehicles to the United States for the first time. Ford and Volkswagenwerk of Germany owned 100 percent of their Mexican subsidiaries. *Maquiladora* plants, meanwhile, continued to expand to the point that 785 operated by 1986.

De la Madrid also stepped up a campaign to shed government-owned firms. Privatization began in March 1984, when the regime began selling stock in 339 nonbanking companies owned wholly or in part by the country's nationalized banks. In effect, the government sold various enterprises back to the original owners. In 1985, the government unloaded hotel chains, a steel complex, a soft-drink company, restaurants, and night clubs. Getting rid of these money losing state companies helped reduce the level of public spending in order to pay off the foreign debt. Nearly 70 percent of Mexico's public sector debt was due to operating deficits of state-owned companies. In many cases, previous governments had bought failing companies to save employment. By 1988, the number of public enterprises plunged from 1,153 in 1982 to barely 400. Although unions and leftists balked, Carlos Salinas de Gortari, the architect of the austerity plan, made it clear that there would be no turning back in the drive to privatize.

By the fall of 1987, de la Madrid smiled more often and an air of expectation permeated Mexico. Automobiles led the way in the growth of exports as well as beer, thanks to a craze for Corona and Tecate beer. Tourism increased from three million in 1982 to five million in 1987. Government-designed resorts such as Cancún, Ixtapa, Zihuatanejo, and Los Cabos generated jobs and tourist revenue. With large monetary reserves, Mexico began to meet the IMF debt targets. Moreover, the population growth rate slowed to only 1.9 percent a year. As in the 1820s, northern regions began to recuperate first. Blessed with natural resources that range from a sprawling coastline to rich copper mines and an industrious population, Sonora did not suffer a recession. It exported tens of thousands of cattle each year to the United States and Japan. With an unemployment rate of only 5 percent, many Mexicans migrated to Sonora to work

in its mines, vineyards, farms, ranches, and factories. The kinds of slums seen in most large Mexican cities were noticeably absent along the palm-tree-lined streets of Hermosillo.

But financial pressures soon led to inflationary levels never experienced. Even though the stock market in Mexico registered the second-highest performance in the world during 1986, many stocks were grossly undervalued. Meanwhile, the battered peso broke the barrier of 1,000 to the dollar in February 1987 for the first time. It had traded at 26 to the dollar only five years earlier. Although the declining peso helped make Mexican goods more competitive to foreign buyers, it also boosted the prices of imported goods needed for manufacturing, adding to the inflationary spiral. One of the most severe peso devaluations in November 1987 soon plunged it to as low as 2,600 against the dollar on the free market. The October 1987 Wall Street crash made its Mexican counterpart suffer its largest one-day decline in history. As the market slid, investors ran to dollars. De la Madrid responded by promising to index wages and prices beginning in March 1988, rather than spending his reserves to defend the peso. The result was that inflation reached 160 percent in 1987. The Banco de México conceded that the government's decision to double the prices of basic goods and services in mid-December 1987 also worsened matters. The index plan to boost wages and prices of various goods and services each month based on projected inflation rates reassured few and never restored confidence. De la Madrid became the first president in 50 years to leave office with the nation becoming poorer during his term.

U.S. Relations. De la Madrid worked with other Latin American nations to try to resolve the insurrection in El Salvador. Mexico also supported Nicaragua and Cuba as part of a Latin American unity campaign. Efforts to arrange new trade initiatives in Latin America, Europe, and Japan resulted in modest success. But the United States opposed Mexican ties with Nicaragua and urged de la Madrid to fight the growing drug trade.

Both Mexico and the United States considered Central American conflicts national security threats but differed on how to respond to them. Mexico rejected the U.S. notion that a civil war in El Salvador was an East-West confrontation and asserted that the turmoil arose from longstanding social injustices that should have been resolved through negotiations. To establish peace, Mexico advocated the withdrawal of all military aid and advisors from the region, followed by direct discussions among the warring factions. Mexico's foreign relations secretary promoted the concept on a tour through Central America. He also pressed home the idea to Secretary of State George Schultz in Mexico City during an April 1983 meeting as leftist demonstrators marched on the U.S. embassy, burning a U.S. flag and chanting, "Yankee worms, El Salvador is our brother." De la Madrid also opposed U.S. attempts to overthrow the Marxist Sandinista regime in Nicaragua, fearing that the conservative Contra rebels might plunge the whole region into a catastrophic war. Mexico advocated talks between Cuba and the United States on regional issues and offered to mediate such discussions, citing its friendship with Cuba and strong ties with the United States. The Ronald Reagan administration rejected this initiative. From desperately needed U.S. spare parts to preferential trade, transportation, communications, diplomatic and propaganda support, Mexico has been Cuba's most staunch ally in the Americas. The foreign relations secretariat believed that its close ties with Fidel Castro represented its only real diplomatic leverage against the United States. De la Madrid urged the United States to become less rigid in its views toward the Cuban leader.

By demonstrating independence and supporting Marxist regimes and the liberation movement in El Salvador, de la Madrid mollified major opposition from the Mexican left, a major governmental concern during the economic crisis. As in past Mexican administrations, de la Madrid found it effective to tranquilize the left by emphasizing pro-Castro gestures. When de la Madrid departed for visits to Colombia, Venezuela, Argentina, and Brazil in March 1984 to gather support for Central American peace negotiations, he struck a popular chord.

The debate over Mexico's role in Central America also produced splits in the U.S. intelligence community. The National Security Council and the CIA believed that Mexico faced a serious threat to its political stability from the left, stemming from the conflicts in Central America and the government's failure to deal with the oil crisis. The defense intelligence agency, low-level CIA staffers, and many in the State Department, on the other hand, rejected that view. Scholars disagreed with the CIA's position that external forces threatened Mexican political stability. In May 1984, the senior Latin American analyst at the CIA resigned after agency boss William J. Casey insisted that he revise a report on Mexico, so his document would support Reagan administration policy. Casey wanted a tough report to help persuade the White House to approve a program of covert and economic pressures on Mexico to induce its support for United States policies in Central America.

The Mexican move to emphasize a regional approach was to pave the way for Honduras and Nicaragua to start formal negotiations to try to avoid war. U.S.-backed Contras attacked Nicaragua from Honduran bases. The other issue pressed by Mexico was to formulate a Central American arms policy to ban foreign weapons and advisors from the area, be they from the United States or Cuba. Colombian, Venezuelan, and Panamanian diplomats backed Mexico's proposal and even planned a trip to Moscow to emphasize its necessity. Mexico sought to change the status quo in Central America, so that the United States would be forced to deal with new conditions that would make Cold War policies obsolete, particularly military advisors, covert operations, and naval exercises. To emphasize its influence over Central America, Mexico, and Venezuela established a San Jose pact by which they provided generous credit terms to ten Central American and Caribbean countries for the purchase of oil. But in August 1984, Mexico and Venezuela announced that they would suspend low-priced oil shipments to Central American and Caribbean nations that "initiate warlike actions" against other countries in the region. Another provision of the 1984 announcement stated that oil supplies would have to be paid for immediately. Using these conditions, Mexico began to delay oil shipments to Nicaragua and Costa Rica.

The determination of the Reagan government to crush the rebels in El Salvador and overthrow the Sandinista regime in Nicaragua even affected domestic Mexican politics. Providing aid to the Contras became such an overriding Reagan goal that it governed nearly all U.S. contacts with its neighbors in Costa Rica, Honduras, Panama, and Mexico. In February 1986, U.S. officials warned their Mexican counterparts that if they lobbied Congress to support Mexican peace initiatives in Central America, the Reagan government would start backing the PAN in Mexico. Reagan was still angry that de la Madrid would not back the United States against Nicaragua. Only 48 hours after meeting with Reagan in August 1986, Contra fund-raiser Carl Channel met with PAN leader Ricardo Villa Escalera at Washington's Hay-Adams Hotel and told him, as well as other PAN officials, that Reagan would help them fight the PRI in return for $20,000 in support of the Contras. The PAN representatives refused to cooperate. As a result of this murky overture, Mexico resumed oil shipments to Nicaragua once the Iran-Contra scandal weakened Reagan and the Soviets stopped supplying oil to the Sandinistas.

Mexico's trade initiatives with South America, Europe, and Japan were modest. Mexico promised to buy $140 million worth of Argentine grain and the two countries doubled their volume of trade in 1984. Moreover, Mexico considered Reagan's decision to side with the British in the Falkland war with Argentina a slap in the face to U.S. neighbors in the Americas. During a June 1985 trip to Europe, de la Madrid obtained new credit lines from Britain, France, and Spain for $240 million. In Germany, Mexico's third trading partner after the United States and Japan, the automobile manufacturer Daimler Benz signed a deal to produce Mercedes commercial vehicles in Mexico. During his state visit to Japan in December 1986, de la Madrid promised to sell more oil while Japan would provide machinery and invest in several *maquiladoras*. Japan and Mexico signed a $1 billion loan agreement that financed a PEMEX pipeline, upgraded a major steel plant, and provided trade credits.

The kidnap-murder of U.S. special narcotics officer Enrique Camarena Salazar in Guadalajara tested U.S. relations severely. He was abducted by state police, handed over to drug traffickers, tortured, and murdered. U.S.officials felt that de la Madrid's government did not act quickly enough to apprehend the killers. Two weeks after the incident, Reagan recalled U.S.Aambassador John Gavin for consultations and ordered exhaustive inspections of Mexican motorists seeking to enter the United States. Camarena had touched a raw nerve in Mexico by investigating allegations that drug traffickers had bribed Mexican officials. Jalisco state police later seized and tortured Victor Cortez, another U.S. drug agent, in August 1986.

Sinaloa is an example of how drug trafficking in Mexican regions became an integral part of daily life and how difficult controlling it could be. Governor Antonio Toledo Corro had been accused of involvement with drug trafficking and selling protection to its operatives. His third son's mother was the sister of Félix Gallardo, a major drug lord, who also operated a stolen car ring. Gallardo was a guest at Toledo Corro's 7,500-acre ranch where they undoubtedly discussed the hundreds of marijuana and poppy fields growing in the mountains that rise in eastern Sinaloa where Durango and Chiahuahua meet.

U.S. charges of corruption sparked protests in Mexico City. During a May 13, 1986, U.S. Senate subcommittee hearing, several Reagan administration officials testified that widespread corruption in the Mexican government was fueling illegal trade in Mexico. U.S. Customs Service Commissioner William von Raab asserted that corruption throughout the Mexican law enforcement system contributed to a sharp increase in drugs being smuggled into the United States. The Mexican government protested the hearings and the PRI organized a march in which 10,000 Mexico City residents walked the one-mile route from the Monument of the Revolution to the National Palace carrying banners that read "Death to Reagan—Long Live Mexico," and "Reagan, We Don't Fear You Because We Are United." The call for the demonstration appeared in Mexico City newspapers in paid advertisements headlined "March in Defense of the National Sovereignty."

Despite the protests in Mexico City, U S. officials noted an increase in drug smuggling and concluded that elements of the Mexican government were involved. They expected de la Madrid to respond. When he did not, U.S. Attorney General Edwin Meese announced the start of a major drug and contraband interdiction program along the border. More than 20 agencies and departments cooperated in Operation Alliance. De la Madrid refused to allow U.S. aircraft to carry out hot-pursuit operations into Mexican airspace, claiming that Mexico was "fully capable" of combating narcotics without the direct involvement of U.S. personnel.

Meanwhile, the highly-publicized Camarena murder began to drive a wedge into U.S. relations. It led to a Senate vote of 63–27 to levy economic sanctions against Mexico in April 1988. But the House of Representatives squashed the measure. The legislators were not satisfied with the arrest of drug lord Rafael Caro Quintero, as well as three of Caro Quintero's associates, incuding a former Mexican police officer. For three years, officials in Washington, D.C. had been wringing their hands, claiming that Mexico's failure to sentence Caro Quintero was evidence of lackadaisical cooperation. Rumors spread that Caro Quintero's cell was equipped with a private phone, whirlpool, and wet bar. Mexico's attorney general, who was governor of Jalisco when Camarena was abducted but who also dragged his feet to investigate the murder, claimed that U.S. legislators did not understand Mexico's legal system. Later a federal grand jury in Los Angeles indicted the former head of the Mexican Federal Judicial Police, the former head of the Mexican branch of the Interpol international law enforcement agency, and 17 others in connection with the slaying of Camarena. The indictments charged that the two high-ranking Mexican police officials had participated in the killing to protect the Guadalajara cocaine and marijuana cartel. But the attorney general of Mexico said that these individuals faced no charges in Mexico and would not be arrested.

The Political Landscape. The real strength of Mexico's political system was its ability to control key domestic forces through corruption, cooptation and repression, thus weakening the emergence of significant antigovernment factions. Threats to stability seemed more likely to come from an explosion of discontent rather than through organized opposition. Therefore, de la Madrid mollified labor, peasants, and opposition parties just enough to stay in power. He tried to polish the tarnished image of the Mexican government by setting an optimistic but low-key tone. A short, serious individual, de la Madrid relied heavily on his cabinet, none of whom had ever held elective office.

Shortly after taking office, de la Madrid created a cabinet position to monitor government corruption and launched a "moral renovation" campaign, aimed at fighting graft and corruption on every level of society. A government report published just before de la Madrid's inauguration stated that López Portillo officials had defrauded Mexico of at least $1 billion. One month after taking office, de la Madrid ordered the dismissal of more than 60 police chiefs throughout Mexico, who had been suspected of condoning corruption. In Mexico City, he dismissed the 1,500-member "delinquency squad," widely believed to be one of the most corrupt organizations in the government. Before 1982, there were no educational requirements to become a police officer. Under de la Madrid, all police officers had to complete elementary and secondary school. For the first time, government officials were required to file statements of their earnings and assets annually. The government enacted new prohibitions against nepotism, both in public employment and in obtaining government contracts.

Responding to calls from opposition leaders, de la Madrid decided to file fraud charges against Jorge Díaz Serrano, former head of PEMEX in 1983. De la Madrid had been reluctant to go after López Portillo's top officials, since he had been a prominent member of that government. But public skepticism about the anti-corruption campaign needed a response and it was critical to make PEMEX more efficient during the economic crisis. Díaz Serrano also had presidential ambitions that offended many. The indignant patrician Díaz Serrano denied charges that he had defrauded the government of $34 million through the purchase of two gas tankers in 1980 and remained under house arrest in his two-story stucco home in Mexico City's fashionable Lomas de Chapultepec neighborhood. Eventually, he was convicted on April 6, 1987, and sentenced to 10 years in prison and ordered to pay $54 million for fraud.

Public outrage against the escapades of Mexico City Police Chief Durazo also forced de la Madrid to take action. Calls for Durazo's arrest began in November 1985, when a former aide published a book detailing Durazo's lavish lifestyle and how he had killed several people on his boss's orders. Durazo cleaned out several bulging bank accounts and fled to Los Angeles, Canada, Europe, and Africa. A federal judge ordered Durazo's arrest and Interpol apprenhended him. When Durazo was finally returned to Mexico, the government's extortion and tax case against him was postponed repeatedly because government witnesses, prompted by threats and bribes, retracted their testimony. Goons even shot at the federal prosecutor handling the Durazo case.

The 1985 Earthquake.

The 1985 earthquakes that rocked Mexico City left deep scars on the sprawling metropolis and shook confidence in the regime because of de la Madrid's inept response. Moments after the first shock struck at breakfast time on September 19, 1985, dust filled the city center air, glass and chunks of cement littered the streets, buildings lurched at crazy angles, while others became piles of debris. People milled about, some gesturing and talking nervously, many stunned into silence; still others wailed hysterically.

Enormous destruction took place in the federal district. The subsoil beneath the center of the massive city—the main area affected—is a soft clay, highly sensitive to seismic movements. Slender buildings between 5 and 20 stories high were subjected to sideway accelerations nearly six times greater than any ever before experienced in Mexico. This is where 10,000 lost their lives and an additional 10,000 bodies were never found. The government-owned baseball park became an outdoor morgue when the main mortuary overflowed with victims. Within 72 hours of the earthquakes, 2,000 bodies covered the outfield. The earthquakes also destroyed or damaged an estimated 3,300 structures, including 800 to 1,000 businesses—mostly modest stores and small factories. The estimated damage was $4.5 billion.

The most urgent problem was the 250,000 people who became homeless after 20,000 housing units, mostly rental, were destroyed or irreparably damaged. Following the tremors, virtually all cities within a five-hour travel radius of Mexico City overflowed with homeless people. Immediately following the quakes, the government called out the armed forces and made public transit and local telephone service free. A few weeks later, the government expropriated several thousand properties in poor downtown neighborhoods and promised to reconstruct them. Meanwhile, the homeless tried to move in with relatives, set up tents and flimsy shacks, or moved into long corrugated metal buildings, some furnished by the government, dubbed "chicken coops" by their residents. Living in small wood-and-carton shelters became difficult because of frigid mornings and the difficulty of keeping things clean as well as getting sick from ill-prepared food.

Many homeless persons remained visible because they opted not to stay in government or private shelters. Traumatized and insecure, they feared they could be evicted at any moment. Eating cold beans and watery rice in shelters became unappetizing. Others resented dormitorylike regulations dictating their schedules while some felt that their presence in clear public view would pressure the regime to keep its promises to reconstruct their homes. Many remained near their former homes to claim their right to live there again when reconstruction would resume. But promises to rebuild lost housing resulted in little progress. The disenchanted homeless began tearing down the flimsy structures they had thrown together in the wake of the earthquakes and erected more permanent shacks. Hundreds of the homeless began to demonstrate on Paseo de la Reforma, shouting "housing yes, eviction no."

Emotional problems also surfaced as federal district residents attempted to rebuild their lives. Distraught over the death of a friend, one lady hanged herself from a staircase in her home. Despondent after the ruinous tremors, a husband started drinking and then shot himself in the head with a semiautomatic pistol. The tedious work of finding corpses still buried in fallen buildings also added stress. Relatives often maintained a vigil at some sites, refusing to leave until a body was found. At some city morgues, people unable to find family members picked out unrecognizable bodies and identified them as those of their missing relatives. Many forced from their homes and apartments became too frightened to return, fearful that the structures could collapse at any moment. Counselors encountered traumatized victims who could not recognize their parents or friends.

The disaster further damaged de la Madrid's weak image because of the government's inability to respond. The lack of leadership demonstrated itself when de la Madrid spurned foreign offers of aid. The European Economic Community appropriated $500,000 for emergency relief in Mexico only hours after the earthquakes but could not release it because de la Madrid would not request it. Although the president heralded the creation of a National Reconstruction Committee, it became largely a ceremonial panel because the government established policy. The entire group did not even meet. The city's government also responded poorly. Its emergency plan was flawed, partly because it did not detail the duties of local and federal departments. Because of confusion about which agency was in charge, relief efforts never materialized or overlapped. After one damaged multistory apartment building in Colonia Juárez collapsed, neighbors could hear cries from entrapped residents six days afterward. Municipal groups that finally showed up argued over how to proceed so pitifully that a French rescue team left in disgust. After a year, the city inspected only a third of the damaged structures in Mexico City. Despite vows to press criminal charges against anyone responsible for faulty construction which contributed to destruction, only one criminal investigation had been conducted by September 1986.

In the aftermath of the earthquakes, past problems became publicized. Supposedly repaired buildings were already falling apart once again. Moreover, some of the buildings destroyed in 1985 had been repaired improperly after quakes in 1957 and 1979. Some of the concrete had air pockets or the concrete had not been washed properly to remove clay particles that weaken the cement's hold. Most of the damaged buildings had inadequate or no structural bracing, such as steel or wooden frames in diagonal supports at regular intervals around the structures. Such bracing helps a building absorb the enormous lateral stress that accompanies earthquakes. Building inspectors were often bribed and did not report many buildings which had previously been private residences and had been turned into offices or even factories. The added weight on older structures caused unexpected stress during the massive 1985 tremors.

The best-known disaster was the collapse of the Nuevo León apartment buildings, 2 of whose 14-story towers crashed like limp accordians, tossing, trapping, and killing 500 of its 1,200 residents in the massive Tlatelolco housing project. Critical design errors, superficial repairs, and overdue maintenance contributed to the deaths. Some U.S. and Mexican engineers questioned whether such an apartment complex should ever have been built on the soft soil. The foundations were too thin and not deep enough. Water seeped in and the towers tilted while the entire structure sank at least 2 feet. Although residents pleaded for repairs, there was little response.

Perhaps the only positive outcome of the earthquake was that the crisis broke down traditional class barriers as many citizens responded heroically. It was not unusual for public accountants, bankers, students, and the unemployed to work together for long hours to pull survivors from the rubble. Others provided housing for the homeless. Some organized masses for the rescue workers and families of those who died in the buildings. One priest used a card table as an altar to honor the saintliness of those who died helping their neighbors. Several congregations wept together and knelt in the streets, rich and poor alike, demonstrating the depth to which many had been touched. Few would forget the unity they experienced. Opera singer Placido Domingo, who lost four relatives in the earthquakes, left the opera circuit to raise money for survivors of the disaster.

Even as de la Madrid's regime dragged on, problems from the earthquake affected Mexico adversely. A shortage of housing and office space in Mexico City boosted inflation. The damaged buildings went unrepaired for several years because of credit shortages. The ongoing financial crisis caused the government to back away from demolishing buildings by means of expensive explosives. Instead, most were torn down slowly with crews using wrecking balls and sledgehammers. Rents for housing doubled and landlords tried to increase rents beyond legal limits. Other apartment owners demanded payment in dollars. Many concluded that the only way to reform the system was to vote out the PRI.

Political Repression. After a promising beginning toward opening up the political process early in his regime, de la Madrid lost legitimacy when he imposed PRI politicians upon disappointed northerners and other regions.

The initial threat perceived by the government was the left. As the 1980s began, Marxists realized that they had to abandon their traditional strategy of organizing workers for revolutionary insurrections. The rise of Eurocommunism in Europe, where Marxists abandoned class conflict and emphasized reformism, as well as the success of the Solidarity movement in Poland, indicated that electoral victories had to become the primary emphasis. Therefore, the small leftist parties organized the Partido Socialista Unificado de México (PSUM) in 1981. PSUM activists now recruited migrants in *colonias*, indigenous peoples, and women. Although the PSUM merger came about without consulting the rank and file, it displayed a certain openness toward differing viewpoints and no longer solved disputes in the PCM tradition of purges. Leftist parties and the PSUM made political inroads during the early 1980s. Their gains increased as Mexico plummeted into financial crisis and discontent in the countryside swelled against the PRI. The PRI was willing to tolerate the PAN getting 15 or 17 percent of the vote in many localities, but not the left since the potential for serious, uncompromising conflict could develop.

The PRI struck against the leftist government in Juchitan, Oaxaca first. In 1981, a grass roots movement in conjunction with the PSUM elected a worker-controlled government in Juchitan which began communalizing land previously held by cacique landowners loyal to the PRI. In July 1983, during the weeks before elections for Oaxaca state legislators, political fervor intensified. The local PRI leader, Teodoro Altamirano, requested Mexican army troops be sent to Juchitan when PRI youth organizations threatened to attack the municipal building if the soldiers did not arrive. Leftist rallies and PRI counterdemonstrations on July 31 resulted in a confrontation that left two persons dead and 20 wounded. Altamirano, seen carrying a machine gun, undoubtedly organized and provoked the killings. Citing the two deaths as their justification, the PRI-controlled Oaxacan state legislature removed the leftist government in Juchitan and installed a PRI-selected alternative body while postponing upcoming municipal elections indefinitely.

More killings in southern Puebla represented the determination of PRI caciques to endure. Several PSUM members in Puebla had been involved in armed conflicts with CNC peasant groups in which members from both sides had died. But the village of San José Miahuatlan represented the new PSUM strategy when the poor farming town elected a PSUM mayor in 1983. Pleas to return water rights had been unheeded before, but the new PSUM government established control of water rights, providing access to running water for all residents for the first time. The PSUM also began a much delayed public works project which previous PRI governments had neglected. Angry landowners did not wait too long before retaliating. Unhappy that PRI national leaders no longer operated through local PRI groups but rather by means of bureaucratic planning, the caciques felt abandoned. Therefore, on September 5, 1984, they unquestionably organized an ambush of PSUM members near San José Miahuatlan, which included a member of the state PSUM committee. After their deaths, the PRI governor of Puebla denied the assassinations were politically based and wrote the incident off as personal feuding.

As the economic-financial crisis intensified, the PRI expanded its domestic control. Violence in Puebla and Oaxaca also resulted in similar incidents throughout Chiapas. The PRI began to manipulate voter lists, deny voter credentials, and set up undemocratic electoral laws. When U.S. Democratic presidential candidate Jesse Jackson brought his Rainbow Coalition theme to Mexico City in 1984, he affirmed Mexico's peacemaking role in Central America but clearly made PRI figures uncomfortable with repeated questions about what role Mexico would assume if the United States unseated the Sandinistas. After Jackson's call for July 4 peace demonstrations on the border by "brothers and sisters from all over the Americas," the government canceled a planned Jackson appearance at the UNAM campus.

The most serious challenge to the PRI hegemony arose in the north. As a protest against the economic crisis, the PAN won mayoral and state legislative positions in 12 northern cities in the states of Chihuahua and Durango in July 1983. PAN victories included mayoral triumphs in Ciudad Juárez and the state capitals of Chihuahua and Durango. The PRI governor of Chihuahua announced that it would be no problem to work with a PAN municipal president in the city of Chihuahua as well as Juárez. Many had interpreted the anticorruption campaign as part of a democratic political opening. They were quickly disappointed when an angry de la Madrid came to Chihuahua to remove the governor.

But times had changed. Northern Mexico had become home to Mexico's business structure in highly industrialized Monterrey. The north also had important agricultural and cattle ranching zones in Sonora and Chihuahua. It was the base for major fishing industries off Baja California, Sonora, and Tamaulipas. *Maquiladores* hummed with activity along the border. More than the rest of Mexico, northerners had become influenced by the United States. Many crossed the border to work, travel, and shop. It was not uncommon to encounter Sonorans who had been in Tucson more often than in Mexico City.

Because of northern ties to the United States, its institutions, its strong middle-class, and vibrant economy, the PAN found more support there than in the rest of Mexico. The PAN gained strength by attracting more middle class Mexicans, angered by the continuing economic crisis. Workers also joined the PAN out of frustration with their sharply reduced buying power, the slow pace of promises to fight corruption, and PRI failure to deliver on its repeated pledges of egalitarianism. U.S. television magnified these issues. In Mexico City, it arrived by cable with commercials taken out. But border residents were treated to a display of U.S. consumerism beyond their southern neighbors' wildest fantasies, much less their pocketbooks.

The PRI attempted a variety of tactics to deal with the PAN threat. PAN mayors became essentially cut off from state governments in budgetary matters as the PRI tried to demonstrate that electing an opposition local government would fall on deaf ears at higher levels. PRI localities became deluged with state and federal projects in an effort to show where the power and money were. In 1984, the PRI selected Irma Cue to be its secretary general, the second most important person in the party and the first woman to attain such a rank.

Relations between the north and Mexico City became hostile as it became clear that the PRI would not let the PAN win the 1985 elections throughout the north. Heavy-handed political maneuvers by the PRI in Chihuahua motivated the PAN mayor of Ciudad Juárez to stage a hunger strike. He drew unexpected popular support. In Sonora, a very popular PAN candidate for governor had been walking across the state for two years, visiting scores of towns as part of an effective door-to-door campaign. His casual speech intrigued many: "I'm an Aries, that's why I have a big mouth." Sensing a defeat, de la Madrid dispatched a cabinet member who had not lived there for 40 years. Running a standard PRI campaign that excited virtually no one, the secretary also offended Sonora's famous reputation for efficiency because his management of telephone and mail systems rated near the police on the list of least-admired public services.

Political violence erupted in December 1984, as a symptom of northern dissatisfaction with the PRI. Protests broke out in Coahuila when the PRI was declared the winner in 35 of Coahuila's 38 municipal elections. The most bitter conflict took place in Piedras Negras, Coahuila, when the PRI-dominated state congress threw out 11 ballot boxes that would have meant victory for PAN candidate Dr. Eleazar Cobos, who won the election based on an early morning count on December 3, until his opponent appealed to the state legislature. PAN protesters reponded by closing the border bridge into Eagle Pass, Texas, for more than 80 hours. After the PRI governor of Coahuila moved the swearing-in date of the imposed PRI municipal president, a strong riot ensued as soon as the ceremony ended. Police attacked 3,000 PAN demonstrators who then burned the Piedras Negras city hall. At least 2 died and another 22 had to be treated for gunshot wounds. De la

Madrid dispatched army troops to restore order. White federal police cars arrived at the work sites of five PAN leaders where agents arrested them. Cobos announced that he would run for a seat in the national Congress during the summer of 1985.

A similar conflict erupted in nearby Monclova, where PAN supporters seized the plaza and municipal building and swore in their own candidate. As in Piedras Negras, Monclova's anger originated from a decision by the Coahuila state legislature to disqualify thousands of PAN votes and install a PRI candidate. Garbage trucks and other municipal vehicles were parked around the city hall to ward off an assault by the state police, who were controlled by the PRI governor. Eventually, the PAN and PRI met in Saltillo, where the legislature discussed new candidates and imposed a compromise PRI mayor who was peacefully sworn in despite a tense atmosphere.

But confrontations continued throughout Coahuila. In Escobedo, PAN supporters seized the newly "elected" PRI leader, stripped him, taunted him, shaved his head, and detained him in a PAN building for an entire night. In Nadadores, the mayor-elect and government representatives were at the municipal building for the swearing-in ceremony but had to flee when they heard shouting PAN members approach, break windows, and puncture tires. A candidate from the Party of the Authentic Revolution staged a dramatic hunger strike in Saltillo that went on for five days. Thus, the PAN platform of free enterprise and clean government had become permanent in northern cities; but the PRI had become unwilling to accept the consequences of De la Madrid's earlier promises of electoral reform.

During the July 1985 general elections, the PRI tightened its control. Of 300 seats up for election to the Chamber of Deputies, the PRI claimed 281, allowing only 5 for the PAN. In Sonora, which had become a PAN stronghold, the state electoral commission declared sweeping PRI victories in all 69 towns and cities, all 18 state legislative positions, the governorship, and 7 federal deputy seats. In Nuevo León, the PAN won one of the state's 11 federal legislative seats, and only 2 of 26 state legislative positions. Although the PRI candidate for governor won, he was considered competent. The largest political demonstrations in Mexico soon unfolded in Monterrey as a result of massive fraud. The PRI had simply decided to endure the short-term problem of PAN discontent rather than allow an honest election. The system had no tradition for working through an opposition governor. De la Madrid made it clear that he would not tolerate political competition on a democratic level in the midst of an economic crisis. Municipal elections held in December 1985 resulted in more ballot stuffing, violence, and attacks on government buildings. The army, with few links to private economic interests and from the same class background as the PRI rather than the PAN, continued to occupy municipalities when unrest broke out.

The increasingly authoritarian determination of de la Madrid to crush the PAN reached a climax in Chihuahua during the July 1986 gubernatorial elections. The PAN had held many state and local offices in Chihuahua since 1982, making it the PAN's biggest stronghold. The PAN's candidate for governor was Francisco Barro Terrazas, a former accountant and charismatic Catholic. The popular Barrio could also count upon activist Catholic communities which received public support from the archbishop of Chihuahua, in itself something of a novelty. Calls for giving priests the right to vote, ending agrarian reform, and terminating federal control of school curriculua had paid off for the PAN. "We are fed up and very tired of all the corruption … the economic situation has worsened," Barrio stated.

The PRI cleverly selected a local politician, Fernando Baeza, who took the unusual step of admitting that the PRI had failed in Chihuahua, accusing the party of inefficiency, unresponsiveness, and corruption while calling for more regional autonomy, frequent PAN demands. But he warned that without ties to the PRI, Chihuahua would collapse, and he registered rural voters to counter PAN strength in the cities. When voting day came, the election was traditional—ballot-box stuffing and voter intimidation prevailed. De la Madrid

had lost a unique opportunity to begin democratizing Mexico as a worldwide trend against authoritarianism seemed to leave Mexico in the dust. De la Madrid later proposed expanding the federal Chamber of Deputies from 400 to 500 seats. This arrangement would have included 200 seats distributed to all political parties based on the proportion of votes won. Previously, only 100 proportional seats had been distributed to minority parties. But the new law ensured that the PRI would never have less than 50 percent of the membership regardless of the percentage of the popular vote. This would prevent minority parties from forming coalitions.

The 1988 Presidential Election. The climax of de la Madrid's electoral tampering was the imposition of his Secretary of Programming and the Budget Carlos Salinas de Gortari. Educated at Harvard, Salinas had been responsible for implementing Mexico's austerity program. Of all the presidential candidates, he was the one closely identified with continuity of de la Madrid's policies. Meanwhile, several leftist parties put aside their differences to unite behind Herberto Castillo of the Mexican Socialist Party, while the PAN continued to expand in the border region, Puebla, and the industrial centers of San Luis Potosí and Monterrey. The PRI had become vulnerable because the middle class had decreased as a result of the economic crisis and was increasingly conservative. Within the PRI itself, labor boss Fidel Velázquez opposed Salina's candidacy but backed down from calling a general strike.

The most viable challenge to the PRI hegemony emerged from the PRI itself in the form of the democratic current faction and Cuauhtémoc Cárdenas. Son of former president Lázaro Cárdenas, Cuauhtémoc had served as PRI governor of Michoacán. With former PRI party chief Porfirio Muñoz Ledo, Cárdenas and the democratic current demanded a limit on foreign debt payments, an increase in worker salaries, a halt to construction on Laguna Verde, and, most importantly, an opening in the PRI's presidential succession procedures. De la Madrid was not interested in ask-

ing for an open registration of presidential hope-
fuls in running for the presidency under the PRI's
banner. In June 1987, the PRI's National Commission of Political Coordination "condemned"
the democratic current and prohibited Muñoz
Ledo and Cárdenas from using PRI funds. In response, de la Madrid opened the *dedazo* selection
process up a bit by publicly naming six PRI stal-
warts in September. They participated in a political format never before seen, each making a
television speech and appearing before PRI forums throughout Mexico to articulate their views.

Cárdenas attacked de la Madrid's maneuvers
and launched his own bid for the presidency. Cárdenas denounced the PRI's selection of six pre-
candidates as a maneuver staged behind the backs
of party members. He said that it would provoke
"abstention in the next election," and would result
in a "social explosion." Appealing to a nostalgic
desire to return to precrisis normalcy, Cárdenas
also called for guarantees of free elections, a
strengthening of political parties, a free press, and
the eradication of corruption. In economic matters, Cárdenas sought to reduce the foreign debt
and high interest rates, as well as eliminate foreign penetration of the economy. The democratic
current also sought a review of U.S. relations in
order to protect Mexico's autonomy.

Cárdenas's bid to reclaim populism and Mexico's sovereignty with an honest government fell
upon millions of receptive, once-apathetic ears
throughout the land. He inevitably insisted that
breaking up the PRI's power was democracy's
first step on the road to significant change. A
spontaneous mass organization behind him made
the 1988 presidential election extremely dramatic. The first strong mobilization of the Cárdenas
campaign took place in rural areas. Cárdenas's
critique of the Mexican political economy and
democracy matured from a vague social democratic reformism into a clear alternative. He fused
four parties and movements into the National Democratic Front (FDN) and gained the support of
Herberto Castillo, who dropped out on June 4,
1988, in favor of the Cárdenas candidacy. Cárdenas's and Castillo's common program called for

replacement of the authoritarian presidential apparatus with a parliamentary system based upon
proportional representation with unquestioned
ethnic, religious, ideological, and sexual liberty.
Under their plan the centralized state would be
federalized with an equitable distribution of resources among the state governments. The secret
forces would been purged and the state would
manage a mixed economy while emphasizing improvements in health, welfare, and mass education. Public enterprises would be cooperatives
owned by the federal government but managed by
workers. The FDN called for the mass media to
be run by independent cooperatives while abolishing indirect controls over the press. Agriculture, whether multinational cooperations, large
and small private property, or ejidos would take
on collective forms, all self-managed by
campesinos with government assistance and marketing. Mexico, in the Cárdenas scenario, would
be non-aligned, nuclear-free, and without foreign
troops or police. Suddenly, the left rather than the
PAN had become the PRI's major threat, as Cárdenas attracted increasingly larger crowds.

But on July 6, 1988, the government orches-
trated a massive fraud in the bowels of the Gobernación Secretariat. Early results from throughout
Mexico indicated that the PRI would lose its two-
thirds majority in the Chamber of Deputies. More
importantly, the votes also carried a convincing
mandate for Cárdenas. He was ahead when the
system went down, but he trailed when it came
back up. Manuel Bartlett, head of the Federal
Elections Commission, claimed that "environmental problems" and computer glitches would
delay final tabulation of the voting. He proceeded
to engineer voting results as he saw fit.

Meanwhile, a battle raged between the PRI old
guard, who insisted upon maintaining the party's
virtual monopoly on public office, and Salinas
supporters, who thought a vigorous opposition
would be healthy for the PRI. As tabulations
dragged on for a week and the numbers slowly
trickled out, PRI politicians openly disagreed
when calling for recounts. Fidel Velázquez, head
of the hard-core "dinasaur" faction, announced

that the PRI would "remain the dominant party." Eventually, the PRI maintained that it had won 60 of the nation's 64 senate seats and 27 of the 31 states. Results released by the government claimed that Salinas had won 50.36 percent of the votes while Cárdenas obtained nearly six million votes or 30.12 percent. The PAN candidate placed third with 17.07 percent, slightly more than it had received in 1982. The PRI's power ebbed in Congress, where it won 260 seats compared with the opposition's 240. Nevertheless, the PRI suffered its greatest losses ever. Even in the official results, which Cárdenas rejected as grossly inflated, the PRI lost to the opposition in 18 of Mexico's 32 state capitals.

Unlike past elections, when the Federal Elections Commission could easily adjust the voting totals, the 1988 elections came under great scrutiny, partially because the new voting law required that each precinct count the ballots at the close of the voting and post the results that evening. But the results announced were different than the posted numbers as the PRI adjusted the numbers. When the newly elected Congress met for the first time to certify election results, shouts, catcalls, bitter exchanges, and insults broke out in what was normally a rubber-stamp process. The election had weakened the PRI so much that when the electoral college's secretary attempted to read the resolution naming Salinas the new president in early September, the disorder was such that the session had to be suspended twice. Finally, near midnight, the secretary read the resolution under guard by PRI deputies and undercover military agents while opposition deputies banged their desktops, tossed ballots into the air, tore copies of the federal electoral code into shreds and shouted, "Total repudiation of the electoral fraud!" nonstop for over two hours.

SALINAS DE GORTARI DISAPPOINTS MEXICO

The Salinas *sexenio* raised Mexico to unusual levels of confidence while also causing devastating anger. Salinas recorded badly needed economic triumphs while continuing to implement the privatization policy initiated by de la Madrid. But in the end, he revealed himself as a shameless, self-serving manipulator.

The Politics of Rising Expectations. After taking office in December 1988, Salinas took charge of the presidency in a decisive, dynamic manner. Only 40 years old, Salinas became Mexico's youngest president in half a century. He was also the best educated. He spoke English and French and held two masters degrees and a doctorate, all from Harvard University. Trim but bald, Salinas was a skillful political infighter, a highly intelligent organizer, and a disciplined stickler for efficiency.

Inaugural ceremonies in the Chamber of Deputies were disrupted by protests indicative of the eroded position of the PRI. When de la Madrid walked into the heavily guarded chamber, the PAN deputies held up signs calling his term "Six Years of Fraud." When Salinas entered, the Cárdenas contingent staged a noisy walkout as one member yelled at Salinas, "you are illegitimate." In his address, Salinas pointed to Mexico's $104 billion foreign debt as the preeminent problem. "The priority will no longer be to pay," Salinas declared, "but to return to growth."

Salinas started the National Solidarity Program, a program for the poor, named after the spontaneous outpouring of citizen self-help following the 1985 earthquakes, the day after he took office. This was a deft move. Under Salinas's direct control, Solidarity was eventually financed through the sale of government-owned industries and represented 35 percent of the federal budget not dedicated to debt payments. During his term, Solidarity provided electricity for 14,000 rural villages, more than 80,000 new school rooms and laboratories, 32 dams, 120 hospitals, 17 airport expansions, and countless clean drinking water projects. Nervous and uncomfortable during his presidential campaign, Salinas became intoxicated with the exhilaration of touching commoners who appreciated his aid. Usually on Thursdays and Fridays, he traveled across the country in shirt sleeves and hiking boots. He discussed local concerns in plain language and avoided promising the impossible.

The Solidarity program made Salinas very popular within only ten months. Everywhere he traveled, Salinas was besieged by people delivering letters with personal requests, imploring him directly for help, or merely touching him. In Torreón, he had been pelted with rotting fruit in 1988; months later, residents cheered after he strode into a crowd of protesters and listened to their complaints. The program aimed to cut red tape and involve ordinary citizens, who would provide labor. Rather than dealing with a graft-ridden bureaucracy, local inhabitants would design devlopment schemes in return for federal seed money. Private financing—from banks, builders, and even from self-imposed business taxes—paid for the rest. Critics claimed that the president visited areas where his popularity was already high or where elections were to take place. No one could doubt that he had seized the initiative in domestic affairs. He became relaxed enough to become romantically involved with one of his economic advisors.

Salinas also confronted Mexico's powerful labor unions by arresting oil workers' union boss Joaquín Hernández Galicia on January 10, 1989. Friction had begun in 1984 when Salinas, then budget director, attacked the union leadership's principal source of enrichment. He ended a long-standing practice which enabled PEMEX to award two-fifths of its drilling contracts and half of the work on all other projects to the union. The union routinely subcontracted much of the business to companies that paid huge fees to bosses like Hernández. In 1987, a bitter Hernández tried to block Salinas's selection as the PRI presidential candidate. Animosity grew when seven leaders serving as congressional deputies voted against the PRI to show their clout. In early 1989, Hernández threatened a nationwide strike if Salinas tried to privatize any aspect of PEMEX. The legendary inefficiency of PEMEX, a bloated work force with leaders suspected of extortion, blackmail, and murder, had to be alleviated in

order to service the export market and meet domestic demand.

Just 40 days into his administration, Salinas ordered police and army troops to arrest Hernández. "Hit the dirt," they yelled at supplicants waiting outside Hernández's Ciudad Madero home. A grenade launcher blew down a wall as authorities apprehended the union leader, just as he finished his morning bath. With 50 of his cronies, he was marched outside shirtless and flown to Mexico City. In one move, Salinas shattered his weak image. In a second display of muscle, Salinas deployed troops to protect oil installations in the face of a short-lived strike by oil workers, which quickly fizzled. Public support shot up when police found a weapons cache, including 200 Uzi submachine guns, inside Hernández's home. One of the few protests came from Fidel Velázquez, who insisted that "As head of the CTM, I cannot accept that this can happen in Mexico." Two days later, however, he met with Salinas and pledged his support. On February 2, the oil worker's union elected a pro-Salinas leader who backed the PRI. To balance the political books, Salinas also jailed Eduardo Legoretta, one of the richest stockbrokers in the country, on charges of fraud and manipulating markets.

Confronted by both conservative and leftist opponents after the 1988 election, Salinas decided to co-opt the PAN while establishing an uncompromising repression of Cárdenas and his new Democratic Revolutionary Party (PRD). This strategy became apparent in 1989 when Ernesto Ruffo Appel of the PAN was elected governor of Baja, California, the first opposition leader governor in the history of modern Mexico. There the PRI also conceded the loss of two municipalities and control of the state chamber of deputies. Although born in San Diego, California, Ruffo became municipal president of Ensenada. When the PRI governor cut off state funds, Ruffo rallied citizens to help clean and pave streets—a move that bolstered his image. He instituted a more democratic government than in any other Mexican state. For the first time in Baja, California, the government's income and expenses were published monthly. Civil service jobs were competitive rather than filled quietly through political contacts. Drug tests helped the police department hire more professional officers. Ruffo stopped the practice of paying journalists for favorable press coverage. He traveled without a vast entourage and banned the purchase of official autos while he drove a used Ford provided by supporters. Perhaps most importantly, municipal governments began to enjoy the autonomy granted them in theory by the 1917 Constitution. Salinas flew to Baja California for Ruffo's inauguration.

During the midterm 1991 elections for governors in six states, the National Chamber of Deputies, and half the Senate, the PAN also emerged triumphant in Guanajuato. Although the PRI won 290 of 300 directly elected congressional seats and 31 of 32 senate posts, Salinas forced PRI Governor Ramon Aguirre to step down after elections took place. PAN opponent Vicente Fox had sent thousands of supporters into the streets and vowed to keep Aguirre from taking office. The usual dirty tricks angered presidential aides who conceded that the vote count of the PRI victor had been grossly inflated. Surprised and pleased, Fox announced that Salinas's move "opens space for democracy and for the electoral process to be fair and equitable." Earlier, he had accused Salinas of using "criminal" methods to steal the election. On September 1, 1999, the Guanajuato state congress selected Carlos Medina, municipal president of León, to serve as interim governor. Fox hailed the selection of Medina as an indication that the next vote would be tallied fairly. Thus, Medina became the second opposition governor as Fox planned another run to become governor.

Salinas courted one of the most fierce anti-PRI leaders, Barrio Terrazas, by permitting him to become elected governor of Chihuahua in 1992. Many of Barrio's supporters considered him a modern-day Pancho Villa. During Barrio's inauguration in Chihuahua City, Salinas stood next to him and shouted "Bravo Pancho, bravo." The next fall, both leaders, along with their families, spent a weekend horseback riding atop Chihuahua's

picturesque Copper Canyon. Barrio reformed the voting process by removing government and party control of election procedures while promoting administrative efficiency. In addition to a struggle against corruption, Barrio revised the state constitution to aid indigenous peoples.

Salinas also pleased PAN leaders by promoting free-market policies, pursuing privatization, and patching up relations with the Church. Salinas appointed an official representative to the Vatican, consulted the Catholic leadership on numerous matters, invited clergy to his inauguration, and welcomed Pope John Paul II to Mexico in 1990. Eventually, Salinas overturned liberal laws by again making it legal for priests to own property, wear their robes in public, and speak their minds on political issues. After 125 years, Mexico and the Vatican renewed diplomatic ties. By the time Salinas finished his *sexenio*, PAN leaders controlled 103 municipalities, thus governing about 13 percent of Mexico's population. PAN party leader Luis Alvarez pursued a policy of cooperation and dialogue with the PRI, avoiding direct criticism of Salinas and supporting government legislation. Although ten key subordinates resigned claiming that Alvarez was selling out to Salinas, the PAN's growth would pay off with complete power at the end of the decade.

Salinas also endorsed a series of overdue political reforms. These included regulation of party finances, limits upon campaign spending, and increased access to media outlets by opposition parties. Although voting machinery remained in the hands of the PRI and the government, the Salinas administration changed voting procedures to make them more credible. Salinas allowed opposition representatives to observe the voting and counting process beginning with the 1991 elections. After taking office, Salinas removed 7 of Mexico's 31 governors after allegations of voter fraud or corrupt business practices. He seemed to legitimize public protests. After peasants from Tabasco and Veracruz marched for 50 days over a 600-mile route to Mexico City as a protest against questionable local elections, Salinas agreed to recognize opposition victories in two contested towns.

Early in his regime, Salinas also enacted civil liberties improvements. Most of these efforts centered around Jorge Carpizo, who initially gained a reputation for integrity when Salinas named him chief of the National Human Rights Commission in 1990. In that position, Carpizo demonstrated a willingness to pressure local and state officials to investigate human rights complaints. After six months, he listed 33 interventions against local officials involving the murder, torture, and kidnapping of citizens by police. This constituted a rare official admission that the judicial system was poisoned by violence.

In response to mass protests decrying police brutality, Salinas legislated restraints upon the police. Among these were a requirement that arrest warrants had to be utilized by the Federal Judicial Police. Detainees were allowed to have an attorney or other advisor present. Suspects could have access to a telephone or other form of communication immediately. Finally, confessions could no longer be the sole evidence brought to bear against suspected criminals.

In 1992, Salinas named Carpizo as federal attorney general. Carpizo shocked the political establishment by declaring the office a "rats' nest" and initiated wholesale dismissals of corrupt federal police officers. Later, he called for the jailing of previously untouchable figures, including Mexican generals. Salinas eventually named the independent Carpizo to become secretary of Gobernación in January 1994.

Repression and Scandal. While Salinas legislated much of the PAN program, he hammered the PRD. Enmity from the 1988 campaign spilled over into the early days of the Salinas regime when Cárdenas supporters occupied nearly half of Michoacán's 113 municipal governments to protest vote fraud and demand replacement of the PRI governor. Similar seizures took place in the tense states of Guerrero, Oaxaca, and Puebla. With minimal PRD organizing support, local citizens often drew upon communal indigenous traditions, experience in independent campesino or labor organizations, or a combination of spontaneity and personal charisma to form their own "popular governments." Citizens in Guerrero took over municipal buildings in 26 communities which they renamed "alternative governments." In Michoacán, the state party leadership agreed to a mutual recognition of 54 PRI municipal presidencies with 51 for the PRD. Guerrero PRI leaders were less generous; there the State Electoral Commission affirmed only three PRD victories during the December 1989 municipal elections. Tension had reached such a level that Guerrero Governor Francisco Ruiz Massieu delivered his state of the state message in the presence of 2,500 soldiers. In several Michoacán cities, the PRI and PRD agreed to share power, but negotiations ended when a police chief in Zitacuaro was killed in March.

Salinas prepared an assault force that routed the PRD supporters in a bold show of force. In April 1990, he sent thousands of troops backed by light tanks and armored vehicles into Michoacán. There the demonstrators surrendered peacefully although military police apprehended dozens. Ten people died in February and March in neighboring Guerrero during a smaller eviction campaign. Military police sought to humiliate and subordinate leftist leaders by beating them, stripping them of their clothes, and marching them through the streets. Cárdenas appeared divided and uncertain and had no intention to retake city governments. Meanwhile, the federal government abandoned projects initiated by Cárdenas when he had served as Michoacan's governor. Particularly costly was an expensive water treatment project for PRD-ruled Morelia. The national development bank refused to extend any credit to the Morelia government beginning in 1992 with the result that the unfinished sewage treatment plant lay in ruin and the water became so dirty that it stained bathtubs.

Salinas continued to hound the PRD, which became increasingly disoriented. Official violence in Guerrero became particularly notorious. Unarmed, bleeding peasants shocked tourists when they took refuge in the lobby of Acapulco's Princess Hotel. In 1990, the PRD presented the U. N. Human Rights Commission and the Organization of American States with documentation of 59 assassinations, 16 disappearances, and 38 political detentions of party militants. In the state of Mexico, the country's most populous and economically important state, the PRI claimed it had won all 34 directly contested seats in the state legislature and 116 of the state's 121 municipalities. This near-total victory flew in the face of the 2-to-1 thrashing the PRD had given the PRI in the 1988 state vote. PRI officials explained that cybernetic engineering enabled them to steal the elections. In many of the PRD working-class neighborhoods ringing Mexico City and in the ramshackle settlements beyond Military Camp Number One, the polls were empty on voting day. The melodrama of fraud against a backdrop of abstention grew to grotesque proportions. The PRD found it difficult to reignite the passions of 1988 in the face of traditional unions, Christian-based communities, and land-hungry indigenous communities. Irma Serrano, the playgirl of PRI officials for many years, even campaigned for the PRD in her bid for a senate seat from Chiapas.

Gradually, the Salinas administration became plagued with corruption. In 1991, the first major scandal to hurt Salinas surfaced when it was revealed that the offices and telephones of the National Commission on Human Rights had been bugged. Although the commission had promised confidentiality to those who would come forward to offer details about official abuse of power, surveillance indicated that such integrity had been breached. After promising to make political competition more fair, Salinas solicited wealthy businessmen for millions of dollars of contributions to the PRI. Particularly notorious was a February 23, 1993, dinner party at which 30 of Mexico's most powerful business people were asked to donate $25 million each. At the dinner was Carlos Slim, benefactor of one of many sweetheart deals. Slim had just paid just $400 million for a portion of the huge $3.9 billion phone company, Telmex. Another who dined with Salinas was a stockbro-

ker who had won the auction for the government's biggest bank, Banamex. Meanwhile, Salinas's older brother Raúl channeled tens of millions of dollars into overseas bank accounts. Raúl Salinas seemed to have ties to drug traffickers. Eventually, it became public knowledge that Carlos Salinas had shot a family maid to death in what was ruled an accident.

Drug-related corruption became a severe problem. U.S. officials tended to turn a blind eye to drug corruption because they did not want to jeopardize U.S. commercial and diplomatic ties with Salinas. The drug trade became serious when U.S. drug agents in the early 1990s began cutting the flow of cocaine into Florida. Mexican cartels picked up the loose ends and constructed a multibillion dollar business. By the end of the Salinas administration, 19 Mexican cartels handled two-thirds of the South American cocaine delivered to the United States; up from about a third. U.S. disappointment with the Salinas decision to name Enrique Alverez del Castillo as Mexico's attorney general should have alerted them to what lay ahead. The Jalisco police knew of the Camarena kidnapping during del Castillo's governorship of Jalisco and even aided drug trafficker Caro Quintero to escape from Mexico after the slaying. Major drug traffickers operated virtually in the open for years throughout Jalisco with the help of many law-enforcement agencies.

At first, Salinas was able to successfully patch up his image in a fake war on drugs. The arrest of Félix Gallardo, a major cocaine operator, helped put Salinas in a positive light during the spring of 1989. Salinas also promised to "make life impossible for drug traffickers." Even U.S. drug agents, who should have known better, served up accolades for Salinas in the following months. Salinas eventually started a "Just Say No" advertising campaign because of rising drug addiction in Mexico, even in rural areas. He even permitted U.S. P-3 radar planes to operate in Mexican airspace, a move criticized by some opponents as a violation of national sovereignty.

Troubling indications of the true reality of government complicity began to appear in the early 1990s. Salinas closed drug checkpoints near the U.S. border in July 1990. When the checkpoints had been created only a year before, U.S. officials had praised them as an important tool in decreasing the northward flow of drugs. Also in 1990, a large drug smuggling tunnel measuring several hundred feet was uncovered in Arizona along the U.S.–Mexican border. A more elaborate, 1,450-foot cocaine-smuggling tunnel was discovered by police in a Tijuana warehouse that was only a few hundred feet from completion to San Diego. Mexican army officers and police were apprehended in significant numbers when they attempted to sell drugs to U.S. undercover agents. Even more bizarre was a two-hour shootout near the Gulf of Mexico when 200 army troops fired on seven federal police officers attempting to intercept a plane laden with 800 pounds of cocaine. Attempting to protect drug smugglers, the army unit in question tried to explain away their role by claiming that low visibility prevented them from sighting who the police really were. But autopsies revealed that two federal agents had been shot in the back and a third had been shot in the mouth. When government authorities did sentence drug traffickers, they often had little to fear. Some ran their drug empires from behind bars; for example, Oliverio Chavez Araujo, was in virtual control of a state prison in Matamoros until shot by a rival during a firefight that killed 18 others.

The most sensational episode involving the drug trade was the May 24, 1993, killing of beloved Cardinal Juan Posadas Ocampo, one of two Mexicans elevated to the rank of cardinal by the Pope, at the Guadalajara airport. According to a government inquiry, Francisco Arellano Felix, head of the Tijuana drug cartel, had killed the cardinal mistakenly as part of an attempt to murder a rival, Joaquin "El Chapo" Guzmán. Most Mexicans and many clergymen, however, believed the killing was part of a conspiracy since Posada was shot at close range 14 times. Revelations that 11 state and federal police officers aided the assassins, particularly in halting a commercial airplane for a successful getaway, embarrassed the govern-

ment considerably. The murder exposed a huge network of drug trafficking and general corruption throughout Mexico. It also shed light on a vicious criminal subculture. Some of the hit men, later captured, told police that they did not intend to kill the cardinal. One participant claimed that he had sought to protect Guzmán because the Arellano gang had killed his wife and sent her head to him in a box. Investigators did not rule out a conspiracy and one arrested murderer claimed that he and the cardinal were riding in the same car when the killers ran up and started firing. Posada had spoken out against drugs and reportedly mediated disputes between the Arellano brothers and Guzmán. Despite friendly relations with Salinas, Mexico's bishops were divided over whether to accept Carpizo's explanation that the Arellanos killed the cardinal when they mistook Posadas for Guzmán.

Far more dramatic was the fate of presidential candidate Luis Donaldo Colosio. Unveiled by Salinas in November 1993 as the PRI nominee for the 1994 presidential election before a somewhat tepid audience, Colosio had served as head of the Social Development Secretariat. A prudent, shadowy politician, Colosio was the son of a middle-class Sonoran farmer. He studied economics at the Monterrey Technical Institute and earned a masters degree in regional development at the University of Pennsylvania in 1977. He began his career at the Secretariat of Planning and Budget before winning a seat in the Chamber of Deputies. He served on the budget committee when Salinas was budget secretary and from there ran Salinas's presidential campaign. He also served as senator from Sonora. Salinas named him head of the PRI where he stated his policy as "Democracy yes, but without excesses." He established such programs as "Operation Tamale," where voters were given big breakfasts and teams of "alchemists" brought the PRI's vote-rigging schemes into the computer age.

Despite his PRI background, Colosio developed into a formidable campaigner who gradually raised expectations for change. Born to a working class family that had only recently advanced beyond peasant status, Colosio connected well with ordinary citizens. Despite his solid education, Colosio had the unusual ability to grasp complex economic concepts and translate them into simple language, a skill that served him well on the campaign trail. While in the cabinet, Colosio went out with Salinas every Thursday and Friday during the Solidarity campaign where he met thousands of people. Thus, Colosio built an extensive network of contacts throughout many regions, not just in Mexico City. On his first campaign trip, Colosio and his wife traveled in economy class while his aides enjoyed first-class luxury and ignored bans on smoking cigars. Colosio also reinforced an austere image by driving himself to events in rented cars and foregoing strict security measures. He emphasized a desire to speak to as many people as possible and not be hemmed in.

Candidate Colosio talked about the need for deep reforms and worried conservatives that he would dismantle the PRI. Despite his administrative credentials, Colosio was a politician rather than a technocrat like Salinas, López Portillo, and Echeverría. He embraced the cause of reform by siding with PRI dissidents in the Democracy 2000 faction. Mostly young, university-educated politicians from the lower echelons of the party, Democracy 2000 sought to open up the ruling party in which a strict hierarchy traditionally limited how far the rank and file could climb the rungs of power. The dissidents complained that *cachorros*, children of the revolution, dominated the PRI's top leadership. Many of these members of Mexico's ruling elite had family ties to Mexican politics that frequently went back to the nineteenth century. Democracy 2000 members argued that party leaders were out of touch with the rank and file. To remedy the situation, these reformers called for new provisions for electing party candidates and ending the cozy ties between the government and the PRI.

Colosio accepted these demands and worked with Democracy 2000 on a stategy for courting voters from outside the PRI. With chapters in 29 states, Democracy 2000 generated debates at a time when Mexicans demanded complete democracy. But their efforts also raised the ire of the PRI's old guard, who considered them traitors. Fidel Velázquez publicly called for the expulsion of Democracy 2000 members. Despite harassment by PRI hard-liners, the democracy campaign made Colosio the front-runner. Perhaps even more controversial was Colosio's embrace of the call for clean elections that rebels in Chiapas demanded.

The Chiapas Revolt. In the 1990s, Chiapas approached a definite crisis. Indigenous peoples began creating their own organizations, a demographic explosion raised demands for land, and hunger increased. Chiapas soon became the second most violent state in Mexico, after Veracruz. It possessed the second highest indigenous population; illiteracy was at 30 percent, two and a half times the national average. High rates of alcoholism and malnutriton compounded social problems.

Perhaps the most controversial cultural problem was the large number of Protestant converts. Often expelled from local communities, many noncatholics emigrated to cities such as San Cristóbol de las Casas for refusing to take part in fiestas and other Catholic traditions. Many Protestants were beaten, had their homes burned, or were killed by local authorities. Since abstinence from drinking alcoholic beverages was a tenet of the Presbyterian church, the converts refused to consume alcoholic drinks, a major source of revenue for the civil-religious hierarchy.

Finally, the policies of Governor Patrocinio González fueled mass discontent. Taking over in 1988, González took credit for various accomplishments. He built more roads and highways than any other governor in a quarter of a century. González also put up more electrical lines in 4 years than previous administrations had in over 15 years. He also punished new arrivals who illegally cleared forests in eastern Chiapas.

But his foes contended that González's failures far outnumbered his successes. He had taken the traditional path of the ruling elite, studying in Europe and using his family connections to rise through government ranks. González began to crack down on Indians who complained about social conditions. He modified the law so that protesters could be considered "terrorists" and "delinquents." In March 1990, 340 peasants marched to Tuxtla Gutiérrez, the state capital, demanding land reform. Authorities told them González wanted to talk with them at the airport. When they arrived, 700 police gassed and clubbed them.

González blamed teachers and leftist priests for inciting the populace. In September 1991, he jailed a Catholic priest and accused him of encouraging rebellion. Thousands of Catholics protested. Human rights abuses mounted. Leaders of peasant organizations were murdered and indigenous farmers jailed. Others protested against rigged elections for municipal presidents. The governor also allowed state police to help ranchers clear out squatters trying to pursue land claims.

The existence of armed rebels in Chiapas had been an open secret for years. Therefore, the August 1991 elections resulted in the PRI winning a stunning 100 percent of the votes in 50 municipalities—the highest margin of any other state. But Chiapas villagers continued to whisper about nighttime training sessions in caves and jungle hideouts. Government intelligence officers discovered a crude weapons factory in 1989; later, they found a rebel training camp in May 1993. In response, Salinas ordered an emergency aid package to cover up signs of rebel activity in order to ensure the PRI's victory in the August 1994 presidential election.

But that strategy collapsed when the Zapatista National Liberation Army attacked San Cristóbol de las Casas and several other Chiapas towns on New Year's Day 1994. Fighting between government forces and rebels continued for weeks in the hills surrounding San Cristóbol. Fears of rebel attacks spread in January 1994 when electrical towers were downed in two states and police in Mexico City beefed up patrols outside banks, public buildings, the subway, and the airport. In a display of support for the rebels, thousands of workers, peasants, and students marched on January 7 in Mexico City, demanding an end to the use of military force to quell the uprising. González, recently elevated to head Gobernación, was forced to resign on January 10, becoming the first casualty of the uprising that shocked Mexico.

Saddled with a terrible crisis, Salinas named close friend Manuel Camacho Solis to head a new Commission for Peace and Reconciliation in Chiapas. The former Mexico City boss, however, experienced difficulty in obtaining a cease fire from rebel leaders who said that they were suspicious of the Salinas peace initiative. Nevertheless, rebels began sending secret messages to Camacho Solis through Bishop Samuel Ruiz, leader of the archdiocese of San Cristobol and trusted by Zapatista leaders. After the rebels seized the governor of Chiapas, Camacho praised the Zapatistas for their willingness to spare his life. Camacho also promised that the Mexican army would remain in its garrisons as a sign of good will. Nonetheless, many smaller villages in remote areas of Chiapas filled up with tanks, heavy artillery, and armored personnel carriers as soldiers stood on high alert.

Rafael Guillen Vicente emerged as the leader of the Zapatistas. The 37-year-old student graduated with high honors from UNAM before earning a master's degree at the Sorbornne in Paris where he studicd philosophy. Then he taught at the University of Nicaragua during the rule of the Sandinistas. Known as Comandante Marcos, Guillen became a colorful spokesman for his insurrection.

The guerrilla demands were extensive. They opposed privatizing formerly state-owned businesses. Particularly objectionable were changes made to Article 27 designed to bring capitalism to the countryside by allowing, for the first time, Mexican peasants to sell commonly held farmland. The poor hated Salinas's curtailment of land distribution. Rebels feared that their poverty would inevitably lead them to sell their small land plots to wealthy Mexican farmers or to United States, Canadian, and European agribusiness concerns that would be able to make direct investments in the Mexican countryside. Another problem was that Salinas withdrew subsidies for coffee growers, which devastated Chiapas when coffee prices collapsed in 1989. With these grievances in mind, the Zapatistas demanded land, work, food, housing, education, liberty, democracy, peace, and justice.

Discussions to resolve the crisis began on an encouraging note. In mid-January 1994, Ruiz began serving as mediator between rebels and the government. Camacho proposed an amnesty and promised that the peace talks would lead to "political recomposition" of Chiapas and "immediate changes" in the judicial system, as well as serious solutions to the problems found in indigenous communities. But Salinas stopped short of recognizing the rebels as a "belligerent force" which the guerrillas demanded. Rebel leaders sought to broaden the talks by inviting representatives of Mexico's political parties to sit in as observers. In an effort to win the guerrillas' trust, Camacho journeyed to the heart of Zapatista territory at Guadalupe Tepeyac for the release of a retired army general, who had been held captive by the rebels for more than 40 days. Camacho even allowed himself to be searched and shook hands with two heavily armed rebels when they delivered the prisoner. And Camacho listened silently as townspeople shouted their unbridled support for the Zapatistas. Meanwhile, the guerrilla demands began to moderate, particularly when they dropped their pleas that Salinas resign immediately.

The peace talks which began on February 21, quickly turned into a battle for the hearts and minds of Mexicans. Under a signed accord, Salinas agreed to hold a special congressional session to enact electoral reforms before the presidential election. Salinas representatives offered a national law which, for the first time, would outlaw discrimination against indigenous people and create a new office to prosecute such cases. In this context, a new federal law would protect indigenous autonomy in family, business, land, and farming matters. Moreover, improved health and education services were made part of the agreement,

which included bilingual education taught in indigenous languages. The rebels would also enjoy an amnesty.

Salinas limited most of his concessions to Chiapas and refused to install a transitional government. Negotiators decided that local governments should serve indigenous communities more directly and that the Chiapas state legislature should have increased indigenous representation. The impoverished state would also enjoy more roads, new housing projects, and expanded electrical power networks. In addition, Chiapas would have new judicial districts with judges trained to respect indigenous cultures. Finally, a new criminal law for the state would outlaw the common practice of expelling people from indigenous communities.

The unprecedented concessions made to the rebels eventually failed. A right wing group threatened to burn the cathedral in San Cristóbol if Ruiz did not resign, although the bishop continued to deny any role in the planning of the guerrilla attacks. Yet he argued that the Zapatista campaign was just—a point of view that infuriated conservative ranchers and entrepreneurs. Then the Zapatistas dealt a major blow to the peace process by flatly rejecting the March agreements. Perhaps even more stunning was the resignation of Camacho as peace envoy, who blamed rivals for blocking his efforts to launch a new peace initiative. Ruiz announced shortly afterwards that he was resigning as a mediator in the negotiations.

Tensions mounted in the aftermath of the stalled negotiations. Worried authorities in Chiapas arrested 127 squatters who had seized several ranches. Chiapas landowners complained that 400 other ranches had become occupied by landless rural inhabitants or guerrillas. At least 19 landowners had been kidnapped and forced to sign documents agreeing to surrender their properties. The guerrillas kept some of the farmers captive for days or weeks, forcing them to earn their freedom by instructing the militants how to operate tractors and other farm equipment.

Worried about the renewal of fighting, Salinas ordered troops to the positions which they had held back on January 12, the day the government ordered a cease-fire as part of a plan to lure the rebels back to the negotiating table. But their movement had not caught on as the rebels had hoped. The populace had not risen up in arms and the PRI remained firmly in power. Moreover, the rebels remained at a military disadvantage, facing 30,000 soldiers. The cease-fire held and the rebellion did not disrupt the presidential elections. Salinas informed Camacho Solis that because he had become popular, he had to declare publicly that he would not seek the presidency. On March 22, Camacho Solis disowned presidential ambitions. The next day Colosio was assassinated in Tijuana.

Deaths of Colosio and Massieu.

The conspirators who killed Colosio provoked confusion and frustration throughout Mexico after the most sensational crime in Mexico since the murder of Obregón. Colosio was shot dead at point-blank range as he left a campaign rally in a poor Tijuana neighborhood on the evening of March 23. The plot began when PRI Tijuana leader Rodolfo Rivapalacio hired bodyguards who organized the killing of Colosio. Mario Aburto Martinez was the individual accused of shooting Colosio, along with six accomplices. The group organized to help with crowd control for Colosio had shadowy backgrounds; they were former police officers of questionable reputations. Some may have been tied to drug traffickers who ordered the assassination to distract attention from their illicit business. Also one of the group was Jorge Antonio Sanchez, a member of Gobernación's Center for Investigation and National Security, who tested positive for powder burns on his hands and had blood on his shirt. The bodyguards cleared a path for Aburto, distracted the security around Colosio, threw themselves to the ground in front of Colosio to block his path moments before the shooting, and were seen speaking to Aburto shortly before the assassination.

Investigators from the attorney general's office focused on Aburto, a somewhat deranged individual who worked at a Tijuana plastics company that manufactured cassette tapes. He had talked about killing himself earlier in the year. He tried to gain attention by attempting to publish political writings concerning his frustration with the political system, although he had no links to the PRD, PAN, or Zapatistas. Three editors turned him down. Living in a tiny brick home in Tijuana, the reclusive Aburto was a devout Jehovah's Witness who had been expelled from school for not showing proper respect for the Mexican flag. Aburto's father believed that his son was set up by the new security team recruited by Rivapalacio. Psychological studies of Aburto demonstrated that he had problems with authority, little self-control, paranoia, and could easily be manipulated.

Although key questions remained unanswered, investigators disbanded their ineffective probe amid new murders. Particularly troubling was that authorities refused to give the assassination commission access to government files in the case. The special procecutor released Rivapalacio while Sanchez was merely suspended by Gobernación. A cardiologist who examined Colosio's body found that the size of the bullet holes varied—one from a 0.22-caliber weapon, the other from a 0.38-pistol. But no ballistics report was made available and authorities could provide only one bullet, thus contradicting the single-killer theory. The Tijuana police chief who aided in the investigation concluded that at least two gunmen participated in the killing. The police chief himself was killed in a mob-style murder a month later. Two men who worked as security guards for the Colosio campaign were gunned down by five shots from a passing car as they drove their Cadillac about 80 miles north of Los Angeles in early May 1994.

To replace Colosio, Salinas selected Ernesto Zedillo Ponce de León, despite the opposition of hard-liners. Like Colosio, Zedillo came from a working-class background. Born in Mexico City, he moved to the border city of Mexicali when he was three. Zedillo attended the National Polytechnic Institute, a university for humble students with few resources. Then he obtained scholarships to study at Yale University, where he received master's and doctoral degrees. Like Salinas, Zedillo became the PRI candidate without having any prior experience running for public office. Both men served in the Secretariat of Budget and Planning, where Zedillo played a key role in reversing Mexico's financial collapse in the 1980s and bringing runaway inflation under control. Zedillo was criticized after being named secretary of public education in 1992 for allowing new history textbooks used in public schools to deemphasize Emiliano Zapata and paint a more positive picture of Mexico's often stormy relationship with the United States. The 1992 texts also included the 1968 massacre for the first time and credited Porfirio Díaz with bringing order and stability to Mexico. The new view of history reflected Salinas's desire to distance Mexico from populist dogma and think of the United States as a friendly trading partner.

Next to die was José Francisco Ruiz Massieu. Considered a key figure in the Salinas regime, he had been named head of the PRI delegation in the Chamber of Deputies, as well as the PRI's secretary-general. On September 28, 1994, he joined 18 other PRI federal deputies for a breakfast at the Hotel Casa Blanca. Afterwards, a young *pistolero* shot Ruiz Massieu as he sat in his car. It is significant that Massieu's brother Mario worked as deputy attorney general at the attorney general's office, and. he and his agents had been targeting the large Gulf Cartel, headed by Juan García Abrego. The assassination was a message from drug traffickers that government efforts should be discouraged. As in the Colosio case, the gunman confessed that politicians in Tamaulipas ordered the killing. The alleged mastermind, PRI congressman Manuel Muñoz, was charged with murder.

What seemed to be an open-and-shut case became bogged down in politics and corruption charges. Mario Ruiz Massieu, put in charge of the investigation of his brother's death, gradually concluded that PRI hard-liners wanted his brother dead because he was pushing to bring further democratic reforms to the political system. Ruiz Massieu began to realize that higher-level officials

of the PRI had been involved. Finally, in November 1994, Ruiz Massieu quit as chief investigator and accused the latest attorney general of obstructing his probe. PRI officials, he claimed, were "more worried about defending criminals" than getting to the bottom of the assassination. His voice cracking with emotion, Ruiz Massieu concluded that "Demons are running around loose and they have won." Eventually, federal prosecutors began to suspect Raúl Salinas was behind the crime. Although few realized it at that time, Raúl was one of Mexico's top drug traffickers.

Economic Growth and Reform. Building upon the legacy of de la Madrid, Salinas engineered a downsizing of the Mexican government in economic life. His administration sold off hundreds of state-owned enterprises, allowed United States businesses to explore for oil for the first time since 1938, privatized the banking industry, and established a regional free trade block among Mexico, the United States, and Canada. Salinas continued to renegotiate the debt, kept up payments, and attracted significant foreign investment.

Debt reduction became one of the early Salinas triumphs. His concern over the crushing foreign debt coincided with the desires of United States President George Bush, whose administration made debt reduction a key component of its foreign policy, believing that the only way to ensure the survival of emerging democracies in Latin America was to find a way to reduce the 1980s slide in living standards caused by the staggering $1.3 billion Third World debt burden. The Brady Plan, named for United States Treasurer Secretary Nicolas Brady, sought to slash this debt by establishing incentives to get commercial banks to voluntarily forgive a portion of their loans. Bush considered Mexico the key test case for the worldwide implementation of the Brady Plan, which it unveiled on March 10, 1989, out of a belief that Salinas had been doing a fine job as president. During his inaugural address, Salinas had insisted upon a reduction in the value of the total debt to bring it more in line with the going market price of the loans, roughly half their value, in addition to extra reductions by means of direct bank writeoffs.

The negotiations worked in favor of Bush and Salinas. The banks did not want debt reduction, which would show up on their books as losses. Nor were they attracted by the idea of making new loans to bad-risk debtors. High-level prodding by Brady, Federal Reserve Chairman Alan Greenspan, State Department officials, the IMF, and the World Bank got them to agree to discussions in return for guarantees that Mexico would make the remaining payments on its debts. The IMF and World Bank agreed to put up $25 billion. Salinas initially insisted upon a 55 percent debt reduction, while the banks offered no more than 15 percent. Mexican Finance Secretary Pedro Aspe claimed that Mexico was paying more in interest payments than Germany had in reparations after World War I. As the negotiators sat down to sort things out, Salinas demanded a 40 percent debt reduction while Brady offered 20 percent. In the summer of 1989, Salinas gleefully announced a new agreement, which was the first time more than 500 banks had been able to agree on a broad reduction to a Latin American Nation. The Lloyds Bank of London and Spanish banks also agreed to debt writeoffs. The eventual agreement reduced Mexico's total public and private debt to foreign lenders to under $80 billion, compared to a peak of $107 billion late in 1987. Debt payments, which amounted to 6 percent of Mexico's gross national product in 1989, were predicted to fall to about 2 percent by 1994.

The money saved by debt reduction allowed Salinas to reduce spending, cut inflation, and generate economic growth. By 1992, Mexico enjoyed a Porfirian-like surplus in public finances. Salinas cut spending and began collecting taxes with zeal. Shaving the deficit also brought down inflation. Inflation fell from 160 percent in 1987 to 19.7 in 1989. In 1993, inflation fell to 8.01 percent, the lowest annual rate in 21 years. These measures significantly encouraged business activity. The capitalized value of the Mexican stock market shot up from $8.7 billion in 1987 to $197.5 billion in early 1994, making Mexico City Latin America's largest market and one of the world's top ten. Cellular telephones sitting atop lunch and dinner tables became a common sight in the thriving business community. Private-sector spending on new plants and equipment enabled much of the economic growth along with lower interest rates. The economy continued to grow until a recession late in 1994. The strategy of bringing inflation down to single digits by cooling off the economy and general belt tightening proved, ironically, too successful. Moreover, the peso had become overvalued, but Salinas refused to consider devaluation.

Attracting foreign investment became vital to the Salinas formula of pushing the Mexican economy further from its inward looking and state-directed past. In 1989, Salinas liberalized formerly strict laws regulating foreign investment in an attempt to attract outside investors to its key tourism industry. Earlier, foreign businesses needed permission from government agencies, often with long delays, before they could invest. Under Salinas, that process melted away. In addition, foreign investors could increase holdings in a Mexican company to a majority stake and profits could be repatriated abroad. By 1990, Salinas opened up two-thirds of the economy to 100 percent foreign ownership. Salinas also scrapped Echeverría's 1973 Foreign Investment Law and sought the advanced technology that United States and European companies could bring in. By the time Salinas left office in 1994, foreign investment had grown from $3.5 billion in 1983 to $120 billion.

Under the dynamic Jacques Rogozinski, privatization accelerated during the Salinas regime. The son of Polish Jews who survived Nazi concentration camps and emigrated to Mexico in 1951, Rogozinski took charge of the fledgling privatization program in 1988. He encountered fierce resistance from bureaucrats and workers. Under Echeverría, for example, the government took over the Cananea Copper Company but proceeded to coddle workers, particularly by granting them up to 100 days for unpaid leave. This meant that the company had to employ vast reserves of workers on salary. Before Rogozinski could sell the bankrupt company, 3,000 troops had to be brought in to subdue the union after negotiations ended.

Rogozinski decided that there had to be a better way to assert control. In 1990, he established the Disincorporation Unit, a 16-member team that served as a holding company for businesses that he targeted for privatization. With himself as chair and cabinet members on his board, Rogozinski finally won the upper hand. By March 1993, he had sold off $22 billion of state-owned companies. In addition to fueling Solidarity social spending, the privatization returns helped pay off the debt.

Rogozinski's biggest deal was the 1991 sale of Telmex. Salinas considered the existing Telmex operation a bottleneck to economic recovery. Its slow service became so notorious that the phone directory was known as the "book of the dead" because its numbers were years out of date. Callers within Mexico City routinely found their discussions interrupted by the abrupt arrival of a third, unwanted party who was the victim of a crossed line. Other conversations ended abruptly when the line went dead. Another distraction was a phone call in which both parties had their ears blasted by either a high-pitched electronic squeal or the sound of a computer tone.

Outside the capital, service fell off to either unreliable or nonexistent. The mayor of Tenejapa, Chiapas had to drive 45 minutes to San Cristobal to make contact with the outside world. So did the municipal judge, since Tenejapa, despite having 1,000 residents, had not one phone. For a family or business person who sought to install a phone, a wait of two or three years was likely. The impact on someone wanting to set up a business is incalculable. Even if they had the talent or capital, no one could call them on a phone.

Because of political concerns about foreign influence on Telmex, Rogozinski designed a public stock offering that would give operating control to Mexicans while attracting the capital that only foreigners had. Telmex required at least $10 billion for the next five years to bring its services and equipment up to date. In December 1990, Salinas announced the sale of its 51 percent ownership to a consortium that included Southwestern Bell, French Telecom, and Carlos Slim for $1.76 billion. Slim obtained majority control. Under the terms of the deal, Telmex's network would be doubled to 10 million lines within four years and the waiting period for installation was to be cut to six months.

Three years later, Bell Atlantic Corporation agreed to pay as much as $1 billion for up to 42 percent of Grupo Iusacell, a major Mexican cellular telephone company. The move put Bell Atlantic, the largest cellular telephone company on the United States east coast, into the middle of Mexico's wireless telephone wars. By then, Mexico had about 350,000 cellular telephone subscribers. Iusacell competed with Telmex for potential customers by employing well-known actresses and soccer coaches to bash their rivals in only slightly veiled references.

Of course, not all privatizations ended happily. Rogozinski sold the government's 58 percent share of Mexicana de Aviación to a tycoon who embezzled so much that the airline bled red ink. A project to build highways grossly overestimated potential traffic. Exorbitant tolls made the highways among the world's most expensive. However, none of the privatizations carried the symbolic weight of the banks. Without an up-to-date, competitive banking system, Mexico would lag in developing its economy, attracting foreign capital, and repatriating money that left after 1982. Labeling nationalization a failure, Rogozinski earned $12.4 billion by selling the banks in an auction that ended in July 1982. But most of the banks were sold to inexperienced people who made bad loans. Poor federal regulations and mismanagement that ranged from fraud to profligacy eventually pushed the banking system to the brink by 1995. Privatization also became popular with state governments. Following Salinas's lead, Aguascalientes sold off 22 companies that it owned, including a furniture factory, textile plant, and a vegetable processing facility.

Salinas transformed PEMEX from the crown jewel of Mexico's public sector to a company merely looking for a profit. Salinas decided to streamline PEMEX in order to increase revenues and boost economic growth. By 1993, 74,000 workers had been laid off and the union's collective contract had been stripped of many of the privileges that made working for PEMEX a cushy job. PEMEX no longer made all of its own equipment and stopped building homes, hospitals, and schools for its workers, as well as operations not directly related to oil production and sales. New directors turned increasingly to private-sector contractors. Salinas also broke a taboo by opening up exploratory drilling and other field services to foreign companies under a strict cash for work contract basis.

A sewer explosion that killed 200 people in Guadalajara in April 1991 was a turning point for PEMEX restructuring. Investigators concluded that the disaster occurred because gasoline had leaked for weeks from a corroded PEMEX pipeline and presented charges of negligent homicide, damage to private and public property, and environmental destruction. Salinas stepped up his attempts to modernize PEMEX, though it had become more a national disgrace than a symbol of pride. Therefore, Salinas split its operation into four subsidiaries which managed their own personnel, operations, investment, and property. Salinas encouraged private investment in the petrochemical operations sector, heretofore prohibited. The new structure copied the organization of international oil companies such as Exxon and Mobil. Each unit was evaluated separately and performance judged against international competitors. One of the most radical adjustments for PEMEX was having to respond to mandatory market pricing between units. In the past, crude oil flowed to the refineries without a price tag attached. That practice however, did not allow for incentives to be efficient.

Compared to past decades PEMEX became a somewhat limited feature of the economy. In 1982, PEMEX's crude oil and petroleum products comprised 73 percent of Mexico's export revenues. By 1989, oil exports had dropped to only 33 percent of the country's exports. Changing international political as well as environmental pressures revealed how PEMEX had fallen behind. Its antiquated production, refining, and distribution systems hampered Mexico's ability to capitalize on the 1991 Persian Gulf crisis. Unlike Venezuela, Mexico could not increase its production in a major way. Besides, growth in domestic demand had lowered exports to about 1.3 million barrels a day by 1992. And, for the first time, PEMEX imported gasoline because it had no unleaded gasoline-refining capacity—desperately needed in order to reduce Mexico City's air pollution.

The NAFTA Accords. Salinas became best known for his efforts to establish the North American Free Trade Agreement (NAFTA). NAFTA initiated the integration of the Mexican, United States, and Canadian economies over a maximum period of 15 years beginning on January 1, 1994. Tariffs had been reduced greatly during the de la Madrid regime; therefore, NAFTA actually inaugurated a harmonization of the laws of each country and sought to institutionalize new policies of openness toward foreign investment.

Salinas initiated the idea of a trading pact with a very receptive President George Bush. During a trip through Western Europe early in 1990, Salinas received merely polite receptions by the Europeans and learned that they would concentrate their resources among themselves. Although he signed a treaty with Spain that provided up to $4 billion in trade and investment credits as well as low-interest loans, Salinas realized that the future for trade lay with the United States. Even though the idea had been considered by United States and Mexican leaders, a United States–Mexico free trade pact seemed esoteric and far away. It had taken the United States and Canada 25 years to work out a free trade pact and by 1990, fewer than 3 percent of imports to Mexico required permits. But in June 1990, Salinas signaled his intent to open Mexico's economy further by endorsing negotiations for free trade with the United States.

It did not take long for Bush and Salinas to discuss free trade thereafter. Salinas decided that hitching Mexico's economic future to the United States would solve many problems. Although Salinas had rejected the idea of such a pact in 1988, he quickly realized Asia did not seriously want to do business with Mexico and a single, unified European market emphasizing new opportunities in Eastern Europe would not work out either. Also, the U.S–Canada Free Trade Pact concerned Salinas because two of Mexico's biggest customers could benefit from closer ties at Mexico's expense. Tying the United States to Mexico would also impose checks on overspending by any future Mexican president because debt crises and balance of payments problems would scare away customers. For their part, U.S. officials themselves competed against the Asians and Europeans. German and Asian exports had grabbed big chunks of the U.S. market with innovative, high-quality products. Bush wanted to revive U.S. competitiveness as much as Salinas; therefore, he jumped on the free-trade bandwagon in September 1990 and quickly established a strong personal relationship with Salinas during a November 1990 visit to Monterrey. Salinas hosted Bush at his Agualeguas hometown community, where they attended a rodeo and ate barbecue. Meeting in the Salinas family home added a personal touch which Bush enjoyed after dealing with difficult confrontations in the Middle East. Their personal interaction seemed to cut through years of misperception and distrust.

Although Bush and Salinas believed free trade had to be achieved, gaining U.S. congressional approval unleashed surprising opposition. Bush sought fast-track authority from Congress to agree on the treaty, which would allow him to negotiate details with Canada and Mexico without consulting Congress on specifics. At the end of the process, the House and Senate would vote to accept or reject the treaty. Rising opposition from organized labor and environmental groups became intense. Union leaders predicted factories would move south of the border in huge numbers while thousands would lose their jobs. Environ-

mentalists feared that U.S. companies would leave to take advantage of lax enforcement of environmental regulations in Mexico. The border region already suffered from toxic waste dumping, serious air pollution, and contaminated water. Others feared that the Mexican market had become flooded with fruits and vegetables bearing residues of pesticides long since banned in the United States. They suggested that the U.S., Canada, and Mexico draw up a long-term management plan such as one developed in Europe.

Even though Salinas had made the achievement of a free-trade accord the central goal of his administration, it faced opposition in Mexico as well. Mexican ecologists warned that the exclusion of environmental concerns from the trade negotiations would extend the border model of rising pollution throughout Mexico. Real incomes had plunged by 60 percent in Mexico since the 1980s and working people feared that free trade would only maintain their cheap labor status indefinitely. Farmers feared that they could not possibly compete with giant U.S. producers who would flood Mexico with massive quantities of grains. At this time, two-thirds of all arable Mexican land was held in plots of less than 12 acres. Tension about the mood in the U.S. Congress rose to such a level that when the *Washington Post* endorsed the free-trade proposal, it became front-page news in Mexico City. Congress eventually voted in May 1991 to extend Bush's negotiating authority for the free-trade agreement.

The three Mexican negotiators blended in smoothly with their Canadian and U.S. counterparts. All three had earned their doctorates from Yale and the University of Chicago. Chief negotiator Herminio Blanco Mendoza had even taught economics at Rice University from 1980 to 1985. Jaime José Serra Puche, who served as secretary of commerce and industrial development, had traveled extensively throughout the United States promoting increased trade. Jaime Zabludovsky Kuper, like the others, had studied the success of countries with free and open markets, as well as the stagnation of countries that relied on protectionism to shield their state-run industries. His views coincided with those of his uncle Jacobo, who was Mexico's most influential television journalist. Jacobo controlled coverage to convince many Mexicans there would only be benefits from the treaty. Top trade officials from all three countries had been meeting informally for several months and were more than familiar with Mexico's overriding desire for investment. Working group discussions on foreign capital yielded promising results. Although not particularly excited about the discussions, Canadian negotiators Michael Wilson and John Weeks felt they had no alternative. Carla Hills and Julius Katz, on the other hand, reflected the Bush desire to hammer out a good deal before the 1992 U.S. presidential election. Bush was concerning himself largely with international events, but strengthening the economy would be a feather in his cap. Polls in Mexico yielded majority backing for a treaty, particularly among the well-to-do and middle-income groups. Northern Mexico, especially managers and merchants, favored the trade accord more than other regions.

After 14 months of talks, the United States, Mexico, and Canada agreed in August 1992 to form the world's largest trading bloc. It created a single market that produces goods and services worth more than $6 trillion annually. The complex agreement treats each economic sector—from automobiles to agriculture to energy—differently. The agreement eliminates remaining tariffs and trade barriers over a 15-year period. Mexico agreed to relax access to its oil patch but stood by its constitutional mandates forbidding foreign ownership of petroleum reserves. PEMEX agreed to designate that 50 percent of oilfield purchases be from Mexican companies, reducing that to 30 percent over eight years, with no special set-asides for Mexican firms by the tenth year. U.S. automakers were pleased overall, although dissatisfied with provisions that require 62.5 percent of parts in a vehicle to be of Mexican origin for production to be classified as North American. But Detroit could begin selling cars in Mexico. Mexico was satisfied that its growing electricity needs could be met by allowing U.S. investors to ac-

quire, establish, and operate electrical generating facilities. Foreigners could now own power plants rather than lease them from the Mexican government. Tariffs were lifted immediately on roughly one-half of all agricultural products traded between Mexico and the United States. Trade barriers were to be gone after 2002 for all but "highly sensitive" products, such as corn and dry beans intended for the Mexican market, and sugar as well as orange juice for the United States. In addition, U.S. banks and securities firms can operate within Mexican banks and insurance companies.

Manufacturing provisions are particularly interactive. The free trade agreement eliminates all tariffs and quotas on textiles and apparel over ten years. Although free trade means more competition, U.S. industry considered Mexico an ally in battles with Asian products. They supported NAFTA because having their production in Mexico lowered overall labor costs and made them more competitive. Six months later, in response to local industry complaints about unfair competition, the Mexican government slapped punitive duties on dozens of Chinese products by as much as 500 percent. Prior to NAFTA, *maquiladoras* were required to export all their production in order to protect Mexican industry. But NAFTA permits *maquiladoras* to sell within Mexico 55 percent of the total value of its annual exports from the previous year. The 55 percent limitation was to be removed entirely by 2001.

Above all, NAFTA encourages foreign investment. Its most fundamental provision states that each member country is to provide investors of the others the same treatment given to local investors. In addition to eliminating direct restrictions upon investment, NAFTA permits investors to transfer payments, particularly dividends, interest, and royalty payments in freely convertible currency or at the market rate of exchange. NAFTA also discourages expropriation. Should nationalization take place, compensation has to be paid quickly, according to the fair market value of the investment.

Should any member nation violate NAFTA provisions, the investor can attempt to have them enforced by means of arbitration. The International Center for Settlement of Investment Disputes supervises arbitration by means of a nonpartisan tribunal. Any arbitration disputes are dictated by either the International Center for Settlement of Investment Disputes or the arbitration procedure of the United Nations Commission on International Trade Law. Should any NAFTA country fail to accept arbitration decisions, which can include payment of monetary awards, it will suffer a suspension of NAFTA benefits.

NAFTA also contains numerous provisions governing intellectual property rights. These laws apply to trade secrets, patents, trademarks, and copyrights. This is something of a deviation from U.S. law, which has no federal trade secret statutes. NAFTA also provides the holder of intellectual property rights with the ability to insist that another NAFTA country detain shipments of infringing goods on that nation's border.

Mexico responded to the need for resolving its environmental problems by enacting the General Law on Ecological Balance and Environmental Protection as well as other regulations. Mexico's desire not to become a dumping ground for others is reiterated in NAFTA, which specifically forbids member countries from lowering environmental standards as part of any attempt to obtain foreign investment. During the ratification debate, however, no issue received as much coverage as the impact of NAFTA activity upon the environment. When Bush lost the presidency to Bill Clinton in 1992, new White House Budget Director Leon Panetta declared that NAFTA was "dead" in Congress. Clinton himself declared that he would not submit the treaty to Congress until environmental concerns were addressed. The heated discussion that ensued prompted the U.S., Mexican, and Canadian governments to include unprecedented environmental provisions in NAFTA and to sign a supplemental North American Agreement on Environmental Cooperation late in the summer of 1993.

NAFTA had further repercussions in Mexico. To mollify critics of low Mexican wages, Salinas raised the minimum wage but pegged it to produc-

tivity. Defining productivity was hard to do because, although some Mexican companies had modern assembly lines employing thousands of workers, the vast majority consisted of shops with fewer than a dozen workers and production methods that harkened back to the colonial era. Too many workers felt they had borne the brunt of anti-inflation policies. Hundreds of former PEMEX workers invaded its corporate office in protest against additional layoffs. Nationalists objected to NAFTA provisions by which Mexico's labor secretary served on a commission with cabinet-level labor officials from the United States and Canada. Many doubted that their wages would improve in that scenario. Conducting company-by-company reviews and then getting small companies to comply with a new minimum wage requirement was a difficult task for Mexico's understaffed Labor Secretariat. But Salinas supporters argued that increasing wages without regard to economic growth was a concept from the past.

Mexico has not been the same. A widespread concern among officials and industry leaders was the loss of many of its "best and brightest," particularly scientists, who studied and then worked in the United States or Europe. To bring home engineers, physicists, and other experts, Salinas offered to pay them to repatriate and increase research funding. About 348 scientists did return by 1993 under this program. NAFTA encouraged faster movement toward democracy and improvement in human rights. It became the first genuine north-south trade agreement that did not have any continuity with the colonial past.

The 1994 Presidential Election. Short on time, momentum, and name recognition, Zedillo played a hurry-up offense, attempting to be all things to everyone in a successful bid to win the surprising August 21, 1994, presidential election. Unlike Colosio, Zedillo did not seem comfortable addressing large crowds of workers and campesinos. His gestures were awkward and mechanical. But when Zedillo talked to business people or academics, he spoke the same language, reeling off statistics and fretting about the gross domestic product. His first breakthrough came in presidential debates, where his intelligence showed. Cuauhtémoc Cárdenas performed poorly. During the campaign, Cárdenas preferred telling his supporters that they had to be prepared to defend their votes to prevent another fraud. His populist, antirich rhetoric called for expanded social programs and rolling back privatization sales. Diego Fernández de Cevallos of the PAN seemed to be the front runner at one point, sparkling in the debates with humor and blunt responses. His theme of "For a Mexico Without Lies" symbolized a propensity to speak his mind, but Fernández often avoided broader issues and did not campaign particularly hard. Moreover, Zedillo received a disproportionate share of media coverage, more than twice the air time of his two chief rivals.

The election was honest and became a refreshing step toward true democracy. Salinas pushed through a dazzling array of electoral reforms, which modernized the electoral machinery and created fraud-resistant voter identification cards. Voterigging became a criminal offense. Election observers, international as well as domestic, monitored the voting. The number of registered voters shot up from 36 million to 44 million, a massive effort in a country where one-fourth of the population had no mailing address other than that of the nearest municipality. Adding to the drama was that few of the people who were supposed to know Mexican politics—intellectuals, political observers, serious newspaper people—expected the result. Only the polls generally succeeded in predicting the election results. This reduced the possibility of fraud and assured acceptance of the exit polls. Voter turnout was also high, nearly 80 percent, which added to Zedillo's victory. The 1994 presidential race was not close at all: Zedillo won 48.8 percent of the vote, Fernandez 26.0 percent, and Cárdenas obtained a mere 16.6 percent.

THE ZEDILLO RECOVERY

Although Zedillo became the fifth consecutive president who had not previously been elected to any public office, he ended the post-1970 tradition of coming in promising reform but going out plundering the treasury and ruining the peso. Zedillo's major task centered upon reviving the economy once again after a devastating financial crisis in the first months of his regime. Most of his regime became a dreary battle to survive, but eventually, the economy kicked into high gear and Mexico enjoyed a monumental presidential election in 2000.

The 1994–1995 Financial Crisis. Financial difficulties began when the new Zedillo government began devaluating the peso on December 20, 1994. Finance Secretary Serra had erred in not talking to and collaborating with Mexico's new NAFTA partners, who might have been able to forestall some of the problems. Zedillo called on the nation to expect more inflation and cuts in social spending as part of an effort to maintain economic growth.

The Zedillo devaluation—Mexico's nineteenth since 1931—was a necessary but painful step that was long overdue because Salinas was spending and borrowing wildly before the 1994 presidential election in order to ensure Zedillo's victory. Mexico's foreign currency reserves dwindled from a high of $30 billion to a low of only $6 billion. In the wake of the NAFTA agreement, imports into Mexico shot up rapidly, far more than Mexico could export. Even before Zedillo took over, Mexico did not have enough to pay its obligations or to sustain the peso's value against the dollar. Prodded by Salinas, the Bank of Mexico had foolishly issued more than $40 billion in dollar-dominated short-term debt, mainly in treasury bonds known as *tesobonos*, which matured in only a year. Because the government provided little warning about the devaluation and concealed its weak financial reserves, investors lost confidence and huge sums of capital, perhaps $5 billion, left Mexico quickly. Three weeks after Salinas had proudly left Los Pinos, the peso had lost nearly half its value.

President Clinton came to the rescue with an aid package worth more than $50 billion in February. Zedillo responded to peso panic with an economic recovery plan that failed to calm financial markets. Emphasizing fiscal restraint, inflation control, privatization, and refinancing, it was a dud in terms of confidence because Mexico could not repay $28 billion in short-term debt that had to be paid in the first half of 1995. That is when Zedillo realized that the debt problem was something he could not handle by himself. Then he sought Clinton's help. Although the crisis was not as severe as the 1982 disaster, Mexico's federal reserve bank was nearly bankrupt and the treasury only days from default. Mexico's problems generated little sympathy on Capitol Hill. Clinton's earlier proposal of $40 billion drew heavy congressional opposition. Eventually, after three weeks of congressional wrangling, Clinton authorized $20 billion in aid on his own and solicited $30 billion more in international support.

The Clinton bailout slowed the Mexican crisis before it became a global panic. Until the peso collapse, little thought had been given to risks associated with capital's free movement. The globalization of financial markets during the 1980s had made money ripple like the wind. By 1994, more than $1 trillion moved electronically between various countries each day. Thus, the devaluation nightmare ricocheted through Argentina, Brazil, Hong Kong, Thailand, and Indonesia without causing other casualties.

The downturn continued late into 1995. During that period, the banking system nearly collapsed under such severe strain. Average interest rates shot up to 82 percent by March. Those who overindulged in credit card payments or had auto notes sometimes faced new interest charges as high as 120 percent. The banks struggled when 20 percent of their customers defaulted on $18.5 billion worth of debts. As a result, the Zedillo government had to bail out nine troubled banks and seize six others. During the deep recession, the peso continued losing its value and the economy actually shrank 6.9 percent in 1995, the largest contraction since 1932 during the Great Depression. By March, the budget had been cut twice. On top of that, Zedillo imposed a severe austerity program that called for increases in taxes, gasoline, and electricity. The overwhelming majority criticized these measures severely. Even billionaires had to suffer; their number dropped to 10 from 24. Meanwhile, new financial obligations increased Mexico's foreign debt to $160 billion.

The 1995 crisis also had a regional factor. State governments, particularly the northern entities of Jalisco, Nuevo León, and Sonora, owed $3.5 billion because of their heavy borrowing during the early 1990s. Interest payments for the Nuevo León government in 1995 swallowed up 79 percent of the state budget. Although state governments did not have the revenues of the national state, they had also embarked on privatization schemes involving roads, water projects, and public buildings. In addition, a five-year drought devastated the northern cattle industry, whose sales and exports fell by 50 percent. The drought also affected farmers, who left millions of acres uncultivated. The drought meant that the Zedillo government had to import more corn, wheat, beans, and sorghum from other countries. Low-cost U.S. beef gained new customers due to reliable handling and slick advertisements.

Social Decline. Severe social problems quickly resulted from the 1994 devaluation fiasco. By 1994, more than 13 million of Mexico's 91 million inhabitants lived in extreme poverty. At least 18 million suffered from malnutrition and more than 45 million were earning less than $10 a day. An estimated 40 million lived in substandard conditions. In an effort to reduce the number of poor people, government hospitals frequently subjected women to intense pressure to accept tubal ligations or intrauterine devices after giving birth. Society became increasingly dependent upon child labor. Between three and five million children washed windshields on passing cars or sold fruit and gum in order to bolster dwindling family incomes.

Conditions worsened from 1995 to 1996. At the most severe point in the new crisis 65 percent of the population fell into the category of being poor, a status attained when a family lived on no more than $9.80 a day. In southern states such as Guerrero, two-thirds of the people lived in one-or two-room shacks without running water, gas, or electricity, except for the kind that is illegally rigged. Only one Mexican in ten owned a telephone. By May 1996, two million had lost their jobs, the highest rate of unemployment in eight years. Purchasing power had fallen another 25 percent since the 1994 devaluation.

The harsh decline in living standards resulted in defiant confrontations. During the spring of 1995, poor campesinos from rural areas began converging daily at the main square in Mexico City to demonstrate support of the Zapatista rebels, as well as to denounce economic problems. To the chant of "people can't take it anymore, the people are rising up," about 5,000 demonstrators marched to Los Pinos. Shortly afterwards, tens of thousands of workers called for the resignation of Zedillo on May 1, instead of staging their traditional march of solidarity in support of his regime. Labor leaders stated that they made their decision because Mexico's economic woes left workers with little to celebrate. Many demonstrators gestured obscenely and shouted curses at Zedillo. A similar May Day protest took place a year later.

Females with their infants could also cause anxiety. On May 31, 1996, a group of mostly women and children from Monterrey stopped an incoming train, unhooked three cars of imported corn, and carried off 50 tons of grain. Police who tried to halt the looting endured a volley of stones until they arrested eight residents at this clash.

Increased crime became another signal that social stability had deteriorated. Many of the growing number of girls and boys who worked on the streets came from one-parent and dysfunctional families where drug addition or alcoholism were common. In addition to the low self-esteem that these young people exhibited, many became criminals. In Mexico City, for example, the number of armed robberies increased by 35 percent within a year after the peso devaluation. Many of these crimes were committed by people as young as ten years old. An average of 58 carjackings

took place each day. From 1993 to the end of 1995, the number of crimes rose from 360 to 550 each day, more than 43 percent of which were violent offenses. In January 1996, more than a dozen banks were robbed. Assailants armed with machine guns often raided businesses, killing anyone who got in their way. Robberies in taxicabs became so common that the U.S. embassy recommended that visitors to Mexico City use only cabs associated with their hotels. Foreigners became favorite targets of kidnappers and murderers. Eight in ten criminal suspects were never apprehended because of police ineptitude. It soon became clear, however, that the police themselves were often the worst criminals. One commander and a group of state police even attempted to carjack an auto driven by the president's son in broad daylight.

Political Confrontations. Handed a government that exploded in his face, Zedillo struggled to contain a power stuggle within the PRI as many of the party's leaders fought over drug money. At one point, the former secretary to Salinas family patriarch Raúl Salinas Lozano declared to U.S. authorities that he was a leading figure in narcotics dealings that also involved Raúl and Jose Francisco Ruiz Massieu, as well as other PRI leaders. The secretary made these revelations during her conviction for 1992 drug deals in Newark, New Jersey. Rumors circulated that Raúl was in league with drug lord Juan García Abrego, who had helped Raúl in an intimidation and wiretapping campaign to ensure his brother's 1988 election. On February 28, 1995, Attorney General Antonio Gracía Lozano, a PAN member and first opposition party official to hold a cabinet position, finally arrested Raúl. Prosecutors charged Raúl with conspiring to kill Ruiz Massieu with former PRI legislator Manuel Muñoz Rocha. Muñoz was last seen driving to Raúl's home after he had telephoned him earlier. He was never found again.

Raúl's arrest immediately made life uncomfortable for his friend, Mario Ruiz Massieu, the deputy attorney general who had been assigned to investigate his own brother's death. He had quit the case, claiming that superiors had protected the guilty party. Some speculated that the crisis was the result of a family spat, since José Ruiz Massieu had been married to a sister of Raúl and Carlos Salinas. In actuality, they had been divorced for 20 years. Mario continued to rant against corrupt authorities as part of a smoke screen to prepare for his stunning departure from the country. The attorney general had evidence that Mario had obstructed the investigation into his brother's death and ordered Raúl's name deleted from investigative testimony. Mario had also apparently fabricated evidence and intimidated witnesses to protect Raúl.

The extent of Raúl's corruption became evident when Swiss authorities confirmed that Raúl had amassed at least $100 million in Swiss bank accounts by means of suspected drug payoffs. In November 1995, Swiss police arrested Raúl's wife in Geneva after she and her brother attempted to use false documents to withdraw money from three accounts totaling nearly $84 million. The money, which the Swiss connected to drug trafficking, belonged to Raúl, who proclaimed his innocence. But brother Carlos, who had earlier engaged in a foolish hunger strike as part of his insistence that Raúl had done nothing wrong, now stated that his sibling should be "punished firmly" if found guilty of laundering drug money. The Swiss began a serious inquiry as support for Zedillo began to rise. The United States became involved when it was learned that Citibank executives had advised Raúl's wife to move the money to Europe, without the legal department's consent. And even when Citibank finally warned U.S. officials about Raúl's suspicious transactions and after Señora Salinas was arrested, Citibank did not tell the government about the network of shell companies and offshore accounts that it had set up to shield Raúl's fortune. In December, British police froze a $22 million London bank account held in Raúl's name. U.S. and Swiss officials began investigating the money's origin as part of a quest to understand money laundering and drug trafficking. Under Swiss law, deposit accounts

can be frozen only if a drug connection is involved.

Meanwhile, Attorney General Lozano announced in October 1996 that human remains had been found on a ranch owned by Raúl near Mexico City. Since Muñoz had now disappeared, it was hoped that his body would implicate Raúl. Investigators had struggled to show that Raúl was involved in José Ruiz Massieu's death, using circumstantial evidence and contradictory testimony. In addition, they had not clearly determined the alleged motive. Several key witnesses, particularly Raúl's bodyguard, changed their testimony amid allegations that attorney general office official Pablo Chapa Bezanilla had bribed one witness with a half-million dollars. Zedillo finally fired Lozano when it became public knowledge that Chapa Bezanilla had hired a psychic to plant the body on Raúl's ranch. The psychic had worked for both Carlos and Raúl Salinas. The bizarre scheme to cement a case against Raúl prompted Lozano to claim that Zedillo knew about the $450,000 payment to the psychic, who was jailed. After dozens of tests, it was revealed that the buried corpse was the father of the psychic's son-in-law.

Even though the corrupt attorney general's office found Raúl not guilty on three separate charges of corruption, tax evasion, and money laundering, Swiss investigators provided embarrassing details of Raul's activities. In April 1997, Swiss prosecutors described solid connections between drug lords and high Mexican government circles. In response, Raúl complained about his jail conditions and insisted that the millions in his Swiss bank account were given to him by wealthy Mexicans for a joint trust fund. But in October 1998, the Swiss researchers concluded that Raúl had received an estimated $500 million in protection money from Colombian cocaine traffickers. Prosecutors said that Raúl used his extensive contacts with army and police forces to provide protection for "multiton" cocaine shipments while officials looked the other way. The Swiss federal police emphasized that Raúl was involved with drug traffickers before his brother became president and habitually protected between 10 and 30 drug shipments per month. The Swiss found 21 of Raúl's bank accounts in Switzerland and 48 in other countries. Some of the witnesses that the Swiss wanted to interview were murdered because they knew too much. Nevertheless, the Swiss based their conclusions upon 78 witnesses and 34,000 documents.

This seemed to motivate Zedillo to wrap up the case against Raúl. At his final hearing, a teary-eyed Raúl reiterated his innocence of the murder charge. Also charged with illegal enrichment, Raúl hoped that speculation about his walking free would become reality. He was the first member of a presidential family to be jailed. Instead, federal judge Ricardo Ojeda found Raúl guilty of masterminding the 1994 murder of José Francisco Ruiz Massieu. The magistrate admitted that he had no direct evidence linking Raúl to the crime but gave him the maximum sentence of 50 years anyway. As consolation, authorities transferred Raúl from Mexico's toughest prison to a lower-security institution in another area of the capital.

Meanwhile, Mario Ruiz Massieu also wound up in jail. U.S. Customs Service agents arrested Ruiz Massieu in early March 1995 as he attempted to board a plane for Madrid. He had failed to declare $45,000 in cash at the Newark, New Jersey, airport. Mexican authorities requested that he be returned after charging that the nation's top antidrug official had set up a franchising operation in key states that generated millions of dollars in kickbacks from drug smugglers beginning in March 1994. Tracing almost $7 million in Texas and another $3 million in Mexico that the government found in Ruiz Massieu's name, Mexican investigators documented an intricate operation in which Ruiz Massieu filled those bank accounts with payoffs from a network of handpicked federal attorneys, who headed narcotics enforcement in various states. Regional prosecutors, in turn, took payoffs from major drug traffickers, including those from the two largest drug cartels in Mexico. U.S. investigators then seized $9 million in Houston bank accounts held by Ruiz Massieu

and concluded that the money came from drug operations. U.S. attorneys also claimed that Ruiz Massieu had stolen a million dolars from a special fund established in Mexico to fight drugs. Ruiz Massieu argued unconvincingly that the money came from family investments as well as bonuses from the president. His remaining brother was a fugitive who had an outstanding arrest warrant for real estate fraud in Acapulco, the family's residence.

As evidence mounted, Ruiz Massieu lied to the end. Nevertheless, a jury's central finding in the case was that the former prosecutor took bribes from narcotics traffickers. One witness had directly tied payoffs to Ruiz Massieu, testifying that he delivered two suitcases full of cash to him. Ruiz Massieu finally killed himself in September 1999 by swallowing a handful of antidepressants rather than serve a long prison term. His death came two days before he was to be arraigned in Houston on charges of laundering $9 million in drug money. His suicide note proclaimed his innocence and accused Zedillo of playing a role in the assassinations of his brother and Colosio.

The Drug Trade Rolls On. Mexican traffickers initiated the narcotics business with low-level production and distribution of heroin and marijuana. Later, they allied with Colombians when U.S. agents blocked the south Florida routes. Then Mexican groups bought cocaine for their own profit and generated a booming trade in methamphetamine. Mexican mafias bought the chemicals, produced methamphetamine, and shipped it across the border. By the early 1990s, Mexican drug cartels threatened the United States more than Colombian producers. More ominously, Mexican drug traffickers gained enormous influence over police and judicial systems. Drugs became tied to several high-profile assassinations while Mexican financial institutions became vulnerable to laundering schemes. Many Mexican businesses sought U.S. investment although they actually belonged to drug cartels.

In response, the Clinton government worked out various plans to cooperate with the Zedillo regime to restrain the drug trade. U.S. drug czar Barry McCaffrey and his delegation met with Zedillo, his attorney general, and other Mexican officials in March 1996. In response, Mexican legislators introduced a bill to fight money laundering and indicated that they might strengthen the bill to meet U.S. concerns. More difficult was whether or not Mexico would extradite its citizens for trial in the United States. The U.S. delegation with McCaffrey carried the names of suspected drug kingpins. Both countries also attempted to plan the training of Mexican soldiers in the United States on antidrug patrols. Proposed military cooperation arose out of a 1995 trip to Mexico City by U.S. Defense Secretary William Perry. But a furor developed when Perry announced that the United States might also consider joint exercises with the Mexican military.

Over several years, drug traffickers stepped up their efforts to buy off Mexico's law enforcement agencies. Some officials became so corrupted that they became "servants" for the drug gangs. Tijuana police commander Ernesto Ibarra confided this to reporters in September 1995; days later, killers assassinated him. Ibarra was one of more than 40 federal agents killed in the line of duty from 1995 to late 1996. Officials described such deaths as part of the sacrifice they made while combatting drug smugglers. Mexico's latest attorney general acknowledged that drug-related corruption remained a problem in his office. In January 1997, he claimed that public confidence in his agency had fallen so low that it was pointless to give speeches promising better days.

The drug issue became acrimonious. By early 1997, the U.S. government obtained considerable evidence that Raúl Salinas and other high-ranking Mexican politicians were more closely tied to narcotics criminals than previously believed. At that time, Drug Enforcement Agency Administrator Thomas Constantine bluntly testified before a congressional committee that corruption had become the central problem for his agents operating in Mexico. In reply, Mexico threatened to expel them. Three months later, it was revealed that Mexico's anti-drug czar was on the payroll of

Mexico's most powerful drug smuggler. General Jesús Gutiérrez Rebollo was arrested as Zedillo defended his use of the military to fight drugs, despite warnings that the army had become as corrupt as other law enforcement agencies.

Economic Revival. Just as important as what Zedillo did to revive the economy is what he did not do. Zedillo maintained the continuity of the past ten years by vowing to meet all of Mexico's obligations under NAFTA, permitting the peso to trade freely, and not opening the treasury to salvage failing businesses or subsidize consumers. Nor would Zedillo give in to demands to stop paying off the foreign debt. By February 1995, trade statistics rose to the point that Mexico recorded its first monthly trade surplus since November 1990. Although unemployment rose in 1995, inflation went down briefly. Steady repayment of short-term debt ended fears that Mexico might default on its loans during the autumn of 1995. By spring of 1996, Mexico was on the way to recovery. The stock market moved at a faster pace than in 1993, while the peso stabilized. The Treasury Department also began paying off the 1995 bailout loan faster than anticipated. By January 1997, the U.S. loan repayment was completed. Highly publicized crackdowns on tax evaders produced more revenue.

After the recession ended in mid-1996, robust growth became evident. Despite economic crises in Russia and Brazil, the gross domestic product grew 4.8 percent in 1998. During that year, the manufacturing sector grew by 7.4 percent, construction increased by 4.6 percent, and services 4.5 percent. Free market forces had not destroyed the ejido. Instead, the ejidos redefined themselves in unexpected ways, particularly in exporting organic coffees and other new ventures. *Maquiladoras* boomed to the point that the General Motors subsidiary Delphi in Ciudad Juárez became Mexico's largest employer with 75,000 workers in plants also located in Chihuahua City, Guanajuato, Los Mochis, Saltillo, Reynosa, Matamoros, and Querétaro. Workers earned an average of $1.90 an hour in wages and benefits. This was low by U.S. standards but compared favorably to Mexico's normal wage of $3 per day.

The privatization scheme also attracted efforts to modernize the railroad system. Zedillo hoped that private as well as foreign investors, who could not own more than 49 percent of any rail line, would spend at least $12 billion to purchase and modernize aging rail networks. Thousands of tracks had not been replaced since the revolution of 1910 began. Union Pacific of Dallas and two Mexican partners bought Mexico's largest rail line, the Pacific North Railway in 1997, after a government auction. The new rail sought to join the surge in U.S.–Mexican trade which jumped from $100 billion to $150 billion in just three and a half years. Railroads were expected to play a large role in U.S.–Mexican commerce because both countries would be moving more goods that could not be carried cheaply by trucks or ships. In December 1997, Kansas City Southern Industries, parent company of Kansas City Railroad, and Mexican partner Transportacion Maritima Mexicana paid $1.4 billion for the Mexican Northeast Railroad, which linked Nuevo Laredo and Matamoros with Monterrey, Mexico City, and seaports on the Gulf of Mexico and the Pacific. It accounted for about 40 percent of all of Mexico's rail freight.

Vital to economic recovery was a healthier banking system. The 1995 crisis pushed the banks to the edge of insolvency then and only a $100 billion government bailout saved them. Foreign bankers swooped in to buy the largest institutions at bargain prices. Mexico's poorly regulated banking industry was on the brink of collapse when the value of the peso dropped in 1995, sending interest rates soaring to rates as high as 120 percent and leaving debtors unable to pay back their loans. Therefore, Zedillo stepped in between 1995 and 1997 with a huge bailout. The regime decided that they could not risk allowing a single bank to fail. The standard deal was that for every dollar of fresh capital that a bank could come up with, the bailout fund, Fobaproa, would buy two dollars of bad loans from the bank in question. Even sweeter deals were available to foreign banks willing to buy entire Mexican institutions. Only four of

Mexico's largest banks survived the crisis with the same owners, while a dozen were sold or taken over by the government. The problem was that Zedilo had never asked Congress for its authorization while the Finance Ministry had bought bad loans and taken over banks suspected of fraud.

Athough the government argued that the cost of the bailout as a percentage of the gross domestic product was smaller (18 percent) than similar bailouts in Chile and Argentina during the 1980s, opposition leaders balked at assuming possibly tainted loans held by high-profile bankers. The PAN and the PRD sought to get the bank bailout program declared unconstitutional, impeach financial officials, and publish names of millionaire business people whose unpaid loans would be passed on to hard-pressed taxpayers. A Canadian audit later revealed that Fobaproa failed to take action against corruption and insider dealing. It also propped up banks that deserved to fail because of gross mismanagement. Despite an eventual cost of $100 billion, Zedillo managed to get congressional approval for continued bailout operations in 1998, the biggest bailout in the nation's history.

But Mexican banks continued to seek out foreign capital because the Zedillo bailout was not enough. Overdue loans remained an Achilles' heel. With a default rate at roughly 12 percent, Mexico's bad debt problem was three times higher than the international standard rate. The banks continued to charge high annual fees and steep commissions for basic services like cash withdrawals and writing more than a set number of checks. Therefore, only 10 percent of the population actually used banks. Sensing an opportunity to use their superior assets to find new customers, foreign banks moved in. The only restriction that Zedillo had for U.S., Canadian, and European banks was that they could not become majority owners of Banamex, Grupo Financiero Bancomer, and Banca Serfín, the three largest Mexican financial institutions. By 1998, 24 of the 49 operating banks had foreign capital. Of those 24, Mexicans were the majority owners in only 3.

As the twentieth century ended, Zedillo could bequeath a far healthier economy to his successor. Five consecutive years of economic growth were a welcome respite from previous chaos. Mexico survived a presidential election without financial chaos for the first time since 1970. By the year 2000, the economy was booming with 7 percent growth, $30 billion in federal reserves, and exports that had grown over 100 percent since 1994. Jobs began to go begging by the summer of 2000, as employers scrambled to find enough workers, often having to advertise bonuses. Talk of a labor shortage was unusual, but the reality was that the thundering U.S. economy continued to boost demand for Mexican-made goods.

The Mexico of burros ambling down dusty streets with bags of corn for the local market did not exist anymore. By 1999, Mexico's integration with global technology and markets enabled shiny new factories to pump out steering wheels, airbags, computers, and most of the televisions sold in the United States. *Maquiladora* employment grew by double-digit rates for five consecutive years, reaching 1.1 million by 1999. That year, Mexico became the eleventh largest car and truck producer in the world with an output of 1.5 million vehicles. Foreign investment went from $11 billion in 1999 to an anticipated $12 billion for 2000. Although Mexico City still accounted for one-third of everything produced in Mexico, the north was clearly driving development and nurturing a middle class that had begun to grow once again. Although purchasing power had shrunk by at least 80 percent since 1977, better times seemed to lie ahead in terms of improving the gap between the haves and have-nots. The Mexican model innovated by de la Madrid and sustained by Salinas as well as Zedillo has paid off. Mexico did the opposite of Japan by cutting tariffs, selling off government-owned industries, and deregulating its economy. The result was that as Tokyo grappled with its own recession Mexico replaced Japan as the second biggest customer of the United States.

Chiapas Stalemated. Zedillo never trusted the rebel leadership in Chiapas to work out a suitable arrangement with him. In a sudden departure from his promise to restart peace talks with the Zapatistas, Zedilo quickly sent 3,000 soldiers and police officers into the rebel strongholds in early February 1995 and arrested more than a dozen alleged rebels. Zedillo had ordered the seizure of the Zapatistas leadership. Soldiers and police met little resistance. Tens of thousands of PRD supporters marched into the capital to demand an end to hostilities. But the PAN and PRI strongly endorsed Zedillo's decision to use force against the rebels. Eight days after the assault, Zedillo vowed not to let the Zapatistas gain the upper hand. This became his major concession to PRI hard-liners as well as to the PAN.

Zedillo, however, proved unable to resolve the crisis. Perhaps his worst mistake was naming hardliner Emilio Chuayffet as secretary of Gobernación. Not long afterward, human rights groups and journalists based in Chiapas warned anyone who would listen that death squads associated with the PRI were carrying out a terror campaign against supporters of the rebels in Chiapas. But complex negotiations finally resulted in the February 1996 signing of the San Andres Accords on Indigenous Rights and Culture. Zedillo, however, set these agreements aside rather than support their enactment into federal constitutional law. Not surprisingly, the rebels walked away from discussions with federal officials in September 1996, after the government withdrew its approval of two key items in the San Andres Accords. Zedillo balked on provisions that would have allowed indigenous peoples to expropriate land, to elect representatives, and decide issues by traditional methods of consensus instead of direct votes. Zedillo then encouraged the Mexican Congress to decide on the issue, hoping the Zapatistas could not reject a publicly supported proposal.

These tensions resulted in the Acteal massacre on December 22, 1997. Several Chiapas villages declared themselves separate from the republic in April 1996, citing negotiated but unratified peace accords calling for indigenous autonomy. The delicate truce between the government and the rebels soon began to disintegrate as killings, burning of homes, and forced expulsions of Indians took place. Finally, gunmen attacked the Chiapas highland village of Acteal on December 22, 1997, and murdered women and children praying in a small clapboard Catholic church. Nearly all were members of an independent peasant group which sympathized with the Zapatistas. In all, 9 men, 21 women, 14 children, and an infant, all unarmed civilians, were shot in cold blood and finished off with machetes. Pregnant women's abdomens were sliced open. More than six hours passed before the police took action, which consisted of cleaning the site and digging mass graves. Amid an international outcry, dozens of arrests were made and the governor resigned along with the Gobernación secretary. The attorney general's office conceded in March 1998 that a pro-government vigilante group had plotted the Acteal massacre for more than two months. State police had aided the attackers by transporting weapons in police vehicles.

Zedillo could not resolve the situation before he departed office. As the Zapatistas suffered ebbing national attention and the PRI celebrated victories in several states previously won by the PRD in 1998, the Zapatistas offered to negotiate. Nothing happened and an attempt to organize sympathy in Mexico City fizzled when masked rebels tried to organize a referendum on indigenous rights in March 1999. Zedillo tolerated the Zapatistas because they enjoyed the popular support of Chiapas and members of mostly leftist circles throughout Mexico and abroad. Their base communities—the mostly Mayan civilians whose welfare the guerrillas claimed to defend—numbered several thousand. Protected by Zedillo's fear of a public relations debacle if he attempted another assault, the Zapatistas continued to hurl their barbed, witty communiques and symbolically sharpen their machetes. Zedillo tried to buy off their base support by spending large sums on hospitals and schools in a state that once barely drew the government's notice.

The Political Panorama. During his presidential campaign, Zedillo raised political reform to the top of his agenda, and as president he grad-

ually made that promise a reality. Zedillo owed much of his electoral victory to the PRI machinery and did not move swiftly. Unlike Salinas, Zedillo began his *sexenio* without a strong cabinet. But from the very beginning, he promised not to select his successor and ended the persecution of the PRD initiated by Salinas. Allowing the PAN to triumph in the February 1995 gubernatorial elections in Jalisco was an early indication of Zedillo's instinct for political reform. Zedillo tried to instill a sense of honesty in government. He also shunned some of the pomp and formality of the presidency, cutting short traditionally long ceremonies and speeches. Zedillo also ventured into the Mexican hinterlands once a week for speeches, ribbon-cutting ceremonies, shaking hands, and kissing babies.

The 1995 crisis, however, produced a certain frustration in Zedillo that lasted until late 1996. Members of the debtors group El Barzon heckled government speakers so mercilessly in Monterrey that it became the first time in many decades that a government official was prevented from speaking at a public forum. The same group briefly took over some of the Gobernación offices in June 1995, including the secretary's private meeting room. Zedillo's approval rating remained stuck at about 20 percent two weeks after his term began because of economic uncertainty and the austerity program. Many speculated that the PRI would force him to step down since it had lost most of the major cities to the opposition parties. Zedillo argued that he was making tough decisions for the good of the nation as a whole. Critics also pointed out that Zedillo's salary had jumped more than 300 percent since he had taken office.

Others charged that Zedillo frequently embraced some of the most backward members of the PRI and allowed them to run various states as their personal fiefdoms. Zedillo defended Tabasco governor Roberto Madrazo, even after documents surfaced showing that Madrazo had allegedly spent $70 million in his campaign, several times the amount of money allowed during his 1994 campaign. That came to about $200 a vote compared to Clinton, who spent about $1 per vote when he was elected president. Zedillo also permitted Guerrero Governor Ruben Figueroa, a PRI hard-liner, to stay in office for eight months after a peasant massacre by police in which the Guerrero government attempted a massive coverup of involvement by leading officials. The sudden arrest of a former Veracruz governor who used his political connections to build a sprawling empire worth millions of dollars took far too long. Another public official to fall in 1996 was Nuevo León Governor Socrates Rizzo, who resigned in April after investigators questioned him about the purchase and sale of a $4 million jet. Dozens of other public officials were fired, disciplined, or arrested in connection with corruption cases after Zedillo took office. The climax came when Morelos Governor Jorge Carrillo Olea resigned on kidnapping charges. Carrillo Olea was the first governor threatened by a political impeachment trial because shortly after he took office, kidnappings, torture, and blackmail fell upon Morelos inhabitants so routinely that ransom payments could be made in convenient monthly payments. Complaints fell upon deaf ears until the commander of the Morelos antikidnapping unit was caught by Guerrero highway police dumping a body alongside a highway. Critics complained that too few crooked officials were ever prosecuted and that those cases which emerged were driven by political expediency rather than good will.

Although Zedillo did not seriously challenge the PRI old guard early in his regime, he kept his promise to generally allow freer elections to take place. In addition to losing Baja California, the first opposition victory to retain a governorship, the PAN triumphed in Guanajuato, placing Vicente Fox in the governor's office. The PAN also took issue with the PRI victory in Yucatán, charging electoral fraud, and refused to negotiate with Zedillo on political reforms.

In November 1996, Zedillo's much-touted electoral reform project ran into trouble when PRI legislators in Congress gutted 16 of its major provisions that had already been negotiated between Zedillo and the opposition parties months earlier. Zedillo seemed to have had little choice but to play it safe for fear of isolating himself politically from PRI members who were impatient and frustrated with new political rules that were already diminishing their power. The modified electoral reform ended an agreement that would have distributed the government's share of free media time more equally among political parties and it reduced sanctions for electoral fraud. The revision also made it more difficult for Mexicans living abroad to vote in Mexican presidential elections without having to return to their home country.

Almost without realizing it, Mexico suddenly became increasingly democratic. Civic action groups rose from only 10 in early 1985 to more than 5,000 by early 1997. They seemed to indicate that the big push for democracy was emerging from common people, who were increasingly fed up with the system. Civic Alliance, the largest of the independent citizens' groups, became a coalition of 400 organizations with 50,000 members nationwide. In 1996, civic groups, the political parties, and Zedillo agreed to make the leader of Mexico City an elective position for the first time since early in the twentieth century. Mexican political campaigns suddenly changed. Instead of relying on wall paintings and perfunctory town plaza rallies, political parties turned to door-to-door mobilization, coffee klatches, wide-open media onslaughts, and hard-hitting advertising. Opposition leaders called for the PAN and PRD to form a coalition against the PRI. Meanwhile, the PAN distanced itself from the PRI as Governor Fox tried to lure dissident PRI and PRD members into the PAN. Meanwhile, the PRD began to gain ground in the PAN stronghold of Jalisco. The political culture mirrored regional attitudes more compellingly as the three parties consolidated. The north continued to be dominated by the PAN, while the center-left PRD continued to make big gains in the south and the PRI, in spite of predictions of its imminent demise, held on to central Mexico.

Zedillo pushed through dual citizenship legislation which allowed Mexican immigrants in the United States to retain Mexican nationality rights. Visiting Dallas early in 1995, Zedillo told Mexican-American politicians and business people that "You're Mexicans—Mexicans who live north of the border." Now immigrants could have Mexican passports and own property, even if they decided to become U.S. citizens. The 51 consultates throughout the United States emphasized programs that educated immigrants about social security benefits, AIDS, and investments in Mexico. Congress also passed a law that granted Mexicans the right to vote in presidential elections, even if they lived abroad. It was an issue that pitted once invisible immigrants against reluctant Mexican federal institutions that had ignored expatriates for far too long. New democratic concepts also allowed millions of Mexican-born people to regain or retain their citizenship even if they were children of immigrants.

The 1997 elections for the head of Mexico City further reflected the opening up of the system. Cárdenas became Mexico City's first elected mayor in July 1997 and promised to expose fraud and conduct a frontal assault upon a horrendous crime wave. However, air pollution, crime, and everyday corruption remained endemic problems in the capital.

Far more dramatic was that the PRI lost control of the Chamber of Deputies during the same July 1997 elections. The PRI controlled only 239 seats, while the PRD won 126 and the PAN captured 121. The exultant opposition parties warned Zedillo to negotiate with them or face dire consequences. Zedillo became the first president to face an opposition legislature since 1913. The opposition deputies included about 40 so-called "external candidates," basically community leaders invited by the opposition to run for office, even though they did not belong to any party. Among them was the first openly gay member of the Chamber of Deputies, indigenous leaders, activists from public organizations, and a journalist. Growing pains were evident. In September 1997, an opposition legislator and a PRI member fought for control of a microphone in a symbolic tussle for controlling economic policies. A PRD deputy screamed at another PRI representative, provoking a fistfight. Debates over critical issues some-

times degenerated into shouting. On the other hand, voters watched congressional sessions more than ever, a healthy sign in itself.

Best of all, Zedillo began to embrace democracy emphatically during the midpoint of his *sexenio*. In 1998, the PRI came roaring back by winning seven of the ten governorships decided that year. This comeback resulted largely from the introduction of party primaries, improving economic conditions, and mediocre performances by opposition governments. The elections were also notable for being basically free from the electoral fraud that had plagued Mexican balloting during most of the twentieth century. As the reform wing of the PRI strengthened its hand, voters infused balloting with more vigor, thus encouraging higher standards of electoral procedures. The primaries also served the purpose of choosing genuinely popular PRI candidates. To shore up its legitimacy and improve its tarnished image, the PRI no longer selected candidates from Mexico City or behind closed doors.

The primary route to power became particularly compelling in Chihuahua. There PAN Governor Francisco Barrio Terrazas seemed to be in an unbeatable position by rooting out corruption and improving overall adminstration. PRI business leader Patricio Martínez convinced party officials that they had nothing to lose by opening up the primary to anyone with a federal voting credential card. About 230,000 people eager to fight crime turned out to vote, a procedure that won the PRI tremendous credibility and made Martínez the frontrunner who eventually won.

Zedillo continued to insist that he would not directly select his successor and urged the PRI to select its presidential nominee by means of an open primary. Eager to preserve party unity and determined to stop bids by discredited traditionalists such as Manuel Bartlett, Zedillo also warned that he would not stand by on the sidelines. But the primary electoral process remained vague until the PRI selected former intelligence chief and hard-liner Fernando González Barrios to manage the historic primary. Zedillo assumed he should prevent a split within the PRI because of his growing competence. Under the new rules, PRI candidates had to fund their own campaigns. The winner would be determined by who won the most electoral districts and not necessarily the greatest percentage of the popular vote. Any registered voter could participate in the presidential primary. Nevertheless, many doubted Zedillo would not pass up the opportunity to indicate who the next candidate should be.

When the PRD attempted to select its leader, the election had to be annulled after massive vote fraud in March 1999. Thus, the party that cried fraud most loudly during the past ten years suddenly had a dirty image of its own. Complaints from the PRD national balloting included charges of ballot box stuffing, theft of electoral boxes, and throwing out polling place observers. This did not bode well for the upcoming elections, which were a true surprise as well as a turning point.

The 2000 Presidential Election. At first, it seemed as though the PRI would maintain its momentum and win the presidency yet again. The PAN and the PRD stepped up their combined efforts in August 1999 to discuss a common political platform, agree on a single presidential candidate, and pick coalition candidates for Congress. Opposition candidates backed by broad coalitions had recently won four governorships. PRI leaders confidently responded that their opponents were desperate and would fail. Cárdenas had begun to slip in the polls because of the PRD's failure to end a crime wave, relocate hordes of street vendors, and improve the chaotic public transportation system in Mexico City. Cárdenas, however, decided to go it alone and run his ill-fated third campaign for the presidency a month later. Although he smiled more than in the past, he continued to rhapsodize about ejidos and PEMEX. Lacking charisma and ignoring modern campaign techniques, Cárdenas was taking a sentimental journey to oblivion.

Meanwhile, the PRI unveiled its new primary strategy that featured many novelties in November 1999. Particularly interesting was an unprecedented debate among the four finalists: Francisco Labastida Ochoa, secretary of Gobernación; Roberto Madrazo, former governor of Tabasco; Manuel Bartlett, former governor of Puebla who also fixed the 1988 election for Salinas; and hardline former PRI president Humberto Roque Villanueva. The debates featured spirited attacks between Labastida and Madrazo. Madrazo accused Labastida of being a hand-picked insider while Labistida responded by calling Madrazo a liar. Both claimed that their opponent had cozy ties with the now-despised Salinas. Bartlett and Roque Villaneuva mumbled traditional formulas and faded away.

Another novelty was the appearance of U.S. style techniques and campaign advisors. Madrazo had shot ahead by means of slick, hard-hitting jabs at Labastida and Zedillo. Mexicans had always appreciated humor and drama, but verbal insults clashed with the traditional Mexican notion of courtesy. Labastida scrapped his somewhat bland offerings and eventually compared Madrazo to Hitler, while laying out an anticorruption pledge based upon a demand that all office seekers list their personal wealth. Although Labastida was a former governor of Sinaloa, where drug business had become a way of life, his law-and-order theme eventually secured him the PRI nomination. With a 20 percent lead in the polls, Labistida appeared to have an unbeatable advantage.

Eventually, Vicente Fox became the major opponent to Labastida. Slowly but surely, he convincingly emphasized the need for change. With his trademark cowboy hat, boots, and oversized belt buckle, the six-foot-five-inch-tall Fox gradually impressed voters with his unorthodox touch and profited from U.S. media consultants such as Dick Morris. Impulsive and tolerant, Fox also had a business person's feel for pragmatic solutions. His insistence upon honest government gradually took hold. Fox did not come across as a career politician either. During the campaign, he used rough language and occasionally lost his temper; but he insisted upon spending every Monday at his Guanajuato ranch to be with his four adopted children, have lunch with his mother, and ride his horse.

As the campaign went on, Fox slowly rose in the polls. By March 2000, he was closing the gap in many opinion polls as he accused Labastida and other PRI members of having links to drug traffickers. Fox claimed that if he won the presidency, he wanted to work closely with the United States, but he said he believed Washington was not doing enough to tackle drug dealers in its home territory. Labastida, who had also been an agriculture secretary, emphasized the traditional rural strength of the PRI; but his stiff style resulted in a tie with Fox among polls taken in April 2000. Fox, a talented speaker, was comfortable on television and performed well in presidential debates when Labastida attacked him. The PRI machinery could only engage in subtle forms of fraud because the newly independent electoral authorities eventually ensured a clean, fair, and credible election. Nevertheless, the Civic Alliance reported incidents where police rounded up citizens in places like San Jeronimo de Chicahualco in the state of Mexico and urged them to vote for Labastida or lose public services. By then, however, Fox had crept a few points ahead of Labastida, although many claimed the race to be a dead heat up to the last few days. Although Zedillo ignored dirty campaign tactics used by the PRI and stepped up pork barrel spending, he made it clear that voting results would be honored.

When July 2, 2000, arrived, many believed the race was still a deadlock. In fact, Fox had picked up strength among younger working class voters and Labastida had weakened in the rural areas. Large numbers of immigrants, many of them Fox supporters, also voted at special polling stations spread out evenly along the border. The result was that Fox won handily, getting 43 percent of the votes while longtime bureaucrat Labastida won 35 percent. Cárdenas obtained only 16 percent but vowed not to cooperate with Fox. In a remarkably fraud-free voting day, Labastida won a majority of the female votes by a slim margin, but Fox presented himself as the person to bring true democracy to Mexico. The PAN also won the most votes for the Senate and Chamber of Deputies. The Fox victory also included two governorships in Morelos and Guanajuato, and the PAN came close to

beating the PRD in the Mexico City mayor's race, even though the PRD entered the race with a huge lead in the polls. A Mexico that had become more urban, educated, and younger had slipped out of the PRI's grasp. Zedillo immediately congratulated Fox and the executive branch began a smooth, friendly transition.

SUGGESTED READING

Azziz Nassif, Alberto. *Territorios de alternancia: El primer gobierno de oposicion en Chihuahua.* Mexico City: Triana Editores, 1996.

Bean, Frank D. *At the Crossroads: Mexican Migration and U.S. Policy.* Baltimore, MD: Rowman and Littlefield, 1997.

Camp, Roderic, *Politics in Mexico*, 3d ed. New York: Oxford University Press, 2000.

———. "Camarillas in Mexican Politics, The Case of the Salinas Cabinet." *Journal of Mexican Studies* 6:1 (1990), 85–107.

———, ed. *Polling for Democracy: Public Opinion and Political Liberation in Mexico.* Wilmington, DE: Scholarly Resources, 1996.

Centeno, Miguel Angel. *Democracy Within Reason: Technocratic Revolution in Mexico.* University Park: Pennsylvania State University Press, 1994.

Erfani, Julie. *The Paradox of the Mexican State: Rereading Sovereignty from Independence to NAFTA.* Boulder, CO: Lynn Reinmer, 1995.

Harvey, Neil. *The Chiapas Rebellion: The Struggle for Land and Democracy.* Durham, NC: Duke University Press, 1999.

Kaufman Purcell, Susan Rubio and Luis Rubio, eds. *Mexico under Zedillo.* Boulder, CO: Lynne Reiner, 1998.

Lustig, Nora. *Mexico: The Remaking of an Economy.* Washington, DC: Brookings Institution, 1992.

Medina Peña, Luis. *Hacia el nuevo estado: México, 1920–1993.* Mexico City: Fondo de Cultura Económica, 1994.

Ronfeldt, David. *The Modern Mexican Military.* Los Angeles: Rand Publications, 1985.

Russell, Philip A. *Mexico under Salinas.* Austin: Mexico Resources Center, 1994.

Schatz, Sara. *Elites, Masses and the Struggle for Democracy in Mexico: A Culturalist Approach.* Westport Ct: Praeger, 2000.

Wise, Carol, ed. *The Post-NAFTA Political Economy: Mexico and the Western Hemisphere.* University Park: Pennsylvania State University Press, 1998.

Glossary

Agrarista   Advocate of land distribution.

Alcabala   Sales tax

Alcalde   Chief constable of a town or city.

Audiencia   Regional system of colonial courts.

Ayuntamiento   Municipal government of an elected town council.

Auto de Fé ("Act of Faith")   Usual punishment handed down by Inquisition tribunal.

Aztlán   The legendary homeland of the Axtecs, probably in Zacatecas.

Barrio   Neighborhood of a town or city.

Batab   Local ruler in the Yucatán.

Bracero   A Mexican worker brought into the United States by means of a labor contract.

Cabildo   Municipal government.

Cacicazgo   Rule of a cacique over a particular region or local area.

Cacique   Local ruler.

Campesino   A rural worker or farmer in the countryside.

Casa del Obrero Mundial   The anarchosyndicalist House of the World Worker.

Casta   Those of mixed blood.

Científicos   Advocates of science who became power brokers from 1876 to 1911.

Cinco de Mayo   The victory of Mexican forces over French invaders at Puebla on May 5, 1862.

Colonia   Small settlement, sometimes part of a town.

CONASUPO   A federal program which provided basic goods, particulary food, to working-class people.

CNC   Confederación Nacional de Campesinos.

CTM   Confederación de Trabajadores Mexicanos.

Cofradía   A religious brotherhood or sisterhood.

Compadrazgo   Godparentage.

Criollo   Spanish person born in Mexico.

Diezmo   The 10 percent church tithe.

Ejidos   Communal land systems on village level.

Empresario   Land grantee required to recruit settlers in order to validate a grant.

Encomienda   A grant of labor and tribune collection.

FDN   National Democratic Front; the 1988 coalition of Cuauhtémoc Cárdenas.

Flota   The Spanish merchant fleet with armed escorts that sailed to Veracruz.

Fueros   Privileges in the form of exemptions from taxation or civil law.

Gachupines   Pejorative term for Spaniards born in Iberia.

Gente baja   Low people at the bottom of society.

Gente de razón   People who reason; respectable persons.

Gobernación   The ministry in charge of elections, security, and public order.

Golpe   A revolt, literally a "blow."

Granaderos   Riot police used from the 1950s to the 1960s.

Hacienda   Large land estate in rural regions.

Hispanic   Spanish.

Hora Nacional (National hour) A government radio program set up in 1942 to inculcate patriotic values.

IMF (International Monetary Fund) A United Nations Agency formed to promote international monetary cooperation, currency stabilization, and world trade expansion.

IMSS Instituto Mexicano de Seguro Social.

Indigenismo The incorporation of indigenous peoples into mainstream Mexican society.

Intendent An eighteenth-century administrator.

Jefes Políticos Persons appointed by national ruler to control regions as a district political chief.

Letrado A "lettered" university graduate.

IRCA Immigration Reform and Control Act of 1986.

Ley Fuga (Law of flight) A term used by authorities indicating a person shot while supposedly attempting to flee.

Los Pinos The official presidential residence.

Machismo Virile manliness, courage, toughness.

Maquiladora Assembly plant with tax exemptions and 100 percent foreign ownership. Derived from the Spanish word *Maquila*, describing how farmers bring grain to a miller.

Merced Land grant.

Mestizaje The mixing of Spanish and indigenous blood.

Mestizo A person of indigenous and European backgrounds.

Mulato A person of African and European backgrounds.

NAFTA North American Free Trade Agreement.

PAN Partido de Acción Nacional.

Pelado ("Peeled one") One who is a rascal or misfit.

PCM Mexican Communist Party.

PEMEX (Petróleos Mexicanos) Mexican national petroleum company set up as Mexico's public utility to drill for and market oil.

PLM Partido Liberal Mexicano.

PNR Party of the National Revolution.

PRD Democratic Revolutionary Party of Cuauhtémoc Cárdenas formed in May 1989.

PRI Partido Revolucionario Institucional.

PRM Party of the Mexican Revolution.

Presidentes Municipales Heads of municipal governments.

Pronunciamiento Appeal for political support.

PSUM Leftist coalition, the Partido Socialista Uníficado de México.

Pulque Alcoholic drink made from the maguey or agave plant.

Puro A "pure" or radical liberal.

Rancho Medium-sized rural property.

Repartimiento Rotational labor system from indigenous villages.

Residencia Administrative review required of all royal officials.

Retablos Religious oil paintings on tin.

Rurales National police established by Juárez.

Sexenio A six-year presidential term in modern Mexico.

UNAM Universidad Naciónal Autónoma de México.

Vaquero Cowboy.

Visita Unannounced inspection of colonial officials in order to investigate misconduct.

Zambo A person of indigenous and African background.

Index

0

Villa, Pancho, *continued*
    reform failures, 226-27
    Zapata *vs.,* 231
Villa de Buentello, Sofia, 268
Villa Escalera, Ricardo, 366
Villages, in ancient Mexico, 2
Virgin of Guadalupe, 78-79, 105, 106,
    113, 143, 165, 183, 190, 332
Visigoths, 20-21
Visitas, 33
Voladores, 46
Voting rights for women, 283-84

W

Wallace, Henry A., 296, 315-16
War of Spanish Succession, 83
Weeks, John, 390
Western Hemisphere Act, U.S., 341-42
Weston, Edward, 263
Williams, Samuel May, 151, 152
Wilson, Henry Lane, 214, 215, 216
Wilson, Michael, 390
Wilson, Woodrow, 214
    anti-Huerta policy, 216-17, 218-19
    Mexican immigration and, 334-35
    Pershing expedition, 227-28, 235
Women
    African, 67
    anti-Zedillo protest, 394
    Aztec, 11, 13
    in Islamic Spain, 22
    Maya, 6
    Mexican
        Bourbon reforms and, 88-89
        Carranza and, 237
        Coalition of Women, 357
        in colonial Mexico, 48-50
        criminals, in Mexico City, 99
        dance and, 330-31
        Díaz and, 193
        in early republic, 136-37
        Echeverría and, 349-50
        feminism, opposition to, 268-69

increasing prominence of, 157
legal protections, 182-83
in liberal period, 173
in Mexican Revolution, 221
mid-twentieth-century, 329-30
Morelos and, 113
Mother's Day and, 330
nuns/convents, 71-72
as royalist supporters, 116
support for oil nationalization,
    287
in U.S.-Mexican war, 162
voting rights, 284, 330
in workforce, 136-37, 330, 350
in Visigothic Spain, 21
Women and the Law (Villa de Buentel-
    lo), 268
World Bank, 386
World War I, Carranza and, 235
World War II, 295-303
    Axis presence in Mexico, 296, 297
    home front, 300-303
    oil sales to Axis, 296
    restrictions against Germans,Ital-
        ians,Japanese, 301
    U.S.-Mexico cooperation, 292, 297
        economic benefits from, 315
Worth, William J., 164
Writing
    convent writing, 71
    Maya, 9-10
    Monte Albán, 5
    Olmec, 4

X

Xixime people, revolt of, 44

Y

Yanga, 68
Yaquis, 91, 189, 274-75, 73210
Yocupicio, Ramón, 278-79
Yrigoyen, Hipólito, 214

Yucatán, 27-28, 44
    autonomy of, 161
    independence of, 159
    in U.S.-Mexican war, 163

Z

Zabludovsky Kuper, Jaime, 389-90
Zacatecas, 58, 60
    Santa Anna *vs.,* 146-47
Zapata, Emiliano, 210, 213, 215, 226
    agrarian revolution, 228-30
    assassination of, 232
    background, 228-29
    decline of, 231-32
    military campaign, 230-31
    Villa and, 231
Zapatista Landscape (Rivera), 250
Zapatista National Liberation Army,
    382-83
Zapatistas, 215, 382, 399, 400
Zapotec insurrection, 45
Zapotecs, 4, 5
Zaragoza, Ignacio, 175
Zavala, Silvio, 326
Zea, Leopoldo, 325
Zedillo Ponce de Léon, Ernesto, 384-85
    Chiapas and, 399-400
    drug trade and, 394-97
    economic revival, 397-99
    1994-1995 financial crisis, 392-93
    1994 election, 391-92
    political confrontations, 394-96
    political reform, 400-403
    social decline, 393-94
Zero
    Maya representation of, 10
    Olmec representation of, 4
Zimmermann, Arthur, 235
Zócalo, 47
Zuloaga, Félix, 173, 174, 189
Zumárraga, Bishop, 78
Zuno, José Guadalupe, 347